RENEWALS 458-4574
DATE DUE

MAY 5			
NOV 8			
DEC 3 1			
MAY 1			
DEC 12			
MAY 0 7			
DEC 1 0			
GAYLORD			PRINTED IN U.S.A.

The
History of Violin Playing
from its Origins to 1761

The first known painting of the violin. *The Madonna of the Orange Trees* (1529–30) by Gaudenzio Ferrari.

The
History of Violin Playing
from its Origins to 1761

and its
Relationship to the Violin
and Violin Music

DAVID D. BOYDEN

London
OXFORD UNIVERSITY PRESS
NEW YORK   TORONTO

Oxford University Press, Ely House, London W.1

GLASGOW   NEW YORK   TORONTO   MELBOURNE   WELLINGTON
CAPE TOWN   IBADAN   NAIROBI   DAR ES SALAAM   LUSAKA   ADDIS ABABA
DELHI   BOMBAY   CALCUTTA   MADRAS   KARACHI   LAHORE   DACCA
KUALA LUMPUR   SINGAPORE   HONG KONG   TOKYO

ISBN 0 19 316315 2

First published 1965
Reprinted 1967 and 1975

PRINTED IN GREAT BRITAIN BY
WHITSTABLE LITHO LTD.,
WHITSTABLE, KENT.

Preface

A N author must be allowed a few vanities in a Preface, among them the customary declaration that his book is a desperately needed contribution. Often this is no mere vanity but an article of faith without which the rigours and exhaustions involved in completing a work of any magnitude simply could not be overcome. In the case of this book, I can claim only that various persons have told me that it is a needed contribution. To be honest, I undertook the research without any grand idea in mind; I was simply trying to find out things about performing violin music to which there were no available answers that seemed to me complete or satisfactory. In this sense, I wrote the book for myself, and surely this is the original impulse of a vast number of books of like nature.

When stated in general terms, the object of this book is deceptively simple. It is to relate the history of violin playing in sufficient detail to illuminate at any given time the evolution of the violin, the relation of this evolution to the development of violin music, and the organic connexion between these factors and the technical problems of playing the instrument. Carl Flesch complained (1923) about the 'little-known history of violin playing', and rightly so, although he did not sufficiently appreciate the reasons for its being little known. Naturally, some of the reasons are obvious enough. The discouraging lack of sources, for instance, particularly in early times, is the first hurdle that the investigator in this field encounters. However, the source material is more ample than might be supposed at first glance; and, among other things, iconography has only recently been properly utilized and its importance appreciated as a primary source of investigation.

The basic reasons for the 'little-known history of violin playing' are concerned rather with attitude and method than with sources. The important question is often 'why' rather than 'what', and the reason for a thing will frequently include the fact of it, but rarely vice versa. In my opinion, the only proper way to approach the 'why' of our subject is through an organic study of the violin as an instrument, the music written for it, and the questions germane to playing it. All these matters are related in one degree or another, and they are mutually illuminating because this is how they happened. We cannot possibly understand the technical details of playing an instrument unless we understand the physical facts of the instrument and the aesthetic conventions that govern the music and musical expression at any given time. Specifically, the articulation of a Vivaldi concerto cannot be understood without a knowledge of the instrument and bow of the time. The long-model Stradivari violin is a mysterious experiment unless we understand the contemporary history of the violin sonata and concerto. And so on. At the same time, I do not mean to deny the importance of the 'what' of facts; I insist only on their proper and organic relation to the context that gives them meaning. To obey the direction to play *staccato* meant something quite different to an eigtheenth-century violinist than it does today, and to play *staccato* with an eighteenth-century violin and bow is still another consideration. In sum the book sets out to give the details of the technique of the violin at any given time and an account of the instrument, bow, and the music which violin technique serves and illuminates.

The book is divided into four main parts of roughly fifty years each, and the chapters within each of these parts are devoted successively to the violin itself, the music, and technical matters of playing the violin. Fifty-year periods seemed to be long enough divisions to show clear developments and changes, and short enough to maintain a certain uniformity of musical style and technical procedure. However, it goes without saying that these periods have to be considered as approximations.

The title makes clear that these periods extend only to the middle of the eighteenth century. The material has proved so much more extensive than I originally expected that it seemed wise at this time to present a history of violin playing only to 1761. This is the date of L'Abbé le fils's treatise, a date as convenient as any to distinguish the period of the 'old' from that of the modern (Tourte) bow. It is a date which also serves to mark the gradual decline of the Italian school of violin playing and the gradual assumption of leadership on the part of the French.

This book does not set out to be a history of the violin or of violin music —only to serve in this respect as a précis of significant developments in these subjects in relation to violin playing. Similarly, general musical matters are discussed only to the extent that the performance of violin music is concerned. On the other hand, the book does intend to be a history of violin playing in the comprehensive sense just outlined. In this respect, it is, as far as I know, the first book of its kind in any language,[1] and if it serves its intended purpose, this in itself will repay the endless labour of gathering and

---

[1] Andreas Moser's splendid achievement, *Geschichte des Violinspiels* (Berlin, 1923), is basically a history of violin music, not a history of violin playing in the sense of the present book. With the possible exception of the first section, Moser's account would be of no real assistance to a violinist or conductor seeking information about the performance of violin music. A number of other excellent studies deal with various

ordering the material—a process that has required more than a dozen years since the project was conceived.

Its purpose is to supply the kind of information just mentioned to those who need it. Who they may be I cannot tell, but I hope among them will be violinists, conductors, musicians generally, scholars, and those interested in music who somehow have ventured with curiosity into the fascinating, arcane, and baffling world of the violin. The audience for a book of this sort cannot be predicted, and I have written it with no particular audience in mind, trying merely to present the material as lucidly as the subject allows. A majority of the statements are documented from original sources, and a large number of musical and visual illustrations have been included to make my points more vivid than any written description could. A number of quotations are cited in the original language and in English translation. The latter are the author's unless otherwise attributed.

A difficult problem of presentation and organization is implicit in my definitions and approach to the history of violin playing. In effect, a way had to be found to describe the development of three different subjects, showing at the same time the organic relations between them. The method finally chosen involves allotting chapters to each of the subjects and connecting them and demonstrating their relationships in introductions and summaries to chapters and parts. This method admittedly has the defects of its virtues. The material is presented systematically within parts and chapters, so that it would be possible for an interested reader to trace (for example) the whole history of the bow by reading the parts concerned with the bow in successive chapters. The principal defect of our plan of organization is a certain amount of repetition, since the same material is sometimes considered in three different contexts, namely that of the violin maker, the composer, and the player. This redundancy, if it is that, is deliberate; and it is actually more apparent than real. By analogy the situation is comparable to the difference the same object undergoes on the stage when illuminated successively by strongly contrasted lights.

A book of this kind must also take into account that it may be used as a work of reference and also (let us hope) that it may be read as a whole. The plan of the book as a complete and continuous narrative has just been explained. To facilitate random consultation and quick reference, considerable pains have been taken. The index is very detailed and it is descriptive. The glossary is an adjunct of the index, and no technical word occurs in the book which cannot be located and defined through the index.

---

specialized phases of the subject, notably Lionel de La Laurencie's *L'École Française de Violon* (3 vols., Paris, 1922–4), and Gustav Beckmann's *Das Violinspiel in Deutschland vor 1700* (Leipzig, 1918), a monograph limited in coverage but admirable in content and method.

Another aim of the index is to permit the reader to find terms in their historical meaning. In short, through the index the meanings of such terms as *tremolo* and *staccato* at any given time can be located immediately. The definition of terms according to historical usage is a feature of this book, and one that has long been needed. I should be the first to admit that terminology is dull stuff as continuous reading, but it is vital information for the man who needs it. Moreover, terminology is often a clue to the change, status, evolution, and inherent character of instruments and the technique of playing them.

The copious cross-references should also prove useful. Their considerable number and the repetition of dates are justified by the usefulness to readers taken as a whole, no matter how such devices may strike readers of the continuous narrative.

While this book attempts to do much, there are some things that it does very little, if at all. Rightly or wrongly, there is very little about folk 'fiddling', and there is almost nothing about the scientific aspects of the acoustics of the violin. Moreover, the book does not attempt to say how the violin music of earlier times should be played today, only to reconstruct as far as possible how it was played through hints of past technical practices, instruments, bows, and attitudes toward expression.

In a matter as subtle and evanescent as the making of music, written accounts can, at best, give a feeble idea of actual performance. Yet hints from the sources often establish how violin music was *not* played and still other sources give us valuable clues as to how it *was* played. Whatever virtue this book may have in general, the information in these pages will be artistically valuable in the degree that it strikes a responsive chord in players today. Naturally what a player does with the information is his own concern. In the last analysis, it will come down to the age-old question as to how far a musician today can and ought to perform violin music of the past according to the intention of the composer. This question, if it becomes a question, must be answered by every performing artist in his own way. To try to bridge the gap between the old and the new, I have contributed a last chapter of practical hints embodying my own thoughts on the subject. These hints have been supplemented by the phonograph recording, included with the book, which illustrates the sound of the 'old' as compared to the modern violin and demonstrates the probable solution to various technical questions. A number of the musical examples in the body of the book have been used for this purpose.

A WORD ON FINGERING AND NOTATION

Violin fingering is indicated in the usual manner: o = open string, 1 = the index finger (not the thumb as in piano fingering).

Where it is consistent with clarity, the pitch of individual notes has been indicated by a letter scheme in common use:

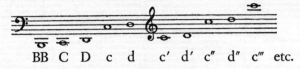

BB C D c d   c' d' c" d" c'" etc.

Under this scheme the notes of the violin tuning are then represented as g d' a' e".

Note to the Third Impression

THIS reprinting of *The History of Violin Playing* incorporates a substantial number of additions and corrections—in fact, as many as it is possible to make within the original pagination and without a new edition. The reprinting of 1967 included corrections of those inevitable typographical and other small errors that were immediately discernible when the book first appeared in 1965.

Besides typographical and simple errors, an author must contend with noticing and incorporating new research and interpretations. In the nine years since the first edition was published, an impressive amount of research has been undertaken by a number of persons either in the specific area of the violin or in the more general field of the performance of music before 1800. Some of this research has appeared in books and articles, and some of it is still in progress or has not yet appeared in published form. To cite two instances in the area of unpublished research, I venture to predict that within ten years we will know much more than we do now about the origins of the violin and the evolution of the bow. Obviously, this third printing can incorporate very little of this new material, published or unpublished, except when the changes are minor and can be effected without a change in pagination. In short, a complete account of this new material must await some future second edition of *The History of Violin Playing*. Nevertheless, the additions and corrections of detail in this third printing are very considerable.

The favourable reception of the book since its first publication has been the source of much gratification to me, and I trust that the changes of detail incorporated in this third printing will make the book more accurate, up-to-date, and useful, within the limitations mentioned.

David D. Boyden
Berkeley
July 26, 1974

Acknowledgements

IT goes without saying that a large project is hardly ever accomplished single-handed, and this history of violin playing is no exception. Many individuals have helped me more than I can say with information, advice, and criticism; and I have been supported and encouraged over a period of years by research grants from various sources, including the University of California at Berkeley, the Guggenheim Memorial Foundation (1954-5), and the Fulbright Commission, whose grant to Oxford (1963) aided me in the final stages of the work.

I am especially grateful to professional violinists and firms of violin dealers and makers who have interested themselves in the subject. In particular, Sol Babitz has provided me with an immense amount of information and violinistic stimulation, so to speak, over a period of years; and, although we have not always agreed, I owe several basic ideas to his acute perception. I am grateful to him also for making the drawing incorporated in Fig. 5. Kenneth Skeaping has contributed numerous ideas concerning the subject in many discussions and letters over the past ten years—an association I greatly prize and remember with the greatest pleasure. Alan Loveday's work with me on a recording to be issued as an adjunct to this book has added new dimensions to my knowledge. At various times, I have consulted and been helped by Robert Gross, Sidney Griller, Sandor Salgo, Joseph Szigeti, the late Louise Rood, Gilbert Ross, the late Philip Burton, Jack O'Brien, and Yfrah Neaman. The firm of W. E. Hill and Sons in London has given me the benefit of its enormous experience and expert knowledge and, together with the officials of the Ashmolean Museum at Oxford, has granted me complete access to the Hill Collection of Stringed Instruments in the Ashmolean—a collection that includes marvellous violins by Stradivari and three generations of the Amati family, among others. The late Rembert Wurlitzer of New York generously contributed photographs of several important instruments, as acknowledged in the plates. The firm of J. N. Aschow of Oakland has also helped me at various times.

I wish to thank Professors Joseph Kerman and Daniel Heartz, my colleagues in the Music Department of the University of California, for reading and criticizing part of the manuscript. Denis Stevens, while Visiting Professor at Berkeley in 1962, read part of the manuscript, and later all of it, with the most careful attention to detail. Robert Donington has read all the manuscript in various stages of its evolution, and I am grateful for his criticism and encouragement. Professor Vincent Duckles, head of the Music Library at the University of California, and his staff (especially Harriet Nicewonger and Minnie Elmer) have done me many favours; and I realize more and more vividly, particularly when I am *in absentia*, the remarkable qualities of the library which Vincent Duckles heads and the many services it performs efficiently and unobtrusively. Roger Levenson and Philip Lilienthal have also devoted time and energy to reading and criticizing the manuscript. Juergen Schulz, Professor of Art at the University of California, has aided me substantially in matters of iconography. For some years M. Marc Pincherle of Paris has responded generously to my requests for his expert advice.

Among a number of research assistants who have performed those endless tasks of searching and checking, I should single out Mrs. Sydney Charles, whose contribution in the field of iconography gave me invaluable clues to the early history of the violin. The last stages of the book were accelerated and bettered by the devoted help of Keith Polk, Jane Bowers, Ellen Amsterdam, Arthur Hills, James Jackman, and Jane Troy Johnson; and briefly, at Oxford, of Christopher Field.

Not least, the secretarial staff of the Music Department of the University of California has contributed so generously of time and typing that I can only hope to acknowledge some small measure of my appreciation by mentioning the long-continued help and association of Helen Farnsworth, Peggy Kauffman, and Jane Imamura.

Lastly, my wife and family have endured it all, but I think they would prefer me to pass over these trials in silence. And I shall.

Berkeley
November 1964

Contents

PREFACE   v

ACKNOWLEDGEMENTS   xi

LIST OF PLATES   xxi

LIST OF FIGURES   xxiv

Part One: The Formative Period, 1520-1600

General introduction   2

I. THE ORIGIN AND DEVELOPMENT OF THE EARLY VIOLIN, 1520-50   6

The early violin. Dates and places of origin. Gaudenzio Ferrari's
   paintings   7
Ancestors: rebec, Renaissance fiddle, *lira da braccio*. The role of the
   viols. Terms   8
Did the viola precede the violin?   15
The 'inventor' of the violin   17
Chronological review of the evidence. Treatises. Historical, political,
   and linguistic questions. Terms   21
Summary   30

II. THE ADVENT OF THE TRUE VIOLIN AND ITS DEVELOPMENT TO 1600   31

The true violin described by Jambe de Fer. Detailed description 31
The emergence of Cremona and Brescia as centres of violin making.
   Andrea Amati, Gasparo da Salò, and G. P. Maggini. Violins shown
   in painting   34
Export of Italian violins to other countries   38
Violin making outside Italy: France. Germany. Poland. Spain. England 39
Treatises. Terminology   42
The violin bow in the sixteenth century   45
Summary   46

III. VIOLIN MUSIC IN THE SIXTEENTH CENTURY   49

The musical functions of the violin   50
The dearth of written violin music   51
The role of the violin in dancing and accompanying voices   52
Instrumental forms. The *canzona*   53
Use of the violin in France. *Le ballet comique de la reine* (1581)   54
In England: records of the court, towns, and private households 57
In Italy: accounts of the Duke of Savoy   59
In Germany: an account of a ducal wedding   61

IV. HOW THE VIOLIN SOUNDED AND HOW IT WAS
PLAYED IN THE SIXTEENTH CENTURY   65

Different methods of playing. The corresponding sound   65
How the violin was played in the sixteenth century   71
Holding the violin and bow   73
Tone, The bow stroke. Ganassi's information. Down-bow and up-bow   77
Pizzicato   84
Fingering. Positions. Shifting   84
Improvisation   89
Multiple stops   90
Expression, including vibrato and dynamics   91
Summary   92

*Part Two: The Development of an Idiomatic
Technique, 1600-1650*

Introduction. Social, political, and artistic conditions. Their impact on
the violin   98

V. THE DEVELOPMENT OF THE VIOLIN AND BOW
IN THE EARLY SEVENTEENTH CENTURY   107

The progress of the violin. Maggini. The Amatis. Details of the
violin and its fittings   107
The bow   111
The violin family as a whole. Terminology   115
Increasing usage of the violin. Its effect on rebec and viol   119

VI. THE NEW VIOLIN IDIOM. VIOLIN MUSIC AND
ITS USES IN DIFFERENT COUNTRIES, 1600–50   121

The implications of the term 'idiom'   121
The development of a new violin idiom   125
Violin music and its uses, 1600–50. The sonata and other forms   126
Contributions of various countries: Italy. Marini   134
Germany   136
France   136
England   138
Other countries   143

VII. THE TECHNIQUE AND SOUND OF THE VIOLIN
IN THE EARLY SEVENTEENTH CENTURY   145

The relation between technique, music, and instrument making   145
The dance style and the sonata style of playing. National styles   147
Holding the violin and bow. The French and Italian bow grips   152
The technique of the left hand: fingering, positions, and shifting   153
The technique of the right hand: bowing and bow strokes   156

Contents

The formation of a bowing discipline in Italy and elsewhere. The
   Rule of Down-Bow. Zannetti 157
Individual bow strokes. Slurring. Francesco Rognoni 163
Borrowing of technique. Multiple stops 166
Special indications: *Tremolo. Affetti* 170
Col legno. Pizzicato 171
The sound of the violin in the early seventeenth century 172

VIII. GENERAL MATTERS AFFECTING THE VIOLIN TO 1650

 175

Ornaments 175
The vibrato 177
Dynamics and expression 178
Rhythm and tempo 180
Pitch. Intonation systems 185
Summary 187

Part Three: The National Schools of the Late Seventeenth Century. The Rise of Virtuosity

Introduction 192

IX. THE DEVELOPMENT OF THE VIOLIN AND BOW, 1650–1700

 194

The influence of Nicola Amati and Stainer 194
Antonio Stradivari (early works). The 'long' model 197
Other makers 198
Details of the seventeenth-century violin. The Talbot manuscript 199
Material and thickness of string. Pitch. Tension. Volume of sound ... 203
The bow. The 'Stradivari' bow 206
Summary 210

X. THE VIOLIN MUSIC OF THE LATE SEVENTEENTH-CENTURY

 212

Introduction: types of music and ideas of expression 212
Contributions of different countries: Italy 216
  Areas of activity. Composers 216
  The Bologna School. G. B. Vitali 218
  Corelli. Works and influence 220
Germany 223
  Biber. Walther 223
  Their music and technique 224
  The *scordatura* 226
France 227
  Lully's use of the violin in dances and the opera 229
  French violinists and the guild system 229

England   229
  The French influence of the Restoration of Charles II. Influx of
    German and Italian violinists, including Baltzar and Matteis   229
  The fancy. John Jenkins   233
  Dances. The variation. *The Division-Violin*   234
  Baltzar as a player   235
  Matteis as a player and composer   236
  Purcell's trio sonatas   237
  Other countries   239

XI. THE TECHNIQUE OF THE VIOLIN, 1650–1700
(I): NATIONAL STYLES OF PLAYING. THE
TREATISES. THE LEFT HAND   241

Introduction. National styles of playing   241
The violin treatises. The rise of the amateur violinist and its consequences 244
The technique of the violin. Tuning the violin   247
Holding the violin   247
Holding the bow   248
The left hand: fingering, positions, and shifting. Rules for the *scordatura* 249
Terms for shifting. Extensions   251

XII. THE TECHNIQUE OF THE VIOLIN, 1650–1700
(II): THE RIGHT HAND AND RELATED
QUESTIONS. THE SOUND OF THE VIOLIN   253

Bowing. The bow stroke   253
Nuanced and sustained bow strokes. Bremner quoted on Corelli's practice   254
The discipline of bowing. The Rule of Down-Bow   256
Muffat and French dances. Terms   257
Types of bowing and their execution: syncopated bowings, *ondeggiando*,
  bariolage, the slurred *tremolo*   262
Multiple stops, their notation and performance   271
The *pizzicato*. Special effects   277
Instrumentation and the ensemble. 'Conducting'   278
The sound of the violin about 1700   281

XIII. GENERAL MATTERS AFFECTING THE VIOLIN,
1650–1700   285

Ornaments   285
The vibrato   287
Improvisation   288
Dynamics   290
Rhythm and tempo   292
Alterations of rhythm: 294
  Lengthening of dotted figures   295
  Alteration of dotted and other figures in the context of triplets 296
  Notes inégales   303
Summary   306

Part Four : The Culmination of the Early History of Violin Playing, 1700-1761

Introduction: the 'evolution of progress' theory. A summary view
of the violin   312

XIV. THE VIOLIN AND BOW OF THE EARLY EIGHTEENTH CENTURY   317

Antonio Stradivari (maturity and old age)   317
The Guarneri family   318
Other makers   318
Details of the violin and its fittings   319
Other members of the violin family. Terminology   323
The bow. Its evolution. François Tourte and the modern bow   324
Summary   329

XV. THE VIOLIN MUSIC OF THE EARLY EIGHTEENTH CENTURY   331

The development of the violin concerto. The *concerto grosso* and solo
concerto   331
The sonata. The variation. Program music   336
The development of the violin idiom   338
Contributions of individual countries   341
Italy: Vivaldi. Veracini. Tartini   341
France: Leclair. Mondonville. Guillemain   344
Germany: J. S. Bach   348
England: Geminiani. Handel. Ariosti   350
Other countries: Sweden. Holland (Locatelli). Switzerland. Poland. Spain 352
Publication, performance, and patronage   354

XVI. THE TECHNIQUE OF THE VIOLIN, 1700–61 (I): THE TREATISES. HOLDING THE VIOLIN AND BOW. THE LEFT HAND   356

Violin treatises, 1700–61   357
The treatises as prototypes: Geminiani, Leopold Mozart, and L'Abbé le fils 364
How the violin was played   366
Conventions of notation   366
Holding the violin. Tuning the violin. Intonation systems   367
Holding the bow   371
The left hand. Fingering   374
Positions, shifting, and the fingerings involved   376
Terminology   378
Shifting   379
Extensions and contractions   381
Harmonics. Combination tones   384
The vibrato   386
Terminology of the vibrato   389

XVII. THE TECHNIQUE OF THE VIOLIN, 1700–61
(II): THE RIGHT HAND. THE BOW STROKE
AND BOW CHANGE. THE RULE OF DOWN-
BOW   391

The bow stroke. The beginning and ending   392
Sol Babitz's theory of the *messa di voce* stroke   393
Leopold Mozart's 'Divisions'   394
How the bow stroke was made. The bow change. Power and tone 397
Bow strokes in general. The Rule of Down-Bow   400
Terminology and signs   403

XVIII. THE TECHNIQUE OF THE VIOLIN, 1700–61
(III): BOW STROKES AND THEIR EXECUTION   404

Introduction. Relation of bowing to the character of the music   404
The individual bow stroke   405
Slurred bowings   407
The violin staccato in the early eighteenth century   408
Terms   408
Signs: dots, strokes, wedges   410
The performance of the individual (unslurred) staccato note   411
Slurred staccato, including 'lifted' bow   416
Slurred *tremolo*, legato and staccato   422
Mixed bowings   424
Vivaldi's bowings and terms   424

XIX. THE TECHNIQUE OF THE VIOLIN, 1700–61
(IV): MULTIPLE STOPS. THE 'BACH' BOW.
SPECIAL EFFECTS. INSTRUMENTATION AND
CONDUCTING. THE SOUND OF THE VIOLIN   427

Double stops   428
Triple and quadruple stops. Their notation   429
The 'Bach' bow, a modern invention. Schering and Schweitzer   431
Multiple stops in actual practice   435
Arpeggios   438
Slurring   441
Special effects, including the *pizzicato*   443
Instrumentation and conducting   445
The sound of the violin in the early eighteenth century   447

XX. SPECIFIC AND IMPROVISED ORNAMENTS. THE
CADENZA   449

The trill   450
The mordent   453
The appoggiatura   455
Improvised ornaments   457
The cadenza   461
Terms. The cadenza in Tartini and Locatelli   464

Contents

XXI. TEMPO. ALTERATIONS OF RHYTHM.
DYNAMICS. EXPRESSION   467

Time signatures. Tempo terms. The 'inherent' tempo   467
Tempo rubato   470
Alterations of rhythm   472
   Notes inégales. Quantz quoted   472
   Double (or triple) dotting   478
   Alterations of dotted and other figures in the context of triplets   482
Dynamics: loud, soft, and the shades between   484
Aesthetics of expression. The *Affetto*   490

XXII. PRACTICAL HINTS TO MODERN VIOLINISTS   495

Introduction: the approach to the performance of old music. The intuitive
   approach. Following the composer's intentions   495
The old violin and the old bow   496
The kind of sound to be produced   497
The bow and bowing   497
Position and fingering   500
Altering the modern violin. Reducing tension   500
Holding the violin   502
Other factors, technical and musical, including expression   502

APPENDIX. Stradivari's birthday   505

BIBLIOGRAPHY   509

GLOSSARY   525

INDEX   531

Plates

(*All, except the Frontispiece, to be found between pages 120 and 121.*)

Frontispiece

The first known painting of the violin. *The Madonna of the Orange Trees* (1529–30) by Gaudenzio Ferrari.

1. The component parts of the modern violin.

2. The violin family: violin (left centre), cello, and viola. Detail of a fresco (1535–6) by Gaudenzio Ferrari in the cupola of Saronno Cathedral.

3a. Two views of a rebec. Modern reproduction by Arnold Dolmetsch (1930).

3b. Angel playing the Renaissance fiddle. Medallion by Memling, *c.* 1500.

4. Two views of a *lira da braccio* made in Venice by Giovanni Maria of Brescia, *c.* 1525.

5. Lady playing a treble viol. A painting by Casper Netscher (1639–84).

6. Neck and fingerboard of the 'old' violin (above) compared to those of the modern violin (below).

7a. A viola by Gasparo da Salò of Brescia, late 16th century.

7b. A viola by Andrea Amati of Cremona (1574), made for Charles IX of France.

8. Detail of the violin and bow from *The Lute Player*, a painting by Oratio Gentileschi (1565–1640?).

9. A portrait of Duiffoprugcar by Woeriot (1562), showing various stringed instruments, none of which is a true violin.

10. A violin in a Spanish painting. *The Death of St. Hermenengeld* by Juan de Roelas (1560–1625).

11. Violin and bow. Detail from *Love as Conqueror*, a painting by Michelangelo da Carravaggio (*c.* 1573–*c.* 1610).

12. A violin and bow (upper left) in a painting *The Madonna* (*c.* 1620) by G. F. Barbieri ('Il Guercino').

13. Dancing *La Volta* accompanied by a string band. A ball at the Valois Court *c.* 1581 (painting in the museum at Rennes).

14. Dancing *La Volta*. Strings at the left (painting at Penshurst Place, Kent).

15. Orlando Lasso surrounded by instrumentalists and singers of the chapel of the Duke of Bavaria at Munich. From a codex (1565–70) illuminated by Hans Mielich.

16. A sketch by Lodovico Caracci (1555–1619), showing the violin and bow grip. Left-handed(!) player, upper right. Tuning the violin with the the right hand(!), extreme right.

17. The violin and bow in a light moment. *The Prodigal Son*, a painting by Dirck van Baburen (*c*. 1590–*c*. 1624).

18. The 'Doria' violin by G. P. Maggini (1580–*c*. 1632).

19. Detail of a violin from a painting by Evaristo Baschenis (1617–77).

20. *The Concert*, an engraving by Picart after a painting by Domenichino (early 17th century).

21. Violin and bow, showing the thumb-under-hair bow-grip. *St. Cecilia* by Bernardo Cavallino (1616–56).

22. Violinist playing in French style. Lithograph of a painting by Gerard Dou dated 1665.

23. A violinist with lutanist and singer(s). An ensemble painted by an unknown Italian of the 17th century (National Museum, Prague).

24. *Vanitas*, still life, showing the violin, by Jacques Grief de Claew (working 1642–76).

25a. Nicola Amati's 'grand' model violin (*The Goding*, 1662).

25b. 'Long' model violin (1693) by Antonio Stradivari.

26. Profile view of old and new violin:

(a) Violin by Jacob Stainer, 1668. Original condition, except for pegs and bridge (and probably fingerboard), all of which, however, have been reproduced in appropriate style. Note the short fingerboard with wedge and the straight neck, which is slightly shorter and thicker than the modern one. Observe also the rapid rise of the arching of the top and the clear view through the sound holes.

(b) Modern violin by J. B. Vuillaume, Paris, 1867 (Stradivari model). Modern elongated fingerboard, no wedge, tilted and narrowed neck, which is mortised into the upper block. Compare the flatter top and back of the Vuillaume with the Stainer.

27. Two views of the bridge of Stradivari's 'Tuscan' viola compared with a modern viola bridge.

28a. A 'Stradivari' bow (*c*. 1700) and (below) a Tourte bow (*c*. 1800).

28b. Detail, showing the nut end of the two bows.

29a. Mechanism of the 'dentated' ('crémaillère') bow.

29b. The slot-and-notch (or clip-in) bow.

29c. Mechanism of the modern bow.

29d. Detail of a bow dated 1694 (cf. Plate 38a).

30. F. M. Veracini playing the violin. Frontispiece to his *Sonate accademiche*, Op. 2 (1744).

31. French violinist. Frontispiece to Corrette's *L'École d'Orphée* (1738).

32. French violinist (playing pizzicato?). From Denis Gaultier's *Rhétorique des Dieux* (c. 1650).

33a. The 'Betts' violin (1704) by Antonio Stradivari.

33b. A violin by Joseph Guarneri del Gesù (1737). Formerly called the 'King Joseph', this violin is known today as the 'Hawley Joseph'.

34. Internal construction of the 'Betts' Stradivari violin: nails in the top block, blocks and linings, bass bar compared to the modern bass bar.

35. Sequence of bows, purporting to represent the development of the bow from Mersenne to Viotti.

36. Frontispiece to Geminiani's *L'Art du Violon* (Paris, 1752(?)).

37. German violinist from J. C. Weigel's *Musikalisches Theatrum* (c. 1720).

38. Stages in the evolution of the bow stick, head, and nut, 1694–c. 1800 (numbering from the top to the bottom):
   (a) Bow dated 1694 (detail given in Plate 29d.)
   (b) Bow by Thomas Smith (d. 1789), probably made between 1760 and 1770.
   (c) Bow by Tourte *père*, c. 1770–80.
   (d) Bow by François Tourte, c. 1800.

39a. Frontispiece of Leopold Mozart's *Violinschule* (1756).

39b. Leopold Mozart playing the violin under his chin (*Violinschule*, Fig. II)

40a. The modern Bach bow.

40b. Compared to the 17th-century French bow and bow grip.

Figures

1. A string quartet of famous personages (1516).   13
2. Places important in the early history of the violin, showing their relation to capital cities.   27
3. Bow with incipient head. Bow and *lira da braccio* suspended by nails from the wall. From Augurellus, *Carmina* (1491).   47
4. Violin and bow and pochette and bow from Mersenne's 'Harmonie Universelle' (1636-7).   113
5. Shifting by 'crawling' downward.   155
6. Bow and bow grip explained. From Corrette's 'L'École d'Orphée' (1738).   372
7. Bow grips from Leopold Mozart's 'Violinschule'. Fig. V shows the faulty grip ('der Fehler').   373

Grateful acknowledgement is due to the following for permission to reproduce photographs and paintings.

Ampliacions y Reproducciones Mas (plate 10)
Ashmolean Museum, Oxford (plates 4, 7a, 7b, 24)
Duits Ltd. (plate 5)
Fratelli Alinari, Florence (frontispiece and plate 2)
W. E. Hill & Sons (plates 6, 25b, 27, 34)
Museum of Fine Arts, Boston (plate 21)
National Gallery of Art, Washington, D.C. (Ailsa Mellon Bruce Fund) (plate 8)
Penguin Books Ltd. (plates 26, 29a, 29b, and their captions)
Publications de la Société française de musicologie (plate 32)
Plate 1 is based on a drawing which originally appeared in the *Scientific American*.

PART ONE

The Formative Period
1520-1600

'And since everyone knows about the violin family, it is unnecessary to indicate or write anything further about it.'

MICHAEL PRAETORIUS,
Syntagma Musicum, 1619, Vol. II, Part II, Chapter XXII.

The Formative Period, 1520-1600

PRAETORIUS wrote the passage just quoted more than three centuries ago, but even at that early time he considered it a waste of time to dwell on a subject as well known as the violin. What everyone knew then, nobody knows now; and today Praetorius's remark makes astonishing and exasperating reading. The early history of the violin and violin playing is veiled by numerous mysteries and obscurities, and in the hindsight of history his well-intentioned brevity has proved penny-wise and pound-foolish. Had he passed on his detailed knowledge of the sixteenth-century violin, oceans of ink and countless hours spent in research might have been saved in the intervening centuries. Although Praetorius could not have described the sound of the violin except in subjective and general terms, his testimony about the construction of the instrument, the music composed for it, and how it was played would be of immense value today. Since his time much has been written about the violin, particularly on its origins and a few well-known makers, but in spite of considerable investigation, relatively little is known about violin music or violin playing before 1600.

The fact is that there are definite limits to what can be discovered about the music and technique of the violin in the sixteenth century—a situation implicit in the state of instrumental music then. Before 1600 only a fraction of the music actually played by instruments was specifically designated for them. Much of the time the instruments were simply doubling vocal parts— that is, accompanying the voices by playing the same notes as the singers— and no separate instrumental parts were made. The amount of music written solely and specifically for instruments was small, and the technical development of the instrumental idiom was relatively limited and unexploited, with the exception of certain pieces for lutes, viols, and keyboards. The principal efforts of the best composers in the sixteenth century were lavished on vocal pieces for the church or chamber: on motets, chorales, anthems, madrigals, chansons, *Lieder*, and the like. For the most part these pieces were considered the common property of any voice or instrument that could perform them, and consequently a substantial part of the music which instruments were called upon to play was basically vocal in character. Instruments which doubled the vocal parts had no independent life, they were employed as additional 'voices' to reinforce the ensemble, and the idiomatic capabilities of the instruments were not considered. In short, where instruments were used as an adjunct to vocal music, no independent body of instrumental music existed and instrumental technique as such did not develop.

Still, the beginning of purely instrumental music and an instrumental idiom *per se* may be traced in the sixteenth century and much earlier. The practice of doubling voices by instruments led naturally to independent instrumental forms derived from vocal models. However, such resulting sixteenth-century forms as the *canzona* were not at first truly independent in *style*. While these forms used no voices in performance, the style of the music clearly betrayed its vocal origin. In short, the idiom was seldom instrumental in character, and the music made no pronounced demands on the technical capacity of individual instruments. For examples of idiomatic instrumental music we must look to occasional preludes, toccatas, and variations written for the lute, viol, or keyboard instruments. Sometimes treatises devoted specific attention to the instrumental idiom. Diego Ortiz's *Tratado* (1553), for instance, explained the manner of playing 'divisions' on the viol, these divisions being more or less elaborate instrumental figurations improvised around a given part or melody.

The early history of the violin must be considered against this background of a great choral tradition and a written instrumental music that was oriented in part to vocal music. The violin probably originated in the third decade of the sixteenth century, corresponding in time to the death of Josquin and the birth of Palestrina; and throughout this formative period of its history the violin family undoubtedly shared in the general practice of doubling vocal music. This in turn explains why a substantial amount of music played on the violin never emerged (and never can emerge) as violin music, and why the technique of the violin, when confined to vocal doubling, remained undeveloped. However, the instruments of the violin family were used as much, if not more, in dance music, as contemporary accounts and iconography make clear. If the violin was used idiomatically in the sixteenth century, as is likely, it must have been in dance music. But since very little of this music was written out or has survived before 1600, further research on this point cannot be pursued very far—certainly not to a decisive conclusion.

The affinity of the violin for dance music may be attributed mainly to its power of rhythmic articulation and to its penetrating, sprightly tone. These features of the new violin explain its general use for dancing, embracing the whole social gamut from the village fete to such Court functions as the French ballet, the English masque, and the Italian *intermedio*. The earliest extant music specifically for the violin dates from 1581, and characteristically this music was written for dancing at a royal wedding in France (see p. 55). Only the greatness of the occasion was sufficient to inspire a written record of the whole affair, which included dance music in passing. But even in this music, specifically composed for violins, the *written* notes call for nothing especially idiomatic to the instrument or technically demanding of it. Possibly these and similar pieces were performed in more complicated ways in the *unwritten* tradition of improvisation, following the example of the viol and other instruments.

The limited fund of information about the sixteenth-century violin and violin playing may also be due in part to its low social position. It was, to be sure, a well-known and popular instrument, as Praetorius implies (1619); and by his time the violin must have been in existence for nearly a century, its popularity being explained by its favoured position in dancing and in the theatre. Nevertheless, it was hardly a respectable instrument, occupying a musical and social position analogous to the saxophone today—also an instrument of relatively recent origin (*c.* 1840), associated mainly with dance music. For the most part, reputable people and musicians in the sixteenth century thought of violins as instruments of lowly origin played mainly by professionals. In comparison, viols and lutes, both belonging to an older and more aristocratic tradition, were played not only by professionals but also by amateurs and gentlemen, who ardently admired these instruments. To play the viol or especially the lute was considered an admissible, even highly desirable, part of the general education of the well-born; and these instruments enjoyed a vogue among persons of social standing, who as amateurs generally regarded music as a commendable avocation, but not as a proper profession. The violin enjoyed none of this social prestige, a point already made clear in the earliest specific account of the violin, written by Jambe de Fer in 1556:

'We call viols those with which gentlemen, merchants, and other virtuous people pass their time . . . The other type is called violin; it is commonly used for dancing . . . I have not illustrated the said violin because you can think of it as resembling the viol, added to which there are few persons who use it save those who make a living from it through their labour.'[1]

The violin, in short, was barely respectable from a social point of view, and compared to the lute, viol, or organ (the instrument of the church), it had practically no musical or social prestige at all. It was regarded as the common instrument of dance music with all the attendant disparaging associations, and it was played largely by professionals who earned 'their living by it' and who were regarded socially as servants.

The musical and social facts of the sixteenth century help to explain the scarcity of written violin music and its elementary technical character—a situation the violin shared with many other instruments of the time. In the sixteenth century the basically neutral and non-idiomatic treatment of the violin and the lack of written music for it prevent our seeing immediately

[1] Philibert Jambe de Fer, *Epitome musical*, Lyon, 1556, pp. 62–63. The full quotation is given below on p. 31.

the potentially close relationship between the evolution of the instrument, its music, and its technique—a relationship that becomes strikingly evident after 1600, when the capabilities of the instrument were exploited in an increasingly idiomatic written violin music. Obviously, what the composer, the violinist, and the violin maker did as individuals depended on the efforts, capabilities, and demands of each other. This mutual relationship, the importance of which has not been sufficiently appreciated, is not negated by the fact that it appears to have been only partly operative in the sixteenth century. In all probability the relationship between maker, player, and composer was actually much closer than is suggested by the available evidence. Whatever the truth may be, the chapters immediately following are devoted to what can be pieced together about the sixteenth-century violin, the music written for it, how it sounded, and how it was played. First we must know something about the origin and development of the instrument itself.

CHAPTER ONE

༄

The Origin and Development of the Early Violin 1520-50

MOST accounts of the 'inventor' of the violin and the precise date and place of its origin bog down in the quagmires of history and terminology. The earliest stages of the violin's emergence are obscured by a process of evolution from earlier instruments, and the date of origin depends on a somewhat arbitrary definition of what a violin is. What structural features must it have? How many strings? And so on. If, among other things, a violin is defined as having four strings, one approximate set of dates may be assigned to its origin; but if three strings will satisfy the definition, an earlier date may be given. However, even if the term *violin* is clearly defined, the date and place of origin can be determined only approximately, since not enough sixteenth-century violins have survived—indeed, only one or two before 1550—and the documentary evidence is scanty and often imprecise. Moreover, should all the instruments involved in the violin's evolution before 1550 still exist, the date and maker of each would be almost impossible to determine. For these reasons, one cannot say *precisely* where, when, and by whom the violin was invented.[1] Nevertheless, by means of a careful study of art objects, documents, and the few extant instruments of the early sixteenth century, these questions can be answered with sufficient clarity and accuracy for our purpose.

In tracing the ancestry and primary stages of the violin, one needs to distinguish the earliest forms of the violin from the 'true' violin. The principal features of the latter are shown and labelled in Plate 1—the violin as it exists today. An instrument embodying these traits, at least in basic forms, emerged about 1550. The earliest type of violin appeared not later than 1530. This differed from the true four-stringed violin by using only three strings (tuned to g d' a', corresponding to the pitches of the lowest three strings of the modern violin) and perhaps a smaller body. At any rate, the

[1] See Renzo Bacchetta, 'Chi inventò il violino?' in *Stradivari non è nato nel 1644*, Cremona, 1937.

existence of a violin of sorts can be established before any specific maker can be credited with having made a violin or before the date of manufacture fixed for any violin now extant.

The early violin. Dates and places of origin. Ancestors

The first indisputable evidence of the emergence of the violin and the violin family is found in paintings and frescoes by the Italian painter, Gaudenzio Ferrari (*c.* 1480–1546), in churches near Milan early in the sixteenth century. The earliest of these paintings, 'La Madonna degli aranci' ('Madonna of the orange trees') in the Church of St. Christopher in Vercelli, where Gaudenzio lived from 1529 to 1536, was painted about 1529–30. It shows a child playing one of these early violins, a small model of rather primitive outline and strung with three strings (see the Frontispiece). Another of Gaudenzio's paintings, in Sacro Monte at Varallo, depicts an angel-child playing a violin, an instrument larger and more developed than that at Vercelli.[2]

The most famous of these representations, however, is found in a large fresco painted in the cupola of Saronno Cathedral in 1535–6 (Plate 2). In this Gaudenzio depicts the three typical forms of the violin family: the treble (discant), alto-tenor, and bass. The discant member (violin) and the alto-tenor (viola) clearly have three tuning pegs and therefore three strings, and all three instruments have a scroll and the outline typical of the violin body.[3]

[2] For these paintings and their dates, see *Mostra di Gaudenzio Ferrari, April–June 1956, Vercelli, Museo Bergogna,* Milan, 1956. Although angels are shown playing the violin, this fact hardly raises the violin to angelic status. In sixteenth-century paintings (and especially earlier), angels are shown playing all sorts of instruments corresponding to medieval notions of the heavenly host. These conventions and representations have little to do with the actual social status of individual instruments or players. Shawms, drums, rebecs, and violins (among others) are all placed indiscriminately in the hands of angelic performers without regard to the great social discrepancy between lutes and viols on the one hand and violins on the other.

[3] As Plate 2 shows, the viola has three tuning peg-heads but, curiously, *four* peg-shanks within the pegbox, and the shanks do not align properly with the peg-heads. Emanuel Winternitz thinks that the presence of four shanks argues for four strings, and he attributes the lack of a fourth peg-head to shoddy perspective or a careless assistant (see Winternitz's article, 'The School of Gaudenzio Ferrari and the early History of the Violin,' note 7, in *The Commonwealth of Music, Writings . . . in Honor of Curt Sachs,* edited by Gustave Reese and Rose Brandel, New York, 1965). However, it is difficult to see how a fourth peg-head could be concealed by any kind of perspective, and a careless assistant can as well add a fourth shank as omit a fourth peg-head. The peg-heads in this viola are consistent in position and number with those in the Vercelli violin by the same painter (see our Frontispiece). It is also worth mentioning that the few theoretical sources of this time which deal with families of stringed instruments related to the violin's evolution allot three strings to the treble and alto-tenor members of the family. In any case, there is no doubt that the violin in the Saronno fresco has three tuning pegs (shanks fortunately concealed!). As to the cello, not all the peg-heads are visible, and therefore the number of peg-heads and strings cannot be determined.

The violin proper has a characteristic bulging back, the viola has f-holes, and the cello f-holes in reverse. Moreover, the violin and viola are apparently being played in third position, the violin perhaps in *pizzicato* fashion. The cello and viola bows are both being played overhand, and the little finger is braced under the bow-stick as in the French grip later on (see p. 75).

The paintings and fresco just mentioned prove that the early violin came into being not later than 1529–30 and that the three principal members of the violin family, including the viola and the cello, must have been 'invented' by 1535–6. Since these paintings are all found in churches in the neighbour-hood of Milan, it is reasonable to assume (although it does not necessarily follow) that the instruments shown originated in northern Italy and were seen there in daily life about 1530 by the painter. Who made the violins represented in Gaudenzio's work cannot be determined, although certain noted instrument-makers of the time are possibilities (see p. 17). In any case, the establishment of the *latest* date that can be assigned to the emergence of the early violin has important consequences.

This date now makes it possible or even plausible that such terms as *violino, violon* (Fr.), and *violetta*, when found about or after 1530, may actually mean 'violin', whereas previously a number of documents and treatises which used such terms in the early sixteenth century have been discounted as evidence of the existence of the violin (see p. 29 for terminology; for terms before 1520, see p. 20). Documents using these and similar terms occur not only in Italy but also in other countries, notably France. In particular, if the term *violon* truly means 'violin' (cf. p. 22), the violin was in existence in France as early as the first Gaudenzio violin paintings about 1530. However, the unambiguous evidence of Italian painting and still earlier Italian docu-ments give to northern Italy the strongest claim as the cradle of the violin and its family.

An account of the ancestry of the violin is not only a matter of great historical interest but it is also vital to an understanding of the principal constructional features and development of the violin and violin family, its musical uses, and technical questions of performance. The violin was not born of a single parent but evolved from several early in the sixteenth century: namely, the rebec, the Renaissance fiddle (G: *Fidel*) and the *lira da braccio* (Plates 3 and 4). It is significant that each contributing instrument gradually became obsolete on the advent of the true violin (*c.* 1550), which combined in one instrument and one family the musical and technical capacities previously distributed among several. Strangely enough, the viols contributed few, if any, features to the violin (see p. 14).

The long history of the ancestor instruments of the violin need not be given here, but a basic knowledge of their construction about 1500 is essen-tial to perceive the contributions each made to the new violin. The rebecs

(Plate 3), which date back to the thirteenth century at least,[4] were a family of instruments in the typical register of soprano (treble, discant), alto-tenor, and bass. The body was shaped like half a pear, and the neck and pegbox were integral parts of the body. There were no overhanging edges. In these respects the bodies of the rebec and violin had nothing in common. However, like the early violins, rebecs had three strings tuned in fifths and to the same notes (g d' a' for the soprano member); and, like the violin, the strings of the rebec were secured and tightened by pegs laterally inserted in the pegbox. The rebec was also played without frets and generally held at breast or neck. The bow was played overhand. Unlike the violin and *lira da braccio*, the rebec had no sound post, a lack that makes an appreciable difference in the quality of sound. To judge by reconstructed modern instruments, the tone of the rebec was somewhat smaller than the violin's, and it was pungent and penetrating, even raucous, with some of the nasal quality of the oboe.

As a rule, the Renaissance fiddle about 1500 had five strings (Plate 3b), one of which might be a drone (*bourdon*), not touched by the finger. In other respects it was similar to the violin, being in the soprano register, of comparable size, and constructed of a top and back with connecting ribs. It also had a separate neck and fingerboard, and it had frets as a rule. However, unlike the violin, it used front pegs in a heart- or leaf-shaped pegbox. The fiddle occurred in both oval and indented forms (guitar-fiddle), and some specimens of the latter type were constructed with the three distinct bouts of the violin. A similar instrument, the Wendish fiddle or *husla*, may also have contributed to the evolution of the violin. The home of the Wends was East Germany or the Slavic countries, and possibly this instrument was the 'Polish' fiddle referred to by Agricola.[5]

The *lira da braccio* (Plate 4), which evolved as a species of fiddle in the fifteenth century, was remarkably close in body outline to the violin, although its body varied in size from that of a small viola to a very large one.[6] Like the violin, the *lira da braccio* had an arched back and top, overlapping edges, ribs, and sound post. The Ashmolean *lira da braccio* has no bass

[4] For details of the history of the rebecs, see Nicholas Bessaraboff, *Ancient Musical Instruments*, Boston, 1941; and especially, H. Panum, *Stringed Instruments of the Middle Ages*, London [1939?].

[5] See p. 28. For a picture of this instrument, see Francis W. Galpin, *Old English Instruments of Music*, London, 1910, Plate 16, p. 84. Significantly, this instrument shown in Galpin has only three strings.

[6] Major Alexander Hajdecki, the first to point out the importance of the Italian *lira da braccio* as an ancestor of the violin (*Die italienische Lira da Braccio*, Mostar, 1892), possessed a *lira da braccio* whose body length was fifteen and a quarter inches (38.7 cm.), the size of a small viola. This instrument or its twin (the dimensions being the same but the label reported by Hajdecki being different) is now in the Ashmolean Museum at Oxford, and two views of this instrument appear in Plates 4a

bar. Unlike the violin, the typical *lira da braccio* about 1500 had seven strings, two of which, the drone strings, were not stopped by the fingers but ran off the fingerboard, as shown in Plate 4a. According to Praetorius (1619), the five stopped strings were tuned to g g' d' a' d", and the drones to d d'.[7] There is no evidence that the *lira da braccio* had frets before 1600. After this they appear occasionally, for instance in Praetorius (Vol. II, Plate XX). Unlike the violin, the tuning pegs of the *lira da braccio* were set horizontally in a leaf- or heart-shaped tuning head. Sometimes f-shaped sound holes and sometimes C-shaped sound holes are found on these instruments. In the course of its evolution in the sixteenth century, the *lira da braccio* developed certain hybrids, such as a three-stringed type and a *lira-viola* (see p. 36), that were probably influenced by the new and developing violin. The same influences may be noted in the development of the body of the *lira da braccio* itself.

Early in the sixteenth century some unknown genius perceived the virtue of combining the greater sonority and more efficient playing potential of the fiddle with the musical advantage of the rebec's stringing and tuning. The flat sound box and sound post of the fiddle (when it had a sound post) had the advantage of a superior sonority. In addition, the indentations of the middle bouts, the flat back, and the separate neck and fingerboard made the instrument easier to play than the rebec. On the other hand, the uniform fifth-tuning of the rebec permitted a more consistent fingering technique, and the fewer strings and the lateral tuning pegs must have made the rebec easier to tune than the fiddle.

In short, the early violin was the result of combining the best sonorous, playing, and musical features of the rebec, the fiddle, and especially of the fiddle's offshoot, the *lira da braccio*. Specifically, the developed form of the *lira da braccio* gave the violin its typical outline, including upper, middle, and lower bouts, the arched top and back supported by a sound post, the ribs, and overhanging edges. Other features are the neck as a part fixed to the body separately, a fingerboard without frets, and sound holes usually of the f-form. A side view of the Ashmolean *lira da braccio* (Plate 4b) shows a

---

and b. The *lira da braccio* shown in Praetorius's *Syntagma Musicum* (Vol. II, Plate XX) is more typical of the size of instruments seen in painting, being eighteen and a quarter inches (46.4 cm.), a very large viola, almost unplayable on the arm. This is why the instruments depicted in certain paintings seem to project in back of the player's neck (see Winternitz's excellent article and pictures under entry *Lira da Braccio* in *Die Musik in Geschichte und Gegenwart* [*MGG*], Vol. VIII [1960]).

[7] Praetorius, Vol. II, p. 26. In 1533, G. M. Lanfranco (*Scintille di musica*, Brescia) gives a tuning for a seven-stringed 'lyra' (= *lira da braccio*) in relative, not absolute, pitches. If Lanfranco's 'tenor' string, to which he relates the other strings, is tuned to d', as it is in Praetorius, the tuning is practically the same as that of Praetorius: drones, d d'; the fingered strings, g g' d' a' e". Note that if we delete the g' from the fingered strings, we have the violin tuning.

profile remarkably close to the violin of the time, including the short neck. The characteristic heart- or leaf-shaped pegbox of the *lira da braccio* is not typical of the violin, which adopted the lateral pegs of the rebec.

Musically, the violins married into the rebec family individually and collectively, not only adopting the three strings but also the tuning by fifths. Moreover, when the *specific* tunings for both the violin family and the rebec family are given for the first time, in Agricola's *Musica Instrumentalis Deudsch* (Wittemberg, 1545), the pitches of corresponding members of each family are identical: namely, the trebles of both are tuned to g d' a', the alto-tenors to c g d', and the basses (with four strings) to F G d a. In both the first and last editions of Agricola (1528-9; 1545) four sizes of rebecs are illustrated: discant (soprano), alto, tenor, and bass, but there are only three tunings, the alto and tenor being tuned the same (that is, in the edition of 1545; no tunings are given in the edition of 1528-9). The instruments of the violin family are not illustrated. Similarly, four sizes and three tunings are also characteristic of the violin family for nearly two hundred years after its origin, and these distinctions have produced many confusions concerning the 'instruments of the middle', especially in the case of the 'tenor' violin.[8]

The violin proper shared the playing position common to all its ancestors among the fiddles, *lire da braccio*, and rebecs of comparable register, the instrument being held at breast or neck, and the bow being played overhand. Some pictures of fiddles and rebecs prior to 1500 show the instrument held across the breast or even downward in the lap,[9] but these positions found no continuing favour among violinists. The cello (bass violin) was, of course, held downward between the knees, the bow being held overhand much of the time, although some pictures show it being held underhand with the viol grip (cf. Plate 5). How bass rebecs were played is not entirely clear, but bass rebecs certainly existed in 1528, because Agricola gives pictures of the rebec family, including the bass. To judge by Agricola's illustration, the bass rebec may have been small enough to play on the arm.[10]

In its musical function the violin was true to the traditions of its ancestors. Like the fiddle and rebec, the violin doubled vocal parts, served to accompany vocal music, or played for dancing of all sorts.

[8] A similar situation existed in the viols. Ganassi (*Regola Rubertina*, 1542-3) speaks of 'tenor' and 'alto' viols which are tuned 'in unison' (Part I, Ch. 15).

[9] For illustrations, see Panum, op. cit. See also Alexander Buchner, *Musical Instruments through the Ages* (London, n.d.). No. 315 shows a Czech folk-fiddler holding the 'violin' across the body and securing it by means of a sling running from the violin to the left arm of the player. This detail makes plausible the few pictures of fiddles and rebecs held in this position.

[10] What may well be a bass rebec being played on the arm is depicted in a painting 'The Muses' by 'Evangelista di Pian di Meleto e Giovanni Santi', done before 1494. Significantly, there are four strings shown, generally characteristic of the bass rebec only.

In the course of evolution from the ancestor forms to the violin there were certain hybrid types, and they should be recognized as such to avoid confusion. 'The Concert', a painting attributed to Lorenzo Costa (1460–1535), illustrates a case in point.[11] The instrument shown has the body of a fiddle with no indentation at all, four strings, a fretted fingerboard and lateral tuning pegs. A rather primitive bow is laid across the instrument.

Another early picture—and an important one (Fig. 1)—provides a missing link between the fiddles and the early violin. This picture, dated 1516, shows four sizes of a family of instruments being played by what is perhaps the most celebrated string quartet in history: Plato, Aristotle, Galen, and Hippocrates. The body outline of these instruments is that of the early violin, but each has a rose hole, not the f-holes of the violin. The alto has three strings; the tenor, four (neither soprano nor bass can be distinguished in this respect). The violin (or rather, soprano member) is being played at the neck, the alto and tenor are held downward in the lap, and the bass between the knees. The soprano and tenor instruments are bowed overhand, and the alto underhand like the viol. Note that this woodcut was done in Paris; but Champier, the author, came from Lyon, a centre of the manufacture of stringed instruments. Unfortunately, we cannot trace any connexion between the author and the artist who made the woodcut. (For further information on Lyon, see p. 39.)

Another example of an early form is represented in a sculpture on Belem Tower, Lisbon, built in 1520. This sculpture affords the rare spectacle of a gargoyle playing a hybrid form of the violin and also holding it under the chin—if a gargoyle properly has a chin—braced on the right side of the tailpiece. The primitive bow rests diagonally across the strings. The instrument itself has certain features of the violin: namely, an outline similar to the violin (although the lower bouts are not clearly differentiated from the indentation of the middle); three or (more likely) four strings; a pegbox with lateral pegs surmounted by a scroll; and primitive f-holes of the general order of those seen on the *lira da braccio* shown in Plate 4. However, the ribs are as deep as those of a treble viol, and there are no overhanging edges.

Several examples of hybrid instruments have been preserved. One, dated *c.* 1500, is now in Vienna. Its body combines features of the fiddle and the violin without being clearly one or the other, and one cannot say how much of the instrument is original and how much was changed or added later—such as the four strings, the fingerboard, scroll, and lateral tuning pegs.[12]

Hybrid instruments continue for some time after the emerging of the decisive features of the violin. Examples are the *lira-viola* of Gasparo da Salò

---

[11] Reproduced in colour in Marc Pincherle, *An Illustrated History of Music*, New York, 1959, p. 33.
[12] Reproduced in Georg Kinsky, *A History of Music in Pictures*, London, 1930, p. 146.

Symphonía Plato

nis cum Aristotele: & Galeni cū Hippocrate D. Sympho=
riani Chāperij.   Hippocratica philosophia eiusdem.
Platonica medicina de duplici mundo: cum eiusdē scholijs.
Speculum medicinale platonicum: & apologia literarū hu=
maniorum.

Quæ omnia venundantur ab Iodoco Badio.

Impressum est hoc opus apud Badiū Parrhisijs. An=
no salutis. MD.XVI.XIIII. Calen. Maias.

Fig. 1. A string quartet of famous personages (1516)

(see p. 36), and the instruments shown in the Woeriot portrait of Duiffoprugcar (1562; Plate 9). Ganassi (1542–3) mentions stringing viols with
only four or even three strings, and Bessaraboff thought that two viols with
three and four strings (now in Modena) were examples of what Ganassi had
in mind.[13]

The viols, which one assumes rose to importance in the fifteenth century,[14] furnished no structural feature really significant to the violin. While
the viol and violin may appear quite similar to the casual eye, especially in
outline, they actually differ in almost every point of construction, stringing,
tuning, and playing technique (compare the viol shown in Plate 5 with the
violin in Plate 1). Compared to the violin, the viol has deeper ribs, a back
that is flat, not bulging, and shoulders that are sloping, not rounded. The
sound holes of the viol are typically C-holes, not the f-holes characteristic of
the violin. Unlike the latter, the viol has no overhanging edges. The true
violin has four strings uniformly tuned in fifths, but the viol usually has six
strings tuned in fourths, or in fourths with a third in the middle. A typical
tuning for the treble viol is d g c' e' a' d", the tenor viol being tuned a fifth
lower, and the bass viol an octave lower, than the treble. On the viol the
fingerboard is fretted for each semitone, while the violin has no frets. As a
rule, the strings and the wood of the viol are thinner than those of the
violin; and for these and other technical reasons of playing, the sound of the
viol is more reedy and less assertive.

The viol and the violin families represent two separate and distinct
entities with respect to their structure, ideals of sound, and corresponding
musical and social context. It was not by chance that the viol family existed
side by side with the violin family for upward of two centuries. When the
viols eventually became obsolete, it was not through a process of absorption
into the violin family; rather, the viols went out of fashion when the kind of
music and social conditions that nurtured their use ceased to exist. However,
a particular instrument of one family will occasionally exhibit a typical
feature of the other family, and in this respect the violin and viol families had
some reciprocal influence on each other. A viol with the characteristic f-holes
of the violin is one example; a cello played with the typical bow grip of the
viol is another.[15]

After the emergence of the early violin not later than 1530, the Italian
term *viola*, used without qualification, could designate a member of either
the viol or the violin family (see below). To avoid this ambiguity, Italian
writers like Ganassi (1542–3) and later (among others) the French theorist

---

[13] For details, see p. 28 below.
[14] When will the mysterious early history of the viols be thoroughly investigated? To
date there is no satisfactory account of the origins and early history of the viols.
[15] For an excellent example see *MGG*, op. cit., Vol. VIII, Tafel 31, opposite col. 737.

Jambe de Fer (1556), qualified the term. *Viola da gamba*, meaning 'viola played at the leg', was used to denote the viol family; *viola da braccio*, meaning 'viola played on the arm', referred collectively to members of the violin family. In Ganassi, *violone* could mean viols as a family.[16] In this way, sixteenth-century terminology reflected the basic difference of position in playing the two kinds of instruments, especially the treble members of the two families. These distinctions were not completely consistent, since the violoncello and double bass of the violin family were not played 'on the arm'. However, all members of the viol family, including the treble (soprano) member, were held downward between the knees and were played 'at the leg'. There was also an important difference in the manner of bowing, the violin bow being held overhand and the viol bow underhand (see Plate 5).

Did the viola precede the violin?

There is a well-established theory that the viola (alto violin) was the first member of the violin family to emerge. Reduced to essentials, the argument is this: the violin was descended from the *lira da braccio*, which was invariably a viola-sized instrument. Hence the earliest 'violin' was a viola. Another argument seeks to equate the tuning of the viola with that of the *lira da braccio*. These arguments are based on insufficient historical knowledge and perspective. The *lira da braccio* was not the only ancestor of the violin, and the tuning of the *lira da braccio* can be equated just as well with the violin as with the viola.[17]

Actually, the violin emerged as a family; and the violin, viola, and cello appeared at about the same time. The Gaudenzio Ferrari fresco in Saronno Cathedral (1535-6) shows the three principal sizes of the violin family all being played together. The evolving hybrids, shown in the engraving of 1516 (Fig. 1) show four sizes of the family (i.e. probably with three tunings). Furthermore all the documentary evidence of early sixteenth-century theorists indicates that rebecs and early violins came in families of three registers; and the first indisputable evidence of the true four-stringed violin, found in the *Epitome musical* of Jambe de Fer (1556) describes the

---

[16] Sylvestro di Ganassi, *Regola Rubertina*, Venice, Part I, 1542, Part II, 1543. Facsimile reprint with a preface by Max Schneider, 1924. For *viola da gamba*, see Part I, Ch. 1; for *viola da brazo* [*sic*], see Part II, Ch. 23. For *viola da gamba* in Jambe de Fer (as in note 1, p. 4 above), see his p. 62. On p. 63, speaking of the violin (Fr. *violon*), Jambe de Fer says: 'the Italians call it *violon da braccia* [*sic*]' (cf. our pp. 32 ff.). For the terms *violette da braccia* in Lanfranco, see p. 25 below.

[17] See Bessaraboff, op. cit., p. 432, note 751. The arguments of Charles Reade in the *Pall Mall Gazette* for 19 August 1872 (reprinted in Ed. Heron-Allen, *Violin Making*, London, 1889, p. 71, note 1) show how the sincere and ingenious reasoning of a connoisseur and 'practical' expert can be completely wrong without sufficient background in the theorists, organography, and iconography.

discant, alto-tenor, and bass members of the violin family with their appropriate tunings. If there is any evidence at all to support the emergence of one member of the family before another, it favours the violin, although such evidence is admittedly incomplete and inconclusive. For example, the earliest picture representing a member of the violin family, the 1529–30 painting of Gaudenzio Ferrari entitled '*La Madonna degli aranci*', depicts a small violin only. In the extensive French inventories of instruments cited by Lesure,[18] violins appear in 1551, violas (*taille de viollon* = tenor violin) in 1553, and cellos in 1570. (For further on these inventories, see p. 38.)

In this context terminology is a treacherous quicksand ready and eager to engulf those who mistake it for *terra firma*. A typical victim of these shifting sands is the argument that the modern term *viola* survives from *viola da braccio*, thus pointing to the viola (alto violin) as the oldest member. This argument is untenable because the term *viola* ('with a bow') is already used by Tinctoris in the fifteenth century to mean a three- or five-stringed fiddle (see p. 50), thus long antedating *viola da braccio*. Besides, the term *viola* is ambiguous in the sixteenth century, having both general and specific meanings. Used as a general term to mean a member of either viol or violin families, *viola* antedates the specific terms derived from it: namely, *viola da braccio* (the violin family), *viola da gamba* (the viol family), and *violino* as diminutive. In its specific sixteenth-century sense, *viola* may have meant *lira da braccio* on occasion; and sometimes *viola da braccio* was used synonymously for *lira*, although it is not certain how old or definite these equivalents were.[19] Nor is it clear whether *viola da braccio* is an older term than *violino*, the latter being used at least by 1538 (see p. 26), *viola da braccio* in 1543 (see p. 28), and *viola in braccio* perhaps as early as 1508–16 (see note 19, below). In any case, there is no evidence that *violino* ever referred to anything save a member or members of the violin family. It usually meant the soprano member and sometimes the alto as well (cf. p. 42); but if there is any proof

---

[18] François Lesure, 'La Facture Instrumentale à Paris au seizième Siècle', in *The Galpin Society Journal*, Vol. VII, 1954.

[19] Baldassare Castiglione's *Il cortegiano* (written between 1508 and 1516, printed 1528, translated into English by Sir Thomas Hoby in 1561 as *The Book of the Courtier*) uses the phrases *cantare alla viola per recitar* and *viola in braccio* in a way that may refer to the *lira da braccio*. Hoby, however, translates *viola* as 'lute'. According to Tinctoris (cf. our p. 50, below), *viola* could mean a species of lute and also a 'fiddle' of which the *lira da braccio* is a species. Manfred Bukofzer thought viola meant 'viol' in this context (*Proceedings of the MTNA*, 1944 [Vol. 38], pp. 233ff.). See also Gustave Reese, *Music in the Renaissance*, New York, 1954, p. 160, note 49). In any case, Castiglione (1478–1529) was a native of northern Italy, and must have known the instruments of his time. He was born near Mantua, educated at Milan, and for a while he served Ludovico Sforza, Duke of Milan. Later, he was attached to the court of Urbino, and his book professes to be an account of discussions held at the Ducal Palace in 1507.

showing that *violino* specifically meant the alto violin (modern viola) to the exclusion of the soprano member (violin proper), it has not come to light (for *rebecchino*, see p. 24).

The 'inventor' of the violin

Who created early violins like those depicted in the paintings of Gaudenzio Ferrari about 1530? There is no definite answer to this question, although certain celebrated makers of the time may have done so. Lanfranco's treatise of 1533, mentioned above and significantly published in Brescia, speaks of 'lutes, viols, lyras and the like' made by Giovan Giacobo dalla Corna and Zanetto Montichiaro, both of Brescia, instruments which 'appear to have been created not by the hands of men but by Nature herself'. This information is valuable for several reasons. It underscores the truth of the observation that sixteenth-century instruments were made expressly to please the eye as well as the ear. It serves to remind us that these early instruments should not be regarded as primitive or inferior in workmanship simply because they are products of change or youth or even because they are represented as comparatively primitive instruments in painting (cf. pp. 37 below). Indeed, a number of 'violins' in the early sixteenth-century must have been made in the tradition of expert craftsmanship for which Brescia and Cremona were already famous. Finally, Lanfranco's testimony identifies two Brescian makers as creators of 'lyras and the like'. In the early sixteenth century the term *lyra* or *lira* might have meant either the *lira da braccio* or a member of the violin family (*viola da braccio*). Some years later Galilei speaks of '*viola da braccio*, which not many years ago was called *lira*',[20] and hence it is quite possible that the makers mentioned by Lanfranco actually produced 'violins'. Unfortunately no extant instrument can be attributed to Giovan [Giovanni] Giacobo dalla Corna (*c.* 1484–*c.* 1550), and the only other known reference (1534) speaks of him as a lute maker.[21] However, a *lira da braccio* made by his father, Giovani Maria dalla Corna, also of Brescia, is now in the Ashmolean Museum at Oxford (our Plates 4a and b). This beautiful instrument bears the label 'Gioan maria bresiano in Venetia', indicating that the instrument was made in Venice by a Brescian maker. The date *c.* 1540, assigned to this *lira da braccio*, for reasons and by persons unknown, seems rather late if the birth date of his son is correct. A more likely date is *c.* 1525.

Zanetto [da] Montichiaro, the other maker mentioned by Lanfranco, was born about 1488 in Montichiaro, a town some seven miles from Brescia. In

---

[20] Vincenzo Galilei, *Dialogo . . . della musica antica et della moderna*, Florence, 1581, p. 147.
[21] 'Che fa lauti [liuti].' Cited in W. L. v. Lütgendorff, *Die Geigen- und Lautenmacher*, 2 vols., 4th ed., Frankfurt am Main, 1922, article 'Dalla Corna'. Could 'lauti' mean instruments in general? In French 'luthier' meant instrument maker in general, hence also violin maker.

1530 he established himself in Brescia, where he died between 1562 and 1568. According to Vannes,[22] Zanetto carried his art to such perfection that he was considered one of the founders of the Brescian school by his colleagues G. G. dalla Corona [Corna?], G. B. Donedo, and Girolamo Virchi. Virchi was born at Brescia *c.* 1523, and was the master of Gasparo da Salò (see pp. 34–36). The son of Zanetto [da] Montichiaro, called 'Pellegrino' (*c.* 1522–1615), was another maker. His first instruments were viols, dating from 1547 (see Vannes). Again, as in the case of Dalla Corna, there is no proof that any of these men made violins, although it is quite likely in view of their reputations as the foremost makers of Brescia at a time when violins were certainly being made in the vicinity.

In modern times a number of special claims have been made for certain favourite sons as the inventor of the violin, the evidence for most of which will not bear close examination. Giuseppe Strocchi, for example, devoted the most intensive efforts trying to prove that Gasparo da Salò did *not* invent the violin, in which he was successful, and to substitute Antonius Bononiensis (= Anthony of Bologna; 1485–1561) in Gasparo's place, in which he was not, since his basic evidence dated from the eighteenth century.[23] The claims for Nicolo Tartaglia as an 'inventor', submitted by Euro Peluzzi, are mentioned only to warn the reader against one of the most preposterous absurdities ever committed to print.[24] Among other 'non-inventors' of the violin are Testator il Vecchio, Leonardo da Vinci, and G. Kerlino. In all this we do not mean that Bologna and Venice (for example) are not likely contributors to early violin making; only that there is no available evidence that they were.

The tangible evidence of actual instruments formed the basis of other claims. For some years it was believed that the earliest violins were made by Gaspar(d) Duiffoprugcar (or Tieffenbrucker), and violins attributed to him with labels dating before 1520 were offered in proof. Vidal showed that these instruments were nineteenth-century forgeries; and the whole claim was exploded by Coutagne, who proved that Duiffoprugcar, born in Bavaria in 1514 and working in Lyon from about 1533 to his death in 1571, was known in his own time primarily as a lute maker.[25] A celebrated portrait of Duiffoprugcar by Pierre Woeriot, dated 1562, depicts several stringed instruments, but none of them is a true violin (see Plate 9).

[22] René Vannes, *Dictionnaire Universel des Luthiers*, Bruxelles, 2nd ed., 1951; Vol. II, Bruxelles, 1959.

[23] Giuseppe Strocchi, *Liuteria—Storia ed Arte*, Lugo, 1937. Specifically, Strocchi thought a 'violin' painted by Francisco Franco of Bologna came from the first half of the sixteenth century. Actually it was done by A. Cossetti in 1744 (cf. Mucchi, as in note 26, Plate IV).

[24] Euro Peluzzi, 'Chi fu l'inventore del Violino' in *Rivista musicale italiana*, Vol. 45 (1941), pp. 25–39.

[25] See Louis-Antoine Vidal, *Les Instruments à Archet*, 3 vols., Paris, 1876–78; and Henry Coutagne, *Gaspard Duiffoproucart* [*sic*], Paris, 1893.

Another controversy of long standing between the adherents of Brescia and Cremona, concerning the respective claims of Gasparo da Salò and Andrea Amati as the inventor of the violin, has generated at least as much heat as light. Part of this controversy can be definitely settled and part must remain in a state of suspension. The evidence of iconography proves conclusively that the early three-stringed violin was in existence by 1530, and therefore Gasparo da Salò, who was born in 1540, could not have invented it.[26] Nor could he have invented the true four-stringed violin, since the earliest known violin of Gasparo dates from 1562 (a year after he moved to Brescia), and Jambe de Fer clearly describes the true violin in 1556. (For more on Gasparo da Salò, see ch. 2.)

The case of Andrea Amati cannot be disposed of so easily. The research of Carlo Bonetti has shown that the previously accepted birth date of *c.* 1520 or 1535 will have to be revised to not *later* than 1511 and quite probably as early as 1500–5. Amati must have died before January 1580, since at that time official documents named his two sons as his heirs.[27] Since Andrea Amati was born not later than 1511, he may well have been making violins about the time of Gaudenzio Ferrari's first 'violin' painting (1530). While there is no record of such early violins by Andrea Amati, two violins, dated 1542 and 1546, are attributed to him, and both are reported to have (or to have had originally) three strings. The 'Amati' of 1542 was presumably still extant at Milan in 1898. In 1800 the 1546 'violin' apparently belonged to an extensive collection of Count Cozio di Salabue, and, according to George Hart, it was converted into a four-stringed violin early in the nineteenth century.[28] The reports of these two instruments, which cannot be affirmed or denied, are given for what they may be worth. Nevertheless, there is nothing at all improbable about Amati's making three-stringed violins in the 1540s. In fact, such a possibility fits in with established historical facts. In any case, the early, three-stringed type of violin probably continued to be made after mid-century. In 1555 Vicentino still speaks of bowed 'violas' with three strings played without frets (*viole d'arco . . . con tre corde senza tasti*).[29]

★   ★   ★

[26] For the date, see A. M. Mucchi, *Gasparo da Salò*, Milan, 1940.
[27] See Carlo Bonetti, 'La Genealogia degli Amati-Liutai e il Primato della Scuola Liutistica Cremonese' in *Bollettino Storico Cremonese*, Series II, Anno III (Vol. VIII), Cremona, 1938. Bonetti's research was published more than twenty-five years ago, but most of the latest reference works still perpetuate the old errors to confuse another generation. Vannes is an honourable exception (see note 22, above).
[28] For the 1542 instrument, see Strocchi, op. cit., p. 117. For the 1546 instrument, see Federico Sacchi, *Count Cozio di Salabue*, London, 1898, Appendix; and George Hart, *The Violin: its famous Makers and their Imitators*, London, revised and enlarged edition, 1884, p. 25.
[29] Nicola Vicentino, *L'Antica Musica*, Rome, 1555, ch. 66, p. 146, verso. Facsimile edition by Edward E. Lowinsky, Kassel, 1959.

The story of the emerging violin has been recounted above at some length, but the impact of this story will be more vivid if an outline of the key information is now presented in chronological order, adding certain corroborating facts to those already mentioned. Two particular advantages accrue from this amplification: (1) a bird's-eye view of the evolution of the violin to about 1550; and (2) a clarification of terminology. Evidence concerning the violin suddenly begins about 1520 and continues consistently thereafter. As Gerald Hayes says, 'The violin . . . is one of the very few important instruments of which it can be said that at a given date it was not at all, and that shortly afterwards it is found full fledged in active life.'[30] The few references to 'violin' that occur before 1520 are probably spurious. For instance, the date and meaning of *violon*, cited by A. Jacquot as occurring in 1490, are suspect, since this term is found in a document of which only an eighteenth-century copy exists.[31] However, because the 'violin' paintings of Gaudenzio Ferrari date as early as 1529–30, it is probable that shortly after 1520 the term *violino* in Italy and comparable terms elsewhere actually meant 'violin' in the sense of the early form with three strings.

In reviewing the following material, one should keep in mind that the main documentary and pictorial evidence concerning the emerging violin emanates from northern Italy, in particular from the geographical areas of Savoy, Piedmont, and Lombardy. The House of Savoy ruled Savoy proper *and* Piedmont. Milan, the chief city of Lombardy, and, as the Duchy of Milan, one of the five city states of Italy, was the primary political and cultural force of the whole area just mentioned. Thus the chief cities and towns connected with the early violin—Saronno, Vercelli, Turin, Cremona, and Brescia (the last ruled by Venice after 1512)—were within the geographical and cultural, if not always political, orbit of Milan. The fact that the area of Milan was the epicentre of intense artistic activity, including instrumental manufacture, is suggestive with respect to the role of France in the early history of the violin. Francis I of France (reigned 1515–47), 'pre-eminently the King of the Renaissance', was motivated by a sincere love of arts and letters and by a foolish and disastrous passion, in the tradition of his predecessors, to possess Milan (the French invasions of Italy had begun in

---

[30] Gerald Hayes, *Musical Instruments and their Music, 1500–1750*, 2 vols., London, 1928–30, Vol. II, p. 160.

[31] See A. Jacquot, *La Musique en Lorraine*, Paris, 1882; and M. Pincherle, *Les Violonistes*, Paris, 1922, p. 12. The term *violinista* of 1462, cited by Signor Rossi in *Giornale di erudizione artistica* (Vol. 5, 1874) and reprinted uncritically by various authors, certainly does not mean a 'violinist'. The passage speaks of 'Quitarrista seu Violinista', and the instruments are described as 'dicta viola seu quitarra'. Hence a *violinista* is a player of the (little) *viola*, and a *viola* in 1462 was, if anything, a medieval fiddle according to Tinctoris (*c.* 1487; see below, p. 50). (For the meaning of 'fiddle', see p. 9, above.)

1494). He sporadically won and lost the city as well as Savoy and Piedmont at immense cost to his kingdom and even at the price of his own liberty (he was imprisoned in Madrid after the Battle of Pavia, 1525). For our purposes, the point of this tangled web of events is that the Hapsburg-Valois Wars undoub⁺edly intensified the already close relationship between France, Italy, and Milan in particular; and a monarch as vitally concerned with the arts as Francis I must have been aware of the latest thing in musical circles. The political facts of the time, taken in conjunction with the events set out below, strongly suggest that the violin was introduced to France from Italy (see also p. 39). Prunières remarks of Francis I, 'He loves the arts passionately and encourages the painters and architects not less than the musicians.'[32] In fact, Francis's reign was marked by an extraordinary Italian invasion which threatened to usurp many of the artistic positions at the French Court. It is not clear to what extent Italian violinists were part of this invasion. About 1530 (see Prunières, as per note 32) most of the Court violinists had French names, but after Francis's death (1547), Henry II saw to it that the violinists were Italian. By 1547 the violin was well established, since six violins took part in the solemnities at the funeral of Francis I (cf. note 32). It was natural that the Italian influence increased under Henry II, because his Queen was Catherine de' Medici, whom he had married in 1533 while still Duc d'Orléans. (For Catherine's introduction of Italian dancers and violinists into France about 1555, see p. 38.) Similarly, political history may account for the introduction of the violin into other countries, notably Germany. Milan and northern Italy were the battleground not only for France but also for the Emperor Charles V, whose possessions included Austria and Spain, and parts of Germany, Italy, and the Netherlands. After 1535 Lombardy, and consequently Milan, fell under Spanish domination, where it remained until 1714. A study of the complex politics of the sixteenth century helps to explain the spread of Renaissance culture from its fountainhead in Italy. Francis I and Charles V repeatedly invaded Italy, but Italy repeatedly invaded their dominions with the stronger and more permanent forces of humanism. Music in all its aspects, players and instruments included, was an important part of this cultural invasion from Italy.

1523

This is the earliest date of a documentary reference to the violin. An official record from the accounts of the general treasury of Savoy shows a payment of six *scudi* on 17 December 1523 for the services of '*trompettes et*

---

[32] See Henry Prunières, 'La musique de la chambre et de l'écurie sous le règne de François Ier' in *L'Année Musicale 1911*, Vol. I, Paris, 1912.

vyollons [i.e. violins] *de Verceil*.[33] Verceil is the French name for Vercelli, a town of some importance in Piedmont (the latter being included in the domain of the Duke of Savoy) about forty miles west of Milan—the same Vercelli in which the earliest of Gaudenzio Ferrari's 'violin' paintings was made (see p. 7).

The appearance of the French term *vyollon* (i.e. *violon* = violin) to describe violinists from the Italian town of Vercelli (and from Paris in 1529; see below) *before* the term *violino* occurs in Italy (1538) is as mysterious linguistically as it is fascinating and baffling historically. As to the latter point, there is not much to be gained by commenting on the priority of the French term, since we cannot actually prove that *violino* was not in use earlier—only that we have not found it earlier. However, it may be significant in this context that Jambe de Fer says that the Italians call the violin '*violon da braccia*' (see below). The use of French in the earliest known reference to the violin does not support a case for French ancestry of the violin. Although the language of official Savoy was French at that time, Vercelli is clearly in Italy. All the reference proves is that violinists and violins must have been in existence in Vercelli before Gaudenzio Ferrari painted a picture containing a violin there six years later (1529–30).

Linguistically *vyollon* (= *violon*) is a genuine mystery, and the obscurity of its etymology defies rational linguistic principles. *Violon* must be derived from Italian sources, the root being *viol-* (i.e. from *viola*). The Italian diminutive is *violin(o)* (= violin); and the augmentative is *violon(e)* (= viols as a class; or later, double-bass viol). In French, too, the suffix *-on* often has augmentative force. How does it happen, then, that the French word first appears in Savoy as *vyollon*—not as *vyollin* or *violin*?

One obvious thought is that *vyollon* does not mean 'violin' at all but *violon(e)* (= viols; double-bass viol). But this cannot be so, because *violon* has a consistent and continuous use after 1523 in contexts where it must mean 'violin'. Furthermore by 1556 Jambe de Fer's definition of *violon* leaves no doubt that he means 'violin'. Finally, there is a French term for viol established in regular usage long before 1523: namely, *viole*. Similarly, among the terms first used for the violin in England is *viollon*, found in court records in 1555 (see p. 41). In the same entries, players of the viols are distinguished by the term *viall*, a term that is already used in England by 1525.

From all this one may reach either a simple or an involved theory to

---

[33] See Stanislao Cordero di Pamparato, 'Emmanuele Filiberto di Savoia, protettore dei musici', in *Rivista musicale italiana*, Vol. XXXIV, 1927, p. 235. At this time French was the prevailing language in Savoy, even in its Italian portions. This was so because northern Italy had been ruled off and on in the recent past by the French and because Savoy was as much a French as an Italian duchy, being predominantly French-oriented, politically and linguistically, in the first quarter of the sixteenth century.

explain the etymology of *violon* = violin. Both theories are based on the probability that the term *violino* (= violin) was not in existence in 1523, but that *violone* was already in common use and meant viols as a class, including the discant viol, as Lanfranco makes explicit in 1533 (see below, p. 25):

1. The simple theory is that the French in Savoy misunderstood the Italian term *violone*, adopting it directly into French. If, as this theory assumes, *violino* was not yet in existence, *violino* obviously could not be adopted into French as *violin*.

2. To understand the more involved theory, which is probably the truth, we must again start with the assumption that *violino* (= violin) was not yet in existence, but that *violone* (or *violono*) was in common use to mean viols as a class (as per Lanfranco, see p. 25 below), including the soprano, alto-tenor, and bass members. The diminutive form was *violetta*, probably meaning the rebec (or, possibly, violin) family as a whole.[34] When the violin family evolved about 1520, the Italians probably first called these instruments *violone da braccio* (= arm viols) to distinguish them from the ordinary *violone* or 'leg viols', or simply viols. This theory accounts for the hitherto inexplicable remark of Jambe de Fer (1556) that the Italians called the violin '*violon da braccia ou violone*' (see below, p. 32). Not long after the origin of the violin, the Italians (e.g. Ganassi, 1542-3) tried to clarify terminology by using *viola da braccio* to mean the violin family and *viola da gamba* to mean the viol family. The term *violino*, the diminutive, was used sometimes for the whole family and sometimes for the soprano and (occasionally) alto members. Later (*c.* 1600) *violone* assumed its true augmentative force, and was restricted to mean double-bass viol only.

When the Court chroniclers in Savoy (or Piedmont) looked for the appropriate French word for the new violin family about 1520 they simply took *violone da braccio* from the Italian; but since in French the word *viole* already meant 'viol', there was no need for the '*da braccio*' which was essential in Italian. Therefore, they called the new violin family simply *violon(e)* or *violon(o)*, or in French simply *violon*; and this term, established from the birth of the violin, was never changed. The advent of the proper diminutive *violino* in Italian had no effect on the previously established French term *violon*; and consequently this term, whose origin has to be traced to the peculiarities of Italian terminology, became rooted in the French language and passed down unchanged through the ages as *violon* to puzzle and confuse future generations by its inherent etymological contradiction.

Violon is still a source of misunderstanding, because the Italian term *violon(e)* is so easily confused with it. In the nineteenth century the distinguished scholar Fétis, for instance, misled a whole generation of

---

[34] See p. 25 below. For the exact linguistic parallel to *violetta* and *violone* in German and for later meanings of *violetta*, see p. 25.

investigators, Vidal among them, by mistranslating Lanfranco's (1533) Italian expression *violoni* (= viols) by the French term *violons* (= violins).

1528–9

At this time Martin Agricola published the first edition of his *Musica Instrumentalis Deudsch* [*sic*] at Wittemberg (for the 1545 edition, see below). In this first edition, Agricola gives illustrations of the rebec family in four sizes, calling them *'kleine Geigen'* (*grosse Geigen* = viols). He says the rebecs have three strings but no frets. The rebecs are tuned in fifths, but Agricola gives no specific tunings. He also illustrates another family of instruments with three strings, 'commonly without frets'. His illustration of these instruments, however, show frets. The tunings are: g d' a' (discant), c g d' (alto-tenor), and F c g (bass). These are also called *'kleine Geigen'*, but the instruments are not clearly violins; they are like his *grosse Geigen*, which in his illustrations are rather strange-looking viols. It is curious that these *kleine Geigen* are assigned tunings, while the rebecs, also called *kleine Geigen*, are not. (For the tunings of the rebecs in the 1545 editions, see below.)

1529–30

The date of Gaudenzio Ferrari's first 'violin' painting at Vercelli.

1529

From about this time one finds the term *rebecchino* (also *ribechino* and other spellings) in contexts which *may* refer to the violin. *Rebecchino* is the diminutive of rebec (*rebeca* or *ribeca*) and perhaps refers to a small instrument such as that shown in Gaudenzio's painting just mentioned. The term is significant if one keeps in mind the role of the rebec in the evolution of the violin or if one considers later terminology applied retroactively. In 1619 Praetorius gives *rebecchino* as a synonym for the violin; and Cerone in 1613 speaks of 'el rebequin ò violino'. In any case a *'rebecchino'* was played at a state banquet at Ferrara in 1529,[35] and much later the same term was used to describe an instrument that played in the *Intermedi* celebrating the marriage in Florence of Francesco de' Medici and Johanna of Austria (1565)—in particular in the *Intermedio* 'Psyche and Amor' by Alessandro Striggio and Francesco Corteccia.[36]

1529, 1533, 1534

These are the earliest dates known of a reference to the violin in France. In 1529, in the reign of Francis I, six French musicians, specifically named

---

[35] See *MGG*, Vol. IV, col. 59.
[36] For a contemporary report in its original and translated form, see O. G. Sonneck, *Miscellaneous Studies in the History of Music*, New York, 1921, pp. 269ff.

and described collectively as 'viollons, haulxbois et sacquebuteurs', received the sum of '41 livres tournois'. The secret accounts of Francis I also mention players 'de violon' in 1533 and 1534, and these accounts imply that 'violinists' travelled with the King on various occasions.[37]

1533

In this year Lanfranco's *Scintille di musica* was published in Brescia. His *Violoni da tasti & da Arco* are, collectively, the soprano, tenor, and bass of the viol family, each member having frets and six strings tuned in fourths and thirds. It is not clear precisely when the meaning of *violone* was restricted to the meaning of double-bass viol only, but the latter meaning was clearly what Praetorius (1619) had in mind.

Lanfranco uses another term which is more puzzling: *Violette da Arco senza tasti* (little violas without frets played with a bow), which he says (p. 137 in his treatise) are played 'on the arm' (*da braccio*). He also describes the *lyra* (= *lira da braccio*) and its tuning by fifths (see p. 10 above). He does not mention the rebecs. Can Lanfranco's *violette* be the unmentioned rebecs? Possibly; but just as possibly they are violins. In 1592 Zacconi in his *Prattica di musica*, refers to Lanfranco's treatise for information about various instruments including '*violini*' (which are not mentioned by Lanfranco!). Did Zacconi consider Lanfranco's *violette* to be violins? Zacconi himself, however, uses the term *violetta picciola* to mean discant viol (in Praetorius, *violetta picciola* is a term either for discant viol or violin!). Lanfranco's *violette* cannot be viols, because he says they are tuned in fifths and the upper two members have only three strings. He gives relative but not specific tunings for three members of the family. If the lowest string of the discant instrument is tuned to 'g', as it is in Agricola (1528-9), the tunings are the same as Agricola's except that Lanfranco has added a fourth string to the bass (tuned to BB flat).

Linguistically, Lanfranco's *violoni* and *violette* are exactly parallel in meaning and usage to Agricola's *grosse Geigen* and *kleine Geigen*, respectively. *Viola* and *Geige* are the general words. *Violoni* = large *viole* = viols; similarly, *grosse Geigen* = large *Geigen* = viols. *Violette* = little *viole* = rebecs or violins; similarly, *kleine Geigen* = little *Geigen* = rebecs or violins.

Much later Cerone defines *La Vihuela de braco* as 'llamada comunmente violeta que es sin trastes' (commonly called *violeta* which is without frets).[38] Cerone, like Lanfranco, gives no specific pitches for his tunings, but again if 'g' is used for the lowest string of the treble (discant), his three tunings are

---

[37] For 1529 see M. Pincherle, *Feuillets d'histoire du violon*, Paris, 1927, p. 7. For 1533 and 1534 see Laurent Grillet, *Les ancêtres du violon*, 2 vols., Paris, 1901 and 1905, Vol. II, p. 9.

[38] Domenico Pietro Cerone, *El Melopeo y Maestro*, Naples, 1613, p. 1057.

precisely the same as those in Lanfranco and Agricola. Apart from this, *violetta* in the late sixteenth century might also mean either a viol (cf. Zacconi, above) or an alto-tenor violin (modern viola). The latter meaning still obtained in eighteenth-century Italy. In 1770 Burney reported that there were (among other instruments) 'four violetti or tenors [= modern viola]' used in the service at the Church of St. Anthony in Padua.[39]

1534

In October 1534 the treasurer of Piedmont paid two *testoni* to the 'Taborins e Viollons de Thurin [Turin]' for furnishing chamber music for 'Madame Catherine Charlocte' [*sic*], the younger sister of Emmanuele Filiberto. Since Emmanuele was born in 1528, they must both have been young children—not older than six years for Emmanuele and still less for his 'younger' sister, tender ages for chamber music. (For this reference see note 33.) (For more on Emmanuele, see ch. 3, p. 60.)

1535–6

This is the date of the Gaudenzio Ferrari frescoes in Saronno Cathedral, showing the three principal members of the violin family (see p. 7).

1538

As far as we know, the term *violino* first appears in this year. It occurs in official records of Pope Paul III (1534–49), who, wishing to impress and please Emperor Charles V and Francis I at a Peace Conference at Nice in June 1538, brought with him trombonists from Bologna, 'violinists from Milan' (*violini Milanesi*) and trumpet, drum, and bombard players from Genoa.[40] It is quite probable that the Papal records used the phrase *violini Milanesi* to refer to violinists in the whole area of which Milan was the cultural centre—an area which would include Brescia, Cremona, Saronno, Vercelli, and Turin (see Fig. 2). It is obvious from this reference, from other documents, and from paintings cited above that Milan and the neighbouring towns produced more than their share of violins and violinists. As we have pointed out, the violin paintings of Gaudenzio Ferrari are to be found in places not far from Milan. Saronno, for instance, is less than fifteen miles away. Later, when Catherine de' Medici imported dancers and violinists from Lombardy 1554–5; see p. 38), their leader was Baldassare da Belgiojoso, Belgiojoso being a small town not far south of Milan. Since the violin and dancing were closely allied in the sixteenth century, the concentration of violinists and violin makers in Milan and its neighbouring towns is significant.

[39] See [Charles Burney] *An Eighteenth-Century Musical Tour in France and Italy*, edited by Percy A. Scholes, 2 vols., London, 1959, Vol. I, p. 103.
[40] See Léon Dorez, *La Cour du Pape Paul III d'après les registres de la Trésorerie secrète, Tome second: Les Dépenses Privées*, Paris, Ernest Leroux, 1932, p. 223.

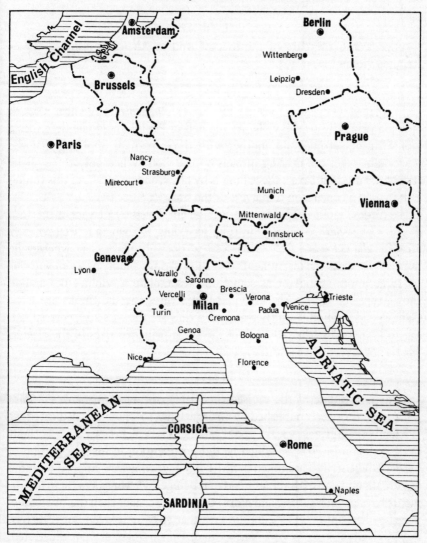

Fig. 2. Places important in the early history of the violin, showing their relation to capital cities.

1542

The term *violino* is also found in personal records. It is used in 1542 and subsequently in the income-tax returns of Francesco da Bertolotti and later in those of his famous son, Gasparo da Salò (b. 1540). The phrase, '*Francesco, violino*', appears to refer to Francesco either as a maker or player of the violin, and in view of the information presented above, efforts to explain 'Francesco, violino' as 'Francesco, maker of *viols*' are most unconvincing.[41]

[41] See Mucchi, op. cit., pp. 16-18.

1542

1542 is also the date of the first of Andrea Amati's presumed three-stringed violins (see p. 19).

1543

In 1542–3 Ganassi published his *Regola Rubertina* in Venice, a work devoted primarily to the viols. At the end of Part II (1543) he describes a viol with four strings and another with three, perhaps implying that the new violin types are making inroads on the viols. When only three of the strings are used (he says), the tuning is by fifths, and he speaks of this tuning as if it were a concession to players of the *'viola da brazo senza tasti'*—that is, of the fretless violins. This tuning 'can be employed by players of the *viola da brazo senza tasti* so as to be in tune according to their practice (*per essere accordati alla sua maniera*)'.[42] Ganassi's text does not make clear whether he himself visualizes the instrument with three strings simply as a viol without its three upper strings or as something resembling a 'violin'. Bessaraboff shows types of viols with three and four strings that he thinks are what Ganassi had in mind.[43] But Bessaraboff's viols are the bass size, corresponding to large cellos, the only one of the three principal sizes of the *viola da braccio* not played 'on the arm'.

1545

This is the date of the revised (and last) edition of Agricola's *Musica Instrumentalis Deudsch*, published by Georg Rhaw (to whom it is dedicated) at Wittemberg. Agricola speaks about another class of *kleinen Geigen* without frets, common in Poland (which he did not mention in his first edition of 1528–9). The strings are tuned in fifths, but the strings are stopped with the fingernails and not with the soft end of the finger. He considers these instruments have a much subtler and more beautiful resonance than the 'Welschen' type (= 'Italian' = viols), and he says that they are played with 'Zittern frey' (= vibrato, see p. 91). These small Polish *Geigen* are not illustrated, nor is another type called 'small three-stringed *Handgeiglein*', also without frets. Agricola says the latter are tuned like the Polish type in fifths, yet are handled differently. 'I suspect that people understand very little about the use of the fingerboard or neck, which is the basis of the whole matter.' Then he gives diagrams to explain clearly the fingering of both types of these fretless instruments. The tunings are the same for both: g d' a' (discant), c g d' (alto-tenor), F G d a (bass). The rebecs are illustrated, just as in the 1528–9 edition, but this time their tunings are the same as the Polish *Geigen*, just given. Agricola clearly distinguishes the rebecs as instruments from the

---

[42] Part II (*Lettione Seconda*), chs. 22 and 23.   [43] Bessaraboff, op. cit., p. 309.

Polish and other *Geigen*—the latter surely being early violins. Much later Praetorius confirms this conclusion (1619) by saying that the *viole da braccio* are called *Geigen* or *Polnische Geigeln*. 'Perhaps this type first originated in Poland,' says Praetorius. Possibly Poland, inspired by the Italians, imported the violins, as they did other things at the time. The fingernail fashion of playing may have been specifically Polish, and the manner of playing may account for the phrase 'Polish violins'.

1546

This is the date of the second of Andrea Amati's presumed three-stringed violins (see p. 19; for French inventories of 1551, see p. 16, above).

1556

In his treatise of this date Jambe de Fer gives the first positive documentary evidence of the true four-stringed violin and the tunings for the three principal members of the family, including the modern tunings for violin and viola (see p. 31). (For other documentary information around the middle of the century, including the violin in connexion with state visits of French sovereigns, see chs. 3 and 4; for Vicentino's three-stringed 'violin' of 1555, see p. 19.)

In view of all the evidence offered above, one can say confidently that the terms *violin*, *violino*, and *violon* generally meant 'violin' from early in the sixteenth century. Such terms as *lira*, *violetta*, and *rebecchino* undoubtedly meant 'violin' in certain contexts. *Viola da braccio* meant the violin family as a whole. From about 1525 to 1550 *violino* (or *violon*) meant the early violin of three strings; after 1550, it meant the 'true' violin, since the meaning must have kept pace with the evolution of the instrument. As just explained, the term *violin* (*violon*) is first connected indisputably with the true violin of four strings by Jambe de Fer in 1556.

In Germany the terminology is more confused. At first the term *kleine Geigen* means 'rebecs'—for example, in Virdung, Gerle, and Agricola (edition of 1528-9).[44] These rebecs have three strings (the bass rebec generally has four), they are tuned in fifths, and are played without frets. The term *grosse Geigen* means the viol family. By the time of Agricola's edition of 1545, *kleine Geigen* refers not only to rebecs but also to the 'little fiddles' of the Polish variety and of still another type. These last two types are undoubtedly violins, all having three strings and tuned in fifths. Later, at least by Praetorius's time (1619), *Geigen* is used alone as a synonym for *viole da braccio*, or violins; and *grosse Geigen* has been displaced by the term *viole da gamba* or *Violen*.

---

[44] Sebastian Virdung, *Musica Getutscht*, Basle, 1511; Martin Agricola, op. cit., 1528-9 and 1545; Hans Gerle, *Musica Teusch*, Nürnberg, 1532.

Summary

The earliest violins were an amalgamation of features of the rebec, the fiddle, and especially the *lira da braccio*, a species of fiddle. The violin adopted the body shape of the *lira da braccio* and the three strings and the fifth-tuning of the rebec. The viols were not true ancestors of the violin. Since the violin proved capable of filling the musical role of all its ancestors, it gradually rendered them obsolete. Certain short-lived hybrids were created in the process.

The earliest violins of three strings preceded the true four-stringed violins by about a generation. Italian painting proves that the early violin emerged not later than 1530, and earlier use of terms like *vyollon* make it likely that the instrument appeared a decade before. The viola and cello, the other principal members of the violin family, were in existence by 1535–6. This and other evidence shows that the old theory of the viola preceding the violin is untenable. Although the violin proper may have appeared a few years before the viola and cello, for all practical purposes the violins emerged as a family.

The weight of documentary evidence indicates that the cradle of the early violin was northern Italy, probably within a fifty-mile radius of Milan. The question of whether Brescia or Cremona contributed more to the early violin cannot be positively decided. If anything, Brescia was the more important in the early sixteenth century.

If any one person 'invented' the violin, no one knows, or can know, his identity. Several Brescian makers are possible candidates, Giovan Giacobo dalla Corna and Zanetto Montichiaro being mentioned as makers of 'lyras' (= violins?) by Lanfranco in 1533. In any case there is no proof that Andrea Amati was the 'inventor' of the violin; and Gasparo da Salò (b. 1540) certainly was not.

The main evidence, documentary and pictorial, suggests that the early violins came into being as a family some time in the 1520s in northern Italy. Nearly as early, a similar instrument may be found in France and Poland. However, from political and cultural history, one may infer that the violin was first imported into other countries from Italy as part of the general cultural invasion of all Europe by the forces of the Italian Renaissance.

CHAPTER TWO

✣

The Advent of the true Violin and its Development to 1600

> *Viva fui in silvis; sum dura occisa securi.*
> *Dum vixi, tacui; mortua dulce cano.*
> (Living I dwelt in the forest;
> Then I was slain by the cruel axe.
> While living I was silent;
> But in death my song is sweet.)[1]

THE true violin came into being about the middle of the sixteenth century, when a fourth string was added to the early three-stringed violin, viola, and cello (the cello may already have had four strings). The change to the four-stringed instrument must have taken place by 1556, since Jambe de Fer, in his *Epitome musical* of that year, specifically mentions these fretless instruments with four strings. He distinguishes the violin family clearly from the viols, mentions their respective social functions, and gives their tunings, the soprano member (*dessus*) being tuned like the violin today: g d′ a′ e″. There is no doubt he is describing the true violin.[2]

Jambe de Fer's description is so interesting and valuable that his treatise is worth quoting at length (excerpts from pp. 61–63):

'The tuning and sound [*ton*] of the violin.

The violin [*violon*] is very different from the viol [*viole*]. First of all it has only four strings, which are tuned in fifths . . . and in each of the said strings there are four tones [*tons*] in such a way that in four strings there are as many tones as in the five strings of the viol. The form of the body is smaller, flatter, and in sound it is much harsher [*rude*]; it has

---

[1] In praise of the wood of instruments. An inscription on the portrait of Gaspar Duiffo-prugcar (1514–c. 1570), etched by Pierre Woeriot, 1562. See Plate 9.
[2] Jambe de Fer's alto-tenor (*hautecontre-taille*) is tuned like the modern viola: c g d′ a′; his bass (*bas*), a tone lower than the modern cello: to BB flat F c g.

no frets . . . [tuning instructions follow] and the French and Italians differ in no way as regards playing the instrument.

Why do you call one type of instrument viols and the other violins?

We call viols those with which gentlemen, merchants, and other virtuous people pass their time.

The Italians call them *viole da gambe* [*sic*] because they are held downward, some between the legs, others on some seat or stool; others [are held] on the knees by the said Italians, although the French make little use of this method. The other type [of instrument] is called violin; it is commonly used for dancing, and with good reason, for it is much easier to tune since the interval of the fifth is easier [*plus douce*] to hear [accurately] than the fourth. It is also easier to carry, a very necessary thing while leading [*conduisant*] wedding processions or mummeries.[3]

The Italians call it *violon da braccia* [*sic*] or *violone*[4] because they support it on the arm, some with a scarf, strings, or other thing; the bass [member of the family] is very difficult to carry because of its weight, for which reason it is sustained with a small hook in an iron ring or other thing, which is attached to the back of the said instrument very exactly so that it does not interfere with the player. I have not illustrated the said violin because you can think of it as resembling the viol, added to which there are few persons who use it save those who make a living from it through their labour.'

The implication of this last statement is that violinists were professionals; they knew what the violin looked like, and nobody else was interested.

Why was the fourth (E) string added to the early violin? The reason probably lies in a combination of several factors. For one thing, the fourth string added a register which emphasized the characteristic soprano qualities of the violin. In this register the sound was especially attractive (significantly the French called this string 'la chanterelle'), and it 'carried'—an important matter to dance violinists. Besides, the additional string expanded the playing range, also something of a consideration since the lowest string, being usually of gut, was not very responsive and was little used. Another possibility is that the range of music in general began to use a somewhat higher

---

[3] A mummery is a theatrical performance usually involving masked figures. Dancing may be a part also. See p. 55, below, for sixteenth-century accounts in France of the violins 'en Muses'.

[4] For the significance of *violon* or *violone* in this connexion, see pp. 22–23, above. The Italian term we should expect is *viola da braccio*, and Jambe de Fer uses (above) the normal term for viol: *viole da gambe* (i.e. his idea of the plural). At this time, the Italian term *violone* means the viols as a family (see p. 25). Later its meaning is restricted to double-bass viol.

register in the upper parts; and assuming that the violins occasionally doubled the parts of vocal music, the added upward range would be a natural development.[5]

However, even though the soprano range was gradually becoming higher, the voice registers were still relatively low-pitched by modern standards, and would have required more instruments in the alto-tenor register than in the soprano. Hence the need for violas was probably greater, numerically speaking, than the need for violins until fairly late in the sixteenth century. This is one reason why Gasparo da Salò presumably made more violas than violins and why a picture of Lasso (painted 1565–70) with the Munich Court Chapel shows more instruments nearer the size of a viola than a violin (see Plate 15 and p. 40). However, this point has no real bearing on the question of which member of the violin family was first to appear (see p. 15). All members of the violin family were needed to double the parts of vocal music.

Although many refinements of detail have taken place from the middle of the sixteenth century to the present day, the violin family was complete in its basic structural features about 1550. This does not mean that the family as a whole was standardized. The viola varied considerably in size, as it still does today, and the dimensions of the cello were not established until the time of Stradivari. Even the violin, the most stable of the family, displayed considerable variety. The body of the modern violin is a standard length of fourteen inches. In the sixteenth century, the violin was made in a small pattern about a quarter-inch shorter than the modern violin, and in a larger one as much as a half-inch longer. Both Andrea Amati and Gasparo da Salò made violins in large and small patterns, while Maggini, a pupil of Gasparo, favoured the large pattern.[6]

Certain details of construction of the old violin, which may be observed in a few extant instruments and in paintings, differ markedly from the

---

[5] It is not clear just when violins began to double vocal parts. Strings and wind instruments in general must have done so fairly early. One of the first documents to demonstrate this is the title-page of Gombert's four-part motets (*c.* 1539), which says they are 'suited to various stringed and wind instruments' ('*lyris maioribus ac tibiis imparibus accomodata*'). In this connexion, *lyra* is the general word for strings, plucked and bowed; *maior* may have the force of the augmentative, possibly suggesting viols as a family (cf. p. 25). It is also possible that *lyra* may mean *viola da braccio* = violin family (see p. 16). *Tibia* is the general name for wind instruments and suggests specifically the flute (recorder), shawm (oboe type), and trombone. Gombert's full title-page is reproduced in facsimile in *MGG*, Vol. 5, cols. 501–2.

[6] Even in a 'standard' size violin of fourteen-inch body, there are many variations in detail, such as the shape of f-holes and of upper, middle, and lower bouts. Variation in these factors, not to mention the manner of cutting the wood, the quality of wood used, varnishes, scrolls, and details of decoration, afford infinite combinations, and distinguish the workmanship of one master from another. In this book, however, we cannot generally pursue such matters. Our account is limited to the general development of the violin as a necessary background and complement to the history of violin playing.

modern violin. The neck is shorter and projects straight from the body, while the neck of the modern violin is bent down at an angle. In the sixteenth century the pegbox describes a much greater downward curve than in later violins. The fingerboard of the old violin is considerably shorter than it is today, and because of the straight neck a wedge is inserted between the neck and the fingerboard to permit the latter to rise in an angle to the bridge. Plate 6 shows the old violin compared to the modern violin. (See also Plate 4b for the short neck, bridge, and short fingerboard of the sixteenth-century *lira da braccio*; Plate 7 shows short fingerboards of two sixteenth-century violas; see also Plate 26). As seen in painting, the bridge is often shown somewhat lower and perhaps less rounded than would be usual now, although these matters are subject to great variation. In some paintings the bridge is placed much farther down toward the tailpiece than it is on the modern violin (compare the modern violin in Plate 1 with the viola in the Saronno fresco in Plate 2); and this feature persists into the seventeenth century, contrary to some observers who have claimed that this position of the bridge was unique to the violin before 1550. With the bridge fitted in this way, the string length is increased, and (according to Sol Babitz) the violin gives a 'silky viola-like tone'.

Our knowledge of the violin after 1550 is much less ephemeral than it is before that date. A few actual instruments are extant, and the names and reputations of certain instrument makers can be clearly established, including those of the celebrated dynasties of violin makers in Cremona and Brescia. Various inventories and records show that the violin was made and used widely throughout Europe. Italy, in particular, enjoyed a flourishing export business in violins and violinists. Iconography is also witness to the evolution of the violin and its popularity, especially in festivals and dancing. Toward the end of the century, first-rate artists, such as Caravaggio, were moved to portray the violin in certain paintings, and sometimes the glowing colours and meticulous workmanship of these instruments reveal the hand of a master craftsman. A few theorists, notably Jambe de Fer (1556) and Zacconi (1592) add precious information about the violin, although Zacconi sometimes confuses as well as helps us in our struggle to penetrate the meaning and mysteries of sixteenth-century terminology (cf. p. 42).

The emergence of Cremona and Brescia as the great centres of violin making is connected with the names of Andrea Amati of Cremona and Gasparo da Salò (1540–1609) of Brescia.[7] Although it is quite probable that

[7] Gasparo da Salò's family name was Bertolotti. He was born at Polpenazze, a small town next to Salò on Lake Garda. According to A. M. Mucchi (op. cit.), he was baptized on 20 May 1540. However, in his income-tax return of 1568 (cited by Mucchi), Gasparo says he is twenty-six; and in his return of 1588 he says he is forty-five—which would seem to show that he was born about 1542. There is no obvious way to account for this discrepancy. At any rate, Gasparo moved to Brescia in 1562 and lived and worked there until his death in 1609.

Brescia played a more important role than Cremona in the first half-century of violin making (cf. p. 38), there is no doubt that Cremona violins became increasingly famous. After the death of the Brescian master G. P. Maggini (the pupil of Gasparo da Salò) about 1632, Cremona violins were unrivalled in Italy, that is to say, the world (for Monteverdi's opinion on the relative merit of Brescian and Cremonese violins, see p. 109). It is likely that Andrea Amati, born not later than 1511 and the founder of the Amati dynasty of Cremona, was the first *famous* maker. He must have been some thirty years older than Gasparo da Salò (b. 1540), the supposed 'inventor' of the violin; and, even allowing for ambiguous and uncertain information, Amati's earliest violins were probably made in the 1540s, while those of Gasparo can hardly have been made before the 1560s. The date of Jambe de Fer's treatise (1556), reporting the four-stringed violin, coincides nicely with the first reported four-stringed violin of Andrea Amati. An Amati violin with four strings and a fourteen-inch body, bearing a label dated 1555, was reported by Strocchi.[8] By 1555 Amati was at least forty-five years old and an acknowledged master craftsman. A few years later Amati had become so famous that (according to La Borde) Charles IX of France ordered from him twelve large and twelve small violins, six violas, and eight basses, a complete string band of thirty-eight instruments.[9] While La Borde's account cannot be confirmed in detail, there are nevertheless two instruments of Andrea Amati in playing condition in the Ashmolean Museum at Oxford: a small violin dated 1564 and a very large (tenor) viola dated 1574 (Plate 7), both with the arms of France depicted on them and inscribed as belonging to Charles IX (reigned 1560–74). According to Van der Straeten, one of the presumed 'Charles IX' cellos [1572?], similarly inscribed, was exhibited and owned in England late in the nineteenth century.[10]

These thirty-eight instruments reported to have been made by Andrea Amati for Charles IX neatly illustrate the uncertainties and doubts surrounding an investigation of the violin in the sixteenth century. The Ashmolean violin of Amati is dated 1564, and if this is correct, the instruments must

---

[8] Strocchi, op. cit., pp. 171–2. For Amati's presumed three-stringed violins of the 1540s, see p. 19, above.

[9] Jean Benjamin de La Borde, *Essai sur la musique*, Paris, 1780, p. 356.

[10] E. Van der Straeten, *The History of the Violoncello*, London, 1915, Vol. I, p. 126. What is possibly another of these cellos is shown in A. Jacquot, *La lutherie lorraine et française*, Paris, 1912, p. 191. This cello, from the 'Collection Snoeck' at Ghent, also exhibits the arms of Charles IX. For still another Andrea Amati cello, thought to contain an original label dated 1569, see *The Strad* magazine for December 1959. For another decorated viola (but not of this set), see the same magazine for August 1959. There are at least two other 'Charles IX' violins extant: one in the city museum at Carlisle (England) and the other privately owned in New York City. The latter instrument, played by Ruggiero Ricci, may be heard in a phonograph record called 'The Glories of Cremona'.

have been ordered prior to 1564. But Charles IX became King in 1560 at the age of ten and was entirely under the domination of his mother, Catherine de' Medici. Charles was a lover of poetry and a patron of Ronsard—possibly he was an amateur violinist—but it was his mother who was genuinely fond of music and dancing. If the violins were ordered of Amati in the early 1560s, it was probably the Queen Mother who commissioned them in the name of the young King. Possibly Beaujoyeulx, the chief of the Italian violinists at the French Court (see p. 38), suggested it. At any rate, by 1573 there were 'some thirty violins' available (all Amatis?) to play in the ballet with which Catherine entertained the Polish Embassy. The latter had come to the French Court for the purpose of offering the Polish Crown to her son, the Duke of Anjou, the brother of Charles, and later Henry III.[11]

Andrea Amati was dead by 1580, and his tradition was carried on by his two sons Antonio (born *c.* 1540) and Girolamo (also called Hieronymus, 1561–1630). These two, known as the 'brothers Amati', often made and labelled instruments jointly. This celebrated family reached its highest point in the seventeenth century in the person of Nicola Amati, the son of Girolamo (see ch. 5).

The life and works of Gasparo da Salò in the context of the Brescian school have been dealt with at length by A. M. Mucchi in a full-scale study, which includes lists of instruments and splendid plates. However, there is considerable confusion as to the dates, and, in some cases, the authenticity of Gasparo's instruments. Probably his early instruments date from the 1560s. A particularly interesting early instrument, combining the features of a *lira da braccio* and viola (this combination is called *lira-viola*), is shown in Mucchi's Plate XL, and another like it, dated 1561, is in the Ashmolean Museum. The *lira-viola* is one of those transient and hybrid forms that accompanied the evolution of the violin in the sixteenth century. A Gasparo viola in the Ashmolean Museum (*c.* 1580, according to Mucchi) makes an interesting contrast with the Amati viola of Charles IX (Plate 7). Both have the short, rather broad neck of the time (only the Amati's is original), and the body outlines are fully developed. These two large tenors exhibit individual differences not uncharacteristic of the Brescian and Cremonese schools as a whole. The Gasparo is rather more massive in appearance and construction, particularly in the upper bouts. The f-holes are also quite different, showing the pronounced individuality of each maker. Unfortunately our plate, being in black and white, cannot give an idea of the beautiful varnishes which make these instruments glow with life and colour—especially the Amati. Finally, some of the Gasparo violins use the double purfling and type

---

[11] For the information on the Polish Embassy see *Oeuvres complètes de Branthôme* [sic], ed. by Mérimée et Lacour, Paris, 13 vols., 1858–95, Vol. 10 (1890), p. 75.

of decorations so characteristic of the instruments of his pupil, G. P. Maggini (see ch. 5).

A few other early Italian violins are extant. There is a violin, dated 1581 and now in Vienna, made by the Venetian, Ventura Linarola (b. about 1550). The body outline is well developed but the f-holes are relatively primitive. This is one of the few surviving instruments of what must have been a flourishing school of Venetian violin making.[12] Craftsmen of other Italian cities continued to make violins, but no maker approached the fame of Amati or Gasparo da Salò.

Italian painting of the second half of the sixteenth century continues to show violinists from time to time. In Veronese's 'Marriage at Cana' (1563) a rather primitive violin is being played in the central background. Similarly, a portrait, thought to be of Monteverdi about the age of twenty-five (i.e. about 1592) shows him playing a viol; while hanging on the wall in the background is an alto violin with f-holes, deeply indented middle bouts, double purfling, and an inlaid fingerboard. The instrument is probably of Brescian manufacture, but it is of no particular distinction. The bow is also partly visible.[13] A sketch by Caracci about 1600, unique of its kind, shows the side (profile) view of a violin as well as sketches of the hand position of the player holding the bow both right-handed (below) and left-handed (above), and (possibly) tuning the violin with the right hand! (See ch. 4 and Plate 16.)

However, not until about 1600 do painters begin to represent the violin in the perfection of form and colour that it must have, in fact, attained some time earlier. In 1533 Lanfranco speaks of Brescian instruments so beautiful that they 'appear to have been created not by the hands of men but by Nature herself' (see above, p. 17). While one might tend to discount this extravagant statement as the natural enthusiasm of a native son (Lanfranco being a Brescian), the fact remains that among the few extant instruments of the time are those which cannot fail to impress the eye with their extra-ordinary craftsmanship and beauty—among them, the *lira da braccio* in Plate 4 and the violas of Gasparo da Salò and Andrea Amati in Plate 7. But there are no paintings of the same time that depict instruments of similar beauty and perfection. This situation began to change only about 1600. Caravaggio, for instance, paints not only the true violin but also the *violino piccolo* with something approaching life-like reality of form and colour. One of the most impressive of these life-like paintings is the 'Lute Player' of Gentileschi (formerly attributed to Caravaggio), which shows a beautiful violin and bow (Plate 8).

[12] This instrument is shown in Kinsky, op. cit., p. 146.
[13] See W. H., A. F., and A. E. Hill, *Antonio Stradivari*, London, 1902. Portrait is reproduced opposite p. 284. For Monteverdi, 'suonatore della vivuola', see p. 108, note 1.

The fame and superiority of Italian violins and players are best attested by records of the flourishing export business to foreign countries. The importation of all sorts of Italian works began about 1496 in the reign of Charles VIII, continued under Francis I, and increased after Catherine de' Medici's marriage to the Duc d'Orléans in 1533 (Dauphin after 1536) and especially after she became Queen in 1547. At her instigation Charles de Brissac, Marshal of France and Governor of Piedmont, sent dancers to France under the Milanese choreographer, Pompeo Diobono (1554), and about a year later, a band of Italian violinists. Their leader was Baldassare da Belgiojoso (a town about twenty-five miles south of Milan)—also called Baltazarini or Balthasar (or Baltasar) de Beaujoyeulx—'the best violinist in Christendom' ('*le meilleur violon de la Chrestiente*')[14] and *maître de ballet*, later responsible for producing the celebrated *Ballet comique de la reine* of 1581 (see p. 55). As mentioned above, Charles IX of France is said to have commissioned a number of violins from Andrea Amati of Cremona; and there is, in addition, another record of Charles IX paying '50 pounds tournois' to one Sieur Delinet to buy a Cremona violin in 1572.[15] Gasparo da Salò from Brescia refers to his export business with France in his income-tax return of 1588, and notes that his French business is falling off—naturally so because of the disturbed political situation in France at that time. The inventories of Parisian instrument makers and dealers, dating from 1551–1625,[16] list the violin (as well as other members of the violin family) in 'the fashion of' Venice, Brescia, and Cremona. It is a moot point whether this phrase means that these violins originated in the Italian cities named or whether they were made in France after 'the fashion of' Italian models. Whatever the truth may be, the majority of those named 'in the fashion of' Italian cities were Brescian, implying a longer tradition of violin manufacture in Brescia than elsewhere.

There are similar instances of Italian imports by other regions and countries. According to Van der Straeten, Flanders, which at that time was in close contact with Italy in everything respecting music (having exported many Flemish composers to Italy), was one of the first countries to introduce the new instruments; and in 1559 Pietro Lupo 'of Antwerp' sold to a repre-

---

[14] According to Brantôme, complete edition of Mérimée and Lacour, Vol. 12 (1894), pp. 151-2. According to A. Pougin (*Le Violon*, Paris, 1924, p. 128), these Italian violinists used violins with five strings tuned in fourths (a d' g' c" f"), 'according to the usage in their country at that time'. This is pure nonsense. There is not a single work of the time that mentions a violin with five strings or one tuned in fourths. Possibly Pougin has confused Jambe de Fer's account of the French viols with the violins. Jambe de Fer says the French use viols of five strings tuned in fourths, but there is no doubt that his violin is a four-stringed instrument tuned in fifths (see p. 31 above).

[15] M. Pincherle, *Les Violonistes*, Paris, 1922, p. 13.

[16] See François Lesure, op. cit., pp. 11-52.

sentative of the Utrecht magistrate five violins (presumably Italian?) and their cases for seventy-two *livres*.[17] By 1590 almost all the players of viols and violins employed by Queen Elizabeth of England were Italian, including various members of the Lupo family headed by Ambrose Lupo of Milan.[18] These imported Italian violins must have commanded considerable prices. Even in Italy violins executed on commission were astonishingly dear. In 1588 Gasparo da Salò reported receiving 102 *lire*, 10 *soldi*, as either the contract price or the deposit on a 'couple of violins' made to order—a sum for each violin more than four times the yearly wage of 12 *lire* he paid to his house-maid![19]

The French inventories mentioned above point also to a considerable native school of violin making centred in Paris after 1550. Other schools were located at Mirecourt, Nancy,[20] and Lyon. The craftsmen at Lyon may have received a real impetus from the immigration of a number of Italians, especially from Milan, a city to which Lyon owed much of its pre-eminence in the silk industry. Through the weaving of silk, Lyon attained great riches and reputation. Francis I actively encouraged this industry. In 1520, for instance, he brought silkworm eggs from Milan to the Rhone valley. (For more information on Francis I and Milan, see p. 21.) Lyon was also on one of the principal trade routes from Venice to Paris. This route passed through Milan, thence to Lyon, and on to Paris; and perhaps this, together with the silk trade, helps explain the fact that the general regions of Milan, Paris, and Lyon are the areas about which we hear the most concerning the manufac-ture of the early violin. A number of concrete events suggest Lyon's impor-tance as a centre of violin making. The true four-stringed violin is first described in Jambe de Fer's treatise in 1556, printed in Lyon. Gaspar Duiffo-prugcar also worked in Lyon from about 1553 to his death in 1571. Although he was known best as a lute maker, and although his 'early' violins have turned out to be forgeries, he may have made violins after 1550.

Woeriot's celebrated portrait of Duiffoprugcar (1562) depicts several instruments (see Plate 9), but none of them is a true violin. Among them (centre) is a four-stringed instrument having several features of a viol as well as certain characteristics of a violin. Those traits typical of the viol are C-holes, no purfling, thick ribs, and no overhanging edges. Those common to the violin are the size, the rounded shoulders, and the lack of frets. Another instrument in the Woeriot portrait (right side) has the typical

[17] E. Van der Straeten, *History of the Violoncello*, London, 1915, Vol. I, pp. 128–9. Also, see Vidal, op. cit., Vol. I, p. 59.
[18] See Walter Woodfill, *Musicians in English Society*, Princeton, 1953, p. 300. For importa-tion into Austria, see Walter Senn, *Musik und Theater am Hof zu Innsbruck*, Innsbruck, 1954.
[19] Mucchi, op. cit., p. 62.
[20] For Mirecourt and Nancy see A. Jacquot, *La lutherie lorraine et française*, Paris, 1912.

f-holes of the violin and is the size of a viola, but otherwise it has the features of a viol: namely, sloping shoulders, frets, and five strings. Finally, some French drawings by Jacques Cellier about 1585, in a manuscript now in Paris, include one of a violin of fairly primitive form together with its bow. The fingerboard is fretted like a viol. This instrument cannot be attached to any school, and is perhaps intended by Cellier as merely representative of the violin as a species.[21]

The violin existed and was presumably made in other countries of Europe, but the records are much more scanty than those concerning the use of the violin and its makers in France and Italy. If there were native schools of violin making in Germany, England, or elsewhere in the sixteenth century, there are no records to prove it. Presumably violins (as well as violinists) were frequently imported from Italy.

In Germany the violin is connected with music at the Bavarian Court by the well-known painting of Hans Mielich representing the Court Chapel at Munich under Orlando Lasso (Plate 15). This picture, done between 1565 and 1570, includes a spinet, wind instruments, and strings. Among the latter are two partially concealed violas and two large-sized violins (or possibly small violas). However, all this tells us nothing about German schools of violin making, and there is a strange lack of such evidence in a country that produced theorists like Agricola during the first part of the sixteenth century. There appears to be only one later reference to the 'Polish' fiddles of which Agricola spoke in 1545 (see p. 28). The burgomaster of the German city Stralsund mentions four *polnische Geiger* in his city in 1555. One other reference connects the violin to the Polish Court. A motet sung during the opening church service at the Parliament of Medgyes in Hungary (1585) was accompanied by a trombone player and a violinist in the service of Stephen Báthory, King of Poland; but the violinist was Italian, and Stephen Báthory himself was educated in Italy,[22] pointing to a foreign art, an imported player, and probably an Italian violin. In short, if there was a native school of violin making in Poland at this time, there are no traces of it now.

And what of Spain, a country with close cultural and political ties to Italy, and whose period of cultural greatness was the sixteenth and seventeenth centuries? After the Treaty of Cateau-Cambrésis (1559), which brought the Hapsburg-Valois wars to a close, all the Italian states except Venice were more or less under Spanish domination. It seems incredible that there should not have been some export of Italian violins to Spain, but if such took place, no documents which furnish particulars are known to exist. Nor do we have information about a native school of Spanish violin making in the

---

[21] See *The Galpin Society Journal*, Vol. X (1957): Plate after p. 62; text, p. 88.
[22] For this see Gustave Reese, *Music in the Renaissance*, New York, 1954, pp. 757 and 725–6.

sixteenth century (or at any other time). Nevertheless, the violin must have been used in Spanish musical life during the sixteenth century, since a few Spanish paintings about 1600 show the violin in developed form. An example is Juan de Roelas's (1560–1625), 'The Death of St. Hermenegild' in Seville. This painting depicts a death scene in which three musicians appear, one playing a large four-stringed violin with double purfling (a characteristic of the Brescian school), another a cello, and still a third a harp (Plate 10). In a country where rebecs and fiddles, those parent instruments of the violin, are portrayed frequently in medieval art, it is strange that the violin is so conspicuous by its absence in the sixteenth century. Perhaps some future and systematic search of Spanish sources will turn up evidence supporting the presence and manufacture of the violin in sixteenth-century Spain.

English documents and paintings afford a number of references to violins and violinists, but a majority of both were probably imported from Italy. The records of 'The King's Musick' list the names of musicians in royal employ, and from 1555 onward the names of Italian violinists appear, and practically all, if not all, come from Italy—to judge by the names themselves or by specific references to 'alien' and being 'of Venice', or 'of Cremona', or 'of Milan'. 'Ambrose [Lupo] de Milan', for instance, appears first (1540) on these rolls as a viol player and later (1555–91) among the players of viols and/or violins. Significantly, not long after the violins appear on these rolls, the rebecs disappear from the lists of the royal musicians.[23]

There are various literary and civic records concerning the use of the violin in festivals and ceremonies (cf. ch. 3), but none refer to native violin makers, although they doubtless existed. Certain inventories of wealthy establishments listed violins among the household instruments (see p. 58), and violins may be observed from time to time in contemporary painting. For example, in a well-known picture, said (probably erroneously, see p. 57) to show Queen Elizabeth dancing with the Earl of Leicester about 1581,[24] the dancers are accompanied by a violin, a viola (or large violin), and cello, all shown as rather primitive (and perhaps locally made?) instruments (Plate 14). This painting may have been inspired by the 'French' painting at Rennes (Plate 13); it is very similar (see p. 56, note 13). Instruments of like but better modelling can be seen in a picture painted in 1590 by the English Court painter, Joris Hoefnagel.[25] This painting depicts a wedding festivity

---

[23] For these lists, see Woodfill, op. cit., and particularly *The King's Musick (1460–1700)*, ed. by H. C. De Lafontaine, London, n.d. (preface dated 1909).

[24] Queen Elizabeth apparently was no stranger to the violins and had employed them in her household much earlier before coming to the throne. According to the *Oxford English Dictionary*, article 'Violin', the accounts of the household expenses for the Princess Elizabeth in 1552 listed a payment of forty shillings to the 'violans'.

[25] This painting is now at Hatfield House. Reproduced in Van der Straeten, *History of the Violin*, 2 vols., London, 1933, Vol. I, opposite p. 65.

H.V.P.–E

of a well-to-do family. At the lower right of the picture is a violinist and viola player (each instrument having four strings), playing for a group of dancers. Another violin and viola (?) can be detected in the background. We have no way of knowing, of course, whether these instruments were produced in England or elsewhere.

Treatises. Terminology

For all practical purposes there are only two treatises that add much to our information about the violin between 1550 and 1600: Jambe de Fer (1556) in France and Zacconi (1592) in Italy. Jambe de Fer's terminology is reasonably clear (see p. 31 for text). His general term for 'viols' is *violes*, and he gives *viole da gambe* [*sic*] as the Italian equivalent. His name for 'violins' is *violons*, which he says the Italians call *violon da braccia* (= *viole da braccio*; cf. p. 32, note 4) or *violone*; and he distinguishes three principal tuning-registers comparable to those of violin, viola, and cello.

Zacconi, on the other hand, is the personification of inconsistency and confusion.[26] Still, his information is valuable, even unique. His is the only source, for instance, that identifies the *violini* with both the violin (g-tuning) and the viola (c-tuning); and this explains why the term *violino* is used by Giovanni Gabrieli in his *Sonata Pian e Forte* (1597) for an instrumental part which descends below the violin register into that of the viola's lowest string. Gabrieli and Zacconi were both Venetians, and this twofold meaning for *violino* must have been peculiar to Venetian usage.

Zacconi's grammatical construction and meaning are peculiarly hard to understand, and consequently he has been badly misunderstood (cf. note 27). At times he seems to distinguish the *viole* completely from the *violini*, but this is only for purposes of generalizing about a whole class of instruments on the one hand (viola = both violin family and viol family) and distinguishing specific instruments (*violino*) on the other. He makes a clear distinction between the viols (*viole da gamba*) and the violins (*viole da braccio*). For the *viole da braccio* Zacconi gives three tuning registers, and although the language is very involved, it is finally clear that he means this:

$$\text{Viole da braccio} \begin{cases} \text{Soprano:} & \text{g} \quad \text{d}' \, \text{a}' \, \text{e}'' \\ \text{Tenor:} & \text{F} \quad \text{c} \, \text{g} \, \text{d}' \\ \text{Bass:} & \text{BB}\flat \, \text{F} \, \text{c} \, \text{g} \end{cases}$$

Then he gives *two* tunings for the *violini*:

$$\text{Violini} \begin{cases} \text{g d a}' \, \text{e}'' \, \text{(in notes)} \\ \text{c g d}' \, \text{a}' \, \text{(in the text)} \end{cases}$$

---

[26] Lodovico Zacconi, *Prattica di musica*, Venice, 1592. Some of Zacconi's information comes from Lanfranco's treatise of 1533, nearly sixty years earlier, and Zacconi explicitly refers to Lanfranco.

Hence the *soprano viola da braccio* = *violino* = modern violin. *Violino* may also mean modern viola.

To understand Zacconi we must keep in mind and accept that

1. *Viole da braccio* is a general term which includes *violino*. Every *violino*, in short, is a *viola da braccio*, but not every *viola da braccio* is a *violino*—any more than every automobile is a Rolls-Royce.

2. Through an oversight Zacconi does not include the alto-register instrument (c-tuning = modern viola) among the *viole da braccio* but only among the *violini*. To him this would have been a matter of no great moment since the alto-violin was one of the *viole da braccio* as a matter of course—just as today it is unnecessary to mention specifically that a Rolls-Royce belongs to the general classification 'automobile'.

3. Zacconi actually admits *four* tuning-registers for the violin family, not the usual three; and rather than assign a single tuning-register to the instruments 'of the middle' (alto, tenor), he assigns two, one each to alto *and* tenor.[27]

The confusion of terminology stems partly from the fact that a number of qualifiers and diminutives are used in connexion with the word *viola*, a term of several meanings, dating back at least to the fifteenth-century treatise of Tinctoris (see p. 50). On the other hand, *violino* never meant anything except a member of the violin family (see below) and, as has been explained *ad nauseam*, the term *viola da braccio* clearly distinguished a member of the violin family from the *viola da gamba* or member of the viol family.

The confusion of terminology simply reflects a considerable variety and confusion of the violin family itself in a state of transition and evolution during the sixteenth century. The four principal sizes of soprano, alto, tenor, and bass corresponded to the four principal parts of the vocal choir, which they often accompanied. But these four instruments were generally grouped in three tuning-registers—the alto and tenor, the 'instruments of the middle', being tuned the same. *In other words, the violin family comprised three principal species but they were often distributed in four or more parts.* In the sixteenth and seventeenth centuries a typical four-part string ensemble might consist of a part for violin, two for viola, and one for cello. In the seventeenth century

---

[27] Unfortunately the late Gerald Hayes (*Musical Instruments, 1500–1750*, 2 vols., London, 1928–30), to whom musicians are indebted for much valuable research, misread Zacconi, assigning the *soprano viola da braccio* exclusively the c-tuning of a modern viola. This error had the effect of setting the *viole da braccio* apart from the violin when, as just explained, the violins were, in fact, part of the *viole da braccio* as a family. Hayes's error, accepted by Bessaraboff and Galpin, has been perpetuated in his article on the violin in the 1954 edition of *Grove's Dictionary*. The late Curt Sachs (*The History of Musical Instruments*, New York, 1940) adopted a similar theory on other, but equally untenable, grounds. For detailed arguments, including texts and translation of Zacconi, see David D. Boyden, 'Monteverdi's *Violini Piccoli alla Francese* and *Viole da Brazzo*' in *Annales Musicologiques*, Vol. VI, Paris, 1958–63.

Mersenne's five-part ensemble was composed of one part for violin, three for viola, and one for cello (see p. 117). The size of the violas assigned to the middle register varied greatly, the smaller violas playing in the alto register and the larger violas in the tenor. Similarly, the bass, roughly corresponding to the present cello (*violoncello* = *violone-cello* = a little double-bass), existed in various sizes. Besides these regular members of the family there was a *violino piccolo*, a smaller instrument than the violin, and tuned a third, fourth, or even an octave above the violin. This instrument (body length of eleven to twelve inches) should not be confused with the small-pattern violin of regular tuning (body length of thirteen and a half inches). Finally, the double-bass violin was an ungainly monster, and the variety of its forms can still be seen in the modern symphony orchestra. At first (in the early sixteenth century), the term *violone* was used to refer to all members of the viol family collectively; later it meant the double-bass viol only (see p. 25).

Happily, the violin itself was the most stable of the family as to form, terminology, and tuning. Although the violin existed in a small and large pattern, as explained above, the differences between the two were not great, and its tuning was consistently the tuning in fifths upward from 'g'. While terms like *rebecchino*, *lira*, and *violetta* might mean 'violin' in certain contexts, the term *violino* never meant anything except a member of the violin family; and increasingly, as the century progressed, it was used in its particular sense of the violin proper or (in Zacconi) the violin *and* viola proper. However, there are those who claim that *violino* may mean either 'viol' or 'violin'. If so, such instances are exceptions which must have resulted from carelessness or ignorance of the clearly understood contemporary meaning of *violino* (*violon*, violin) in the sixteenth century. The terminology used in inventories, records, and in the theorists is unusually clear in this respect. At Queen Elizabeth's coronation in 1558 there were three 'vyalls' and six 'violons'; and such phrases as 'viol or violin or both' leave no doubt that there was a clear distinction between the two families and that the two terms were quite separate and distinct.[28]

More specifically, in England *viol* (*viall*, *vyall*) is clearly distinguished from *violin* (also spelled: *violen*, *viollen*, *viollon*, *violine*, *vyoline*, *viallin*, *violan*, *violand*, *violent*, *vyolon*), and the individual members of the families are described by such expressions as *bass viol*, *tenor violin*, and so on.

In France *viole* is quite separate from *violon*, and, as Jambe de Fer says (see p. 31), 'the violon is very different from the viole'. As in English, the individual members of the family are specifically referred to by such terms as *taille de viole* (tenor viol), or *haute-contre de violon* (alto violin = viola). Other qualifiers are: *dessus* (discant, treble, soprano), *basse* (bass), and *basse contre* (double-bass).

[28] For the phrase, see Woodfill, op. cit., p. 85; also pp. 183 and 299.

In Italy, the basic terms, *viola da braccio* and *viola da gamba* are qualified by the terms, *soprano*, *alto*, *tenor*, and *bass*. Thus *soprano viola da braccio* = *violino* = violin.

In Germany the situation is somewhat more confused. The *kleine Geigen* refer not only to rebecs but violins. The usual qualifiers are *discant*, *alto-tenor*, and *bass*. Later, the specific Italian terminology of *viola da braccio* and *viola da gamba* with its appropriate qualifiers may be found in Germany. By the early seventeenth century, *Geige* may be used for the violin proper, and it is not long before *Brazzo* (from *braccio*) becomes *Bratsche*, the latter being the modern German term for viola.

The violin bow in the sixteenth century

There is no reason to think that the bow used with the earliest violins differed significantly from those used by their ancestors among the rebecs, fiddles, or *lire da braccio*. However, all these bows varied greatly in shape and length, the rebec bow and bows for dancing being generally shorter than the *lira da braccio* bow. It is a striking fact that in Agricola (ed. of 1545) the bows illustrated for the *grosse Geigen* (viols) do not differ markedly from those for the *kleine Geigen* (rebecs, violins; only the rebecs are shown).

We are entirely dependent on iconography for our knowledge of the sixteenth-century bow. When this type of bow became obsolete in the eighteenth century, such old bows as had survived were almost all discarded. A few from the seventeenth and eighteenth centuries survived, but apparently none from the sixteenth. Unlike the violins, it was easier to make new bows than to alter and preserve old ones to conform to changed conditions.

All bows, whatever their length and appearance, were generally convex in shape, that is, outwardly curved like a hunting bow. In general, the degree of curvature of the bow stick was fairly considerable in the early part of the sixteenth century, but it began to decrease at the end of the century. Some of the bows are represented as clumsy; others as well balanced and relatively efficient, even elegant.

In general, the ribbon of hair appears somewhat narrower than it is now. At any rate, one of the main problems in making the bow was how to secure the hair. The early bow had no head at the point (as a rule), but was fastened directly to the point in one of various ways. Similarly, the hair was secured at the other end by various devices of tieing or slotting; and given sufficient curvature to the bow stick, the hair was held away from the bow stick satisfactorily. The pronounced curvature of the bow stick, however, made the bow hard to manage, and consequently the bow stick began to be straightened. As this happened, some way had to be found to keep the hair away from the stick for efficient playing. The first development was a kind of horn-shaped nut which held the hair away from the stick at the lower part of the bow where it was grasped by the player's hand (see Plate 11). However, at the point the stick and hair still came together in an apex, and this feature of the bow actually reduced the amount of hair available for playing. This difficulty was settled eventually by making a 'head' which held the hair away from the bow stick at the point. A head of sorts appears on some bows shortly after 1600 (Plate 12), and may even be seen in a woodcut of the late fifteenth century (Fig. 3), which shows a bow with both head and horn-shaped nut. Note that both the bow and the instrument are hung up by a nail. The instrument, a *lira da braccio*, displays one unusual feature: the bourdon strings run off the *right* side of the fingerboard, not off the left side as is usual. Undoubtedly the artist cut the woodblock as he saw the instrument, and thus the image was reversed in the printing, switching the position of the bourdons.

Another problem was tightening the hair. For the most part the bows were fixed in tension, the hair being attached firmly to the point at one end and to the horn-shaped nut at the other (cf. Plate 11). It is possible that some other devices to regulate and adjust the tension of the hair, involving slots and wedges, were used in the sixteenth century and had been earlier. But for the most part the sixteenth-century bow was fixed in tension, and successful attempts to solve the problem of adjusting the bow hair to different tensions did not occur until the end of the seventeenth century, when the movable nut, involving thread and screw, was invented (for more on the bow and its action, see ch. 4; also cf. the bows in Plates 2, 8, and 16; for a primitive slip-knot tightening device, see Bessarraboff, op cit., p. 348.)

Summary

About 1550 a fourth string was added to the early three-stringed violin. The four-stringed instrument, which gave an additional fifth in upward compass, became the standard violin.

The principal structural features of the true violin must have been established about the middle of the sixteenth century. At the same time, considerable experimentation was taking place, the violin being made in a small and a large pattern for some years; and various details of construction and fitting of the violin altered it in one way or another through the centuries and up to the present day.

There is an encouraging increase in our knowledge of the violin after 1550. The first of the great makers appear, among them, Andrea Amati of Cremona and Gasparo da Salò of Brescia. At the same time, the violin was used more and more throughout other European countries. We may presume, although we do not know, that violins were made by native makers in every country that used them. Duiffoprugcar's portrait by Woeriot (Plate 9) and the Paris inventories (p. 16) point to a native school in Lyon, Paris, and else-

*Fig. 3. Bow with incipient head. Bow and lira da braccio
suspended by nails from the wall.*

where in France. Records in other countries are very scanty in this respect. One may also assume that a certain number of violins were imported from Italy into various countries. In any case, Italy enjoyed a flourishing export business in violins and violinists, notably to France. The best of the Italian violins commanded very high prices relative to living standards.

To judge by the few extant violins before 1600, the violin 'in the flesh' was considerably superior in beauty and craftsmanship to the rather inferior and primitive specimens that appear in sixteenth-century paintings. After 1600 painters like Gentileschi began to paint the violin with the beauty of lifelike reality (cf. Plate 8).

While the terminology of the violin and violin family is confused and confusing, the word *violin* (It., *violino*; Fr., *violon*) seems to have meant 'violin', and, as far as is known, seldom if ever 'viol'. The term *violin* unqualified might refer to any member of the violin family, but it was used more and more in its specific meaning of the soprano member (that is, the violin proper) as time went on. There is one elaboration to this particular meaning. In Venetian usage, *violino* as a specific term might mean either the violin proper or the viola proper at the end of the sixteenth century.

At first early violin bows did not differ significantly from those used with rebec, fiddle, *lira da braccio*, or viol. Our knowledge of the early bow comes almost entirely from iconography. These bows varied considerably in shape and length, but at first they all had a pronounced outward curve like a hunting bow, a curve that was gradually decreased. At first the bow was simply secured by the hair at the two ends. Gradually a horn-shaped nut emerged at the lower end, and a head at the upper. Most bows were fixed in tension. Some bows, however, could be adjusted by dentation, by slots, or by wedges. The type of movable nut used in the modern bow did not appear until the end of the seventeenth century.

By 1600 the violin had come a long way from the three-stringed violins depicted about 1530 by Gaudenzio Ferrari. Almost from its origins and certainly by 1550 the violin had attracted first-rate craftsmen in Italy; it was exported and probably manufactured throughout Europe, and its best examples were eagerly sought and highly prized by the knowing and the wealthy. The external grace and beauty of the violin was such that by the end of the century eminent artists were moved to paint the instrument in the glowing colours of varnishes fresh from the workshops of master craftsmen. By 1600 the popularity of the violin had increased to the point where the rebec and the *lira da braccio* were rapidly becoming obsolete. For the requirements of dancing, the sprightly tone of the violin proved particularly suitable, and in this field the violin was much sought after, whether for peasant dancing in the meanest tavern or for the aristocratic Court ballet in the palace of a king.

CHAPTER THREE

❧✠❧

Violin Music
in the Sixteenth Century

MUCH of the specific information about the origin and development
of the violin, related in the first two chapters, raises provocative
and tantalizing questions. What kind of music was composed for
the violin during the first century of its existence? Who played it, how was
it performed, and under what conditions? Was the music written for the
early violin of three strings different from that for the four-stringed violin
after 1550—or, for that matter, from music for the viols? Was the violin used
to accompany voices in such prevailing forms as the masses, motets,
chansons, and madrigals? To what extent did the violins usurp the place and
role of their ancestor instruments?

In some cases the questions suggested by particular events are even more
interesting since they often focus on important occasions and personalities.
If Charles IX of France commissioned Andrea Amati of Cremona to make
violins, violas, and basses for a whole string orchestra of thirty eight players
—for which he must have paid a princely sum—to what use were these
instruments put, and what music did they play? Has any of this music
survived? Is any music extant for the dancing, weddings, and 'mummeries'
which Jambe de Fer associated with the violin? (cf. p. 32). What music did
the *violini milanesi* of the Pope play at the Peace Conference with the Emperor
at Nice in 1538? How were the violins (or violas) employed in the Court
Chapel at Munich under Orlando Lasso? Or at the Parliament of Medgyes in
Hungary in 1585? What has happened to the dance music played by the
Italian violinists imported by Catherine de' Medici about 1555? Does this
music exist in print or in manuscript? What was the ballet and ballet music,
played by 'violins', with which Catherine de' Medici entertained an
Embassy from Poland in 1573? What violin music was used in the *Ballet
comique de la reine* of 1581 on the occasion of the marriage of the Duc de
Joyeuse to the Queen's sister? Or, again, what was the serenade which the
'wretched violins and small rebecs' played, unbidden and unwelcome, to

Mary Queen of Scots, shortly after her arrival in Edinburgh from France in 1561? (cf. p. 59).

Not all these questions can be answered satisfactorily. To those that can, a few general remarks will serve as a useful prelude and common denominator of essential background. For one thing, the violin in its earliest stages served two principal functions: to play for dancing or entertainment and to double vocal music literally or to accompany it. There is no evidence that this dual function changed basically before 1600, and consequently there is no pronounced difference in the kind of music played by the early three-stringed violin and the true four-stringed violin in the first fifty years of its existence and development. For another thing, it is a fairly safe assumption that the violin took over the musical role of its ancestors since it made the rebec rapidly obsolete and the *lira da braccio* gradually so. How the music was performed by the violin is the subject of the discussion in the next chapter.

What was the musical function of the ancestors of the violin? Tinctoris's *De Inventione et Usu Musicae* (c. 1487) is our principal witness in this matter. What he has to say about the lute, 'viola', and rebec is of great interest; and while the lute is not an 'ancestor', his remarks on the lute are quoted for their relevance to what he says about the other instruments. The lute (says Tinctoris) was used

'at feasts, dances, and public and private entertainments, and in this many Germans are exceedingly accomplished and renowned. Thus some will take the treble part . . . and improvise marvellously upon it . . . Furthermore, others will do what is much more difficult: namely, to play a composition alone, and most skilfully, in not only two parts, but even in three or four . . . While some play every sort of composition most delightfully on the lute, in Italy and Spain the viola without a bow [i.e., the guitar-like *vihuela de mano*] is more often used. On the other hand, over the greater part of the world the viola with a bow [here Tinctoris means a species of fiddle but not a rebec or viol] is used not only in this way but also in the recitation of epics . . . my predilection for the rebec I will not conceal, provided it is played by a skilful artist, since its strains are very much like those of a viola. Accordingly, the viola and the rebec are my two . . . chosen instruments . . . those that induce piety and stir my heart most ardently to the contemplation of heavenly joys. For these reasons I would rather reserve them solely for sacred music and the secret consolations of the soul, than have them sometimes used for profane occasions and public festivities.'[1]

[1] See Anthony Baines, 'Fifteenth-century Instruments in Tinctoris's *De Inventione et Usu Musicae*' in *The Galpin Society Journal*, Vol. III, 1950.

Tinctoris admits the 'profane occasions and public festivities', in which the fiddle and rebec must sometimes have taken part, and this suggests that occasional playing for 'profane' dancing and feasting, similar 'public festivities', sacred music, and recitation of epics were among the functions of bowed stringed instruments before the appearance of the violin. These same functions were undoubtedly shared by the violin in varying degrees during the course of the sixteenth century.

There is one important fact that conditions an answer to any of the questions that have been posed above: namely, only a handful of pieces of sixteenth-century violin music has survived in written form, and all of these date from the last twenty years of the century. Consequently, a discussion of the music of the time often becomes a thing of shadow rather than of substance; and we must rely on reports of the nature and function of the music rather than on the music itself.

Certain musical and social reasons help explain a situation in which so little music survives in written form compared to the considerable amount of music actually performed on the violin. As we have noted before (p. 4), the violin occupied a low social and musical position in the sixteenth century. It was played predominantly by professionals, not by aristocratic amateurs; and Jambe de Fer pointedly says, when comparing viol and violin, that the viols are those with which 'virtuous people' pass their time. Violin music, unlike the masses, motets, madrigals, or keyboard literature of the time, was considered of little moment *per se*, and for the most part it was mentioned, written down in manuscript, or printed only in so far as it was part of some important occasion whose purpose it served. Thus two dances for the violins in the *Ballet comique de la reine* survived simply because the dances were part of a royal wedding festivity in 1581. When the music was published in 1582, the dances were included as a matter of course (cf. p. 56); and it is to this circumstance that we owe the preservation of this work, the earliest known violin music surviving in written form. Besides, one should remember that many string players performed dance music from memory. Moreover, a number of players, even so famous a violinist as Bocan in the seventeenth century (see p. 149), could not even read music; and such considerations, which seem incredible to musicians today, effectively reduced the demand or need for written violin music. In short, while paintings, inventories, and contemporary accounts prove that a great deal of music was played on the violin in the sixteenth century, very little of it was written down for the reasons mentioned, and almost none of it has survived in print before 1600.

Almost every specific instance of the violin in sixteenth-century records can be explained in terms of the functional, utilitarian, or incidental to something else—principally dance music or entertainment, or doubling vocal parts. The French passion for dancing, for example, must have kept many a violinist busy, including on the one hand those who played in lowly taverns and, on the other, those royal musicians who played the Andrea Amati(?) violins at the court of Charles IX for such celebrated occasions as the Polish Embassy entertainments (1573), royal weddings, or related festivities.

From its birth the violin seemed fated for the embrace of dance music, and each was drawn to the other by the ardour of a natural and mutual attraction. The rhythmic demands of dance music were eminently satisfied by the violins and, as Maurice Emmanuel has so neatly said, 'their salient quality was placed at the service of rhythm'.[2] The piquant gaiety, penetrating tone, and power of the violins were particularly suited to the demands of dancing at the court and elsewhere.[3] In the area of dancing the violins gradually drove the rebecs from court, eventually making them obsolete. Jambe de Fer in 1556 considered the violin primarily suited for dancing. However, Thoinot Arbeau's dance treatise of 1589, cast in the form of a dialogue, names the violin only as one among several kinds of instruments used for dancing:

> '*Capriol* (after introducing the pavane *Belle qui tiens ma vie*): Is it necessary to use the tambourin and the flute in pavanes and basse dances?
> *Arbeau*: not necessarily: for one can play them with violins, spinets, flutes, recorders, oboes, and all sorts of instruments: [or] even sing [them] with the voice.'[4]

Apart from its role in dancing, the sixteenth-century violin lived under the overpowering shadow of a dominant vocal music. Much of the time the violin served anonymously, doubling the parts of the voices or sometimes playing vocal pieces with instruments alone—one reason why a substantial amount of music actually played by instruments does not appear as instrumental music. It may have been in some such subordinate capacity to voices that the *violini milanesi* were taken by the Pope to Nice in 1538 (cf. p. 26), although the violins were more likely used to enliven the proceedings of the

---

[2] Maurice Emmanuel, 'The Creation of the Violin and its Consequences' in *The Musical Quarterly*, October 1937. It was probably in the second quarter of the sixteenth century that the old wind bands were displaced by string bands for playing dance music.

[3] While violins are clearly associated with dance music in all classes of society, it is not easy to say to what extent they were employed by one class of society as opposed to another. In two engravings by Jan Théodore de Bry (1528–98) aristocrats are dancing to plucked and bowed strings (including an instrument resembling a small violin), while peasants are dancing to bagpipe and wind instruments. See Curt Sachs, *World History of the Dance*, New York, 1937, Plate 24.

[4] Thoinot Arbeau [Jehan Tabourot, *c.* 1519–*c.* 1595], *Orchésographie*, Langres, 1589 ('Privilège' dated 1588), fol. 33v. Translated by C. W. Beaumont, London, 1925; also by Mary S. Evans, New York, 1948.

Peace Conference with dancing and other festivities. Similarly, the instruments, including members of the violin family, shown in the picture of the Munich Chapel under Lasso (Plate 15) were probably doubling the vocal parts. The same procedure might be expected on social occasions in the home.

The practice of doubling voices led, naturally enough, to a notion of playing vocal pieces by instruments alone, a practice recognized and regularized by typical directions reading 'for voyces and viols' or 'for all sorts of instruments'. In this way instrumental forms like the *canzona* sprang from vocal models and began their separate instrumental existence.[5] However, in sixteenth-century instrumental music, even in the 'sonata'—a form inspired more by instrumental than vocal considerations—the violin is rarely specified. Giovanni Gabrieli's *Sonata Pian e Forte* (1597), which calls for a single 'violin' among the wind instruments of the ensemble, is one of the few specific instances (see p. 42). On the other hand, the *Concerti* of Andrea and Giovanni Gabrieli ten years earlier (1587) are more typical of general usage in that no instrument is specified, the whole thing merely being marked 'per cantar e sonar' (to sing and play). Even in Giovanni Gabrieli's *Sonata* of 1597, just mentioned, the 'violin' part is not particularly idiomatic to the instrument. The technical capacity of the violin is not exploited, and the music could have been played equally well by another string or wind instrument of the same register. In dance music the violin is used primarily for the rhythmic possibilities of its clear, penetrating voice, not for its agility or range; and extant violin music is very simple technically (cf. Ex. 1, p. 56). In all this we must allow for the possibility that the violin played elaborations not suggested by the score itself. The practice of improvisation and ornamentation of this sort was well established and documented in music for the voice, lute, and viol (cf. p. 89).

Unless it was in unwritten and improvised music, the real potential of the violin was not developed until the seventeenth century when the Italians began to exploit its idiom in the sonata and related forms independent of the dance. In any case, in the first century of its existence the violin inspired little written music, printed or manuscript, and no great composer wrote for the violin with the possible exception of Orlando di Lasso (see note 11, below) until the time of Gabrieli and Monteverdi at the end of the sixteenth and beginning of the seventeenth century.

On the other hand, it is well to emphasize again the discrepancy between the volume of music performed by the violin and the scarcity of violin music in written form. The rarity of written violin music in the sixteenth century

[5] Sometimes folksongs were arranged for instrumental performance, although no case is known of such an arrangement for violins in the sixteenth century. Hans Gerle gives two such pieces in four parts for rebecs in his *Musica Teutsch* of 1532.

gives no hint of the popularity of the violin whose widespread and increasing use in musical activities of the time can be more than amply documented by paintings, inventories, and records. Court and aristocratic circles employed violinists to play dance (and other) music at festivities, private and public dinners, royal marriages, and state visits. The *ballet de cour* in France and its later imitator, the English masque, include court dances. Civic archives prove the existence of town musicians, including violinists,[6] and records of private households point to the use of the violin at home. Incidental references in literature and the evidence of paintings indicate that the violin was also to be found in lower strata of society, leading a thriving existence in taverns (cf. Plate 17 for a seventeenth-century example) and at rustic weddings. There are references to the use of the violin in the theatre, in the Italian *intermedio*, and in the church service (cf. p. 60).

The use of the violin in France

A great deal of French dance music for ensembles was printed in the sixteenth century but no printed dance music can be linked specifically to the violin before 1581 (see p. 55). Collections of dances, often printed under the name 'Danceries', contain many a *basse danse*, *branle*, *pavan*, and *gaillarde*, but, as their titles often proclaim, they are intended for 'all sorts of instruments' or even to be sung (cf. the quotation from Arbeau, p. 52 above). These 'Danceries' were apparently aimed at amateurs, probably not at the typical professional, such as the violinists, who played for actual dancing. Significantly, in pictures of the time, dance musicians are shown playing without music (cf. Plate 13).[7] Furthermore, there is nothing in the music of these dances that is uniquely idiomatic to the violin. They could be played just as well by wind instruments, or sung. A representative case is Gervaise's *Sixth Book of Danceries in four parts*.[8] However, in the contratenor part (of a set of parts in Paris) there is a handwritten addition following the title of the dance *Pavanne des dieux* reading: 'which is well made for the violins' ('*qui est faict bonne* [?] *pour les violons*'). When this phrase was added is perhaps of less importance than that someone thought the piece was 'well made for the violins'. This does not necessarily mean that the piece was not well made for other instruments.

---

[6] For elaborate accounts of the English town musicians ('waits') see Woodfill, op. cit., chs. 2 and 4 (references to violins in the latter).

[7] See Daniel L. Heartz, *Sources and Forms of the French Instrumental Dance in the Sixteenth Century*, unpublished Ph.D. dissertation (Harvard University), 1957. See especially Chapter III ('The Danceries'). These dance musicians may also have played from ·violin tablatures. For a rare surviving example, see François Lesure, 'Les orchestres populaires à Paris vers la fin du xvie siècle' in *Revue de Musicologie*, July 1954, facing p. 53.

[8] *Sixième livre de Danceries mis en musique à quatre parties par Claude Gervaise*, Paris, 1555.

Although practically no music, either in print or in manuscript, can be ascribed solely to the violin before 1581, we can establish the extent and variety of violin music by examining its use in various countries. In France, records of court life contain numerous references to the use of violins about and after 1550 (for earlier references, see p. 24). After Henry II came to the throne in 1547, he and his Queen, Catherine de' Medici, paid state visits to Lyon (1548) and Rouen (1550); and on these occasions, violinists took part in open-air festivities, which apparently included dancing. At Rouen the violinists were disguised 'en Muses'—perhaps one of the 'mummeries' mentioned by Jambe de Fer (cf. p. 32 above). In 1565 celebrations were held in Bayonne in honour of a visit of Catherine de' Medici, now the Queen Mother. Among the provincial groups appearing were the 'Bourguignonnes et Champenoises' dancing to the 'small oboe, the violin (*dessus de violon*) and *tambourin de village*'.[9]

After the importation of the dance band of Italian violinists and their leader Balthasar de Beaujoyeulx about 1555, dancing to the violins must have been increasingly common in the French court. The Queen Mother was and always had been fond of dancing, and so was her daughter-in-law, the equally celebrated and notorious Mary Queen of Scots, briefly Queen to the sickly and youthful Francis II (d. 1560). In August 1573, Catherine de' Medici, as Queen Mother under her son Charles IX, entertained the Polish Embassy with *Le Ballet Polonais* (cf. p. 36), an elaborate affair which was composed of sixteen of the most beautiful ladies and young girls representing the sixteen provinces of France. The music, according to Brantôme, was the 'most melodious one had ever seen' ('*la plus melodieuse qu'on eust sceu voir*') and the ballet was accompanied by some thirty (*trentaine*) violins 'playing very pleasantly a somewhat warlike tune' ('*sonnans quasy un air de guerre fort plaisant*').[10] The music, alas, has not survived.[11]

Dance entertainment of this sort reached a high point under Henry III (reigned 1574–89), whose favourite, the Duc de Joyeuse, married Mademoiselle de Vaudemont, the Queen's sister, in 1581. Among the festivities on this occasion was the most famous ballet of the period, *Circe ou le ballet comique de la reine*. This incredibly lavish production cost 3,600,000 francs, a King's ransom and a sum that could be justified less by a royal wedding than by the political desire of the French court to impress the world with its

[9] Marc Pincherle, *Les Violonistes*, Paris, 1922, p. 19.
[10] For this see Brantôme, complete edition of Mérimée and Lacour, Vol. 10 (1890), pp. 74–75.
[11] According to Gustave Reese (*Music in the Renaissance*, New York, 1954, p. 571), Lasso was commissioned to write part, if not all, of the music. One selection, a *Dialogue à 8*, is extant. See Orlando di Lasso, *Sämtliche Werke*, Leipzig, 1894, Vol. 19, p. 138. There are no instruments indicated in this piece for double chorus, entitled '*Unde revertimini, Pax Religioque sorores?*'

solvency. The general production was entrusted to Balthasar de Beaujoyeulx, the leader of the Italian band of violinists brought from Piedmont by Marshall Brissac about 1555. Balthasar was also described as *maître de ballet*. The music was composed by Lambert de Beaulieu and Jacques Salmon (the latter was probably a violinist). Le Chesnaye, the King's almoner, wrote the libretto, and Jacques Patin, the court painter, designed the magnificent costumes and decorations. To violinists, the most interesting pieces are two sets of instrumental dances expressly designated for ten 'violins', the five parts of the music presumably being distributed equally among violins I and II, violas I and II, and bass.[12] This is the earliest *printed* violin music known. Ex. 1 shows the beginning of the first ballet. The contemporary

Ex. 1

account describes the entrance of the elaborately dressed musicians as follows: 'then there entered the hall by the two arbors ten violins, five on one side and as many on the other, dressed in white satin enriched with golden tinsel, feathered and provided with egret plumes; and in this ornamental dress they began to play the first *entrée* of the ballet'. In the museum at Rennes there is an interesting painting (Plate 13) that may depict another event that was part of the same wedding festivities.[13] The

[12] The text and music of the ballet (originally spelled *Balet comique de la Royne*) were printed in 1582. A copy is in the British Museum, among other places. The music was reprinted in the series, *Chefs-d'oeuvres classiques de l'opera français*, with an introduction by J.-B. Weckerlin, Paris, n.d. [1882?].

[13] Louis Dimier (*Histoire de la Peinture de Portrait en France au xvie siècle*, 2 vols., Paris, 1925, Vol. 2, p. 195), dates this painting (Museum de Rennes, No. 331) about 1581, and credits it to Herman van der Mast, a painter of Dutch origin who came to the French Court between 1570 and 1580. This attribution has been contested. The 'Elizabeth-Leicester' picture (see our Plate 14 and p. 57), now at Penshurst Place, probably has nothing to do with either Elizabeth or Leicester. According to Francis M. Kelly ('The Master of the Valois Revels' in *The Connoisseur*, Vol. 88, July–December 1931, pp. 296–301), this painting depicts a ball at the court of Henry III of France—the costumes, figures, and halberdiers at the back all being typical of the French Court of Henry III. Kelly maintains that this painting is an old copy or adaptation of a sixteenth-century original, probably lost, and he points to still another painting of similar grouping, but from a different hand, in Gaesbeck Castle, Belgium. It seems quite possible that both these pictures were adapted from the painting at Rennes. In a recent article Lucienne Colliard points to still a fourth painting (at Blois) of similar subject and grouping. This author labels both the 'Gaasbeck' [sic] painting and the Penshurst Place painting as '*Le Bal du duc de*

painting shows an aristocratic couple, possibly the wedding couple themselves, dancing *La Volta*. In the left background is a lively string band that is furnishing the music. The instruments include a small and a large violin, a viola, and a double bass. The small violin and the viola appear to have three strings and the double bass, four (for additional details, see p. 66).

Patronage of this sort did no harm to the violin's popularity or its social position. At some time during the reign of Charles IX the band of violins moved up a social step on the royal rolls of employed musicians from the *'écurie'* (literally, 'stable') to the chamber. By 1609 there were twenty-two *'violons ordinaires de la chambre du Roy'*—the forerunner of the famous 'Twenty Four Violins of the King', formally recognized as such under Louis XIII (see ch. 6).[14]

In England

In England references to the use of the violin in social life are equally numerous. By 1555 violins were part of the English royal establishment. On January 18, 1561 the play *Gorboduc* (later called *Ferrex and Porrex*) by Norton and Sackville was first acted by members of the Inner Temple before Queen Elizabeth, and 'Musicke of Violenze' [violins] preceded Act I. If the painting in Plate 14 represents Queen Elizabeth, as is unlikely (cf. note 13), the festive occasion may have taken place in connexion with her visit to the Earl of Leicester at Kenilworth in 1575. If so, there is no mention of the violin in the records of that illustrious affair. However, the Queen danced on this occasion, and instruments, unnamed but probably including the violins ('excellent music of sundry sweet instruments') played for the dancing.[15] The Earl of Leicester certainly had violins at Kenilworth later, since an inventory of 1583 lists a 'chest of five violens'.[16]

The English Court masque, like the French Court ballet and the Italian *intermedio* (cf. p. 59), featured music for dancing, but there is no

---

Joyeuse', while she calls the Rennes painting '*Bal à la cour des Valois*' and the Blois painting '*Bal à la cour de Henri III*'. Colliard believes that the painter may have been Jacques Patin rather than Van der Mast and that none of the personages in these paintings are identifiable as historical figures. However, Colliard gives a detailed analysis of another painting in the *Louvre* which is definitely related to the royal wedding of 1581. This painting depicts the wedding couple dancing and, among the spectators, Henry III, his Queen, and Catherine de' Medici, the Queen Mother. The instruments shown accompanying the dancing in this painting are lutes, not violins. See Lucienne Colliard, 'Tableaux représentant des bals à la cour des Valois' in *Gazette des Beaux-Arts*, March 1963, pp. 147–56.

[14] For this see Henry Prunières, 'La musique de la chambre et de l'écurie sous le règne de François Ier in *L'Année musicale 1911*, Vol. I, Paris, 1912, p. 247.

[15] See W. Dugdale, *History of Warwickshire* (1656), section entitled 'The Princely Pleasure of Kenilworth Castle'. See also John Nichols, *The Progresses and Public Processions of Queen Elizabeth*, London, 1823, 3 vols., Vol. I, p. 435.

[16] Woodfill, op. cit., p. 277.

H.V.P.–F

specific record of the violin's use in the masque until the seventeenth century
(see ch. 6). In these court activities it is a noteworthy fact that music formed
a regular part of court life—indeed, even of the daily life of a number of
sovereigns, who were moreover able and eager participants in the musical
activities themselves. There is no mention, however, of such exalted persons
playing the violin. Queen Elizabeth played the virginals, and King Henry
VIII played, sang, composed, and danced; but the violin was far beneath the
musical and social consideration of a nobleman, not to mention a king or
member of the royal family.

Besides the royal records, the inventories of English towns and private
households suggest a considerable activity with respect to violin music. In
1572 Sir Thomas Kytson, in whose service the madrigal composer Wilbye
worked for many years, bought a violin [from Italy?] for twenty shillings—
more than a year's wages for a servant (cf. Gasparo da Salò in a similar
situation; see p. 39 above). Thirty-one years later (1603), the inventory of
Kytson's household mentions, among other instruments, six 'violenns' and
the same number of viols. Town records specify the violin, but not the use
to which it was put. About 1585 the Norwich town musicians played 'viol
or violin or both', and about 1590 the town musicians of Chester played the
'violens'. As the century progressed, the number of foreign musicians in
England increased. By 1590 nineteen of twenty-nine musicians in the King's
Musick were immigrant from Italy, the well-spring of both makers and
players.[17]

While the English records are usually not specific, there is hardly any
doubt that the violins listed in private inventories and town records were
used primarily for dancing. There is one printed collection of sixty-five
dances late in the century (1599) in which the violin is specifically mentioned
in the title: A. Holborne, *Pavans, Galliards, Almains, and other short Aeirs [sic],
both grave and light in five parts for Viols, Violins, or other Musicall Winde
Instruments.* It is possible that the violins were used by amateurs in chamber
music at home. The Holborne collection, for example, may well have been
used in this way. However, in chamber music the violins were clearly second-
best to the viols whose presence is regularly specified in the English 'broken
consort'. The latter generally consisted of the lute, pandora, bass viol,
cittern, treble viol, and flute. Significantly, this is the instrumentation of
Thomas Morley's *The First Booke of Consort Lessons* (1599). The fine modern
edition of this work[18] contains as a frontispiece the reproduction of a famous
painting, executed about 1591, showing scenes from the life of Sir Henry

[17] See Woodfill, op. cit., p. 85, for Norwich and Chester; p. 278 for the Kytson inven-
tori.., ... p. 300 for 'alien' musicians.
[18] *The First Book of Consort Lessons Collected by Thomas Morley 1599 and 1611.* Reconstructed
and edited by Sydney Beck, New York, 1959.

Unton, Queen Elizabeth's ambassador to France. The nuptial banquet scene is accompanied by a broken consort with the same six instruments just mentioned except that an instrument played on the arm—either a rebec, a fiddle, or just possibly a violin—is substituted for the usual treble viol (which was invariably played between the knees). The painting, the original of which is in the National Portrait Gallery in London, is not clear enough to let us decide on the exact instrument intended. In a later engraving (1776) of the original, the instrument in question is clearly portrayed as a violin, but this is merely a later interpretation.[19]

There is even a reference, although scathing, to violins in Scotland, at the time when the young Mary Queen of Scots returned to her native country, already the widow of Francis II at the age of 19. Concerning an event on the night of her arrival in Edinburgh (August 1561), Brantôme, who accompanied her on the journey from France, says:

> 'In the evening as she [the Queen] wished to sleep, five or six hundred scoundrels [*marauts*] of the town serenaded her with wretched violins and small rebecs, of which there is no lack in this country; and they began to sing psalms than which nothing more badly sung or out of tune could be imagined. Alas, what music and what repose for her night!'[20]

Presumably the 'scoundrels of the town', thinking to honour the Queen known for her vivacity and love of dancing, got small reward for their pains, even if they played dances, as is probable. Brantôme says 'they began to sing psalms', but he does not say that they were accompanied by violins and rebecs; and it would be interesting to know what the violins and rebecs 'of which there is no lack in this country' played in general. Undoubtedly it was dance and vocal music, as it was everywhere else.

In Italy

As might be expected, the Italians used the violin in a variety of ways. The violin must have been employed extensively in Italian dance music. This was surely the case by 1550 since Beaujoyeulx, the leader of the Italian dance band cited earlier, was sent from Italy to France about 1555. After mid-century, the violins also played in the Italian theatre, notably in the *intermedio*. The latter included pieces of music, dances, and madrigals together with pantomime or spoken parts, and were used between the acts

---

[19] This engraving appears in Joseph Strutt, *A Compleat View of the Manners, Customs, Arms, Habits . . . of the Inhabitants of England*, London, 1776; also in Sydney Beck's article ' "Broken Music" Made Whole Again' in the *Bulletin of the New York Public Library*, October 1959.
[20] Brantôme (see p. 55, note 10), p. 127.

of a play, generally a comedy. These plays and their *intermedi* were associated with the sumptuous festivities of northern Italian courts, including elaborate weddings, reception of distinguished guests, and other ceremonial occasions. In 1589, for example, the wedding of the Grand Duke Ferdinand de' Medici and Christine of Lorraine, celebrated at Florence, included six *intermedi*, and among the forty-one important musicians who took part, Alessandro Striggio played the *sopranino di viola* [= the violin? the discant viol?]. An account of these proceedings was printed in 1591, including a five-voiced *sinfonia* by Marenzio, which introduced the second *intermedio*. Marenzio's music, which is very simple, was played by a harp, two liras, a *basso di viola*, two lutes, a *violino*, *viola bastarda*, and a *chitarrone*.[21]

Besides elaborate occasions of this sort, the Italians found the violin acceptable in church and elsewhere for the performance of sacred music, the vocal parts of which were often doubled by instruments. Violins may have been used in this way early in the century (cf. the *violini milanesi* of Pope Paul III in 1538; see p. 26). At any rate, Montaigne says that violins and organs were used to accompany the Mass in the great church at Verona in 1580; and in 1586, one Antonio Beltramin, a violinist, was engaged by the Padua church authorities for the '*concerti* which are played in this sacred Temple'.[22] Sacred music used at important weddings was sometimes accompanied by strings and sometimes performed by them alone.

The violin must also have been used frequently to furnish music at dinner or in the chamber for persons of rank and importance. A good example is Emmanuele Filiberto, Duke of Savoy (1528–80) about whose relationship with musicians we have relatively extensive records. As Prince (until 1553, when he became Duke of Savoy), Emmanuele Filiberto was a celebrated soldier, who served on the side of the Emperor in the suicidal wars which decimated Italy in the first part of the sixteenth century. As Duke he was an admirable ruler who succeeded in freeing his duchy from foreign domination. From our point of view, Emmanuele Filiberto is interesting for his protection of musicians; and his records reveal many payments to them even from his childhood (cf. p. 26 above). In the course of his travels, which were extensive, there are numerous entries (all in French) of which the following are sample references to payments to the 'violins' (see p. 240, note 2 of Pamparato's article, mentioned on p. 22 above, note 33):

(1) 1543—'Journey from Nice to Genoa, Milan, and Vercelli . . . to the violins (*violons*) who came to play at the dinner of Mons. the Prince.'

21 See Otto Kinkeldey, *Orgel und Klavier in der Musik des 16. Jahrhunderts*, Leipzig, 1910, pp. 172ff. The music of the *sinfonia* is printed on p. 312.
22 For Verona, see Michel de Montaigne, *Journal du Voyage*, 1774, Vol. II, p. 555. English translation by W. G. Waters, 1903. For Padua, see *Padova, Archivio Antico della Veneranda Arca del Santo*, Vol. 8 (old numbering), fols. 157v.–158r. For the last-mentioned information, I am indebted to Pierluigi Petrobelli.

(2) 1544—'Journey to Milan . . . for wine for the violins (*violons*); for four violins (*violons*) who played this evening.'

(3) 1544—[another journey to Milan] 'for four violins (*viollons*) who played this morning in the room (*chambre*) of Mons. the Prince . . . for four violins (*viollons*) and in the evening for four other violins.'

(4) 1545—[on a trip to Germany] 'Kempten . . . another "fillie" who played the viol (*vyolle*)'—one of the few references to viols (or women players) in these accounts.

(5) 1551—'Trent . . . a company of violins (*viollons*).'

(6) 1551—'Barcellona . . . a player of the "citara" .' No violins are noted on this Spanish trip.

(7) 1557—[on a trip to the Netherlands] 'to violins (*violons*) of the city of Brussels.'

These accounts give us a glimpse of a Duke who encouraged music because it was a natural part of his public and private existence. Consequently he heard music in his court not only during public festivities but also in his private chambers, at dinner, and even in his extensive travels.

As a final note to the social and political context of the violin and violinist in Italy about the middle of the sixteenth century, it will not be amiss to quote the vivid report of the Venetian ambassador to the Court of Savoy on the conditions of Piedmont about 1560 as a result of the devastation of the Hapsburg-Valois wars and the terrible antagonism between Protestants and Catholics:

> 'Uncultivated, no citizens in the cities, neither man nor beast in the fields, all the land forest-clad and wild; one sees no houses, for most of them are burnt, and of nearly all the castles only the walls are visible; of the inhabitants, once so numerous, some have died of the plague or of hunger, some by the sword, and some have fled elsewhere preferring to beg their bread abroad rather than support misery at home which is worse than death.'[23]

In Germany

German accounts of the usage of the violin in the sixteenth century are scanty, but there is one extremely elaborate printed account of the music and festivities at a ducal wedding in 1568, which gives us a detailed picture of the contemporary use of instruments in Germany, including the violin. On 22 February 1568, Wilhelm V, Duke of Bavaria, married Renée of Lorraine, and the festivities, which had started the day before, lasted until

[23] See *The Encyclopaedia Britannica*, 11th ed., Cambridge, 1910, Vol. 9, p. 341: article 'Emmanuel Philibert'.

9 March.[24] Orlando Lasso was charged with the musical direction of the whole affair; and we can do better than guess what the instruments (including the stringed instruments) and players looked like. The music for the whole festivity was furnished by the Munich Court Chapel under Lasso, and Hans Mielich, the court painter and Lasso's son-in-law, painted the players and singers (most of whom were probably Italian) about this time performing under Lasso (Plate 15).

The nuptial banquet was an exceedingly elaborate affair with a number of courses, each of which was accompanied by different music. Included were several pieces that employed the violins alone or in combination. In particular, a six-part motet of Cipriano de Rore was performed by six *viole da brazzo* (members of the violin family); and a twelve-part piece of Annibale Padovano, by six *viole da brazzo*, five trombones, a *cornetto*, and a *regale dolce*. Note that the piece for violins alone was a piece of sacred vocal music simply performed by instruments.

Troiano's account also makes clear that the violin was commonly played during dinner (cf. the Duke of Savoy, p. 60 above), and this was true of other instruments. A kind of hierarchy ruled the order of instruments and voices heard at the repasts of Wilhelm V. Troiano tells us that after the first dish is served and 'all are seated at table and the noise has ceased', the wind instruments played French chansons and other pieces of joyful character. Then (with the serving of the second dish), 'Antonio Morari and his companions,[25] with their violins, sometimes also with viols and various other instruments, play French chansons, motets of refined style and some exquisite madrigals . . . and that up to the last course'. When the fruit arrives, the singers perform under Orlando Lasso's direction 'new compositions which the master offers each day [i.e., of this special festival] to his audience. One often hears also beautiful quartets and trios, interpreted by experienced and selected singers'.

[24] A contemporary account of the whole affair was published in Munich in 1568 by Massimo Troiano (an Italian singer at Wilhelm's Court) under the title *Discorsi delli trionfi, giostre, apparati . . . nelle sontuose nozze dell' Illustr. e Eccell. Signor Duca Guglielmo*. For a full discussion of this and Lasso's part in the ducal marriage festivities, see Charles van den Borren, 'Orlande de Lassus et la musique instrumentale' in *Revue Musicale*, May 1922, pp. 111–26. For a contemporary picture of the wedding banquet, see H. Besseler, *Die Musik der Mittelalters und der Renaissance*, Potsdam, 1931, p. 230.

[25] See Adolf Sandberger, *Beiträge zur Geschichte der bayerischen Hofkapelle unter Orlando di Lasso*, 3 vols., Leipzig, 1895. The documents in Vol. III give us a record of payments made to violinists at the Munich Court under Lasso from 1554 to 1587. The number of violinists varied, but did not exceed nine (in 1569). 'Anthonj Geiger' (= Antonio Morari), an Italian like several of the others, appears early on these rolls (at least by 1568), and he must have advanced rapidly, becoming the leader of the violins. By 1572 his salary was 270 florins when others were receiving 150 to 180. By 1581 he was receiving 450.

From this we may conclude that both in status and repertory the instrumentalists were secondary to the singers. The former, even when playing alone simply played the vocal repertory, not pieces specially composed for instruments; and the finest treat which Lasso can offer his Duke and guests on this especially distinguished occasion—the musical dessert, so to speak, which coincides with the actual dessert of fruit—is *a cappella* vocal music by a small choir and, especially, quartets and trios by the best soloists of the Chapel. On other occasions during these nuptial festivities voices and instruments joined together, a usual procedure; and it would not be difficult to show that vocal pieces were often performed vocally *or* instrumentally, or vocally *and* instrumentally in various combinations. In daily practice, it is probable that the instruments in the ducal court played a less prominent role than on festive occasions. (For additional references to music in Hungary, Poland, and Spain, see p. 40ff.)

Violin music in the sixteenth century is like a person or object silhouetted against a strong light. The main outlines are clear but many of the details are in shadow and cannot be perceived. Similarly, the corpus of sixteenth-century violin music is clearly silhouetted by the kind of reports, inventories, records, and treatises which have been cited above. Collectively these documents tell us about the violin in various European countries, the kind of music it played, its function in dancing, and its generally subordinate role to sacred and secular vocal music. But the details of the music, its actual musical substance, are obscured by the almost complete lack of written music and also by the distinct possibility that those few pieces of extant music represent only an approximation of what was played in the tradition of sixteenth-century improvisation. Taken at face value, however, the few pieces of music, as well as the documents mentioned, suggest that the idiomatic potential of the violin was relatively little exploited, especially when the violin served a subordinate role to vocal music.

Toward the end of the century the conditions just described began to change. The growth of an instrumental tradition in general and a few specific instrumental forms of ensemble music encouraged greater independence for the instruments. The trend may be seen in the late sixteenth-century concerto in which instruments sometimes accompanied and sometimes competed with voices. The independence of all instrumental forms and idioms was not far off—that of the keyboard and plucked instruments having already been attained earlier. The ensemble sonatas and canzonas of Giovanni Gabrieli showed the rapid and independent growth of instrumental music in Italy, and by the early seventeenth century, Monteverdi was already using independent parts for violins in his madrigals and in his opera *Orfeo* (1607). A few years later (1610) the first sonatas for the violin appeared in Italy.

From then on, the violin rapidly came into its own musically and technically, and the amount of written and printed violin music increased enormously. These developments, in turn, were predicated on a basic, although rather elementary, tradition of violin playing in the sixteenth century, the subject of the following chapter.

CHAPTER FOUR

❦

How the Violin Sounded and how it was Played in the Sixteenth Century

'How often have I said to you that when you have eliminated the impossible, whatever remains, however *improbable*, must be the truth?'

Sherlock Holmes to Dr. Watson in A. CONAN DOYLE'S
The Sign of the Four (Chapter 6.)

ALTHOUGH Sherlock Holmes's remark to Dr. Watson would not survive the scrutiny of the strictest student of logic, his principle of investigation has its uses in searching for the details of anything as confused and elusive as violin playing in the sixteenth century. *Reductio ad absurdum* is a negative method which may lead to positive results. Consider the matter of the sound of the sixteenth-century violin. How can we possibly know what the violin sounded like four centuries ago? Obviously we cannot know absolutely, even if there were adequate words to convey an accurate notion of sound. However, it is useful to establish the fact that the old violin could not possibly have sounded like the modern violin; and thus, having eliminated the impossible, we can go on, by more positive methods, to show what must have been the truth—however improbable (cf. p. 67).

In essence, much of our investigation of sixteenth-century violin playing has to start with comparable methods of subtraction. All the information that can be assembled from pictures and documents will not tell us half of what we want to know about the technique of the violin and nothing definite about its sound. Therefore, we start with what we wish to learn, posing those questions that would naturally occur to any player or musical person; and what cannot be answered directly from the evidence of documents and pictures must be inferred or determined by experiment. This

procedure involves examining and interpreting the relatively few available
pictures of sixteenth-century violinists, the information found in the
theorists, and a substantial body of additional information already presented
in the preceding chapters concerning the origin and development of the
violin, its music, and its social function. The proper use of all this material
often gives positive results through a process of triangulation, as it were.
Finally, actual experiments with violins and bows, reconstructed from this
information and played according to the technique and spirit of the sixteenth
century, must give a fair approximation of the truth in so far as it can be
discerned in the deep obscurity of the past.

It is probable that not one but several methods of playing were in vogue
in the sixteenth century, and these in turn were related to the several social
and musical functions of the violin. The band of violinists performing for the
festivities and dancing at the Valois Court, possibly in connexion with the
marriage of the Duc de Joyeuse in 1581 (Plate 13), are playing with short
bows in rhythmically animated style to suit the dance *La Volta*; and indeed,
the viola player with his instrument ecstatically raised suggests the gyra-
tions of a modern saxophone player and something roughly equivalent to a
French 'Dixieland' style in the sixteenth century. In short, the players are
'jamming', there is no music in sight, and the musicians, the dancers, and
spectators are 'with it'. The music must have been very animated rhythmically but restricted in range, and holding the instrument at breast position
suggests that the music stayed within the limitations of first position.[1]

The atmosphere of *La Volta* explains the animation of the players. With
respect to this dance, Curt Sachs says:

'Instead of dancing alongside or opposite each other . . . the *volta*
dancers, in close embrace, turn constantly and without separating
leap high into the air. This lively dance brings into the refined ballroom an unwonted influx of power and primitivism, of impetuous
energy, meridional *gaillardise*, and self-confident vigor. . . . We cannot blame the German zealots of that time when they call the "shameful way" in which the lady is held "indecent" and the entire dance
"filthy" . . . Arbeau is less exercised about it. . . . The "shameful"
touching disturbs him as little as does that indiscreet flying of the
skirts which so delighted Brantôme, the chronicler of the immoralities
of the Paris Court about 1570. . . .'[2]

---

[1] Compare the strikingly similar picture (Plate 14), said (probably erroneously) to
depict Queen Elizabeth of England and the Earl of Leicester (cf. p. 56, note 13)
dancing *La Volta*, 'a series of veritable springs in the air in which Her Majesty takes
pleasure'.

[2] Curt Sachs, *World History of the Dance*, New York, 1937, pp. 374–5.

Compare this gay milieu of the French Court with the picture of Lasso surrounded by his sombre singers and players in the Court Chapel at Munich about 1565 (Plate 15). Here the players are decidedly serious in mien and action. Their attitude recalls the remark of Tinctoris (see p. 50) that he would rather reserve the 'viola' and rebec 'solely for sacred music and the secret consolations of the soul than have them sometimes used for profane occasions and public festivities'—thus acknowledging their dual role. The music lies before Lasso's players, and they may be playing learned chamber music (*ricercar*?) or doubling the vocal parts of some mass, motet, chanson, or madrigal that the choir is singing. The bows are longer than those seen in the French picture, and the violins (or violas) are held at the shoulder or neck in an attitude of dignified restraint.

The sound of the two groups must have been different, and the two pictures just cited point up the contrast of the ways of playing dance music on the one hand, and doubling vocal music on the other—the two principal functions of the violin in the sixteenth century.[3] Form follows function in this as well as other aspects of life and art, and over and over again one could duplicate such instances and intermediate shades between them. Such shades are more than probable, especially in view of the lack of standardization of instruments and bows, the discrepancy between the master instruments of Amati and the instruments of a village maker, the difference of talent of individual players, and the evolving and unsettled state of the technique of the violin. We do not expect Balthasar, 'the best violinist in Christendom' and perhaps one of the violinists playing for *La Volta*, to sound the same as a tavern fiddler. In any case, the violinist who doubled the vocal parts of the solemn motets and masses must have performed and sounded differently when he played the sprightly tunes usually demanded for 'dancing, weddings, and mummeries'.

Can any valid observation be made about the sound of the violin in the sixteenth century? Yes, within certain limits. As suggested above, we first eliminate the impossible by showing that the sound could not have been like the violin today. This conclusion is inevitable on both negative and positive evidence. Since the violin, bow, and technique of the sixteenth-century instrument differed from the modern instrument, the general negative conclusion is that the sound was different. But more positive methods are needed to identify and define the truth in this negative residue. By using the principles of what was rather than what was not, we can, as far as available

---

[3] There may have been still other uses of the violin in connexion with vocal music. What of the 'viola with a bow' played in 'the recitation of epics' of which Tinctoris speaks in the fifteenth century (see p. 50)? Was this practice transferred to the violin in the sixteenth century? If so, what was the music like and how was it played? Unfortunately, there is no way whatever to satisfy our curiosity on these points.

information permits, reconstruct instruments and bows; and by playing on them with the old technique we must arrive at a fair approximation of the sound of the sixteenth-century violin. What the violin sounded like at any given time is a function of the character of the violin, bow, and technique of the same time.

In particular, the sixteenth-century violin was decidedly different from the modern instrument, it varied in size and model to a notable extent, and it was strung with gut strings at lower tensions at varying standards of pitch and over a different type of bridge, neck, and fingerboard. By modern notions there was little standardization in the instrument, methods of playing, or the bow. The latter was fundamentally different in style and shape from the modern bow (cf. pp. 45ff.). Unlike the modern bow, the old bow was made in a variety of shapes and length, and all of these old bows produced a bow stroke different from the modern bow. Finally, both the violin and bow were held in one of several ways, all differing from modern methods. Consequently, the sound must have been different. However, in spite of all these diversities, one may come to certain general conclusions. By experiments using a reconstructed violin, an 'old' bow, and the old technique, one finds that the gut strings, the different bridge (possibly placed closer to the tailpiece than today), lower tensions, properties of the old bow (see p. 75), the different ways of holding and playing the instrument and bow, and the sparse use of vibrato, all produce a tone less intense, purer, more reedy, and smaller than is generally created by the violin today.[4]

However, one has to allow for some latitude on the last point in other members of the violin family. The alto violin (viola), for example, probably produced a larger tone in the sixteenth century than its soprano sister, the violin proper. Many violas of that time were made in a large pattern—for example, those of Andrea Amati and Gasparo da Salò—and must have had considerable power, although less than the same instrument strung up today under modern fittings and tensions. A large viola was doubtless what the Venetian composer Giovanni Gabrieli intended to be used in his *Sonata Pian e Forte* (1597), where one choir of instruments comprises a *cornetto* and three trombones, and the other choir, a *violino* and three trombones. Gabrieli's *violino* uses the register of the lowest string of the viola and hence must have been a viola (for *violino = viola* in Venetian usage, see p. 42). The violin proper of the sixteenth century would probably not have been sufficiently powerful to balance the *cornetto* or the trombones in the *forte* passages of

---

[4] Rabelais says: 'The sound of the rustic bagpipe pleases me more than the subdued voices (*fredonnemens*) of the lutes, rebecs, and violins of the court (*aulicques*)'—an interesting passage because it classifies the violin as a relatively soft instrument and because it admits the violin to court at that early time (1546). See *Fait et dits héroiques du bon Pantagruel*, Book III (1546), ch. 46.

Gabrieli's sonata. On the other hand, Gabrieli may have doubled his 'violino' part with more than one instrument.

There are several other points to keep in mind. For one thing, the violin music of the sixteenth century was restricted in range, for the most part keeping within the register of first position (g—b″), and even so, making little use of the lowest string. The sixteenth-century musicians heard none of the brilliance of the high positions of the E string and very little of the dark richness of the G string, so characteristic of modern violin playing. Another point is that the sound of the sixteenth-century violin must have varied a good deal: the French dance musicians playing at the Valois Court surely sounded quite different from the violinists under Lasso in the Munich Court Chapel. Finally, the words used above to describe the sound of the violin are all poor approximations and are all relative to the sounds we know today; and it is extremely doubtful if musicians and theorists of the sixteenth century, accustomed to the rather self-effacing tone of the viol, would consider our description of the sound of the sixteenth-century violin at all accurate. Indeed, regarding the violin from their vantage-point and in their own comparative terms, they labelled the tone of the 'upstart' violin as penetrating, powerful, and assertive. The violin, says Jambe de Fer in 1556, is '*beaucoup plus rude en son*' compared to the viol; and it was undoubtedly to its relatively penetrating and sprightly tone and its powers of rhythmic articulation that the violin owed its popularity, especially in dance music.

On the other hand, everything being relative, the modern string player would hardly apply such terms to the sound of the early violin, since things have changed a good deal over the centuries. Nowadays we use steel or wound strings for the most part, strings are strung at higher tensions, and the strings are played more powerfully with stronger bows tightened to greater tensions. The need for a big sound, essential today in large concert halls, did not exist in the sixteenth century. Besides, modern violin tone is intensified by a continuous vibrato, which today is considered an organic part of string playing. In the sixteenth century vibrato was used only occasionally as an ornament; and merely in itself, this difference in usage makes a notable difference in the sound. Since a continuous vibrato, especially of the wide and wobbly variety, tends to prevent perfect clarity of intonation by obscuring the centre of pitch, the texture of sixteenth-century violin music must have been rather more transparent than is the case today. These factors all lead inevitably to the conclusion that the sixteenth-century violin sounded different from the modern instrument: it was less powerful and less 'expressive', however assertive and penetrating it may have been regarded by musicians accustomed to the viol; and by today's standards the tone of the sixteenth-century violin must have been comparatively light, pure, and transparent.

Some of the points touched on above are worth amplifying in more detail. The matter of violin strings is a case in point. How to select and test good strings was a matter of considerable concern to early players, judging by remarks in the theory books of the sixteenth century, among them those of Agricola, Gerle, and Ganassi, who explain how to distinguish false from true strings. If experiments today mean anything, a gut G string could not have given a clear response, a fact that may account for the infrequent use of the lowest string of the violin until the later seventeenth century. Not before the early eighteenth century did violinists use a G string overspun with silver, although, even at the beginning of the seventeenth century, Praetorius comments on the advantages of strings of steel or brass from which he says 'a tranquil and almost lovely resonance, more than from other strings, is produced'. But no one seems to have paid him serious heed. We cannot tell the exact gauges of violin strings, although treatises of the time comment that they were stronger and thicker than viol strings.

The standards of pitch fluctuated to a degree difficult for modern musicians to imagine. Although pitches were assigned to the tunings of instruments, there was no accepted standard of pitch, such as a' = 440. Agricola (1528) tells the player of the discant viol to tune his top string as 'high as it can bear', and this direction is repeated with studious monotony in contemporary lute instructions and in various violin methods up to the early eighteenth century. Naturally, such a situation could not exist when and if the strings played with keyboard instruments of fixed pitch. Even so, there was no international pitch, and the standard of pitch varied from country to country and even from town to town. This chaotic situation was by no means limited to stringed instruments. Surviving sixteenth-century recorders at Verona 'sound a good semitone above modern pitch. . . . Many other specimens also sound about this pitch, though yet others are lower, probably having been built (as many inventories reveal) to suit the pitch of some church organ'.[5] Nor was there a standard tuning system, such as the equal temperament used today.

Similarly, the sixteenth-century bow was quite unstandardized in a number of respects and remained so for over two centuries until the time of François Tourte about 1780. The length, weight, and shape of individual bows varied greatly, and the old bow in general differed from the modern bow in several important points of construction (see Plate 11 and p. 45). The stick of the old bow curved outward and away from the hair, although the degree of curvature was an individual matter; and the hair was probably strung at fixed tension, not adjusted or adjustable by a screw as in later bows. Compared to the modern bow, the ribbon of hair on the old bow was

[5] Anthony Baines, *Woodwind Instruments and their History*, New York, 1957, p. 242.

narrower, and this, combined with lower tension and the (generally) shorter length of the bow, made for a smaller volume of tone. The shape of the head and the nut of the old bow also differed from our bow today. Besides, the yielding hair of the old bow naturally tended to produce a somewhat yielding bow stroke from the player, and this method of tone production contributed to the more relaxed and smaller tone of the old violin, as well as to a more clearly articulated sound. The bow was rubbed with rosin, just as it is today. Gerle, in a passage that has a timeless ring, warns the player about a bow that is too smooth to play. In such cases, the player should clean the bow and rub it with colophane of English rosin which, Gerle quaintly says, 'can be procured at the apothecary'.[6]

How the violin was played in the sixteenth century

Owing to the kind of bow and to the fact that the violinist commonly played for dancing, the run of violin music was probably played in a somewhat more articulated and non-legato style than would be usual now. As just explained, the yielding hair of all these outwardly curved bows gives a greater natural articulation than a modern bow. The balance of the old bows is generally more toward the frog, and therefore the point of the bow is lighter. Consequently bow strokes played in the upper third of the old bow have less momentum than similar strokes produced by a modern bow; and this property, combined with the inherent yielding properties of the old bow, gives naturally a greater degree of articulation or separation between the notes or phrases produced by individual bow strokes. As a rule the old bow, while unstandardized, was appreciably shorter than the modern bow; and the bows being generally shorter, the bow strokes were also shorter than in modern playing. As far as musical requirements went, dance music needed precise, well-defined rhythms, and a clear non-legato articulation between bow strokes was better suited to this need than the pronounced legato bow-change which is in vogue today. In violin music of the sixteenth century, therefore, there would doubtless have been a greater feeling of light and air, greater breath between the phrases, a kind of non-legato style suitable to rhythmic animation. A clear articulation, which corresponds to the breathing of singers on whose art the tone-production of violinists was modelled, was more natural to violinists of earlier times. They were not beset by the modern mania for the 'endless bow'—a smooth and seamless bow change which has preoccupied violinists more and more since the nineteenth century.

The playing of the best violinists of the sixteenth century gave much satisfaction to their contemporaries. The composer Peri, in the foreword to his opera *Euridice* (1601), speaks of 'Messer Giovan Battista Jacomelli, most

[6] Hans Gerle, *Musica Teusch*, Nürnberg, 1532, Bii recto.

excellent in every part of music, who has almost changed his name to Violino, being a marvellous violinist, and who, for the three successive years in which he has appeared at the carnival, was heard with the greatest delight and was received with the universal applause of those who attended'. M. A. Ingegneri, the teacher of Monteverdi, was known as a 'famous violinist' ('*violino di grido*').[7]

No pronounced differences of national styles yet existed. Jambe de Fer, the earliest (1556) to make specific reference of this kind, says there is no difference in the ways of playing the violin in France and Italy in his time (see p. 32). There must, however, have been some differences, as explained above, but these were not so much along the vertical lines of nations as the horizontal ones of class or function, such as dancing. In retrospect, Jambe de Fer's statement implies that there was one general style, probably that of the Italians, which the French, among others, adopted. The latter, as well as other nations, imported Italian instruments, violinists, and dancers (see p. 38), and undoubtedly adopted the Italian style of playing as well as dancing. At the French and English Courts, for instance, there were numerous Italian violinists, but we do not hear of any instances of 'foreign' violinists being imported into Italy, at least until the seventeenth century. It is a fair inference that playing styles were formed by the Italians, especially in dance music. (For the possibility that there were certain characteristic national differences in holding the violin and bow, see p. 74.)

In any case the technique of the violin was slowly developing. It must have evolved as the instrument evolved, and it must have borrowed heavily from the technique of its contemporary and ancestor instruments, notably the *lira da braccio*, rebec, and viol. From this reasonable assumption and from pictorial evidence, practically all we know about sixteenth-century violin playing must be deduced, there being treatises on the viol, but none on the violin as such in the sixteenth century. However, stray references to the violin and scraps of information on the violin do turn up here and there in treatises devoted primarily to other instruments or to matters of general musical interest. Contemporary records show that violinists were sometimes players of liras or viols, and the probability is that they transferred the technique of the older instruments, where possible and advantageous, to the violin. Ganassi goes to some trouble to describe a practice of using the viol with only three strings, which are to be tuned in fifths for the convenience of players of the *viola da brazzo* (violin family); and about 1600 Alessandro Striggio is mentioned both as a *lira* player and as a violinist.[8] A number of

---

[7] For the Jacomelli quotation, see Oliver Strunk, *Source Readings in Music History*, New York, 1950, p. 375. For Ingegneri, see Leo Schrade, *Monteverdi*, New York, 1950, p. 79.

[8] See E. Van der Straeten, *The History of the Violin*, 2 vols., London, 1933, Vol. I, p. 34.

players at the English Court are listed variously among the violins *and* viols
(see p. 41). Since there are certain details of string technique common to
several bowed instruments, it is a workable assumption that the technique
of the rebec, *lira da braccio*, and viol (about which we have the most, and best
documented, information), was adapted to the violin where practical and
appropriate, at least by those violinists who played one or several of the
older instruments just mentioned. In later centuries the borrowing process
was sometimes reversed, notably by the viol, which borrowed from the
violin. In L'Abbé le fils's important violin method (*Principes*, Paris, 1761), the
author says on his title page: 'Those persons who play the *par-dessus de viole*
with four strings can utilize these principles [i.e. of the violin] observing
only to give the letters T and P [i.e. *Tiré* and *Poussé* = down-bow and up-
bow, respectively] a meaning contrary to that found in this book.'

Holding the violin and bow

Whatever the extent of the transfer of technique from viol to violin, it did
not include methods of holding the instrument or bow, in which the viol and
violin were fundamentally opposed. The violin was held 'on the arm', while
the viol, even the smallest, was held between the knees or legs, and this
basic distinction was reflected in the terminology of *viola da braccio* (arm
viola) for the violin, and *viola da gamba* (leg viola) for the viol. There were
also pronounced differences in bow grip and bowing. The bow of the violin
was held palm downward with the weight of the hand transmitted to the
bow stick. The natural fall of the player's arm in this grip produced a
greater weight and accent on the down-bow than on the up-bow. On the
other hand, the viol bow was held palm upward (cf. Plate 5), with the
pressure not on the bow stick but on the bow hair, which was controlled by
the second and third fingers, the bow stick being lightly grasped without
much arm weight by the thumb and the first finger. The natural distinction
in accent between down-bow and up-bow is therefore not as great on the
viol as on the violin, and such natural accent as results from the viol bow
occurs in up-bow, not down-bow. For the viol players the natural stroke to
begin a measure of music is, if anything, up-bow; for the violinist it is
decidedly down-bow (cf. p. 79).

For information about holding the violin and bow in the sixteenth
century we are largely dependent on pictures. According to them, the
violin was held in a variety of ways, reflecting the practices of the rebec
and *lira da braccio*, the violin's ancestors (cf. Plates 3 and 4): (1) against
the left breast as was common with rebec players, or even in the middle
of the breast; (2) at the shoulder, slightly higher than the breast; or
(3) at the neck, in the usual fashion of *lira da braccio* players, with the
pegbox end of the violin often, although not always, below the level of the

tailpiece. The player's neck is customarily at the right side of the tailpiece.[9]

Although the violin sometimes appears to be held under the chin in the last-mentioned method, it is doubtful if the chin really gripped the instrument except possibly on those occasions where the violin played in the second or higher positions, and especially where it was essential to steady the instrument in downward shifts. In the Gaudenzio Ferrari fresco at Saronno (Plate 2) the angelic viola player is playing in third position, but she holds the instrument high on the shoulder, not at the neck, much less gripping with the chin.

If any conclusion can be drawn from all this information, it is, very generally, that the violin was probably held at the neck in the degree that it was a large instrument and at the breast when it was smaller or used for dancing. The *lira da braccio* was invariably held at the neck because of its size, and the alto violin (viola) was usually held in a like manner for the same reason. On the other hand, the Galen 'Quartet' (Fig. 1) uses the neck position for the smallest instrument, but it is the only one held 'on the arm' and it is not clearly in the violin tradition. The Italians probably preferred the neck (or high shoulder) position for most music, judging by their quick gravitation to this position after 1600. A position midway between breast and shoulder position may be seen in Veronese's 'Marriage at Cana' (1563)—a fascinating picture in which Veronese and Tintoretto play the viols, Titian the double-bass, and a young man the violin.[10] Dance players commonly used the breast position, as shown in the French and English *La Volta* pictures (Plates 13 and 14). On the other hand, the violin and viola shown in the 'Hatfield House' picture of an English wedding (1590) are playing for dancing and their instruments are held loosely at the neck, the chin being to the *right* side of the instrument (see ch. 2, p. 41, and note 25, above). However, the breast position is the usual one for dance violinists, and it was quite satisfactory for music in first position. This grip is also associated with the relatively short bows and the clearly articulated rhythmic bow stroke appropriate to dance music.

[9] See Max Sauerlandt, *Die Musik in Fünf Jahrhunderten der Europäischen Malerei*, Leipzig, 1922. Page 49 shows Rafael's 'The Coronation of the Holy Virgin' depicting two angels, one with a rebec played at the breast and the other with a *lira da braccio* held at the neck. Page 8 shows a number of *lira da braccio* (or fiddle) players in the second part of the fifteenth century, all holding the instrument at the neck or even under the chin. On p. 30 there is a painting of Fra Angelico (1387–1455) in which an angel is playing a rebec held at the neck. In Edward Heron-Allen, *De Fidiculis Bibliographia*, London, 1890–4, 2 vols., Vol. 2, p. 288, there is a picture of G. Grotto, *La Violina* [*sic*], about 1550, showing a species of *lira da braccio* held at the neck and at . the *left* side of the tailpiece (i.e. the modern method).

[10] For the identification of the figures see Patricia Egan, ' "Concert" Scenes in Musical Paintings of the Italian Renaissance', in *The Journal of the American Musicological Society*, Summer 1961, p. 192, note 32.

Holding the bow

Similarly, the manner of holding the bow was doubtless related to its musical function from the beginning of the violin: that is to say, the thumb-under-hair ('French') grip was probably preferred for short bows and dance music, and the thumb-between-hair-and-stick ('Italian') grip was used for longer bows and more 'serious' music. However, these distinctions cannot be clearly maintained until the seventeenth century. The difficulty is that in the sixteenth century there are no descriptions of these grips, and we must rely on pictures, which are not numerous and which seldom show the hand position in all its details. Just as today, the bow was undoubtedly held in a way that achieved the most effective grip and pressure with the individual bow, considering the musical purpose involved. Since bows differed considerably in length and balance, the results were also variable, especially in such matters as whether one held the bow at the frog or at some distance above (cf. Plates 16 and 13).

The details of the two principal methods of holding the bow in the sixteenth century are these: (1) the bow is held with the thumb under the hair and (generally) with three fingers above the stick. This is the so-called 'French' grip used in French violin playing until the middle of the eighteenth century. This grip can already be observed in 'fiddle' players late in the fifteenth century (Plate 3b). The persistence of this grip may be related to the fact that the hair of most bows before 1700 was fixed: the thumb-under-hair grip could be used to tighten the hair—something of an advantage as the hair gradually slackened. (2) The bow is held with the thumb between the hair and the stick, the so-called 'Italian' grip, a splendid impression of which is afforded by a unique sketch (Plate 16) by the artist Lodovico Caracci (1555–1619). In this grip, the basis of that used in modern times, the four fingers and the thumb grip the stick. The thumb does not grasp the hair of the bow, as in the French grip. Caracci's sketch shows the bow held at its lowest extremity; but in the actual practice of violinists as a whole the distance of the grip from the frog must have varied considerably, and was doubtless determined for the individual player by the length of the bow and its balance. Plate 16 is also remarkable in that the two sketches in the right corner seem to concern a left-handed violinist, one holding the bow, the other tuning an instrument. A painting of Cima da Conegliano (first quarter of the sixteenth century) depicts a player of a large *lira da braccio* with a very long bow held well above the frog. Obviously the bow is too long to be played with the player's hand at the lowest extremity of the bow.[11]

Actually we have very little information concerning such details of bow

[11] For this painting see G. Adler, *Handbuch der Musikgeschichte*, 2 vols., Berlin, 1930, Vol. 1, p. 597.

grips as whether the stick was grasped loosely or tightly or at the first or second joint of the first finger of the bow hand. In the Saronno fresco (Plate 2) the players, especially the viola player at the right, appear to be holding the bow firmly but not tightly, and the bow stick is held approximately at the first joint of the index finger. The little finger is braced under the stick in the cello and viola grips, as it is in certain pictures showing the French grip in the seventeenth or even early eighteenth century (Plate 31). On the other hand, some pictures of the French grip show the little finger quite free of the bow stick (Plates 22 and 23). In the Caracci sketch (Plate 16), an example of the Italian grip, the hand is at the lowest extremity, practically enfolding the bow stick, which must be against the second or even third joint of the index finger. Presumably increased pressure from the index finger was the usual means of increasing volume of tone. Ganassi implies this in his description of the bow grip of the viol, although the grips are not directly comparable (see p. 84).

Paintings and iconography in general are helpful to the extent of the details just given, but other points of string playing cannot be deduced from such sources. For further information we must turn elsewhere, principally to those theorists who furnish the details of playing the viol. In spite of the great differences between viol and violin, there are (as we have remarked already) certain principles, common to all string playing, that apply to both instruments. It is a striking fact that some of these principles, which are not formulated specifically for the violin before the seventeenth century or even later, are anticipated by teachers of the viol before the middle of the sixteenth century.[12] The most remarkable of these theorists is Sylvestro di Ganassi, whose two treatises, one on the viol and one on the flute, set forth a great deal of valuable information regarding playing in general and string playing in particular.[13] Ganassi was born in Venice, and he became a teacher of the recorder and the viol, a chamber musician of the Doge, and an instrumentalist at San Marco, where he must have known and played the music of such famous contemporaries and colleagues as Willaert, among others. His books must reflect the professional aspects of his own experience.[14]

---

[12] We do have one record of a violinist promising instruction on the violin to another player (1582), but we do not know of what the instruction consisted. See François Lesure in *The Galpin Society Journal*, Vol. VII (1954), p. 35.

[13] Sylvestro di Ganassi, *La Fontegara*, Venice, 1535 (facsimile reprint, 1934) is concerned with the flute (recorder). *Regola Rubertina*, in two parts (or, more properly, '*Lettioni*'), Venice, 1542 and 1543 (facsimile reprint, preface by Max Schneider, 1924), is basically concerned with the viol and the lute.

[14] Cf. Hans Gerle, *Musica Teusch*, Nürnberg, 1532. Gerle, although well known as both performer on the lute and as a maker of lutes and viols, says explicitly that his book is written for amateurs, and he implies that it is for those who cannot afford a teacher. Hence this book is one of the first of a long line of 'self-instructors' or 'do-it-yourself' manuals which became so popular later (see ch. 11).

Ganassi's *Regola Rubertina* is the only really detailed treatise on string playing in the sixteenth century, and in spite of the extraordinary difficulty, obscurity, and redundancy of its language, it is one of the most precious and revealing documents of the time. His treatise is especially remarkable in that he gives musical pieces in a notation which indicates quite precisely details of fingering, shifting, and bowing for the viol; and from this we can see that Ganassi was aware of all sorts of colour possibilities of the strings. Moreover, he is among the first to expatiate on the innate difference of individual instruments (Part II, ch. 16). From this treatise one can almost reconstruct a method of string playing that must have been central to instruction for years afterwards, and a number of its precepts are basic to all string playing ever since. Violinists undoubtedly adopted and adapted certain technical procedures or principles derived from the viols (as well as other instruments and the voice) long before they were described specifically in connexion with the violin. Indeed, the rapid advance of violin playing in Italy in the seventeenth century may be attributed not only to natural aptitude but also to the sound and extensive foundation of string playing in general developed by the viol players, and especially by Ganassi, in the sixteenth century.

Tone. The bow stroke

The voice was the model of tone, and it remained so for centuries. 'Just as the painter imitates nature,' says Ganassi, 'so wind and string players should imitate the human voice'.[15] Tone is also related to bowing. In the *Regola Rubertina* Ganassi says the bow is to be drawn at right-angles to the string (but compare Ganassi's actual practice; see p. 80), and the distance of the bow from the bridge is determined by the kind of effect and tone desired: well away from the bridge and near the fingerboard for sad effects; near the bridge for stronger and harsher sounds; and in between for normal playing. There is no evidence that Ganassi was thinking of *sulla tastiera* and *sul ponticello* in the modern sense (as has been claimed) when he spoke of 'near the fingerboard' and 'near the bridge', respectively. Energetic bowing is recommended for lively pieces, and more relaxed bowing for music of greater expression, which may also be accompanied by vibrato and by a '*tremar*' of the bow. Long and short strokes are also related to the length of the note-values: the longer note-values are played with a long stroke using the arm—'*sonar soperbo*' (to sound gloriously)—and the shorter note-values with a short stroke using the wrist (Part I, ch. 6).

Ganassi puts a dot under a note to indicate that the bow is to be drawn away from the viol, *normally* called 'down-bow' (and indicated by ⌒). 'Up-bow' (∨) is assumed if no dot is used (Part II, ch. 15). From these bowing indications, especially as they are found in Ganassi's music in Part II,

---

[15] Ganassi, *Fontegara*, ch. 1.

certain conclusions follow concerning single strokes, the use of several notes in one stroke, and the ordering of the down-bow and up-bow relative to musical context.[16]

The single stroke for a single note is the basic and most usual procedure. In these strokes, down-bow and up-bow are usually alternated (but see below). We may infer that the individual strokes were basically non-legato in character—that is, clearly, although barely, separated—because the yielding hair of the old bow favoured an articulated stroke, as explained above, and because instrumental music at that time was generally played in a more detached manner, if we may judge by studies of fingering of sixteenth-century keyboard music.[17]

Ganassi does not know the legato slur as such, but in the music his system of dots for 'down-bow' makes clear that two or three consecutive down-bows may be used; or the same (or perhaps greater) number of consecutive up-bows. These consecutive downs or ups do not amount to a legato slur, but rather to a species of *portato* in which two or more notes are played with the same bow but perceptibly articulated. That Ganassi means a *portato* and not a pure legato is implied by his description (Part II, ch. 15), and by his statement that this binding together cannot be done in rapid passages (Part II, ch. 18), a statement that would be senseless in connexion with a pure legato.[18] It would seem that in Ganassi a 'legato' has to have the element of articulation the *portato* affords, articulation being characteristic of single strokes and perhaps of this music in general. On the other hand, Ortiz[19] seems to allow for a legato of 'two or three semiminims' in one bow, and similarly Richardo Rogniono (see p. 83) mentions two notes in one bow stroke (*in una arcata*), but in connexion with establishing the proper bowing pattern. This is probably Ganassi's intent also in using two or more consecutive down-bows or up-bows, as will be explained presently.

First, however, there is a difficulty of terminology in general and one

[16] In Part II, the music includes four *ricercari*, an unnamed piece probably for lute, and a madrigal for voice accompanied by viol, mostly in double stops, but with some triple stops. Part I has four additional *ricercari*.

[17] See Newman Powell, *Early Keyboard Fingering and its Effect on Articulation*, unpublished M.A. thesis, Stanford University, Palo Alto, Calif., 1954. See also an abstract of a paper on the same subject by the same author in *The Journal of the American Musicological Society*, Fall 1953, p. 252.

[18] There are certain ambiguities in Ganassi's use of dots under notes to indicate bowings. For one thing he sometimes uses dots under notes for fingering in connexion with multiple stops. A more serious difficulty is this: since the lack of a dot under a note means up-bow, must we conclude that all consecutive notes without dots are to be played with consecutive *portato* strokes, all in one bow? If so, the music yields as many as nine such notes—rather inconsistent with the maximum number of specifically designated consecutive down-bows, which is three.

[19] Diego Ortiz, *Tratado de glosas*, Rome, 1553; reprint edited by Max Schneider, Kassel, 1936.

related to Ganassi in particular that must be cleared away. On the violin, the terms down-bow (⌐) and up-bow (v) make sense because the strokes are literally 'down' and 'up'. These terms are used also on the viol, but they are not really applicable. Far better terms would be 'out-bow' and 'in-bow', respectively, since in 'down-bow' the viol bow is drawn roughly parallel to the floor, 'out' from the instrument; and in 'up-bow' the viol bow is pushed 'in' toward the instrument. Furthermore, down-bow and up-bow on the violin have musical associations different from so-called down-bow and up-bow on the viol. *From a musical point of view, violin down-bow is roughly equivalent to so-called viol up-bow (and vice-versa)*; and this equation is related to the anatomy of the bow stroke and its weight relative to musical weight or accent. For the violinist the weight of the arm gives the down-bow a greater emphasis compared to up-bow, and therefore down-bow is the stroke that the violinist naturally uses to play a note on an accented beat (or even part of a beat, tempo permitting); and consequently, down-bow is normally the first bow-stroke of the measure. On the other hand, for the viol player the down-bow (out-bow) and up-bow (in-bow) are nearly equal in weight, because the pull of gravity and the weight of the arm are not factors in the horizontal plane of the bow stroke or in the underhand bow grip generally used. Nevertheless, the players must have felt that viol in-bow (up-bow) had a slight preponderance of weight (or perhaps afforded an easier way to commence the stroke) compared to out-bow (down-bow). At any rate, in-bow is the stroke favoured by the viol players to begin a measure or to play an accented note. Hence, musically speaking

violin down-bow = *viol up-bow* (*in-bow*),

violin up-bow = *viol down-bow* (*out-bow*).

In his text Ganassi follows the general principles of down-bow and up-bow just given, although he is not completely faithful to these principles in the music, occasionally using viol down-bow on the accented note for no discernible reason. However, this inconsistency presents no special barrier to perceiving the general principle, and an artist must be allowed some latitude, a foolish consistency being the hobgoblin of little minds. But Ganassi's terminology is a nightmare of nightmares, and only the tough-minded reader will want to follow the next few paragraphs devoted to discovering the meaning and sense (if any) of this particular terminology. Not only does Ganassi use the terms *down-bow* and *up-bow* in a meaning the reverse of the usual meanings just explained, but he does so in language which occasionally and maddeningly employs technical terms couched in his local dialect.

Ganassi's terms are *in su* (or *in suso*), whose literal Italian meaning is 'up-bow'; and *in giù* (or its colloquial equivalent *in zoso*), literally meaning 'down-bow'. These two terms are common Italian terms for *up-bow* and *down-bow*, respectively, and are used by Italian violinists for centuries afterwards either alone or more explicitly as *pontare in su* and *tirare in giù*. In Ganassi, however, the meanings of these two terms are reversed. His text makes absolutely clear that *in su* means not 'up-bow' (its literal meaning) but 'out-bow', that is, down-bow; and *in giù* (or *in zoso*) means, not down-bow (its literal meaning), but in-bow (up-bow). The reason seems to be this —and this helps to remember the meaning: the viol players shown in the frontispiece of Ganassi's book are drawing the bow in such a manner that the frog of the bow is somewhat higher than the point. Hence to draw 'out-bow' (i.e. normally called 'down-bow') is actually to draw the bow uphill, even though slightly—hence, literally 'up-bow'. Similarly an in-bow (normally called 'up-bow') is to push the bow downhill slightly—hence, down-bow.[20] Therefore, all Ganassi's down-bows and up-bows have to be reversed in meaning *compared to the normal terminology of the viol strokes*, and by a kind of double reverse, his basic meaning is such that *as far as the weighted stroke is concerned* his term 'down-bow' (*in giù* or *in zoso*) has the same effect as violin down-bow. This all means that in Ganassi the viol bow-strokes are equated as follows:

His term *down-bow* = *in-bow* = the musical effect of violin *down-bow*.

His term *up-bow* = *out-bow* = the musical effect of violin *up-bow*.[21]

Ganassi's most ardent admirers would be compelled to admit that his terminology, general confusion of vocabulary and syntax, and redundancy of language are perfectly capable of reducing the most determined and strong-minded reader to a state bordering on hysteria or delirium tremens. Nevertheless, Ganassi deserves the credit for establishing a workable, although elementary, discipline of bow strokes for the viol—a discipline that anticipates in its main principles the so-called 'Rule of Down-Bow', central to the bowing discipline of the seventeenth and eighteenth centuries (see p. 157).

[20] A more vivid example is furnished by Hans Judenkünig, *Ain schone . . . Underweisung*, Vienna, 1523, the frontispiece of which shows a bass (or tenor) viol being played by a man in standing position, the bow being played crosswise at a diagonal of about forty-five degrees.

[21] Ganassi also uses the same terms '*up-stroke*' and '*down-stroke*' in his explanation of the action of the right (plucking) hand of the lutanists: *in suso* is the 'up' action of the index, middle, or ring finger striking the strings in an upward motion, thus engaging the strings from the highest-sounding string to the lowest; and the reverse *in zoso* or 'down' motion, normally with the thumb striking downward, engaging the lowest-sounding strings first. From this it would seem that the terminology of 'down' and 'up', used by bowed stringed instruments, came originally from the lutanists, was then adopted by the viol players, and still later, by violinists. This last point was first noted by Martin Greulich, *Beiträge zur Geschichte des Streichinstrumentenspiels in 16. Jahrhundert*, Berlin Ph.D. Dissertation, 1933, p. 44, note 60.

The viol in-bow is recommended by Ganassi as the normal beginning stroke, which is presumed to be on the accented note. He also tells the player to begin *passaggi* by 'always drawing the first bow stroke inward', although he also recommends practising out-bow for the same situation, just as a swordsman must (he says) be able to use the blade in his left hand if his right hand is incapacitated in battle—a vivid reminder of the disturbed state of Italy at that time.

As already explained, Ganassi normally alternates in-bow and out-bow, but he also allows for consecutive in-bows and consecutive out-bows, played *portato*. Apparently he thinks of *portato* in connexion with regulating the bow stroke so that the in-bow will again coincide with the accented note, as in Ex. 2 (a), first full measure.[22]

Ex. 2

Ex. 2 serves also to emphasize certain ways in which Ganassi's bowing discipline differs from that of later times. For one thing, he does not use the so-called 'replaced bow'. The latter term refers to a situation where (let us say) two consecutive down-bows are played not by a *portato*, as in Ex. 2 (a), or by being smoothly phrased together as in a pure legato, but are played by lifting the bow and actually replacing it for two separate and distinct down-bows. Ex. 2 (b) illustrates the replaced bow, typical of a later time. Ganassi explicitly rules out this bowing by saying in effect that when one connects two consecutive down-bows or up-bows the bow does not leave the string.

In a bowing discipline in which the weighted stroke is related to musical accent, there is no problem when one encounters an even number of notes in a measure (2, 4, 6, 8, etc.). Individual down-bows and up-bows, played alternately, are the simple and normal solution; and in Ganassi's passages involving an even number of notes of the same value, alternate down-bow and up-bow are commonly indicated by him. In this respect the first four notes in Ex. 2 (a) could be bowed equally well with alternate down-bow and up-bow; Ganassi's indications here are simply for musical variety. But in the

[22] Ex. 2, transcribed for bass viol, is taken from the last line (m. 2–3) of *Recercar Primo* in Part II, ch. 20. In all examples ⊓ = weighted bow, and v = unweighted bow *irrespective of whether the viol or violin is concerned or what the bow stroke is called.* This procedure is essential to give some uniformity to the examples, to conform to the accepted violin notation, and to get around the pitfalls and inconsistencies of terminology like Ganassi's.

following measure there is the unequal number of seven notes, and some
device has to be found if the weighted bow-stroke and accented beat (or
parts of beats) are to coincide. In this case he uses the *portato* for the first
two notes of the measure. Another solution is shown in Ex. 3. In this
example[23] the *portato* is indicated from the weak to the strong beat. The
musical implication of this bowing is interesting. The dissonant seventh on
the third beat of the first measure is not slurred to its resolution; rather, the
leading tone is slurred to the tonic. Does bowing discipline or the drive to
the tonic take precedence over the resolution of a dissonance? The bowing
discipline is probably not a factor here, since other passages show that
Ganassi's application of the discipline is by no means rigid. Indeed, the last
note in measure 2 of Ex. 3 shows flexibility in this respect, since a strict

Ex. 3

application of the bowing discipline would require this note to be played
up-bow so that the following measure would naturally begin down-bow.
Sometimes Ganassi bows two successive measures of uneven notes with
alternate individual strokes, thus coming out down-bow at the beginning of
the third measure. While in practice Ganassi deals with the problem of equal
and unequal numbers of notes in a measure, he does not mention this
phenomenon as such. The first to do so explicitly is Cerreto,[24] although
Richardo Rogniono implies a similar usage nearly ten years before him.

Rogniono is also the first to mention the discipline of bowing for players
of 'violins', and his treatise, also published in Venice, does not appear until
1592, fifty years after Ganassi's—perhaps a significant time-lag in comparing

---

[23] Taken from *Recercar Secondo* (labelled 'R. S.') in Part II (ch. 15), and transcribed for
alto-tenor viol (tuned: A d g b e' a'). Also given in Davison and Apel, *Historical
Anthology of Music*, 2 vols., Cambridge, Mass., 1946–50, Vol. I, No. 119. However,
the latter source has no bowings and it uses longer note values in certain chords than
are justified by the original.

[24] Scipione Cerreto, *Della prattica musica*, Naples, 1601. However, Cerreto says the
opposite of what we should expect. He tells us to begin a passage involving an even
number of notes with (unweighted) 'out-bow', and vice versa. This is the reverse of
normal practice. The only explanation that seems at all probable is that since the
weight of the two bow strokes on the viol is nearly equal (as explained above),
Cerreto simply and arbitrarily chose one instead of the other. Another bare possibility is that violists were playing with the overhand grip of the violinists; and it is
worth mentioning that a viol player shown in the border of Cerreto's portrait in his
treatise is playing with the overhand grip. But this would not explain the inconsistency of Richardo Rogniono's information where the bowing of viols and violins is
the same in one place and the opposite in another (see p. 83).

the technique of the viol and violin in the sixteenth century.[25] By the end of the sixteenth century the violins are presumably becoming important enough to be included with the viols, and Rogniono mentions down-bow and up-bow in connexion with both viols and violins. His terms are: *tirar* = down-bow, and *pontar* (*puntar*) = up-bow. Rogniono's information is clear enough in relation to the violin, but it is confused in one point with respect to the viol. He speaks of the difficulties of making the down-bow and up-bow strokes at the beginning of 'the sound'. Then he says that the viol (*Viola da Gamba*) and also the violin (*Viola da Brazzo*) should always begin by 'drawing' the bow ('*tirar*' = down-bow on the violin = out-bow on the viol). This is as puzzling as Cerreto's information (cf. note 24), and it is inconsistent with what Rogniono himself says a sentence later in his preface: namely, that long 'diminutions' of eighths and sixteenths should begin up-bow (*pontar*) on the viol but down-bow (*tirar*) on the *Violino da Brazzo*, as we should expect.

Rogniono also deals (at least by implication) with the problem of bowing passages or measures that contain an even number or odd number of notes: 'Replace the bow when you find quarter-notes in the midst of eighth-notes or eighth-notes in the midst of quarter-notes, or take two notes in one bow-stroke' ('*repigliar l'Arco quando si trova semiminime nel mezo delle Crome ò Crome nel mezo delle Semiminime ò far due note in una Arcata . . .*'). This passage implies that since the insertion of eighth-notes into passages of quarter-notes (or vice versa) often gives an unequal number of notes in the passage or measure, the passage must be bowed either by (1) replacing the bow, or (2) slurring two notes together in legato or *portato*. Although Rogniono's instructions are very brief, and not to be compared with Ganassi's as a whole, Rogniono goes beyond Ganassi's concept of bowing discipline, and he significantly relates it to either viol or violin.

Rogniono's precepts are also valuable in the context of the few examples of violin music that we have in the sixteenth century. His instructions can be applied readily to Ex. 1, given earlier (cf. p. 56), from the dance music for violins in the *Ballet comique de la reine* (1581). The opening measures of this music are quoted in Ex. 4 (first-violin part only). In measure 1, eighths

Ex. 4

25 Richardo Rogniono, *Passaggi per potersi essercitare nel diminuire terminatamente con ogni sorte d'instromenti*, Venice, 1592. Most of this work is devoted to music of the *passaggi*. The text of the quotations below is contained in a short preface entitled 'A i Virtuosi Lettori L'Autore'. Rogniono's treatise, thought to have been destroyed in World War II, has recently been rediscovered.

occur in the 'midst' of quarters, giving the 'uneven' number of five notes. Consequently, on beat two the bow, depending on speed or context, would either be replaced, as at (a), or played legato (b), or portato (c).

Pizzicato

Plucking the string by the viol player is also mentioned by Ganassi, although he calls this device simply '*percotere la corda*' ('striking the string'). He does not use the term *pizzicato*.[26] It was only natural for players of bowed stringed instruments, who heard lutes and guitars everywhere, to imitate them by plucking the string as a special device; and violinists probably used the *pizzicato*, although not the term, almost from the origin of the instrument. The violinist in the Saronno fresco (1535) may be playing *pizzicato* (Plate 2).

One word of caution about all the treatises of the sixteenth century with respect to their technical information: it is a mistake to read modern meanings into the old terms unless explicit directions show that this is so. *Spiccare* and *calcare* are two cases in point. The first of these refers simply to a detached style of playing and cannot be equated with *spiccato* in its modern sense. We do not know precisely what *calcare* (literally, 'crush') implies. It may have meant that the bow was pressed heavily on the string for greater volume. In any case, it is most unlikely that it is the modern equivalent of *martelé*, as has been suggested.

Fingering. Positions. Shifting

While intended for viol players, Ganassi's sections on the management of the bow and the discipline of ordering the bow strokes can be translated into terms of violin playing. His information on fingers, positions, and shifting is similarly suggestive; and although many of the details are not directly applicable to the violin, Ganassi's treatise shows how much was understood about alternative types of fingerings, the use of high positions, the individual colour of the strings, and even the details of shifting. We cannot prove that violinists availed themselves of a string technique that was well known, but it would be astonishing if there were not some transfer of Ganassi's viol technique to the violin by players who were accustomed to play on both instruments. However, there is no proof of such a transfer in any extant music or document specifically connected to the violin.

In the first place Ganassi's fingerings cannot be transferred directly to the

[26] Part II, ch. 11. Ganassi's instructions for plucking the viol are mixed up with his instructions for plucking the lute and with which finger is to be used. It is by no means clear whether his different dots, indicating different fingers of the lutanist, also apply to the viol. On the lute, fingers one, two, or three were generally used for an up-stroke, thumb for a down-stroke. Cf. p. 80, note 21, above.

violin. Each semitone of the viol is fretted, and the fingering is calculated basically by semitones for adjacent fingers. For the reason of the resulting stretch of the hand, the viol is tuned in thirds and fourths (a fifth being too great a stretch). In Part II Ganassi gives fingerings very exactly by a system of dots next to the arabic number that indicates the fret. His music is put in tablature, the six lines of the tablature represent the six strings of the viol, and the top line is the lowest-sounding string of the viol. The following shows how (as an example) the fifth fret of a given string would be played by different fingers in Ganassi's special notation (o = open string):

fret with dots: –o—·5—·5—5:—5.

finger meant: o   1   2   3   4

The violin is unfretted, tuned uniformly in fifths, and the fingering is calculated basically with adjacent fingers on adjacent notes of the diatonic scale—that is, mainly by whole-tone steps mixed with some semitones (cf. Ex. 5). Even in Ganassi's last chapter (Part II, ch. 23), where he gives tunings for a three-stringed instrument tuned in fifths without frets for the convenience of the '*viola da brazzo*' players, he still gives fingerings that are basically related to viol fingerings (Ex. 5).

Ex. 5

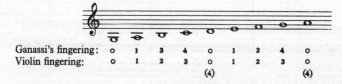

Ganassi's fingering: o 1 3 4 o 1 2 4 o
Violin fingering: o 1 2 3 o 1 2 3 o
                              (4)   (4)

Unfortunately we have practically no information about violin fingerings before 1600 even for such simple music as is extant.[27] We may infer from Ganassi and from information in the seventeenth century that in first position the open string was regularly used in the sixteenth century; and from the ranges of extant violin music we may suppose that fingering was no great problem in music limited to first position. The lack of response of the lowest (gut G) string must have prevented effective use of that string, and this string is not much used until late in the seventeenth century. Consequently, the range of sixteenth-century violin music was limited largely to the upper three strings, and if restricted to first position, the resulting range (d'—b" or c''') was less than two octaves, corresponding closely to the typical range of the soprano voice.

While Ganassi's elementary fingerings are practically of no value for violinists, his information on advanced technique and his sophisticated

---

[27] In 1545 Agricola speaks of using the fingernails to stop the strings [sideways to the strings?] of the early violin or rebec under certain conditions, but such information about fingering, even of such a general and esoteric sort, is rare.

attitude toward the upper positions, shifting, and tone colour are all very
suggestive of the wide horizon of string playing in general even before the
middle of the sixteenth century. Ganassi and others refer to playing 'beyond
the frets' for the best players (there being normally seven frets, each representing a semitone); and he gives explicit numbers and signs for fifteen frets
of which he uses fourteen in his music.[28] If translated into terms of the
unfretted violin and its diatonic fingering, the fifteenth fret implies the use
of the sixth position, a range not known to violin music until about 1650,
more than a century later. Jambe de Fer (1556) who treats viols as well as
violins, speaks of playing on the viols four, five, and six *diatonic* scale-steps
(*not* the semitones of the frets) above the open string or even higher, but
'this would be most unusual'—undoubtedly so in Jambe de Fer's own experience in France. But Ganassi speaks of those players who play at the extremities of the fingerboard of the bass viol, and he names the most expert:
Alfonso da Ferrara, Joanbattista Cicilian, Francesco da Milano, and Rubertino Mantoano. From this we conclude that although Ganassi appears far in
advance of his time, he is following the example of the best contemporary
Italian players—an example which, as a professional viol player, he
thoroughly understood and appreciated himself.

Ganassi's information covers far more than extending the range to the
extremity of the fingerboard. In retrospect it is much more remarkable that
he uses the upper positions on other strings to exploit the tone colour of
their upper register. In his music he requires the tenth fret on all upper three
strings (equivalent to violin third position), and, in addition, at least the
fourteenth fret on the highest string.

Furthermore, Ganassi is aware of such alternate possibilities as (1) playing scales in first position, using open strings, or (2) avoiding open strings,
using the upper positions for a more equal (and sometimes richer) tone
colour. In Part II (ch. 17) he deals with 'mutation of the fingers and strings',
by which he means alternate possibilities of fingerings, positions, and shifts.
He gives six examples of the same passage, each with different fingerings and
positions (also with different rhythms and a few bowings). These examples
are given in tablature and involve anywhere from two to four of the upper
strings, depending on the fingerings and positions used. Using the tunings
of the bass viol, we transcribe two of the examples, as shown in Ex. 6 (the
fingering and note values given above the example are from Ganassi's Ex. 1;
those below, from his Ex. 5). In Ex. 6 the upper fingering is quite elementary: it uses open strings, and it shifts only to extend the range. By contrast,
the lower fingering is quite sophisticated. It calls for the same (upper)

[28] Judenkünig, op. cit., speaks of playing beyond the fifth fret (which is normally the
limit of first position) to the equivalent of the eighth fret.

position throughout, starting and remaining in what is equivalent to third position on the violin. The advantages are that the fingering is uniform, there is no shifting, and the colour is not only richer but more homogeneous than in the first example.

Ex. 6

Whereas Ex. 6 shows a simple and a sophisticated method of playing the same scale passage—either of them quite acceptable and both technically easy for the right and left hand—Ganassi quotes passages of really awkward fingering, involving open strings and the exchange of strings, which he inveighs against (Ex. 7, upper fingering). As an alternative he gives a fingering (Ex. 7, lower fingering) that avoids the open string and stays in one position on the same string, an alternative (or one like it) which must be employed to make the passage practical to play—not to mention making it satisfactory from a musical point of view. (Ex. 7 is transcribed for discant viol.) In the passage shown in Ex. 7 one may recognize a written-out trill

Ex. 7

approached by a turn. The upper fingering is, as Ganassi says, excessively awkward. It involves a rapid exchange of adjacent strings (and consequently tone colour) on the trill figure. Ganassi's solution (Ex. 7, lower fingering) is simplicity itself: everything is played on one string, completely avoiding open string and string exchange. A solution of this kind would be essential if the notes in Ex. 7 were played at all rapidly, as they would have been in *passaggi* and diminution figures used by the advanced players of the time.

Ganassi says relatively little about the details of shifting, commenting merely that sometimes it is essential to move the hand up one fret. However, the music itself is more instructive. In it Ganassi commonly takes advantage of an open string to shift either up or down a number of frets. Other common ways of shifting, indicated by the fingerings in the music, are: 12–1 (see

Ex. 6, upper fingering), or 124–1 (a larger movement of the hand). In a few special cases, the shift 1–1 is used.

Two more things may be said about Ganassi's fingering and hand position. The hand may be contracted or expanded in position, depending on whether whole or half tones are used by successive fingers and in what combination. Finally, Ganassi has a special sign (1) which he inserts in the tablature to guide the first finger to the new (adjacent) string—a form of 'finger preparation'; and this usage may be extended in double stops by placing the finger flat across several strings.

To what extent did the violinists take advantage of the horizon of advanced technique opened by the viol players, especially as represented by Ganassi? This question can be answered only in a general way, since no written violin music of the sixteenth century calls for playing above first position, much less requires the other sophistications mentioned above in the remarkable treatise and music of Ganassi. Nevertheless, well before the time of his treatise, various paintings show rebec, and especially *lira da braccio*, players using third position (or thereabouts). The fresco in Saronno Cathedral (1535) depicts the viola (i.e. the alto violin) playing in third position and probably the violin in second or third position as well. About the middle of the century Rabelais mentions the violin in a passage that may refer to shifting: 'All the furr'd [law] cats began to play with their claws as if they were shifting on the violin.'[29] At the end of the century (1592) Zacconi mentions position playing for the *viola da brazzo* (violin family): 'The violins ascend through 17 *voci* [steps of the diatonic range, that is, through the first position] . . . besides some other tones which are produced by artifice and judgement in the same way they are produced by the players of the [other] *viole da braccio* and *da gamba*.'[30] In view of the evidence of the Saronno fresco in the first part of the sixteenth century and that of Zacconi at the end, one must conclude that the best violinists, at least, used positions above the first from the beginning of violin playing, and that in spite of the simplicity of existing music and its first-position range, this extension of range was a common property of string playing as a whole throughout the sixteenth century.

On the other hand, it must be admitted that an attitude as advanced as Ganassi's toward positions and tone colour[31] can hardly be found in the violin treatises until the time of Leopold Mozart in the middle of the eighteenth century. Furthermore, the construction of the sixteenth-century

---

[29] '*Commencèrent tous les Chats-fourréz joüer des gryphes, comme si fussent violons démanchéz*' [*démanchéz* = shift]. See *Faits et dits héroïques du bon Pantagruel*, Book V, ch. 13. Quoted in Laurent Grillet, op. cit., Vol. II, p. 11.

[30] Lodovico Zacconi, op. cit., Part I (1596), fol. 218r.

[31] An attitude possibly shared by Agricola in his edition of 1545; see fol. 35r.

violin was not specially suited to playing in positions above the third even on the highest string. The short, straight, and relatively fat neck did not encourage still higher positions. The latter were easier on the viol, since, in playing an instrument held between the knees, the position of the left hand of the viol player was much less constricted above third position than the left hand of the violinist. Violinists of that time may also have been timid about accurate intonation in the higher positions; but in this respect the viol player had an equal problem, at least in theory, since the frets which helped him in the lower positions were usually limited to seven and would have been no comfort from the eighth to the fifteenth semitone—a region truly 'beyond the frets'.

Improvisation

If the violinists approached the elaborate technique of the viol players anywhere it must have been in the realm of the unwritten improvisation. For information about the latter we are again indebted to treatises concerned with the viol and the voice for a detailed exposition of a tradition of performance that is seldom reflected in written music. Elaboration of the bare bones of the score through added ornaments or through improvised *passaggi* is commonly discussed and illustrated in treatises of the viol, lute, and voice in the sixteenth century and even earlier. In the late fifteenth century Tinctoris speaks of improvisation on the lute and 'viola' (a species of fiddle; see p. 50), and Ganassi discusses improvisation in both his treatises, especially in *La Fontegara*.[32] Ortiz wrote mainly about improvisation on the bass viol, and there are various other authors concerned with vocal ornamentation and improvisation.[33]

Improvisation of this sort on the violin is not specifically mentioned until Mersenne in 1636 (see p. 127), but it may well have been practised by violinists in the sixteenth century. The preface of Richardo Rogniono's *Passaggi* (1592; see p. 83) speaks of the violin (*Violino da Brazzo*) in connexion with *passaggi*; and in his exercises for 'all sorts of instruments', an instrumental style is systematically explored and developed. It is significant that Agazzari (1607), less than a generation later, characterizes the style of the violin in these words: 'The violin requires beautiful passages [*passaggi*], distinct and long, with playful figures and little echoes and imitations repeated in several places, passionate accents, changing strokes of the bow,

---

[32] On the other hand, Ganassi also speaks in a way that shows he someti.nes wished the player to follow the written score strictly, 'not augmenting or diminishing what the composer has specified' (*'non accrescere ne mancare di quello chel compositore l'havera ordinada'*). *Regola Rubertina*, Part II, ch. 16.

[33] For improvisation on the bass viol, see Ortiz, op. cit. For vocal improvisation, see Max Kuhn, *Die Verzierungs-kunst in der Gesangs-musik des XVI. und XVII. Jahrhunderts*, (*1535–1650*), Leipzig, 1902.

gruppi, trilli, etc.'[34] The end of this quotation calls to mind the fact that many ornaments, such as trills and turns, were not indicated by stereotyped signs as they are today, but were written out in the music (cf. Ex. 7).

Multiple stops (cf. p. 166, note 23)

Double stops may also have been a part of the 'lost' tradition of violin playing; and multiple stops were certainly used by the viol players and especially by performers on the *lira da braccio* and *lira da gamba*.[35] In his music Ganassi gives two- and three-part chords for the viol, playing alone, and also in his madrigal setting ('*Io vorei Dio D'Amor*'), in which the player sings and accompanies himself in two and occasionally three parts on the viol. In this connexion he mentions two players who were particularly skilful at this special type of performance: Juliano Tiburtino and Lodovico Lasagnino Fiorentino (Part II, ch. 16). Ganassi speaks also of chord playing as being more natural to the lute and 'lyra of seven strings' (*lira da braccio*, presumably), but he allows the possibility of a piece of music in five parts, one of which is to be sung, and the other four played on the viol. In this case, however, a longer bow than usual is needed, and the fingerboard and bridge are to be less convex (and possibly the hair of the bow looser) than usual (Part II, ch. 16). Some years later there is a reference to four-part playing on the *lira da gamba*, the larger, bass cousin of the *lira da braccio*. In 1567 Cosimo Bartoli praised Alessandro Striggio (the elder) 'who is . . . even more than excellent in playing the "viola", and he plays on it in four voices at one time with such elegance and fullness of tone that he amazes the listeners'. Striggio's 'viola' was a large *lira da gamba* of many strings, as we learn from a contemporary letter.[36]

Sometimes an apparent double stop is written out for instruments that is probably not intended as a double stop. A number of motets exist in instrumental version that are identical with the vocal version except that the text

[34] Agostino Agazzari, *Del sonare sopra il basso*, Siena, 1607. For the English translation, see Oliver Strunk, *Source Readings*, New York, 1950, p. 429. But note that the phrase *arcate mute* in Agazzari means 'changing strokes of the bow', not 'mute strokes of the bow' as Strunk would have it.

[35] With respect to the *lira da braccio*, see the interesting and ingenious article by Benvenuto Disertori—'Pratica e tecnica della lira da braccio' in *Rivista musicale Italiana*, XLV (1941), pp. 150ff.—in which he works out the chords resulting from the hand position of various players of the *lira da braccio* shown in a number of paintings of the fifteenth and sixteenth centuries. Page 156 of this article includes an especially interesting cut of a painting by Eusebio da San Giorgio ('L'Adorazione dei Magi'), in which two angels are shown. One is tuning a *lira da braccio* held on the left knee, while bowing at the same time; the other is in normal playing position with an instrument (rebec?) on the arm. Both are bowing with the Italian grip (thumb between hair and stick), the bows being held at the extremity of the frog.

[36] For all this, see Alfred Einstein, *The Italian Madrigal*, 3 vols., Princeton, 1949, Vol. II, p. 762.

has been discarded and except that in some cases the final note of one or more parts is a 'double stop'. According to E. H. Meyer, a motet of this kind is 'Dum transisset', by John Taverner (*c.* 1495–1545), in which 'several parts have double stoppings in the final chord!' However, an examination of the manuscript concerned shows that the extra note which constitutes the double stop is actually a 'custos', that is, an indication of the first note which the part will play (or sing) on repeating part of the music; and hence, our double stop is more apparent than real. There is no clue to the identity of the instruments which played the Taverner motet. Quite likely they were viols.[37]

Expression including vibrato and dynamics

It is obvious from Ganassi's remarks that technical devices were dependent on the emotional effect to be achieved. Bowing, for instance, is related to expression: heavy and light bowing (and the appropriate movements of the body) are related to corresponding emotional effects, and playing near or far from the bridge is related to tone with its emotional connotations. In his flute method (*La Fontegara*, see above, p. 76, note 13), Ganassi speaks in a similar vein. In ch. 24 he says, 'Your expression should vary from the most tender (*suave*) to the most lively (*vivace*)'; and in the same chapter he speaks of 'the dexterity needed for the extremes of expression. To modify these, blow with moderate force and increase more or less as required . . . In any case it is always essential that you be guided by good taste and discretion.' Ganassi's general remarks concerning expression in viol and flute playing are similar, and in both cases he joins technique to expression. There is no reason to believe that he would take a different attitude toward the violin in music of like character.

Vibrato and dynamics were certainly used occasionally to intensify expression. Early descriptions of the vibrato in Agricola doubtless refer to the rebec or the early violin, and the ubiquitous Ganassi describes the same effect on the viol. Agricola says:

> 'Auch schafft man mit dem zittern frey
> Das süsser laut die Melodey
> Denn auff den andern geschen mag.
> ('Who, while their stopping finger teeter,
> Produce a melody much sweeter
> Than 'tis on other fiddles done.')[38]

[37] See Ernst H. Meyer, *English Chamber Music*, London, 1946, p. 83, note 1. The vocal parts of the motet may be found in *Tudor Church Music*, 10 vols., London, 1922–9, Vol. III, pp. 37–45. For pointing out this 'custos' to me I am indebted to Denis Stevens.

[38] Agricola, op. cit., ed. of 1545, fol. 42r. Translation by Curt Sachs, *Our Musical Heritage*, New York, second ed., 1955, p. 134. Sachs thinks this passage shows that the vibrato was introduced by 'Polish fiddlers'.

Ganassi describes the vibrato on the viol in these words:

'Alle fiate tremar il braccio de l'archetto, e le dita de la mano del manico
per far l'effetto conforme alla musica mesta & afflitta . . .'
('At times a trembling of the bow arm, and [of] the fingers of the hand
that holds the neck [of the viol] to make the mood conform to sad and
afflicted music.')[39]

However, vibrato was generally used as an ornament applied occasionally,
not continuously or as an intrinsic part of technique, as today.

Among dynamic effects, the *messa di voce* ($\smile$ $\frown$), particularly on long
notes, must have been in vogue in vocal instruction by the last years of the
sixteenth century, to judge by Caccini's preface to *Le Nuove Musiche* (1601);
and the violin, which took the voice as its model, may have imitated the
messa di voce in the sixteenth century. It certainly did so in later times.
Similarly, the tradition of performing vocal music with added *piano*, *forte*, and
intermediate nuances may have been transferred to violin music. Of composition in general Vicentino says (1555) that it would be impossible to
notate compositions 'as they are' or better as they must be played 'with their
piano and *forte*, *presto* and *tardo*, in accordance with the words'.[40]

The much earlier manuscript lute book (*c.* 1517) of Vicenzo Capirola is
not only the oldest extant lute manuscript but in it is 'the earliest occurrence
of legato and non-legato, of two kinds of trills and of dynamic indications'.
Capirola came from Brescia, a fact of interest with respect to the use of
dynamics in the early history of violin playing.[41]

Summary

In the discussion of the violin in the preceding chapters we have tried to
show that the development of the instrument and bow, the music, and the
technique and sound of the violin are all functions of each other. Although
there are many obscurities and shadows in the whole picture, sufficient
details do emerge to confirm this thesis, the truth of which becomes more
apparent after 1600, when the information is more abundant and precise.
Without the central notion that styles of playing are functions of instrumental development and musical usage, it would be quite impossible to
make any sense of the scraps of diverse information available to us about the
violin in the sixteenth century. We could not explain anything as different
as the practice of the gay dance musicians on the one hand and those

[39] *Regola Rubertina*, Part I, ch. 2.
[40] Nicola Vicentino, op. cit., fol. 94v.
[41] For the quotation see the summary of a paper on the manuscript by Otto Gombosi in
The Journal of the American Musicological Society, Spring 1948, p. 58. The manuscript
is now printed: *Compositione di Meser Vincenzo Capirola. Lute-Book (circa 1517)*, edited
by Otto Gombosi, Neuilly-sur-Seine, 1955.

solemnly accompanying voices or playing chamber music on the other. The dance violinists at the Valois Court of Henry III certainly played quite differently from the violinists at the Munich Chapel under Lasso. Styles were determined less at this time by national differences than by differences of musical usage.

The diversity of instruments and bows was partly a matter of the confusion and experiment that normally accompanies birth and growth, but this variety may also be explained in terms of function. The same diversity is reflected in holding the violin variously at the breast, shoulder, or neck, and in holding the bow in the 'French' or 'Italian' manner. Presumably the resulting violin sound differed somewhat, but this difference would not be as striking as the contrast in sound between the 'average' sixteenth-century violin and the 'average' modern violin. The reason for this contrast lies in the pronounced differences in tension, gut as opposed to metal or metal-wound strings, the sparse use of vibrato, the different action of the bow, and a marked dissimilarity in the technique of the right and left hand. Consequently, if any generalities can be made at all (particularly when anything as unstandardized as the sixteenth-century violin and bow is involved), the old violin must have sounded more reedy, purer, and more transparent in tone than the modern violin; and the action of the bow and the musical aesthetics of the time must have worked together to produce a somewhat more articulated sound than is usual today.

Such matters have to be determined by experiments with reconstructed violins and 'old' bows. There is no other way to determine the approximate sound. The information which permits us to reconstruct instruments and bows has to be pieced together from the evidence of a few extant instruments, paintings, and documents, the latter being mainly theoretical works in general and treatises on the violin in particular. The last phrase is something of a misnomer. There are no treatises devoted exclusively to the violin in the sixteenth century, although random references to the violin and its practices do occur in other treatises. There is so little sixteenth-century violin music, either printed or in manuscript, that this source of information is, for all practical purposes, a book with seven seals. If all we could learn about the violin in the sixteenth century came from extant music, we would have to conclude that the music and technique of that time existed only on the most naive and primitive level. To be sure, such a conclusion is a bare possibility, but the truth is probably somewhat different, if only because of the extraordinary craftsmanship which such makers as Andrea Amati and Gasparo da Salò lavished on the violin, at least after 1550, and because of the enthusiastic endorsement of these instruments, in the form of hard cash, by celebrated players, aristocrats, and even kings. These facts are not compatible with a primitive instrument or technique. While the technique may well have been relatively simple, the resulting music must have been more than satisfactory from the point of tone and rhythm. It is quite likely that the early history of the violin is comparable in certain respects to the early history of jazz, whose documented narrative would be sparse indeed without the phonograph record. Remove this source of information and blur the focus of history with four centuries of time, and we have the situation of the violin in the sixteenth century. In point of fact, the dance violinist of the sixteenth century may have occupied a social and musical position not much different from the saxophonist today; and, similarly, not only was the music of both infrequently written down, but the manner of performing may well have been practically impossible to notate with any accuracy. Those violinists who accompanied serious vocal music undoubtedly stuck much closer to 'the book', but this book was the singer's score, and, as a rule, no separate parts were needed or made for the violinists.

To perceive the true magnitude of the string player's horizon in the sixteenth century we must look to the lutanists and especially to the viol players whose instruments were admired and respected by solid citizens in a position to support and demand written music and treatises for instruction. To this circumstance we owe a fairly respectable amount of information, which reveals a far broader extent and advanced technical level of string playing than is generally recognized, and which could have been, and perhaps was, adapted by the sixteenth-century violinist of talent and ambition. The most advanced information of this sort comes from Ganassi in 1542–3, hardly more than a generation after the birth of the violin. In his instructions to the viol player, he advocated principles of string playing, a number of which are valid today; and his notions of fingering, position playing, and string colour cannot be found in the violin treatises until two centuries later. He was the first theorist known to establish a workable, if rudimentary, discipline of bowing, including the ordering of the down-strokes and up-strokes and the use of *portato*. He also admitted the *pizzicato* (although not by that name) and the vibrato. In his treatise, bowing and tone are related to expression; and from other sources we get the notion that nuances of tone, as well as louds and softs, were used in the interest of expression. Ganassi used a number of multiple stops, and he and others like Richardo Rogniono give examples of *passaggi*, usually improvised. Toward the end of the century there are a few references in the theorists like Rogniono and Zacconi to the discipline of bowing on the violin and to playing above first position—a state of affairs that must have existed in violin playing early in the century, to judge by the evidence of pictures such as the fresco at Saronno Cathedral (Plate 2).

The important and really unanswerable question is to what extent the violinists availed themselves of the possibilities opened to them from the developed and advanced technique of the other string players, notably the best players of the viol. In short, did the violinists of the sixteenth century adopt the advanced technique, the ornamental elaborations, and the devices of expression used on occasion by the best and most adventuresome viol players of the time? We do not know. It is quite possible that a few violinists, the best and boldest of their time, did so in their own practising or in the privacy of chamber music in their own homes. On the whole, however, the majority probably followed such practices to a comparatively limited extent. Violinists were largely professionals engaged mainly in playing for dance music or in doubling vocal parts. For neither of these pursuits were violinists required to master more than the first position and simple bowings—much less the diminutions and *passaggi* of Rogniono and particularly the extremities of the fingerboard and subtleties of positions and tone colour known to viol players like Ganassi. The demands of dance music were chiefly rhythmic, not those required to delineate vivid or expressive texts or to satisfy the groping fantasies of an art music developed in purely instrumental terms.

Later the expressive and experimental attitudes of the seventeenth century gave birth to a new music for whose performance the violin was eminently suited. Not long after 1600 composers, especially in Italy and Germany, began to exploit the inherent potential of the violin to rival the human voice in expression and especially to achieve an exceptional variety, range, and brilliance in passage work. In these matters, violinists built directly on the remarkable achievement of the viol players of the sixteenth century. At the same time, the violin continued its role in dance music and as an accompaniment to vocal music, particularly in the new operatic forms. Even in vocal pieces, Monteverdi treated violin accompaniments in a manner that was usually idiomatic to the instrument and, comparatively speaking, fairly advanced in technique. With the advent of the Italian sonata about 1610, the development of the violin had to proceed beyond the simple demands of the dance or vocal accompaniment. The true nature and idiomatic treatment of the violin began to be realized by composers who were bound only by the confines of their own imagination and by the new instrumental forms and abstract designs in which they worked. With these developments a new period began. The formative period of the violin had come to a close.

PART TWO

The Development of an
Idiomatic Technique, 1600-1650

The Development of an Idiomatic Technique, 1600-1650

FROM the outset the seventeenth century showed numerous signs of breaking with the Renaissance traditions of its immediate past. This was as true in music and the fine arts as in other fields of thought and endeavour. An experimental frame of mind and a desire for individual and personal expression characterized a number of musicians and thoughtful men everywhere, and instrumental music as a whole began to develop its own idioms and forms. The violin was associated very closely with these developments. It inspired composers and players to develop a new and particular style, idiomatic to its own nature and potential, and it spurred composers to the invention of new forms of purely instrumental music, notably the sonata. At the same time, the violin continued its traditional roles in dance music and entertainment, furnished the backbone of the orchestra used in the new opera, and accompanied various types of vocal music such as the concerted forms of the madrigal and sacred music.

All these changes were far from fortuitous. Rather they were part of a much larger change in society as a whole. The frontiers of geography and the mind had been greatly expanded during the sixteenth century, and they were to expand incomparably more in the seventeenth century. Exploration enlarged human knowledge of the physical boundaries of the world; and more important, the most adventuresome spirits of the seventeenth century realized that the horizons of the mind were potentially infinite, not to be limited by tradition or authority. This attitude, in marked contrast to the prevailing thought of the sixteenth century, was anticipated earlier by a few universal spirits like Leonardo da Vinci, and certain manifestations of it inspired the Reformation in Germany. In the seventeenth century, however, a truly experimental and exploratory attitude characterized an age for the first time. The exploration of the world was pushed into the universe of space by astronomers and mathematicians like Galileo and Kepler; and other scientists like Francis Bacon, Descartes, and Isaac Newton founded a new inductive method based on fresh experiments, overturning a scholasticism in science that had rested so long on the ancient findings of Aristotle. Science, mathematics, and philosophy went hand in hand in this respect, and the seventeenth century discovered many laws of external and internal nature, including those of gravity and motion (Newton) and the circulation of the blood (Harvey).

There were other changes in social and political organization. In the Middle Ages society was organized along the horizontal lines of feudal class, all united by a universal Church and by Latin, the universal language. The Reformation in Germany in the sixteenth century and the questioning, experimental, and philosophical attitude of the seventeenth century hastened social and political changes which were to result in a new vertical alignment into modern nations. Realignments on such a scale are never accomplished without strain and conflict; and the numerous wars in the seventeenth century, involving the growth of nations, the conflict of Church and State, the emphasis on the secular rather than Church authority, and the savage religious conflicts of Protestants and Catholics, were all witness to a fundamental change. Included in this change were certain religious divisions within individual nations, and, more generally, a cleavage in Europe between the nations in the north, which became predominantly Protestant, and those in the south, which remained Catholic.

These physical and mental transformations, and especially the intellectual and philosophical attitudes that fostered them, had a profound effect on the arts. Just as scientists were overturning and questioning the validity of accepted dogma in science, artists and musicians were reacting with more than their usual iconoclasm to the gods and mores of their ancestors in art and music. Whereas previous generations had been satisfied to rearrange the rules of their predecessors here and there, the musicians of the seventeenth century were prepared to discard the rules themselves for an artistic result they considered essential. In the Preface to *Alceste*, Gluck wrote 'there is no rule which I have not thought it right to set aside willingly for the sake of an intended effect'. Gluck's words were published in 1769, but they could have come as well from Monteverdi early in the seventeenth century in his controversy with G. M. Artusi, who, as the conservative voice of the musical past, had taken Monteverdi to task in a treatise characteristically entitled 'Of the Imperfections of Modern Music' (1600). In short, the artists and musicians of the early seventeenth century began to claim an unprecedented freedom from authority and tradition. This was the attitude of individuality and personal expression that permeated the early phases of the so-called Baroque—an age which began in music about 1600 and which was often confusing and contradictory by virtue of its very individuality. The flamboyant, bizarre, and exaggerated often appeared side by side with works whose lasting beauty stemmed from controlled imagination, freshness of idea, and perfection of execution. A new technical virtuosity was a conspicuous trait of some Baroque art.

In music the pre-eminence of the personal and individual encouraged a new attitude toward the voice and particularly toward the independence and individuality of instruments. The most obvious manifestations were the rise of the opera and the development of the idioms and forms of instrumental music. New forms, new manners of expression, and a new technical virtuosity were encouraged in both opera and instrumental music. After 1600 the development of instrumental music and those figurations idiomatic to it was little short of spectacular; and this remark applies especially to the violin. To perceive this point, one has only to compare Monteverdi's violin figuration accompanying the aria 'Possente Spirto' in his opera *Orfeo* of 1607 with the simple melodic lines in the *Ballet comique de la reine* of 1581 (see Ex. 1, p. 56). The idiom of a few instruments had been developed earlier, but for the most part instrumental music before 1600 was secondary to vocal music. In the Renaissance the musical focus of development was the voice and vocal music, especially in the Church. Not until the seventeenth century, when a new spirit began to manifest itself (including the gradual subordination of religious to secular authority) were instruments as a whole released from their confining subordination to the voice.

The treatises of the seventeenth century were characteristic of the new change in attitude. The musical theorists of the sixteenth century devoted relatively few words to instruments, generally at the end of their discussion. In the early seventeenth century treatises like those of Praetorius and Mersenne described all the instruments of the time in elaborate and meticulous detail. Mersenne's *Harmonie Universelle* is a particularly good example of the new spirit and age. It is symptomatic of the times that Mersenne was both mathematician and musician; and in his treatise music, science, and mathematics come together in substance and form. In substance, Mersenne is interested in acoustical questions of all sorts, which he treats with mathematical exactness. The form of the book itself is arranged in the fashion of a geometry treatise with propositions and corollaries, and it uses geometric figures to demonstrate the solutions to various problems. This is hardly surprising in a man who was a close friend of Descartes (who wrote a treatise on music which had some influence on Mersenne); and when Descartes went to Holland to avoid religious persecution, Mersenne acted as his correspondent and agent. Mersenne also quotes Kepler in his treatise, and he dedicates the section on the organ to Etienne Pascal, the father of the philosopher and mathematician.

Of all the instruments at the beginning of the seventeenth century the violin was the one with the greatest undeveloped potential for personal expression throughout a wide range of diverse use. As Robert Donington has aptly said:

'The qualities which have bestowed on the violin family its present leadership are not so much its beauty of tone as its extraordinary flexibility. Except for the voice, few instruments have quite the same power of modifying their quality and loudness in the course of a single note. The violin can sustain its tone still more tirelessly; it can attack each note with a still wider variety of styles, ranging from the smoothest legato (bonded style) to the most delicate staccato (detached style). Its range of notes is much greater, and it can jump about throughout this range with an almost unparalleled agility. It has an astonishing choice of different tone qualities: it has perfect control of pitch, enabling a good player to be always properly in tune. Finally, its normal, basic tone is of a satisfactory and fascinating kind that can be listened to almost indefinitely without palling.'[1]

Nor were theorists of the seventeenth century unaware of the violin's beauties, and some of their sentiments are quoted below (for Mersenne, see p. 174; for G. B. Doni, see p. 121). With such an instrument at hand it remained only for the composers and players of the time to develop the violin in range, figurations, melodic possibilities, and other devices (cf. ch. 6). Violin music was now written down and sometimes printed—a situation which permits us to describe the style of the music without the qualifications necessary in our account of sixteenth-century music (cf. ch. 3).

The development of nationalism in the seventeenth century had no uniform effect on music although one obvious result was the formation of a national French style, especially after 1650. During the seventeenth century France gradually became a strong nation, the strongest power in Europe, beginning with Louis XIII and Richelieu in the early part of the century and reaching a vast crescendo of power under Louis XIV at its end. The focus of political life around the French monarchy undoubtedly resulted in a concentration of artistic life about the Court, which in turn solidified and defined the French spirit in arts and letters. In music it produced a specific style as the antithesis of the Italian style, and these two styles were the poles of a musical conflict for two centuries. Other nations tended to be attracted or repulsed by the French and Italian styles in music, which acted like magnets.

Neither Italy nor Germany made any special progress toward political unity in the seventeenth century; and in England a civil war dangerously divided the nation. Like Germany and England, Italy was torn by strife, but it overcame these disasters to assume musical leadership throughout the seventeenth and eighteenth centuries. Italy owed its pre-eminence in music to the traditions of its past, to the prodigality of natural talent, and to diverse centres of wealth and culture in cities like Venice, Milan, Florence, Bologna, and Rome. In these centres music was supported by the Church, by religious orders like the Jesuits, by municipalities, or by dukes and popes, themselves passionately interested in music or deeply committed to it for State or propaganda reasons.

The Italians developed a musical style central to which was the cantabile of the solo voice reinforced by a passionate mode of expression and by a

[1] Robert Donington, *The Instruments of Music*, London, 1949, p. 46.

harmony and rhythm that sought to illuminate the text. In violin music the Italian style was characterized by a singing type of melody modelled on the voice and by abstract figurations and designs idiomatic to the violin and to the new forms of instrumental music. In France the style was more restrained emotionally and technically. In opera, for example, the voice was treated in a far less expressive way than in Italy, and instrumental music was largely functional, with particular emphasis on its rhythmic properties. The theatre and dancing, those twin poles of French artistic life, required the almost exclusive service of instrumental music, and as a result violin music was largely synonymous with dance music. However rhythmically gay and sprightly, French violin music in the seventeenth century was relatively confined, narrow in its horizons, and simple in its technical development compared to Italian violin music, which expanded the idiomatic and technical capacity of the instrument in the new forms of instrumental music (see ch. 6).

The Germans were primarily followers of the Italians. Heinrich Schütz (1585-1672) went to Italy to study with Giovanni Gabrieli in Venice and later with Monteverdi, and his style was greatly influenced by the Italians. He even describes approvingly the practices of Italian violinists in one of his prefaces (see p. 136). Schütz was a symbol of the fate of German musicians in the early seventeenth century. He had great native gifts and was magnificently trained in Germany and Italy, but his music and life and those of his colleagues at the Dresden Chapel, which he headed, were completely disrupted by the Thirty Years' War in Germany (1618-48). In the late seventeenth century the Germans developed an advanced style in violin music; and while it was still indebted to the Italian style, it possessed a marked individuality of its own, surpassing the Italian style in certain technical respects (see ch. 11).

The number of English violinists actually increased after 1603 during the reign of the Stuarts, but the players were predominantly from families of foreign extraction, as they had been under the Tudors. When a 'composer for the violins' was appointed for the first time in 1621, the post went to Thomas Lupo, a member of an Italian family that had entered the Royal service in the sixteenth century (cf. p. 39). The principal function of the violin was playing for dancing, and the models upon which the dance style of playing was based were Italian and French. A distinctive English style appeared in vocal music and in instrumental 'fancies' for the viols. In a few cases, where the violins were admitted to chamber music, the instruments were treated with an individuality idiomatic to the violin or that akin to the English style of viol music. Nevertheless, the technical level of all English violin music remained relatively simple compared to that of the Italians.

In the seventeenth century the violin must have filled a greater number of social and musical roles than previously. Traditionally the instrument was connected with dancing of all sorts, with entertainments, including playing at feasts and dinners, and such special occasions as weddings, festivals, and Christmas celebrations. The violin had also been used extensively in connexion with sacred and secular vocal music and also to some extent in chamber music. These traditional uses certainly continued in the seventeenth century, probably in amplified form, and in addition the violin became the backbone of the new opera orchestra and it developed its own independent instrumental forms. Besides, in its traditional accompaniment of vocal music, the violin was used in new ways. The concerto-like settings that characterized many vocal pieces in both sacred and secular music (e.g. Gabrieli, Monteverdi) treated the violin, not as an instrument to double the vocal lines, but to play an independent, *obbligato* part (see ch. 6). Finally the public concert made a tentative appearance in England, and the violin must have had some part in these activities.[2] The English public concert was far in advance of its time, since the European public concert can hardly be found before the late eighteenth century.

The musical flexibility of the violin and its immense potentiality for development explain the increased vogue of the violin in the seventeenth century, and this popularity is amply attested in painting. Dutch genre painting is a good example. In a carefully documented study of instruments depicted in seventeenth-century Dutch paintings, Ian F. Finlay says of the violin:

'The violin was almost as universal as the lute. It was played at peasant gatherings, either as a solo instrument or as an accompaniment to dancing. It was also found at family gatherings and popular festivals. Violins often occur in still lifes and are found as accessories in many paintings, either hanging on the wall or lying on tables.

There are a few examples of the instrument being tuned and in one case a violin is being played resting on a table. There is one case of a left-handed violinist and several elaborate string-holders. As with the gamba, ribbons were sometimes tied round the tuning pegs. The instrument seems to have been played more often by men than by women.'[3]

Finlay also shows that certain combinations of instruments frequently played together, and, in order of popularity, these combinations were: bass viol and violin; lute, bass viol, and violin; lute and violin (cf. Plate 20). According to Finlay, 'the violin was almost as universal as the lute', but the

---

[2] For this see Woodfill, op. cit., p. 50.
[3] Ian F. Finlay, 'Musical Instruments in 17th-century Dutch Paintings' in *The Galpin Society Journal*, July 1953, p. 56.

violin turns out to be considerably more popular than either the lute or the bass viol in the fifty-four group-combinations cited by him in his article. One may add that group-combinations of instruments that include the violin appear in Italian and French as well as Dutch painting (cf. Plates 20 and 23). Besides, a number of still-life 'violin' paintings illustrate the 'Vanitas' theme of 'life is futile', 'we are here today and gone tomorrow'. A globe, a skull, an hour-glass, or ancient texts are characteristically part of these compositions (see Plate 24). Does this association imply that the violin is an instrument of 'Vanitas'?

A study of art objects of the seventeenth century makes clear that the violin had permeated all ranks of society to a greater degree than in the sixteenth century. Possibly violins were cheaper and easier to procure. In any case, Dutch genre painting, which is especially faithful in its realistic portrayal of daily life in all classes of society, depicts the violin increasingly in the hands of peasants and amateurs, and tavern scenes and those featuring low life are far more numerous (cf. Plate 17). At the same time, the violin is often painted in scenes laid in the homes of wealthy Dutch burghers. It was the latter who were responsible for many of the Dutch paintings of musical interest, having encouraged their families to pursue music and having commissioned the excellent Dutch artists to depict scenes from their family life through paintings and prints. Royal and aristocratic patronage of the violin and violinists continued and increased. In France a formal band of *Twenty-four Violins of the King* was founded (1626), and a similar group existed in England. Without a doubt the English sovereigns were England's greatest patrons.[4]

The various uses of the violin, explained above, can be fitted, with certain overlaps, into the three categories of chamber, church, and theatre, established by the theorists of the seventeenth century. In the Church, for instance, one expects to encounter sacred music for the service, but it is more surprising that purely instrumental music, in the form of the 'church' sonata, should be found (cf. pp. 133-4). The word 'chamber' presumably covered considerable territory, and under the term 'chamber music' could be included violin music used for dancing, for instrumental music played at home for amusement, and possibly dinner music. In this connexion, it is tempting to quote a contemporary document concerning the use of music at great feasts, noting at the same time its remarkable resemblance to the description of music at the Munich Court under Lasso (see p. 62). This description is taken from Richard Brathwaite's *Some Rules and Orders for the Government of the House of an Earle* (1621), and reads as follows:

'At great feasts, when the earl's service is going to the table, they [the

---

[4] For details, see Woodfill, op. cit., p. 241.

musicians] are to play upon shagbut [= sackbut = trombones], cornetts, shawms, and such other instruments going with wind. In meal times to play upon viols, violins, or other broken music . . .'[5]

In the theatre the violin was mainly used in the operatic orchestra. It must also have been employed in incidental music for the theatre, for dancing in this connexion, and for quasi-theatrical productions, such as the masques in England, a central feature of which was dancing.

In general the social position of the violin and violinists improved in the seventeenth century. The increased use and acceptance of the violin in many ranks of society were bound to ameliorate the position of an instrument which had originally been employed largely by professionals to play dance music. By the same token the lot of violinists had also been bettered, although the social position of the individual professional violinist varied, according to the circumstances of his employment, from the relative well-being of Royal musicians to free-lance fiddlers who were merely 'one cut above a beggar'. As a class, musicians generally fell into the category of the lower middle class; and they often belonged to families that were tradition-ally musicians for generations. In one sense musicians as a whole belonged to no class because individuals varied greatly in rank according to whom they served; and because many musicians, being called upon to play for all ranks of society, conformed to none.

Court musicians, encouraged and supported by sovereigns for personal and State reasons, had several important advantages. As members of a Royal establishment, they had better social positions, better salaries, and a species of security not enjoyed by other musicians. In addition they had still other advantages often overlooked: namely, the best available instruments and gorgeous costumes. The finest instruments were generally in the hands of Royal musicians, either because they could afford them or because such instruments belonged to the Court (cf. p. 35 concerning the Amatis allegedly ordered by Charles IX of France); and the Royal musicians were frequently attired in magnificent costumes as part of the retinue of the sovereign or the occasion they served. From the accounts of the *Ballet comique de la reine* (1581; see p. 55) or those of the French and English Courts in the seventeenth century, one sees that the players of violins and other instruments were dressed in a style to which they could hardly have aspired as private and ordinary citizens. In spite of all this, however, musicians were still regarded as servants in the great household of which they were a part, and this fact was basic to the employment of musicians until the end of the eighteenth century, including one so famous as Joseph Haydn.

[5] Quoted in Woodfill, op. cit., p. 235.

H.V.P.–I

This does not mean that musicians of the seventeenth century were without some measure of protection in professional matters. Both the French and English enjoyed the kind of collective bargaining that is associated with unions today. The musicians' companies or guilds banded together for mutual support and succeeded in obtaining concessions that protected their interest. In England, for instance, the Musicians' Company in 1606 adopted a by-law that set the minimum number of musicians to be hired at any engagement. No group 'under the number of four in consort or with violins' was to play at a gathering upon threat of a fine of three shillings, four pence for each offender.[6]

All this has a strangely modern sound to a musician today; and indeed it was in the early seventeenth century that the violin left behind its formative stages and started to develop the idiomatic style of music and technique of playing upon which modern violin music and technique were ultimately founded.

[6] See Woodfill, op. cit., p. 19. For organization of French musicians, see p. 137 below.

CHAPTER FIVE

The Development of the Violin and Bow in the Early Seventeenth Century

B Y the early seventeenth century the violin was so well known, according to Praetorius, that nothing more needed to be said about it. With our advantage of hindsight, one further thing might be said about it now: at the beginning of the seventeenth century the capabilities of the violin and probably the bow were well in advance of the demands made upon them by composers and violinists, who needed to catch up with the musical and technical possibilities inherent in this remarkable instrument. Consequently only a few changes had to be made in the violin in the early seventeenth century; and it is noticeable that new changes in violin design were largely decorative rather than functional (see below, p. 108). Certain refinements took place in the bow, as will be described presently, to meet demands of players for new effects.

What was new were the efforts of composers of instrumental music in particular, who were inspired by the experimental frame of mind described above and more specifically by the new style in the opera and in the 'modern' madrigal. Formally, these composers built upon the old *canzona* and the imitative *ricercar*, and in the course of the next fifty years they changed these forms greatly, largely adapting them to the new sonata and to forms of imitative counterpoint. Technically, violinists were ready for a new music, and they already had at hand a great reservoir of technique from the players of the viols (see ch. 4). To develop this technique, to adapt it to the needs and nature of the violin, and to bring out the true idiom of the instrument was the work of the seventeenth-century violinists, especially the Italians and, later, the Germans.

In northern Italy conditions were ripe for a massive advance by maker, player, and composer in developing the idiom of the violin. The pre-eminence of the schools of violin making in Cremona and Brescia, begun in the sixteenth century, continued (as already explained) along traditional lines with Maggini and the Amati family; and at the same time composers and players emanated from these and neighbouring cities to give a strong impulse to new forms of violin music and the technique of the instrument. Monteverdi, himself a professional string player who used the violin copiously in his operas and vocal music, was born in Cremona and spent his working years successively in Mantua and Venice.[1] Biagio Marini, the most important composer of violin music in the early seventeenth century, and G. B. Fontana, another violin composer of note, were both born in Brescia. Carlo Farina, one of the first virtuosi on the violin, was born in Mantua. The most important centre of publishing violin music was Venice, where many important musicians were concentrated, including the Gabrielis and, later, Monteverdi. These examples show the importance of northern Italy as a centre of violin makers, composers, and players.

This is not to say that other countries were unimportant in the development of the violin and its music. Compared to Italy, however, they produced fewer renowned violin makers and contributed less to the new forms and idioms of violin music (see ch. 6, p. 131). On the other hand, documents and paintings reflect the widespread use of the violin and its increased prestige in other European countries, the Low Countries being especially prolific in genre paintings that depict the violin (cf. p. 103). It is also significant that the most encyclopedic information about instruments, including the violin, emanated not from Italy but from Germany and France in the treatises of Praetorius (1619) and Mersenne (1636), the former being particularly well informed about developments in Italy.

The violin continued to develop along lines begun in the sixteenth century. The international fame of the makers in Brescia and Cremona remained unchallenged for another fifty years, and during this time the Brescian school maintained its prestige under the leadership of G. P. Maggini (1580– c. 1632), the pupil of Gasparo da Salò. Maggini refined the model of his teacher, and added certain particular traits of his own, notably double purfling and, occasionally, striking ornamentation on the back of his instruments (Plate 18).[2] In Cremona, the two sons of Andrea Amati, Antonio and Girolamo (Hieronymus), continued the tradition of their father, often sign-

---

[1] Monteverdi began at Mantua as a '*suonatore di vivola*'. In Bottrigari (*Il Desiderio*, Venice, 1594), the *vivola* is a viol. Later Praetorius speaks of the *vivola* in connexion with the *viole da braccio* (members of the violin family). Monteverdi's brother speaks of the composer's duties as a player of the *viola bastarda*, which, according to Praetorius, was an outsized species of tenor viol, or, according to F. Rognoni, of a size between tenor and bass.

[2] See Margaret L. Huggins, *Gio. Paolo Maggini: his Life and Work*, London, 1892.

ing their instruments together.[3] Nicola Amati (1596–1684), the son of Girolamo, was the most important of all the Amatis, and his violins had a profound influence outside Italy, especially in France and the Low Countries. By the time of Nicola Amati, Cremona violins were long since established as the best in Italy or, what amounted to the same thing, in the world. In a fascinating correspondence during 1637–8, one Father Fulgenzio Micanzio of Venice advises Galileo, the astronomer, on the choice of a violin for his nephew. Father Micanzio, relying on the opinion of Monteverdi, strongly recommends the 'incomparably better' Cremona violins rather than those from Brescia, and he cites prices as an indication: twelve ducats for a Cremona violin but four or less for one from Brescia.[4] Painters of the time, such as Gentileschi, Caravaggio, and Baschenis (1617–77), painted violins and other instruments which they saw all about them (cf. Plates 8, 11, and 19).

No French, German, English, or Dutch maker of international repute had yet appeared. Jacob Stainer, for example, born in Absam in the Tyrol about 1617 (not 1621), achieved his great reputation largely after 1650. The same may be said of Jacobs in Holland. Nevertheless, the number of violins depicted in the paintings in countries other than Italy—for example, in the Low Countries and Czechoslovakia—shows the considerable amount of activity involving the violin.[5] While some of these instruments were doubtless of Italian origin, many must have been of domestic manufacture.

Existing instruments that date from the early seventeenth century are far more numerous than those from the sixteenth century. However, one cannot be certain of all the details of the seventeenth-century violin merely by examining surviving instruments. The body shell itself has usually remained unchanged, but the fittings and various details of construction have invariably been altered in the intervening centuries, including the neck, fingerboard, bridge, bass-bar, and strings. Furthermore, all modern instruments have been fitted with a chin rest and a tuner for the E string

[3] Contrary to the information in most reference works, Antonio was born about 1540 (death date unknown). Girolamo was born in 1561 and died in 1630. For these dates, see Carlo Bonetti's article mentioned in note 27, p. 19, above. If Bonetti is correct about these dates (and he seems to be supported by documents), Antonio was twenty-one years older than his brother Girolamo. This discrepancy of age may account for the fact that in 1588, eight years after the two brothers inherited their father's business (1580), Antonio sold out to his younger brother. Under these circumstances, it seems likely that most of the instruments coming from the Amati workshop in the early seventeenth century were the work of Girolamo, who is today generally considered somewhat more gifted than his older brother.

[4] For this correspondence, see W. H., A. F., and A. E. Hill, *The Violin Makers of the Guarneri Family*, London, 1931, pp. 150–1.

[5] For the Low Countries, see note 3, p. 103. For a few in Czechoslovakia, see the paintings in Czech museums shown in Alexander Buchner, *Musical Instruments through the Ages*, London, n.d.

(and sometimes for all the strings); and old violins have invariably been modernized in the same manner.

In the early seventeenth century the body length of most violins was approximately fourteen inches, just as it is now. Nevertheless, by modern notions the violin was less standardized with respect to length and arching of the body. For example, a number of the Maggini violins were made on a large pattern, and the Brescian and Cremonese instruments used a higher body arching than is usual in the later model of Stradivari. Pegboxes sometimes end in carved heads instead of scrolls. The old-style neck of the sixteenth century (cf. Plate 16), projecting straight from the body and short by modern standards, persisted until about 1800. The fingerboard began to lengthen, but not appreciably, since the music did not yet require the high positions. Even in the case of Uccellini, who calls for the sixth position (see p. 125), a position relatively rare at that time (1649), the fingerboard would still have been two and a half inches shorter than it is now. Because of the relatively low tensions on the bridge, the seventeenth-century violin at that time did not need the heavy bass-bar and sound post of the modern instrument, and consequently the bass-bar was shorter and lighter, and the sound post was probably thinner in diameter than it is today.

The old bridge was also different. Sometimes it had an arch rather than a bar across the lower part. However, a more typical bridge about 1600 had the bar somewhat as it is now, but the upper part was cut differently from the modern bridge (compare Plates 8, 16, and 19 with Plate 1). Bridges varied so much that it is very difficult to make a general statement about them. This applies to their height and contour. About 1631 Pierre Trichet describes the bridge as a semicircle, a half-moon crescent, 'so that the bow can touch each string separately'.[6] In general, the bridge was probably a bit lower in height and somewhat flatter in contour than that used now, but, judging from paintings and theoretical works of the time, the contour was subject to a number of variations. The bridge may have also been somewhat narrower and thicker, but this cannot be proved one way or the other. A surprising fact is the position of the bridge relative to the belly. Frequently the bridge depicted in paintings is placed not in line with the notches in the middle of the f-holes, as it invariably is today, but appreciably farther down toward the tailpiece (see Plate 20). The numerous examples of this placement shown in paintings and the theorists cannot be purely accidental, and, in fact, this placement of the bridge persists from similar usage much earlier in the sixteenth century. The reasons for this position are not entirely clear. Possibly a longer length of playing string was being aimed at, a condition

[6] See François Lesure, 'Le Traité des Instruments de Musique de Pierre Trichet' in *Annales Musicologiques*, Vol. III, 1955, Paris; continued in Vol. IV, 1956. Trichet's treatise was also published separately (ed. by Lesure), Neuilly-sur-Seine, 1957.

later achieved by lengthening the neck slightly; possibly a difference in tone quality was being sought (see p. 34).

Finally, the strings were still all gut—a bad thing as regards the response of the lowest (G) string. Strings must have been a source of considerable anxiety to the player. Mersenne (1636) tells us how to test good and false strings, and explains at length how strings are made, their lack of uniformity, where the best strings come from (Rome, particularly), and the properties of gut and metal. Kircher (*Musurgia Universalis*, Rome, 1650) mentions strings made of silk as well as metal and gut. Mersenne explains that gut gives a softer tone than copper or steel; and Praetorius (1619) remarks on the 'tranquil and almost lovely resonance' of brass and steel strings compared to that of gut (cf. p. 70 above). This wistful remark of Praetorius apparently had no influence on violin stringing, which, as a rule, continued to be entirely gut at least until 1700, shortly after which gut strings wound with silver were introduced to improve the response of the lowest string. Mersenne writes copiously about the relative diameters of strings, and he says violin strings are thicker than the corresponding strings of the viol. Unfortunately, he tells us nothing about the absolute diameters of either violin or viol strings.

To sum up, the violin of the early seventeenth century was basically the instrument developed in the late sixteenth century. Italy still dominated violin making. The prevailing models were those established by the schools of Cremona and Brescia, and the traditions of these schools were carried on by the Amatis and by G. P. Maggini, among others, in the seventeenth century. These beautiful violins were still awaiting the day when composers and players would discover and exploit their full potential. In the meantime violin makers needed to do no more than to improve details here and there, such as slightly elongating the fingerboard and adding decorative touches like double purfling and ornamental designs to the backs of instruments (see Plate 18).

The bow

Surviving specimens of early seventeenth-century violin bows are much rarer than extant violins of the same time. The best violins were precious commodities and were carefully preserved by constant repairing or by alterations to suit the changing musical and technical demands of successive generations. Not so the old bows. The modern Tourte bow, perfected about 1780 and based on different principles of design, rendered the old bows obsolete, reducing their commercial value to zero. Consequently these pre-Tourte bows were generally discarded by players, who probably were in the habit of replacing their bows anyway, since in many cases (and quite unlike the violin) it was hardly more expensive to buy a new bow than to alter or repair an old one extensively. As a result and just as in the sixteenth century (cf. p. 45), our main information about early seventeenth-century bows comes from treatises or iconography, infrequently from the actual bows themselves.

These old bows were far from standardized with respect to length, shape, and elegance of appearance. The bow for dance music was generally quite short. The playing hair of the violin bow shown in Mersenne is barely as long as the body of the violin beside it, which would presumably make the playing hair a scant fourteen inches (Fig. 4). The comparable length of the modern bow is twenty-five and a half inches. The violin bow shown in Praetorius's *Syntagma Musicum* is not wholly visible, and therefore cannot be measured accurately. However, a fair approximation is fifteen inches of playing hair. The Italians who played sonatas generally used longer bows. Assuming that the violin body in Caravaggio's painting 'Love as a Conqueror' (Plate 11) is about fourteen inches in length, the playing hair of the Italian bow shown is about nineteen inches long, still six inches less than the modern bow. The advantages of a longer bow were appreciated in principle, however, although a long bow is seldom seen in illustrations of the violin at this time. In describing the bow of the pochette (shown in Fig. 4) Mersenne says, 'I have made the bow very long (*grand*) so as to observe that the bows are as much better as they are longer, provided they are not inconvenient, because the movements (*traits*) and strokes (*coups*) last longer.'

The ribbon of hair was considerably narrower than that of the modern bow, and this explains why Mersenne specifies only eighty to one hundred hairs in the seventeenth-century bow as compared to one hundred and fifty to two hundred today. For the most part, the bow appears to be fixed in tension, there generally being no way to tighten or loosen the hair. Nevertheless, in pictures knobs may occasionally be seen at the nut-end of the bow stick, as in Mersenne (Fig. 4) and Praetorius; and while these knobs may be ornamental (some appear white as in ivory), they may also be the screw knobs that adjust a movable frog as in modern bows.[7] The matter cannot be proved one way or the other. However, neither Praetorius nor Mersenne, in whose treatises such knobs are illustrated, say anything about a device to loosen or tighten the bow hair. Had such existed, it would have been a curious coincidence and oversight that both Praetorius and Mersenne, the two most encyclopedic writers on instruments of the time, failed to say anything about it. According to present knowledge, the first bow that we can confidently say was equipped with a screwknob and movable frog dates from 1694 (see p. 114 and Plate 29d). Other devices to adjust the hair, involving notches or slots and wedges, may also have been used (cf. p. 46 above).

[7] For knobbed bows in Praetorius, see his *Syntagma Musicum*, Vol. II, Plate XX, Nos. 1 and 2, bows of treble and tenor viol. Curiously, none of the bows in his illustrations of the violin family (Plate XXI) have these knobs.

Fig. 4. *Violin and bow (lower right) and pochette and bow (middle left)
from Mersenne's 'Harmonie Universelle' (1636–7).*

In typical bows of the early seventeenth century the hair was well separated from the bow stick at the lower end by the horn-shaped nut, but at the upper end of the bow the bow stick and the hair met in a point (Plate 20), the bow generally lacking a distinct head. Consequently there was a gradually decreasing distance between the hair and the bow stick from nut to point. The playing length of such bows was effectively reduced, since one cannot play to the extreme point of the bow because the hair hits the bow stick. Such considerations spurred the formation of a distinct bow head, and the latter may occasionally be observed in embryonic form in certain bows depicted in paintings before 1650 (see Plates 12 and 17, and Fig. 4). However, the distinct bow head did not become common until the late seventeenth century.

The bow stick was generally convex (outwardly curved) but not greatly so, and in some cases it was nearly straight. In Plate 21 the bow has a healthy convexity, but there is no distinct head, the bow itself curving down to meet the hair. In Plate 20 the bow stick is practically straight, and the hair and the stick converge almost in straight lines to a headless point. Some of these bows were relatively clumsy in appearance, while others were executed with care and artistry. The bow stick, which was either round or octagonal, was sometimes fluted, a feature of considerable elegance and practicality, making the bow somewhat lighter and more flexible, while retaining its strength. The fluting extended part of, or sometimes nearly all, the length of the stick.[8] The result was a bow combining beauty, strength, and lightness; and such bows compare favourably in strength to the modern bow in the upper third of their length. In short, the best bows were probably extremely good and very efficient, being constructed for the musical purposes of that time.

The best players must have used bows made of the best woods and materials available. It is generally claimed today that the preferred wood for early bows was snakewood ('specklewood'). However, a recently discovered treatise of the seventeenth century proves that even 'brazilwood'—supposed to have been used first in the bows of François Tourte in the late eighteenth century—was being used a century and a half earlier. In Pierre Trichet's *Le Traité des Instruments de Musique* (*c.* 1631) we read: 'bows . . . of brazilwood, ebony, or other solid wood, are best and most esteemed.' (Cf. note 6, above.)

Bows varied a great deal from maker to maker and from nation to nation. Consequently it is difficult to generalize about the bow of the early seventeenth century. Furthermore, it is almost impossible to date early bows with any accuracy. Bows were seldom, if ever, signed or dated by their makers before 1700, and the first dated bow (1694, in the Hill Collection, in their

[8] For a good example, see Gerald Hayes, op. cit., his Plate 8. See also our Plate 28a.

shop, 140 Bond Street, London) is an object of the greatest rarity (Plate 29d). Not until mid-eighteenth century did bow making become an independent art, and even then as celebrated a master as François Tourte never signed his bows. John Dodd, his English contemporary, was one of the first to do so. However, even today, although bows are usually signed, they are rarely dated.

The gradual changes in the seventeenth-century bow included a lengthening of the bow stick, a gradual reduction in the convexity of the curve, the selection of finer woods, and the shaping of the bow stick with the idea of combining strength with elasticity. The gradual formation of the bow head was related to balance, to extending the length of the bow, and to utilizing the whole of it. The device of the modern screw nut, used to tighten the bow hair to the desired tension, must have been known and in use by the end of the seventeenth century. All these changes were ultimately caused by musical requirements, especially in Italy, where new instrumental forms like the sonata inspired bow makers to produce a longer bow capable of more subtle bow strokes, greater variety of tone, and an increased range of expression and dynamics.

The violin family as a whole. Terminology

The great variety of bows had its counterpart in the numerous types of instruments that comprised the violin family in the early seventeenth century. The terminology was correspondingly rich in variety, inconsistency, and confusion. The old Italian distinction between *viole da braccio* (violin family) and *viole da gamba* (viol family) was still valid and usual. Used without qualification, the term *viola da braccio* included the 'small violin' (*violino piccolo*), the violin proper, the viola, and the cello, and, on occasion, an instrument whose register lay between the modern viola and the cello. What corresponds to a modern viola (c-tuning) was variably called an 'alto' or 'tenor' (*viola da braccio*). The violin proper could be referred to as a soprano (treble, discant) *viola da braccio*, as a *violino da braccio*, or simply as *violino*.

Considerable confusion has arisen from the fact that, although the prevailing ensemble of the time used a four- or five-voiced texture, the basic tunings of the violin family were three, just as they were in the sixteenth century (cf. p. 43):

1. Soprano (i.e. the violin proper) g d a' e"
2. Alto-tenor c g d' a'
3. Bass (cello) C G d a (Praetorius)
   or BB♭ F c g (Mersenne)

The difficulties of terminology and register are especially acute in the case of the 'tenor' (i.e. when it was not a viola), an instrument with a register between alto-tenor and bass. This instrument, tuned upward from F or G was sometimes called a 'tenor' (Zacconi) and sometimes a 'bass' (Praetorius); and on occasion it was treated like a low tenor and at other times like the true bass of the ensemble (Banchieri, 1609). At any rate, this instrument looked like a small cello and must have been played like one. It never attained the standing of a full partner in the violin family, and by the end of the seventeenth century it had pretty well disappeared, its musical function being shared between the modern viola and cello.

Praetorius gives the fullest description of terms under the heading '*Violn de Bracio*' [*sic*].[9] As equivalents to this term, he gives *vivola, viola da bracio,* and *violino da brazzo*. He defines the latter as '*eine Geige . . . Discantgeig* which is called *Violino,* or *Violetta picciola,* also *Rebecchino*'.[10] Earlier in the same volume (p. 4), Praetorius gives as synonyms: '*Violino, Rebechino* [*sic*], *Fides, Fidicula, kleine Geigen,* otherwise called *Viol de bracio*'. In his table of tunings (p. 26) under *viole de braccio* and under *Geigen* he gives the violin tuning g d' a' e", which he labels '*Discant Viol.* [= *viola da braccio*]. *Violino*'. In his Plate XXI, showing the violin family, Praetorius calls the violin '*Rechte Discant-Geig*' (the treble violin proper); and his drawings, all to scale, show that the body of the violin was almost exactly fourteen inches long, as is usual today. Praetorius also illustrates a type of *Discant-Geig* tuned a 'fourth higher'[11] as well as *Geigen* an octave higher than the violin proper. Praetorius reaffirms much of this information in Vol. III of the same work (p. 142), where he equates 'small or *Discant Geig*' with '*Rebecchino, Violino, Fidicula*'. He adds: '*Tenor-Alt Geig* and all *Geigen* which are held on the arm, both *Discant* and *Bass-Geigen,* are generally called *Viole de braccio* or *Viole da brazzo.*'[12] In 1620, Francesco Rognoni speaks of '*Viole da brazzo,* particularly the violin' (see p. 164), which shows that Rognoni classified the violin as one of the family of 'arm violas'. From all this it cannot be doubted that:

(1) *viole da braccio* = *Geigen* = violins as a family; and

(2) the soprano *viola da braccio* (*bracio, brazzo*) = the violin.

In France Mersenne explains the terminology of the violin relative to ordinary ensembles and to the *24 Violons du Roy,* the latter formally estab-

---

[9] *Syntagma Musicum,* Vol. II, p. 48.

[10] If *violetta* in Lanfranco (1532; see p. 25) means the rebec (or possibly the violin) family as a whole, then *violetta picciola,* the diminutive, means the soprano of the family. A similar relationship exists between rebec and *rebecchino*.

[11] This tuning was typical of the *violino piccolo* in the seventeenth century. However, the *violino piccolo* used by Bach was generally tuned to b flat, a minor third above the normal tuning of the violin proper.

[12] J. H. Schein uses the corruption '*Figlin*' for violin (1617). See Andreas Moser, *Geschichte des Violinspiels,* Berlin, 1923, p. 38.

lished by Louis XIII in 1626. According to Mersenne (1636), the Royal players were ordinarily distributed in a five-part ensemble, six players being allotted to each of the treble and bass parts, and four players each to the three middle parts. These five parts of the *24 Violons du Roy* were called in descending order of register: *Dessus*, *Haute-Contre* or *Haute-Contre Taille*, *Taille*, *Quinte* or *Cinquiesme*, *Basse*. In ordinary ensembles the highest and lowest parts were called the same as those just given, but the terminology of the middle parts was reversed: *Dessus*, *Quinte* or *Cinquiesme*, *Haute-Contre*, *Taille*, *Basse*. Mersenne's five parts must have worked out to violin, three violas (of varying sizes, different playing registers, but *the same tuning*), and bass (cello). Van der Straeten[13] concluded that Mersenne's ordinary *cinquiesme* part (next below the *dessus*) must be a part for second violin, but this cannot be so, because Mersenne says that all the 'instruments of the middle', which he explicitly lists as *cinquiesme*, *haute-contre*, and *taille*, are tuned 'in unison', and all these instruments are larger than the treble. Furthermore, one of these 'instruments of the middle' has the viola (c) tuning, and the range of none of the parts of the 'middle' goes below 'c'. Hence the three middle parts are all played by violas of varying sizes, each tuned to 'c' like the modern viola but playing in different parts of the same register. The typical five-part ensemble in France in the seventeenth century consisted, then, of violin, viola I, II, and III, and bass (cello). This situation remained unchanged at least up to the time of Brossard (1703), who says under '*Bracio ou Brazzo*': '*Braz. 1.⁰ 2.⁰ 3.⁰ . . .* are the bowed instruments which correspond to our *Haute-Contre*, *Taille*, and *Quinte de Violon*'.[14]

In this connexion, it is well to point out that in the early seventeenth century, particularly when the violins were used to accompany, the clef employed is no true indication of the instrument intended. Monteverdi, for instance, uses both the G clef second line and the C clef first line for the violin. There is a corresponding variety in the other parts. The alto-tenor uses C clef third or fourth line; in a set of Monteverdi's *vivola da brazzo* parts, one part uses the C clef first line, another the C clef third line.[15] It is the range of the parts and the desire to avoid ledger lines, not the instrument concerned, that determines the clef. In France the usual clef employed for the violin is the G clef first line not G clef second line, as is usual elsewhere.

Occasionally tablatures are used for dances, but this practice was never widespread in violin playing, and hardly more than seven or eight violin tablatures are extant today. In the first part of the seventeenth century the

---

[13] E. Van der Straeten, *The History of the Violin*, 2 vols., London, 1933, Vol. I, p. 79.
[14] Sébastien de Brossard, *Dictionnaire de musique*, Paris, 1703. The same terminology occurs in the German treatise of Daniel Merck (*Compendium*, 1695).
[15] See Monteverdi, *Tutte le Opere*, edited by G. F. Malipiero, 16 vols. (1926–42), Vol. XIV, p 123 (opening of the 1610 *Vespers*, 'Domine ad adjuvandum').

only theorist to use violin tablature is Gasparo Zannetti in his *Il Scolaro* (Milan, 1645). However, violin tablature is mentioned by others, including Mersenne.[16]

The distinctions and definitions involving the violin family, made by theorists like Praetorius, are implicit in music of the time. In particular, one can see that the soprano *viola da braccio* is the violin. In Monteverdi's *Combattimento di Tancredi e Clorinda* (1624), the foreword refers to '*quattro viole da brazzo*', but in the music itself the two upper parts of the four-part string ensemble are both marked 'violino'. Similarly, at the head of the score of his opera *Orfeo* (1607), Monteverdi lists the instruments required. For the violin family he specifies two *violini piccoli alla francese* and ten *viole da braccio*. Monteverdi does not list *violini* separately, but *violini* are explicitly called for in the score, and the parts are in the first-position violin register, including passages on the highest string. This can only mean that the violins proper are included among the ten *viole da braccio* and that they are the soprano members of the *viole da braccio*, since none go higher except the *violini piccoli alla francese*, which are listed separately. The latter are treated in this way because they are not usual among the *viole da braccio*, although they are played on the arm and although Praetorius, with typical thoroughness, includes these small violins in his catch-all category of *Violn de bracio*. The ten *viole da braccio* are commonly used by Monteverdi in an ensemble of five-part music in *Orfeo*, and, as Professor Westrup has shown, the distribution is probably two players each for violin I and II, viola I and II, and cello.[17]

Monteverdi's terminology at the beginning of Act II of *Orfeo* has been the cause of considerable confusion and speculation. The particular terms in question are the *violini piccoli alla francese* and *violini ordinarij da braccio*. Both these terms are used uniquely in this part of the opera—indeed, they do not occur again in Monteverdi's works—and both are used in special ways and for very special reasons. According to Curt Sachs[18] these 'small violins' are our 'ordinary' violins, and the 'ordinary' violins in Monteverdi's score are violas. In light of more recent research, Sachs's opinion is no longer tenable. The 'ordinary violins' of Monteverdi turn out to be, not so surprisingly, ordinary violins. The 'small French violins' are not (as is generally believed) small violins tuned a fourth above the usual violin, but small boat-shaped

---

[16] For a full account of violin tablatures, see Johannes Wolf, *Handbuch der Notationskunde*, 2 vols., Leipzig, 1913 and 1919, Vol. II, pp. 232–40. See further, Dragan Plamenac, 'An Unknown Violin Tablature of the early 17th Century' in *Papers of the American Musicological Society*, 1941, pp. 144–57. Also, Gustav Beckmann, *Das Violinspiel in Deutschland vor 1700*, Leipzig, 1918.

[17] J. A. Westrup, 'Monteverdi and the Orchestra' in *Music and Letters*, July 1940. For the opinion of Gerald Hayes and others that the discant *viola da braccio* = the modern viola, see above, p. 43, note 27.

[18] Curt Sachs, *The History of Musical Instruments*, New York, 1940, p. 358.

violins or pochettes (cf. Fig. 4), tuned an octave above the ordinary violin and treated as octave-transposing instruments.[19]

Nicholas Bessaraboff, however, whose excellent book[20] is a major contribution to the study of instruments, maintained that the *violini piccoli alla francese* were small violins tuned a fourth above the violin—the conventional opinion. His conclusion was based on a study of the ranges of the violin parts in *Orfeo*, which convinced him that Monteverdi never used the lowest string, as would be necessary to play the lowest written note (c′) in the parts of the *violini piccoli alla francese*. However, Bessaraboff's painstaking work on ranges was limited to *Orfeo*, and an examination of Monteverdi's other works shows that Bessaraboff's conclusions cannot be applied rigorously to Monteverdi's works as a whole. Actually, Monteverdi does use the lowest string of the violin in other works of the same time (e.g. *Scherzi musicali*, 1607) and in later works as well.

Increasing usage of the violin. Its effect on rebec and viol

The variety of types within the violin family in the early seventeenth century is simply a sign of confusion that often accompanies vigorous growth. An appreciation of the qualities of the violin and its increasing usage and popularity are implied by its establishment in Royal favour in France and England, by the gradual obsolescence of the rebec, whose capabilities the violin far surpassed, and by the gradual inroads made in the popularity of the aristocratic viol.

The rebec was still heard in the land—as in Milton's *L'Allegro*: 'When the merry bells ring round and the jocund rebecks sound.' But it was rapidly being pushed into the background by the violin; and a number of theorists, including Mersenne and Trichet, make this point explicitly. By 1650 the heyday of the viols *as a family* was coming to a close, and the ranks of the viol makers and players began to diminish. When André Maugars, the celebrated French violist, who had studied the viol in England about 1620-4, visited Rome in 1639, he found no Italian viol players of any importance left in that city.[21] This was to be expected in a country where the violin was enjoying a phenomenal success and an unprecedented development. The viols continued in favour longer in England and still longer in France, where a direct line of famous bass-viol players descended from Maugars and culminated in Marin Marais (1656-1728), a man who possessed genius both as a virtuoso violist and as a composer of viol music. In England the 'fancy' for an ensemble

[19] For detailed argument see the author's article cited above on p. 43, note 27. For a picture of the 'small French violin', see Praetorius, op. cit., Vol. II, Plate XXI, No. 2.
[20] Nicholas Bessaraboff, op. cit., p. 433, note 769.
[21] See Arnold Dolmetsch, *The Interpretation of the Music of the XVIIth and XVIIIth Centuries*, London [1916], p. 465. For the title of Maugars' report, see below, p. 137, note 19.

of viols was an archaic breath of the past after mid-seventeenth century, and the Purcell Fantasias of 1680 are the real end of this genre. After Purcell, the only member of the viol family to play a vigorous role was the bass *viola da gamba*, which persisted as a *continuo* instrument until 1750, and in some cases functioned brilliantly as a solo instrument still later. In 1667 Mace writes bitterly about the violin *vis-a-vis* his beloved viols; and when he berates the 'scolding Violins' and complains of their 'High-Priz'd Noise fit to make a man's Ear Glow, and fill his brains full of frisks', he is recording a situation that has existed for some time in England. Mace concedes that a pair of violins may be added to the chest of viols 'for any Extraordinary Jolly, or Jocund Consort-Occasion'.[22]

By Mace's time the best old days of the viols had gone, and he was waging a futile battle for an instrument whose great moments were past and whose appealing and noble qualities were more suitable to the quiet delight of friends at home than in the tavern, dance hall, or theatre. In the theatre, particularly where the opera was in vogue, the more powerful and expressive violin prevailed. To Mersenne, the tone of the violin was the 'most ravishing' of the stringed instruments. Obviously he was not alone in his extravagant admiration, for composers of the time were inspired to create an idiomatic music conceived purely in terms of the violin, whose immense potential for a cantabile style and brilliant passagework the seventeenth century was just beginning to perceive.

[22] Thomas Mace, *Musick's Monument*, London, 1676, ch. IV, p. 246.

PLATE I

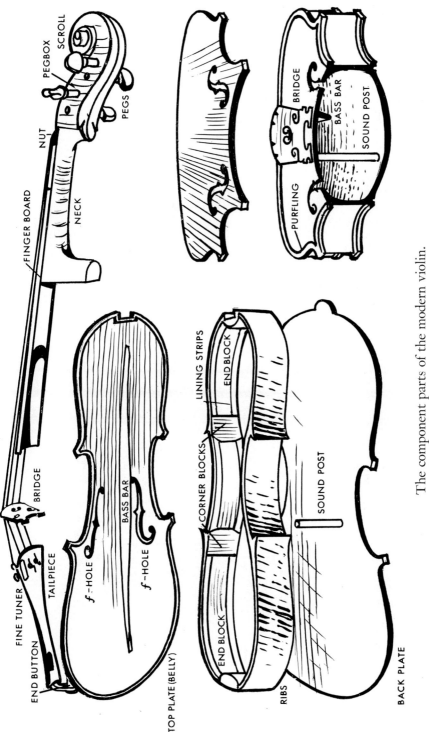

The component parts of the modern violin.

PLATE 2

The violin family: violin (left centre), cello, and viola. Detail of a fresco (1535–6) by Gaudenzio

PLATE 3

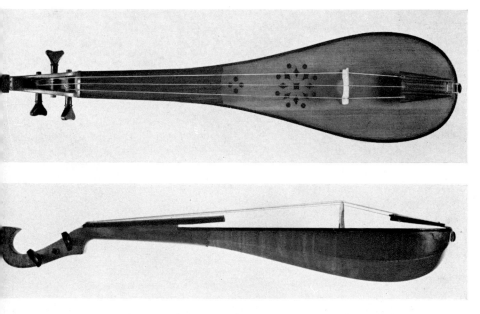

(*a*) Two views of a rebec. Modern reproduction by Arnold Dolmetsch (1930).

(*b*) Angel playing the Renaissance fiddle. Medallion by Memling, *c.* 1500.

PLATE 4

Two views of a *lira da braccio* made in Venice by Giovanni Maria of Brescia, *c.* 1525.

PLATE 5

Lady playing a treble viol. A painting by Caspar Netscher (1639–84).

PLATE 6

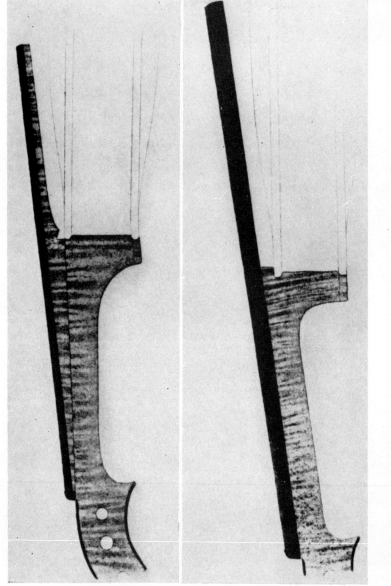

Neck and fingerboard of the 'old' violin (above) compared to those of the modern *violin* (below).

PLATE 7

viola by Gasparo da Salò of Brescia, late century.

(b) A viola by Andrea Amati of Cremona (1574), made for Charles IX of France.

PLATE 8

PLATE 9

A portrait of Duiffoprugcar by Woeriot (1562), showing various stringed instruments, none of which is a true violin.

PLATE 10

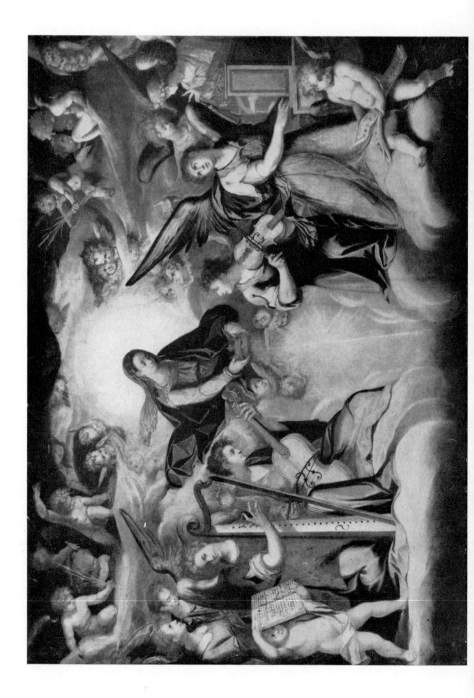

PLATE II

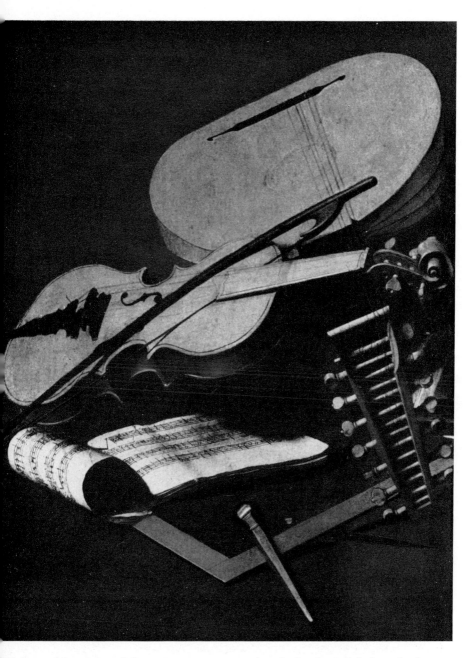

Violin and bow. Detail from *Love as Conqueror*, a painting by Michelangelo de
Caravaggio (*c*. 1573–*c*. 1610).

PLATE 12

A violin and bow (upper left) in a painting *The Madonna* (*c.* 1620)
by G. F. Barbieri ('Il Guercino').

PLATE 13

Dancing *La Volta* accompanied by a string band. A ball at the Valois Court *c.* 1581 (painting in the museum at Rennes).

PLATE 14

PLATE 15

Orlando Lasso surrounded by instrumentalists and singers of the chapel
of the Duke of Bavaria at Munich. From a codex (1565–70) illuminated by
Hans Mielich.

PLATE 16

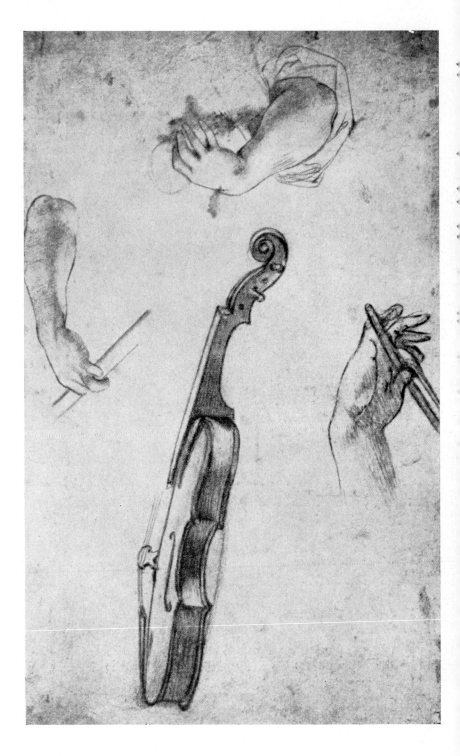

PLATE 17

The violin and bow in a light moment. *The Prodigal Son*, a painting by Dirck van Baburen (*c.* 1590–*c.* 1624).

PLATE 18

The 'Doria' violin by G. P. Maggini (1580–c. 1632).

PLATE 19

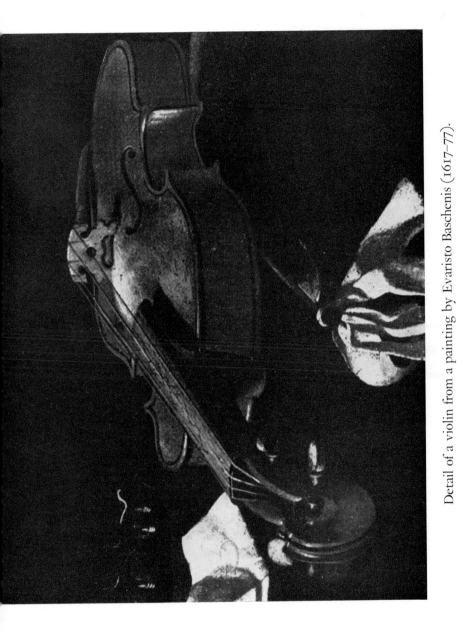

Detail of a violin from a painting by Evaristo Baschenis (1617–77).

PLATE 20

The Concert, an engraving by Picart after a painting by Domenichino (early 17th century).

PLATE 21

Violin and bow, showing the thumb-under-hair bow-grip. *St. Cecilia* by
Bernardo Cavallino (1616–56).

PLATE 22

Violinist playing in French style. Lithograph of a painting by Gerard Dou, dated 1665.

PLATE 23

A violinist with lutanist and singer(s). An ensemble painted by an unknown Italian of the 17th century (National Museum, Prague).

PLATE 24

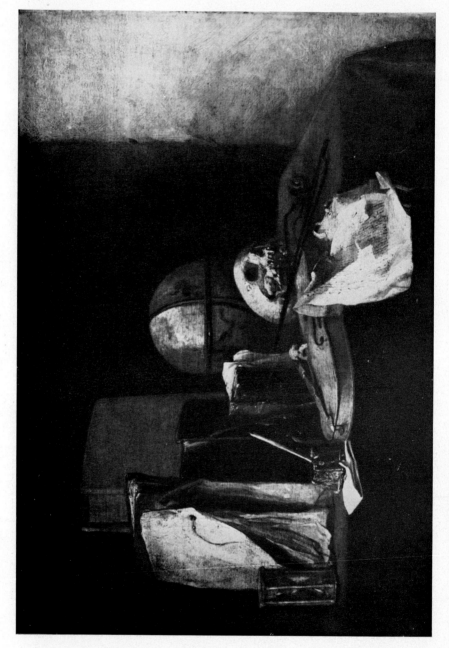

Vanitas still life, showing the *richtekenkunst* Clothes for her face of her face of color for color of

PLATE 25

(*a*) Nicola Amati's 'grand' model violin (*The Goding*, 1662).

(*b*) 'Long' model violin (1693) by Antonio Stradivari.

PLATE 26

Profile view of old and new violin:

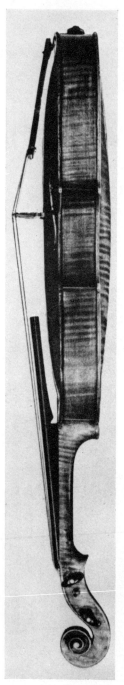

(*a*) *Violin by Jacob Stainer, 1668. Original condition, except for pegs and bridge (and probably fingerboard), all of which, however, have been reproduced in appropriate style. Note the short fingerboard with wedge and the straight neck, which is slightly shorter and thicker than the modern one. Observe also the rapid rise of the arching of the top and the clear view through the sound holes.*

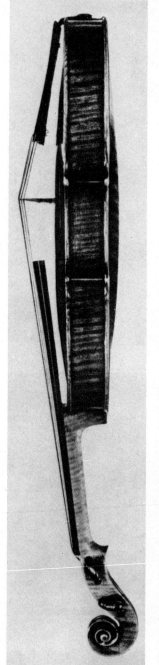

(*b*) *Modern violin by J. B. Vuillaume, Paris, 1867 (Stradivari model). Modern elongated fingerboard, no wedge, tilted and narrowed neck, which is mortised into the upper block. Compare the flatter top and back of the Vuillaume with the Stainer.*

PLATE 27

Two views of the bridge of Stradivari's
'Tuscan' viola, compared with a
modern viola bridge (below).

PLATE 28

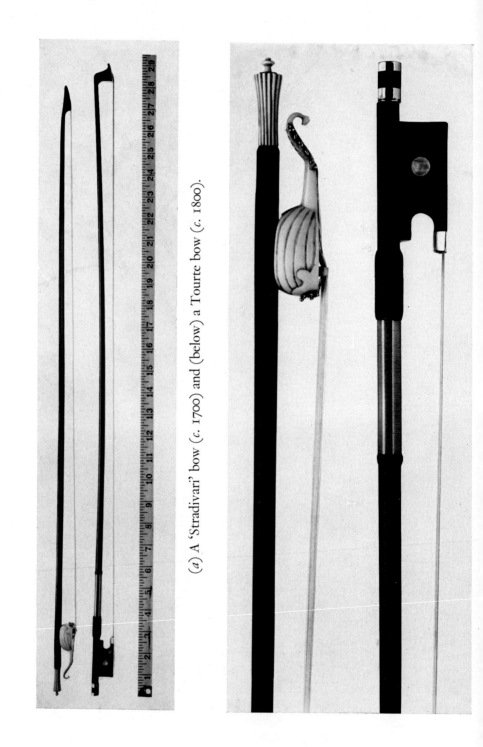

(*a*) A 'Stradivari' bow (*c.* 1700) and (below) a Tourte bow (*c.* 1800).

PLATE 29

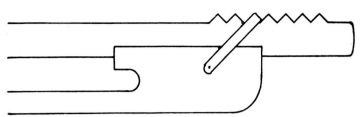

(*a*) Mechanism of the 'dentated' ('crémaillère') bow.

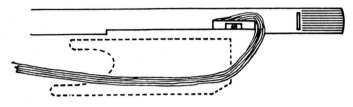

(*b*) The slot-and-notch (or clip-in) bow.

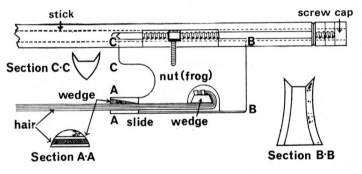

(*c*) Mechanism of the modern bow.

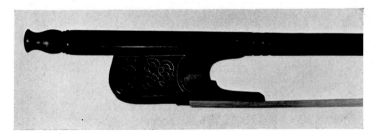

(*d*) Detail of a bow dated 1694 (cf. Plate 38*a*).

PLATE 30

F. M. Veracini playing the violin. Frontispiece to his *Sonate accademiche*, Op. 2 (1744).

PLATE 31

French violinist. Frontispiece to Corrette's *L'École d'Orphée*, 1738.

PLATE 32

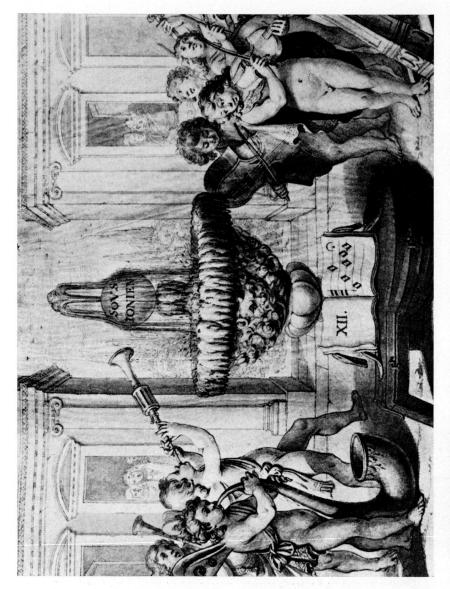

PLATE 33

he 'Betts' violin (1704) by Antonio
Stradivari.

(*b*)   A violin by Joseph Guarneri del
Gesú (1737). Formerly called the 'King
Joseph', this violin is known today as
the 'Hawley Joseph'.

PLATE 34

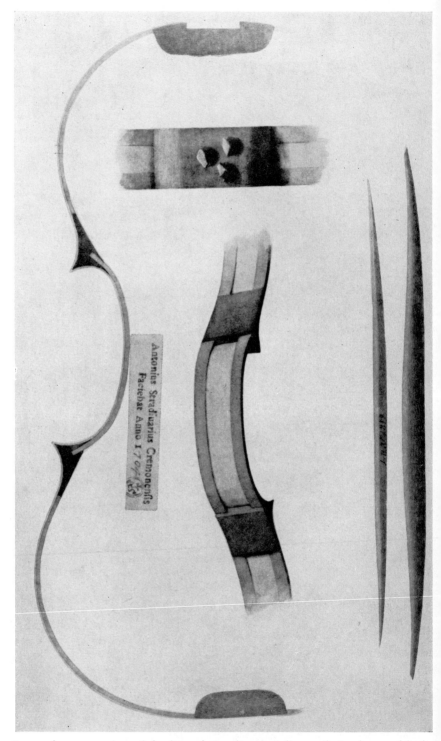

Internal construction of the 'Betts' Stradivari violin: nails in the top block, blocks and linings, bass bar compared to the modern bass bar.

PLATE 35

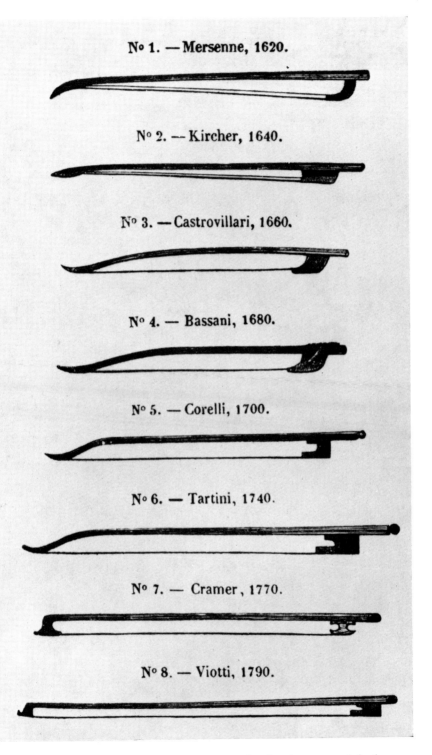

Nº 1. — Mersenne, 1620.

Nº 2. — Kircher, 1640.

Nº 3. — Castrovillari, 1660.

Nº 4. — Bassani, 1680.

Nº 5. — Corelli, 1700.

Nº 6. — Tartini, 1740.

Nº 7. — Cramer, 1770.

Nº 8. — Viotti, 1790.

Sequence of bows, purporting to represent the development of the bow
from Mersenne to Viotti.

PLATE 36

Frontispiece to Geminiani's *L'Art du Violon*, Paris, 1752 (?).

PLATE 37

German violinist from J. C. Weigel's *Musikalisches Theatrum*, *c.* 1720.

PLATE 38

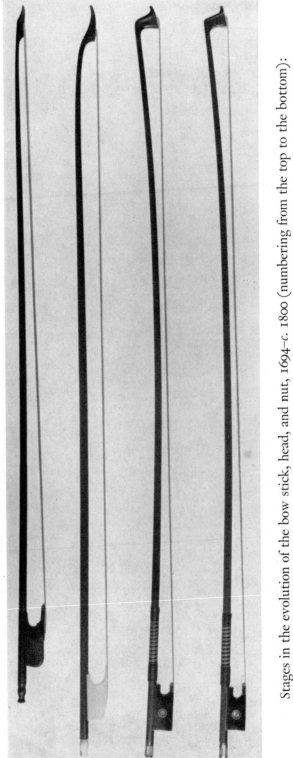

Stages in the evolution of the bow stick, head, and nut, 1694–*c.* 1800 (numbering from the top to the bottom):

(*a*) Bow dated 1694 (detail given in Plate 29*d*).
(*b*) Bow by Thomas Smith (d. 1789), probably made between 1760 and 1770.
(*c*) Bow by Tourte *père, c.* 1770–80.
(*d*) Bow by François Tourte, *c.* 1800.

PLATE 39

(b) Leopold Mozart playing the violin under his chin (*Violinschule*, Fig. II).

(a) Frontispiece of Leopold Mozart's *Violinschule* (1756).

PLATE 40

(b) Compared to the 17th century French bow and bow

(c) The modern Bach bow

CHAPTER SIX

꩜

The New Violin Idiom.
Violin Music and its Uses in
Different Countries, 1600-50

'In sum, in the hand of a skilful player, the violin represents
the sweetness of the lute, the suavity of the viol, the
majesty of the harp, the force of the trumpet, the vivacity
of the fife, the sadness of the flute, the pathetic quality of
the cornett; as if every variety, as in the great edifice of
the organ, is heard with marvellous artifice.'

G. B. DONI,
Annotazioni sopra il Compendio de' Generi, e de' Modi della
Musica, Rome, 1640, p. 338

G. B. DONI'S enumeration of the violin's many expressive possibilities may seem extravagant. Nevertheless his statement, however regarded, is a clear tribute to the progress of the violin and to the appreciation of its inherent qualities by musicians in the first half of the seventeenth century. What is true of the violin is true of all instruments in one degree or another, the specific and idiomatic capabilities of individual instruments being realized more and more clearly after 1600. Mersenne expressed the new attitude very clearly: 'While each instrument can be used to play such pieces as one desires, nevertheless experience shows that some pieces are more successful than others when they are played on certain instruments, and what is good on one is not so agreeable or so fitting on another.'

The meaning and implication of the key terms 'idiom' and 'idiomatic' are matters of some importance in the context of a rapidly developing violin music and technique. An 'idiomatic' style of violin music or violin playing involves those traits which are particularly characteristic or 'agreeable' on the violin. This is not to imply that what is idiomatic to the violin is always a unique property of it. Double stops in themselves are idiomatic to the violin, but they are also idiomatic to the viol and to other bowed stringed instruments. However, there are certain double stops that are not only idiomatic but also unique to the violin, not to the viol—and vice versa.

In written or printed music the elements of the violin idiom that are relatively easy to identify are types of melodic lines, figurations, double stops, and certain special effects. Any violinist who examines a page of seventeenth-century violin music for ten minutes can say how well the passage will sound on the instrument with respect to sonority and register, and how well the figuration will fit the hand of the player. But he could not say accurately how much of this same music would be grateful to the viol player unless he also played the viol himself.

What cannot be indicated in the music is the variety, beauty, or volume of tone of the violin, its timbre in general, or the varieties of tone colours through its different registers. These are particular properties of the violin and presumably part of its idiom, considered *in toto*; but, unlike the idiom of melodies and figurations, these tonal characteristics are not recognizable in written or printed form, since they cannot be notated in score. Yet these tonal features are especially striking to the ear in performance, and G. B. Doni, in the statement quoted above, remarks on the tonal versatility of the violin and its ability to imitate a number of other instruments in one respect or another.

When we speak of such matters as tonal qualities, it is difficult to say whether we are talking about what is idiomatic to the violin or rather what is appropriate to it. In the sixteenth century the violin was considered appropriate to dance music because of its relatively penetrating, powerful tone and its affinity for clear rhythmic articulation. Two dances from the *Ballet comique de la reine* of 1581 (see Ex. 1 and pp. 55ff.) were obviously considered appropriate to the violin, since they are so designated—the first extant violin music specifically labelled for violins. However, this music is idiomatic not only to the violin; it could as easily be played by wind instruments of the same register—or, for that matter, sung. By way of contrast, a few years after 1600 an astonishing development of the violin idiom, especially of figurations, took place, inspired by that same experimental and exploratory frame of mind described earlier (cf. p. 98). Many of Monteverdi's violin parts, for example, not only could not be sung but neither would they have sounded as well or been played as easily on other instruments. As a rule, it is more with the idea of melodies, figurations, and special effects in mind that we apply the word 'idiomatic' to violin music and violin playing; and although 'idiomatic' is generally used in this sense, we wish on occasion to take advantage of its broader meaning relative to characteristic types of tone, timbre, and volume.

Idiomatic writing for the violin, in the sense of melodies and figurations, was developed very quickly after 1600, actually preceding those instrumental forms, such as the sonata, whose origins were closely identified with the violin. This prior development of a characteristic violin idiom was only natural. As soon as players and composers turned their attention to the violin as a medium of expression, its idiom was exploited just as much in connexion with vocal as instrumental music, and often first in vocal music. Monteverdi's *Orfeo* (1607) already exhibits certain highly developed violin figurations long before the sonata crystallized. The sonata, one of the chief new forms of instrumental music, did not evolve exclusively in violin music, and the musical needs that prompted the creation of the violin sonata were essentially common to all instrumental music, only incidental to the development of the violin idiom. That is to say, the creation of purely instrumental music involved the manipulation of abstract patterns of tone so as to produce coherence and variety over a considerable time-span. The idiomatic development of any particular instrument was incidental to these considerations.

After 1600 particular instruments were increasingly specified by composers, and the close and traditional relationship between the violin and dance music was explicitly acknowledged by writing dances 'for the violin'. Nevertheless, in the tradition of the past, a number of pieces were still indiscriminately labelled for 'all sorts of instruments'; and sometimes the upper parts were indicated as 'Canto I' and 'Canto II' to take advantage of the various alternative instruments of treble register suggested in certain titles. Even the new forms of abstract instrumental music, such as the sonata and canzona, were often labelled for 'violin or cornett' in the early seventeenth century. In these cases, however, a good business reason may have prompted offering the choice. The violins belonged to one guild and the cornetts to another; and by signifying that his music was suitable for either instrument, the composer broadened his market. It is possible but less likely that the pieces were equally idiomatic for both instruments. At any rate, such alternatives occurred less and less frequently after 1625, and music was labelled specifically and solely 'for the violin' in the degree that violin technique became more and more idiomatic. In some pieces the style and technical demands of the music itself show that the violin must have been intended even when the pieces are ambiguously labelled.[1]

---

[1] The practice of alternative labelling persisted into the eighteenth century, whether for 'business' or other reasons. Handel's Op. 1 (1731) is entitled *15 Solos for German Flute, Oboe, or Violin* in spite of the fact that these alternative instruments cannot be taken very seriously in certain solos which call for double stops. Similarly, various orchestral scores call for oboes or flutes to double the violin part, although on occasion neither the flute nor the oboe can perform the figuration or play in the register called for by the part.

Although '*violino ò cornetto*' seems to have been a common alternative in the early seventeenth century, the choice of 'viol or violin' was largely restricted to music neutral in style—a kind of generalized instrumental style playable by several instruments—such as Dowland's *Lachrimae* for lute, viols, or violins in five parts (1604; see p. 139). By way of contrast, the choice of violin or cornett is often stipulated for pieces written in fairly advanced violin style. Apart from this rather mysterious and permissive attitude toward '*violino ò cornetto*', the particular nature of the violin idiom seems to have been recognized distinctly and very soon after 1600, especially in Italy. In general, one can say that after this date a piece specifically labelled 'for violin' meant that it was intended primarily for the violin as the instrument best suited to play the music, either for reasons of tone or those of figuration. If a piece of instrumental music was not marked for any particular instrument, we assume either that it was written for 'all sorts of instruments' or that the style of the music indicated *per se* the particular instrument for which it was intended.

Like the violin, the viol went its way in the development of its own idioms and forms, the violin gradually associating itself with certain types of music and the viol with others. In general, the violin established a partnership with 'new' music and the viol with traditional music. The violin continued its relationship with music for social and ballet dancing (as already explained); it became the backbone of the opera orchestra, and it often joined in the concerted forms of vocal music (for 'concerted' see note 9 below). Used alone, the violin was a central contributing force to the development of the sonata, among other instruments. The viol, generally played in 'consort', was associated with the polyphonic fancy (*fantasia*), the *In Nomine*, and other *cantus firmus* forms, all of which looked to a past tradition. The viol also played dances, but these dances were generally intended as abstract music for chamber-music ensembles. After 1600 viols seldom played music for actual dancing, this function being increasingly the province of the violin.

Naturally there were good reasons for these musical associations of the viol and violin. The expressive qualities of the latter made it more suitable for the expressive music of the seventeenth century in general; and its variety of tone and mood and its properties of rhythmic articulation made it the preferred instrument for the vocal and instrumental forms mentioned above. In certain instances, the viol had the advantage of the violin, notably in the clarity of the voice parts of the ensemble. The relatively thinner, smaller, and reedier tone of the viol produced a more clearly etched sound and a more transparent texture than obtained in an ensemble of violins; and these features were more suitable to the clarity of the texture and part writing necessary in the performance of polyphonic music. Consequently, the viols were particularly appropriate in the polyphonic and *cantus firmus* forms like the fancy and *In Nomine*. These associations, traditional from the sixteenth century, were continued in the seventeenth. However, the violin occasionally invaded the traditional strongholds of viol music, such as the fancy, an example being a *Fantazya* by William Lawes (d. 1645) for two violins, bass viol, and organ or harp.[2]

It is difficult to distinguish *in detail* the precise technical idioms of the viol from those of the violin. These distinctions are based on the differences between a fretted viol with six strings tuned in fourths and thirds and an unfretted violin of four strings tuned uniformly in fifths. As a result, the viol and violin use different types of figuration and different open notes. And, of course, the tone of the viol and the violin is quite different, a factor in which the respective bodies of the instruments, the frets, the tension of the strings, the bow, and types of bowing all play a part.

The development of a new violin idiom

The tone and cantabile properties of the violin were among its most characteristic traits, and made the instrument a formidable rival of the human voice. However, tone quality and its varieties cannot be deduced from written music, and can only be mentioned, not discussed in detail, as part of the violin idiom. On the other hand, it is both possible and necessary to analyse the principal features of the new violin style, as shown in the written music of the early seventeenth century. At first the Italians were the most active in exploiting the idiomatic potential. Strangely, although the Italians were acutely aware of the tonal and singing properties of the violin, they paid relatively little attention to beautiful melodies *as such* in the first part of the century. Not until the late seventeenth century were composers like Corelli fascinated by the singing melody *per se*. Before 1650 composers of violin music seem to have concentrated more on figurations and scale passages, expanding the range of the instrument, and on special effects.

Previously the range of the violin had been limited largely to that of the soprano voice. Now it was extended in both directions: into the register of the lowest (G) string, and higher into the register of the highest (E) string. By 1649 Uccellini called for the note g''' in his Op. 5—a tenth above the open E string and requiring the sixth position (see Ex. 17). The use of the G string was restricted to occasional passages, probably because of the poor response of the string itself (cf. p. 70). At first Monteverdi was conservative

[2] See E. H. Meyer, *English Chamber Music*, London, 1946, p. 187 and p. 271, where the music is printed in full. For a short excerpt, see Ex. 15 below. Murray Lefkowitz (*William Lawes*, London, 1960, p. 88, note 1) maintains that this piece was for two violins, bass viol, and organ (*not* organ or harp).

in his use of the violin range. In *Orfeo* (1607), for example, he avoids the G string and he does not exceed the range of the first position. Nevertheless, within these restricted ranges, he wrote for the instrument interestingly and idiomatically. In other and later works, Monteverdi occasionally ventured into the region of the lowest string and also as high as e''', an octave above the open E string—that is, fourth position (see the *Magnificat* of 1610). Third position was fairly common in Italy at this time. Whether the upper positions were commonly used on the lower three strings is doubtful, although Mersenne speaks of such matters (see pp. 154–5 below).

A good comparison of old-style and new-style melody and figuration for the violin is afforded by Ex. 8a, which shows the opening subject of Giovanni Gabrieli's 'Sonata for Three Violins' (posthumously published in 1615), and by Ex. 8b, that of Marini's 'Sonata for Three Violins' (Op. 22, 1655). The

Ex. 8a

G. Gabrieli (1615)

Ex. 8b

B. Marini (1655)

Gabrieli subject can be played just as well on another instrument of the proper register, or even sung. Ex. 8a exhibits a narrow range, uses only the two upper strings of the violin, and is not particularly interesting or idiomatic as violin music. As a whole, the Gabrieli piece is clearly instrumental in style and concept—a number of its short phrases and sequences not being vocal in character—but it is in the generalized instrumental style mentioned earlier, not in the specific idiom of the violin. On the other hand, the Marini subject (Ex. 8b) is all dash and fire in terms of the violin. Its rapid passage-work fits the hand of the violinist, and it uses all four strings of the instrument, including the open G of the lowest string. In these few measures, Marini calls for broken chords and passages across the strings in a way grateful to the instrument, and boldly passes from one string to another in an idiomatic and resonant manner. All this is accomplished without departing from first position. In short, the Marini passage is calculated in terms of the violin and would be less effective on another instrument.

The mere expansion of the range of the violin is in itself no guarantee of idiomatic technique. It is simply a sign of a new freedom in exploiting fundamental resources of which increased range is one. It is quite possible to develop an idiomatic style within the limits of first position (cf. Ex. 8b).

Violinists and composers of the time began to use scales which are characteristic of the instrument and other figurations suggested by experience with the violin. Some passage work proceeds rapidly in sixteenth notes and even in thirty-seconds; and such passages are sometimes slurred and sometimes not (Ex. 9). Where these rapid notes are imitated by the *basso continuo*, a good player of the cello or bass viol may be taken for granted.

Ex. 9   Uccellini (1649)

Scale passages and figurations had been common to music for some time as a result of an elaborate 'division' technique and the use of *passaggi* in the voice, viol, and keyboard. These are now transferred to the violin, and theorists begin to mention *passaggi* as one of the violin's prerogatives. Francesco Rognoni comments: 'One sees today many who play cornett, violin, or other instrument who do nothing but play *passaggi* . . . ruining the canto'.[3] Mersenne gives a piece by Henry Le Jeune, and shows how the violin part may be elaborated (Ex. 10). Incidentally, a more elaborate species of *passaggi* is given by Mersenne for the organ. The practice of adding *passaggi* extemporaneously to the written score became so widespread and general that composers were occasionally obliged to indicate that the score was to be played as written. One finds such directions as '*come sta senza passaggi*' ('play as it stands without adding *passaggi*').

Ex. 10

(ornamented version)

(original)

If, as Rognoni says, instrumentalists were continually playing *passaggi*, no one was more to blame, or encouraged this practice more, than Rognoni himself. In Part II of his treatise (cf. note 3 below), he gives page after page of *passaggi* formulas, elaborating given melodies in various note values, and incorporating a bewildering variety of patterns idiomatic to instruments. These *passaggi* formulas are specifically for bowed stringed instruments and wind instruments (just as in Part I he has given *passaggi* for the voice); and,

---

[3] Francesco Rognoni, *Selva de varii passaggi secondo l'uso moderno*, Milan, 1620. Part I deals with *passaggi* for the voice; Part II, with *passaggi* for instruments. The above quotation is found on p. 2 of Part II. For the variant spellings 'Rognoni' and 'Rogniono', see p. 158, note 14.

while not specifically intended for the violin only, these 'passages' are often idiomatic to the violin within the limitation of a kind of common denominator of instrumental style. In this respect, it is characteristic that the idiom is explored thoroughly and systematically without exceeding the first-position range of the violin. Rognoni has passed well beyond the limitation of a style 'for voyce or viol' or even 'for *all* sorts of instruments'. His idioms are those of the strings and winds. In a preliminary section of text and music, he makes clear that the winds have certain special problems; and the strings, others. As a specific property of the violin idiom he includes slurring of two or more notes, and he implies that 'smooth' bowings of this sort are essential to temper and soften the tone of the violin which (he says) is, of itself, 'crude and harsh' (cf. p. 164, ch. 7).

The formulas that one perceives in Rognoni's treatise have their counterparts in violin music. Among them are scale passages, which move by step, and many others, which move by leaps of various sizes, including those of the octave, ninth, tenth, and even eleventh and twelfth, some of which force the player to skip over strings (Ex. 11). These leaps are sometimes used

Ex. 11

systematically and consecutively in broken thirds and sixths and in sequences of descending or ascending octave skips with their surrounding figuration. Other resources are arpeggios or broken chords (Ex. 8b), figurations involving playing back and forth across two or more strings (Ex. 12), and repeated notes in subjects and figuration.

Ex. 12

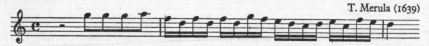

The most advanced technique may be unknown to us, either because it was used only occasionally and never written down, or because technical novelties were regarded as professional secrets. The theorists occasionally mention technical matters before they can be found in music. Mersenne, for instance, describes the violin mute in 1636, but no surviving music calls for it until Lully's time, some years later.

Naturally, violin music shared a number of the effects in general use. Among them is the so-called 'Lombard' rhythm or 'Scotch' snap (♪♩). Quantz, more than a hundred years later (1752), claims that this 'snap' was invented in the early eighteenth century. The fact is that passages of this kind of rhythm, slurred and unslurred, are common in the violin music of the early seventeenth century (cf. Ex. 27, p. 163). Another typical device of music in general is the 'echo' effect in which a passage is literally echoed more softly on repetition. In Marini's Op. 8 there is a 'Sonata in Echo' for three violins, 'the first to be seen and the other two are not'.[4] The theorists, too, furnish examples of the echo. Francesco Rognoni expressly marks the '*ecco*' in certain of the examples in his valuable treatise (Part II, p. 66).

A number of the conventional ornaments, especially the trills, are written out in full (Exx. 9 and 10); and they are often indicated with slurs. While the practice of indicating ornaments by signs had not yet become general, there were nevertheless signs and terms for them. The 't' or 'tr' is sometimes used for our trill (see p. 177). Neither consecutive trills or trills on syncopated notes are common but they may be found occasionally. (For trills in thirds and sixths, see p. 167.) The vibrato and even the legato slur are usually classified among the ornaments at this time.

Pizzicato begins to turn up in violin music, but it must have been used in violin music long before it is specifically indicated. Viol players used *pizzicato* in the early sixteenth century (see p. 84), and string players, surrounded as they were by guitars and lutes, would have had to be blind and deaf not to think of plucking the strings. Monteverdi, so prolific in everything, specifically calls for the *pizzicato* in his *Combattimento* (1624) in these words, addressed to the string players collectively: 'At this point put the bow aside and pluck the strings with two fingers' ('*Qui si lascia l'arco e si strappano le corde con duoi dita*')—not the usual method today. And for the return to bowing (*arco*) Monteverdi directs: 'Here one retakes the bow' ('*Qui si ripiglia l'arco*').

Monteverdi also claimed (1638) that he invented the measured *tremolo* by writing a number of repeated sixteenth-notes, played in strict time, to express the warlike passions in a 'style of excitement' ('*stile concitato*'). But Marini had already used this kind of measured *tremolo* in his Op. 1 of 1617, and there are much earlier examples in other vocal and instrumental music, in particular such pieces as Jannequin's descriptive chansons, or, in the realm of purely instrumental music, Andrea Gabrieli's *Aria della Battaglia* for eight wind instruments (1590).[5] Establishing the priority of the use of

---

[4] For an example of the echo effect (and another of the 'Scotch' snap), see the 'solo' sonata of Marini (Op. 8) given as No. 183 in Arnold Schering, *Geschichte der Musik in Beispielen*, Leipzig, 1931.

[5] For the Gabrieli, see *Istitutioni e monumenti dell'arte musicale italiana*, 7 vols., Milan, 1931–41, Vol. I, p. 93. Adam Carse, *The History of Orchestration*, London, 1925, p. 29, says that *Guidizio d' Amore* (1599) by Baldassare Donati contains the earliest known instance of quickly repeated notes in violin playing. This work is apparently in manuscript.

repeated notes is largely a game of finding written sources. A device of this kind is a natural resource for descriptive music, and it is natural to the violin. Consequently, it was probably used from the beginning of the violin's history.

In the seventeenth century the interesting thing is in what form the simple repeated-note formula (*tremolo*) will appear. At first, the *tremolo* was rhythmically measured, as in Monteverdi. In Farina's *Capriccio Stravagante*, that regular grab-bag of violin tricks, the composer is probably calling for a true modern ('unmeasured') *tremolo*. Another species of *tremolo* is required (1639) by the German composer, Andreas Hammerschmidt, when he indicates that a series of repeated notes are all to be executed in one bow stroke (*portato*). His directions are quite clear: 'four notes must be taken in one bow stroke' ('*sollen vier in einen Strich seyn*').[6]

A number of devices were used sporadically by violinists for descriptive effect although they did not become a part of regular technique for some time. These devices included the *portamento, glissando, col legno,* and *sul ponticello,* all of which are suggested by Farina. The so-called *scordatura* (literally, 'mistuning'; *accordatura* = tuning)—a tuning of the violin that departs from the usual tuning—also made its début, following earlier practices of the lute. These *scordature* had advantages: they made some passages easier to play; they made certain double stops possible; and they changed the tone colour by introducing different tensions to the strings. In addition, a *scordatura* tuned to the tonic chord of a piece helped to reinforce the principal overtones of the main key. Marini is among the first to call for this 'mis-tuning' in his *Sonata Seconda per il Violino d'Inventione* (Op. 8, 1626-9). He directs the player to retune his E string a third lower during seven measures of rest, and then proceeds to use the *scordatura* to play rapid passages in double-stopped thirds, including four measures in sixteenth-notes (Ex. 13). After this, Marini expects the player to retune to normal pitch within the space of six measures of rest. Such procedures are hard on the player's nerves, and for this reason the șame *scordatura* is usually preserved throughout the entire piece. Marini's *scordatura* piece is notated at pitch, and the player must work out the fingerings. Most later *scordatura* pieces were in 'hand-grip' notation (cf. p. 250). The Germans later specia-

---

[6] See Gustav Beckmann, *Das Violinspiel in Deutschland vor 1700,* p. 17. Note that in the above discussion we have been using the term *tremolo* to mean repeated notes. However, in the seventeenth century, *tremolo* was susceptible of various meanings. To the keyboard player (for instance, Diruta, 1593), *tremolo* meant a species of trill in the modern sense. On the other hand, the word *trillo* meant a series of repeated notes to the early seventeenth-century singer! About 1600 the repeated-note passage was most aptly described as *trillo,* although there were instances of repeated notes being described as *tremolo* or *tremulo* (F. Rognoni, 1620). In the eighteenth century, to compound the confusion, the term *tremolo* usually meant 'vibrato' in Italian violin music. For details on seventeenth-century terms, see pp. 176–7.

lized in *scordatura* pieces, and there are many varieties of these tunings in the music of Biber (see p. 226). The *scordatura* persisted well into the eighteenth century and even later.[7] The disadvantages of the *scordatura* prevented its general acceptance: among them, intonation problems arising from a lack of a 'set' tuning, and still other difficulties relative to special rules of fingering, string tensions, and notation.

Ex. 13

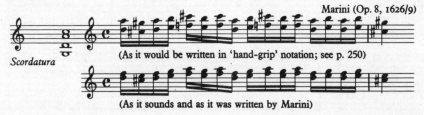

Scordatura

(As it would be written in 'hand-grip' notation; see p. 250)

(As it sounds and as it was written by Marini)

Finally, one finds numerous double stops in the new idiomatic writing for the violin. Marini uses them extensively in his Op. 8; and he experiments with triple stops in a piece with the significant title, *Capriccio per Sonare il Violino con tre corde a modo di lira* (Capriccio to play the violin with three strings in the manner of a lira). (See Ex. 14.) Marini is not alone. Farina and O. M. Grandi (1628) use double stops about the same time. Collectively, the music from 1600 to 1650 affords numerous examples of interesting double stops, including trills in thirds and (rarely) sixths, and an occasional triple or quadruple stop. The unison double stop, composed of a stopped and open string, also dates from this period. Taken as a whole, these double stops present a considerable variety of musical effect and a corresponding range of difficulty for the violinist. After Marini and Grandi the Italians mysteriously cease to write double stops for approximately fifty years. By 1671 at least, double stops appear once more in Italian violin music (in G. M. Bononcini's Op. 4, which also calls for the *scordatura*); and thereafter both Germans and Italians make notable use of them.

Ex. 14   Marini (Op. 8)

Violin music and its uses, 1600–50

About 1600 violin music is remarkable for its experiments in idiom, form, and expression; but it does not follow that novelty and experiment are always synonymous with the best artistic results. The most interesting

[7] For the history of the violin *scordatura*, see Theodore Russell, 'The Violin Scordatura' in *The Musical Quarterly*, January 1938. See also the article 'Skordatur' in *MGG*. For basic rules governing *scordatura* playing, see p. 250 below.

piece violinistically is not necessarily the most interesting musically, and the exploration of the violin idiom sometimes advances the technique of the instrument more than its musical ends. Farina's much-mentioned *Capriccio Stravagante* of 1627 is a classic case. This piece calls for relatively exotic devices like *col legno, sul ponticello,* and even *glissando* in the interests of depicting barking dogs, yowling cats, and crowing cocks. All this is good fun for the violinist—and was probably intended as such by Farina—but musically such pieces cannot be considered seriously except in so far as they advance the technique of the instrument. Farina's *Capriccio* is by no means unique in this respect. Falconieri, one of the first violin composers to emanate from Naples (or, for that matter, southern Italy) published a battle piece of similarly descriptive intent: *Battalla de Barabaso yerno de Satanas* (1650)—the Spanish title reminding us of the Spanish rule and influence in Naples.[8] At the same time the violin's potential variety of tone and expression is recognized by composers like Farina and others when they write a species of descriptive violin music 'in the manner of' the trumpet, *lira,* fife, and so on, in the vein suggested by the remarks of G. B. Doni quoted above (p. 121).

The violin made great advances in the new trio sonata and especially in the sonata for solo violin and *basso continuo* (see p. 133). Besides, as has been noted above, the violin family figured prominently in the opera orchestra and in other forms of sacred and secular music. In many types of 'concerted' music[9] the violin was used to double the vocal part(s), but just as often the violin was assigned an *obbligato* part of its own, quite distinct from the voice part and written with an eye to the violin idiom. The increasing number of *obbligato* parts for violin is a sign of the developing idiom of the instrument.

Monteverdi provides the best example of the use of the violin in large and small forms involving the voice, and his usage is especially instructive because he was himself a professional string player (cf. p. 108). In his operas Monteverdi uses the violin to accompany voices, either by doubling choral parts or in *obbligato* fashion (cf. the aria 'Possente spirto' in *Orfeo*), and also to play alone in instrumental interludes (*ritornelli*) and independent pieces (*sinfonie*). Monteverdi assigns *obbligato* parts to the violin in his 'modern'

[8] For the Farina piece, see W. J. von Wasielewski, *Instrumentalsätze vom Ende des XVI. bis Ende des XVII. Jahrhunderts,* Berlin, n.d. For the Falconieri, see Luigi Torchi, *L'Arte Musicale in Italia,* 7 vols., Vol. VII, G. Ricordi, Milan, n.d. [1897].

[9] The term *concerto* or *concertato* had a much vaguer meaning about 1600 than it does today. Basically it meant either 'ensemble', conveying nothing more than that the voices and instruments were playing together, or it conveyed the idea of opposition and struggle involving soloist(s) and ensemble or involving two (or more) ensembles. The purely instrumental concerto was not a factor in violin literature until the end of the seventeenth century. See David D. Boyden, 'When is a Concerto not a Concerto?' in *The Musical Quarterly,* April 1957. See also *MGG,* Vol. 7 (1958), article 'Konzert'.

concerted madrigals of Books VII (1619) and VIII (1638), and also in some of his sacred music (for example, the 'larger' *Magnificat* of 1610). In his *Combattimento* of 1624, he uses the violin to emphasize the dramatic and descriptive effects of the text, employing the *pizzicato* and the measured *tremolo* (see p. 129) to that end, among other devices. Monteverdi makes a significant remark in the same context: 'The instruments should be played to conform to the emotions suggested by the text.' Monteverdi had already associated the violin with certain emotional states, at least by inference. In *Orfeo*, the violin is used for the gaiety of dancing and, together with the flutes, to portray the mood of pastoral scenes. Mersenne assigns '*le mode gay et joyeux*' (the gay and joyous mode) to the violin; but (he adds) it can also imitiate all the instruments and the voice. Thus it can suggest sadness as the lute does or become animated like the trumpet (cf. the quotation from G. B. Doni, p. 121).

Italy and to a lesser extent Germany were in the vanguard of the technical and musical advances of the violin in the seventeenth century. England and France, on the other hand, were treating the violin primarily as an adjunct to dancing, the theatre, and to such Court activities as masques and 'magnificences'. Occasionally they used the violin in chamber music, which included dances in its repertory. Because of these limitations, England and France lagged behind Italy and Germany in violin technique and violin music throughout the seventeenth century.

The new forms of instrumental music, notably the sonata and *canzona*, were important vehicles for the continuing development of the idiom and technique of the violin. The variation, an older form, also served the cause of the violin very well, particularly in developing violin figuration. In the variation composers could draw on the old 'division' or *passaggi* technique already explored in music for the voice, viol, lute, and keyboard in the sixteenth century. The *ostinato* forms—in which a persistent melodic pattern recurs in one of the parts, usually the bass—were a species of variation, and the *ostinato*-inspired forms like the *romanesca*, chaconne (*ciaconna*), *follia*, and so on, occur from time to time in the literature of the violin in the seventeenth century.

All these forms were composed primarily for small chamber-music ensembles of strings accompanied by a keyboard instrument. The favoured settings were: (1) the trio, in which two violins were accompanied by a *basso continuo*, the latter being played by the cello or the bass viol and being 'realized' by the keyboard instrument to form an accompaniment; and (2) the 'solo' setting (really a misnomer) in which a solo violin was similarly accompanied by a *basso continuo*. (For the true solo sonata '*senza basso*', see p. 213 and 336.)

The chief new form was the sonata, which took its point of departure from the *canzona*, an older form. The *canzona* tended to use more voice parts and a more conservative instrumental technique than the sonata. The *canzona* was sectional, but the sections were played continuously, not with definite breaks between them as in movements. The texture was indeterminate: either homophonic or contrapuntal, usually imitative. As it developed, the sonata gradually reduced the number of voice parts of the *canzona*, so that the typical result was the trio or solo sonata. In these sonatas the sectional character of the *canzona* was replaced by distinct movements, the internal dimensions of these movements were gradually expanded in length, and the technical demands on the violin were notably increased. By the middle of the century the sonata generally had four or five movements, usually in the order: slow, fast, slow, fast. The second movement (fast) often retained the traditional imitative counterpoint of the opening of the old *canzona*. By mid-century, too, the sonata had distinguished its function either as 'church sonata' or 'chamber sonata'. The church sonata (= *sonata da chiesa*, a term used by Merula as early as 1637) was purely instrumental in its musical development and patterns, essentially as described above; the chamber sonata was based on the forms of dance music and paralleled the development of the dance suite. A passion for dancing actually generated an art literature of instrumental music, and the numerous *balletti*, *correnti*, and similar dances, found in violin music of this time, are witness to the transfer of dances from the ballroom to the chamber.[10]

Italy

After 1600 the Italians continued to compose reams of dance music both for actual dancing and for chamber music (cf. Zannetti, p. 154, below). The use of the violin in vocal music and the opera, especially in the imaginative hands of Monteverdi, has been mentioned above. In the purely instrumental forms, the *canzona*, *capriccio*, and sonata received increasing attention after 1600. These early pieces are characterized to some extent by descriptive effects (cf. p. 130), but, for the most part, by attempts to work out new forms and idioms in abstract patterns. The first sonata for solo violin and *basso continuo* to appear in print (1610) was composed by G. P. Cima.[11] Giovanni Gabrieli wrote a Sonata for Three Violins and Bass (see p. 126),

---

[10] This book is not concerned with a detailed history of violin music, only with the essential background of the history of violin playing. For a detailed account of violin music, see, among others, Andreas Moser, *Geschichte des Violinspiels*, Berlin, 1923; W. J. von Wasielewski, *Die Violine und ihre Meister*, 6th ed., Leipzig, 1920; and for a particular phase of the music, William S. Newman, *The Sonata in the Baroque Era*, Chapel Hill, N.C., 1959. The sources of the music itself are given in these publications and mentioned in particular instances below.

[11] Given in Gustav Beckmann, *12 Sonaten für Violine und Klavier*, Berlin and New York, 1921.

published posthumously in 1615, but both his and Cima's sonatas are more interesting for their groping toward new forms, in which the violin is incidentally concerned, than for advancing the technique of the instrument. For this we must look to G. B. Fontana (d. 1630 or 1631), about whom little is presently known, to Carlo Farina (*c.* 1600–*c.* 1640), and especially to Biagio Marini (*c.* 1597–1665). The latter, like Farina, Salomone Rossi, and G. B. Buonamente, began as one of the violinists under Monteverdi at Mantua.[12]

Marini, born in Brescia, appears to be the most important composer for the violin in the early seventeenth century. His earliest music (*Affetti musicali*, Op. 1, Venice, 1617) consists of dances (including *correnti*, *balletti*, and *gagliarde*), 'symphonies', canzonas, and sonatas for a variety of instruments including the violin. From 1623–6 he served the Court of the Wittelsbachs in Neuberg, Germany; and at the end of his stay there, his Op. 8 was published in Venice (1626 or 1629), although it must have been composed in Germany.[13] Like Farina, who served as concert-master to Schütz in Dresden, Marini learned from the German style, especially in the matter of double stops (see p. 130–1 and Exx. 13 and 14), and the violin pieces found in his Op. 8 are among the most interesting in the early seventeenth century. Marini served again in Germany—this time in 1640—in the service of Wolfgang Wilhelm at Düsseldorf, and he must have returned to Italy for good about 1645, dying in Venice in 1665, apparently well-to-do, a '*cavaliere*', and '*nobile di Brescia*'. The technical demands of Op. 22, his last work (1655) do not exceed those of Op. 8. However, Op. 22 does distinguish between *sonate da chiesa* (church sonatas) and *sonate da camera* (chamber sonatas), although this distinction may already be found in works of others some years earlier (for instance, in Merula, 1637).

Marini has been mentioned at length because of his intrinsic importance and his relation to the German school. In addition to Marini there were a number of Italians (who can be mentioned only in passing) composing interesting violin music during this period, among them, Dario Castello, Salomone Rossi, Maurizio Cazzati, and Marco Uccellini. Some of these

[12] See Dora J. Iselin, *Biagio Marini: sein Leben und seine Instrumentalwerke*, Hildburghausen, 1930. For Marini's music and others of the time, see the invaluable Einstein collection housed at Smith College: a manuscript collection of Italian and German instrumental music of the sixteenth to eighteenth centuries prepared in score by Alfred Einstein (*c.* 1899–1903) and presented to Smith College Library. For an important source of printed Italian instrumental music, see Claudio Sartori, *Bibliographia della musica strumentale italiana stampata in Italia fino al 1700*, Florence, 1952; and Denis Stevens, 'Seventeenth-Century Italian Instrumental Music in the Bodleian Library' in *Acta Musicologica*, Vol. XXVI (1954), p. 67.

[13] The preface to Op. 8 is dated 1626 in Neuberg. The printed copy is dated Venetia, MDCXXVIIII, the final 'III' being inked in. This accounts for the different dates (1626, 1629) assigned to this work.

composers have been mentioned in the earlier discussion of the new idiom and technique of the violin.[14]

Germany

The German contributions to violin music were less important than those of Italy in the early seventeenth century. The Italians, Marini and Farina, constituted a bridge from the relatively simple German style at this time to the advanced style of J. J. Walther and Heinrich von Biber at its end (cf. p. 223-6 below). In the first part of the century the Germans, such as Hassler, Praetorius, and Schein, were more concerned with dances than with the new sonata and the new violin technique. Praetorius's *Terpsichore* (1612) contains French dances in four and five parts, including *branles, sarabandes, courantes, voltas,* and *balletti.* England as well as Italy contributed to instrumental music in Germany during this period. Walter Rowe and William Brade, both Englishmen, travelled abroad, influencing the instrumental music of North Germany. Nicholas Bleyer (b. 1590), for instance, was a pupil of William Brade. However, in certain cases, the technical demands of individual German composers for the violin, notably Johann Schop (*c.* 1590–1667), are most impressive. Andreas Moser considered Schop the German counterpart of Marini as a musician and Farina as a technician.[15]

Heinrich Schütz was a pupil of Giovanni Gabrieli and Monteverdi. Like the latter, Schütz wrote in the modern Italian manner in concerted vocal pieces, and he advised the musicians who were not acquainted with the 'black [i.e. fast] notes and the continually sustained musical stroke on the violin' to acquire this technique by private practice before performing this 'modern' music in public.[16] Schütz, of course, was inspired by Italian practice, and his remarks imply that the level of violin technique was lower in Germany than in Italy. A factor in all this was doubtless the political and social state of Germany in the early seventeenth century. The Thirty Years' War (1618–48) exacted a terrible toll in lives, in property, and in frustrated artistic endeavour.

France

In France the violin gained in respectability, but its musical and technical advances were not noteworthy. The violin increased its prestige when Louis XIII made the *24 Violons du Roy* a formal organization in 1626. This action of the King simply recognized a long-standing situation in which the

[14] Representative music is printed in W. J. von Wasielewski and Luigi Torchi (cf. note 8) and in Gustav Beckmann (cf. note 11). For Cazzati and Uccellini, see William Klenz, *G. M. Bononcini.*

[15] See Andreas Moser, op. cit., p. 105.

[16] See his *Symphoniae Sacrae*, Part II, 1647, and see especially pp. 3–6, Vol. VII, of his complete works: Heinrich Schütz, *Sämtliche Werke*, 18 vols., edited by Philipp Spitta, Leipzig, 1885–1927.

violin already had an important role in the dance and other activities of the Court (cf. p. 55). Mersenne was one of the first (1636) to recognize the pre-eminence of the violin, bestowing on it the accolade 'the King of Instruments', a title previously reserved for the organ. In France, too, the guild of minstrels and players were highly organized, recognized by the King himself, and headed by its own 'King of the Violins'—at that time by a violinist named Louis Constantin (*c.* 1585–1657) to whom Mersenne admiringly refers.[17]

French violin music of the seventeenth century was essentially dance music, not only at court but in all ranks of society. According to Trichet (*c.* 1631): 'The violins are principally used for the dance, balls, ballet, *mascarades*, serenades, *aubades*, feasts and other joyous pastimes, having been judged more appropriate for these types of recreations than any other sort of instrument' (cf. p. 110, note 6).

French violin music at this time was of the simplest kind, limited to first position for the most part, and it required nothing new from the violinist except in so far as new dances demanded new rhythms. Nevertheless, some violinists must have been capable of playing more complex music. Mersenne says, 'The excellent violinists who master this instrument can ascend each string up to the octave on the fingerboard' (i.e. through the fourth position). On the other hand, Mersenne also notes that French violinists played almost exclusively on the upper two strings of the instrument, a very limited range.[18] If one may judge by the accounts of French travellers and musicians on hearing violinists play in Italy, the technical achievements of the French were modest indeed by comparison. The French violist, André Maugars (see p. 119) was astonished by the 'chromatic' (fast) manner of violin playing in Italy. At first, Maugars found this fast playing unrefined, but later it gave him much pleasure.[19]

---

[17] See E. Thoinan [Antoine Ernest Roquet], *Louis Constantin, roi des violons 1624–1657*, Paris, 1878. In his capacity as 'King of the Violins', Constantin was obliged to see that the statutes and dignity of his guild were upheld and that violators were punished. In response to one such action, the Civil Lieutenant who dealt with the matter ruled in Constantin's favour (27 March 1628), forbidding (among other things) 'the playing of the treble, bass, or other members of the violin family except the rebec [*ains seulement du rebec*], that is the three-stringed violin, in cabarets and places of ill repute [*mauvais lieux*], all this [to be enforced] under penalty of a prison sentence, a fine of twenty-four *livres*, and destruction of their instruments.' (Thoinan, p. 9.)

[18] Marin Mersenne, *Harmonie Universelle* [1636], *The Books on Instruments*, English translation by Roger E. Chapman, The Hague, 1957, pp. 237–8 and p. 241. The above quotation is translated from the original (Fourth Book, Proposition I, p. 179).

[19] A. Maugars, *Responce* [*sic*] . . . *sur le sentiment de la musique d'Italie* (Paris?), 1639. German translation by W. J. von Wasielewski in *Monatshefte für Musikgeschichte*, Vol. 10, 1878, pp. 1–9. Maugars employs the expression 'chromatic' not in the sense of the chromatic scale but in the older sense of *croma* = an eighth note—that is, the smallest 'black' note value—hence, fast.

H.V.P.–L

From the accounts of Maugars and Mersenne it appears that the French violin style was a simple one, and we have no reason to believe that the situation was otherwise in the Low Countries. Very little music of either region has survived from that time,[20] and certainly no violin music has come to light that demonstrates anything approaching the Italian advances in purely instrumental music and the technique of the violin. On the other hand, the violin must have been played at various functions in all classes of society throughout the early seventeenth century because paintings show the violin again and again taking part in festivals, dances, in tavern scenes, and in the home. How can we account for the discrepancy between the volume of music played by the violin and the apparent dearth of written music for it? The explanation of a similar situation in the sixteenth century doubtless still applies: most violin music was dance music played without notes, and when the violins doubled voice parts, no parts for them were made or needed.

From the evidence of iconography and treatises we may imagine that a distinct dance style emerged from this period and that violinists developed a style of playing appropriate to it (cf. ch. 7). This was certainly the case after 1650, when Lully, originally a violinist and dancer himself, created a mannered and highly disciplined style of violin playing to meet the needs of French dancing and the operatic orchestra (see pp. 146–7).

England

In certain respects, the situation in England resembled that in France, since the violin was associated with dancing at every social level. At Court the violin figured in the King's private entertainments, and by 1621 the violin was in the Royal favour. In that year Thomas Lupo was appointed 'composer for the violin' by James I (reigned 1603–25) that the band might 'be better furnished with variety and choice for our delight and pleasure in that kind'. By 1631, during the reign of Charles I (1625–49), there were fourteen players of 'violins' in the Royal band: three trebles, two contra-tenors, two tenors, three low tenors, and four basses.[21] Very early in its history, the violin had been used in England in connexion with the theatre for incidental music to *Gorboduc* by Norton and Sackville (1561; see p. 57). In the early seventeenth century, another species of entertainment, the English masque, combined dancing and theatrical representation. These masques enjoyed an immense vogue, and since dancing occupied a central position in their presentation, the violin was a favoured instrument. The

---

[20] At one time the so-called 'Philidor Collection', housed in the Paris Conservatory and Versailles, contained music of the *Violons du Roy*. This music is now lost (see p. 228, note 20). See also Jules Écorcheville, *Vingt suites d'orchestre*, Paris and Berlin, 1906.
[21] See Woodfill, op. cit., pp. 186–7.

masques were lavish and brilliant spectacles, combining dancing, drama, elaborate costumes, and exotic disguises (i.e. 'masques'—hence the name), the participants being drawn from the Court and sometimes from the Royal Family itself. Certain of these festivities have been described in detail. Thomas Campion wrote an account of the masque given in celebration of the marriage of Lord Hayes (1607), and he specifically mentioned the participation of the violins in particular dances and in the 'consorts' that played for dancing. In one consort of ten musicians there were two 'treble violins', and in another consort of twelve players nine were violinists.[22] A contemporary account of a later masque, Ben Jonson's *Pleasure Reconciled to Virtue*, presented on Twelfth Night 1617–18, says: 'The violins, in number certainly more than twenty-five or thirty and all in one box, commenced their airs.'[23] Whether 'air' is used in the sense of 'dance music' is not entirely clear. In any case, these 'airs' were sometimes collected and published separately, as in John Adson's *Courtly Masquing Ayres* (1611 and 1621), which call for 'violins, consorts and cornets [cornetts]' and were 'framed onely for Instruments; of which kinde these are the first that have beene ever Printed.'

The violin was also specified occasionally as an alternative to viols or other instruments. A famous example is John Dowland's *Lachrimae or Seaven Teares Figured in Seaven Passionate Pavans, with divers other Pavans, Galiards, and Almands, set forth for the Lute, Viols, or Violons [sic], in five parts* [1604].[24] However, as we have already pointed out (p. 124), Dowland's music is in an idiomatically neutral style which could be played as well by one instrument as by another of the proper register.

Enough has been said to establish the active role that violins played in English dance music. However, it is more difficult to judge how widely the violin was used elsewhere in English music of the time. A considerable amount of chamber music, in which the violin is specified, is in manuscript (a few of these pieces have recently been published; see notes 27 and 28 below); and some violin music may be camouflaged in 'fantasies' whose precise instrumentation is not clear.[25] There are still other examples of

[22] For this see Woodfill, op. cit., pp. 192–3. Woodfill also mentions (p. 195) the use of Cremona violins at Court, but not the date concerned. Music for the songs from this masque, but not the dances, may be found in G. E. P. Arkwright, *Old English Edition*, London, 1889, No. 1.

[23] See Mary Sullivan, *Court Masques of James I*, New York and London, 1913.

[24] The date is also given variously as 1605 or 1603. A modern edition, scored for two violins, viola, and two cellos (and lute) was published by Peter Warlock [Philip Heseltine], Oxford, 1927. Another edition may be found in Nagels Musik-Archiv. If these parts were truly conceived as optional violin parts, and if Parts I and II are assigned to Violins I and II, the fact emerges that the violin uses the register of the lowest (G) string, especially in the Violin II part (cf. previous comments on violin ranges in Monteverdi, p. 119).

[25] See Thurston Dart, 'The Printed Fantasies of Orlando Gibbons' [c. 1620] in *Music and Letters*, October 1956.

chamber music which call for the violin together with viols in the fantasia, a form traditionally associated with the viols. A good example is William Lawes's *Fantazya*, mentioned earlier (p. 125), for two violins, bass viol, and written-out part for organ (probably not for 'organ or harp'). According to Meyer, this piece was 'obviously written during the last years of his life'.[26]

Actually Lawes's 'Fantazya' may be called more accurately a 'fantasia-suite' consisting of a 'Fantazya' followed typically by two dances, an *Alman* and *Galliard*, both of which are often camouflaged in similar pieces under the non-committal title 'Aire'. This species of 'fantasia-suite' is a distinct English genre, often associated with the violin; and it represents an amalgam of the polyphonic tradition of the viol fancy and the dance tradition associated so closely with the violin. Typically these pieces are set for one or two violins, bass viol, and (in Lawes) a partially or completely written-out part for organ. Coperario is a pioneer of the 'fantasia-suite', having written at least fourteen involving one violin and twelve more involving two violins;[27] and Coperario, having studied in Italy, was one of the first to introduce a taste for the violin in English chamber music. In this instrumentation they parallel roughly the Italian solo and trio sonata, although the written-out organ parts are unique to the English species. Coperario's 'fantasia-suites' inspired those of William Lawes, of which there are eight for one violin, bass viol and organ, and eight more for two violins, bass viol, and organ. The 'Fantazya' of one of the latter set has been referred to above, and one of the former set has been published complete by Lefkowitz.[28]

It is unfortunate that Lefkowitz, in his valuable book on William Lawes, has used the term 'sonata' to describe the 'fantasia-suite'. The English themselves did not use the term 'sonata' before 1650; and these 'fantasia-suites' are not part of the Italian sonata tradition, nor are they influenced by it. It is not until the sonatas of William Young (1653; cf. p. 237) that the Italian tradition clearly enters English violin music.

Lefkowitz argues that the 'fantasia-suites' consist of dances, the Italian *sonate da camera* (chamber sonatas) also consist of dances; and therefore the English pieces can be called 'sonatas'. This line of argument is not compelling. The principal developments in the sonata as to form and instru-

---

[26] See Meyer, op. cit., p. 186. Lefkowitz (see note 28, below) dates these pieces *c*. 1630–5. Lawes was killed in the Civil War in 1645. The music mentioned above is reproduced in full in Meyer, pp. 271ff. For 'organ or harp', see our note 2, p. 125, above.

[27] Two of each type have been published in full. See Thurston Dart and William Coates, *Jacobean Consort Music*, Vol. IX (1955) of *Musica Britannica*, 20 vols. to date, London, 1951–62. The four pieces are Nos. 98, 99, 102, and 103. For a more general account, see Cecily Arnold and Marshall Johnson, 'The English Fantasy Suite' in *Proceedings of the Royal Musical Association*, 1955–6.

[28] Lefkowitz, op. cit., pp. 293–316, disguised under the title 'Sonata No. 8 in D Major'. There are various other works of Lawes which use the violin. Lefkowitz says that 75 per cent of the instrumental works allot the violin a prominent part.

mental technique took place in the *sonata da chiesa* (church sonata), consisting of 'abstract' movements (see p. 134, above). Unhappily, the Italian term 'sonata' can refer either to suites of dances or to pieces consisting of abstract movements; but there is no point of introducing this confusion of terminology and meaning into English. Above all, the use of the term 'sonata' to describe the 'fantasia-suite' obscures the fact that the English development was valid, even unique, in its own right, and it should not be confused with the Italian tradition to which it owed little, if anything, before 1650.

In these pieces the chief technical development as regards the violin idiom and technique is found in the 'fantazya' proper, although in the contrapuntal tradition of the form, the violin shares the musical interest with the bass viol and organ part, which is often fully written out. In some of these pieces the violin part, doubtless inspired by the 'division' technique of the viols, has quite elaborate figuration, while still remaining in first position, and is written in real violin style. Both of the Lawes pieces specifically mentioned above (as per notes 26 and 28) are examples, and the point will be made clear by examining a few measures of the music, shown in Ex. 15. Music of this sort is entirely in the spirit and idiom of the violin, and

Ex. 15

W. Lawes (c. 1640)

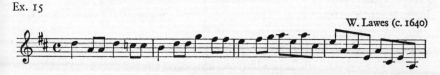

is technically far ahead of dance music. It is probable, also, that composers like Lawes, influenced by the encroaching violin, tended at times to strain their treble viols toward the idiom and technique of the violin.

Much of this chamber music is quite fascinating as music. But it is unlikely, both for musical and political reasons, that in England before 1650 there existed a substantial body of violin music that treated the violin in a way comparable to the advanced practices of the Italian composers of sonatas. Apart from dance music, the violin had a limited place in the English scheme of things in the early seventeenth century. Chamber music or 'consort' music was devoted largely and by tradition to the viols,[29] and the remarkable polyphonic literature of fancy and *In Nomine* is composed primarily for them. The fact that a certain number of fantasias by Coperario, Gibbons, William Lawes, and others make idiomatic use of the violin does not substantially alter the point relative to the large amount of music for the viols.

Moreover, the musical situation in general was quite different from that in Italy. The English did not adopt the opera, and consequently there was

[29] See Thurston Dart and William Coates, as per note 27, above.

no need for the kind of orchestra or the violins that the opera required. The only approximation to the opera in England at this time was the masque, but here the violin was not used systematically, as in the Italian opera, but largely to play dance music in ensembles as the occasion required. It is also noticeable that in England (and in France) violins were used infrequently as solo instruments in the early seventeenth century. While the Italians were developing violin technique, especially through the medium of the solo sonata, the English were writing polyphonic ensembles in which a violin or violins were sometimes included as one of several parts but which were mainly intended for the viols. In these ensembles extraordinary harmonies and rhythms were exploited in fascinating ways; and on the whole it is fair to say that the experimental, the subjective, and the personal were lavished primarily on music for the viols, much less on music for the violins. The reverse was true in Italy, and it is significant that the Italian sonata proper was practically unknown or uncopied in England before 1650. The first English sonatas were written for ensemble, not solo, being composed by William Young and printed in Innsbruck in 1653 (see p. 237).

Neither the Italian opera nor the expanding violin technique and its typical forms seem to have gained much of a foothold in England during the early seventeenth century. The reasons were undoubtedly compounded of national temperament, of resistance on the part of musicians to change and to foreign encroachment, and, especially, of political events. These events included a civil war, the beheading of a king, and the period of the Common-wealth under Cromwell—periods of instability and unrest not conducive to music in general and especially not to the newfangled and foreign idiom of the violin. It was not until the Restoration of Charles II in 1660 that the fantasias were generally displaced by the 'light and airy music' of the violins. After this time a number of composers such as John Jenkins (1592-1678), trained in the polyphonic tradition of the viol, used the violin with greater frequency in their ensembles, and made greater technical demands on the violin.

The reaction of the English to the playing of foreign violinists is a fair indication of the state of violin music and technique in England before 1650. When Thomas Baltzar, a German violinist from Lübeck, arrived in England about 1655, he astonished English musicians and violinists with what was undoubtedly a normal technical standard of playing in Italy and probably in Germany; and he easily overshadowed Davis Mell (b. 1604), the best violinist in England. Baltzar seems to have created a furore simply by playing in the upper positions, by using the Italian bow grip (see p. 153) rather than the old French bow grip favoured in England then, and by playing faster than English violinists. Similarly, English violinists and musicians were still capable of astonishment about 1672, when the Italian violinist and composer

Nicola Matteis arrived in England. Had anything comparable to Italian standards of violin playing obtained in England, neither Matteis's playing nor his printed music could have made the overwhelming impression they did. One can only conclude that the technical capacity of English violinists was comparatively limited before 1650 and that the advanced figurations found in the fancies of Lawes and others failed to inspire violinists to raise their standards of playing above those required for dance music.

Other countries

What was the state of the violin and its music in other countries? As we have remarked about sixteenth-century Spain, little is known about the violin in that country during the seventeenth century—a strange fact, since the Spanish Empire, although declining, was still one of the strongest in Europe and must have been in constant touch with the Low Countries and particularly with Italy, parts of which it ruled.[30] About the middle of the sixteenth century, when Queen Maria of Hungary, sister of Charles V, returned to Spain, she brought a number of instrumentalists with her, and the chapel lists mention, among others, players of viols and violins. Yet the violin seems to have been a true novelty in Spain at the beginning of the seventeenth century. In a description of the festivities at the court of Philip II, Cerone says in his *El Melopeo* (1613) that he heard the guitar, lute, harp, cornet, trombone, vihuela, cello, and even violins. Lists of the Chapel Royal in 1608 do not mention violinists at all,[31] but this is not surprising since violins were not used in the liturgy. There are one or two Spanish paintings of the time showing members of the violin family. A large violin (or viola) and cello are portrayed in Juan de Roelas's (1560–1625) painting 'The Death of St. Hermenengild' (see Plate 10), and Murillo's 'Vision of St. Francis of Assisi' (painted 1645–50?) shows a violin being played.

There are also a few extant paintings of seventeenth-century violins and violinists in Czechoslovakia,[32] and there are occasional and tantalizing references to Polish musicians in connexion with the violin (cf. note 33). There are very few pieces of Polish violin music published which date from

[30] All trace of the violin method *Lyra de Arco ou Arte de tanger Rabeca*, Lisbon, 1639, by the Portuguese musician, D. Ágostinho da Cruz, seems to have vanished. Rafael Mitjana in his article 'Espagne' in the Lavignac *Encyclopédie de la musique et dictionnaire du conservatoire*, Part I, Vol. 4, p. 2089, says: 'The publication of this didactic treatise is only four years after the admission of the violins to the Royal Chapel at Madrid (1635), an example immediately followed by the Royal Chapel at Lisbon.' Mitjana gives no evidence for this assertion. There is some reason to question whether this treatise was ever published.

[31] For this see Lavignac, op. cit., pp. 2083ff.

[32] See Alexander Buchner, op. cit., cf. No. 255 (second half of the seventeenth century). Various Italian violinists, including Buonamente, were active in Prague in the early seventeenth century.

this time, one such being a 'Tamburetta' for violin, two *viole bastarde*, and *basso continuo*. The music is rhythmically vigorous in the style of the Italian canzona, on which it is based, but it does not exceed first position in range.[33] From time to time one finds evidence of the spread of the violin to little-suspected places. Dragan Plamenac cites the presence of a dance tablature for violin in Dalmatia in the early seventeenth century (cf. p. 118, above, note 16), and this may be regarded as a tribute to the influence and strength of the Italian violin school. In addition, there must have been considerable interest in the violin in Scandinavia. In 1647 Queen Christina of Sweden is said to have imported six French violinists for the Court orchestra.[34] A few years later the Swedish Queen must have taken Baltzar (b. 1630) into her service. He was a highly paid chamber violinist at her Court immediately before settling in England about 1655.

Lacking sufficient records we cannot yet comprehend the full extent of the panorama of the violin in all Europe in the early seventeenth century. However, it is clear that the fruitful imagination of the Italians developed the idiom of the violin and advanced its technical and musical capacity in an abundance of descriptive and 'abstract' music written for the instrument before 1650. At the same time, violin makers were producing beautiful instruments, some of which exist, and doubtless beautiful bows, which do not, to serve those players whose services were the indispensable link between the written score and the living phenomenon of music. The technique of these players and the contemporary attitudes toward rhythm, dynamics, and expression are the subjects of the following two chapters.

[33] See H. Opienski, *La Musique Polonaise*, Paris, 1918, p. LXXXII–XCI. This piece is drawn from a manuscript collection, *Canzoni e Concerti* by Adamo Harzebski, 1627.

[34] According to Carl Nordberger, 'Violin Making and Violin Playing in Sweden' in *Violins and Violinists*, July–August 1960. The same author says that in 1534 the Court orchestra got its 'fiedel-players' from Poland, and these players were supplanted by Italians twenty years later.

CHAPTER SEVEN

The Technique and Sound of the Violin in the Early Seventeenth Century

I N any technical advance, the *status quo*, the dead tradition of the past, is altered only by some compelling need or fresh idea from the present. In the sixteenth century the violin was inseparable from vocal accompaniment and dance music, which, being simple, demanded little except rhythmic animation from the player. It is not surprising that where violin playing was so restricted the technique of the violin remained static at an elementary level. A classic case was France, whose devotion to dance music and whose scorn of the new Italian sonata inhibited her technical progress throughout the seventeenth century.

The compelling need which changed this situation was the advent of the opera, the new instrumental forms, and the concerted vocal forms of the seventeenth century (cf. ch. 6). In turn, the performance of this music required a more expressive, idiomatic and technically advanced style—and all this can be related to the experimental attitude of the seventeenth century described earlier (see p. 98). In the present chapter we shall consider how this music was performed and how new styles of playing changed the playing tradition of the sixteenth century.

In the first place, it is well to insist again on the organic relationship that exists between technique, music, and instrument making. Violinists, makers, and composers are all influenced by each other, and ideally, men of great ability in each of these fields work together for similar ends. While the simultaneous appearance of gifted men is presumably fortuitous, it is a striking fact that great violin makers, violinists of note, and imaginative composers of violin music may all be found together in seventeenth-century Italy. Is it merely by chance that similar combinations do not appear in France until late in the eighteenth century?

Shortly after 1600 the situation in Italy was favourable to a new advance in violin technique. Italy had an established tradition of violin making in the north, including craftsmen of genius like Maggini and the brothers Amati, who could respond to the needs of composers and players. At the same time Italian composers like Monteverdi were using the violin extensively in the forms of vocal music, including the opera and sacred music; and others like Marini were experimenting with purely instrumental forms. Composers of violin music were frequently violinists—Farina and Marini are examples—and the musical idea or figuration was suggested to the composer by the technical knowledge and imagination of the player in the composer. In short, the musical desire for something new and expressive, which animated the early seventeenth-century composer generally, was supported and nourished by technical experiment and insight, often on the part of the same person who was both composer and performer. These composer-violinists had an ample reservoir of string technique to draw on from the viol players of the sixteenth century, who had already expanded the technique of their instrument well beyond that of the violinists of their time (cf. ch. 4). The sixteenth-century violists had already exploited the higher positions; they were critical and selective in their attitude toward tone colour and toward open and stopped strings; they had worked out more uniform and easier fingerings; and they were interested in a greater variety of shadings and expression. In a word, an advanced technique of the viol was ready at hand to be adapted to the technique of the violin in the early seventeenth century.

All this led to a new violin idiom that, among other things, extended the range and amplified the kind of scale passages and figurations used in violin music (cf. ch. 6). Naturally, musical and technical changes go hand in hand. A new musical idiom often requires a new technical solution from the player. Extension of range implies playing in the upper positions, new problems of fingering and shifting, and a more secure hold or grip on the instrument, especially in downward shifts. Similar changes take place in the bow grip and bowing. An amplified range of expression requires new attitudes concerning tone colour, vibrato, bowing, ornaments, dynamics, rhythm, and tempo. Some of these matters, such as rhythm, are general to the performance of all music of the time, and their particular relation to the performance of violin music will be discussed later (ch. 8).

While the effect of the new instrumental idiom on violin technique is fairly obvious, the effect of the new opera on the violin is more subtle and indirect. The opera required the formation of an orchestra of sorts, quite unstandardized by modern notions, but still a loose collection of instruments, the backbone of which was the strings. In fact, the only 'standardized' orchestras that existed in the seventeenth century were established string bands like the *24 Violons du Roy* (see p. 104). When a substantial number of strings played together, a discipline of bowing was necessary to achieve uniformity in phrasing and accentuation.[1] This necessity already existed in dance music, and certain fundamental principles of the rules of bowing were well understood early in the sixteenth century by violists like Ganassi (see p. 81) and, partially at least, by violinists at the end of the century (see p. 83). Until 1600, however, string ensembles were generally small, and the need to formulate and enforce a bowing routine was not pressing. In the seventeenth century a bowing discipline became imperative for the enlarged opera orchestra and the large groups which played for dancing. As one might readily predict, this bowing discipline, as it concerned the violin, appeared in Italian sources of the early seventeenth century, already foreshadowed (as just mentioned) by others in Italy late in the sixteenth century and by the viol treatises before 1550. After 1650 various bowing rules were formulated in connexion with Lully's dance and opera orchestras. This need of a bowing discipline made the violinist amplify the technique of the right hand, and it also required the bow maker to introduce somewhat longer, stronger, and more responsive bows. All this shows that technique cannot be understood or appreciated in a vacuum. The why and wherefore of the player's technique are intimately related to the why and wherefore of the composer and the maker of instruments and bows.

How did all these developments change the basic style of violin playing inherited from the sixteenth century? The latter styles were chiefly two: a rhythmically animated style of dance music clearly instrumental in style though technically simple; and a vocally oriented style derived from the practice of doubling voice parts (cf. ch. 4 and Plates 13 and 15). The situation changed after 1600, but there was one constant in a field of variables—namely, the dance style. The other style, the literal doubling of vocal parts, began to die out. While the violin still served to accompany vocal music, it was characteristically assigned an independent (*obbligato*) part, and the style, if not specifically violinistic, was at least instrumental, not vocal, in character. This was true whether the music was sacred or secular, whether it was intended for the church or the theatre. The use of the violin in the opera is typical of its expanded role in accompanying. In Monteverdi's opera *Orfeo*, for example, the violins were sometimes used to play independent pieces, sometimes to accompany pieces in *obbligato* style, and sometimes to double vocal parts.

Besides the styles used in dancing and accompanying, another violin style emerged. This third and most important manner of playing was developed as a twin of the new instrumental forms, especially the new violin

---

[1] The uniformity essential to discipline in an orchestra extended to those players who bowed left-handed—a breed that may be seen occasionally in paintings of the time. These paintings become increasingly rare, and we must conclude that the left-handed violinist perished or was converted to right-hand custom.

sonata[2] in which composers wrote most idiomatically for the violin and made the greatest technical demands on the players. This new style is a fine example of artistic alchemy—in this case, the application of an expanding instrumental technique to vocal forms. The sonata, which came to be the most 'abstract' of instrumental forms, originated in the *canzona*, which in turn grew from the old practice of doubling vocal parts of a *chanson*, one of the principal vocal forms of the Renaissance.

In the sixteenth century, the formative period of the violin, one may distinguish playing styles most easily according to their function in dancing or in accompanying. In the seventeenth century national styles of playing begin to emerge, and they can be distinguished roughly along the lines of the musical developments just mentioned. The focal points are the French and the Italian styles, the former being directed primarily toward dance style and the latter toward both dance style and the new violin idiom of abstract instrumental music. That there was already a marked difference between French and Italian style is implicit in the astonishment expressed by Maugars, the great French viol player, when he heard Italian violinists play in Rome in 1639 (see p. 137). In particular, the Italians used an advanced technique and expressive style in such instrumental forms as the sonata and the variation, including the *ostinato* forms (see p. 133); and the Italians had already transferred the new violin style to *obbligato* parts in the opera and the concerted forms of vocal music. In all this, the Germans followed the Italians as models.

Although the dance style came to be identified later in the seventeenth century as a primary interest of French violinists, the dance style, with certain local variants, must have been common to all countries. It was certainly a strong musical factor and clearly recognized in Italy. Indeed, a bowing discipline was first formulated in Italy to establish a uniformity of stress and articulation in connexion with such dances as the *saltarello*, *gagliarda*, *allemanda*, and *corrente*, whether for actual dancing or for chamber music (see pp. 157ff., below). It is significant that Beaujoyeulx, so influential as a leader of the violins and as dance master at the French Court late in the sixteenth century, was imported from Italy; and in seventeenth-century France the case of Lully himself was not dissimilar, since he was an Italian by birth and both a dancer and violinist.

But everything is relative. While the dance tradition in Italy continued in strength, the new development of the instrumental forms and corresponding advances in violin technique were more important. It is striking that the most important violinists in Italy were more often composers than dancers,

[2] By 'sonata style' is meant the style associated primarily with the church sonata (*sonata da chiesa*) rather than the chamber sonata (*sonata da camera*), which consisted mainly of dances. When the chamber sonata is meant, this specific term will be used.

whereas the reverse was true in France. Bocan (Jacques Cordier), highly praised by Mersenne as one who played the violin 'perfectly', was equally renowned as a dance master and choreographer to the French and the English Courts (masque productions, 1610–11), and as dancing master to queens in Spain, Poland, and Denmark. The French became closely identified with the continuity and development of dance style in violin music, and throughout the seventeenth century the discipline and limitation of this manner of playing characterized French violin music to the exclusion of sonata style.

The developments in England and the Low Countries paralleled those in France and Italy, the English masque being an obvious counterpart of the French *ballet de cour*. One visible sign of their relationship was the connexion of Bocan, just mentioned, with the English masque. At the same time, there are some traces in England of an instrumental style, often idiomatic to the violin, found in certain of the fantasias (and fantasy-suites), a form of ensemble music most closely identified with the viols. This style is also distinguished by the angular themes and modal harmonies characteristic of English instrumental music of the early seventeenth century (cf. ch. 6). The technical demands of this music, compared to those of the Italians, were relatively slight. There was also a substantial literature of *fantaisies* in France in the early seventeenth century, but this type of music was not regarded as especially appropriate to the violin, being typically played by viols and sometimes by keyboards, both separately and together.[3]

Between them, the new and the traditional styles of violin playing generated a great variety in the instruments and techniques from one player to the next, and this fact is reflected in paintings, other art objects, and treatises of the time, especially with respect to the violin and bow and how each was held. In all this, however, it is still possible to reduce the variety to two main prototypes: the dance style, represented primarily by the French; and the sonata style, by the Italians. Certain pictures afford visible evidence. Plate 20, an Italian print of the early seventeenth century, is probably a fairly close approximation of the Italian style; while Plate 22 (dated 1665) is close to the French dance style. One might even think of Plate 20 as typical of the playing positions of Italian violinists like Marini, Castello (Monteverdi's 'concertmaster' in Venice), or Uccellini in Modena; and Plate 22, of French violinists like Bocan or Lazarin in Paris.

For the most part Italian sonata players used a longer bow than the French dance players (cf. p. 112), although this point is not at all evident in comparing Plates 22 and 20. Indeed, the French bow in these plates appears if anything longer than the Italian bow. (At the same time, we must

[3] See Albert Cohen, 'The *Fantaisie* for Instrumental Ensemble in 17th-Century France' in *The Musical Quarterly*, April 1962.

remember that the French bow in Plate 22 is depicted in a painting about fifty years later than the Italian print in Plate 20.) The Italian players used the 'Italian' grip (cf. p. 153); and the French, the thumb-under-hair grip long associated with dance music of the past and illustrated very clearly in Plate 22.

To achieve a greater volume of sound, the Italian sonata players probably used a violin more strongly strung than the French counterpart, and they doubtless held the violin at the neck, as the player is doing in Plate 20. By way of contrast, dance musicians held the violin at the breast (Plate 22) or collarbone.[4] The discipline of bowing central to the dance style (cf. pp. 157ff.) must have been the starting-point for the more varied and flexible Italian bowing which was developed to meet the demands of the sonata. Because of a common denominator of dancing, the Italian and French bowing had elements in common, but the Italian style, which included the sonata style, exceeded the French in variety and subtlety. This point cannot be illustrated from our plates, and neither can other differences in our prototypes, such as the greater speed and higher register of Italian playing, the greater diversity of expression (and probably, volume), the amplified use of double stops, and other technical devices to be described presently. The following discussion of violin technique elaborates on many of the technical details just mentioned, making clear, where appropriate, the characteristics typical of national styles.

Two additional points need to be made here. First, there is relatively little violin music extant that we know specifically was intended for actual dancing in this period. On the other hand, there is a lot of violin music which *may* have been used for dancing, especially in Italy (cf. Zannetti, p. 154 below), and if not, certainly for chamber music. Because of the new uses of the violin in Italy, there is, in addition to dances, a substantial literature of sonatas and variations for the violin, not to mention other violin music in the form of *obbligato* parts to vocal music. It is significant that, unlike the sixteenth century, a considerable number of pictures of violinists in the seventeenth century show music spread in front of the players, as in Plates 20 and 22.

What music is being performed by the players shown in these plates? The French player is alone, and he may well be playing a dance for his private edification or possibly for an unseen audience or group of dancers. The Italian picture suggests a solo sonata with the *basso continuo* being realized by the bass lute (*chitarrone*) player, who is tuning with his left hand and strumming the strings with his right. And can we define the role of the precocious child in the right foreground who, with an air both charming and

---

[4] For this see a picture (dated 1688) of one of the *24 Violons du Roy* in Lionel de la Laurencie, *L'École Française de Violon*, 3 vols., Paris, 1922–4, Vol. 3, p. 95.

mischievous, implores our silence? Is he preparing to join in the ensemble with the violin just visible in his left hand? Perhaps after the solo sonata is finished he will take part in a trio sonata with the other players.

Finally, what of the sound of the French, as opposed to the Italian, violin? One would imagine that the latter was far more varied and expressive for the several reasons of greater variety of musical forms and the more elaborate technique of the right and left hands. This is quite consistent with the tonal variety reported by G. B. Doni (see p. 121). One would expect the French violin to be relatively limited in expression because of its fairly rigid limitation to dance music and the simple technical demands concerned. Yet it is difficult to avoid the uncomfortable feeling that some part of the picture has been obscured from view. Mersenne speaks so glowingly of the violin as the 'King of Instruments', of its 'ravishing and powerful tone', and the 'thousand different manners' of playing the string with the bow, that one must beware of undervaluing the virtues and potential of French violin playing at this time. Nevertheless, it is not clear whether Mersenne's remarks, especially the 'thousand different manners' of playing the string, are based solely on French playing or rather on the best violin playing anywhere, which meant the Italian style. Unless it can be shown that Mersenne's remarks apply specifically to French style, one can only conclude that the Italians used the violin in a more varied way than the French and that the tonal variety and volume were correspondingly greater. However, the best of the French players like Bocan and Lazarin who, according to Mersenne, played the violin 'perfectly', must have done something to justify Mersenne's praise. We imagine that they produced a beautiful tone managed with a neat, effective, and disciplined technique within the musical limitations of French dance music. (For more detailed comments on the sound of the violin, see p. 172.)

To describe prototypes of French and Italian violin playing is to give the central facts about the two styles of playing, but there are still other details which must be added to complete the picture as a whole. For these we turn (as we have before) mainly to theory books and the evidence of iconography for further instruction. The scores of the time yield few indications about violin playing or the indispensable expression which is central to the life of any music.

In this connexion one wonders how much weight to attach to individual descriptions in the theorists even when the expositions are detailed. Praetorius, after describing various methods of tuning, makes the following wry comment:

'I do not consider it very important how each player tunes his violin or viol as long as he is able to play his part correctly and well.

Some persons get special notions about such things, and are wont to scorn organists who do not use this or that fingering. But this, it seems to me, is not worth discussing. Let one run up and down the keyboard with the front, middle, or rear finger, and even with his nose if it helps, for as long as what one plays sounds fine and pure, and is correct and pleasant to the ear, it is not very important how one accomplishes it.'[5]

And this from a man who generally gives the most meticulous details!

Holding the violin and bow

Paintings of the early seventeenth century show that the violin was held variously at the breast, shoulder, or neck, much as it was in the sixteenth century (see pp. 73-4 above). In the early seventeenth century, however, there was a preference for shoulder and neck position (cf. Plates 20, 21, and 23), especially in Italy,[6] breast position being used principally by dance violinists (Plate 22) and in conjunction with the 'French' grip (see below). In neck position, presumably used by the most advanced players, the instrument was braced against the neck, but played with little chin support. By modern notions, all these positions were insecure. There was no chin rest, and the main support of the violin came from the left hand grasping the rather fat neck. The hand was held at a lower level than it is today, and consequently the level of the scroll was markedly lower than that of the tailpiece. The violin was sometimes held nearly parallel to the floor and sometimes tipped at an angle, ranging from a small to a large one, so that the E-string side of the instrument tipped correspondingly. For simple dance music in first position, which does not require the hand to shift position, any of the hand grips described above were reasonably satisfactory. More advanced music that often required upward and downward shifts of the hand, especially from third to first position downward, must have needed some bracing at the neck or a special technique of the left hand (see p. 155). In the sixteenth century Jambe de Fer speaks of supporting the violin on the arm with a sling or scarf, but it is unlikely that this reference has any relation to shifting.

The types of bow grips were also variable. One may even see violinists bowing left-handed in contemporary paintings (see note 1 above). The two basic manners of holding the bow, both of which existed in the sixteenth century (cf. pp. 75ff.), continued their existence in the seventeenth century and even into the eighteenth. Of these the thumb-under-hair 'French' grip afforded firmness without much subtlety or nuance, it gave the player a direct contact with the bow hair (as in viol playing) and, above all, it was

---

[5] Praetorius, op. cit., Vol. II, Part II, ch. XX.

[6] For a good picture of shoulder position in Italy, see the representation of a violinist in a Roman fresco of Guido Reni (c. 1608), reproduced in *MGG*, Vol. 4, 1195-8. In the same fresco, see also a tenor violin (?) played like a cello or viol.

very effective for a straightforward rhythmic and articulated bow stroke needed in dance music. In spite of its name (probably applied later), this bow grip was not limited to the French at this time, being widespread in Italy and elsewhere (cf. Plates 21 and 23). The other basic grip was later called the 'Italian' grip, the thumb being placed between the hair and bow stick (cf. Plate 16). This grip was better suited to the more varied and subtle strokes of the advanced Italian technique, especially of the sonata players. The French grip probably became obsolete in Italy before the end of the seventeenth century, but it prevailed in France until the Italian sonata gained a firm foothold there about 1725. In both these grips, the arm, elbow, and wrist were apparently held freely and loosely. The resulting stroke must normally have been a light and articulated one, rather than powerful and heavy. Nevertheless, the ideal stroke was played well into the string. Francesco Rognoni (1620) speaks of the bow being 'well pressed to the *viola da brazzo* as the good players do'. He also rails against those who raise the bow violently so that they make as much noise with the bow as comes from the instrument. The position of the fingers with respect to the frog (nut) is dependent on the length of the bow and its balance. With the short bow, which generally prevailed in this period, the hand usually gripped the bow at the frog itself (cf. Plate 16). In the eighteenth century, particularly with longer bows, a typical grip was several inches above the frog (cf. p. 371). The volume of sound was presumably controlled by pressure from the first finger, which usually gripped the stick at the first joint.

The technique of the left hand: fingering, positions, and shifting

The open string was used where possible, as fingering from Mersenne (Ex. 16) and Zannetti show (Exx. 22–23 and 25–26; cf. note 7 below). Indeed, the old fat neck made it harder to use the fourth finger than on the modern violin, and, in addition, there was not as much difference between the sound of the open and stopped strings then as there is today. In any case,

Ex. 16

if the violin was tuned to special tunings in *scordatura* (see pp. 130 and 250), the player had *always* to play the open string unless the fourth finger was expressly indicated. This was a fundamental principle of *scordatura*-playing, and the composer depended on it when writing the score. In more complicated music of normal tunings, especially where rapid notes and figurations occurred, the fourth finger, instead of the next-higher open string, could be used for the sake of convenience. At any rate, finger four had to be used in certain double stops. Semitones were played, as they usually are today, by sliding the finger or by using the fourth finger. Mersenne shows how the note 'b' on the lowest G string (Ex. 16) is 'made into' b flat by drawing back the second finger toward the pegbox; or how the c' sharp is produced by advancing the third finger of c' a bit toward the bridge; and similarly for the other strings. Finger four was used on the three lower strings for the chromatic notes d' flat (Ex. 16), a' flat, and e" flat, the last being the only one frequently called for (Ex. 21). In the general practice of the time fourth finger on the highest (E) string was extended by a semitone upward to c'''. This is shown clearly in Zannetti (1645) where the music, consisting of dances, is given both in regular notation and in tablature so that the precise fingering is furnished for every note. In these tablatures Zannetti assigns the figure '5' to the extended fourth finger, and the same extension is used occasionally in the viola part. Zannetti's dance pieces are set in four parts for violin, two violas, and cello (except a single piece for two violins, viola, and cello, labelled 'Correnta à tre soprani'), and all string parts stay within the limits of first position. Even so, the range is still further limited, since Zannetti calls only occasionally for notes on the lowest string, and he does not use the open note of the lowest string at all.[7] Moser, citing another Italian tablature of unspecified date (but probably from this time), implies that, for reasons of tone colour, open strings were used in ascending passages, while finger four was used in descending passages.[8] The short example Moser gives is not conclusive, and no other source of the time bears him out. We conclude that for dance music, limited to first position, open string was used wherever possible. Indeed, fourth finger was actually avoided, even though it would have been easier to use in certain cases (cf. Ex. 25, m. 1; for the sound of Ex. 25, cf. our recording).

Theory books of the time have little to say about playing in the higher positions. However, Mersenne comments that the best players reach an octave above the open strings (that is, fourth position or, perhaps, third plus

---

[7] Gasparo Zannetti, *Il Scolaro di Gasparo Zannetti per imparar a suonare di violino et altri stromenti*, Milan, 1645. This work has been little described and its importance even less appreciated. Nevertheless, it is remarkably significant. Its dances—mainly *Saltarello, Gagliardo*, '*Alemanna*', '*Correnta*', and *Balletto*—are of great interest, and the fact that the regular notation is also reproduced in tablature permits us to study the violin fingerings and to determine the pitch of the open strings of the instruments concerned. In this way we are certain that the *canto, alto, tenore*, and *basso* are intended for violin, two violas, and cello, respectively, following the old tradition of the alto and tenor of the violin family both being violas (see p. 43). The tablature also shows that the violin and viola have the usual modern tunings, but the cello is tuned upward from BB flat (not from C as it is today). Zannetti is also an important key to bowing in the early seventeenth century (see below, p. 159).

[8] Andreas Moser, op. cit., pp. 62–63.

an extension) on *all* strings, and this is very unusual information as regards the three lowest strings, although in double stops one must occasionally use second or third position on the lower strings. But he says nothing whatever about how this is accomplished, giving the note d''' (third position), but neglecting to say what the fingering is. Mersenne's fingering implies that the highest notes on the E string are reached simply by advancing the fourth finger step by step as needed. This 4–4–4 fingering would not be satisfactory for the virtuoso pieces in Uccellini's Op. 5, which ascends into the sixth position as in Ex. 17. In this example, what of the return to the lower posi-

Ex. 17

tions from the note c''' to c''? Here the instrument will fall from the hand without some support, which must come either from the chin or the left hand. It seems unlikely that those players who used the neck position would not have steadied the violin with the chin from time to time, particularly since there was no chin rest. The need for steadying is somewhat reduced by taking advantage of open strings to shift and by a special technique of crawling downward, particularly from third to first position, by an adroit manipulation of the thumb, first finger, and wrist, in combination (Fig. 5).[9]

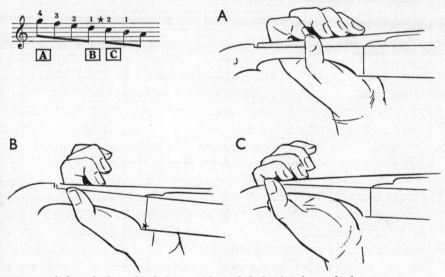

Fig. 5. Shifting by 'crawling' downward. At 'B' the thumb goes back in preparation for the shift, then the second finger jumps into place with some leverage from the thumb and some from the wrist at contact★.

[9] Today Sol Babitz of Los Angeles has been able to revive this method of shifting successfully, and he has drawn Fig. 5 to show how this shifting is done.

Leopold Mozart decries this old position and method of shifting when, years later (1756), he describes the best methods of his time (see p. 369).

We can only guess at the precise details of fingering and shifting in the more complicated music of the Italians and Germans. Violinists must occasionally have used the second or third position on the lower strings in double stops or in complicated figurations. Ex. 18 is an interesting case of figuration which requires either (1) skipping strings in eighth- and sixteenth-notes for the large leaps, or (2) extensions (see Index) of tenths plus successive shifts (cf. m. 2, Ex. 18).

Ex. 18

Frantz

The technique of the right hand: bowing and bow strokes

Early in the seventeenth century bowing was becoming a complex matter. Mersenne speaks of the 'sweetness and delights of the strokes of the bow with which the excellent players of viols and violins, like Maugars, Lazarin, Bocan, Constantin, Leger, and some others, delight the mind of the listeners'.[10] As already noted, Mersenne maintains that the right hand serves for playing the strings in a 'thousand different manners', and he adds that the right hand ought to be at least equal to the left in speed of movement. There is a surprising number of references to long bow strokes; and even if we assume that the bow was relatively short by modern standards, the 'long bow stroke' can only mean that the player was using all of it. Thus Praetorius speaks of the 'long, quiet bow strokes' (*'stille, lange Striche'*), and Monteverdi of 'long and smooth bow strokes' (*'arcate lunghe e soavi'*). With reference to the viol, Cerreto says one ought to make as long a stroke in down-bow (*tirare*) as in up-bow (*tornare*);[11] and Schütz mentions the 'steady extended musical stroke on the violin' (*'stäte ausgedehnte musicalische Strich auff dem Violin'*). Long strokes using all the bow must have been employed for long notes and for long slurs, the very short strokes for rapid sixteenth and thirty-second notes. The wide range of note values in some pieces—from dotted whole notes to sixteenths in Gabrieli's Sonata for Three Violins— would require a corresponding range of bow strokes from the full length of the (rather short?) bow to the smallest manageable stroke. Theorists and composers speak not only of the length of the bow stroke but also of its 'smooth' (*soave*) qualities. Monteverdi's 'long and smooth bow strokes' have just been mentioned, and F. Rognoni (1620) uses the phrase 'a bowing sweet

[10] Mersenne, op. cit., Chapman translation, p. 159.   [11] Scipione Cerreto, op. cit., p. 325.

and smooth' ('*un' arcata dolce e soave*'). These phrases imply that tone was closely linked to bowing and was always in the minds of the players.

The basic bow stroke was the single down-bow and up-bow stroke. In the tradition of the sixteenth century the bow was held at right-angles to the strings, and it was carefully regulated in its distance from the bridge, depending on the desired loudness, softness, and tone quality; and, as explained earlier (p. 71), this stroke was clearly articulated, especially in dance music. However, neither dots (·) nor strokes (ı) were used as yet, either in the music or in the treatises, to indicate the degree of separation. A distinction was made between the individual bow stroke and groups of two or more notes taken in one stroke as indicated by slurs; and considerable attention was paid to the regulation of the down-strokes and up-strokes of the bow.

The formation of a bowing discipline in Italy and elsewhere. The Rule of Down-Bow

The ordering of the down-bow and up-bow, already a matter of concern in the sixteenth century, was clearly developed in the seventeenth century, and this discipline was known later as the 'Rule of Down-Bow' from one of its central principles: namely, that down-bow is used for stress.[12] Consequently the first beat of a measure in a piece of music normally begins down-bow. For the violinist, down-bow is the naturally weighted stroke (cf. p. 79), and it was inevitable that this stroke should be related to normal musical accent or stress, as in the first beat of a measure; and, *per contra*, that up-bow should be related to unaccented beats or parts of beats (time permitting). These physiological facts of natural weighting explain the Rule of Down-Bow, and the basic relationship between musical stress and down-bow must have existed from the beginning of violin playing. The necessity of establishing a strong, clear beat and regular stress is obvious in dance music, and through the entire sixteenth century the violin and dance music were practically synonymous. Even if no records of bowing discipline existed in the sixteenth century (cf. pp. 77ff.), we could predict the existence of some rudimentary Rule of Down-Bow, and it would require no crystal ball to prophesy an amplification of this discipline under conditions of the enlarged dance and opera orchestras of the seventeenth century.

The relationship between stress and the proper bow stroke was first hinted at in the sixteenth-century treatises on playing the viol. It was already implicit in Ganassi's indications (1542-3) of up-bow and down-bow (cf. p. 77). Similar indications and rules were stated for the violin, apparently

---

[12] It is not clear when the phrase 'The Rule of Down-Bow' was first used explicitly. Since the principle of down-bow is constant irrespective of its name or when that name was first used, we will employ the term hereafter as a convenience, although, to our knowledge, the explicit phrase is not used in the theoretical literature of the early seventeenth century.

for the first time, by Richardo Rogniono in 1592 (see p. 82 above). By 1601 Cerreto had carried the simple principle of stress to more sophisticated lengths in relating down-bow and up-bow on the viol to an even and uneven number of notes in the measure (see p. 82).

· Hitherto, the French have been credited with being the first to develop a discipline of violin bowing. Mersenne describes it as follows in 1636:

> 'One ought always to draw the bow downward on the first note of the measure and the bow must be pushed up on the following note . . . the bow is always drawn downward on the first note of each measure composed of an even number of notes, but if a measure is composed of an unequal number . . . one draws the bow upward on the first note of the following measure so as to draw it down again on the first note of the third measure.'[13]

Georg Muffat also describes the principles of the 'Rule' in the preface to his *Florilegium Secundum* of 1698 (see p. 260), a detailed exposition of Lully's style of bowing and playing. However, it is hardly reasonable to believe that more than a century would elapse after the invention of the violin before rules of bowing were formulated. Undoubtedly players understood the main principles from the beginning of their instrument, and the 'inventor' of these principles was not necessarily the same person who first wrote about them. In any case, the Italians, not the French, were the first to give us written clues about a bowing discipline, just as they were first in practically everything connected with the violin. The role of Richardo Rogniono has just been mentioned. Nearly thirty years later (1620), his son, Francesco Rognoni, elaborates on his father's information.[14]

Francesco Rognoni gives this fundamental rule: 'the manner of managing the bow is that one always uses a down-bow at the beginning of the melody' ('*la maniera di portar l'arco e questa che sempre si tira l'arco in giù nel principiar del canto*'). The implication of this remark deserves a brief digression. By itself Rognoni's statement embodies the basic principle of the Rule of Down-Bow for the *violin*, yet it occurs in a section labelled 'concerning the nature of the

---

[13] Mersenne, op. cit., Fourth Book of Stringed Instruments, Proposition IV.

[14] Francesco Rognoni, op. cit., Parte Seconda . . . Milan, 1620. An earlier work of 1614, *Aggiunta del scolare di violino*, apparently lost, may conceivably contain similar information. There is a difference of spelling of the surname on the title-pages of the two treatises (1592, 1620)—the father being given as Rogniono, the son as Rognoni. There is no doubt that Francesco was the son, because, on the last page of his treatise, he speaks of 'Ricardo Rognoni padre dell'autore'. In a section entitled 'Instructions for bowing and slurring the bowed instruments' ('*Instruttione per archeggiare ò lireggiare gli instromenti d'arco*'), Francesco Rognoni says that 'T' stands for '*tirare in giù*' (down-bow) and 'P' for '*pontar* [i.e. *puntare*] *in sù*' (up-bow). This is the same *lettering* used later by the French: 'T' = *tiré* = down-bow; 'P' = *poussé* = up-bow.

viols'. The normal initial stroke for the viols is up-bow—that is, the bow starting at the point and being pushed toward the body—while the normal initial stroke for the violin is down-bow. Hence Rognoni's statement, assigning initial down-bow to the viol, is confusing, since it is contradictory to accepted practice. Yet there can be no doubt that by 'down-bow' he means the bow stroke in which the bow starts at the frog and is drawn out and away from the body. (For similar contradictions and confusions in Richardo Rogniono's treatise and in Cerreto, see pp. 82–3.) In his section on the violin family, Francesco Rognoni reflects further on the management of the bow (*portar l'arco*): after a whole rest, take down-bow, but after a half-rest or a quarter-rest (*sospiro*), take up-bow. In a *passaggio* beginning directly with sixteenths or thirty-seconds (says Rognoni), use down-bow, but if preceded by an eighth-note, play up-bow, and 'this is the natural thing whether in a madrigal, motet, or canzona with diminutions . . .'

These remarks of Rognoni were fundamental in formulating a discipline of bowing, and they were copied by others. In Germany, J. A. Herbst adopted Rognoni's bowing rules, acknowledging in his title the Italian origin of his information—'Everything from the most distinguished Italian Authors' (*'Alles aus den furnemsten Italienischen Authoribus'*)—and crediting (p. 19) certain examples to 'Franc. Rognoni'.[15] Herbst's musical examples and particularly those of Gasparo Zannetti (1645) show certain refinements and modifications of these bowing principles in practice. Zannetti's work, the real significance of which has so far escaped attention (cf. note 7 above), gives a large number of four-part ensembles for 'Violin and other instruments' that are explicitly marked with 'T' and 'P'. While this music has no bar lines, there is little difficulty putting them in, working backwards from the cadences in doubtful cases. Furthermore, Herbst's examples, which have bar lines, are perfectly consistent with Zannetti's, and they both emerge as continuations of Rognoni's basic formulas. Rognoni's and Zannetti's works were both published in Milan, and Rognoni, at least, and probably his father, were active in the musical life of that city. (For the importance of Milan in the early history of the violin, see pp. 20, 26, and 30.)

From the three sources just mentioned, certain bowing principles can be formulated:

1. Down-bow is used normally on the first note of a measure that does not begin with a rest. This is the basic Rule of Down-Bow, related to stress.

2. In practice, this basic rule may be superseded by a more important rule, or rather, procedure. (While these procedures or principles will be called 'rules' here, they were not formulated as such until later.) According to this second rule or procedure, the first note of a measure, especially the

---

[15] J. A. Herbst, *Musica Moderna Prattica*, Frankfurt, 1653. This work appeared earlier in a shorter form (Nürnberg, 1642).

initial measure, begins with a down-bow if there is an even number of notes —or more accurately, bow strokes—in a measure. The corollary is that the measure begins with an up-bow if an uneven number is involved. (Cf. Cerreto's explicit but confusing remark, p. 82, note 24 above). *Notes are to be played with individual bow strokes unless slurs are explicitly marked.*

Rule 2 is important in practice because it may nullify Rule 1. Ex. 19, taken from Zannetti, is an excellent illustration of the application of Rule 1 in the bass and of Rule 2 in the treble (dotted bar lines added by the author).

Ex. 19

Zannetti (p. 22)

two middle parts omitted

In the first measure the bass starts down-bow (T = *tirare* = down-bow) because it conforms to Rule 1 and because there are an even number of four notes in the measure. (The modern indication for down-bow is ⌐ ; and for up-bow, ∨.) The bowing at the beginning of measure 2 then comes out down-bow as it should. But the treble part presents another situation. Normally it should conform to Rule 1, but Rule 2 proves stronger: Zannetti marks the first note up-bow (P = *pontare* = up-bow) because there is an uneven number of five notes in the measure and because the main pattern, beginning in measure 2, ought to start with a down-bow.

Rule 2 may also nullify Rognoni's rules for rests, given above. In Ex. 20, for instance, Zannetti marks down-bow after a half-rest which, according to Rognoni's rules, should be followed by an up-bow. The reason is that the rest is followed by an even number of six notes, and it begins down-bow in accordance with Rule 2. This example is also an interesting case of a syncopation, the first half-note in the passage being taken up-bow. In Ex. 21, which begins with two half-rests, Rognoni's rules are followed, since the first note after the half-rest is marked up-bow, a procedure that also satisfies Rule 2. Ex. 22 is a normal case of up-bow after the quarter-rest.

Rule 2 is rarely violated, but there is one instance in Zannetti's music that is interesting in relation to triple time (cf. Rule 3 and Exs. 24-26, below). In Ex. 23 the beginning up-bow specified by Zannetti is required in order to make the bowing come out down-bow on the whole-note (semibreve) of measure 3. If the piece is barred in 3/2 time, as it is here—no bar lines being given by Zannetti—Rule 1 and Rule 2 are both violated in measure 1 by Zannetti's up-bow indication. However, if one bars Ex. 23 in 3/1 or 6/2 meter, Rule 2 applies, since there are an uneven number of five notes in the initial measure (i.e. the first two measures shown in the example). However, Rule 1 is still disregarded. *Rules 1 and 2 apply with particular force to initial measures, but they are the guiding principles throughout.*

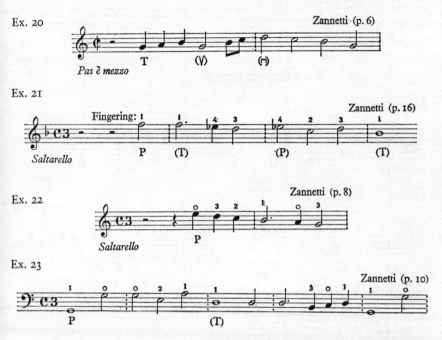

3. Once the bowing pattern is established, down-bow and up-bow are normally alternated (subject to the conditions given in Rule 4 below). This means that in triple time (to which the later treatises, especially in the eighteenth century, devote much attention) down-bow occurs on the first note of every other measure if there are three bow strokes in each measure (cf. Ex. 21).

4. In practice the rhythmic pattern or phrase may fall in such a way that a stressed note may be followed immediately by another stressed note, resulting in two consecutive down-bows; or two such down-bows may be essential to readjust a musical pattern. Two consecutive down-bows may be performed either by slurring (i.e. in effect, one down-bow), by a kind of *portato* (the down-bows made consecutively but articulated), or by replacing the bow for two separate and detached down-bows. Similarly, the musical patterns may work out so that two unstressed notes come together or so that the pattern needs adjustment. The result is two consecutive up-bows, done with the same alternative bowings just mentioned. Ex. 24 and Ex. 25, both from Zannetti, illustrate these points. Ex. 24 is particularly fascinating because it uses two consecutive down-bows to bring out the *hemiola* rhythm, essentially separating and emphasizing alternate measures in 3/2

and 6/4 times. (For more on *hemiola*, see p. 185.) In this case, the articulation probably demands a *replaced* bow (bowings in parentheses added by the author). In Ex. 25 Zannetti calls for consecutive up-bows on the dotted-quarter figure (♩ ♪) of measures 3-5, which seems to imply a slur or a *portato* rather than replaced bow.[16] Ex. 26 is a rather unusual example of a long initial down-bow occupying a whole measure (and requiring a long bow stroke), after which the bow must be replaced to begin the next measure down-bow. (For the sound of Ex. 25 cf. our recording.)

Ex. 24

Ex. 25

Ex. 26

Zannetti's markings, which are in accord with those of Herbst, are of great historical, musical, and technical interest. Without Zannetti's explicit bowings, one would bow his music in rather different ways according to modern notions. Zannetti's pieces are mainly dances, but it is likely that at first the sonata players adopted the same basic principles. The Rule of Down-Bow and its related bowing principles, set forth above, undoubtedly were inspired primarily by the needs of dance musicians, and their formula-

---

[16] In an undated violin tablature (but probably early seventeenth century), contained in MS. 33748 in the German Museum at Nürnberg, a dot under the tablature means up-bow (cf. Ganassi, p. 77 above). The accompanying tablature shows that the Rule of Down-Bow was clearly operative and also that the two consecutive up-bows, as explained in Rule 4 above, must be employed. For this tablature, see Johannes Wolf, *Handbuch des Notationskunde*, 2 vols., Leipzig, 1913 and 1919, Vol. 2, p. 233.

tion in the present instance depends on the explicit markings in dance music. Unfortunately, there are no similar markings in the sonatas of the same time. Yet the sonata players must have based their bowing technique on these same dance principles of bowing, considering dance bowings carefully before rejecting or amplifying them. We do not know in what respects, if any, the sonata players before 1650 deviated from the basic bowing principles of the dance violinists. At the end of the century Muffat shows how differently a minuet is bowed in the French style on the one hand and in the Italian-German style on the other (cf. p. 261 and Ex. 82), but there is some reason to think that his report is not very reliable on this point as regards Italian-German style, and, in any case, this bowing concerns a minuet, not a sonata. By the eighteenth century the Italians had discarded the strait-jacket of the Rule of Down-Bow, which came to be associated more and more with the French style of dancing, and Geminiani calls it that 'wretched Rule of Down-Bow' (see p. 401). As regards the early seventeenth century, we must be content with the principles and details of bowing described in this chapter, which will serve as a basic guide to the bowing of European dance music at that time. In the case of the Italian sonata, we must adapt these principles to the musical context as our taste and knowledge of the time dictates. Marini, Farina, Uccellini, and other violin virtuosi among Italian players of the time must have done the same.

Individual bow strokes. Slurring

The above bowing rules are based on the premise, obvious enough from Zannetti's examples, that each note receives an individual bow stroke unless a slur is marked, or unless two consecutive down-bows or up-bows are applicable (here, too, depending on execution, each note may get a separate and distinct stroke, as in *portato*). Under certain conditions, some allowance must be made for inserting slurs, but the scores should be played as written unless there is some good reason to do otherwise.[17] This same remark about slurring applies to Lombard rhythms, which may be found slurred as well as unslurred (cf. Ex. 27), to individual sixteenth and thirty-second notes, and to written-out trills, including those in rapid notes and those of some duration. The speed at which these individual notes were played must have been

F. Rognoni (Part II), p. 5

Ex. 27

[17] Gustav Beckmann, *Das Violinspiel in Deutschland*, Leipzig, 1918, Anhang No. 6, gives two different versions of the slurs in Uccellini's Op. 5, one from manuscript and one from the printed score. For the whole piece, see Beckmann, *12 Sonaten*. Beckmann thought that certain features of the rhythmic notation of the violin tablatures in Anhang No. 2 (*Violinspiel*) implied the addition of slurs. This is doubtful.

considerable. Mersenne puts the limit to the number of movements of the bow hand at sixteen to a second for the best players.[18] This speed would tax good players today, and unslurred trills would sound remarkably fast, not to say loud and brilliant.

There are certain instances where the composer may have intended slurs to be added *ad libitum* without specifically indicating them. Richardo Rogniono (the father, 1592) speaks of 'taking two notes in one bow stroke because one cannot make a diminution of any length if the bow does not claim its rights (*se l'Arco non va al dritto*)'.[19]

When the violin exactly doubles long vocal melismas or echoes them, it is tempting to consider slurring the violin part to the corresponding vocal syllabification (Ex. 28). However, no contemporary treatise mentions such a

Ex. 28

possibility and the length of such a slur as that on the syllable 'Glo-' in Ex. 28 would seem to rule out this possibility for any music louder than *piano*.

In a number of cases, slurs are already indicated, and they occur with increasing frequency as the century progresses, especially in music for advanced players. Cerreto (1601) indicates that in viol music, two, three, or four notes may be slurred in one bow stroke (*in una arcata*), and Ganassi uses slurs (i.e. *portato*) in viol music before the middle of the sixteenth century (cf. p. 81). Francesco Rognoni says in 1620: 'the *viole da brazzo*, particularly the violin, is [*sic*] an instrument crude and harsh [*crudo e aspro*] by itself if not tempered and sweetened by smooth bowing [*soave archata*].' (Rognoni, by the way, uses *arcata* and *archata* interchangeably.) Whether Rognoni refers to slurring several notes in one bow stroke in this particular passage is not evident; but at any rate he takes pains to see that the violinist has instructions elsewhere in his text on slurring as many as fifteen notes in one bow stroke. His father, Richardo, had already given slurrings by two (see p. 83). For slurred bowing, Francesco Rognoni gives a special term, *lireggiare*, and he furnishes examples that are both instructive and puzzling.[20] In particular, there are slurs for groups of notes by 2, 3, 4, 5, 6, 8, 10, 12, and 15. Ex. 27 shows the 'Lombard' figures, some slurred by twos and some unslurred.

[18] Mersenne, op. cit., Chapman translation, pp. 190–1.
[19] Riccardo Rogniono, op. cit., in his preface entitled *A I Virtuosi Lettori L'Auttore* (To the Virtuous Readers from the Author).
[20] In J. G. Walther's *Musicalisches Lexikon*, Leipzig, 1732, *lireggiare* (*lirare*) is still defined as two, three, or more notes in one bow.

Ex. 29 is an instance of a type of syncopated bowing; and Ex. 30 is a syncopated figure within a bow stroke. In Ex. 31 the repeated note, contained within the slur, implies two slurs within this slur to articulate the repeated note; and the second measure of this example, with three repeated notes, is even more curious for the same reason. Ex. 32 with twelve notes under a slur, is a slurred trill with 'afterbeats'. Ex. 33 and Ex. 34 are illustrations of a special bowing called *lireggiare affettuoso* by Rognoni. He describes it as 'with *affetti*' being

> 'the same as the above [i.e. *lireggiare* = slurred bowing] . . . but it is necessary that the motion of the bow arm beat every note as if it were skipping along (*saltellando*), one for one, and this is hard to do well; therefore this requires much study to be able to maintain the time in conformity with the value of the notes, taking care not to make more noise with the bow than with the sound.'

Can Rognoni actually be describing a species of slurred *staccato* (or possibly *sautillé*) at this early date? When Farina in his *Capriccio Stravagante* (1627)

instructs the player to slur several notes, his wording—'to slur the notes with the bow in the manner of a *lira*'—recalls Rognoni's term *lireggiare*. Farina also uses syncopated bowings (Ex. 35). Castello has as many as twelve notes under one slur,[21] and Mersenne gives the astounding information that 'one can play a courante or several other pieces of music with a single bow stroke'. Could this mean: 'using one particular kind of bow stroke', rather than that a whole piece was performed in one bow stroke? No wonder that Scheidt in his *Tablatura Nova* for organ (1624) labels a passage of sixteenth-notes, slurred in groups of four, 'Imitatio Violistica'.[22]

Ex. 35

"Il Pifferino"   Farina

Borrowing of technique. Multiple stops

In the situation just mentioned, Scheidt is a self-confessed 'imitator', transferring string technique to the organ. This is perfectly normal. All the instruments were inveterate borrowers from each other and from the voice. Later the voice returned the compliment and imitated certain figurations of the violin concerto and sonata. In the early stages of developing its own idiom, the violin drew heavily on the technique of older instruments. The figurations and *passaggi* of viols, voice, and keyboards were adapted to the peculiar needs of the violin, and certain devices, now regarded as basic to the violin idiom, were developed from long-standing practices of the viols and even the lutes. Two good examples are the vibrato and multiple stops.[23] Of these, vibrato will be discussed among the ornaments, since it was classified as one in the seventeenth century (see p. 177).

The history of multiple-stop writing is fairly old. Ganassi gives a number of examples for the viols in his treatise of 1542-3 (see pp. 90-1, above), and such instruments as the lyra viol and *lira da gamba* specialized in this kind of playing. The lute also developed chord-playing both for accompanying and for solo performance. In the fifteenth century Tinctoris in his *De Inventione et Usu Musicae* (c. 1487) speaks of lutanists playing 'most skilfully, in not only

---

[21] Moser, op. cit., p. 58.

[22] For the music, see Archibald Davison and Willi Apel, *Historical Anthology of Music*, Cambridge, Mass., 1950, No. 196, last line.

[23] In this book the term 'multiple stops' is used as a general term to describe collectively all chords written for the violin irrespective of the number of notes involved. Today the term 'double stops' is often used to mean not only a two-note chord but also a three-note and four-note chord as well. To avoid this confusion, the term 'multiple stops' is used here as the general term; 'double stops', 'triple stops', and 'quadruple stops', as specific terms.

two parts, but even in three or four. For example, Orbus, the German, or
Henry who was recently in the service of Charles of Burgundy; the German
was super-eminent in playing in this way.'[24]

From the beginning of the seventeenth century, violinists vigorously
exploited multiple stops (see p. 131). Some of these stops require a considerable technique to perform. It is true that the isolated stop of two notes
presents no problem as a rule; it is the passage of continuous double stops
that requires attention, particularly where speed of movement, rapid
fingering changes, or shifts of the hand are involved. Apparently with the
intent of simplifying this problem, Marini resorts to the *scordatura* to play
continuous passages in thirds (cf. Ex. 13). He does this by lowering the E
string a third to c″, so that the intervallic relation of the two upper strings
(E and A) is a minor third. In this way the violinist can play consecutive *minor*
thirds simply by putting the same finger across the two upper strings. But
Marini's music calls also for *major* thirds, and this involves the player in
fingering problems, especially when executed in sixteenth notes. (In Ex. 13
the upper staff shows how the passage must be written for the player; the
lower staff shows the actual sound.) Even if the tempo is no faster than
moderato, the fingering and shifting at beat two (presumably to second or
third position) would require a nicety of technique to play this passage in
tune.

Another excerpt in sixths and thirds is shown in Ex. 36. This example,
from an interesting piece by an obscure composer, Stephan Haw, 'Dance-
master to the Princess of Heydelberg', is not in *scordatura*, but it is in
sixteenth-notes and, judging by context, no slower than moderato.[25] The

S. Haw

Ex. 36

fingering must be changed accurately at every sixteenth note, and some of
these changes are difficult. The third sixteenth, for instance, involving the
interval e′-g′, must either be played in first position with the fourth finger
extended a full whole tone to play the note e′, or the passage must be played
by shifting to second or third position. Note also the two octave-intervals
called for. Presumably all these stops are played with an individual bow
stroke to each sixteenth.

In this period no new principles are involved in trills in thirds or sixths.
It is quite astonishing, however, even to find the trill in sixths. This trill

[24] Quoted in Anthony Baines's article (p. 24), as per p. 50, note 1, above.
[25] Given in Beckmann, *Violinspiel*, Anhang No. 10 (*c.* 1640?).

(Ex. 37) is found in a work, probably composed before 1646, by the German violinist, Johann Schop (d. 1667), who was obviously a virtuoso. Over a hundred years later (1756) Leopold Mozart comments on the great difficulty of the sixth-trill. The fingering of this trill involves a rocking motion of the first finger (and hand) back and forth from the D string to the A string.

J. Schop

Ex. 37

Probably this particular trill would be slurred to reduce the right-hand problem to the minimum, concentrating on the extreme difficulty of the left. Mersenne seems to imply that ornaments could be slurred or unslurred.[26]

The double stops just cited are written in note-against-note style, but other consecutive double stops occur in which the two voices are rhythmically different and independent. In passages such as Ex. 38 (taken from a

Ex. 38

O. M. Grandi

piece of O. M. Grandi, 1628), the matter of adding slurs becomes a vexing question. The passage cannot be played exactly as written. At the beginning, the g″ of the upper part must either be shortened to conform to the dotted eighth of the lower part, the sixteenth-note b′ of the lower part then being played with another bow stroke; or the lower part must be slurred to conform to the time value of the upper part, the whole first beat being taken in one bow. And so on throughout the passage.

This particular problem of double (and multiple) stops is a thorny one at least to the middle of the eighteenth century, and there is very little direct evidence which suggests contemporary solutions to it. Presumably, everyone knew how to do it then, did not remark on such a commonplace, and, therefore, no one knows how to do it now. It can only be said that slurring was a well-known type of bowing (cf. Rognoni's *archata lireggiare*, p. 164 above), and it is probable that such passages were left to the discretion of the player to slur or not, as taste, convenience, or context dictated. On the other hand, it can be shown that the notation of the seventeenth and eighteenth centuries must have been approximate, and certain passages would not have been played as written. In Ex. 39, for instance, Marini (Op. 8) writes a passage that is virtually impossible to perform strictly

---

[26] See Mersenne, op. cit., Chapman translation, p. 240.

according to all the written note values (cf. Bach's solo sonatas and similar problems of notation, pp. 429ff., below).

Not content with double stops, composers and violinists explored the possibilities of triple and quadruple stops. The latter usually occur as isolated chords, but the former, sometimes as consecutive chords. Where

Ex. 39

triple and quadruple stops are written as single chords (Ex. 40 and Ex. 41) they were probably arpeggiated swiftly, starting with the lowest note. The swiftness of the arpeggiation and the resonance of the lower notes gave the impression that the notes of the single chord sounded briefly together. Where the chord is of some duration (Ex. 41), it is probable that only the top note was held, judging by later instructions in the theorists (cf. p. 436). However, with the more yielding hair of the old bow (and particularly if the bridge is flattened somewhat), it is physically possible to sustain triple stops at *forte* more easily than on the modern bow.

Ex. 40   Ex. 41

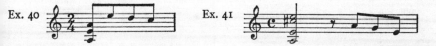

Consecutive triple stops were viewed as something special and experimental. Marini calls for such a *tour de force* in his astonishing Op. 8. His *Capriccio per sonare il Violino con tre corde a modo di lira* (Capriccio to play the violin with three strings in the manner of the *lira*) is explicit in its use of the three strings and its imitation of the *lira* (*da gamba*), an instrument of many strings and flat bridge, specializing in the playing of chords (see p. 90 above). Marini gives special directions for playing these triple stops (Ex. 14): 'the two largest [lowest] strings must be close together' ('*bisogne che le due corde grosse sijno vicini*')—the implication being that triple stops could not normally be executed consecutively as chords without the adjustment called for. Later treatises (see p. 436) make clear that triple stops were not played simultaneously as chords; the technique of triple and quadruple chords was basically one of swift arpeggiation under normal circumstances. Mersenne notes that the same finger, touching two neighbouring strings, 'always produces the fifth at all points of the fingerboard'; and he continues, 'if the violin were tuned otherwise, for example, in fifths and fourths, the same finger would be able to make a perpetual chord by always playing two or three strings, but it would be necessary for the bridge to be lower than it is

and for it to imitate that of the lyre, of which I shall speak in another
place.'[27] In 'another place' he says that the 'lyre' (which he illustrates) has
fifteen strings and 'it must still be noted that the bridge is longer, lower,
and flatter than that of the viols, because it bears a greater multitude of
strings, which must be played three or four at a time by a single stroke of
the bow, so as to produce chords'. This implies that triple stops on the
violin called for exceptional treatment because the normal rounded bridge
and tense bow made them difficult to play; and only under conditions
similar to those prevailing on the lyre could triple stops be made to sound
like full chords. What is true of triple stops in this respect is even truer of
quadruple stops.

Special indications: Tremolo. Affetti

Besides the bowing problems connected with multiple stops, there are
several puzzling indications in the music that may involve bowings. In a
canzona of Merula (1639) the indication 'tremolo' occurs under all parts in
relatively long note values in a passage some twenty measures in length
(Ex. 42). This 'tremolo' probably means 'vibrato', although it could con-

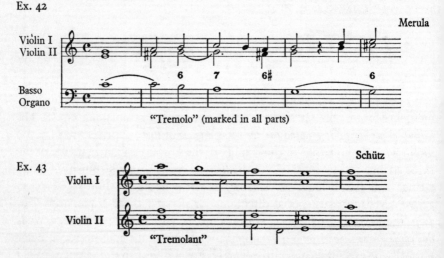

Ex. 42

Violin I
Violin II   Merula

Basso
Organo

"Tremolo" (marked in all parts)

Ex. 43   Schütz

Violin I

Violin II

"Tremolant"

ceivably mean a regularly measured *tremolo* in the modern sense, perhaps of
repeated sixteenth notes (Francesco Rognoni uses *tremolo* in this latter
sense). Two passages in the works of Schütz cast some light on this problem,
and suggest the correct solution. They are shown in Ex. 43 and Ex. 44,
taken from his *Symphoniae Sacrae*, Part II of 1647.[28] Here Schütz distinguishes

---

[27] For this and the following quotation, see Mersenne, op. cit., Chapman translation,
   p. 240 and p. 263.
[28] See Schütz, *Sämtliche Werke*, Vol. VII, p. 182 and p. 174.

between 'Tremolant' (Ex. 43) on the one hand, which is similar to the
Merula passage in Ex. 42 and seems clearly to imply vibrato; and, on the
other, 'Tremulus' (Ex. 44) which gives slurs over repeated notes (and
others), implying a species of legato *portato*—that is, repeated notes barely
separated but in the same bow stroke as indicated. (For more on *portato*
and *tremolo*, see the Index.)

Ex. 45 is more puzzling. Under a passage of twelve measures of half-notes
Marini has written *Affetti*. This passage serves as a bridge from a somewhat
free passage to one in strict tempo. Schering[29] has suggested that this should
be performed as a continuation of the figures of the preceding measure or a
'staccato eighth-note repetition of the tone, in the sense of the old *tremolo*'.

Ex. 45

This may well be. It may also be a suggestion to the player merely to add
such *affetti* as he pleases—that is, improvised ornaments. To Caccini (1601)
the *affetti* meant collectively repeated notes (*trilli*) or a species of trill (*groppi,
tremoli*; see p. 176.) Perhaps Rognoni's special bowing, the *lireggiare
affettuoso*, is applicable. Rognoni equates this special bowing with the
affetti and with the special *saltellando* motion of the bow arm described above
(p. 165). However, it is a fair guess that Marini's term *affetti* is simply an
invitation to the player to improvise *ad libitum* with *affetti*. This is doubtless
the sense of Torelli's instruction *Adagio e con affetto* in his solo concerto,
Op. 8, No. 7, published in 1709.[30]

Col legno. Sul ponticello. Sulla tastiera. Pizzicato

Exceptional types of bowing include striking the string with the wood of
the bow (*col legno*), bowing very near to the bridge for a glassy, brittle
sound (*sul ponticello*), and bowing over the fingerboard (*sulla tastiera*). Such

---

[29] Arnold Schering, *Geschichte der Musik in Beispielen*, Leipzig, 1931, remark to No. 183.
[30] For this and the music, see Schering, op. cit., No. 257.

effects, required by Farina's *Capriccio Stravagante* in the interests of description, present no special problem of performance. These bowings are worth mentioning here only as examples of the inventiveness of early seventeenth-century violinists. They had little use for some time afterwards.

The *pizzicato* is a different matter. It was already in use in the sixteenth century (cf. p. 84), and in the seventeenth century it became a standard, although special, effect on the violin in imitation of the plucked instruments. There was as yet no regular method of performing it. Monteverdi speaks of plucking the string with 'two fingers' (see p. 129), and Farina asks the player to hold the violin under the right arm, plucking the string 'as if it were a regular Spanish guitar'. The latter method would naturally be impractical unless an entire piece were to be executed *pizzicato* or unless there were a few seconds to change from this to a bowing position. In Tobias Hume, '*The First Part of Ayres* (1605) for lyra viol, one finds the use of both *pizzicato* and *col legno*. The latter effect is called for in a piece 'Hark, Hark' in connexion with a passage in multiple stops under which are the directions 'Drum this with the back of your bow'.[31]

The sound of the violin in the early seventeenth century

Since its origins in the early sixteenth century the violin had progressed and changed rapidly. After 1600 its development was increasingly swift. Compared to the sixteenth-century violin, the seventeenth-century instrument began to be heard more and more in the brilliance of its upper registers and occasionally in the deepest registers of the G string. The agile properties of the violin were exploited in scale passages and figurations across the strings that took advantage of the idiomatic possibilities of the instrument. A new sonority from these passages, especially in the keys of the open strings and from double stops of all kinds, was soon evident; and the special effects of *pizzicato*, the mute, and even *col legno*, *sul ponticello*, and *sulla tastiera* could occasionally be heard. The violin *cantabile* was modelled on the voice, and as such it took on the dynamic nuances characteristic of its model.

The old rhythmic bow stroke of the sixteenth-century dance music continued, and from the music we judge that to this were added strokes of increasing subtlety and variety developed by the Italians. The latter began to discipline the order of down-bow and up-bow and the legato slurring, and when Mersenne speaks of 'playing the string in a thousand different manners', he is probably thinking at least as much of the Italians as the French. G. B. Doni is eloquent in his praise of the variety of violin tone (see p. 121), and this variety is based on different kinds of bowing and tone production. Francesco Rognoni remarks on the link between tone and

[31] See *Musica Britannica*, Vol. IX, p. 202.

bowing when he says that by itself the violin is 'crude and harsh unless tempered and sweetened by a smooth bowing'. Tonal variety is produced by the many types of bow strokes. An additional variety may be assumed from the expressiveness of nuanced tone and the occasional use of vibrato.

Tone and quality of sound cannot be described in words, but such descriptions are not wholly useless if they can be related to our common vantage-point of the modern violin. By comparison, the tone of the seventeenth-century violin was smaller and less brilliant because the strings were gut and because they were under less tension. Besides, the bow and bow strokes were probably lighter, and the bow strokes were more naturally articulated than is the case today. For the same reason the tone of the seventeenth-century violin was doubtless sweeter and less metallic. As we have explained above, the variety of tone was considerable in the seventeenth century, but this variety was a product more of the types of articulated and legato bow strokes than of the use of the complete register, the high positions, or the tone colour of individual strings. Compared to modern playing, violin tone in the early seventeenth century depended far less on the use of the lowest (G) string and especially the throaty sound of the high positions of the lowest strings. Similarly the brilliance of the highest registers and such things as the flute-like tone of harmonics were little used, even if known. The special tone colour of individual strings was understood and appreciated, but the elaborate usage of tone colour as an effect was less common than in today's playing. Vibrato was not an organic part of violin technique as it is today, and its expressive qualities were utilized in the seventeenth century largely as an occasional ornament. As a result the tone, lacking the shimmer of constant vibrato, was more focused in its pitch, and there must have been greater clarity of individual lines in ensembles.

All this is to say that the modern violin is a far more developed instrument than its seventeenth-century ancestor. In the long process of its evolution the modern violin has gained much in power and in range of variety and expression. It has also lost something in sweetness of tone and in natural articulation, and its varieties may be different but no greater than the seventeenth-century violin. Many of these questions are largely matters of interesting speculation.

Comparing the tone of the seventeenth-century violin to the modern instrument is useful largely as a point of reference. However, this comparison tells us nothing about the relation of the seventeenth-century violin to its predecessor in the sixteenth century. In this case, there must have been a very rapid, not to say spectacular, change in the early seventeenth century to judge by the types of music written for the violin after 1600, the generally expressive manner of performance, the documented witnesses to the swift progress of the violin, and the beautiful violins and bows that resulted.

By the middle of the seventeenth century the capabilities and prestige of the violin were such that it had clearly become the instrument *par excellence* of the time, and Mersenne summed up its qualities with this supreme accolade:

> 'the beauties and graces that are practised on it are so great in number that it can be preferred to all other instruments, since the strokes of the bow are sometimes so delightful that one has a great discontent to hear the end, particularly when they are mixed with ornamentation of the left hand which force the listeners to confess the violin to be the king of the instruments.'[32]

Mersenne's words are equally remarkable for their praise and their implied prophecy. 'The king of instruments' had established a royal line, and it remained only to perpetuate and strengthen the succession. The extraordinary achievements of the violin which prompted Mersenne's words were to be extended and its promise brilliantly fulfilled in the generations and centuries to follow.

[32] Mersenne, op. cit., Fourth Book of Stringed Instruments, Proposition I. See also Chapman translation, p. 235.

CHAPTER EIGHT

⟨∽∾⟩

General Matters affecting
the Violin to 1650

To understand the history of violin playing involves more than a narrow focus on the mechanics of manipulating the violin and bow. In earlier chapters we have dealt with the historical 'why' of many matters relative to the progress of the violin, violin music, and the technique of playing it. In this concluding chapter to Part II we consider those questions of a general musical nature which are pertinent to our subject. The performance of violin music belongs to a larger context of musical performance in general, and such matters as ornaments, including the vibrato, often need special discussion in connexion with violin music. In addition, certain general musical facts of the time are imperfectly understood—for instance, rhythm and tempo in the early seventeenth century—and in so far as these questions affect the performance of violin music, we will report any significant results of the most recent investigations.

Ornaments

Two types of ornaments may be distinguished: first, stereotyped ornaments that have specific names may often be represented by signs, and indicate to the player a definite musical formula or procedure. Typical ornaments of this class are trills, mordents, and (at this time) the violin vibrato. The second type of ornament is more general, being in reality ornamental melodic figures, often improvised. Ex. 10 (ch. 6) is an instance where Mersenne shows how a simple part is elaborated by the addition of ornamental melodic figures. In general, 'divisions' and '*passaggi*' may be classed among these ornamental figures, a species of variation or elaboration. These melodic figures have to be written out or improvised at the discretion of the player—they cannot be reduced to conventional signs or names—and, although ornamental figures of this type will be noticed from time to time in later chapters (cf. pp. 288 and 457), we need not consider them further at this point.[1]

[1] For a detailed discussion of such melodic ornamental figures in relation to improvisation, see Ernest T. Ferand's article 'Improvisation' in *Die Musik in Geschichte und Gegenwart*, Vol. 6, 1957.

In the case of stereotyped ornaments, the violinist needs to know what the signs and terms of the early seventeenth century mean, whether to slur the ornament, and, especially for those indicated merely by signs, their duration and how fast or slow to play them. Unlike later practices, typical ornaments, such as trills and mordents, were often written out, not indicated by signs, in the early seventeenth century (see Ex. 10 for the written-out trill in m. 2). However, conventional signs gradually came into vogue in the course of the century, especially after 1650. Before that time there was a great deal of confusion with respect to the notation of ornaments. The most typical, irrespective of their notation, were: (1) the trill starting with the main note (cf. Ex. 46); (2) the trill starting with the *upper* note ('upper accessory')—

Ex. 46

Tremolo ("Tremulus Ascendens")

that is, starting with the note above the written note over which the trill indication was placed (Ex. 47); (3) the mordent—the trill starting with the written note and alternating rapidly with the tone or semitone below (Ex. 48); and (4) the old *trillo*, consisting of repeated notes. Agazzari and Praetorius, among others, specifically associate certain ornaments (*gruppi*, *trilli*) with the violin (see p. 89 for quotation from Agazzari).

Ex. 47

Conforto

Groppo ("Groppo di sopra")

Ex. 48

Praetorius

"Tremulus Descendens"

When the ornaments were not written out but designated by specific terms, the following distinctions were generally valid in spite of some confusion and inconsistencies:

1. *trillo:* repeated notes.
2. *tremolo (tremulo):* a trill starting with the main note (Ex. 46).
3. *tremoletto:* the same but shorter.
4. *groppo (gruppo):* trill starting with the upper note (Ex. 47). *Groppo* sometimes means 'turn'.
5. mordent: there are several terms for the mordent as defined above.

Praetorius calls the mordent *Tremulus Descendens* (Ex. 48), which he considers inferior to the *Tremulus Ascendens* (the main-note trill; Ex. 46). Conforto[2] calls the *groppo* proper (Ex. 47) *groppo di sopra*, and the mordent proper (Ex. 48) he calls *groppo di sotto*. Shorter ornaments he qualifies with *mezzo* (*mezzo groppo*) as in Ex. 49.

Conforto

Ex. 49

"Mezzo groppo"

In early seventeenth-century violin music, 't' or 'tr' usually stands for '*tremolo*' in the sense of a main-note trill. When Marini writes '*groppo*' and 'tr' in the same piece, he means the main-note trill by 'tr', and an upper-note trill by '*groppo*'. One such direction in Marini is hard to interpret: the term '*groppo all'alta*' (Ex. 50). By this he probably means simply '*groppo* with the note above' (i.e. *groppo di sopra*, the upper-note trill as in Ex. 47, the normal procedure) as opposed to '*groppi di sotto*', the lower-note trill or mordent (Ex. 48). A number of trills are shown with typical terminal notes or 'after-beats' (Ex. 47). These are discretionary and more usual in the longer trills. The number of repercussions and the speed of the trill were apparently left to the performer's judgement in the context of the music and the effect to be achieved. Herbst, interestingly enough, shows trills which increase in speed; and he adds this comment to a trill in sixteenth notes: 'make the number of percussions according to your own wishes' ('*si batte quante si vuole*').[3]

Marini

Ex. 50

"groppo all' alta"

The vibrato

Throughout the seventeenth and eighteenth centuries, the vibrato was generally treated by violinists as an ornament to be used occasionally. In the sixteenth century we hear about the vibrato from time to time (cf. p. 91), and in the seventeenth century there are one or two references to it. Our best source is Mersenne. He equates the violin ornaments with those of the lute. Among the lute ornaments is the vibrato, which he calls *verre cassé*, and, in view of what he has said, his description applies likewise to the violin:

'As to the *verre cassé*, I am adding it here, although it is not used so much now as it was in the past, inasmuch as it has a very great charm when it

---

[2] G. L. Conforto, *Breve et facile maniera d'essercitarsi . . . a far passaggi*, Rome, 1593 (or 1603).

[3] Herbst, op. cit., p. 59.

is made quite properly. And one of the reasons that the moderns have
rejected it is because the older ones used it almost all the time. But since
it is as vicious to use it not at all as to perform it too much, it must be
used in moderation. Its notation is ͵. the preceding comma followed by
a dot.

And to perform it well, the finger of the left hand ought to be placed
at the point indicated; and although the string will be played with the
right hand, the left hand must swing with great violence, while raising
it towards the head of the lute, and bringing it down towards the
bridge without lifting the tip of the finger off the string in any fashion.
But the thumb of the left hand must not touch the neck of the lute,
when this ornament is performed, so that the action of the hand may
be freer in it.'[4]

This passage is fascinating in itself and for what it implies. What players
were the 'older ones who used it [the vibrato] all the time'? When was this
extensive usage in force? And did the 'older ones' include violinists as well
as lutanists?

We do not know under what conditions and in what musical situations
violinists of the early seventeenth century used the vibrato. From later
information we assume that it was used occasionally on long notes (cf.
Ex. 42), combined with some dynamic nuance. In any case, it does not appear
to be particularly appropriate to dance music, and it would be somewhat
difficult to execute freely, holding the violin in the breast position characteristic of those violinists who played dance music.

Dynamics and expression

After 1600 a desire for the personal and the expressive dictated a greater
use of loud, soft, and the gradations between. *Piano* and *forte* were well-
known resources in the sixteenth century, but we know more about their
presence than their precise use. In the early seventeenth century, *piano* and
forte are expressly indicated with increasing frequency, especially to indicate the 'echo' effect, and refinements begin to appear. Monteverdi, for
instance, gives the direction '*tocchi pian piano*' ('play very softly') in his
Orfeo, and Mersenne recognizes some eight degrees of loudness and softness
by 1636.

Passing gradually from one dynamic degree to another is a natural consequence, but specific signs for *crescendo* and *diminuendo* are rare in the music.
However, about 1600 and thereafter these gradations are found in the
theorists, in composers' prefaces, and sometimes in the music. Caccini's

[4] Mersenne, op. cit., Second Book of Stringed Instruments, Proposition IX. See also the
Chapman translation, p. 109.

preface to *Le Nuove Musiche* (1601) explains various ways of increasing and decreasing the sound under the general name of *esclamazione*. Francesco Rognoni (see p. 158 above) directs the singer 'to begin long notes with the voice soft and low, raising it bit by bit to the maximum in words of grief because the true effect consists in knowing how to diminish the voice and to raise it where there is need'. In his madrigals of 1638 Mazzochi speaks of the sound dying away to nothing, and his eighteenth madrigal closes with a *diminuendo* expressed by *forte—piano—pianissimo*. Similarly, Benedict Lechler (*c.* 1640) uses the signs p—pp—ppp—pppp for a still subtler effect.

While dynamic nuance appears first as an ornament for the solo voice, the melodic instruments, most of which looked on the voice as a model of expression, rapidly followed suit. Monteverdi indicates a *diminuendo* for the violin in his *Il Combattimento* (1624) by writing over the last measure of the piece 'this last note is played with a diminishing bow stroke' (*'questa ultima nota va in arcata morendo'*); and in the same work, the marking *'forte piano'* with one bow stroke' (Ex. 51) suggests a short *diminuendo* from *forte* to *piano*—not *subito piano*. This *forte piano* marking of Monteverdi is probably the ancestor of a little-known and misunderstood sign 'f p', used as late as W. A. Mozart to indicate a short *diminuendo* (see p. 488). Fantini's trumpet method of 1638 uses the most characteristic of all singing nuances, the *messa di voce* (already employed by Caccini and Mazzochi), consisting of a *crescendo* to the middle of a note and then a *decrescendo* to its end (—⟨⟨ ⟩⟩—). The *messa di voce* was quite probably used on the violin also, although we do not know of its specific application until later.

Ex. 51

"arcata sola"
"forte piano"

The violin's power of increasing and decreasing the sound is considered an important asset by the theorists, and some of them begin to comment on the dynamic limitations of the keyboard instruments compared to the voice and melodic instruments like the violin. Praetorius is a case in point. He quotes with approval from a booklet, dated 1610, in which its author, Hans Hayden of Nuremberg, explains that he invented the '*Geigenwerk*' (or 'violin-clavier'; see Praetorius, op. cit., Vol. II, Plate III) to remedy the disadvantage of all keyboard instruments with respect to *crescendo* and *diminuendo*. 'The player of keyboard instruments is thus restricted in that he cannot give expression to his Affections [i.e. emotions or moods], showing whether sad, joyous, serious or playful thoughts are in him; while this can all be indicated

quite clearly on violins . . .'⁵ Salomon de Caus is another who comments on
the flexibility and advantage of the fretless violins, as follows: 'One can lower
or raise the sound according to the will of the player not only from low to
high or high to low but louder or softer. The organs and harpsichords do
not have this effect.'⁶ Mersenne says much the same thing: 'One can still
note many things which are particular to the bow. For example that one
holds the same tone as long a time, or as softly or loudly as one wishes. This
the organ does not have, for it cannot decrease or reinforce its sound according to the desire of the organist.'⁷

All this amounts to saying that violinists of the time must have recognized a number of degrees of loud or soft and the gradations between. The
crescendo, diminuendo, and the *messa di voce* were probably used on single notes
or phrases of relatively short duration. However, there is no evidence of long
crescendi or *diminuendi* until late in the seventeenth century (see p. 291).⁸
Exactly how and where these dynamic levels and gradations were used is
not certain, the markings in the music being mainly limited to *forte* and
piano. Long notes were probably graced with dynamic nuance accompanied
by vibrato, but for the rest, the player must have played loud or soft, and,
within these general terraces of dynamics, increased or decreased the sound
as the mood of the piece struck him. This nuanced style would doubtless
have been more characteristic of the sonata players than of dance musicians,
whose first duty was to the steady clear beat of the *gagliarda* or *corrente*, not
to the changing expression of which the new instrumental forms were
capable.

The use of dynamics is an important element in an expressive performance. Rhythm is another (see below). On occasion, composers simply
gave a general indication of expression, leaving the execution solely to the
player. Thus Tobias Hume contrasts two styles of performance in his piece
'Death' for lyra viol. Under measures 9-11 he has the direction: 'Play this
passionate after every strain.' And following this comes the direction: 'Play
this [m. 13 ff.] as it stands.'⁹

Rhythm and tempo

About 1600 the situation with respect to rhythm and tempo began to
change as it did in so many other musical matters. In the late Renaissance the

---

⁵ Praetorius, op. cit. Vol. II, Part II, XLIV. See the edition of Harold Blumenfeld, p. 69,
    who translated the first two parts of Vol. II, printed by Yale University, 1949.
⁶ Salomon de Caus, *Institution Harmonique*, Francfort [*sic*], 1615, p. 55.
⁷ Mersenne, op. cit., Chapman translation, p. 256.
⁸ Possibly Monteverdi means a long *crescendo* in his opera *Ulysses*, where three dotted
    breves are tied together and marked *piano*, the three following tied breves are
    marked *forte*, and the last three tied breves are marked *più forte* (see Monteverdi,
    Tutte le Opere, Vol. XII, p. 88).
⁹ *Musica Britannica*, Vol. IX, p. 202.

central unit of time was called the *tactus,* meaning a 'beat' in the sense of a measure of time and also of the 'conductor's' beat, the latter comprising a down- and an up-motion of the hand to each tactus. In binary divisions of the tactus, the motions were equal in duration; in ternary divisions (e.g., *tripla;* see 'proportions', below), two counts were generally allotted to the down-motion and one to the up-motion. The speed of this time-unit of the tactus was generally stable, probably about M.M. 60, and was usually represented in the basic duple notation by a whole note (semibrevis).[10]

Thus the seventeenth-century musician inherited a system which had a more or less stable tempo tied to the note values of the notation. In this system tempo changes were effected by a series of proportional signs, such as the *alla breve* (𝄵), which generally meant to play the note values twice as fast as when written with the signature (C). Later, *alla breve* sometimes meant merely to play faster. In *tripla* (3 or 3/1), the notes were played three times as fast as the written values suggested; in *sesquialtera* (3/2), 3/2 times as fast as written. In modern note values, these proportional relationships come out to those shown in Ex. 52.

Ex. 52

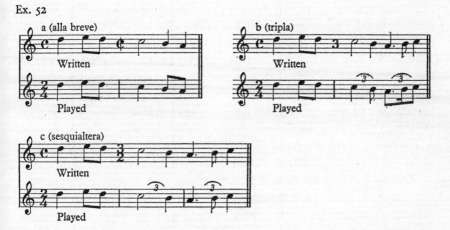

The essential point is this: to a modern performer, unacquainted with the proportional signs and their meanings, a *tripla* section (for instance), written in longer note values, *looks* as if it should go at the *slower* pace suggested by the longer note values (cf. Ex. 53). Actually, the reverse is often the case, since the note values in the *tripla* proportion are meant to go three times as fast as they are written. But the *tempo is not necessarily faster because*

---

[10] The whole note as tactus was simply a measure of time or beat, not necessarily the time-unit basic to harmonic change. In the early Renaissance (e.g., in the music of Josquin), whole notes were the normal values of harmonic change or movement. After 1550, the comparable unit was the half note (minim), and after 1600, a quarter note (semiminim), as is often true today.

the note values are played faster than written. This is an important distinction. In numerous cases, it is true that playing the note values faster than written (as a result of the proportional signs) results in a faster tempo. On the other hand, the resulting tempo may sometimes be *slower* because the pace of the music depends not on the proportions themselves but on the length of note values used after the proportional signs and, in vocal music, on the number of syllables set to the notes in the different sections. Specifically, in Ex. 52b, the speed of movement of the note values after the tripla sign (3) and,

Ex. 53

consequently, the tempo are increased since, in effect, a measure of 6/8 (although appearing as 6/4) is played in the same time as the previous measure of 2/4. But in measure 4 of Ex. 53 the *tripla* section, although subject to precisely the same laws and proportional relationships, is heard as a slowing down of the syllables that strike the ear. The three whole notes of the *tripla* section are played three times as fast as the written note values: that is, in the same time as one whole-note of the preceding section. But, because of the way the syllables are set, the *tripla* section calls for three syllables (m.5) sung in the same time as the preceding four (m.2)—that is, a slowing of the tempo of the individual syllable, which is what the ear hears.[11]

The proportions mentioned above are among the most common ones, but there are many others such as 4/3, which means that four notes are performed in the time of the three preceding of the same written value. These proportions, a vestige of an older system, may still be seen in the seventeenth century. The puzzling 8/6 in the violin music of Corelli, for instance, simply means to play eight notes in the time of the preceding six, and 6/8 restores the original relationship. In the *tripla* sections the tempo will alter, generally to a faster one, as explained above.

Another important feature of sixteenth-century notation was the mensural division of the notes. Thus C, meaning 4/4 today, meant something

[11] Although musicians sometimes get intuitive feelings that these proportions are not correct, there is no doubt about the *tripla* proportion just explained as far as the written note-values are concerned. For a particularly striking and decisive proof in the works of Schütz, see Arthur Mendel, 'A Brief Note on Triple Proportion in Schuetz' in *The Musical Quarterly*, January 1960.

quite different under the old system, where note values could be subdivided either by triple or duple division. Today only duple division is normally used: a whole note is subdivided into two half-notes, two halves into two quarters, and so on. We take duple division for granted, and our time signatures are basically indications of meter, showing how many notes of what value are contained in a measure. But the older mensural system used these 'time signatures' as an indication, not of meter, but of the manner of subdividing note values into duple *or* triple divisions as the case may be. C3, which occurs frequently in the seventeenth century (and appears in our examples), is a relic of this sytem, the 'C' meaning essentially that the large note division is duple, and the '3' meaning that the smaller division is triple —hence, for practical purposes, approaching our concept of 6/8 or 6/4 time. Occasionally the old mensural C turns up in seventeenth-century music, and under this guise the music may actually be in triple-meter, as can usually be seen by the musical groupings. A good example is Marini's *Romanesca* (Op. 3, 1620), given by Wasielewski with the sign C, and barred by him in duple time (Ex. 54). His barring in duple time masks the intent of

Ex. 54

the music, which is obviously in triple time. In Ex.54 the duple time of Wasielewski is retained, the obvious triple groupings being suggested below. When one realizes that C is a mensural sign, having nothing to do with modern 4/4 time in this case, the fact of triple meter can be realized and appreciated. Marini's *Romanesca* then makes musical sense, the main notes of the *romanesca* bass coming out on the strong beats of the triple measure, as shown by arrows.[12]

The new expressive demands of the seventeenth century required a more

[12] For the whole piece, see W. J. von Wasielewski, *Instrumentalsätze*, No. 10.

flexible system than the old *tactus* and its proportions. Gradually the note
values were divorced from tempo meanings and began to approach the
modern system where note values may be assigned to any tempo. As a
result of this divorce, tempo markings became essential in the seventeenth
century, and these markings sometimes had mood connotations as well as
those of tempo. *Allegro*, for example, meant 'cheerful' as well as 'fast'. The
first tempo indications were those for fast or slow, not for *moderato*. *Moderato*
was the normal speed inherent in the old *tactus*, and there was no need to
indicate the norm. Thus Banchieri gives terms that are either slow or fast,
not moderate:[13] *adagio, allegro, veloce, presto, più presto, prestissimo*. The situation is the same in Praetorius (1619): *presto* (defined as fast, *not* very fast),
adagio, and *lento*. Even in 1652 Herbst is still giving terms for fast and slow
only: *adagio, lento, largo, tardo, presto*. The markings in the music conform
to the limitations suggested in the theorists. Where no tempo markings
are given, *moderato* may be assumed, modified as needed by vestiges of the
old system, such as *alla breve* or *tripla*.[14] The tempo markings for fast and slow
are relative to an implied norm of *moderato*. It was inevitable under the new
system that some attempt would be made to fix the relationship of the unit
of beat to a definite tempo. In such matters we can almost always depend
on Mersenne for some appropriate comment, and he suggests a species of
pendulum by means of which the composer can fix the time of his piece.

With few exceptions the old system of the sixteenth century presupposes
a steady tempo throughout a piece, but the seventeenth century, with its
penchant for emotional representation, began to alter the old system.
Flexible tempo is naturally suggested by an emotional representation of
words, and Caccini (1601) wishes certain pieces to be performed 'without
measure' (i.e. in free time). Monteverdi, in his madrigal *Non havea Febo
ancora* (Book VIII, 1638), directs the singers to perform the first part in the
'tempo of the hand'—that is, the strict measure of the old *tactus*—and the
second part (entitled *Amor*) in a tempo dictated by the emotional spirit of
the piece, 'not in the tempo of the hand'. Frescobaldi intends his keyboard
toccatas of 1614 to be performed freely in the spirit of the 'modern' madrigal
(cf. Monteverdi), and he says in his preface:

> '*Passaggi* and expressive sections in toccatas and partitas must be played
> in slow tempo, while the other sections can be played somewhat *allegro*.
> The player's taste and judgement should be the arbiters. It is upon the
> correct tempo that the spirit and perfection of this style depends.'

[13] Adriano Banchieri, *L'Organo suonarino*, Venice, 1605, 2nd ed., 1611.
[14] For further details, see Curt Sachs, *Rhythm and Tempo*, New York, 1953; and (for music
before 1600) Willi Apel, *The Notation of Polyphonic Music, 900–1600*, Cambridge,
Mass., 1942, and later editions.

In the original, these remarks are printed in bold-faced type, and the importance of this statement deserves such emphasis. A violin piece of Marini[15] calls for '*tardo*' and '*presto*' in short successive phrases, almost in the manner of a rhythmic echo; and Farina suggests a species of *allargando* with his direction *sempre più adagio*.[16] However, free tempo (or tempo *rubato* in any form) is more appropriate to those pieces of violin music of rhapsodic or ornamental character than to those in strict forms, such as fugal movements, which should be performed in the strict 'tempo of the hand'.

In the ferment and experiment taking place during this time, strict forms mixed freely with those of rhapsodic character, and the old *tactus* alternated with the new *tardo* and *presto*. In playing seventeenth-century music we should not allow ourselves to be dominated by the tyranny of the modern bar line but rather be musically attentive and sensitive to varying accents and rhythmic patterns inherent in the music. One of the favourite patterns of the time was the *hemiola*, in which six notes are divided alternately into

Ex. 55

two groups of three or into three groups of two. These patterns are recognizable in the music, and sometimes the composer takes pains to notate them in a way that makes the *hemiola* more apparent. In Ex. 55 this is done by underlining the pattern in the bass: measure 1 is clearly in 6/4, and measure 2 in 3/2.[17]

It is probable, too, that the emotional character of certain pieces was emphasized by rhythmic alterations of the written notes: for instance, dotted notes sometimes elongated to doubly dotted notes, and sometimes notes written evenly played slightly longer or slightly shorter than the written values (for such rhythmic liberties, see p. 294).

Pitch. Intonation systems

Today we take for granted the security of the equal temperament of the piano, and depend on a pitch fixed at $a' = 435$ or 440. Only in recent times

[15] See Schering, op. cit., No. 183.
[16] See Beckmann, *Das Violinspiel in Deutschland*, Anhang No. 3.
[17] Taken from Andrea Falconieri's *Ciaconna*, 1650. The whole piece is printed in Luigi Torchi, *L'Arte Musicale in Italia*, 1897, Vol. VII, pp. 122ff.

H.V.P.–O

have such standards obtained. In the seventeenth century the standard of pitch varied enormously from one place to another, and even in the same town two churches might have organs tuned to different pitches. There were different types of pitch, such as 'chamber-pitch' and 'cornett-pitch', and we sometimes learn of pitch being lower or higher in one country than in another. Mersenne speaks of pitch being a tone lower in English viols than in French 'so as to render the harmony softer and more charming'.[18]

This chaotic situation was particularly hard on wind-instrument players, but less so on violinists, who could adjust more easily to circumstances. The treatises of the sixteenth century (cf. p. 70) often tell players of lutes and viols to 'tune the top string as high as it will bear', and similar instruction for the violin turns up in the seventeenth century and even in the eighteenth. When violins played with keyboard instruments, they must have conformed to the fixed pitch of the latter. Whether seventeenth-century violinists generally played at a higher or lower pitch than prevails today cannot be determined, since practices varied enormously.

Theorists commend the fretless violin on its superior flexibility compared to that of the viol and lute, which, because of fixed frets, had to play fixed intervals of pitch, presumably in equal temperament. The fact is that viols can adjust temperament, and frets do not fix the pitch absolutely. Nevertheless, everything is relative, and the fretless violins could adjust more easily to individual intervals that were 'pure' (i.e. in just intonation) or play in the meantone system prevailing in many keyboard tunings.[19] Similarly, the violin could accompany the voices more flexibly than the fretted instruments. Mersenne notes that the violin, not being restricted to frets, can play any kind of music, enharmonic, diatonic, or chromatic, and he gives the violin the highest marks as an accompaniment for the voice or other instruments.

With this flexibility seventeenth-century violinists could and probably did make distinctions between notes of enharmonic pairs, such as C sharp and D flat. Mersenne seems to imply this in his instructions on violin fingerings. The modern violinist makes these subtle distinctions, too, but with an important difference. Today, C sharp, as a tendency tone to D, is usually played higher than D flat, as a tendency tone to C. The reverse was true in earlier times, and this distinction of sharps being lower than corresponding enharmonic flats prevailed until about 1800. The change at that time may have been related to the sharp third of equal temperament or possibly to a striving for greater brilliance of effect.

[18] For a lengthy discussion of pitch, see Arthur Mendel, 'Pitch in the 16th and 17th Centuries' in *The Musical Quarterly*, January–October (four parts), 1948.
[19] See J. Murray Barbour, *Tuning and Temperament*, East Lansing, Michigan, 1951, 2nd ed., 1953.

Summary

The history of violin playing in the early seventeenth century was one of rapid change and development; and this situation reflected an era and environment which took an avid interest in experimentation, personal expression, and exploration of the physical and intellectual world. Political as well as social changes laid the foundation of modern society and nations.

Musical changes after 1600 were quite considerable. To these changes Monteverdi contributed greatly; and, as far as the violin was concerned, Marini was an important pioneer. The development of new idioms and national styles for the violin, and the corresponding change in the instrument, bow, and playing styles were all related to the rise of the opera, the concerted forms of vocal music, and especially the rapid development of instrumental music. Instrumental music, which felt especially the liberating effect of a contemporary attitude that encouraged individuality of expression, experimented extensively with new forms such as the sonata, developing new idioms in these forms and in such old ones as the variation and even the fantasia. Besides, descriptive music was often a factor in stimulating the discovery of special instrumental effects. The old interest in dance music continued and increased, and the new instrumental forms and idioms shifted the general emphasis from vocal to instrumental music in the course of the seventeenth century.

The violin proved capable of an almost infinite capacity to meet and exploit these new opportunities of musical expression. This potential for development had several important results. Now the violin began to fill a greater social role than formerly, being used more widely in the church, chamber, and theatre; and, in addition, the violin spread through practically every class of society, a fact reflected in art objects of the time, especially in Dutch genre painting. In particular, the violin was played not only in taverns and at home but also in the palace. The formation of the *24 Violins of the King* in France was symbolic of the increased social and musical prestige of the violin and violinists in the seventeenth century. The lot of violinists varied considerably, of course, the Royal musicians being the best off. On the other hand, lesser players enjoyed a measure of protection from the musicians' guild.

As in many other things of the time, changes in the violin idiom after 1600 were rapid and profound, and the technique of playing advanced correspondingly to meet the new conditions. It may seem a paradox that relatively few changes took place in the violin and bow. The reason is that its musical and technical potential were already in advance of the demands made upon them in the sixteenth century, and consequently the violin of the early seventeenth century had to make relatively few adjustments in the instrument which had come down from the late sixteenth century. The changes in the violin were, in fact, largely matters of detail and decoration, as one can see by comparing the violins of the brothers Amati with those of their father, or the work of Maggini with that of his teacher, Gasparo da Salò. There were still no violin makers of international reputation outside Italy.

Changes in the bow were more extensive. Though quite unstandardized, it began in general to lengthen and straighten, and some attempts to make a distinct bow head may be observed. The use of better, stronger, and more flexible woods is a sign of the importance attached to the bow in the interest of greater volume, expression, and variety of bow strokes.

The terminology of the violin reflects the variety and change in instruments and bows, mixing terms derived from the sixteenth century with those proper to the seventeenth, to the general confusion of everyone today. The problem of distinguishing between terms for families of instruments and terms for individual members of families is especially great. Every violin, for instance, is a *viola da braccio*, but not every *viola da braccio* is a violin. A number of terms, as well as instruments, became obsolete with the passage of time. In particular, the function of certain instruments was usurped by the violin, and gradually fell into musical disuse, notably the rebec, and, to some extent, the viol, especially in Italy.

New musical conditions after 1600 included the rise of the opera and the development of specific instrumental forms; and these conditions required a greater and greater use of the violin, which was increasingly specified in the scores. The natural result was a rapid development of an idiom of expression peculiar and natural to the violin. This idiom included an increased range, especially in the upper register, melodic lines and species of figuration grateful to the violin, multiple stops, the amplified use of trills and other ornaments, experiments with the *scordatura*, and special effects such as the *pizzicato*, vibrato, and *col legno*. The expansion of the idiom proper must have been accompanied by an increasing variety of tone, a matter noted by contemporaries like G. B. Doni and Mersenne. The rhythmic possibilities of the violin were developed in dance music particularly. While the idiom advanced considerably in the sonata and related forms (as we can tell by the music that has come down to us), it is quite probable that an even more advanced technique was practised by those among the virtuosi who extemporized— roughly, the hot-jazz boys of the early seventeenth century.

Technical changes go hand in hand with musical changes, although it is not possible to say whether one preceded the other or whether the changes were simultaneous. Extensions of range, for example, require technical changes in holding the violin and bow, not to mention playing in the upper positions and shifting. New types of expression require new attitudes toward such matters as bowing, vibrato, and dynamics. Similarly, technique varies according to function. The technical requirements for playing dances may be quite different from those needed to play sonatas. These functions correspond roughly to the principal national styles which developed, the French being oriented toward a dance style and the Italians toward a dance *and* sonata style.

The advancing technique and the necessity of uniformity in large ensembles required the formation of a bowing discipline, which took place first in Italy in connexion with dancing, and was later extended and developed by the sonata players. This discipline, afterwards known as the 'Rule of Down-Bow', soon appears in other countries, especially in France, and is subject to certain local variants. Bowing and various types of slurring are related to this central discipline and also to tone production. Bowing and other matters, like multiple stops, result in a considerable playing variety, so that Mersenne could speak of bowing the string in a 'thousand different manners'.

Compared to the sixteenth-century violin, the seventeenth-century instrument must have increased in variety of tone and expression, and perhaps in volume. However, compared to the modern violin, that in the seventeenth century was smaller in tone, although probably sweeter and less metallic. These differences are the result of differences in the violin and bow and the technical manner of playing.

For a modern violinist there are a good many musical problems of a general nature in the early seventeenth century. In particular, ornamentation, including the vibrato, is often confusing as to names, signs, and meaning with respect to performance. Signs for dynamics and expression are seldom indicated in the scores. This does not mean that the music was intended to be without expression—only that there were special conventions of the time which were clearly understood by early seventeenth-century violinists. Similarly, usage with regard to rhythm and tempo is very confusing to a modern musician; yet these conventions must be understood to discover the intentions of the composer.

There is no doubt that the early seventeenth century was a time of intense experiment and rapid change for the violin, just as it was for the society which supported it. The idiom of the violin expanded rapidly after 1600 to meet the new musical conditions, and consequently the technique of the violin and, to some extent, the violin and bow changed and advanced correspondingly. By 1650 the idioms associated with the sonata and the dance were sufficiently contrasted so that we can discern quite clearly an Italian sonata style on the one hand and a French dance style on the other, corresponding to the techniques involved. These distinctions were emphasized still further in the last part of the seventeenth century, and the result was an amplification of national styles, as we shall see.

PART THREE

The National Schools of the
Late Seventeenth Century.
The Rise of Virtuosity

National Schools. Virtuosity

IN the early seventeenth century the violin idiom developed at such a rate in the forms of instrumental music that a pronounced cleavage between the new progressive style of violin playing and the older conservative manner, suited primarily to dance music, became more and more apparent. After 1650 these distinctions, originally based on function, became identified with national styles, and the contrast between the resulting Italian and French schools of violin playing was noticeably intensified at the end of the seventeenth century. Violin playing in other countries was modelled to a greater or lesser extent on the Italians and the French.

A new virtuosity in violin playing was also associated with the formation of national styles. The extensive technical advances of the Italian school in the early part of the century were carried still further: the interest in a *cantabile* style increased, and earlier technical experiments were more carefully worked out. On the Italian model, the Germans created a style of violin playing that was still more advanced with respect to range, bowing, double stops, and the use of the *scordatura*. The French, within the limitations of a conservative dance style, developed a sophisticated manner of bowing suited to the rhythmic articulation of their dances.

All technical advances and changes are related sooner or later to musical changes and (in violin music) to the instruments and bows required. While certain traditional functions of the violin—such as playing for dancing and accompanying vocal music and the opera—required little technical change, the new forms of the sonata, the variation, and later, the concerto, prompted an expanded technique and certain corresponding changes in instruments and bows. The instruments of Nicola Amati, especially his 'grand' pattern, coincide in time with technical advances in Italy; and their beauty of tone and ease of response must have been enthusiastically received by players. Similarly, the 'long' model Stradivari violin appeared just at the time (1690) when the concerto was appearing in Italy. It is also a sign of the times that the marked progress in German violin playing coincided with the appearance of Stainer's instruments in the Tyrol, the first time that a great violin maker had appeared outside Italy.

As the seventeenth century advanced the social position of the violin improved. This amelioration was related to various factors. One was the widespread use of the violin in all classes of society. Another was the fact that, on the one hand, the violin had long since ceased to be associated exclusively with dance music; and, on the other, that it was in the forefront of progressive musical developments in instrumental music, engaging the attention of the best players and composers. A final and decisive factor was its rapid adoption by amateurs in the last part of the seventeenth century, who turned from the viol to the violin as the old polyphonic music associated with the viol went out of fashion. The advent of the violin treatise toward the end of the seventeenth century was essentially due to the rise of the amateur violinist, and the simplicity of the tunes printed in these tutors shows the gulf that divided them from advanced players of the time. Ironically, many of these tunes were dances, but this was a consideration of no moment—the violin in the hands of amateurs was respectable no matter what was played.

CHAPTER NINE

༄༅

The Development of the
Violin and Bow, 1650-1700

IN the art of violin making the extraordinary advances in violin music
and technique were paralleled by an equal if not more spectacular
advance. The three great makers just mentioned dominated the field:
Nicola Amati, Jacob Stainer, and, at the end of the century, Antonio
Stradivari, whose productive years extended well into the eighteenth
century. While Stainer is the only figure outside Italy in a class with Amati
and Stradivari, Hendrik Jacobs in Amsterdam may also be mentioned as an
outstanding maker.

Prior to Stradivari the most influential maker was unquestionably
Nicola Amati (1596-1684), the great master of Cremona.[1] After Maggini's
death (c. 1632), the Brescian school ceased to produce masters of the very
first rank, and the supremacy of the school of Cremona was unchallenged
from then until the middle of the eighteenth century. (For Monteverdi's
opinion of the relative merits of the violins of Cremona and Brescia, see
p. 109.) The embodiment of Cremona's supremacy was Nicola Amati, and
between the demise of Maggini and the advent of Stradivari's 'long' model
(1690)—and perhaps even as late as 1700—Amati held absolute sway as the
first among European *luthiers*. His influence was decisive on the whole
Cremona school and indeed throughout Europe during the eighteenth
century. As Lütgendorff says, 'Almost every master of first rank from the
beginning of the eighteenth century was directly or indirectly his pupil.'[2]
In the early eighteenth century the prices paid for the Stainer violins sometimes surpassed the Amatis, but Stainer's influence as a maker was less. The
list of Amati's pupils in Cremona reads like an honour roll, among them his
son, Girolamo (II), Andrea Guarneri, Giambattista Rogeri (who died at

---

[1] For detailed information on individual makers, see René Vannes, *Dictionnaire
Universel des Luthiers*, 2nd ed., Brussels, 1951, Vol. 2, 1959; and W. L. von Lütgendorff, *Die Geigen- und Lautenmacher vom Mittelalter bis zur Gegenwart*, 2 vols., Frankfurt, 1904, 3rd ed., 1922. For instruments of Amati, Stainer, and Stradivari, see our
Plates 25, 26a, and 33a.
[2] Op. cit., Vol. II, p. 16.

Brescia), Francesco ('Il Per') Ruggieri, Paolo Grancino (later, at Milan), and, presumably, Antonio Stradivari (see p. 197).

Characteristically, Nicola Amati's violins had highly arched tops, and the tone was a bright, woody soprano, lovely rather than big and full. Apparently with increased volume of tone in mind, Amati began to produce his 'grand' model about 1640 (Plate 25a), widening the upper and lower bouts rather than lengthening the body appreciably. Later, Amati preferred a somewhat smaller model. No maker in the seventeenth century surpassed and few equalled his violins with respect to beauty and finish of craftsmanship and varnish, ease of playing, and beauty of tone. As long as a large volume of sound was not essential, the violins of Nicola Amati remained the ideal of the player and listener; and it is significant that even in the late eighteeenth century his violins cost far more than those of Stradivari.

Jacob Stainer (*c.* 1617–83), born in Absam near Innsbruck in the Tyrol, was the first great Austrian maker. He is a prime example of the effect of time and change on reputation. By the early eighteenth century his fame was so great that his violins commanded prices considerably higher in the London market than either Nicola Amati or Stradivari—a fact that simply reflected esteem and demand. Francesco Maria Veracini (1690–*c.* 1750) and Pietro Locatelli (1695–1764), two of the greatest violin virtuosi of the early eighteenth century, both owned and used Stainer violins; and although Locatelli, at the time of his death, possessed a violin by the brothers Amati (as well as a Stainer of 1667), there is no record of his having a Stradivari. According to Burney, Veracini had two Stainers, 'thought to have been the best in the world. . . . He used to call one of his violins St. Peter, and the other St. Paul.' Burney also reports that Veracini lost both violins in a shipwreck shortly after 1745.[3] On the other hand, Corelli is said to have preferred his Andrea Amati (d. before 1580) above all others, and he also possessed a violin by Matthias Albani, who, like Stainer, was a maker from the Tyrol.[4] According to Van der Straeten, Leopold Mozart is holding his 'beloved' Stainer in the frontispiece of his *Violinschule* (1756). Heinrich von Biber, who (like Leopold Mozart) lived and worked in Salzburg, must have known Stainer's violins very well. At one time, Biber had commissioned a set of Stainer instruments for his former master, the Bishop of Olmütz; and Stainer mentions in his letters that the 'eminent virtuoso' Biber could and would testify to the excellence of his work. We know that J. S. Bach owned a

---

[3] Cf. Plate 30 of Veracini playing the violin (1744; a Stainer?). For the quotation concerning Veracini, see Charles Burney, *General History*, op. cit., reprint, Vol. II, p. 451. For the information about Locatelli, see the inventory of his possessions printed in Arend Koole (in Dutch), *Pietro Antonio Locatelli da Bergamo*, Amsterdam, 1949.

[4] The case of Corelli's Amati violin was supposed to have been painted by A. Caracci according to W. H., A. F., and A. E. Hill, *Violin Makers of the Guarneri Family, 1626–1762: their Life and Work*, London, 1931, p. 109.

Stainer. The inventory compiled of his possessions lists a Stainer violin valued at four times his 'ordinary' violin.[5] As late as 1774, Löhlein, a German theorist, remarks that the Stainers and Amatis with their flute-like tone were preferred to the Stradivaris with their more penetrating and oboe-like tone; and Löhlein himself obviously holds the Stainers and Amatis in highest esteem.[6] He notes their great popularity and remarks that all these instruments are in the hands of connoisseurs and therefore very hard to obtain. Löhlein's high opinion of Stainer is corroborated a few years later (1776) by Hawkins, who says, 'the violins of Cremona are exceeded only by those of Stainer, a German, whose instruments are remarkable for a full and piercing tone. . . .'[7]

Contrary to the usual opinion, Stainer took but one apprentice, and we do not know his name.[8] Apparently Stainer trained no successors, but nevertheless his work served as a model for makers in Austria and Germany as well as those in France, England, and even Italy. There is no proof that Stainer was a pupil of Nicola Amati, although the work of these two famous makers has points of construction in common.

Like the Amatis, the Stainer violins are highly arched in the modelling of the top and back, but they are usually a bit narrower and shorter in the body. One Stainer of 1668 (now owned by the firm of W. E. Hill and Sons of London) has never been opened, and it has been preserved in original condition for the most part (Plate 26a). In particular, the neck, the tailpiece, and the bass-bar inside the instrument are all original. The pegs, bridge, and fingerboard, while not original, have been reproduced in appropriate style. In Plate 26a note the typical straight neck of the time (cf. also Plate 6), and the fingerboard 'wedge'—necessary to make the fingerboard rise at an angle from the straight neck in order to parallel the strings which must rise to the bridge. The neck, however, is not perceptibly shorter than a modern neck. The fingerboard is short (as usual) and the nut is placed nearer the pegbox by about a quarter-inch. The highly arched modelling of the top and back are obvious here—so much so that there is a clear view through the f-holes, made possible by the slight bass bar of the time. Note also the

---

[5] For the Leopold Mozart reference, see E. van der Straeten, *The History of the Violin,* op. cit., Vol. I, p. 160; and cf. our Plate 39a. For Bach, see Philipp Spitta, *The Life of Bach,* English translation, 3 vols., London, 1899, Vol. III, p. 352.

[6] G. Löhlein, *Anweisung zum Violinspielen,* Leipzig, 1774, pp. 129–30.

[7] Sir John Hawkins, *General History,* 5 vols., London, 1776. For the quotation, see the reprint (London, 1875), Vol. II, note at the bottom of p. 688.

[8] See Walter Senn, *Jacob Stainer der Geigenmacher zu Absam,* Innsbruck, 1951. Senn (p. 15) is the source for the revised birthdate, c. 1617, thought for a long time to have been 1621. For another interesting study on Stainer, see Kenneth Skeaping, 'Some Speculations on a Crisis in the History of the Violin' in *The Galpin Society Journal,* Vol. VIII (March 1955). For Stainer labels, see E. N. Doring in *Violins and Violinists,* March–April 1955, pp. 44–50.

beautiful scroll. Sometimes in a Stainer violin (and others of the time) the scroll is replaced by the head of a lion or even by a gargoyle.

The old type of neck was not mortised into the top block, as it is today, but simply glued on and then fastened by nails driven through from inside the block into the base of the neck (see Plate 34). The old neck was less capable of withstanding modern string tensions than the mortised neck bent back at a slight angle (cf. Plate 26 and Plate 6). The nailing also explains the fatter base of the old neck.

The Stainer violins, so sought after in their own time and throughout the eighteenth century, were inspired by ideals of violin making shared by the Nicola Amatis, and both suffered the same fate after 1800, when all violins were subjected to certain constructional changes to increase their volume and brilliance. The highly arched and sweet-toned Stainers and Amatis, intended for chamber music, did not respond to these changes sufficiently to be used by soloists in large halls or in competition with a symphony orchestra in concertos. Consequently their reputation declined in the nineteenth century among violinists who found the flat-modelled Stradivaris and Guarneris more adaptable to altered circumstances and to their needs for brilliance and power (cf. Plate 26).

In spite of intensive efforts of a number of scholars, there are still numerous obscurities about the life and origins of Antonio Stradivari (1644?–1737). It cannot be proved, for instance, that the most famous son of Cremona was actually born in Cremona, although there is no doubt that he was married and spent his entire long and productive life there. We are wholly dependent on two violin labels of 1665 and 1666—the latter, at least, apparently genuine—for the statement that Stradivari was the pupil of Nicola Amati. Although Andrea Guarneri is named in a document as the apprentice of Nicola Amati, there is no such proof in the case of Stradivari. His birthdate has also been the subject of prolonged investigation and controversy (for this, pro and con, see the Appendix).

At first Stradivari's instruments came under the influence of his supposed teacher, Nicola Amati, including those fashioned after the model of Amati's 'grand' pattern (1684–90). But all his work exhibited a strong personality. His violins were more masculine than the Amatis, and they gradually tended toward the flat-modelled body that later became characteristic. The beautiful workmanship, quality of wood, and varnish were obvious from the beginning. The instruments made up to the year 1690 are today generally called 'Amatisé' to indicate that they were still, broadly speaking, under the influence of Nicola Amati.

Even before 1690, Stradivari's experiments, which distinguished his work throughout his life, had been extensive; and from c. 1690, these experiments were probably related increasingly to the musical demands of a small but important minority of virtuosi who were seeking greater reserves of power than the Amatis and Stainers afforded. Significantly, this was the time of rapid advances in the sonata and the new instrumental concerto. One thinks immediately of Corelli, Albinoni, and Torelli, not to mention Walther and Biber, all of whom were writing new and advanced works during the last twenty years of the seventeenth century. In the concerto, especially, the soloist needed increased power to compete with the orchestra, and in some cases to fill larger halls. The violin maker's problem was to furnish greater power while retaining beauty of tone and ease of playing. Stradivari's many experiments must be viewed against this background.

At any rate, after 1690 Stradivari's efforts took a new form in his so-called 'long' pattern. To satisfy the needs described above, and probably inspired by the earlier and powerful Maggini violins of Brescia, Stradivari increased the length of the violin body from fourteen inches to a typical fourteen and five-sixteenths. But he kept the upper and lower bouts somewhat narrower in proportion, giving the appearance of an elongated instrument (Plate 25b). This model did not give all the desired results, and about 1700 he abandoned it, returning to a model about fourteen inches in length. With the 'Betts' violin of 1704 Stradivari succeeded in producing an instrument of classic proportions, which became the model for his later violins and for many other makers thereafter. The so-called 'golden' period had begun.

A few of Stradivari's violins had special embellishments on scrolls and ribs, and some had inlaid purfling. The earliest of these ornamented instruments was the 'Hellier' violin of 1679. Stradivari also made a few violas, and he succeeded in establishing a standard model for the cello.

After the death of Nicola Amati (1684), Stradivari's reputation rapidly increased. His instruments were highly prized, although not above those of Stainer and Amati. The majority of players were still using violins in private homes and small halls to which the tone of the Amatis and Stainers was perfectly suited. Stradivari violins did not become the rage until the end of the eighteenth century, when they were introduced to Paris by Viotti. After 1800, for reasons already suggested (p.·197), the violins of Stradivari and Guarneri became the first choice of concert violinists. (For the eighteenth-century violins of Stradivari, see p. 317).

In addition to the great makers, there was a number of distinguished makers of the second class. Paolo Albani from Cremona is a good example. Goffredo Cappa, who assiduously copied Amati, and his pupil, Carlo Giuseppe Testore, worked in nearby Saluzzo. In Milan, the Grancino family made noteworthy instruments, and the same may be said of the Tononi family in Bologna. In Rome, the German-born David Tecchler modelled his violins first on Stainer and later on Amati. The famous and numerous Gagliano clan originated in Naples at the end of the seventeenth century. In

Mittenwald in the Tyrol, the Klotz family began with Mathias I (b. 1656), and from him date a long line of makers whose mass production earned their instruments (and especially imitations of these) the name of 'Midwalders' in the eighteenth century. Matthias Albani (1621–1712) whose models were based on those of Stainer and Amati, also came from the Tyrol. In Holland, Hendrik Jacobs (1629/30–99) was an imitator of Amati, frequently using the 'grand' pattern.[9] The day of the great makers in France had not yet come, although Nicholas (III) Médard (b. 1628) of Nancy may be mentioned as a superior maker. In England no violin maker of more than local importance can be cited until the advent of Barak Norman (b. about 1678).

A special kind of 'folk' violin makes its appearance in Norway in the seventeenth century. It was called *Harding fele* (meaning, in Norwegian, 'fiddle from Hardanger', a Norwegian province), and the oldest known specimen is dated 1651. Besides the regular four strings, this instrument has four 'sympathetic' strings (early specimens have only two or three such strings). The latter are not bowed but vibrate in 'sympathy' with the four bowed strings. The bridge is flatter than in a regular violin, making polyphonic playing easier. The bowed strings for the *Harding fele* may be tuned in several ways, for example: a d' a' e″ (or transposed literally a third higher: c' f' c″ g″), and c' g' c″ e″. The body of a typical *Harding fele* is a bit smaller than that of the standard violin, and from its inception the instrument was commonly decorated with inlays and other ornaments.[10]

Details of the seventeenth-century violin. The Talbot manuscript

Today we are obliged to study the instruments of the old makers as we find them after centuries of use and alteration. Some old violins are still in excellent condition, but even so a violin that has not been altered to meet the varying needs of violinists over the years is a rare exception (cf. the 1668 Stainer, mentioned above). On the other hand, art objects and records of the time furnish valuable evidence of the state of the violin as it existed in the last years of the seventeenth century. A precious document of this sort is the James Talbot manuscript, found in Christ Church Library, Oxford.[11] It was written between 1685 and 1701, and contains detailed measurements of wind and bowed stringed instruments. Talbot's information is sufficiently rare to

[9] Cf. Plate 25a. For photographs of violins by Jacobs and other Dutch makers, see Max Möller, *The Violin-Makers of the Low Countries*, Amsterdam, 1955. The frequent appearance of the violin in Dutch painting of the time proves the use of the instrument in Dutch social life, but not necessarily that the instrument was of native make.

[10] For this see *Sohlmans Musiklexikon*, Stockholm, 1950; and Gurvin and Anker, *Musiklexikon*, Oslo, 1949. For a photograph of the instrument, see Buchner, op. cit., No. 314. In the photograph just mentioned, one peg of the instrument is missing, giving only seven tuning-pegs instead of eight.

[11] See 'James Talbot's Manuscript' in *The Galpin Society Journal*, Part I by Anthony Baines, Vol. I, 1948; Part II (on bowed stringed instruments) by Robert Donington, Vol. III, 1950.

deserve attention; and while we cannot know that it is completely accurate, the copious corrections in the manuscript imply that the author intended it to be as accurate as possible. Some of the information can easily be corroborated. When Talbot says that the violin body is fourteen inches in length, we know this is correct from the measurements of many instruments of the time; and it is also the modern measurement. Similarly, pictorial evidence confirms Talbot's measurement of eight inches for the length of the fingerboard, about two and a half inches shorter than the modern one.

There are some surprises. From the end of Talbot's fingerboard to the bridge is five inches, and this, added to the length of the fingerboard, makes the length of the playing string thirteen inches, as it usually is today. This length, which is as much as a half-inch longer than one would expect about 1700[12] cannot have been achieved by moving the bridge back toward the tailpiece, as was sometimes done (cf. p. 110). Talbot says explicitly, 'Place Bridge even wth [*sic*] Notch or [of?] *f* of the Sounding holes'. Consistent with the modern length of playing string, Talbot reports that the length of neck from 'nutt to belly' is five and a quarter inches, a length very close to the modern measurement, the violin neck about 1700 being generally shorter than this. The width of Talbot's fingerboards appears to be about an eighth-inch wider at the nut than the modern one (intimating that the strings at this point were a trifle wider apart?) but about the same width as the modern one at the point where the old fingerboard ends (that is, the old fingerboard was about eight inches long, the modern one about ten and a half). These fingerboard dimensions are also characteristic of the Stainer mentioned above (pp. 196–7). Talbot's bridge, however, is slightly narrower than the modern bridge, perhaps (but not necessarily) implying that the strings were set somewhat closer together at the bridge-end. The most surprising figure is the one-inch measurement given by Talbot for the height of the bridge—the modern bridge is about one and a quarter inches high—particularly in conjunction with the three and a half inch figure for the depth of the violin under the bridge (that is, the height of the violin from belly to back). The latter measurement seems preposterous. The corresponding measurement of the typical modern flat model is hardly two inches, and Talbot's measurement would make a regular tub of the violin. It is possible that Talbot meant two and a half inches, which would be more consistent with a model of fairly high arch, such as the Stainer and Amati models prevalent in England about 1700. Judging by the evidence of pictures, the height of the bridge varied considerably, but Talbot's height of one inch seems to be too low, even for these early times. On the other hand, the

---

[12] The treatise *Nolens Volens* (1695; see our p. 245) says, 'First cause the length of the Strings extended between Nut and Bridge to be the same as that in the Example.' The 'Example' is a fingerboard, and the length between nut and bridge is 12 ⅟₁₆ inches.

lower bridge is compatible with the relatively low tensions on the strings. Lower tension is implied by the slenderer and shorter bass-bars removed from these early instruments. With such weak bass-bars the tops of the violins would eventually have collapsed under the increased tensions to which they were subjected after 1800. Significantly, Talbot's sound post is the 'thickness [of a] goosequill'—a diameter that would hardly be sufficient to support modern tensions. Talbot adds: 'Sound post under treble string . . . between back & belly under bridge or there about accordg. to discretion of Artist.' He says of the 'Barr' [Bass-bar] merely that it is 'glewd on the bass side of the same wood within the belly'. By the 'same wood' he must mean the wood he has just described as composing the belly: 'Belly of Cullin Cliff' [see note 14 below]—in his mysterious words. Talbot continues: 'Back, Neck & Ribs of Air [= Airwood = oriental maple].[13] Pegs of dryd Box Ebony or any hardest wood: Finger-board finest Russian Ebony very hard wood & brings forth clearer sound of Instrt by hard stopping: commonly of Air wood. . . . Tail-piece same wth Finger-board . . . Button same wth Pegs as the Nutt is. Bridge same wth back. . . . Best strings are Roman 1st & 2d of Venice Catlins: 3d & 4th best be finest & smoothest Lyons all 4 differ in size. Ag[utter].'[14]

[13] George Hart (*The Violin*, London, 1887, p. 62, note 1) explains the derivation of 'air-wood' as follows: plane-tree = 'oriental maple' = 'morgenländischer Ahorn'. From 'Ahorn' is probably derived the term 'airwood', often corrupted into 'hairwood'. Respecting the lute, Thomas Mace says, 'the airwood is absolutely the best; and next to that our English maple'.

[14] A catling is a gut string, and this name was used for the smallest string on a lute. As to 'Cullin Cliff', Bessaraboff (op. cit., p. 223) quotes Mace (p. 49): 'The *Best Wood* [for Lute bellies] is called *Cullin-Cliff*; and it is no other than the finest sort of *Firr*, and the choicest part of *That Firr*. I have seen some [bellies] of *Cyprus very Good*, but none like *Cullin-Cliff*.' Bessaraboff (p. 419, note 488) then cites Canon Galpin: 'Cullin-cliff is the wood of the Silver Fir (*Pinus Picea*) which abounds in the forests of Central Europe. It is soft, white, light with little resin and was especially used for the sound-boards of musical instruments. The name, which is a corruption of "Cologne-cleft" would imply that it was prepared in the Rhineland for that pur-pose.'
'Ag.' doubtless refers to Ralph Agutter, a violin and instrument maker of the time, who must have supplied James Talbot with much of the above information concerning the violin. We can identify Agutter through the pages of the newspapers of the time. The *London Gazette* for 24 September 1683 speaks of 'Ralph Agutter, violin-maker' [in the Strand]; and the same magazine for 12 June 1685 has a notice by Ralph Agutter offering a reward for news of a lost 'black Leather Violin-case, with a Violin in it, that is all inlaid on the sides with Grayhounds and Birds, and within it a printed Inscription in Latin of the place where it was made; and on the Finger-board is engraven on Mother of Pearl the Howards Coat of Arms'. Agutter appears again in the same journal for 23 September 1695, advertising the sale of 'Twelve Sonata's [*sic*] (newly come over from Rome) in 3 Parts . . . by A. Corelli . . . 1695'. For this, see Michael Tilmouth, *A Calendar of References to Music in News-papers published in London and the Provinces (1660-1719)*, published as 'R. M. A. [Royal Musical Association] Research Chronicle No. 1', Cambridge, 1961.

H.V.P.–P

The Talbot manuscript is the most detailed document concerning the violin at this time, and Talbot's information is typical of the violin about 1700 with respect to the body length, the bass-bar, the sound post, and the kind of woods used. Talbot's figures for the width of the upper and lower bouts (six and three-quarters and eight and three-eighths respectively), the depth of the 'Rimms' (one and a half), and the depth under the bridge, all point to an instrument resembling the 'grand' pattern Amati. This is hardly surprising in view of the fact that a number of Cremona violins were purchased for the King's Musick shortly after the Restoration, and these fine instruments were the focus of much admiration by players and imitation by makers.[15] The length of playing string and the length of neck are very close to modern measurements, while the bridge is exceptionally low.

Bridges of this time must have varied a good deal in height, shape, and placement. In his *The Division Viol* (1665), Christopher Simpson shows a rounded bridge for the viol, which he recommends so that each string 'may be hit with a bolder touch of the bow'. The fingerboard is to be of a proportionate roundness to the bridge. The old-style bridge had an interior arch (cf. p. 110), but at the end of the seventeenth century this arch was supplanted by a bar across the lower part, much as it is now. Among the surviving bridges is one that Stradivari made (1690) for the 'Tuscan' viola (Plate 27). Stradivari's bridges approach the modern one, but they are a little thicker, lower, and narrower, and somewhat more open in design.[16] A particularly interesting feature of the 'Tuscan' viola bridge is the ornamentation front and back (Plate 27). It shows that the bridge has not been cut down, since the black outline at the top of the bridge remains intact. From the purely decorative point of view, the two figures holding up the bridge convey the sense of arrested motion so typical of Baroque art. *En passant*, the shape of the violin itself has certain correspondences to the typical arches, curves, and ornamental features characteristic of Baroque art in general. Could it be that the outlined 'S' in the middle of the 'Tuscan' bridge is a deliberate Stradivari initial?

It is almost impossible to generalize about the arch of the violin bridge. Judging from iconography, some are flatter in curve than that used today. Still others use a curve very similar to the modern bridge. In any case, the bridge is ordinarily placed on a line with the notches in the middle of the f-holes, as recommended by Talbot (just as it is today), but it is sometimes placed farther down toward the tailpiece (cf. Plate 20 and p. 110).

[15] See H. C. De Lafontaine, *The King's Musick*, entry for 24 October 1662: £40 to John Bannister 'for two Cremona violins bought by him for his Majesty's service, and also £10 for strings for two years'. £20 was a high price, ordinary violins being nearer half this cost.

[16] For other examples of Stradivari bridges, see Hill, *Stradivari*, op. cit., p. 206.

Material and thickness of string. Pitch. Tension. Volume of sound

Presumably violin strings were all gut, although it is hard to believe that players could have been happy with a gut G string, which gives a poor response. The use of this lowest string increased markedly in the music of the late seventeenth century, but if players at this time changed to a silver-wound G string, there is no mention of it in the sources. In his *Traite de la viole* of 1687, Rousseau reports the use of brass- and silver-wound strings, but he does not approve of putting them on the viol. He notes their use in England on the *viole d'amour*, but he says nothing about them on the violin. If satisfactory wound or metal strings were available for any or all the violin strings, violinists did not see fit to use them; and one assumes that their preference was based on very good reasons, such as the tone quality, cheapness, and availability of gut strings. Other things being equal, metal or wound strings would have been preferable since, quite apart from the poor response of the gut G, gut strings as a whole are not as durable as metal and they vary considerably in trueness. That gut strings broke frequently, even under the lower tensions of those days, is shown by the considerable sums spent for their replacement (cf. note 15 above).

The thickness of strings used on these old violins is all but impossible to determine. In the Talbot manuscript the principal centres of string making are named, but nothing is said about the gauge of the strings—merely that they were all different in size. Actually, we know next to nothing about the exact thickness of violin strings at this time, obviously because there were no clear standards. Thickness or thinness of string depends on individual instruments (which then, and even now, exhibit great variety), on standards of pitch, and on the individual needs and situations of players. All these factors made necessary a variety of gauges for the same string. This is doubtless the reason that the thickness of strings is described in relative terms by contemporary writers. In his *Comparison between French and Italian Music* (1702), François Raguenet, a French author, says of the Italians:

'Their violins are mounted with strings much larger than ours; their bows are longer, and they can make their instruments sound as loud again as we do ours. The first time I heard our band in the Opera after my return out of Italy, my ears had been so used to the loudness of the Italian violins that I thought ours had all been bridled.'[17]

Raguenet does not mention the relative pitch or the tensions of strings in France and Italy, but these must have been factors also. Perhaps the new 'long' model Stradivari violins as well as the longer, larger, and stronger bows had something to do with the power of the Italian instruments.

[17] From the English translation attributed to J. E. Galliard (1709), reprinted in *The Musical Quarterly*, July 1946, p. 431.

Georg Muffat, a German musician of Alsatian extraction, who spent six years in Paris studying Lully's style (cf. p. 257, note 7), relates thickness (strength) of strings to pitch in his *Florilegium Secundum* of 1698. Even so, we cannot be entirely sure of the implication of his words:

'The pitch to which the Lullists [the French] ordinarily tune their instruments is, in general, about a whole tone, and in the Opera, about a minor third, below our German pitch. The so-called [German] Cornett-pitch appears to them [the French] too forced and squalling. If I were free to choose without hindrance, I should choose before others the so-called Choir-pitch which has sufficient sweetness mixed with vivacity, using strings that are a little stronger.'
('Der Thon nach welchem die Lullisten ihre Instrumenta stimmen, ist ins gemein umb einen gantzen, ja in Teatralischen Sachen umb ander-thalb Thon niedriger als unser Teutscher. Der so genante Cornett-Thon scheinet ihnen gar zugezwungen and schreyig. Wann mir frey wäre bey kein entgegen-stehenden Respect, so wurde ich den soge-nanter Chor-Thon wegen gnugsammer der Lieblligkeit eingemengter Lebhafftigkeit mit wenig stärckern Seiten vor andern erkiesen.')

'Cornett-pitch' was often the same as 'choir-pitch', but not necessarily so. Here Muffat implies that choir-pitch is lower than cornet-pitch and that his first choice would be a pitch between that of France and Germany—perhaps a semitone above French pitch. In any case, he would use stronger (= thicker) strings. Presumably he means 'thicker' than the strings normally used by the Germans playing at cornett-pitch—not 'thicker' than those used by the French. Other things being equal, thicker strings go with lower pitch.[18] Obviously, such things as tensions were not always equal, because otherwise the French with their lower pitch would have thicker strings than the Germans; and the Italians, having much larger strings than the French, would have strung their violins with regular ropes.

The truth is, of course, that both pitch and tension fluctuated exceed-ingly. Pitch was so variable from country to country and even from town to town that it is impossible to deal with it in any absolute sense. When Raguenet speaks of the 'Italians' he is being ambiguous, perhaps purposely and necessarily, about relating thickness of string to pitch in a country where some cities had a high pitch and others a low one (e.g. Venice and Rome, respectively). As to tension, the details of construction of the violin, such as the slighter bass-bar, argue that the violin was generally under less tension than it is now. However, these lower tensions were not uniform nor

---

[18] Later Reichardt (1776) and Schindler (1855) both relate low pitch in orchestras to thicker strings. See Arthur Mendel, 'On the Pitches in Use in Bach's Time—II' in *The Musical Quarterly*, October 1955, p. 471 and p. 474.

did they *necessarily* imply lower pitch, because a number of factors contributed to tension in relation to pitch—among them: the gut strings, their thickness, the relative height of the bridge, and the angle of the neck and fingerboard. Nor is there a direct relationship between the amount of tension and the resulting volume of sound. However, lower tensions do tend to argue for less brilliance, and this is one of the attributes which doubtless distinguished the sound of the violin about 1700 from that today.

Indeed, for us the valuable part of Raguenet's and Muffat's testimony is not so much what they say about pitch as what they suggest about the sound of the violin. Their accounts emphasize the important point that there were marked differences in the degree of volume and brilliance of violin sound in different countries about 1700. From the accounts of Muffat and Raguenet it becomes clear that the volume produced by French violins was much less than that of the Italian violins strung with thicker strings, presumably under higher tensions. Similarly, the sound of the French violins was softer and less brilliant than the German violins which were tuned a whole tone or even a minor third above the pitch used by the French. The Germans and Italians were simply striving for greater volume and brilliance than the French, and this tendency was in accord with their advanced notions about violin music and technique. In this respect they exhibited symptoms and inclinations that seem to be common to virtuosi of every time and place.[19]

By the end of the seventeenth century, as the violin strengthened its position, there was less diversity in the models that comprised the family. Stradivari's 'classical' model established a standard for the violin from 1700 on, and his modification of the size of the cello had a similar stabilizing effect. The viola, made in alto and tenor sizes, presumably to correspond to the tone qualities of those registers, tended to be smaller than the instruments made before 1660, when large violas were the rule. The viola not only diminished somewhat in size during this period but also in quantity of production. The demand for it was considerably less from 1650 to 1750 than it had been earlier. The reason was that the musical texture of a typical ensemble was now in four parts, which used one (or two) viola, rather than in five parts, which normally used two (or three) violas. Furthermore, the

---

[19] Perhaps loudness and brilliance were incompatible with the use of the mute, which is not called for in the advanced music of the Italians or the Germans during this period. The mute is first mentioned by a Frenchman, Mersenne (1636). It is used occasionally in the opera or vocal music of the late seventeenth century: specifically in Purcell's *Fairy Queen* of 1692 ('violins with sourdines'), in Lully's *Armide* of 1686 ('*Il faut jouer cecy avec des sourdines*'), and in Schmeltzer's *Memorie Dolorose* (1679; '*con sordini*'). The fact that the last is German music does not disturb the point, since the violin in this case serves as accompaniment to vocal music of sombre character, quite removed from loudness and brilliance.

most prevalent form of chamber music, the trio sonata, generally used no viola part at all.

The rapid evolution of the violin as an instrument and the accompanying musical developments tended to push the viol family still further into the background, although an exception should be made in the case of France, where a strong school of viol playing and viol music culminated in the figure of Marin Marais in the early eighteenth century. However, even this viol school centred primarily about the bass viol. The latter instrument, which alone of the viol family survived the popularity of the violin after 1700, was also influenced at times in certain points of construction by the cello.

When Mace's *Musick's Monument* appeared in 1676, the violin had been in existence long enough so that one could speak of 'old' violins, and this was still truer of the more ancient viol. The perennial argument of the relative value of old as opposed to new instruments already makes its appearance in Mace, who extols the advantages of old viols and their varnishes with arguments that, except for their archaic language, could have been written yesterday (old spelling, punctuation, and italics retained):

> 'The *Reasons* for which, I can no further *Dive* into, than to say; I Apprehend, that by *Extream* Age, the *Wood*, (and *Those Other Adjuncts*) *Glew*, *Parchment*, *Paper*, *Lynings of Cloath*, (as some use;) but above All, the *Vernish*; *These* are *All*, so very much (by *Time*) *Dryed*, *Lenefied*, *made Gentle*, *Rarified*, or (to say *Better*, even) *Ayrified*; so that *That Stiffness*, *Stubbornness*, or *Clunguiness*, which is *Natural* to *such Bodies*, are so *Debilitated*, and made *Plyable*, that the *Pores* of the *Wood*, have a *more*, and *Free Liberty* to *Move*, *Stir*, or *Secretly Vibrate*; by which means the *Air*, (which is the *Life of All Things*) both *Animate*, and *Inanimate*) has a more *Free*, and *Easie Recourse*, to *Pass*, and *Re-pass*, &c. Whether I have hit upon the *Right Cause*, I know not; but sure I am, that *Age Adds Goodness* to *Instruments*; therefore They have the *Advantage* of all our *Late* [i.e., modern] *Work-men*' (pp. 245–6).

The Bow

In the second half of the seventeenth century the violin bow was the object of intense experimentation, corresponding to the musical ferment at the same time (see ch. 10). The national differences in types of music account for differences in types of bows: the relatively straight bow stick for French dance music, the straight (or slightly outward curved) and longer bow of the sonata players in Italy, and, among the Germans, bows of varying lengths with a more pronounced convex curve, perhaps related to their penchant for multiple stops.

It has long been an article of quaint belief that the violin bow prior to the time of Tourte (*c.* 1780) was a clumsy implement unworthy of the wonderful violins of Stainer, Amati, and Stradivari with which it must have been used. This is a typical example of those folk tales which are uncritically passed down from one generation to another. On the face of things, it makes no sense that a great maker, having lavished the most intensive effort on perfecting a beautiful instrument, would neglect the bow, the 'soul' of the violin and the principal means by which the beautiful tone of his instrument must be produced.

In the Ansley Salz Collection of stringed instruments and bows, housed in the University of California at Berkeley, there is a bow probably made about 1700, perhaps by Stradivari, which as a playing stick must be considered the equal of a fine Tourte bow.[20] Furthermore, this bow (Plate 28a and b) is made of Pernambuco wood (a superior variety of brazilwood), although current mythology credits the first use of this wood to François Tourte about seventy-five years later. The 'Stradivari' bow must have been executed on special commission, and it probably owes its very existence to its external beauty, exceptional playing qualities, and commercial value. The frog is made in the form of an ivory pandurina (resembling a lute), between whose golden strings the bow hairs are interleaved (Plate 28b). The ivory pandurina is movable by a screw arrangement similar to that used today, being regulated by a fluted screw tip, also carved in ivory. The stick itself is fluted in the upper three-quarters of its length. The total length of the bow is twenty-eight and a quarter inches, the free (playing) hair measuring a scant twenty-four.

Compared to the modern bow (which is normally twenty-nine and a half inches with free hair of twenty-five and a half), the 'Stradivari' bow is lighter and shorter, and it has less momentum; but it has similar remarkable qualities of balance and response. The balance, however, is different, the balance point being lower toward the frog, since, among other things, the head is lighter and less massive. These differences have interesting consequences. Using the 'old' bow in experiments, modern concert violinists have been able to produce certain types of bowings with greater technical ease and with better musical results than by using a genuine Tourte bow; and this is true not only of 'old' music, where the result could be predicted, but also in certain rapid passages and bowings in Viotti and even in Beethoven and Mendelssohn. In particular, the 'Stradivari' bow is superior to the modern bow in articulation of detached notes in the upper third of the bow.

[20] Henri Poidras in his *Critical and Documentary Dictionary of Violin Makers old and modern,* Rouen, 2 vols., 1928–30, Plates 49–50, Vol. 2, opposite p. 200, illustrates this bow, calling it unequivocally a 'Stradivari' bow. There is no documentation nor further text concerning this bow. For positive evidence that Stradivari made bows, see p. 328.

In effect, the bow produces a crystal-clear *spiccato* sound of its own free will, without actually bouncing, and the brilliance of sixteenth-note passages when played near the point is especially noticeable. For a virtuoso there is no difficulty in producing the 'flying staccato'.

Because of the 'give' of the bow hair, it is somewhat easier to produce triple stops with this bow than with the modern bow, but hammered chords at the frog cannot be brought out with the same force. The modern bow has the advantage in a long cantabile line of melody. The 'old' bow is more difficult to control in its upper third in a drawn-out cantabile, and, being lighter, shorter, and using a narrower ribbon of hair, the 'old' bow is not able to sustain the singing phrase with as much power or with as long a bow stroke as the modern bow. In these 'old' bows there is no ferrule, as there is in the modern bow, to spread out the hair in a firm ribbon.

There was a far greater variety of lengths, shapes, weights, and balances among the early bows than obtains in the standardized bow today. There were undoubtedly many poor 'old' bows, and an inexpensive modern bow, standardized on the Tourte model, is quite likely a better bow than a bow of comparable quality and cost in early times. However, the 'Stradivari' bow serves to underscore the important axiom that no player, composer, or maker worth his salt will permit his artistic and expressive efforts to be cancelled by one weak link; and it is unthinkable that the finest craftsmen of earlier times would allow their beautiful instruments to be played to disadvantage for want of bows of comparable effectiveness, subtlety, and beauty. The fact that bow makers remained anonymous before 1700 does not mean that they made bad bows or were unaware of the importance of the bow to the player.

The 'Stradivari' bow may be viewed as a triumph of bow making which represents not only the achievement of perfect balance but also the culmination of certain tendencies that had long been discernible (cf. p. 112): namely, the straightening of the bow stick, the formation of a distinct bow head, and the development of a movable nut to facilitate tightening the hair at variable tensions. The bow head had been developing for some time (cf. Plate 12 and p. 46); and by 1700, the approximate date of the 'Stradivari' bow, its shape resembled a pike's head. This is the typical head of the early eighteenth-century bow. The 'hatchet' head (Plate 35, No. 7), transitional to the modern, Tourte-designed head (Plate 28a), appears some fifty years later.

The movable nut of the 'Stradivari' bow represents a considerable advance in design. Prior to the last years of the seventeenth century, the bow nut was either unmovable, being strung up at fixed tension, or it could be tightened in one of several ways. The dentated (*crémaillère*) bow must have come in some time between 1650 and 1700. In the dentated bow (cf. Plate 29a) the nut is movable and is held tight in one of several positions by engaging the iron catch over one of the teeth. The slot-and-notch bow

(Plate 29b), although less satisfactory, was also in existence. A beautiful bow of this sort is in the Ashmolean Museum (Hill Collection) at Oxford. The modern screw to move the frog and tighten or loosen the hair as desired (cf. Plate 29c) must have been invented in the last years of the seventeenth century. In the Hill Collection of bows (London), a bow in original condition has the date 1694 stamped on its movable frog, which is adjusted by a screw (Plate 29d).

The typical wood used in the bow during this time was snakewood, also called 'specklewood' by Talbot and others. Rousseau refers to a current belief that the best wood for bows was 'bois de la Chine',[21] but he says it is not indispensable as some claim. The 'Stradivari' bow described above is made of Pernambuco (brazil) wood, a wood that was recommended by Trichet about 1630 (see p. 114). The hair of the bow comes invariably from white horses (bass bows often use black hair).

About 1700 the bow was, for the most part, shorter than the modern bow. Nevertheless, in the experimental spirit of the times, there were also a few bows of considerable length, exceeding in isolated cases that of the modern Tourte bow. Tourte, therefore, not merely lengthened the bow but in some cases shortened it—or more exactly, he standardized the bow and brought to it his unexcelled craftsmanship. Just as in the last years of the seventeenth century Stradivari produced a 'long' model violin, a few bow makers also produced a 'long' model bow, and probably for similar experimental reasons, related to increased variety and volume of sound. Simpson speaks of a viol bow of about twenty-seven inches of hair between the two places where the hairs are fastened at each end; and if by this he means 'free' hair, this measurement would make the playing hair of his bow substantially longer than that of the Tourte bow which averages twenty-five and a half inches.[22]

Simpson is speaking of a viol bow, but in the eighteenth century Veracini's violin bow, represented in a portrait of 1744 (see Plate 30) was perhaps as much as twenty-eight inches of playing hair in length, if the picture of

[21] Rousseau, 1687, p. 39. The context makes clear that Rousseau really means 'wood from China'. Could it have been a wood resembling brazilwood? The answer is probably 'no'.

[22] Christopher Simpson, *The Division-Viol*, 2nd ed., London, 1665, p. 2. First edition entitled *The Division-Violist*, 1659. Facsimile of 2nd ed., published in London, 1955. Gerald Hayes (*Musical Instruments 1500–1750*, op. cit., Vol. II, p. 63 note, p. 122 note, and p. 37 note) claims that other measurements of Simpson are too large to be reasonable, on the grounds that he was speaking of a smaller inch than is used today. Therefore, in Hayes's view, the twenty-seven inches was somewhat less. This is a possibility, but there is no evidence that the standard British inch in Simpson's time deviated appreciably from modern standards.

Dutch paintings of the seventeenth century show a number of long viol bows. See *The Journal of the Galpin Society* (Vol. VI), July 1953, following p. 48, especially Plate 5. The player is gripping the bow-stick several inches above the frog.

him is in true proportion. This is two and a half inches longer than a modern bow, and such lengths are exceptional, of course, even by the standards of the Italian sonata players. As a matter of fact, the twenty-four inches of playing hair of the 'Stradivari' bow is probably a bit above average, the latter being closer to twenty-one or twenty-two. Roger North reported that the Italian violinist Nicola Matteis used 'a very long bow', and elsewhere North calls Matteis's bow 'bipedalian' (= two feet)—significantly, the length of the 'Stradivari' bow.[23] The dance bow of the French was shorter; and very short bows appear in some pictures and treatises (e.g. Playford's *Introduction*, 1658). The bow shown in the Dou painting of a violinist (1665; Plate 22) is about twenty-one inches of playing hair. The Weigel bow (cf. Plate 37) measures about nineteen inches of playing hair, and two bows with *cremaillère* in Vienna, about twenty-one inches. Finally, the Talbot manuscript gives lengths for bows, but does not specify whether these measurements apply to the total length of the bow or to the playing (free) hair. Talbot says the 'hair should be full. Bow of violin not under 24 [inches] from there to 27 1/2 at most. 27, 26–25 1/2 Solo-Bow'. On the whole, it is unlikely that English violinists were using bows with twenty-seven and a half inches of free hair (in spite of Simpson's explicit measurement of the viol bow) when the majority of advanced Italians were using not more than twenty-four or twenty-five inches of playing hair in their bows. If these figures of Talbot refer to total length, the playing hair of the bow measured about twenty to twenty-three and a half inches, which would be more likely and usual. Talbot does not mention a device for regulating the tension of the hair. He says simply 'Bow of fine Speckled-wood has two mortises to wch the hair fastened and one at the head the other towds the bottom or back part of Nutt'.

Summary

In the half-century after 1650 both violin and bow made considerable progress, commensurate with musical demands and changes. Even though there were some failures in this period of arduous experiments, the violin benefited greatly from the attentions of first-rate craftsmen. In the best efforts of Stainer and Nicola Amati, the violin reached a state of perfection in terms of the musical needs of the time that could hardly have been surpassed. The numerous experiments of Stradivari in the last years of the seventeenth century did not mean that he was unappreciative of the wonderful violins made by his predecessors. Rather, Stradivari's experiments meant that the musical needs of his time were undergoing a rapid change. His 'long' model of 1690–1700 was one attempt to supply these needs; and while this model was not entirely successful, its partial failure was doubtless necessary to

[23] See *Roger North on Music*, edited by John Wilson, London, 1959, p. 168 and p. 309.

show Stradivari the way to his magnificent 'classical' model, first embodied in the 'Betts' violin of 1704. About 1700, then, the Italians were still in the forefront of violin making, as they were in violin music and violin playing, but it is symptomatic of the musical and technical advances in German-speaking countries that a great maker appeared for the first time outside Italy in the person of Jacob Stainer, an Austrian.

If anything, the progress of the bow was more marked than the violin's. Equally significant is the fact that the bow was clearly recognized as the 'soul' of the instrument. The bow was still far from standardized; and the variety of its lengths and shapes reflected uses as diverse musically and technically as the simplest dance music in France and England on the one hand and the complex bowings of the sonatas and concertos in Germany and Italy on the other. A shorter bow for dance music still persisted in all countries as a distinct type for a specific purpose. However, with the gradual development of the sonata and concerto, longer and longer bows came into use, and the workmanship became more elegant, reflecting the makers' concern with the needs for better balance, flexibility, and response to a far larger variety of bow strokes. The devices for tightening the bow hair were also greatly improved. In the best bows of the time, such as the 'Stradivari' bow (*c.* 1700), described earlier, violinists must already have possessed advantages comparable to those enjoyed by Viotti with a fine Tourte bow a hundred years later.

The last fifty years of the seventeenth century witnessed more than physical changes in the instrument and bow. By 1700 the violin had become relatively respectable. It had ceased to be the exclusive property of a professional class of servant-musicians, and was now being played by amateurs in sufficient numbers to inspire a theoretical literature for their instruction (see p. 244). A primary reason was the expanded musical function of the violin. Violin music was no longer so closely identified with dance music, and the violin and violinist no longer suffered the corresponding social stigma. The remarkable progress of the sonata, the new concerto, and other forms of instrumental music, which are about to be described, were important factors in the increased social and musical prestige of the violin at the end of the seventeenth century.

꙳

CHAPTER TEN

The Violin Music of the
Late Seventeenth Century

T HE intensive experimentation that distinguished the early seventeenth century produced an idiomatic violin music and technique,
and it laid the foundation on which these gains were consolidated and
pushed to new heights by 1700. In the last quarter of the seventeenth century Germany enjoyed a hitherto unparalleled development of violin
virtuosity, and Biber and Walther exploited the resources of the violin to
such a point that Walther in particular could justly be called the Paganini of
the seventeenth century. In Italy Corelli was the first violin composer to
attain lasting stature in the world of music, and in his works violin music
reached a point of genuine maturity where musical and technical considerations were in perfect union.

The technique of the violin advanced rapidly in Italy and Germany, and
the attitudes toward music in these and other countries accentuated national
differences. The Italians had the most numerous and the best makers and
composers, and they experimented most widely with the forms of music,
especially the sonata, the variation, the dance forms, and, at the end of the
century, the concerto. The Germans sympathized with the musical aims of
the Italians for the most part, surpassed them technically, and were particularly fond of the variation and descriptive music. The French were
mainly interested in dances, although they exhibited some interest in the
sonata after 1690. This preoccupation with dance music tended to inhibit
the development of the violin idiom although, at the same time, it required a
highly mannered bowing discipline to satisfy the rhythmic requirements of
the different dances. The English imitated the French in certain respects,
and they did so increasingly after 1660 under the Restoration rule of
Charles II, a thoroughly Frenchified monarch. At the same time, the English
exhibited a more international concern than the French, imitating the new
Italian sonata as well as composing dances, variations, and music in the old
fantasia tradition. However, English musicians were rather more concerned

with dances for the violin than with its use in fancies or sonatas. The prevalence of dance style is implied by the reaction to it. In a 'Note' to his first set of trio sonatas (1683; see p. 237), Purcell says that his models are Italian; and he continues "tis time now . . . to loath the levity, and balladry of our neighbors' (i.e. the French and their dance style).

In any case, violin music enjoyed an increased vogue throughout Europe. It permeated the Church, the theatre, and the chamber, being prominent in the opera, the secular cantata, and in accompaniments to church music; and it was one of the chief agents in advancing the cause of instrumental music as a whole. With some exceptions in the opera, the most important developments in violin technique took place, naturally enough, in the instrumental forms, especially in the sonata, the variation, and, to a lesser extent, the dance; and the development of the violin idiom in these instrumental forms, rather than in the vocal forms, will be the main consideration in what follows. Descriptive music often encouraged the use of certain special effects on the violin (cf. p. 130), and after 1700, the concerto became an increasingly important factor in the development of violin technique (see pp. 333ff.).

In the sonata the violin served the cause of music as much as its own technical development—a necessary distinction at certain times and places. Composers, attracted by the figural and melodic possibilities of the violin, lavished much of their best efforts on the violin sonata, chiefly the trio sonata for two violins and *basso continuo* (cf. p. 133) and the 'solo' sonata for violin and *basso continuo* (the latter type of sonata was much less frequent until 1700). The variation and the related *ostinato* forms—*chaconne, passacaglia, folia (follia)*, and others—were also favourite forms of composition, often stimulating composers to a high degree of technical display. The same is true of the relatively rare *sonata senza basso*, the real solo sonata without accompaniment.

Dance music, traditionally the special province of the violin, continued to be closely associated with it both in social dancing and the more formal ballet and masque. In addition, certain dances ceased to be used for actual dancing. Instead they became 'art' music, and were grouped in suites and in the Italian *sonate da camera*, having, as it were, been kicked off the dance floor and into the more dignified and detached surrounding of private chambers, where as 'chamber' music they amused the players, their friends, and patrons. This dance music still displayed the modesty of its origins, and contributed little to the new violin technique except an articulated style and a mannered bowing discipline. While dance music was an inherent part of the musical life of all countries, it was the primary concern of France and, to a lesser extent, England. This fact helps to explain the relatively low technical level of violin playing in these countries until the eighteenth century. Sporadic efforts in such forms as the individual violin prelude, cultivated largely in England and Germany, or the violin duet for beginners, do not change the perspective of the main developments.

The general evolution of all this music depended on the growing understanding of tonality and modulation. These resources, basic to unity and variety, were essential to pieces of any length that were dependent solely on the abstract designs of purely instrumental music. The one exception was the theme and variations which generally remained in the same key throughout. However, by means of the diversity of successive variations of contrasted character, the theme and variations sought to avoid the monotony inherent in a single tonality. The immense vogue of the variation in the early seventeenth century is a monument to the limited understanding of tonality and modulation at that time. However, as tonality developed in the late seventeenth century, the variation did not immediately and markedly decline in popularity, because it had such inherent musical possibilities and because composers and players recognized its great value as a vehicle for the development of instrumental idioms.

Shortly after the middle of the seventeenth century musical divergences in French and Italian music created an elaborate polemical literature, both amusing and acrimonious, which later degenerated into musical 'wars' in France during the course of the eighteenth century. As far as the violin was concerned, the interests and efforts of the French were firmly centred in the dance, and they were hardly able to comprehend the passionate expression of the Italians or their intense preoccupation with forms like the sonata, whose abstract designs represented nothing to them but pure patterns of tone. To the French the latter were as cold and inexpressive as marble. Fontenelle's question, '*Sonate, que me veux-tu?*' ('O, sonata, what do you wish [to tell] me?') is a clue to the different musical worlds in which the French and Italians moved. Isolated 'sonatistes' such as François Couperin, Rebel, and La Guerre appeared in France in the last years of the seventeenth century, but it was not until the time of Leclair about 1720 that the French really began to follow the model and lead of the Italian sonata.[1] The French were animated by the idea of music as an expression of something, and their music, rooted in the doctrine of imitation of nature, took such tangible and concrete forms as dancing and descriptive music. When Geminiani complained later (1751) of the imitation of the 'Cock, Cuckoo, Owl, and other

[1] However, it is quite likely that professional musicians admired the Italian sonatas and played them at home—as opposed to the general public who 'knew what it liked'. Le Cerf de La Viéville says (*Comparaison de la musique italienne et de la musique françoise,* Brussels, 3 vols., 1704–6, Vol. I, p. 44): 'A great deal of France likes and admires the music of Italians. There are not only professional musicians but persons of quality and prelates who sing and have performed in their houses nothing but Italian pieces and sonatas.'

Birds', he was referring to a lowly manifestation of nature-imitation most commonly found in France and Germany (cf. p. 337, including note 11).

Thus Fontenelle's question was quite natural, but its implication was somewhat misleading. The purely musical patterns of the Italian sonata were 'cold as marble' only in the emotional vacuum of the printed page, for in reality the Italians brought a passionate expression to their music in actual performance. A contemporary wrote of Corelli, 'I never met with any man that suffered his passions to hurry him away so much whilst he was playing on the violin.'[2]

No one country had any particular monopoly on ideas of expression. The attention paid to the strongly contrasted notions of the French and Italians has had the effect of obscuring many an English commentary on the role of music as emotional expression, ranging from the highly personal to the deeply philosophical, although these sentiments are rarely expressed specifically in connexion with the violin. Mace relates a homely and charming tale about his Lute Lesson called 'my Mistress', so named because Mace composed it when his future wife was 'wholly in my fancy, and the chief object, and ruler of my thoughts', and because in retrospect, this piece seemed to express all the qualities of his beloved, the 'Perfect Idea of my living Mistress'.[3] In a less personal vein (p. 152), Mace compares music to language as being unbounded and unlimited in its power of expression in the same way that oratory has powers to move the emotions.

Such ideas are much older than Mace, and so are those notions, also expounded by him, in which music is related to the universe. The ratios of intervals, as the 2 : 1 of the octave, are connected with and symbolize the mysteries and unity of the universe; the basic triad of three notes in harmonious relationship is symbolic of the Trinity itself; and good and evil have their counterparts in the good and bad ratios of concord and discord. Christopher Simpson, a fellow Englishman and contemporary, speaks of similar things in his *The Division-Viol* (1665), and he adds his speculations on the correspondence of the seven notes of the diatonic scale, the seven-stringed lyre of Orpheus, and the seven days required by God to finish the universe (p. 23). Such mysteries, the music of the spheres, and the relations between intervallic ratios and purity of expression were all real enough to the seventeenth century; and its speculations on these matters show that the mind and emotion of that time, if not its ear, were appreciative of an 'inaudible order' in the unseen world of the intangible and metaphysical. But these were matters more for the learned and philosophical among musicians than for the ordinary run of practising violinists.

[2] For the full quotation and source, see p. 243.
[3] Thomas Mace, *Musick's Monument*, op. cit., pp. 122–3.

Italy

Between 1650 and 1700 the contributions of different countries to violin music differed greatly in extent and kind.[4] From a purely musical point of view, Italy still held the centre of the stage, although the German virtuosi surpassed the Italians in the development of violin technique. In this period the Italians seemed more interested in solidifying their gains musically and technically than in expanding the technique of the instrument itself. In their music a clearer understanding of tonality is noticeable in the use of themes and chord progressions that clarify key. The material is extended by the use of the sequence and, in fugal pieces, by exploiting the episode. The new violin figuration itself constitutes an element of novelty and variety. Variety is especially welcome in a tonal system where relatively few modulations are available (see p. 219); and variety is particularly important in the variation, where generally there is no true modulation at all. Even in the fugue, short sections of free figuration are sometimes introduced, often in the manner of a free fantasy or cadenza, as *divertissements* between entries of the subject or answer. By the end of the century the sectional character of the sonata (especially the 'church' sonata) has been replaced by well-defined movements, fewer in number (four or five as a rule) than previously, but amplified internally and better constructed; and the musical character of the movements themselves is also more clearly defined. In the harmonic textures, the voices often move in note-against-note fashion (Ex. 56). The polyphony is usually imitative, and the *basso continuo* frequently becomes a melodic part, imitating the soloist(s) or vice versa, as in Ex. 57.

Ex. 56

Violin I
Violin II

Violone
Organo

Corelli, Op. 3, No. 4

Significantly, the main area of activity was northern Italy. The greatest makers (cf. ch. 9), composers, and players were centred there, and in addition composers of violin music were themselves mainly string players. In the last quarter of the century Rome became an important focal point about Corelli

[4] Examples of violin music from this period can be found in the general collections of Schering, Torchi, Wasielewski, and Davison and Apel (see the Bibliography). Some publishers have devoted special series to 'old' music, such as Nagel's *Musik-Archiv*. In some cases there is a complete edition of an individual composer, an example being Corelli. For detailed discussions of the music, see the authors mentioned on p. 134, note 10,

and his circle. Later, Naples assumed importance as a leading musical centre. In the north there was considerable activity in Venice, Modena, Ferrara, and particularly Bologna.

Ex. 57

Antonii, Op. 5, No. 3

The enumeration of a few characteristic composers will be helpful, and excerpts from their music will show the violin idiom. Giovanni Legrenzi (1626–90) lived in Venice, where from 1685 he was *Maestro di Cappella* at St. Mark's. Ex. 58, taken from a Legrenzi trio sonata of 1655, is a good example of a disciplined fugal subject, clearly defining the tonality of the head of the subject and affording variety with its chromatic notes. At the same time, the

Ex. 58

Allegro

Legrenzi (1655)

passage is idiomatic to the violin but modest in technical demands. Marco Uccellini (1603–80), G. M. Bononcini (1642–78), and T. A. Vitali (*c.* 1665 to at least 1734) lived in Modena.[5] The latter composer, the son of G. B. Vitali (see p. 218), is identified with a famous *Chaconne*, known to every violinist in one of the several arranged versions.[6] Antonio Veracini (*c.* 1650–after 1696), was a prominent composer in Florence; and among those in Ferrara, G. B. Bassani (*c.* 1657–1716) and G. B. Mazzaferrata may be mentioned. Bassani, incidentally, was certainly *not* Corelli's teacher, as is often said. Ex. 59, from a

---

[5] For Uccellini, Bononcini, and the importance of the 'Modena' school, see William Klenz, *Giovanni Maria Bononcini of Modena*, Durham, N.C., 1962.

[6] There is substantial doubt that T. A. Vitali composed the '*Chaconne*'. The original version exists in a manuscript for violin and figured bass entitled merely '*Parte di Tomaso Vitalino*'. From this Ferdinand David (1810–73) arranged the piece known today as the Vitali '*Chaconne*', and he made extensive changes in the original as well as furnishing an accompaniment from the figured *continuo*. For a restoration of the original, see the edition of G. Benvenuti: 'T. Vitalino (?), Passacaglia, Violino e Pianoforte', Milan, 1938. See also Mario Rinaldi, 'Sull'autenticità della "Ciaconna" di Tommaso Antonio Vitali' in *La Rassegna Musicale*, April–June, 1954, pp. 129–34. Rinaldi admires the '*Chaconne*', but, on the basis of musical style, he sees no resemblance to the known works of T. A. Vitali. Consequently he assigns the '*Chaconne*' (which he classifies as a *passacaglia*) to an anonymous composer of the eighteenth century.

H.V.P.–Q

Mazzaferrata trio sonata of 1674, shows typical idiomatic violin figuration, motives in sequence, and (in the presto) the broken chord structure of a subject that uses the register of the G string, including the open note. Ex. 60, the opening of a trio sonata of Bassani's Op. 5 (1683), shows the typical short motive of dramatic character, consisting of repeated notes and octave leaps downward. The rest of the subject continues in sixteenth-notes including more repeated notes and figurations across the strings.

Ex. 59

Ex. 60

The activity in Bologna, centring about the San Petronio Chapel, was such that it constituted a veritable school. The great period of this school began when Maurizio Cazzati (*c.* 1620–77), a Venetian, was appointed director in 1657 and organized a chapel orchestra. In 1671 Cazzati left Bologna and went to Modena; and toward the end of the century the musical organization of San Petronio was dissolved, its members going elsewhere. Among the violin teachers in Bologna was Ercole Gaibara. Two of Gaibara's pupils were Benvenuti and Brugnoli, and the young Corelli studied in Bologna with them (1666–71) before he moved to Rome. Among the violinist-composers at Bologna were G. B. Vitali (*c.* 1644–92), Pietro degli Antonii (1648–1720), who made the 'solo' sonata his principal field of activity, and Giuseppe Torelli (1658–1709), so important in the early history of the concerto.

G. B. Vitali, the most talented pupil of Cazzati, is one of the most interesting of the *Bolognesi*. Among his works are trio and solo sonatas and a large number of dances in trio settings. The dances include many a *balletto* and *corrente* as well as a certain number of *allemande, gagliarde, sarabande, ghighe,* and others. In his *balletti* of Op. 3, Vitali labels six of them 'per ballare' (for dancing) and four others 'per camera' (for the chamber), implying a distinction between actual dance music and dances used solely as chamber music. Moderate in technical demands, although very well written for the violin, his pieces are frequently more significant musically than technically. They also reflect an experimental turn of mind. His *Artificii Musicali* (Musical Artifices; Op. XIII, 1689), one of the most important collections of the Bologna school, contains a *Passagallo* for violin and bass which modulates through the following keys: E flat, F, C, G, D, A, and E, on which it ends, although it began in E flat! Vitali must have been deliberately experimenting with the notion of expanding the limited range of keys available in the prevailing 'meantone' temperament. The title of this piece reads: *Passagallo per Violino che principia per B. molle, e finisce per Diesis (Passagallo* for violin which begins in the flat [key = E flat] and ends in the sharp [key = E]).[7]

The significance of meantone temperament in relation to the range of modulation needs explaining. Equal temperament is general today (i.e. as used on the modern piano), but it was not common in the seventeenth century, when the meantone tuning prevailed. The latter system of tuning used 'pure' thirds and appreciably flat fifths. Meantone temperament worked well provided that enharmonic notes like G sharp and A flat did not both occur in the same piece. In meantone, G sharp is not the same pitch as A flat, and, in keyboards at least, one had to tune the 'black' keys to one or the other. This means that if one starts a piece in E flat major (as Vitali does in his *Passagallo*), which requires the note A flat, one cannot (as Vitali does) use A major in the same piece, which requires the note G sharp;[8] and therefore Vitali could not have been using the meantone temperament. More likely it was a species of equal temperament.

In another piece from the same collection Vitali experiments with different time signatures, using 4/4 (C) for Violin I, 12/8 for Violin II, and 3/4 for the *basso continuo* (Ex. 61). In spite of the strange appearance and the bar-

Ex. 61

G. B. Vitali (1689)

ring of this music, there are no real ensemble problems of performance, since the quarter-note *beat* is common to each part. At the head of this piece, Vitali says: 'the first violin sounds in *tempo ordinario* [4/4], the second violin in *dodecupla* [12/8], and the *violone* sounds in *tripla* [3/4].' The implication of

---

[7] For this piece, see Torchi, *L'Arte musicale in Italia*, op. cit., Vol. VII, p. 159. See also *Giovanni Battista Vitali*, '*Artifici Musicali*', *Op. XIII*, edited by Louise Rood and Gertrude P. Smith, Northampton, 1959, p. 59.

[8] For such questions, see J. Murray Barbour, *Tuning and Temperament*, East Lansing, Michigan, 1951; 2nd ed., 1953.

this passage is that the three notes of the triplet figure are to be played as written against two eighths, and that the dotted eighth figure (♪. ♪) is to be played as written—or perhaps with the dot slightly lengthened—but not as (♪ ₃ ♪). (For more on this point, see pp. 296 ff.)

With the Bologna school, double stops return to Italian violin music after the absence of a half century (cf. p. 131), and the *Bolognesi* display an interest in expressive melody and harmony. The return of double stops may have had something to do with the increased interest in the sonata for solo violin and *basso continuo*, which was cultivated relatively little until the last quarter of the century. In any case, double stops are associated more closely with the 'solo' sonata, whose technical demands are naturally greater than those of the trio sonata. Ex. 62, taken from a piece of Torelli, shows double stops typical of Corelli and later masters, the soloist being required to play the subject of a fugue together with its countersubject.

Ex. 62

While G. B. Vitali wrote few solo sonatas, Pietro degli Antonii specialized in them, and his music is notable for its lyricism and expressive chords. In the short passage already quoted in Ex. 57, both the *basso continuo* and the solo part are melodic, imitating each other; and at (*) the expressive melody is supported by the correspondingly expressive Neapolitan-sixth chord. The Bologna school also included virtuosi on other instruments, notably the cellist Domenico Gabrielli, and the presence of cello virtuosi explains the frequent difficulty of the parts written for the *continuo*.[9]

The Bologna school played no pioneering role. The path of violin virtuosity suggested by the earlier Italians was followed by the Germans, not by the *Bolognesi*, whose violin music is marked by restraint in technical demands, by increased clarity of form, and by expressive melody and harmony. This is the style of music that Corelli inherited from the school of Bologna. Moving to Rome at the age of eighteen, Corelli still called himself '*il Bolognese*', but he remained in Rome the rest of his life, surrounded by the urbane, the sophisticated, and the music-loving from the highest ranks of an aristocratic and clerical society.

[9] For specialized literature on the Bologna school, see: Jean Berger, 'Notes on some 17th-Century Compositions for Trumpets and Strings in Bologna' in *The Musical Quarterly*, July 1951; and Henry G. Mishkin, 'The Solo Violin Sonata of the Bologna School' in the same journal, January 1943. The latter article contains excellent background material for the Bologna school as a whole. For the Modena school, see Klenz (note 5, above).

Corelli's total *oeuvre* was not large, but its influence was immense. The trio sonatas, consisting of twenty-four church sonatas and twenty-four chamber sonatas (primarily dances), totalled forty-eight works as well known to the eighteenth century as Bach's forty-eight preludes and fugues were to the nineteenth. The twelve sonatas for solo violin and *basso continuo* (actually, eleven sonatas plus *La Follia*) made an even greater impact, and they formed a staple of the diet of all violinists for years. The publication of the twelve *concerti grossi* (1714) in the year after Corelli's death was significant in itself. Some of these concertos must have been composed thirty years earlier, according to the testimony of Georg Muffat, but Corelli, continually polishing, was unwilling or unready to publish them until the end of his life, leaving instructions for their publication in his will. Corelli's concertos constitute his only real pioneer work. (Corelli's concertos and those of Torelli and Albinoni will be discussed in ch. 15 with concertos of the early eighteenth century.)

In the trio and solo sonatas he clarified the form, and he brought the sonata a new musical stature, calculating his music in terms of maximum sonority without resorting to extreme technical demands or violinistic tricks. This is not to say that all his works, particularly the solo sonatas, were easy for his contemporaries to play. He exploits various bowings, including the *bariolage* (Ex. 63, m. 1; for the meaning of the term, see p. 265),

Ex. 63

but the range is modest, third position being the usual limit. An occasional fourth position is called for, and rarely fifth position (in the *concerti grossi* only). The greatest difficulties occur in the solo sonatas, where the violinist encounters double-stop passages, including thirds in sixteenth-notes, polyphonic playing of the two parts of a fugue, arpeggios, and *perpetuum mobile* movements. The incipient cadenza occurs occasionally as an interlude or extended cadence (Ex. 63; for the sound of Ex. 63, cf. our recording). The twelfth solo sonata, *La Follia*, is a real exposition of the art of bowing as practised in Italy at the end of the seventeenth century; and it include's a variation consisting entirely of long-held notes in the violin part, presumably played with expressive *messa di voce* (see p. 291).

The lyrical slow movements must have been played with ornamental additions ('graces') at least part of the time. An edition of the Corelli solo sonatas published by Etienne Roger in Amsterdam includes ornamental versions, as 'Corelli played them' (see Ex. 112). The Amsterdam edition 'graces' the adagios of the first six sonatas only. Other and more elaborate versions appeared later in the eighteenth century. Geminiani, Corelli's pupil, added ornaments to all the movements of one sonata (No. 9). Matthew Dubourg, a pupil of Geminiani, adds 'graces' to the adagios of Sonata No. 5, and to both slow *and* fast movements of Chamber Sonatas Nos. 7–11 (cf. Ex. 113). The latter are not ornamented in the Amsterdam edition at all. Of the Matteis ornamentations to the Corelli sonatas, mentioned in passing by Quantz (1752), no trace exists.[10]

There must have been numerous violinists in Rome prior to Corelli. Celebrated makers like David Tecchler (*c.* 1666–1748) would not have been attracted to Rome or stayed there without the prospect of customers. But none of these violinists seem to have attracted international, or even national, attention as players, composers or teachers. All this was changed with the advent of Corelli.[11] His music and teaching founded a Roman school whose influence touched practically every violinist in Europe. The numerous

[10] Until recently the Amsterdam edition of Roger was dated *c.* 1715—that is, after Corelli's death (1713). However, John Walsh advertised his edition of Corelli's Op. 5 with 'ye Graces' in December 1711 (see William C. Smith, *A Bibliography of the Musical Works published by John Walsh during the Years 1695–1720*, London, 1948, pp. 119–20). If Walsh issued his edition *after* Roger's, as seems almost certain, the Amsterdam edition could not have appeared later than 1711. Andreas Moser thought these 'Graces' were spurious. Schering accepted them as genuine; and Marc Pincherle has shown, beyond reasonable doubt, that they are authentic (see Marc Pincherle, *Corelli*, Paris, 1933, 2nd ed., 1954; English version: *Corelli: His Life. His Work*, New York, 1956). For Geminiani's ornamentations to Sonata No. 9, see John Hawkins, *A General History*, 1776 (reprint of 1875, Vol. II, pp. 904–7). A unique manuscript copy of the Dubourg ornamentations was part of the library of Alfred Cortot in Lausanne.

[11] There was, however, one composer in Rome who probably had some influence on Corelli's trio sonatas: namely, Lelio Colista (1629–80). Colista was not a violinist but a lutanist, guitarist, and composer of chamber cantatas, arias, and trio sonatas. The latter were written mostly in the 1660s. Colista should doubtless be included among those '*più valorosi professori musici di Roma*' who were followed as models by Corelli according to his own statement (1685). For Colista's influence on Purcell, see p. 238. Two of Colista's trio sonatas have recently been published: one, in A major, edited by Helene Wessely-Kropik, in the *Hortus Musicus* series (No. 172), Bärenreiter, Kassel, 1960; and the other, Sonata No. IV in D major, edited by Michael Tilmouth, Stainer and Bell, London, 1960. See also Helene Wessely-Kropik, *Lelio Colista*, Vienna [1961?].

Italian and foreign editions of Corelli's music are witness to his immense and widespread appeal as a composer; and Corelli's lasting fame as a teacher was assured through his pupils, among them, Geminiani, Locatelli, Veracini, and Somis. Somis, in turn, was the teacher of Leclair, the chief and most important French violinist-composer of the early eighteenth century. Corelli, in short, exerted a profound influence on the history of violin music and violin playing through his music, his teaching, and his pupils.

Although Corelli's technical demands were quite modest compared to those of Biber and Walther, these demands were more realistically geared to the ability of his contemporaries; and Corelli's pieces were so idiomatically written for the violin that they almost played themselves. Moreover, his music as music represents a greater achievement than that of Biber and Walther. Corelli's contributions in advancing the sonata and the concerto can hardly be appreciated simply by examining his music, since the magnitude of his success in combining a number of disparate elements can be grasped only through a detailed study of the instrumental music of the seventeenth century. That is to say, Corelli's music represents a perfect working out of the musical and violinistic problems posed by his predecessors.

Germany

In the history of violin technique Corelli's works cannot claim to be landmarks. Still, they achieved a musical reputation that has survived change and fashion to the present day. Almost the reverse can be said of Biber and Walther, Corelli's German contemporaries. Their fertility in inventing new violin sonorities and technical innovations produced music requiring a virtuosity unequalled up to their time with respect to extended range, double stops, special bowings, the *scordatura*, and descriptive effects. Compared to Corelli's music, however, that of Biber and Walther was less worthy of the effort required to perform it. Nevertheless, technical advances must begin somewhere, even if the implied horizons are not reached for years. Some of the most elaborate efforts of the Germans, especially in the *scordatura*, proved to be a cul-de-sac, but it is difficult to imagine the unaccompanied violin solos of Bach without the previous essays in multiple stops which the works of Biber, Walther, Bruhns, and others contain.

If Walther was the Paganini of the seventeenth century, Biber was, in certain respects, its Ludwig Spohr. Just as Paganini and Walther were specialists in the violin, Spohr and Biber, both professional violinists, were interested in all kinds of music. Besides the central figures of Heinrich von Biber (1644–1704) in Salzburg and J. J. Walther (*c.* 1650–1717) in Dresden, there were numerous others. J. H. Schmeltzer (*c.* 1623–80) worked in Vienna, and was quite probably Biber's teacher. Schmeltzer's sonatas for solo violin and bass emphasize the variation form, which serves as a vehicle for a virtuoso technique of runs, figures, arpeggios, some double stops, and a range through the sixth position.[12] J. P. von Westhoff (1656–1705), an associate of Walther's at Dresden and called by Moser the 'greatest master of polyphonic music for violin prior to Bach',[13] had the further distinction of introducing the German violin style to Paris, of having some of his pieces published there, and of pleasing Louis XIV. Westhoff is also one of the few composers in the seventeenth century to write a solo sonata for unaccompanied violin.[14] Georg Muffat, who worked in Salzburg and later in Passau, is largely remembered today as an astute observer of the instrumental style and practice of Lully, with whom he studied for six years in Paris (see p. 257). In north Germany the great organist Buxtehude transferred his dramatic style to a few works involving the violin, including seven sonatas for violin, viola da gamba, and cembalo (Op. 1, 1696).

These composers and many others represent a considerable variety of styles. However, the chief technical advances of the German school can be summarized in three printed collections: Biber's 'Mystery' (or 'Rosary') Sonatas (*c.* 1674), consisting of fifteen sonatas with *basso continuo* plus an unaccompanied *passacaglia*; and two collections of Walther: the *Scherzi* of 1676 and *Hortulus Chelicus* of 1688.[15] Collectively, these three works comprise solo violin pieces (plus *continuo*), many of which have descriptive interest. Formally they consist of sonatas, suites of dances, and variations. In the *Hortulus Chelicus* some easier pieces are intermixed with those of great technical difficulty.

While Corelli developed the sonata to a classical perfection, the Germans paid zealous attention to the large-scale variation, probably as a natural device for the cultivation of diverse and difficult experiments in technique from one variation to the next. Walther's *Hortulus* No. 27 consists of fifty short variations over an *ostinato* of the descending C major scale, and (as Gustav Beckmann remarks) this work exhibits the whole art of the violin,

---

[12] Six of Schmeltzer's sonatas—'*Sonatae unarum Fidium*' of 1664—were reprinted in Vol. 93 of the *Denkmäler der Tonkunst in Österreich* (Vienna, 1958), together with three additional sonatas and two suites. One of these three sonatas entitled 'Sonate [*sic*] "Cucu" ' shows an interest in descriptive music common at the time.

[13] Moser, op. cit., p. 136.

[14] Published in Beckmann, *12 Sonaten*; see also the facsimile of part of another piece in Kinsky, *The History of Music in Pictures*, p. 183, No. 3.

[15] There are modern critical editions of two of these collections: Walther's *Scherzi* complete in *Das Erbe Deutscher Musik* (Vol. 17), Hannover, 1941; and Biber's 'Mystery' Sonatas complete in *Denkmäler der Tonkunst in Österreich* (Vol. 25), Vienna, 1905 (the *scordatura* of Sonata XI, wrong in the 1905 edition, was corrected in a later and separate issue of this sonata). In addition, Beckmann, *12 Sonaten*, contains two of the *Scherzi* and two pieces from the *Hortulus*. There is no complete modern edition of the latter.

hardly surpassed in the seventeenth century as a virtuoso piece. The Biber *Passacaglia* for unaccompanied violin is a worthy predecessor to Bach's unaccompanied violin sonatas.

Biber and Walther share a number of the same technical characteristics. Both are fully at home in the complete range of the violin from the open G string to a''' (seventh position); and the upper positions must have been used on the lower strings, at least in certain multiple stops. Their music demands a variety of bow strokes, including individual strokes of every speed, and numerous slurred bowings. Biber and Walther are among the first to use dots (·) and/or stroke (ı) over notes to indicate staccato. Groups of notes over which dots or strokes are placed may also be slurred, and some of these are quite astonishing (see p. 270). Syncopated bowings are frequent, and other types, such as the *bariolage, arpeggiando,* and *ondeggiando* (cf. p. 265), make their appearance from time to time. Figurations are spread out over a wide range of the instrument (Ex. 64), and they may consist of figures

Ex. 64

skipping strings or of repeated notes.[16] Whole movements are to be played *pizzicato*. There are double, triple, and quadruple stops, not only as isolated stops but in continuous polyphony, and some stops require extensions of the fingers.

In certain respects Biber and Walther differ, not merely as every artist must, but in their fundamental outlook. Much of their music is pictorial in character. Biber's is the subtler music of a mood suggested by a title; Walther's typically and rather naively seeks to paint a picture by depicting realistically such physical sounds as those of the cuckoo (Ex. 65), the nightin-

Ex. 65

Walther (*Scherzo* No. 10)

"Cuc - cu"

gale, the trumpet, the bagpipe, the guitar, and the harp. The title of the last piece in his *Hortulus Chelicus* is a case in point: *Serenata A un Coro di Violini, Organo Tremolante, Chitarrino, Piva, Due Trombe e Timpani, Lira Todesca, et Harpa Smorzata, per un Violino Solo* [and figured bass] (Serenata for a string choir, organ tremolant, small guitar, the bagpipe, two trumpets and timpani,

---

[16] For large leaps in C. H. Abel, see Moser, op. cit., p. 110.

German *lira*, and *Harpa smorzata*, for violin solo). In this piece, Walther has turned the violin into a one-man orchestra. By way of contrast, Biber's 'Mystery' Sonatas are each prefaced by a picture representing an episode in the life of Christ, but the music itself generally seeks to create the suggested mood and atmosphere rather than to paint a musical picture in the realistic, physical manner typical of Walther.

Biber and Walther differed conspicuously in their attitude toward the *scordatura*. Biber developed it to an amazing point that has never been surpassed. Walther detested and never used it, and one can sympathize with his probable objections. The *scordatura* is often a nuisance, since changing tunings makes it difficult to set the tuning and to play accurately in tune. Besides, the farther a *scordatura* is from the normal tuning (called *accordatura*), the less the violin sounds like a violin. On the other hand, the *scordatura* has some remarkable possibilities. It may simplify a passage technically, it may be used for sonority reinforcing the principal notes of the key, or it may accomplish the difficult or even the otherwise impossible with relative ease.

Biber's love of the *scordatura* is seen at its most intense in the 'Mystery' Sonatas. In them he specifies fourteen different tunings of this kind; and these tunings are related either to the main notes of the tonality in question, thus reinforcing the sonority, or they are geared to the solution of technical problems. Biber's varied use of the *scordatura* shows a fertility of imagination for sonority that anticipates violin technique of a later time. Some of the effects had not yet been thought of in his own time, and others can hardly be

Ex. 66

achieved without the use of the *scordatura*. For example, Biber must have imagined the sound of octaves and tenths, which were not yet part of the violin idiom, and he produces them easily with the astounding tuning and in the manner shown in Ex. 66 and Ex. 67. What strings were used in achieving the tuning in Ex. 66 or what the sonorities were when certain strings were tuned above or below normal pitch are questions which will be left to the reader.[17]

[17] For peculiarities of playing and notating *scordatura* pieces, including the signatures, see p. 250. For detailed information, see the author's review of the complete recording of these sonatas, *The Musical Quarterly*, July 1963.

Ex. 67

France

The technical demands of the German school stand in sharp contrast to the unassuming simplicity of the French. Except for a few trio sonatas in the last decade of the century,[18] French violin music was largely synonymous with dance music. We must remember that interest in the viol, especially the bass viol, was still strong in France, and that during the last quarter of the century some of the best efforts of French composers were expended in compositions for the viols. Marin Marais's first set of *Pièces* (for one or two viols) dates from 1686, and Rousseau's viol method (*Traité de la Viole*) was published in the following year.

Lully's influence was as strong in violin music as it was everywhere else in musical France. Trained as a violinist and dancer himself, Lully was able to impose a bowing and rhythmic discipline on French dance music that gave it a special, if mannered, style, the details of which, ironically enough, were recorded by a German, Georg Muffat (see p. 257). Under Lully, French musical life was highly organized and disciplined. The *24 Violons du Roy* had been established by Louis XIII long before, but Lully, infuriated by their ignorance and routine playing, persuaded Louis XIV to create a new band of sixteen players. This new group, first appearing publicly in 1656, was called *Les Petits Violons* in contrast to the *Grande Bande* of twenty-four, and was later expanded to twenty-one players.[19] *Les Petits Violons*, also called *Violons du Cabinet*, were suppressed at the beginning of Louis XV's reign, and the *Grande Bande* met a similar fate in 1761. It was with the small 'band' that Lully effected the style of bowing and piquant rhythms that Muffat describes. Lully also insisted on doing away with the custom of adding improvised ornaments, rejecting (as Muffat says) 'immoderate runs as well as frequent and ill-sounding leaps' both in vocal and instrumental music. Lully's manner of performing was highly disciplined, but his music was technically simple, the 'test' piece which he required for his violinists being

[18] For example, those of François Couperin (*c.* 1692), J. F. Rebel (1695), and Mlle de La Guerre (1695). See La Laurencie, op. cit., Vol. III, p. 229. See also Marc Pincherle, 'La Technique du Violon chez les Premiers Sonatistes Français (1695-1723)' in *Bulletin Francais de la Société Internationale de Musique*, August-September 1911 (Vol. 7, Nos. 8 and 9), pp. 1-32.

[19] For this see La Laurencie, op. cit., Vol. I, p. 23.

a fair sample (Ex. 68). Most of this dance music stayed in the first position, and it used the G string very little. It contained none of the multiple stops and few of the fingering and bowing difficulties of the Italians and the Germans. Relatively little music of the *24 Violons du Roy* or *Les Petits Violons* has been preserved.[20]

Ex. 68

Besides dance music, the violin was employed in sacred music (for example, by Lalande) and especially in the operas of Lully where the strings were used to play in such pieces as overtures, dances of various sorts (*minuet, gavotte, gigue,* and so on), chaconnes and passacaglias (both of which could be of very considerable length), music for interludes, and descriptive pieces.[21] Typical examples of the latter are 'les Vents' in *Alceste* (1674) or 'Air pour les Démons et les Monstres' in *Amadis* (1684). Instrumental *ritournelles* were sometimes used in connexion with vocal solos, and instruments sometimes doubled the choral parts or furnished accompaniments, including obbligatos,

[20] Originally the Philidor Collection in Paris, made by André Philidor, the copyist of Louis XIV, contained at least one volume of music of the *24 Violons.* This volume, along with others containing dances, has disappeared. See E. H. Fellowes, 'The Philidor Manuscripts' in *Music and Letters,* April 1931. The best sources for these French dances are the *Florilegium Primum* (1695) and *Florilegium Secundum* (1698) of Georg Muffat, whose pieces are based on the Lully model (these two works are published in the *Denkmäler der Tonkunst in Österreich,* Vols. 2 and 4). In addition, Écorcheville published a manuscript found in Cassel, which contains a substantial repertory of French dances modelled directly on, or taken from, the French dances found in the ballets and operas of Lully. See Jules Écorcheville, *Vingt Suites d'Orchestre,* Paris and Berlin, 1906. Écorcheville (Vol. I, p. 5, note 4) mentions André Philidor, *Suites de danses pour les violons et hautbois qui se jouent ordinairement aux bals chez le roi, dont la plupart sont de la composition de M. Philidor l'aisne.* A MS. in the Bibliothéque Nationale (Vm⁷3555) of 120 pages is very similar to this. The printed title dated 1707 is corrected in ink to 1712. This MS. contains only the *dessus* part. There are about 250 pieces, some composed by members of the *24 Violons.* See also Praetorius, *Terpsichore . . . Darinnen allerley Frantzösische Däntze und Lieder . . .* 1612, for older types of French dances (published as Vol. 15 of the *Gesamtausgabe . . . von Michael Praetorius,* 20 vols., Wolfenbüttel, 1928–40).

[21] Apparently there was a distinction between the strings used in the opera orchestra and the *24 Violons du Roy* and *Les Petits Violons.* These last two groups devoted their energies to playing for dancing, particularly in connexion with Court functions. *Les Petits Violons,* in particular, played during the King's repasts, as he retired, for balls at Court, and during journeys of the sovereign. The opera orchestra was 'carefully selected and strictly drilled by Lully himself' (D. J. Grout, *A Short History of the Opera,* New York, 1947, p. 124), but it is not clear whether it was a regularly constituted orchestra or one assembled for particular occasions. See also Henry Prunières, *La Vie illustre et libertine de Jean-Baptiste Lully,* Paris, 1929, pp. 183–4.

for soloists. The technical demands on the violin, however, were relatively slight, the range being limited and rarely if ever exceeding c''' (that is, the first position extended by a semitone). There were no problems of fingering, shifting, or double stops, and none of the complex bowings of the Italians and Germans. The complications were chiefly rhythmic in this mannered style which specialized in dotted rhythms. At the same time, Lully understood the strings at first hand, and the result was a beautiful sonority suited to the monumental grandeur of his operas whose setting was the magnificence of the Court of Louis XIV.

The old five-part ensemble of strings, described by Mersenne, was still typical of French string music. Thanks to Lully and his pupil Muffat, the French style of violin playing, formulated primarily to articulate and emphasize dance rhythms, spread to other parts of Europe, particularly to England, Germany, and the Low Countries. Until 1750 at least, the special style of Lully's operatic French Overture had an immense vogue in Europe, not only in opera and oratorio, but also as a prefatory *pièce de résistance* in orchestral and keyboard suites of dances. Lully, backed by the most powerful of French kings, wielded an absolute authority over French music, and the influence of this great musician and master intriguer carried its impress to other parts of Europe for many years after his death.[22]

French violinists were highly organized. A species of musicians' 'union' grew out of the guild system, headed by a '*Roi des Violons*' recognized by the King of France himself. Legal statutes regulated the length of apprenticeship, the details of registering pupils with the 'King of the Violins' (naturally requiring a fee!), the amount of payment of the violinist on becoming a 'master', and the privileges of master violinists, including the sole right to play in certain places.[23] This system served as a protection to musicians and particularly to violinists, who, even at the end of the seventeenth century, were held in less regard in France than lutanists, organists, and harpsichordists. The violin was still considered a noisy instrument in France, suitable largely for dancing, and consequently violinists were low in the social scale even among musicians. The musicians' guild, in short, protected musicians from each other and from a society that thought little of musicians and even less of violinists.

England

With the Restoration of the monarchy in England in 1660, French influence became increasingly strong in the English Court. After the disruption of English national life during the Civil War and Commonwealth

---

[22] See Charles Cudworth, ' "Baptist's Vein"—French Orchestral Music and its Influence from 1650 to 1750' in the *Proceedings of the Royal Musical Association*, 1956–7.
[23] See F. J. Fétis, 'Du Roi des Violons' in *Revue Musicale*, 1827, p. 173.

(1649–60), the Stuart line in the person of Charles II was restored to the throne. Charles had spent his long exile in France and there was French blood in his veins, which meant, among other things, dance music in his ears. At the beginning of his reign Charles II established the *24 Violins of the King*, directly imitating the *Grande Bande* of Louis XIV and using it in much the same way. Pepys, in a diary entry of 23 April 1661, mentions the *24 Violins* in his description of the Coronation Dinner of Charles II; and Evelyn in the next year (24 December 1662) related that the '24' were introduced into the Christmas Eve Service—to the consternation of the pious who equated the violin with the Devil and dancing.[24] Like Louis XIV, Charles also created a small band, called the 'Private Musick', appointing John Banister on 19 August 1663 'to make choyce of twelve of our four-and-twenty violins to be a select band to wayte on us whensoever there should be occasion for musick'.[25] Obviously the small band was directly inspired by *Les Petits Violons* that had been created a few years earlier by Lully (see p. 227) and with whose function Charles II must have been familiar during his exile in France. As in France, the English dance bands of the King played for Court functions and dancing, including masques, one of which took place in 1674. These Court affairs must have been sumptuous, and the dress of the court musicians was similar. The Royal accounts for 20 March 1664–5 speak of 'habitts of several coloured silkes for four and twenty violins', and a few days earlier (18 March) of 'habitts for the twenty four violins like Indian gowns but not so full, with short sleeves to the elboes, trymmed with tinsell about the neck and bottom and at the sleeves'.[26]

Charles II naturally set the tone of his Court, and his immediate influence was noted by contemporaries. 'King Charles II', says Roger North in his *Memoirs*, 'was a professed lover of musick but of this kind onely [dance music] and had an utter detestation of Fancys.' And in his *Musicall Grammarian*, North remarks, 'After the manner of France, he [Charles] set up a band of 24 Violins to play at his dinners, which disbanded all the old English musick at once.'[27] Charles imported French musicians and he also sent English musicians to Paris to study, including one of the leading English violinists, John Banister (1661–2), and the composer, Pelham Humphrey, the teacher of Purcell. Among the imports was Louis Grabu, who later displaced Banister from the King's favour and became Master of the King's Musick

---

[24] The typical ensemble of the English '24' was usually composed of four, not five, parts, as among the French. The English 'band' consisted of six violins, six counter-tenors, six tenors, and six basses. See W. Sandys and S. A. Forster, *History of the Violin*, London, 1864, p. 146.

[25] Lafontaine, *The King's Musick*, p. 159.

[26] Lafontaine, op. cit., p. 176.

[27] For these quotations, see *Roger North on Music*, op. cit., p. 350 and p. 300 respectively.

(1667). The obvious *parti pris* of the King gave a noticeable impetus to French dances, instrumental overtures (*Simphonies*) in French style, and the French manner of performing. However, this pronounced French bias was not highly regarded by a number of English musicians (for Purcell's comment, see p. 213).

Charles's preference for dance music and the violin, and his 'detestation of Fancys' hastened the downfall of the viol in England, but actually it was only a question of time before more fundamental changes in music would have undermined the viol's position. The old polyphony, so closely associated with this instrument, was going out of fashion, and the new styles and forms of music were far more suited to the more expressive, flexible, and powerful violin. After Purcell's Fantasias of 1680, new composition for the viols practically ceased, and this date is as convenient as any to mark the end of the English fancy. Three years later Purcell turned to the trio sonata for violins, and he did not return to the fancy again. Mace sadly and bitterly comments on the unequal struggle (see p. 120), and a contemporary, William Turner (1697), writes quaintly, 'The Treble Viol also is much out of Doors [i.e. out of fashion], since the Violin came so much in request. The Base, and Lyra Viol . . . keep pretty well in repute, especially the first, because it cannot be wanted well [dispensed with] in Consort, etc. . . . The Violin is now arrived to a great Perfection of Performance.'[28]

There was still another reason for the triumph of the violin in England. The advent of German and Italian violinists opened the eyes and ears of English musicians to the real possibilities of the instrument. Thomas Baltzar from Lübeck (via the Swedish Court) came to England by 1655, making a profound impression on the English; and when the Italian violinist, Nicola Matteis, appeared early in the 1670s,[29] he made a similar impact. The high standards of playing of these true professionals made the playing of amateur performers on the viol and even of native professional violinists seem a rather dull affair except to the most hardened amateur enthusiasts and lovers of the viol like Mace. Furthermore, the opportunity to see and hear such gifted and brilliant players was increased by the founding of music clubs and public concerts, though on a small scale, not long after the Restoration.[30] Significantly, Italian violin music began to be published by enterprising English publishers, who were also responsible for the first violin tutors.

[28] William Turner, *A Compleat History* (Part III, 'The Curiosities of Art'), London, 1697. Quoted in Michael Tilmouth, 'Some Improvements in Music noted by William Turner in 1697' in *The Galpin Society Journal*, May 1957.

[29] According to Michael Tilmouth, 'Nicola Matteis' in *The Musical Quarterly*, January 1960, p. 22.

[30] See Michael Tilmouth, 'Some Early London Concerts and Music Clubs, 1670–1720' in *Proceedings of the Royal Musical Association*, 1957–8.

The latter, printed in considerable numbers in the last years of the seventeenth century and first quarter of the eighteenth century (see p. 244), point to the rise of a potent number of amateur violinists and to the voracious appetite for violin music. Each violin tutor and each subsequent edition of the same tutor used entirely different pieces of music—obviously to satisfy the demand for new, if easy, music. The amateur viol player was a phenomenon of long standing. The amateur violinist was something new, and the origin of this novel species may have been related to the increase of chamber music during the Commonwealth when, as North says, there was a great spurt of music 'in private society, for many chose rather to fidle at home, than to goe out & be knockt in ye head abroad'.[31]

The marked success of Baltzar and of Matteis after him casts into sharp relief the impress of foreign musicians on English musical life. The same sort of thing had begun earlier, but it had been much less obvious in effect. The new trend reached a great crescendo in the early eighteenth century, when Italian musicians in particular, including many violinists, dominated the English scene. A number of these 'foreigners', Geminiani for example, remained in England for most of their lives. Foreign musicians were attracted to England by opportunity and by the prospect of substantial cash rewards. According to Roger North, they soon found out 'the Grand secret that the English would follow Musick and drop their pence freely'; and early in the eighteenth century Mattheson in Germany noted that 'he who in the present time wants to make a profit out of music betakes himself to England'.[32]

After the Restoration, English violin music is influenced by three main considerations: the participation of the violin in the briefly continuing fantasia, the introduction of the Italian sonata, and the traditional association with the variation and the dance. The new French influence is a part of the emphasis on the literature of dances for the violin. All this shows that the outlook of English musicians was more international than that of the French, and the violin repertory of the English was more varied, consisting of dances, 'airs' (often dances in disguise), fantasias, sonatas, and different species of variations, such as 'chacony' (*chaconne*) and divisions on a ground (*ostinato*). English violinists and composers were thoroughly familiar with the basic idioms of the violin, but the music as a whole varied a good deal in its degree of difficulty—the dances being simple and some of the 'violin' fancies and the sonatas being fairly advanced in character. Much of this music has a strong English flavour of angular themes, modal harmony, and often (in the fancies and sonatas), rather elaborate polyphony.

[31] Roger North, *The Musicall Grammarian*, edited by Hilda Andrews, London, n.d. [1925], p. 19. See also *Roger North on Music*, op. cit., p. 294.
[32] Johann Mattheson, *Das Neu-eroffnete Orchestre*, Hamburg, 1713.

The contrast between the French and English attitude toward the violin may be observed in the treatment of the fantasias in both countries. Apparently the French did not use the violin in their *fantaisies*, restricting the violin to the simple idiom of dance music. On the other hand, the English occasionally wrote violin parts in their fancies, in which the violin was sometimes treated in a technically advanced manner.

The English fancy began to change character. The strict polyphony of the early seventeenth century was often replaced by a pseudo-polyphony in which the parts were not only reduced in number but were also written in a concerted or *concertante* style, stressing virtuosity and individual brilliance— in contrast to the old, sombre, polyphonic style in which each part had an equal musical interest. This new trend began earlier in the fantasias and fantasia-suites of William Lawes (see p. 140), and it continued with similar pieces by John Jenkins, Christopher Simpson, and Matthew Locke. An example is Simpson's fantasias *Months and Seasons*, for violin, two bass viols, and *basso continuo*.[33]

John Jenkins (1592–1678), 'the ever Famous, and most Excellent *composer*, in all Sorts of *Modern Musick*', is the best example of the change from the old-style fancy to the new.[34] Certain of his new-style fancies use one or two violins, and some of them are modelled on the Italian style, using rather elaborate figuration. The three-part fancies for two violins and bass viol are influenced by Italian models in which two treble instruments of equal range

Ex. 69

Jenkins

are set against the bass, as in the trio sonatas. There are also fantasia-suites for violin, bass, and organ; and still others for two trebles, bass, and *continuo*, in which the *fantasia* is followed by a single *ayre*. These 'trebles' are undoubtedly violins, and it is in these pieces that sections in rapid 'divisions' occur (Ex. 69) and in which the Italian trio-sonata style penetrates the English fancy most strongly.

---

[33] For one of the fantasias from this set, see Meyer, op. cit., p. 227. For a study of pieces for violin and gamba, see Peter Evans, 'Seventeenth-Century Chamber Music Manuscripts at Durham' in *Music and Letters*, July 1955.

[34] The quotation is from Simpson, *The Division Viol*, op. cit., p. 61. For a representative selection of Jenkins's music, see *John Jenkins Fancies and Ayres*, edited by Helen Joy Sleeper, Wellesley College Editions, No. 1, Wellesley, Mass., 1950.

H.V.P.–R

The violin music of an early English tradition was associated especially with the variation and the dance. Some of these dances were English and some adopted from France, especially after the Restoration. Both dance and variation had deep roots in English instrumental music, and the violin had been associated with dance music from its beginnings. In the seventeenth century, many dances for the violin appear in collections. There were two famous ones published by John Playford. First to appear was *The English Dancing Master*, a collection of airs used for country dances and intended primarily for the violin. The great popularity of this work is attested by numerous editions between its first appearance in 1650 (actually dated 1651) and 1728. Some years later (1669 and later editions) Playford issued *Apollo's Banquet, containing Instructions, and Variety of New Tunes, Ayres, Jiggs, and several New Scotch Tunes for the Treble Violin. To which is added, the Tunes of the Newest French Dances* (this is the title of the fifth [1687] and sixth [1690] editions; the exact title of the first edition of 1669 is not known). Dances also appear in instruction books for the violin. At the end of *The Self-Instructor on the Violin* (1695; see p. 245), one of the first extant tutors devoted solely to violin instruction, are thirty-one complete pieces for violin, including Ayres, Marches, Scotch tunes, Trumpet tune, and dances such as *Boree* (or *Bore* = *Bourrée*), *Saraband, Gigg, Minuet*, and *Hornpipe*, including an unacknowledged one by Purcell. The last of the pieces in this tutor is a gesture to the new fashion: a 'Sonata Solo of Mr. Courtiville'. It is typical, however, that the opening adagio of this sonata has variations.

The English variation has a long history. By 1600 the English virginalists had brought it to a high point of development. The 'division' technique, so dear to the viol players, was naturally exploited in the variation, and a substantial part of Simpson's *The Division-Viol* is devoted to the role of 'divisions' in the variation. Apparently the success of *The Division-Viol* inspired the publication of similar works for other instruments. The ubiquitous John Playford brought out *The Division-Violin* in 1684, and it was reissued in 1685, 1688, 1693, and even later (presumably by his son Henry, John Playford having died *c.* 1686). There was even a *Division-Flute* published by Walsh in 1706. With the possible exception of Matteis' *Ayres* (see p. 236), *The Division-Violin* contains what is technically the most advanced violin music published in England in the seventeenth century. It has, collectively, rapid notes, double stops, and passages on the lowest (G) string. However, with the exception of pieces by the two foreigners in the collection (Baltzar and van Schmelt), who use third position freely, the music stays mainly in the first position (nevertheless, No. 2, an anonymous piece entitled 'Duke of Norfolk or Pauls Steeple', calls for the note e''' or fourth position). The majority of pieces are dances and 'grounds' (variations). No. 5 is particularly interesting. It is called 'Faronells [*sic*] Division on a Ground', the same music

Corelli used fifteen years later as *La Follia* for the last of his twelve 'solo' sonatas of Op. 5.[35]

Among the composers represented are Christopher Simpson, Davis (or Davies) Mell (the best of the English violinists), 'Senior Balshar' (= Baltzar), Cor. van Schmelt, and John Banister. All but two of the twenty-six pieces are set for violin and *continuo*, No. 24 being for two violins to a 'ground', and No. 25 being a duet (*Ayre*) for two violins by Banister. Mell and Baltzar each contribute a 'division' on the same tune, 'John come kiss me now'; and a comparison of these two pieces as a whole (Nos. 11 and 12) is a comparison of German and English style and technique. Ex. 70a and Ex. 70b are parallel passages from these two pieces. In proportion as Mell's piece is technically superior to contemporary dances, Baltzar's flights of figuration and double stops are above the level of Mell's.

Ex. 70

The Division-Violin

Tune: "John come kiss me now"

Mell-variation 10

Baltzar-variation 14

The dance, the variation, and the fantasia were forms of music deeply embedded in the English past. Something new was added with the invasion of foreign violinists and the music of the Italian sonata, which must have reached England in increasing quantities in the last quarter of the century. Of the foreign violinists, Baltzar and Matteis were the most influential, because they came to England and settled there. Their technique of playing in the positions, facility in double stops, and the manner of holding the violin and bow were all quite novel to the English, and their example was doubtless imitated by those English violinists anxious to play Italian sonatas.

[35] Michel Farinel (baptized 1649), the son-in-law of the French composer, Cambert, was born in Grenoble. He travelled to Spain and Portugal, being intendant to the Queen of Spain (see p. 239). In a register of 1690 (according to the article on 'Farinel' in *Grove's Dictionary*) he is described as a 'gentleman pensioner to the King of England' and signs himself 'Michel Farinelly'. His name survives in history as the arranger of *Les Folies D'Espagne*, known in England as *Farinel's Ground*. This ground is used earlier in Simpson's *The Division-Viol* (p. 65). See also Otto Gombosi, article 'Folia', in *MGG*.

Some musicians, however, found things to criticize in Baltzar. Roger North reported that 'his playing like his country was harsh and rough'. But this was one small dissenting voice. Anthony Wood met Baltzar in 1658 and recorded in his diary that he saw Baltzar 'run up his fingers to the end of the Finger-board of the violin, and run them back insensibly, and all with alacrity, and in very good tune, which [neither] he nor any in England saw the like before'. And Wood continues in a more social and personal manner: 'being much admired by all lovers of musick, his [Baltzar's] company was therefore desired: and company, especially musicall company, delighting in drinking, made him drink more than ordinary, which brought him to his grave.' And again, 'after Baltzar came into England and shew'd his most wonderful parts on that instrument, [Davis] Mell was not so admired, yet he played sweeter, was a well bred gentleman, and not given to excessive drinking as Baltzar was'.[36] Poor Baltzar! His excesses caught up with him, and this gifted violinist died in 1663, still in his early thirties.

Not until the arrival of Nicola Matteis about ten years after Baltzar's death did the English exhibit the same kind of astonishment they had displayed over the phenomenon of Baltzar. Roger North's *Memoirs* say that Matteis 'was an excellent musitian, and performed wonderfully upon the violin. His manner was singular, but in one respect excelled all that had bin knowne before in England, which was the *arcata* [i.e. long bow stroke with *messa di voce* and possibly vibrato]; his *stoccatas, tremolos*, devisions, and indeed his whole manner was surprising, and every stroke of his was a mouthfull.'[37]

Matteis composed four books of 'Ayres of the Violin', and the title of the first of these books (1676) describes the contents: *Preludes, Fuges, Allmands, Sarabands, Courants, Gigues, Fancies, Divisions. And likewise other Passages, Introductions, and Fugues for Single and Double Stops, with Divisions somewhat more Artificial.*[38] These pieces represent an effort on the part of Matteis to write various titbits in the different styles and forms current in England at that time. The music of these *Ayres* is composed in a moderately advanced technique, but North comments that these lessons 'shew much of his air & skill, but nothing of his manner of playing, wch made them much richer than ye prints shew and now it is Impossible either to find out or describe the musick he made of them'.[39] The *Ayres* display one especially interesting

---

[36] See Anthony Wood, *Diary of his Life*, as quoted in *Memoirs of Musick by the Hon. Roger North*, edited by E. F. Rimbault, London, 1846, pp. 100–1.

[37] *Roger North on Music*, op. cit., p. 355. The editor, John Wilson, thinks the last phrase of this quotation 'probably refers to a manner of gracing'.

[38] See Michael Tilmouth, 'Nicola Matteis', op. cit. According to Tilmouth, Book I and II were issued in 1676, and a second impression came out before 1679. The title of the original issue was in Italian and that of the reissue was in English. Books III and IV were published in 1685, and a new edition with second treble appeared in 1687.

[39] *Musicall Grammarian*, op. cit., pp. 35–36. See also *Roger North on Music*, op. cit., p. 310.

feature: the addition of alternate versions containing double stops, the added notes engraved as dotted lozenges, or, as Matteis said, 'the pointed notes are made for masters that can touch two cords for want of a second treble' (Ex. 71). In the Bodleian Library at Oxford there is an interesting manuscript (Mus. Sch. c. 61) containing a number of 'divisions' and other works. Various dates (1676 to 1693) appear in the manuscript, and pieces by Purcell and Corelli are included. There is also a 'Division on a ground' (pp. 16–19), labelled 'N.M.'—surely, Nicola Matteis—and a sample of its style of violin writing is shown in Ex. 72. The last measure of Ex. 72, with its extension of a ninth, is particularly interesting.

Ex. 71

Matteis

Ex. 72

(The Ground)

"N. M."

Purcell's *Sonnata's of III Parts* of 1683 are the first genuine break with the past. The flavour of their themes and harmonies is English, but the texture and forms are those of the Italian trio sonata; and Purcell himself says in a prefatory note 'To the Reader' that they are composed in 'just imitation of the most fam'd Italian masters'. (For a matter concerning the instrumentation of these sonatas, see p. 279 below.) If one compares the Purcell fantasias of 1680, the end of that genre in England, with the new trio sonatas three years later, a great difference of form and feeling is at once apparent. It is true that there had been earlier 'English' sonatas by William Young (1653), but his eleven sonatas for two, three, and four parts and *continuo* were published, not in England, but in Innsbruck, where Young was living at that time; and these sonatas are certainly the result of continental influences.[40]

---

[40] All these sonatas are published by Oxford University Press, edited by W. G. Whittaker. See also W. G. Whittaker, 'William Young' in *Collected Essays*, London, 1940.

Like the Purcell sonatas later, these ensemble sonatas by Young have, in general, the texture and order of movements of the Italian church sonata, and they have single movements in imitative counterpoint labelled 'canzona'. Young's pieces are simple and are limited to first-position range. John Jenkins is said to have composed twelve trio sonatas for violins (1660), but no trace of them has yet been found.

Purcell may have known the sonatas of Young and Jenkins, but the real models for his sonatas were the Italians, as he says himself. These models doubtless included pieces by Cazzati, G. B. Vitali, Lelio Colista, Nicola Matteis, perhaps G. M. Bononcini and just possibly Corelli, whose Op. 1 was published in 1681. In any case, in the last years of the seventeenth century and through the eighteenth, Corelli's music enjoyed a tremendous vogue in England, not to mention achieving numerous editions there.

The influence of Matteis on Purcell was evidently slight, but that of Colista was strong. Purcell quotes from Colista's music in 1683, the same year that Purcell's first trio sonatas appeared. The quotation may be found in 'The Art of Descant' (p. 114), published as Part III of the tenth edition of Playford's *Introduction to the Skill of Musick*. In this, under 'Double Descant', Purcell says, 'Of this sort, there are some Fuges used by several Authors in *Sonata's*; a short One I shall here insert of the famous *Lelio Calista* [*sic*], an *Italian*'.[41]

Purcell's two sets of trio sonatas—twelve in 1683 and ten more in 1697 (the latter set probably composed about 1683 also but published posthumously)—reveal their background in the polyphony and thematic economy of the viol fantasia; and individual sonatas and movements sometimes emphasize the devices of counterpoint or other technique of the past. The sixth sonata of the first set, for instance, opens with a canon by twofold augmentation in the fifth and octave above; and the sixth sonata of the second set is an extended chaconne. The rhythmic complications of counterpoint are also present. However, the framework of his trio sonatas as a whole is derived from the Italian church sonata with respect to the number and order of movements and the texture of two violins of equal register plus *basso continuo*. This framework is a break with the old tradition of the viol fantasia and it is a break with the tradition of the dances that often follow the fantasia proper. Purcell's sonatas are also a reaction against the prevailing French style and taste of the English Court.

While these sonatas are Italian in inspiration and are idiomatic to the violin, they are also good examples of angular themes and English, Purcellian

[41] The section quoted is from the first *allegro* of Sonata No. IV in D (see p. 222, note 11, above). For much of this, see Michael Tilmouth, 'The Technique and Forms of Purcell's Sonatas' in *Music and Letters*, April 1959. See also J. A. Westrup, *Purcell*, London, 1937.

harmony (often of a chromatic or modal sort), grafted on the Italian model. Purcell also uses the archaic word *canzona* to describe his fugal movements. Purcell's sonatas are not more than moderately difficult for the violinist. A fair variety of bowings and a considerable amount of rapid figurations occur, but there are no multiple stops, and the range rarely exceeds extended first position (c'''). Above all, the musical values are obvious on every page, and the complex counterpoint of the *canzonas* and the expressive harmony of the slow movements are musically impressive.

In addition, there is a single 'solo' sonata for violin, bass viol, and *continuo*.[42] This, too, is based on the Italian sonata as regards order, number, and texture of movements. However, the bass-viol part is an independent part, serving as an equal partner to the violin, by no means slavishly doubling the *continuo*. In this respect, Purcell's sonata reminds us of the instrumentation and behaviour of William Lawes's fantasias for violin, bass viol, and organ (see p. 140), or Buxtehude's pieces for violin, bass viol, and *continuo*. This particular sonata of Purcell has no technical complications; if anything, it is simpler than the trio sonatas.

By the end of the seventeenth century the English had been exposed to the advanced schools of violin playing in Germany and Italy by the example of violinists like Baltzar and Matteis, and they must have known a certain amount of Italian violin music. When the flood of Italian violinists inundated England in the eighteenth century any astonishment the English felt at the new virtuosity of a Veracini or Geminiani must have been one of degree and not of kind.

Violin music in other countries

Little is known of the progress of the violin in other European countries at this time. The Dutch were undoubtedly following the Italians in violin making, but in violin music and technique they followed the tradition of the French, as one can deduce from remarks by Georg Muffat about the Low Countries and their imitation of Lully's style. In addition, Dutch paintings of the time show violinists using the typical French method of holding the violin and bow (cf. Plate 22). The French style was also known in Spain, at least in the Spanish Court. In 1679 the niece of Louis XIV, the Princess Marie Louise, married the Spanish King, and she took with her to Spain a number of musicians, including ten violinists among whom was Farinel of *Farinell's Ground*.[43] After her death, some of these musicians returned to

---

[42] Published in *The Works of Henry Purcell*, Vol. 31, London, 1959, pp. 95ff., where it is called 'Trio Sonata'.
[43] See Marcell Benoit, 'Les musiciens français de Marie-Louise d'Orléans, Reine d'Espagne' in *Revue Musicale, numero special, 226* (ed. Dufourcq), Paris, 1955. For the *Sarabande* in Spain, see below, p. 292 and note 13.

France, but we do not know what temporary or lasting influence this body of musicians had on Spanish instrumental music. It is not until the time of Herrando (1756) that a Spanish violin treatise appears (see p. 362), and at least until then our judgement of Spanish violin music and its technique are shreds and patches of guesswork.[44]

At any rate, we possess sufficient music of the time from European countries as a whole to show that violin music had made significant progress in the last half of the seventeenth century. Moreover, the tastes and prejudices of different areas asserted themselves in distinctive national styles of music and playing technique. The development of the latter and its relationship to the instrument and the music itself is a matter which we must now consider at length.

[44] Op. 1 of the Spanish composer D. F. G. de Castro was published in Bologna in 1695. Entitled *Trattenimenti armonici da camera*, these works are imitations of Cazzati and Corelli, and are in pure Italian style. Cf. A. Lavignac and L. de La Laurencie, *Encyclopédie de la musique et dictionnaire du Conservatoire*, pp. 2081ff.

❧

CHAPTER ELEVEN

The Technique of the Violin, 1650-1700 (I): National Styles of Playing. The Treatises. The Left Hand

B Y the late seventeenth century, national styles of violin music emerged more and more clearly, and inevitably there appeared corresponding differences in instruments, bows, and playing technique. Two sharply contrasted ways of playing, the French dance style and the Italian sonata style, were the focal points and inspiration for followers and imitators in Germany, England, and the Low Countries. Between these sharply drawn prototypes there must have been a good many intermediate styles of playing, and, with certain local variants, dance style must have been very similar in all countries, crossing national lines.

The dominant influence was Italian; and in proportion as Italian violins and violin music spread over Europe, the playing style which this music required made its influence felt, even in France. Longer bows appeared in both France and the Low Countries; and in England the Italian violinist, Nicola Matteis, showed the advantages of the Italian bow grip to the English, 'no small revelation' (see p. 249). The use of Italian violins throughout Europe was nothing new, and this usage continued. A number of Cremona violins were purchased for the *24 Violins* in England, as the records of the King's Musick show (see p. 202, note 15, above); and the measurements in the Talbot manuscript (see p. 202) reveal that the typical English violin was modelled on the instruments of Nicola Amati. In Holland the leading violin maker, Jacobs, followed the lead of the Italians, just as Stainer did in Austria.

The contrast of French and Italian style of playing dates from earlier times (cf. ch. 7), but the disparity between the two increased in the last part of the seventeenth century. The French were still playing dance music in a conservative style from the past, although carefully and even elegantly worked out; on the other hand, the Italians had developed the sonata and, by the end of the century, were composing concertos. The Germans, following the Italian style, carried certain technical features of the latter still further.

However, it is not easy to draw the main lines of these contrasting prototypes with assurance. We know too much about the simple technique of the amateur and not nearly enough about the advanced style of the professional. With the rise of amateur violinists, treatises for them appear; yet methods which reflect the practices of professional violinists cannot be found until well into the eighteenth century. There was a market for do-it-yourself manuals for amateurs, but none for the professional, the ambitious, or the exceptional player, all of whom went directly to a master. Ironically, in a time when so much experiment was taking place in both music and technique, the information of documents reflected practices of times past whose exponents were chiefly amateur and dance players.

Iconography, another source of information, is strangely lacking in this period. There are portraits of Corelli, but none of him playing the violin. Nor are there any pictures of German virtuosi like Biber or Walther. Dutch genre painting still contributes some examples of violins and violinists, and there are a few French pictures in which violinists are shown in playing position. However, to judge from the music being composed at that time in France and Holland (and from music that may occasionally be deciphered in such pictures), violinists in these countries must have been playing quite simple music, intended largely for dancing.

Taken as a whole, the Italian style varied greatly in difficulty and character. On the one hand were the dance violinists; on the other, violinists like Corelli playing sonatas on his Andrea Amati or Albani violin; or still others playing concertos and perhaps experimenting with the new 'long' model Stradivari violins. Compared to our prototype in the early seventeenth century, embodied in the Domenichino picture (Plate 20), a good Italian violinist at the end of the century was using a longer bow, and his instrument was more strongly strung. The bow was manipulated by the Italian grip (see p. 75); and his violin, probably an elegant one from Cremona, was held at the shoulder or neck in such a way to facilitate playing in the higher positions with a variety of bow strokes. This style was probably not far from that of the Italians in the early eighteenth century, as shown in a celebrated picture of Veracini playing the violin (Plate 30). If such figures could come to life and actually play for us, we would also be impressed by the expressive qualities of their playing. Galliard gives us a verbal description of Corelli's playing—a description that is quite astonishing in view of the seeming calm and nobility of Corelli's music:

'I never met with any man that suffered his passions to hurry him away so much whilst he was playing on the violin as the famous Arcangelo Corelli, whose eyes will sometimes turn as red as fire; his countenance will be distorted, his eyeballs roll as in an agony, and he gives in so much to what he is doing that he doth not look like the same man.'[1]

The German style was modelled on the Italians, and Biber and Walther developed it to the nth degree (see p. 225); but, just as in Italy, there are no satisfactory accounts or pictures which explain or describe the practices of these advanced players.

Within its technical limitations, the French style had become polished and sophisticated, thanks to the standards of ensemble playing demanded by Lully. The playing principles were the same as those in the early part of the century, but they were more refined and regulated, as Muffat makes apparent to us in his *Florilegium Secundum* of 1698 (see p. 260). Moreover, it appears likely that the French had been somewhat influenced by the Italians over a period of time. Pictures show the violin held at the shoulder or neck, the customary Italian position, but relatively little at the breast, the position traditional to the French in the past. A comparison of the Dou picture (Plate 22), used to illustrate breast position, with the later one of Corrette (1738; Plate 31) will make the point clear. Perhaps the influence of Lully's fine Italian hand is to be seen here. The French bow is also longer than previously, although it is shorter than that of the players of Italian sonatas or concertos; and it was held with the French grip, a grip which continued to be used by dance players in all countries until the early eighteenth century. The English followed the French, at least during the Restoration. In 1661 John Banister, a leading English violinist, was sent to Paris to study the ways of the *24 Violons du Roy*, and a few years later 'Mons. Louis [Lewis] Grabu', a Frenchman, became 'master of his Majesty's musick in the place of Nicholas Lanier deceased' (see p. 230).

Ultimately, differences in music and technique argue differences in sound and expression. In general, the Italian and German violinists sounded louder, more brilliant and varied, and more expressive, than the French. The latter were distinguished by uniform bowing, whose precise rhythmic style gave a special articulated sound, suited to the dances concerned. However, since the particulars of these differences are related to the details of technique, the

---

[1] François Raguenet, op. cit., notes and translation by Galliard (?), printed in *The Musical Quarterly*, July 1946, p. 419, note 15.

matter of the sound of the violin in the late seventeenth century will be discussed later (see p. 281).

This brief description of the two main contrasted styles of playing serves the useful purpose of introducing the subject and putting certain features in simplified form. To describe in detail each national style of playing has the disadvantage of repeating those features common to several styles. Consequently, the details of violin playing will be described as a whole, and specific references will be made to those national traits that distinguish one style from the other in the late seventeenth century. First we must say something about a new phenomenon, the violin treatises.

The violin treatises

By the end of the seventeenth century instruction books devoted solely to violin technique began to appear. On the surface of things it seems strange that these treatises were aimed primarily at amateur instruction and were far below the level of superior players. Under the circumstances that obtained at the time, it was really not strange at all. Those who were sufficiently expert to describe the new and advanced technique were practising virtuosi and, for the most part, they had no time or literary skill for such an effort. More important, written instructions were completely contrary to prevailing tradition, according to which the best players were taught orally and individually by a master as in the guilds. Under this system, details of advanced instruction were regarded as priceless trade secrets, not to be written down and printed—probably the fundamental reason why no treatise of the time explains the practices of the *avant-garde* schools of Italy and Germany. It is true that Georg Muffat's *Florilegium Secundum* describes the professional methods of the French violinists under Lully, but this technique was relatively simple compared to that of the Germans and Italians, and it was geared primarily to the performance of dance music.

The first treatises came from England and Germany, where the amateur violinist flourished. There was only one violin treatise in the seventeenth century that explained the practices of professionals—that of Georg Muffat, just mentioned. Not a single violin tutor concerned with the practices of professional violinists in Italy or Germany appeared in the seventeenth century. The first violin treatises were directed to amateur players; the first instruction books which reflect professional practice appear long after 1700. Instruction always tends to lag behind the best efforts of creative and performing artists, and the gap was particularly noticeable in violin playing at this time.

However, one should not imagine that the early violin treatises, although directed to amateurs and beginners, were without interest or significance. On the contrary, they have a very particular value. Collectively, they furnish us with a kind of information which, though elementary, can at least be documented.[2]

Perhaps more important, the appearance and continuing publication of these elementary manuals show that the violin had ceased to be the sole property and concern of professional violinists and that it had begun to appeal to a far broader social group among players. The elementary character of the first violin treatises is not indicative of the level of violin playing as practised by superior or professional violinists, but rather of the violin's popularity among amateurs on the decline of the viol. As a consequence, the violin gained rapidly in respectability, usurping most of the musical prerogatives of the viol and, in the process, acquiring something of the social esteem that the viol enjoyed. The adoption of the violin by amateurs in the late seventeenth century and the new developments in violin music (apart from the dance) account together for the greatly improved social position of the violin and the violinist by the end of the seventeenth century.

Information about violin playing often occurs first in works addressed to musicians as a whole, not specifically to violinists. A case in point is John Playford's *A Brief Introduction to the Skill of Musick*. Nothing about the violin appears in the first edition (1654), but the second revised edition of 1658 includes a section entitled 'Playing on the Treble Violin'.[3] Similarly, in Germany Georg Falck's *Idea boni Cantoris* (1688) has a section on the violin in a work of general musical instruction.

In 1695 three works appeared that are typical of new developments. The first of these was Daniel Merck's *Compendium Musicae Instrumentalis Chelicae*, published in Augsburg and containing elementary instructions, mainly for the violin, but with brief additional sections on the viola and viola da gamba. Two others were published in London: one with the charming and paternalistic title, *Nolens Volens or You shall learn to Play on the Violin whether you will or no*, 'Printed and Sold by T. Cross'; and the other, *The Self-Instructor on the Violin or the Art of Playing on that Instrument*, published by Miller, Walsh, and Hare. Of these three, the last two are devoted solely to violin instruction,

---

[2] The first violin tutors were essentially 'do-it-yourself' books. Often regarded as a modern phenomenon, such books flourished during the seventeenth and eighteenth centuries not only in music but in many other fields as well, and they furnish a vivid social commentary on the times. They 'told the seventeenth and eighteenth century how to rig a ship, fire a gun, beat a drum, lacquer a vase, get a husband, brew some beer, and beget a handsome child. The fact that few copies of them have survived is proof that they were read. In fact, they are far rarer today than the literary works of the time, which were bought and often preserved unread—even as now.' See Lawrence Clark Powell in the *University Bulletin* of the University of California, 22 June 1959, p. 191.

[3] The date 1658 is still within the period of the English Commonwealth, and the amateur instruction for the violin is a natural accompaniment to the growth of chamber music, noted earlier (p. 232).

and *Nolens Volens*, having been published about six months earlier than *The Self-Instructor*, may be regarded as the first violin tutor exclusively for the violin extant in any language.[4]

The level of instruction in all these violin tutors is elementary, and Merck, writing for German amateurs, confesses as much. He says that terms like *spiccato* and *harpeggiato* (*arpeggiato*) are not mentioned, although they are used by famous violinists like Walther, Biber, and Westhoff; and he tells us that this is because his work is for beginners, not for advanced violinists. Similarly, Falck, also a German, leaves the *scordatura* to the 'masters', and his section on the stringed instruments is labelled 'for beginners'. The burden of instruction was left to the teacher and even to the ingenuity of the pupil. In his *Traité de la viole* (1687), a relatively advanced work for viol, J. Rousseau says that his manual cannot take the place of a teacher; and Daniel Speer, in his *Grund-richtiger . . . Unterricht* (Ulm, 1687), leaves the matter of holding the violin and the bow to the student's discretion and imagination! It is no wonder that Leopold Mozart regarded his complete and systematic *Violin-schule* (1756) as the first true book of instruction for the violin. However, it is unlikely that Leopold Mozart knew any of these elementary works from the seventeenth century, including the descriptions of the 'professional' practices of Lully's violinists by Georg Muffat.

In all this, it is well to emphasize, as the treatises sometimes do, the importance of the teacher and the advantage of individual demonstration and instruction, compared to the written word alone. It is more than doubtful whether any fine violinist, in the past or present, ever learned to play solely from a book. This point should be kept firmly in mind in judging and using violin treatises, particularly those of early times, when the old guild relationship of master and pupil was so strongly in force and when the gap between the amateur instruction of the violin methods and the practices of professional violinists was so considerable.

The education of violinists probably began with playing simple dances and tunes, which might be elaborated by variations, then proceeding onward to ornaments, violin figurations of various sorts, and work in the positions and double-stop technique. The methods of the seventeenth century would suffice only for the early stages of this instruction and for beginners and

[4] There may be certain 'lost' violin tutors that antedate *Nolens Volens*—for example, John Lenton's *The Gentleman's Diversion* (1693)—but it is unlikely that any of them exceeds its level of instruction. For this and for the relationship of these two English tutors to Peter Prelleur's *The Modern Musick-Master* (1731) and to Geminiani's *The Art of Playing on the Violin* (1751), see David D. Boyden, 'Geminiani and the first Violin Tutor' in *Acta Musicologica*, fasc. III–IV, 1959, and 'A Postscript to "Geminiani and the first Violin Tutor" ' in *Acta*, fasc. I, 1960. A complete, revised list of English violin tutors, 1658–1731, is given in the latter article. The large number of these tutors is also a witness to a continuing amateur tradition of violin playing.

amateurs. More advanced violinists and professionals had to acquire their training by their own efforts or from a master. The violin tutors give a limited amount of basic information, but for a detailed picture of violin playing we must rely in addition on iconography (where possible), hints and deduction from the music itself, and on other treatises, including those of the viol and those from the eighteenth century, which may sometimes be related backwards in time to the practices of the seventeenth century.

The technique of the violin. Tuning the violin

The violin was normally tuned to g, d', a', e", just as it is today. The specific exception was the *scordatura* (see pp. 130 and 250). The pitch of the usual violin tuning, however, must be considered a relative matter, not necessarily that of modern pitch. John Playford (1658), still harking back to the sixteenth century, advises the player to tune the highest (treble) string 'as high as it will conveniently bear without breaking'. The testimony of Muffat (1698) shows that the violin in France was tuned a whole tone or even a minor third below that in Germany (see p. 204). Obviously Playford's relaxed notions about pitch would not do where ensembles with instruments of fixed pitch were concerned. The violins were normally tuned in pure fifths, but a typical keyboard tuning of the time used the flat fifth of meantone temperament. Falck recognized this situation, and proposed that the A string of the violin be tuned to the 'A' of the keyboard. According to Falck, tuning with the D string—which seems to have been the more usual method at that time—makes too great a pitch discrepancy on the E string; and by this he means that adding the two pure fifths, D-A and A-E, makes the highest string (E) of the violin noticeably sharper than the corresponding 'E' of the keyboard instrument. By tuning to 'A', the discrepancy becomes noticeable on the lowest (G) string, but this string was not used nearly as much as the upper strings. *The Self-Instructor* (1695) tells the violinist to tune upward from 'G'!

Holding the violin

The same variety and experiment, noted in the development of the violin and its music in the late seventeenth century, appear in the technique of the instrument. The methods of holding the violin and the bow are apt illustrations. The violin is still held variously at the breast, the shoulder, or the neck, much as it was earlier (cf. p. 152), but there have been refinements and improvements to cope with new technical and musical demands. Falck's instructions (1688) are typical of the elementary information in the methods, all of which describe breast or shoulder position.[5] Falck's comments are more

---

[5] Most of Falck's information about the violin is still being repeated for beginners over fifty years later by J. F. B. C. Majer in his *Neu-eröffneter theoretisch- und practischer Music-Saal*, Nürnberg, 1741, 1st ed., 1732 (the latter prefaced by the phrase *Museum Musicum*).

specific than most. According to him, the violinist should hold the violin between the left thumb and the ball of the forefinger, not too tightly in case it is necessary to play in the upper positions (*in der Höhe*) and return. The violin is to be placed on the left breast and inclined downward a bit to the right so that the right elbow will not have to be raised too high in playing the lower strings. The arms should be held freely and not tight against the body, and the fingers should be curved above and close to the fingerboard. In Simpson's *The Division-Viol*, almost thirty years earlier, the author makes this interesting point: the player ought to keep his fingers on the strings until they must be raised. This, he says, simplifies the fingering and continues the sound of the note when the bow has left it, and he gives a specific sign ($\diagdown\diagup$) where he wishes the player to do this. Simpson's instructions are explicitly addressed to the viol players, and while similar precepts do not appear in violin treatises until the eighteenth century, his sensible method, equally effective and applicable in the case of violin playing, may well have been adopted by violinists of the same time.

Breast or shoulder position was the customary one for dance musicians, being generally used in France, the Low Countries, England, and Germany for music limited mainly to first position. But pictures show increasingly that the violin was also held or possibly braced at the neck, a position more suitable for an advanced technique. Breast position or shoulder position was satisfactory for simple music without shifts. For difficult pieces, advanced players must have adopted methods suitable to their needs, which included shifting the hand through the upper positions and back again, and some firm manner of holding the violin in downward shifts must have been used to prevent its falling. Two chief methods were used to accomplish this: holding the instrument against the player's neck and bracing it with the chin; or developing a special technique of 'crawling' downward, especially from third to first position (cf. p. 155, and Fig. 5).[6]

Holding the bow

The methods of holding the bow are similar to those of the early seventeenth century (see pp. 152–3). However, the thumb-under-hair (French) grip is losing ground to the Italian method of gripping the wood of the bow between thumb and fingers. When Matteis came to England early in the

[6] Roger North says Matteis 'was a very tall and large bodyed man, used a very long bow, [and] rested his instrument against his short ribbs . . .'; and, at another time North confirms this information, saying, 'He [Matteis] held his instrument almost against his girdle . . . and I have found very few that will beleeve it possible he could performe as he did in that posture' (*Roger North on Music*, op. cit., p. 309 and note 63). Matteis's method of holding the violin still does not seem possible; and the incredulity of Matteis's contemporaries proves that his playing position was unusual to the point of incomprehensibility.

1670s, 'He taught ye English to hold ye bow by ye wood only & not to touch ye hair which was no small reformation.'[7] Falck advocates the French grip: the right thumb presses into the hair directly at the frog (*Härpflein*) so that a deep stroke and sound can be produced from the strings. Hold the bow between the first two joints of the [index] finger, says Falck, and not too near and not too far from the bridge. Pressure on the bow stick presumably controls volume. The French grip is still basic to France, England (cf. Playford), the Low Countries, and, in part, to Germany. The Italian grip is used in Italy and probably among advanced players elsewhere, especially in Germany (cf. Plates 22 and 31 for the French grip; Plate 30 for the Italian).

Falck clearly recommends holding the bow at the frog (nut). But, as pictures show, the hand was frequently held from one to three inches above (cf. Plate 36). The considerable variation in bow lengths, weights, and balances makes this variety of holding understandable. A short bow, as in the typical dance bow, would normally be held with the hand at the frog to take advantage of its full length. This is obvious from descriptions and pictures. An old bow, probably from the late seventeenth century and now belonging to the firm of W. E. Hill and Sons of London, has a worn place near the frog, where the fingers habitually gripped the stick. The *crémaillère* bow (Plate 29a) must have been held above the dentation for reasons of comfort. Christopher Simpson used the entire length of a very long bow (see p. 254), and the picture in his treatise shows his hand at the frog, not several inches above. Mace (1676) cites Simpson's instructions for holding the bow, and then adds this interesting and significant comment: 'I must confess, that for my own Part, I could never Use It [the bow] so well, as when I held it 2 or 3 Inches off the Nut (more or less) according to the Length or Weight of the Bow, for Good Poyzing of It: But 'tis possible, that by Use I might have made It as Familiar to My self, as It was to Him [Simpson].'[8] In all this the fundamental factors were undoubtedly the balance of the bow itself, the effects to be achieved, and the technical ability of the player.

The left hand: fingering, positions, and shifting. Rules for the scordatura

Fingering and position-playing, discussed in the treatises of the time, are rudimentary indeed—there is scarcely any advance beyond the early seventeenth century (cf. pp. 153ff.). First-position fingering, with an extension to c''', is often the only one given, and open string is used consistently, indicated by 'o', as it is today. As we noted earlier (p. 153), open string was easier to play because the rather thick violin neck made it somewhat more

---

[7] Roger North, *The Musicall Grammarian*, op. cit., pp. 35–36. See also *Roger North on Music*, op. cit., p. 309.
[8] *Musick's Monument*, op. cit., p. 248.

H.V.P.–S

difficult to play the same note with the fourth finger on the lower string. Besides, with gut strings the contrast between the open and stopped string is not as great as it is with the metal or wound strings used today. Fretted fingerboards are still recommended occasionally for 'learners', but this was only a crutch for intonation, and was soon abandoned by players of any ability. Chromatic scales through the first position are given in these elementary treatises, the sharped notes being reached by sliding a finger toward the bridge, and flatted notes by sliding a finger toward the nut (Ex. 73). But c′ sharp, g′ sharp, and e″ flat are often taken with the fourth finger (Ex. 73).

Ex. 73

The Self-Instructor (1695)

```
o    1    1    2    2    3    4    4    o    1    1    2    2    3    3    4    4    4
```
(Two upper strings only)

Note the fingering distinction in Ex. 73 between a″ sharp and b″ flat, the former presumably being lower in pitch. Yet d″ sharp and e″ flat are both given as the fourth finger—perhaps a typographical error. Since the treatises deal largely with elementary technique, we have very little information about fingering as used by advanced players (see, however, p. 248 for Simpson's advice to viol players).

When playing with a *scordatura* tuning, there are special fingering rules. In the first place, the appropriate 'mis-tuning' is invariably indicated at the beginning of the piece (cf. Ex. 66). Out of consideration for the player, whose fingering is tied to normal tuning, *scordatura* pieces are generally written, not at sounding pitch (as in Marini: see p. 130), but so that the player reads the music, and fingers, just as he would if playing in the normal tuning. In effect, the usual *scordatura* notation is a 'hand-grip' notation, a species of tablature for a kind of transposing instrument. To make this notation work, there have to be special provisions: (1) first position is used wherever possible; (2) open string *must* be used unless the contrary is expressly indicated; (3) the accidentals in the signatures apply only to the note in question, not to the octave above or below. Some strange key signatures result (see Ex. 66 and Ex. 67). Through trial-and-error we know that these rules of *scordatura*-playing are fundamental, given a 'mis-tuning' and a 'hand-grip' notation. Further proof is afforded by the explicit 'tablatures' used by Ariosti in his 'Lessons' for viola d'amore in the early eighteenth century (see p. 352; for further on the *scordatura*, see our Index).

A good violinist of the time was accustomed to playing in the third and fourth position in Italy, and in Germany a virtuoso confidently navigated the sixth and seventh position. The eighth position is called for on a few rare occasions, as in Alessandro Scarlatti's opera, *Laodicea e Berenice* (1701). Ordinarily, the upper positions were restricted to the highest string, largely to extend the range; but in double stops particularly, the upper positions must have been used on other strings as well. Almost all of Corelli's music can be played with the first three positions, allowing for an occasional fourth, and a rare fifth, position. The positions mentioned specifically in the treatises are usually the third and the sixth, the latter, significantly, by a German (Falck). The second position is not described at this time, although it must have been used in sequences and double stops (cf. Ex. 62, last beat). Almost all French music remains in first position, and it hardly exceeds third position until the time of Leclair in the eighteenth century.

The actual details of shifting are not discussed by the theorists, but we may deduce from the fingering given that the first finger was usually the shifting finger, and that, as a rule, the number of shifts was kept to the minimum. In ordinary scales, one shift is sufficient to arrive at fourth position and one shift likewise to get back to first (Ex. 74). The downward shift in Ex. 74 requires the hand to move through the large shifting-interval of the fourth, and implies a firm grip on the instrument. In the music some sequences by steps must have been played by corresponding shifting by step

Ex. 74

(Ex. 75). Shifting is simplified when an open string occurs in a passage. The shift can then be made while the open string is being played, and this method of shifting must have been prevalent. Leopold Mozart later discusses the specific advantages of using open string and repeated notes to help effect a shift of position (cf. the repeated note in Ex. 75). In all this we must keep

Ex. 75

in mind the facts of the old violin. Its thick neck and lack of chin rest tended to dictate the way the hand held the instrument. In addition, when playing up to the seventh position, the player got more hand support from the old thick neck than from the modern counterpart. Above the seventh position the modern neck is essential to play comfortably.

Terms for shifting begin to appear. *Applicatur* or *Application* is the general term in Germany. In Italy the word *manico* is connected with shifting. Torelli's violin concerto Op. 8, No. 7 (1709) contains the direction *sopra il manico tutto* for playing a specified passage, apparently meaning to play all the notes included by the direction above the first position. In a remark made much later, Quantz confirms this interpretation:[9] 'The so-called *mezzo manico* which calls for placing the hand a semitone, whole tone, or several tones further up the fingerboard, gives a great advantage not only in avoiding open strings . . . but in many other places, especially in cadenzas.' Note that Quantz speaks of using shifts to *avoid* open strings—doubtless referring to passages where the contrast of colour between open and stopped strings would be too disparate, and presumably showing that even with gut strings he was sensitive to the difference of colour involved.

To avoid shifting, the fingers are sometimes extended ('extensions') to reach certain notes, the commonest being the fourth finger extended a semitone to reach c''' on the E string from the first position. In double and triple stops a whole-tone extension is sometimes called for in the music (Ex. 76).

Ex. 76

No reference to harmonics appears in the music or in the treatises of the seventeenth century. They were used in playing the *tromba marina*, but not by violinists until the eighteenth century (see p. 337).

Today the vibrato is considered an organic part of left-hand technique. In the seventeenth century it was treated as an ornament, and it will be discussed as such later (p. 287). So will other technical matters concerning the right hand of the violinist.

[9] J. J. Quantz, *Versuch*, Berlin, 1752, ch. 17, sec. 2, para. 33.

✼

CHAPTER TWELVE

The Technique of the Violin, 1650-1700 (II): the Right Hand and Related Questions. The Sound of the Violin

I N his *Traité de la viole*, Rousseau observes that if the viol is the body of the instrument, the bow is its soul; and from this time violinists and other string players seem to be increasingly aware of the manifold possibilities of bowing for expression and variety.[1] In the seventeenth century, as in the sixteenth, the most detailed descriptions of bowing occur in accounts of the viol. These descriptions often apply in principle to the violin and were doubtless adapted by violinists to their purposes. In the instructions for the viol player in his *Musick's Monument* (1667), Mace emphasizes the necessity of a good 'Stroak', and he tells the player 'to draw your Bow just Cross the Strings in a Direct line, endeavouring to Sound one Single String, with a Long Bow, well nigh from Hand to Point, and from Point to Hand Smoothly . . .' (p. 248). Mace also discusses the bow change and the function of the wrist in it. This is done, he says, 'by causing the Hand, at the very Turning of the Bow (either way) to incline to a Contra-Motion; the Arm (as it were) leaving the Wrist behind It, seems to draw It again after It . . .' (p. 249). Simpson, in his *The Division-Viol* (1665), is more specific about the role of the whole arm, the elbow, and the wrist of the viol player. The shoulder joint is used in playing long notes, but this 'must be avoyded' in playing quick notes, using the wrist. Simpson explains a divergence of opinion concerning the wrist and the elbow. Some, he says, contend that only the wrist should be used, 'keeping his Arm streight and stiff in the Elbow Joint'. 'Others

---

[1] The French also call the sound post 'the soul' (*l'âme*); but which meaning came first or whether the French would bestow two souls on the violin are mysteries which we prefer to leave unresolved.

contend' that the wrist must be assisted by the elbow. Specifically, Simpson adds that in thirty-second notes the wrist 'chiefly' is used, but in sixteenths and eighths 'we must allow so much stiffness to the Wrist as may command the Bow on, and off the String, at every Note, if occasion so require' (pp. 7–8).

The treatises recommend that the bow be kept parallel to the bridge. Playing close to the bridge is advocated for loudness, for the upper string, and for thin strings; farther from the bridge for soft passages, the lower strings, and for thick strings. The hand and especially the first finger are the means of making the bow produce a louder or softer sound. The speed of the bow stroke as a factor in loudness or softness is not mentioned before Leopold Mozart's *Violinschule* of 1756 (see p. 396).

The increasing length of the bow seems to be related to an increased consciousness of tone quality, and string players begin to take more and more advantage of the whole bow-length and the full length of the extended arm. 'Give as much bow to every Quaver [eighth], as the length thereof will permit,' says Simpson; and he tells the player to make 'each several String yield [*sic*] a full clear sound'. Roger North speaks of '*arcata* or long bow', thus implying that the basic bow stroke is long.[2] Even with the shorter and stiffer dance-bow, an ideal of beautiful sound is pursued. Muffat, although describing the practice of French violinists in particular, says that the best masters of every nation agree that 'the more the stroke (*trait*) is long, firm, equal, and sweet, the more it is esteemed'. Even 'in so many successive down bows (*reprises de l'archet en bas*), one never hears from the Lullists anything disagreeable or rude'.

By 1700 tone production, bow change, and the use of the whole bow were closely related by the theorists, as they doubtless had been by players from earliest times (cf. p. 77). In any case, producing a beautiful tone was obviously much in the mind of performers in the last half of the seventeenth century. The lack of much explicit information on tone production in the violin treatises is far less significant than the continuous and zealous experiments of violin makers to achieve an instrument capable of beautiful tone, ease of playing, and reserves of power. The experiments of Nicola Amati and Stradivari are eloquent testimony to these aims, and the increased length of the bow points inevitably in the direction of greater variety, expression, and volume.

Nuanced and sustained bow strokes

The application of nuances of *crescendo* and *diminuendo* is considered in the category of ornaments in the late seventeenth century. Simpson, for

---

[2] *Roger North on Music*, op. cit., p. 164. For the quotations from Simpson, see his *The Division-Viol*, pp. 5 and 3 respectively.

example, classifies each of these nuances as an 'ornament of the Bow'. But it is probable that violinists applied the *messa di voce* ($\Longleftarrow \Longrightarrow$) to long notes in imitation of the voice, the model of violin *cantabile*. One entire variation in Corelli's *La Follia* (Op. 5, No. 12) is devoted to long notes; and in the tradition of the time, it is almost certain that these notes were played with the expressive *messa di voce*, probably graced with vibrato. Geminiani, the pupil of Corelli, says in 1751 that long notes are always played with *messa di voce*; and although a pupil need not necessarily follow his master slavishly, much of Geminiani's information is in the direct tradition of Corelli. Roger North (*c.* 1695) also would have a long note filled and softened '*insensatim* [imperceptibly], so as to be like also a gust of wind, which begins with a soft air, and fills by degrees to a strength as makes all bend, and then softens away againe into a temper [moderation], and so vanish'. This is North's picturesque way of describing the *messa di voce* on which he would 'superinduce' the vibrato, 'a gentle and slow wavering', which he also calls a 'waived note'. A generation later he questions the use of a wrist-shake (vibrato) 'upon every note that gives time for it'.[3]

A little-known work of the greatest interest reports on Corelli's practices with respect to evenly sustained and nuanced bowing. Robert Bremner, a highly regarded English publisher, wrote *Some Thoughts on the Performance of Concert-Music*.[4] Bremner says that he was a violin pupil of Geminiani (d. 1768), and presumably his information represents the Corelli tradition as reported by Geminiani. According to Bremner, nuanced bowings and addition of ornaments and improvised passages are the province of the soloist, not of the orchestral violinist, who should play what is written. In this context Bremner may be commenting only on the practice of his own time, not Corelli's, but he also speaks specifically of the performance of Corelli's works (p. vii):

'The practice of the swell, as there instructed [in Tartini's *Letter* to Lombardini, see p. 361], is of the utmost consequence to those who wish to send a melodious Adagio, or any air home to the heart; but such slow movements as are composed more for the effects of harmony than melody, like those in the trios of *Corelli*, and many modern compositions, claim, in most instances, a steady equal pressure of bow. A daily practice of this manner of bowing is of equal importance with that of the swell, if not more so, to those who wish to be useful in concert; as it accustoms the student to have at all times length of bow to spare, of which every good performer makes a point. These two, namely the

---

[3] For these quotations, see *Roger North on Music*, op. cit., p. 18 and pp. 164–5.
[4] Bremner's *Thoughts* are concealed in a preface to his edition of *Six Quartettos for two violins, a tenor, and Violoncello . . .* by J. G. C. Schetky, Op. VI, London, 1777.

swell, and *sostenuto*, or sustained bow, may be said to be the roots from whence all the other powers of the bow spring.'

In a footnote, Bremner adds this important comment:

'I have been informed that *Corelli* judged no performer fit to play in his band, who could not, with one stroke of his bow, give a steady and powerful sound, like that of an organ, from two strings at once, and continue it for ten [*sic*] seconds; and yet, it is said, the length of their bows at that time did not exceed twenty inches.' [Bremner must mean 'twenty inches' of free playing hair.]

Bremner's remarks point to the presence of two styles of bowing, the nuanced and the evenly sustained. In this connexion, it should be pointed out that the term *sostenuto* is used ambiguously in violin playing. *Sostenuto* means literally 'sustained' or 'held out' and it is sometimes used merely in this sense without connotation as to dynamics. At other times, *sostenuto* may imply the addition of various types of nuance. Bremner obviously means *sostenuto* in the sense of 'evenly sustained' without dynamic nuance. To avoid confusion in this context, we will distinguish the two types by the terms 'evenly sustained' and 'nuanced' bowings. (For *enfler le son*, see the Index.)

According to the above quotation from Bremner, the 'swell' is used for expressive melody, while the evenly sustained style is more appropriate for passages whose effects depend on harmony. Bremner's distinctions are perfectly valid. However, general practice at the end of the seventeenth century as regards the use of the 'swell' may be stated more broadly: namely, that the nuanced style was commonly used not only for melodious and expressive movements but also for long notes. Hence Corelli's direction, unique in his entire works, *Arcate sostenute e come sta* (sustained bows and [play] as it is written) at the head of the *Grave* movement of his 'Christmas Concerto' (Op. 6, No. 8), implies exceptional treatment: namely that the long notes of this movement are to be bowed in evenly sustained style, and they are to be played as written without the addition of ornaments or improvisations. Otherwise one assumes that a nuanced style would have been used on these long notes as a matter of course, and the ornamental additions would have been made *ad libitum* according to prevailing convention.

The discipline of bowing. The Rule of Down-Bow

In the early seventeenth century the Italians developed a discipline of bowing, regulating the conduct of down-bow and up-bow (see p. 157). The continuation of this bowing discipline is inherent in reports of Corelli's practice. Muffat, in the foreword to his *Auserlesene . . . Instrumental-Music*

(1701) says that he heard Corelli's concertos in Rome 'some time ago [1681–2] . . . beautifully performed with the utmost accuracy by a great number of instrumentalists'. The 'great number' was sometimes as many as one hundred and fifty players according to another account,[5] and the 'utmost accuracy by a great number' implies a discipline and system of bowing. According to Geminiani, 'Corelli regarded it as essential to the *ensemble* of a [string] band, that their bows should all move exactly together, all up, or all down, so that at his rehearsals, which constantly preceded every public performance of his concertos, he would immediately stop the band if he discovered one irregular bow.'[6] However, in this period the most explicit details about the discipline of bowing and the so-called Rule of Down-Bow come from Muffat, a German reporting on the practices of the French.[7]

Muffat's remarks have received considerable attention, since they are the only real source of the practice of professional violinists at this time. One must remember that the French style is a conservative one, largely devoted to the requirements of playing dance music; and, although highly mannered and worked out in sophisticated ways, the French style is actually based on the principles first enunciated by the Italians in the early seventeenth century, if not before. In view of the advanced practices among the Italian and German violinists at the end of the century, about whom we have so little information, it is ironic that much of our knowledge about bowing in the late seventeenth century has been based on the details of the French style as related by Muffat. It is true that Muffat shows certain bowings in relation to *allegro*, *adagio* and so on, possibly indicating some relationship to the sonata style; but we may assume from his title that what he says is directed primarily to the performance of dances in general and the French ballet in particular. There are a few German and English treatises of the time, as already explained, but they are addressed to amateurs and dance violinists, who employed a style based on the French.

Lully, under whom the French style developed, was Italian-born, and

---

[5] See *Grove's Dictionary of Music and Musicians*, 5th ed., London, 1954, Vol. II, p. 439. For the quotation from Muffat, see Strunk, *Source Readings*, op. cit., p. 449.

[6] See Charles Burney, *A General History*, op. cit.; the quotation is taken from the reprinted edition (New York, 1935), Vol. II, p. 443.

[7] Muffat's principal statement is contained in the explanatory material in his *Florilegium Secundum*, op. cit., 1698. This material, cited here in French but published in four languages, consists of: (1) *Preface*; (2) *Premieres Observations de L'Autheur sur la maniere de Jouër les airs de Balets à la Françoise selon la methode de feu Monsieur de Lully*. According to the *MGG* article on Muffat, he was born in 1653, and studied in Paris from 1663–69. If this is so, Muffat's information was gathered as a boy aged ten to sixteen; and it was not committed to print until nearly thirty years after he left Paris. These remarks are not intended to cast doubt on the reliability of Muffat's testimony, only to put it in historical context. Although certain features of Lully's style must have developed after 1669, Muffat probably knew about them, because the French style was well-known in Germany.

possibly some of his practices may be traced to Italian violinists of a considerably earlier time (cf. pp. 157ff.). Not the slightest hint of the details of Italian bowing of the late seventeenth century is recorded by Italians themselves, there being no Italian treatises known. Even though Geminiani, a half-century later (1751), speaks scornfully of that 'Wretched rule of down-bow', there must have been a disciplined routine of bowing widespread in Italy which continued the bowing practices of the early seventeenth century. Geminiani is reacting against the cut-and-dried rationale of French dance bowing developed under Lully.

The treatises of the time tacitly acknowledge the importance of the Rule of Down-Bow by including it with monotonous regularity, and Merck comments in 1695 that proper bowing rules are essential, otherwise 'there will be gross errors such as one sees in those who have had no instruction'. The workings of the Rule of Down-Bow have been treated in some detail in an earlier chapter (pp. 157ff.). Nevertheless, we restate the Rule here, showing certain of its applications in general, in the French style, and in other treatises of the time. To review: in essence the Rule prescribes that a down-bow is normally used on the first beat of a measure unless it begins with a rest. This rule, being related to stress, is also applied to the accented parts of single beats, tempo permitting. A complementary rule is that up-bow is used on unaccented notes, such as up-beats, and on unaccented parts of beat if the tempo is not too fast. Initial rests are considered as down-bow, and the following notes are bowed accordingly. Playford states the 'Rule' in the following rather quaint way: 'If there be an odd note at the beginning of a Lesson or Tune, as usually there is in Ayres and Corants, then you strike it with drawing the Bow backwards; and if there be no odd Note, then your first Note is strook [*sic*] with the Bow put forward.'[8] Playford is speaking of the viol, but there is no difficulty in translating his statement to the language of the violin: for 'backwards' read up-bow; and for 'forward' read down-bow.

Whether there is an even or uneven number of notes in a measure also affects the bowing, since down-bow is normally used at the beginning of each measure. In Ex. 77a, the first note is taken down-bow according to the Rule, and alternate up-bows and down-bows follow. In Ex. 77b, on the other hand, the first sixteenth-note of beat two would be taken down-bow in slow or moderate tempo because the odd number of seven notes in the measure would result in the following measure beginning with an up-bow if the normal alternation of up-bow and down-bow is continued. Besides, the down-bow on beat two may be rationalized as coming on the strong *part* of the beat, and it is so heard in slow or even moderate time. In rapid tempo the

[8] John Playford, *A Breif [sic] Introduction to the Skill of Musick for song and viol*, London, 1658, p. 74.

four notes of beat two would normally be slurred and taken up-bow, as shown below the example. In Ex. 77c, the initial rest is regarded as a silent down-bow, and the following note is taken up-bow according to rule. Ex. 77d is similar in principle to Ex. 77b.

Ex. 77

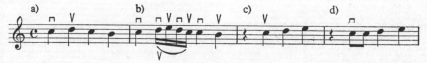

When two down-bows or two up-bows follow each other the bow must either be replaced or successive regions of the bow must be used, the latter procedure being normal (cf. Ex. 81b). As Rousseau says, 'Go to about the middle of the bow and continue in the same direction without re-drawing'.

If a measure contains an even number of notes, the normal procedure (in the absence of slurs) is alternate down-bow and up-bow. Since measures of duple time more often contain an even number of notes—and triple time, an odd number—the treatises frequently discuss the matter according to categories of bowing in duple and triple time, as, for example, in *Nolens Volens* (1695, see p. 245). The real factors, of course, are whether a note is to be stressed and the fact that the violin down-bow is, by its very nature, the stroke normally used for stress. These two considerations explain the normal rule of starting each measure down-bow.

The rules are not always easy to apply since different tempos complicate the matter. Ex. 78 would normally start up-bow according to the rule, and

Ex. 78

the normal bowing would be that shown at (1). But at a fast tempo, it would be easier to slur the sixteenths as at (2) or even to start down-bow as at (3). The difficulty in Ex. 78 is that there is an isolated group of two sixteenths, which complicate the bowing if each of the notes in the measure is taken with individual, alternate bow-strokes. On the other hand, sixteenth-note

Ex. 79

patterns may work out so that each note may be bowed separately and alternately with down-bow and up-bow, and still naturally result in down-bow at the start of the following measure (Ex. 79).

Muffat makes the point that there is no uniformity of bowing except in France. Nevertheless, it is clear that players and composers like Corelli insisted on a definite uniformity in their music (cf. p. 257 above). The Germans admit that there are different opinions about bowing. With respect to the music shown in Ex. 80, Merck says that the usual method of bowing

Merck

Ex. 80

this passage is two down-bows and one up-bow as shown (N = *Niederzug* = down-bow; A = *Aufzug* = up-bow). Nevertheless, he continues, there are some who use one down-bow and two up-bows, thereby rendering the bowing complicated (*verzurket*), since the up-bow is ordinarily shorter than down-bow. Hence the first method is preferable. Falck (see p. 245) also admits there are different opinions about bowing. For a measure containing an odd number of notes he gives either down-up-down *or* down-up-up. To him it is a matter of indifference which one is used—or indeed whether the player starts down-bow or up-bow—provided that the composition is not 'defamed' thereby (cf. Praetorius's similar remark, p. 151 above).

The rational mind of the French will have none of this shilly-shallying. Dance music, the speciality of the French, must be clearly accented and articulated, and the Rule of Down-Bow does this admirably. Muffat gives the usual Rule as applied to initial beats and rests and to even numbers of like notes in duple time. But where there are odd numbers of notes in triple time, he gives such examples as Ex. 81a. Each measure of this example, labelled *Grave*, is bowed down-up-down. The down-bow which begins measure 2 is presumably performed by replacing the bow. Ex. 81b shows how similar patterns in fast triple time are bowed, beats two and three being taken as two consecutive up-bows. This bowing, played in successive regions of the bow, is distinctly articulated and is called *craquer*. The same type of bowing is applied to similar passages in fast 6/4, 6/8, and 9/8 time. (But see Ex. 81e for a different 6/8 bowing.) In Ex. 81c, also in triple time, the initial rest in measure 2 is followed by a down-bow because there is the even number of two notes in the measure. In Ex. 81d, a down-bow is indicated for each of the single notes that fills the entire measure. Each of these is presumably a 'replaced' bow. In Ex. 81e, down-bows and up-bows are used in alternation in a *gigue* in 6/8 time. Sometimes this principle of alternation of down-bow and up-bow is applied over two measures of triple time, coming out down-bow every other measure. In Ex. 81f, the *craquer* bowing is used in duple time, the tempo by implication being fast; and in Ex. 81g, two down-bows come together because there are an uneven number of notes in the measure and because the second note, on beat three, requires some stress. Muffat also admits a number of slurred bowings, especially in fast time (see below). One of Muffat's most interesting, as well as most quoted, examples

Ex. 81

is a minuet fully bowed according to French style, shown above Ex. 82. The bowing given below Ex. 82 is the Italian-German style for the same music, according to Muffat. However, in view of the Italian and German bowings described in the early part of the century by Rognoni, Herbst, and Zannetti (see pp. 157ff.), Muffat's simple up-bows and down-bows in alternation for Italian dance music must be an oversimplified approximation of the real thing. At any rate, the implications of Ex. 82 are manifestly absurd as a bowing discipline for the complexities of the advanced German and Italian style of music.

On the other hand, the French bowing of Ex. 82 is extremely instructive in its proper context of French dancing. An important point is that the pattern of a given dance step may take two measures of the music. The

Ex. 82

menuet is a case in point, the pattern requiring six beats covering two measures. In other words, a marked articulation comes after every sixth beat, not after every third beat, and a heavy stress is normal at the beginning of every *second* measure only. Ex. 82 is a classic case of bowing arranged to suit the dance pattern of the *menuet*. The first measure is really an up-beat or warning signal; the real pattern starts in measure 2, and the bowing is worked out in uniform groups of two measures, each group being bowed as follows:

Pattern

m.2:   m.3:
down-up (*craquer*) | down-up-down | | down (replaced bow), etc.

In this two-measure pattern, the bowing is arranged so that at the beginning of each new pattern the down-bow must be lifted and replaced ('replaced' bow), since the last bow stroke of the old pattern is also down-bow. The result is a real articulation between patterns and a heavy stress at the beginning of each new pattern. The down-bow at the beginning of the second measure of the pattern also gives some stress, but there is no articulation, since the down-bow comes after an up-bow played with the *craquer* bowing (for the sound of Ex. 82, cf. our recording). In fast dances like the *gigue* (Ex. 81e), the six beats, all in one measure, are taken by alternate down-bow and up-bow, 'as it comes'. The other dances for which Muffat furnishes specific bowings are the *courante*, *bourrée*, and *gavotte*. On the whole, dances in duple time have simpler bowings than those in triple.[9]

Terms and abbreviations for down-bow and up-bow are as follows:

	Down-bow	Up-bow
Italy	T (*tirare*)	P (*pontare; puntare*)
German (Merck)	N (*Niederzug*)	A (*Aufzug*)
England	d (down)	u (up)
France (usual)	T (*tiré*)	P (*poussé*)
France (Muffat)	l	v
	n (*nobilis*)	v (*vilis*)

Muffat's first usage is his normal one. The 'n' and 'v' are not really bowing signs; they stand for 'good' (stressed) and 'bad' (unstressed) notes, normally played with down-bow and up-bow, respectively. His sign (ı), a vertical stroke, is very confusing for down-bow, because he gives the same sign for *détachement* (staccato). Any connexion between 'n' and 'v' and the modern signs, n and v, for down-bow and up-bow, is apparently fortuitous.

Types of bowing and their execution

The simplest form of bowing is the individual bow stroke, but such strokes may be connected in varying degrees of legato and staccato. There are also numerous types of slurred bowings, including those with staccato

[9] The whole question of the relation of French dances to bowing has been studied carefully and in detail. See Barbara A. G. Seagrave, *The French Style of Violin Bowing and Phrasing from Lully to Jacques Aubert (1650–1730)*, Ph.D. dissertation, Stanford University, 1959, available through University Microfilms, Inc., Ann Arbor, Michigan.

dots under slurs. The relative length of the individual bow stroke depended on context and, to some extent, on the dictates of national style, the short stroke being usual in French music. A concert master in Ansbach, Germany, is said to have left his post in 1683 because he was not comfortable in the French manner and did not wish to conform to 'this very short stroke'.[10]

As far as one can generalize, individual bow strokes of the seventeenth-century violinist were normally somewhat more articulated than modern strokes. The properties of the old bow and the use of the old bow grips produced a kind of non-legato stroke. In modern violin playing a legato bow change is assiduously cultivated, and the result is a very smooth connexion between individual notes. Nevertheless, this modern legato bow stroke is frequently called *détaché* (detached), a very misleading term. Today *détaché* may mean 'detached' in the sense of 'separated' or 'disconnected'; more commonly, it means an individual stroke connected legato-fashion to the following stroke.

When degrees of separation greater than the non-legato of the normal seventeenth-century bow stroke were required, they were indicated either by terms such as staccato or spiccato (which were apparently synonymous at that time), or by special signs, the two commonest being a dot (·) or vertical stroke (|) placed above or below the notes. Today *staccato* has a special technical meaning to a violinist (see the Glossary). In the late seventeenth century dots and strokes usually meant the same thing, but if both occurred in the same piece, the stroke generally meant a more vigorous and pronounced degree of separation than the dot. At a moderate speed the staccato sign implied shortening the sound of the written note by half of its value, or, in the case of dotted notes (that is, notes followed by the dot of addition) by a third (Ex. 83). Strokes and dots to indicate staccato appeared in the music of advanced players after 1675.[11]

Muffat calls this detaching or separation of notes *détachement*, and he gives both dots and strokes without distinction, using only the dot in his musical

Muffat

Ex. 83

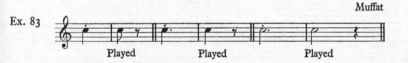

Played   Played   Played

[10] See Andreas Moser, op. cit., p. 118, note 2.
[11] The meaning of dots (or strokes) above or below notes is sometimes ambiguous. Generally their meaning is *staccato*, as just described. Sometimes dots (or strokes) mean to play the notes as written, not as *notes inégales* (see p. 303). In the latter case, it is not clear whether both meanings may apply: that is, can the dots (or strokes) mean not only to play the notes as written rhythmically, but also to play them detached (staccato)? Presumably, the primary meaning of dots and strokes was a detaching or separation of some sort. If so, it follows that the notes were played as written since *notes inégales* were not appropriate to detached notes.

examples. His degree of detachment follows the rules just given (cf. Ex. 83). The staccato dot or stroke also appears in the music of the Bologna School.[12] Ex. 84 shows the staccato dot as it appears in a piece of Walther. Neither staccato dot nor stroke is to be found in Corelli's music and this insertion or use must have been left to the player's judgement.[13] Interesting descriptions of the staccato occur in accounts of other instruments. Mace, for instance, describes the lute staccato under the picturesque name of 'Tut', as follows: 'The Tut is a Grace, always performed with the Right Hand, and is a sudden taking away the Sound of any Note, and in such a manner, as it will seem to cry Tut; and is very Pritty, and Easily done . . .'.[14]

Ex. 84

"Gallina"

The actual amount of separation depends on the kind of notes and the tempo. Ex. 85 is marked staccato for a whole section to avoid putting in all the dots or strokes. In these rapid notes the degree of separation would be small, and a light wrist stroke would effect it clearly. The old bow lacked the momentum of the modern bow and would articulate such passages with natural clarity. In notes of longer duration, the staccato separation must have been made by a lifting motion of the bow. In the foreword to his

Ex. 85

"staccato"

Ausserlesener . . . Instrumental-Music (1701), Georg Muffat discusses the manner of performing these concertos, and instructs the players to follow the 'Italian style' in the opening sonatas, the fugues, and expressive graves; and Muffat describes a feature of the Italian style in these words: 'in the suspension, the note tied over, the note sounding the dissonance in another voice, and the note resolving the dissonance . . . are to be played at all times with the same full tone, lifting the bow (in Italian, *staccato*), detaching them rather than weakening them by prolonging them timidly'.[15] The term 'lifting' in this context must really mean a lift of the bow, and is not the same as 'bounding' bow. As to the latter, Rousseau says: 'one ought never to prac-

---

[12] See *The Musical Quarterly*, July 1951, opposite p. 363 and p. 359 (Ex. 4).
[13] In Corelli's Trio Sonata, Op. 1, No. 12, movement two, the term *Largo e puntato* may mean 'slow and dotted' in the sense of the staccato dot (·).
[14] Mace, op. cit., p. 109.
[15] See Oliver Strunk, *Source Readings*, op. cit., p. 452.

tise these *passaggi* from high to low or low to high with bow strokes which one calls *Ricochets* [bounding bow] and which one hardly ever allows (*souffre*) in violin playing . . .'[16]

In simple slurred (legato) groups, the principles of down-bow and up-bow are the same as stated above in the Rule of Down-Bow; the down-bow is related to stress, and the ordering of the strokes is related to the number of notes and their grouping in the measure. The slur, originally classified as an ornament, now occurs more frequently. Sometimes the music does not include slurs, but they must be added by the player. Examples have already been cited in connexion with the Rule of Down-Bow where added slurs are sometimes admissible or necessary at rapid tempo and in triple time (cf. Ex. 78 and Ex. 81b). Little need be said about the performance of slurred notes. The slurred group is simply played in one bow according to the Rule, perhaps with a slight emphasis on the first note of the group.[17]

There are, however, certain particular types of legato bowings and slurred groups that need definition and explanation:

1. Syncopated bowings—syncopated in the sense that the bowing produces a rhythmic syncopation (Ex. 86).

Ex. 86

2. *Ondeggiando* (*ondulé*), indicated by a wavy line under a slur (Ex. 87a). *Ondeggiando* refers to a 'wavy' motion—in this case, the motion of the bow arm crossing two strings back and forth. In Ex. 87a, eight sixteenth-notes are taken in one bow stroke alternating from the A string to the open E string (that is, slurred *ondulé*). Without this indication the player might bow these eight notes entirely on the A string. Ex. 87b has the wavy sign below, but no slur; and above, the wavy line under a slur. Ex. 87a and b show two ways of indicating the same thing, the effect being the same. The term *ondeggiando* may also be used to indicate the 'wavy' motion involved in playing arpeggios (Ex. 87c). *Ondulé* may be slurred or unslurred.

3. *Bariolage* (French term, meaning 'curious mixtures of different colours'). Ex. 87d calls for the *bariolage*, an *ondulé* bowing of a special kind:

---

[16] J. Rousseau, op. cit., p. 73. For the actual sound of the non-legato and the different staccatos, cf. our recording.

[17] J. Rousseau, op. cit., pp. 103-4, defines *tenue* as two or more notes slurred in the same degree (i.e. tied notes); and *liaison* as different notes under one slur. Rousseau also notes that if the *tenue* is too long to hold in one bow stroke, then the bow change must be made as imperceptibly as possible. The puzzling indication 𝄐 at the end of Biber's 'Biblical' (or 'Mystery') Sonata No. 7 probably means to slur the two notes as eighths (♫).

H.V.P.–T

repeated notes played alternately on two strings, one stopped, one open.[18] In this example, the bow arm undulates from one string to the other, playing the lower (A) string stopped and the upper (E) string open. In this effect, the note 'E' is repeated and articulated by means of a legato bowing, the *timbre* of the stopped and open notes being slightly different (hence *bariolage* = mixture of colours). Although *bariolage* is included here for convenience, it is not necessarily a slurred bowing; it may be executed with individual bow strokes.

Ex. 87

4. The *slurred tremolo*, our general term for the legato repeated note on the same string. Ordinarily two notes of the same pitch bound by a slur are tied and played as one note. In violin music the slur (or wavy line) is sometimes placed over groups of notes of the same pitch, usually four or eight (Ex. 88b). Unlike the *bariolage*, the repeated notes are played on the same string, and each note of the group is very slightly articulated in the same bow stroke. The bow is not really stopped between impulses (cf. the *portato* and its different signs, below),[19] but gives just enough articulation to each note to suggest a throbbing or trembling. Indeed, this is the name for the effect in French and Italian: respectively, *trembler* and *tremolo*. But note the confusion: in Italian, *tremolo* also means vibrato and sometimes trill, and similar confusions exist in French. In this book the term *slurred tremolo* is used to avoid these confusions. In Ex. 88a, Walther gives the specific direction *tremolo*, and in the context of repeated notes there is no doubt what he means. However, he omits the customary slur or wavy line, and therefore he does not define the

---

[18] *Bariolage* is a relatively modern term, probably appearing well after 1750. It does not occur in such eighteenth-century dictionaries as those of Walther or J. J. Rousseau (the philosopher, not the violist cited frequently above). The term is interpreted to mean different things. The most inclusive definition is found in P. Baillot, *L'Art du Violon*, Paris, 1834, p. 126. His definition of *bariolage* includes: (1) our meaning given above; (2) a passage of notes played on different strings for contrast of colours; (3) a passage played in such a way that one hears an open note where ordinarily it would be played as a stopped note, thereby resulting in a new colour effect.

[19] When the *tremolo* is indicated by a wavy line, it has no dots or strokes, and we cannot distinguish between legato and staccato slurred *tremolo*, as in the eighteenth century (see p. 422). See also Ex. 88e, marked 'Tremolo spiccato adagio'. This example, however, has no slur.

number of notes to be taken in one bow stroke (by twos?). This example is
also an instance of double stops using the *tremolo*. Ex. 88b, also from Walther,
requires sixteenth-notes in groups of eight, as the wavy line makes clear, and
this particular effect is used to imitate the 'organo tremolante'.[20] Ex. 88c
shows a passage taken from Purcell's *Ode to St. Cecilia's Day* (1692). The word
tremolo is indicated over the typical wavy line; and all string parts have the
tremolo at the words 'jarring, jarring'.[21] In Ex. 88d, from Lully's opera *Isis*, the
orchestral parts are marked with the wavy line where the word *trembler* is
used in the text. Ex. 88e and Ex. 88f show two examples from the Swiss
composer Albicastro's Op. VII (probably printed between 1700 and 1705),
Concertos III and IV, respectively. The first example has repeated quarter-
notes in groups of six, labelled *tremolo spiccato adagio*; and the other has

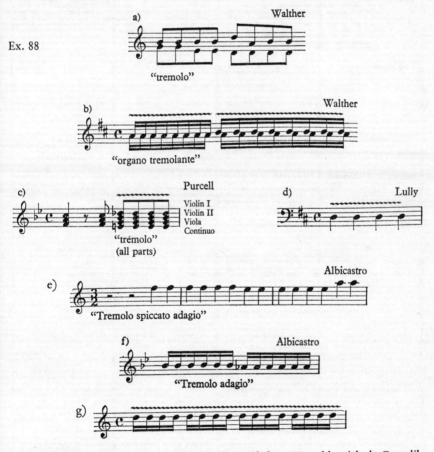

Ex. 88

---

[20] Simpson, op. cit., p. 10, says, 'Some also affect a Shake or Tremble with the Bow, like
the Shaking-Stop of an Organ, but the frequent use thereof is not (in my opinion)
much commendable.'

[21] See *The Works of Henry Purcell*, London, 1878–1928, Vol. VIII, p. 35.

repeated sixteenth-notes, also in groups of six, labelled *tremolo adagio.* Presumably these are slurred in groups of six although no slur is given. Ex. 88g includes twelve notes under the wavy sign of the tremolo, here called *Schwermer* or *Bombi.*[22]

So much for the special types of slurred bowings. Like the *bariolage*, the effect of repeated notes may be produced by individual bow strokes. In this case, however, neither the term *tremolo* nor the wavy sign is indicated in score, the notes involved are to be played rapidly, and each is performed with an individual bow stroke as written (Ex. 89a). A species of figuration, involving repeated notes, is shown in Ex. 89b. In all this there looms the pit-

Ex. 89

fall of terminology. The seventeenth-century term *tremolo*, as explained and illustrated above, refers to groups of slurred repeated notes, and hence our term *slurred tremolo*. This distinction is necessary because the modern term *tremolo* refers to unslurred repeated notes.

Individual notes are played with various degrees of detachment or articulation, sometimes indicated by special signs and sometimes without. There is no special sign for playing arpeggios across the strings; the general direction is simply the word *arpeggio*. In Walther's *Scherzi*, a type of lightly articulated bow stroke is suggested by his direction *arpeggiando con arcate sciolte* (arpeggios with unshackled bow), and the rapid arpeggios shown in

Ex. 90

"arpeggiando con arcate sciolte"

Ex. 90 could be performed with this light, slightly bounding bowstroke.[23] Detaching the notes is sometimes inherent in the nature of the figuration. This is the case in Ex. 91a, where the first note must be detached slightly to cross the string intervening between it and the repeated notes. The latter

---

[22] See W. C. Printz, *Musica modulatoris vocalis*, Schweidnitz, 1678, p. 51. *Schwermer* (German) and *Bombi* (Italian), the terms given by Printz, continue to mean string *tremolo* well into the eighteenth century. For the slurred *tremolo* in Bononcini, see Klenz, op. cit., pp. 198–9 and elsewhere.

[23] Arpeggios are often to be played legato. Cf. the term '*Arp. legato*' in Beckmann, *Violinspiel*, Anhang No. 19 (Ex. XII). Ex. 90 could also be played legato. For the sound of Ex. 90, cf. our recording.

are detached as a matter of course. Ex. 91b would require an even more vigorous detaching of the first note of the sixteenth-note groups, since the following notes are separated by *two* strings.

Ex. 91

Still another type of bowing articulates each of a group of two or more notes, all with one bow stroke. This type of bowing, which may be called *slurred staccato*, is indicated by a slur over groups of notes each marked with a staccato dot or stroke. (Today this effect, as written, is simply called *staccato*; but the performance of a modern staccato [see Glossary] is quite different from the seventeenth and eighteenth-century variety.) A simple example is Muffat's *craquer*, used by him in triple time (Ex. 81b), the two notes being played in successive regions of the bow with a just perceptible pause between. Another on-string type of bowing is the *portato* (later called the *louré*), executed at moderate speeds, often on repeated notes (Ex. 92a); and in this case it resembles the slurred *tremolo* played with a greater degree of detachment. Ex. 92a is executed up-bow, but Ex. 92b, consisting of two or more of these short groups, is played down-bow *and* up-bow alternately. According to the testimony of Leopold Mozart much later, the notes in this bowing are detached 'by means of lifting the bow'. This type of bowing, seldom used today, is somewhat easier to execute with the old bow.

Ex. 92

In demonstrating how to fill intervals with shorter notes, Muffat contrasts legato and detached bowings under a slur. In view of the slurred bowings just explained, Muffat's special marking shown in Ex. 92c is rather confusing. The bowing with strokes under a slur Muffat calls *coulement droit*, and the passage is played as shown. On the other hand, the bowing with dots *above* the slur (Ex. 92d) means a *pétillement*, literally, a 'crackling or sparkling'. Muffat says that the *pétillement* differs from the *coulement* in that it expresses the notes distinctly, making them '*craqueter*' in the same bow stroke. Muffat also allows for filling intervals of this kind with individual bow strokes in a device called *tirade*, indicated as shown in Ex. 92e.

The German school of virtuosity developed the staccato-under-slur to a high point. An early example (1664) from Schmeltzer is shown in Ex. 93 (see p. 165 for still earlier types in Rognoni's *lireggiare affettuoso*). As might be expected, still more elaborate examples occur in the music of Biber and especially Walther. Biber uses as many as twenty notes with *staccato* dots

Ex. 93

under one slur, and Walther has the incredible number of thirty-two, taken up-bow (Ex. 94; for the sound, cf. our recording). Such elaborate bowings may well have been the kind of thing Leopold Mozart had in mind when he explained a bowing involving twelve notes similarly indicated, as follows:

> 'Play the twelve notes . . . in the up stroke, separating them by a quick lift of the bow. . . . This style of performance will be somewhat difficult to the beginner. A certain relaxing [*Mässigung*] of the right hand is necessary for it, and a retarding of the bow. . . . The weight of a violin bow contributes much, as does also in no less degree its length or shortness. A heavier and longer bow must be used more lightly and retarded somewhat less; whereas a lighter and shorter bow must be pressed down and retarded more. Above all, the right hand must be made a little stiff here, but the contracting and relaxing of the same must be regulated according to the weight and length, or the lightness and shortness of the bow. The notes must be played in an even tempo, with even strength, and not over-hurried, or, so to speak, swallowed.'[24]

Ex. 94

Mozart's explanation appears to be applicable to Walther's bowing; and Mozart's statement is doubly interesting because it emphasizes the unstandardized state of the bow, and relates these differences to technical solutions.

The treatises of the time, which are principally concerned with elemen-

[24] Leopold Mozart, *Violinschule*, Augsburg, 1756; translated into English by Editha Knocker as: *A Treatise on the Fundamental Principles of Violin Playing*, London, 1948; 2nd ed., 1951, p. 119.

tary instruction, do not mention such bowings. Nevertheless, the music of advanced players contains a large number and variety of complex (and perhaps experimental) examples. In the course of variations, elaborate bowings are often systematically called for. Corelli's *La Follia*, a theme and twenty-four variations, is a true 'Art of Bowing' for good players of the Italian school of the late seventeenth century. The more complex technique of the Germans is likewise summarized in variations, and Walther's fifty variations in his *Hortulus Chelicus* of 1688 is a worthy anticipation of Tartini's fifty variations in his *L'Arte del Arco* in the middle of the eighteenth century.

Multiple stops, their notation and performance

The long development of multiple stops, begun early in the seventeenth century, reached a high point in Germany at the end of the century. The Italians, after abandoning multiple stops about 1625, began to use them again after 1671. In performing these stops, there are two particularly difficult problems: (1) understanding the meaning of the notation used in triple and quadruple stops; and (2) the implication of the notation with respect to arpeggiating the notes and inserting bowings, especially legato slurs.

First, let us summarize what has been said in an earlier chapter (see especially, pp. 167ff.): difficulties with multiple stops arise from a conflict between what the written notes call for and what is actually possible on the violin. Two-note stops are normal and (usually) easy. Today with the concave modern bow and curved bridge, the three notes of a triple stop can be played simultaneously only if they are played briefly and loudly. Four-note chords cannot be played at all in this manner. Consequently, in modern violin-playing triple and quadruple stops are broken, usually starting just before the beat (Ex. 95), and then only two of the three or four notes are

Ex. 95

Played

sustained (but see note 26, p. 275 below). It is possible to strike three or four notes together and *sustain* them only if the bridge is perfectly flat; and then it is impossible to sound single notes by themselves. It is often claimed that the old violin had a very flat bridge, and that, in conjunction with an outwardly curved (convex) bow, the flat bridge would allow the violinist of early times to sound triple and quadruple stops together and sustain them in a contrapuntal manner. The fact is that the old bridges shown in pictures and in treatises are not markedly and uniformly flat—some are relatively flat and others quite curved in arch—and the bows used in Italy and France after 1650 are generally straight, not curved. In Germany, typical old bows do

have something of an outward curve, but it is not sufficient to play quadruple stops simultaneously without hitting the stick. The fact of the matter
is that with the greater 'give' of an old bow and with a moderately flat
bridge, a player can play triple stops in a somewhat fuller and easier manner
than with a modern bow. Whether a seventeenth-century violinist tried to
play the three notes of a chord simultaneously is another question. However,
no bow, German or otherwise, can play four notes of a chord simultaneously,
provided the bridge is curved enough to play single notes.

Nevertheless, the fact remains that scores of the time indicate *sustained*
three-part and four-part chords. The answer to this puzzle lies in an understanding of the notation and the tradition of violin playing. To a modern
player the score means just what it says, and the so-called *Ur-text* is sacro-
sanct. On the other hand, in older times many scores were simply sketches
of what the composer intended, and a modern player, trying to play the
notes exactly as they appear on the printed page or manuscript, may actually
be violating rather than fulfilling the composer's intentions. The rhythmic
notation must have been approximate in certain respects, because it is sometimes physically impossible with any bridge or bow to play or sustain the
notes as written. In Ex. 96a, the 'E', whether played stopped or open, cannot
be held while playing the open 'G', because another string intervenes on
which nothing is to be played. In Ex. 96b the passage is written to be played
pizzicato, and consequently the half-notes of the score are a fiction or merely
a convention.

Ex. 96

Pizzicato

Why was the score written in this approximate way? Probably because
previous performing traditions left much to the judgement and artistry of
the player. The composer of violin music wrote out the polyphonic progressions in an idealized way to show the true counterpoint, but he left the
actual 'realization' of the score to the violinist according to his desires and
abilities. Moreover, this idealized version of the music helped the player to
understand the musical progression otherwise concealed in the figuration.
The liberties permitted performers were far greater in earlier times, and
ideally the violinist was an artist of sufficient stature to rise to the level of
his opportunities. Compared to the seventeenth-century player, the modern
performer is bound hand and foot to the printed score, and to regain the
flavour of earlier times one needs to approach an old score in the spirit that
created it.

This is not easy, and a number of puzzles and inconsistencies are the reward of the conscientious player who would divine the composer's inner spirit. In double stops there are numerous passages that are very puzzling with respect to the insertion of slurs and the duration of notes. If there were clear conventions on these points, the theorists of the time have failed to mention them. Consider Ex. 97a and Ex. 97b. These two examples, containing two identical measures from different parts of the same piece by Corelli, have inconsistencies with respect to the bowing and length of the notes; and the two measures that are identical in notes in both examples have different bowing. Ex. 97a raises the question whether the lower notes of measures 2 and 3 should be played as written. If so, the addition of a slur to the upper part will be required. This is quite possible in measure 2, but in measure 3 the b' flat cannot be held in first position while playing the d'', since both come on the same string. This passage can be played as written only by a

Ex. 97

sudden shift to another position, a procedure that hardly seems likely in this piece of Corelli. Our solution, admittedly somewhat inconsistent, aims at simplicity and at coming out down-bow at the cadence. The lower notes of the second and third measures are shortened to quarter notes, and a slur is added to the first two notes of the upper part of measure 3 as shown.

Ex. 97b, a passage later in the same piece, contains identical music (m. 3–4 of Ex. 97b = m. 2–3 of Ex. 97a). But measure 3 of Ex. 97b is slurred differently from the corresponding music in Ex. 97a. The probable reason is that the previous context is slightly different, and Corelli makes the adjustment with the notion of down-bow on beat one of the following measure. In this connexion, one may speculate whether consistency was a very important factor in Italian music at this time, or, for that matter, how important and binding the Rule of Down-Bow was.

Chains of suspensions present another difficulty, as shown in Ex. 98a. Obviously this music cannot be bowed exactly as written. It is possible that this passage implies one long slur for the whole series of suspensions, since the tempo is *vivace*; and one might be able to play the passage with one bow at that tempo, although not loudly. Or, again, the first four measures might be taken in one bow, a bow change being suggested at measure 5 at the triple stop. The latter (as opposed to a double stop) is essential at that point to avoid shifting. But it is more likely that the bow is changed at every measure. In this case, the bowing of the upper part can be preserved by shortening the lower part in one of several ways (Ex. 98b); or conversely, the lower notes can be played as written by shifting the slurs of the upper

Ex. 98

parts (Ex. 98c). The latter method of performance, however, violates the suspended dissonance. The fact that arpeggios are often written out in tied-note versions to show the voice leading and chord structure is indicative of another fiction in notation (Ex. 99). Here, of course, the ties are meaningless in terms of sound.

Ex. 99

"arpeggio"

Sometimes slurs are specifically added, and this may imply that the composer generally indicates slurs only where he wants them (cf. Ex. 100a and Ex. 100b). In fugue subjects or imitative phrases, the bowing of the first statement is normally preserved on repetition. This point is sometimes

Ex. 100

applicable to double stops. In Ex. 101, for instance, the figure that begins the example is played with individual strokes, and since the repetition of the figure requires the same bowing, the upper note a'' of the first double-stop must be shortened to a dotted eighth. There are many such examples where the context of bowing and simplicity of execution suggest that notes are not sustained their full written length, even when it is possible to do so.

Triple and quadruple stops involve the further complication of performing the individual stop itself, as explained above. In the seventeenth century, the player conventionally broke triple and quadruple stops from bottom to top. The viol treatises speak explicitly of this method, although the violin treatises, being of elementary character, say nothing about it. Simpson says, 'When two, three, or more Notes stand one over another . . . they must be

Ex. 101

play'd as One, by sliding the Bow over those Strings which express the sound of the said Notes. . . . be sure to hit the lowest String first (insisting thereon so long as need requires) and let the Bow slide from It to the highest, touching in its passage those in the middle betwixt them.'[25] Simpson writes all sorts of chords, including one with *six* notes (the viol has typically six strings). For single chords, Simpson uses down-bow; for consecutive chords he alternates down-bow and up-bow.

The information just quoted from Simpson is quite contrary to modern practice. It suggests that the lowest note be emphasized and played by itself, the following notes then to be played rapidly one after the other, dwelling on the top note.[26] Simpson's methods of playing multiple stops must have been widespread, and this sort of information occurs in the eighteenth century in violin instruction (cf. Quantz, our p. 436). In such cases as Ex. 102,

Ex. 102

Simpson's way is obviously the right way. The lowest note must be shortened, the chord swiftly broken, the top note briefly dwelt on, and the repeated notes articulated with separate bows. In this case, the second triple stop would be played up-bow or by a replaced bow. In Ex. 103, from Playford's *The Division-Violin*, the top notes are printed in the lengthened manner

[25] Simpson, op. cit., p. 9.
[26] There is a good deal of variety in the modern practice of performing multiple stops. The French school today generally rolls chords with overlaps from one note to the next. Some also hold only the top note. A few modern players try to play all notes of the chord as one. Spivakovsky has been able to achieve or approximate this ideal in triple stops. Heifetz breaks chords; Oistrakh usually rolls them. Casals seems to have returned in essence to the method recommended by Simpson three centuries ago, as just cited.

that they would actually sound according to Simpson's method of performing multiple stops.

Ex. 103

Simpson's instructions leave something to be desired when the melody is not in the upper voice. In Ex. 104 the melody (or rhythmic motive) goes successively from the bottom to the middle to the top part, and the player must find some way to bring out the melody part in its successive occurrences in different voices. Simpson's method would not work very satisfactorily in the first two statements of the melody, and one can only conclude that violinists tried to play the chord members rapidly and as much together as possible, retaining and emphasizing the melody note to bring out the

Ex. 104

subject. Breaking from bottom to top is still the basic technique. Dynamics help to accent the main note. In this connexion we should consider further that many violin pieces of the time were played in small rooms or halls whose walls, often hard and bare, produced a maximum resonance and reverberation. Under such conditions, a suggestion of the sound of the chord would be enough to convey the harmonic progression indicated without actually sustaining the chord by the pressure of the bow. The resonance of these small rooms, for which the volume of sound of the old violin was often more than ample, is a factor often overlooked. (For the sound of Ex. 104, cf. our recording.)

Sometimes one must allow for the fact that triple and quadruple stop notation is simply a sketch for an arpeggiated passage. A model for the proper procedure is often written out for a few measures, and the rest of the passage is then indicated as multiple-stop chords (Ex. 105). Sometimes there is no model for the arpeggios, the term 'arpeggio' simply being written over passages of triple and quadruple stops. When no arpeggio is expressly indicated the player must decide whether this manner of performance is appropriate.

Ex. 105

Three final examples are worth a comment. In Ex. 106 the rhythmically syncopated bowing is not only interesting in itself, but it implies that the accompanying note cannot be held full value. Ex. 107 suggests that the half-notes must be shortened to eighth-notes, and the lower notes played with individual bow strokes. Ex. 108a could not be executed as written unless all four strings could be sustained. Since this is impossible, the passage must be played in a way similar to Ex. 108b.

Ex. 106

Ex. 107

Ex. 108

The pizzicato

Indications of the *pizzicato* are found largely in the German school, where it is used extensively in the interests of description. A typical indication is *senz'arco*. There is not a single *pizzicato* called for in Corelli's works, but in those of Walther there are several complete *movements* entirely in *pizzicato* (for example, *Hortulus Chelicus*, No. XXII). Walther describes the usage and manner of performing the *pizzicato* in a note following the Index of the *Hortulus Chelicus*: 'In those cases where we imitate the harp, lute, small guitar, timpani, or similar things, one uses the tip of the finger instead of the bow, and one touches the strings of the *basso continuo* [instruments?] simply with a single finger, and the Violoncino [*sic*] likewise *senz'arco*.' An illustration found in a collection of lute pieces by Denis Gaultier, entitled *La Rhétorique des Dieux* (*c.* 1650), suggests that the violinist and violist are plucking the string with the first finger while holding the bow in the fist (Plate 32). However, this may simply be an illusion in which the first finger is considerably extended in regular bowing.[27] The position of the cello (?) strains the imagination, although the same position occurs in another illustration in the same collection. An elementary 'left-hand' *pizzicato*, intriguingly called 'Thump', is mentioned in Playford's *Musick's Recreation on the Viol lyra-way* (1669; earlier editions: 1652, 1661), but only for open strings.

Special effects

Col legno, sul ponticello, and *sulla tastiera*, called for by Farina and others early in the century, seem momentarily to have disappeared. If these effects were in use by violinists, it is curious that no notice of them appears either in the theorists or in the music. On the other hand, the mute, mentioned earlier by Mersenne, is occasionally called for in the music. Lully and Purcell specify it in connexion with music for the stage (see p. 205), but there is no known use of it among the advanced violin music of the Italians and Germans. As far as we know, it is not used in sonatas or concertos before 1700.

Instrumentation and the ensemble. 'Conducting'

Which instruments and how many were used to perform the violin sonatas and concertos? In the first place, terms such as *sonata a tre* mean, not 'sonata for three players', but 'sonata for three voice parts': two solo parts and the figured *basso continuo*. The latter normally served two players: the keyboard player (sometimes, the lutanist), who 'realized' (improvised) an accompaniment according to the figures, and a stringed instrument, generally the cello, bass *viola da gamba*, or *violone*, which played the *basso continuo* itself. Therefore, the trio sonata was ideally performed by four players, and, significantly, trio sonatas were invariably printed in four part books and the 'solo' sonatas in three. However, in the absence of ideal performing conditions, a trio sonata might be performed with three players, dispensing with the cello or gamba; or perhaps it might be performed with two players, the soloist and a keyboard player. The latter then played the other solo part in the right hand, filling in chords with his left.

The harpsichord was generally used for chamber sonatas, which consisted largely of dance movements; the organ was usual in church sonatas. The keyboard was regarded as indispensable, and there is no evidence in contemporary treatises that the keyboard accompaniment was ever considered

---

[27] This collection is edited by A. Tessier and printed in *Publications de la Société Française de Musicologie*, l⁰ série, Vols. VI and VII, Paris, 1932–3.

optional. Indeed, the keyboard was taken so much for granted that there was nothing inconsistent in the term *solo sonata* for a piece in which a soloist is accompanied by a keyboard player and a gambist. A true solo without accompaniment had to be given a title like that of Bach's unaccompanied violin sonatas: *Solo a Violino senza basso*, specifying that the *basso continuo* was to be omitted.

In view of the indispensability of the keyboard according to the treatises, the title of Corelli's Op. 5 is something of an enigma: *Sonate a Violino Solo e Violone ò Cimbalo*. The significance of the phrase *Violone or Cimbalo* (harpsichord) is puzzling. F. T. Arnold, the authority on the figured bass, says, 'no great stress was laid on the choice of the word *e* or *ò* . . . in Italian works. . . . That the co-operation of *both Organ and Violoncello* was intended in these works is sufficiently proved by the fact that in them, as in so many others, the Bass part is *in duplicate*.'[28] Arnold's explanation is comforting, but in accepting it we must also be prepared to concede that Corelli either did not know or did not care what his title-pages said. Op. 2 and Op. 4 use phrases similar to Op. 5, above, while the title pages of Op. 1 and Op. 3 call clearly for *Violone and Organ*. A typographical error may be involved in Op. 5—unlikely in view of its occurrence in Op. 2 and Op. 4—or the title-page in Op. 5 and the others may refer to the unusual and little-known practice of omitting the keyboard. This is suggested by a remark of Bononcini with respect to his Op. IV, the title of which read *Arie, Correnti, Sarabande, Gighe, & Allemande A Violino, e Violone, over Spinetta . . . per diverse accordature*. The setting specified by the wording is the same as Corelli's, and apparently *violone* was given the preference to *spinetta* by Bononcini, since at the head of p. 3 of the *violone* part one finds this: 'It should be noted that the *Violone* will make a better effect than the *Spinetta*, since the Basses are more appropriate to the one than the other.'[29]

In the preface to his *Sonnata's of III Parts* (1683), Purcell explains the delay in publication by saying that the music would have been 'abroad in the world much sooner, but that he has now thought fit to cause the whole Thorough Bass to be Engraven, which was a thing quite besides his first Resolutions'. This ambiguous remark should not be taken to mean that Purcell had ever contemplated omitting the Thorough-Bass part in the sense of omitting the harpsichord. It doubtless meant that Purcell finally decided to make the Thorough-Bass part, from which the keyboard player improvised the accompaniment, a simplified form of the *continuo*, which was played by the cello, gamba, or double bass. Since this simplified form was 'a thing quite besides his first resolutions', he had to engrave a separate Thorough-Bass part for the use of the keyboard player. Hence his remark

[28] F. T. Arnold, *The Art of Accompaniment from a Thorough-Bass*, London, 1931, p. 329.
[29] For this see Klenz, op. cit., pp. 52 and 66.

and the delay in the appearance of the four [*sic*] part books of these *Sonnata's of III Parts.*

About 1700 a *concerto grosso* was normally printed in seven part books: three for the solo parts of the *concertino* (violin I and II, and cello) and four for the *ripieno* (violin I and II, viola, and bass).[30] Both *cello-concertino* and *basso-ripieno* were figured, the implication being that two keyboard instruments were used, one to accompany the *concertino* and another, the *ripieno* (see also Muffat's remark to the same effect, below). In small groups of players placed close together, one keyboard instrument would be sufficient; but two keyboard instruments would be necessary if the concertinists were separated from the ripienists, or if large forces were employed. When there were only seven part books, the keyboard and bass player must have shared the same part. This inconvenient arrangement would have been possible only so long as there was one player to the bass part. Similarly, if a keyboard accompanied the *concertino*, the solo cellist must have read his part (which was often difficult) by peeping over the shoulder of the keyboard player.

The number of players used in the *concerti grossi* varied greatly—from eight or nine players (that is, one player to a part) to as many as one hundred and fifty on special occasions. Such large forces would, of course, need far more part books than the usual seven. Forces were amplified by increasing the number of players in the *ripieno*; the concertinists were soloists, and only in the largest ensembles were the soloists doubled in the *concertino*. In his preface to Op. 6 (1698) Torelli says: 'Note that wherever in the concerto you find the word *Solo* written, it is to be played by one violin alone. For the remainder, the parts may be doubled, or even re-enforced by three or four instruments apiece'.[31] Torelli says much the same thing in the preface to his Op. 8, published posthumously in 1709.

The foreword to Muffat's *Auserlesene Instrumental-Music* (1701) contains valuable information, especially regarding large ensembles. Muffat tells us about the 'number and character of the players and the instruments' and also 'the manner to be observed in performing these concertos'—directions that should be read by every musician interested in the music of this time. Among other things, Muffat makes allowance for trying over the concertos with instruments of the *concertino* only, 'should you be short of string players'. But if there is a large number of players,

'you may assign additional players, not only to the first and second violin parts of the great choir (concerto grosso), but also to the two

[30] The parts used in the *concertino* and *ripieno* may depart from this norm. Muffat, for example, generally uses three parts in the *concertino* (as above) but five parts in the *ripieno* (violin I and II, viola I and II, and bass). For other combinations in the eighteenth century, see pp. 445–6.
[31] Quoted in Abraham Veinus, *The Concerto*, London, 1948, pp. 11–12.

inner viola parts [Muffat used two, not one] and to the bass, further ornamenting this last with the accompaniment of harpsichords, theorbos [large lutes], harps, and similar instruments; as to the little choir or trio, for it is always to this that the word "concertino" refers, let it be played singly, but at the same time superlatively well, by your three best string players with the accompaniment of an organist or theorbo player, never assigning more to a part, unless in some unusually vast place where the players of the great choir are exceptionally numerous, then assigning two at the most.'[32]

The small ensembles of eight or nine players got along without a conductor, being led by the first violin of the *concertino* (no score for a conductor is included with the customary part books). Presumably the same arrangement applied to large ensembles, even those of large forces of over a hundred players, although the difficulties involved make one question the efficiency of the result. However, Muffat says nothing about a conductor of large forces in the passage just quoted, and when, in a later section, he speaks of 'directing the measure or beat', the implication is that the usual arrangement of the leader-violinist obtained (for Quantz on this point, see p. 446).

The sound of the violin about 1700

By 1700 the changes in construction of the violin and bow must have made the instrument capable of a still more powerful and carrying sound than previously. Moreover, the development of a violin technique and a violin music that exploited the greater resources of the instrument contributed to a more brilliant and sonorous sound from those 'old' violins which fifty or even a hundred years earlier had been accustomed to speak in more subdued voices. Nor were new instruments lacking whose primary aim was increased power and sonority. It is probable that the Stainer violins and the 'grand' pattern Amatis had this aim in view, although they were still geared to chamber music. It cannot be a mere coincidence that Stradivari's experiments with the 'long' model of 1690–1700 occur at the same time the concerto was beginning, when a small but important minority of virtuosi were demanding greater power to compete with the concerto 'orchestra' and to fill the 'vast spaces' of public gatherings. The lengthening and strengthening of the bow was caused by the need for power and by a more complex and varied bowing technique. Other factors affecting volume and brilliance were the greater thickness of the strings in certain countries (see below), the tension at which they were strung, the height of the bridge and the pitch.

Even in the hands of virtuosi, however, the violin about 1700 must have

[32] Translation from Strunk, op. cit., pp. 450–1.

produced less volume than the modern violin fitted with a high bridge and strung with steel and wound strings at considerably greater tension. In the seventeenth century the use of gut strings, the slighter bass-bar and sound post, weaker neck, the thicker bridge, the type of old bow, which was generally shorter and lighter than the modern bow, all point to this conclusion. In an interesting article[33] Walter Senn reports on a series of experiments made on the same instrument successively fitted in different ways and played with different bows, chosen to reflect fundamental changes over the centuries: first with an old bow, thin strings, and light sound post [and light bass-bar?]; then with the addition of a heavier sound post; then with thicker strings; and finally with modern bow, sound post [and bass-bar?], and steel strings. Senn's experiments demonstrated a gradual increase in volume and change in tone colour from the first to the last, and the divergence was so marked that the identity of the violin could scarcely be recognized as the same. Senn does not mention the bridge in these experiments, but earlier in his paper he says that the old bridge was somewhat thicker than the modern one and that this accounts for a weaker, although more transparent, tone.

The difference of the tone is related to the factors already mentioned and, of course, to the manner of playing the instrument. In this the 'old' bow was a most important factor. The shorter, rather stiff, dance bow played with the French grip gave a clearly articulated sound, well suited to dancing. Many descriptions of the time which speak of string tone use the adjective 'clear'— 'a full clear sound'[34]—and it may be that this word best describes the tone produced by the short bow of the dance musicians. The same description, however, is applicable to the sound produced by the longer sonata bow played with the Italian grip; and, in addition, the sonata bow and the more advanced technique which it implies were capable of more varied effects: among them, chord playing of a greater fullness and ease of execution than the modern bow enjoys, brilliant passage-work of rapid notes executed in the upper third of the bow, and a considerable variety of *staccato* and mixed bowings.

The use of gut strings was also important to the sound, and so was the manner of using the vibrato—that is, occasionally as an ornament but not continuously, like the modern vibrato. The vibrato must have enjoyed an increasing vogue in the late seventeenth century. It is described more frequently in the treatises as an important ornament, and for the first time a

---

[33] 'Der Wandel des Geigenklanges seit dem 18. Jahrhundert' in *Congress-Bericht, Gesellschaft für Musikforschung*, 1957, held in Hamburg, 17–22 September 1956. For the actual sound of the 'old' as compared to the modern violin, cf. our recording.

[34] Simpson, op. cit., p. 3; see also Playford, *Introduction*, ed. of 1667, p. 94; also, Mace, op. cit., p. 248.

specific sign (m) may be found occasionally in theorists and the music (see p. 287). The violin vibrato was doubtless first inspired by the viol players, whose vibrato was varied and elaborate.

After 1650 violinists were increasingly interested in volume, sonority, and colour. They seemed less concerned with such exotic sounds as *sul ponticello* and *col legno*, concentrating rather on the singing qualities of the violin, on its brilliance in running passages, and on the sonority to be obtained from figuration, double stops, and arpeggios. The intensive use of multiple stops and the *scordatura* in Germany was inspired, at least in part, by the possibility of new sonorities and colours. The colour of the violin tone was also modified occasionally by the mute. Strangely enough, although the mute is required in a few ensemble pieces of the late seventeenth century (see p. 205), no example of its use in solo violin music—that is, in sonatas and concertos as a whole—is known before the eighteenth century. But other colour possibilities of the violin were exploited by soloists, notably an increased use of the registers of the highest and especially the lowest (G) strings and of the *bariolage*, alternating the colour of the stopped and open string.

In all this the formation of national schools was naturally accompanied by different kinds of music, which in turn demanded different types of sound. As the testimony of Muffat and Raguenet show (see pp. 203-4 above), the volume of sound and brilliance of effect were far less marked among French violinists than among the Italians and Germans. Compared to the French, the Italians strung their violins with thicker and stronger strings, presumably at a greater tension. The Germans achieved a greater degree of brilliance and sonority from a higher pitch than the French. These tonal characteristics can only reflect the musical needs and *Klang-ideal* inherent in the sonatas and the concertos of the Italians and Germans as opposed to the dance music of the French.

Thus theorists about 1700 noted the difference of the sound of the violin in various countries. By another touchstone of comparison the sound of the violin is contrasted to that of the viol. The treble viol, says a contemporary, is played in a subdued manner, not like the violin, which is characteristically animated. Simpson, when describing the quick notes on the viol, says 'the sound should be quick and sprightly like a violin'.[35] These descriptions, however, account only for the most obvious contrasts of the sound of viol and violin.

By 1700 the violin was capable of a vast range of tone and expression. Its inherent capabilities were being appreciated more and more by the average and amateur violinist. Certain virtuosi and composers of the time were spurring makers to produce an ideal instrument that would combine power

[35] Simpson, op. cit., p. 1.

with beauty of tone and ease of response, an instrument finally achieved by
Stradivari shortly after 1700. The importance of the bow is reflected in the
variety of types and in the many experiments with different woods, weights,
and lengths. As a result, the best of these 'old' bows were worthy of the
finest instruments, which, after all, could realise their full potential only
through a fine bow in the hands of an excellent player. By 1700 all these
conditions obtained, and the sound of the violin made an increasing impression on the musical public. Players of exceptional gifts knew how to make
their wonderful instruments sing; and to beauty of tone they added the
sonority of double stops and the brilliance of dramatic passage-work
throughout the range of the violin, expressed in many varieties of bowing.

Pronounced differences in social and musical conditions in different
countries contributed to the rise of national schools which had different
musical aims and different notions of instrumental sonority. Among the
Italians the rapid development of the violin under the great masters of violin
making proceeded apace with the development of the violin technique and
an expanded range of dynamics and expression required to play the new and
growing literature of sonatas and concertos composed by a Vitali, a Corelli,
or a Torelli. In German-speaking countries a great maker appeared for the
first time in the person of Jacob Stainer; and the German school under Biber,
Walther, and Westhoff achieved a new virtuosity on the violin, surpassing
the Italians. The German technique was geared to music in which the forms
of the variation, descriptive music, and the sonorities of multiple stops and
the *scordatura* were all featured. French music was practically synonymous
with the dance and with the corresponding mannered and disciplined bowing style of Lully's dance musicians, a style restricted in a technical and
expressive sense, but perfectly suited to its function. The English were
partly influenced by the French dance and bowing style, partly by the new
Italian sonata, and partly by the tradition of their past with respect to polyphony, the variation, and the dance. Foreign musicians, whose numbers and
influence were so great in the eighteenth century, had already begun to
come to England in substantial numbers; and Baltzar and Matteis introduced
the English to the German and Italian styles of violin playing.

The ground work of violin playing was laid in the seventeenth century
through a happy combination of remarkable players, makers, and composers. Their attainments were solidified and expanded, perhaps even more
remarkably, by those who followed in the eighteenth century. To this period
belong the greatest instruments of Stradivari and, late in the century, the
superlative bows of Tourte. The names of Vivaldi, Bach, Tartini, Viotti, and
Mozart are only a sampling of those distinguished composers and players
whose efforts, joined to those of superb craftsmen, made the eighteenth
century one of the greatest periods of the violin.

CHAPTER THIRTEEN

⌒⟡⌒

General Matters
affecting the Violin, 1650-1700

I N the early seventeenth century ornaments were frequently written out
in the music; and the terms, occasional signs, and execution of these
ornaments were nearly as varied as the individual composers who used
them. About the middle of the century the French lutanists and especially
harpsichordists began to introduce a more rational order into this chaos,
standardizing the ornaments and the names and signs for them. As a consequence, ornaments were less commonly written out, and instead, stereotyped conventional ornaments were indicated by signs which gradually
came to have a more uniformly understood meaning. This state of affairs
first became general in seventeenth-century France, and the lead of France
was followed elsewhere in the eighteenth century. In Italy few specific
ornaments were indicated by signs, the performance of the unadorned notes
being left mainly to prevailing tradition and the discretion of the performer.
Trills, for instance, were conventionally inserted at cadences, and vibrato on
long notes. In France improvised ornaments and passage-work decreased in
favour as specific ornaments and their signs became conventionalized. On
the other hand, the Italians seldom indicated the specific ornaments they
played, and as a rule they improvised additions to the written notes in the
slow movements.

Musical ornaments were rationalized in contemporary treatises by liken-
ing their purpose to those on buildings: not absolutely essential but nevertheless agreeable to the sight. In the same vein various theorists pointed out
that ornaments in music served a function similar to seasoning in food.
Rousseau speaks of ornaments as melodic salt which seasons the melody and
gives it taste, without which the melody would be flat and insipid. But, he
adds, as salt must be used prudently, ornaments must be used with moderation, and one must be able to discern where they would be excessive and
where too little.[1]

[1] Rousseau, *Traité*, p. 75.

In performing ornaments, two basic procedures are generally observed after 1650: (1) ornaments are usually slurred in whole or in part; (2) if an ornament is used in one part, the same ornament is used on repetition in an imitating part.

The subject of ornamentation is a complex, detailed, and confusing one, and the discussion here centres on general usage in violin music.[2] In Italy composers were often content merely to indicate where an ornament was appropriate, usually by a cross (+), and the specific ornament was left to the player. A similar usage occurs in French violin music from time to time well into the eighteenth century (see p. 450), although such examples are much less frequent in French than in Italian music.

Trills (shakes, *tremblements*) are typically indicated by t, tr, or ∿, but there are numerous personal variants (=, //). The trill generally starts from the note above the written note, but in long or medium-length trills (Ex. 109a) there may be (1) a dwelling on the upper note, (2) the repercussions proper, and (3) an ending with notes called 'afterbeats' (G.: *Nachschläge*). Ex. 109b shows written out 'afterbeats' of a common variety, and they are incorporated smoothly at the end of the trill in this example. The length of the trill is roughly that of the length of the written note. The speed of the trill corresponds to the speed of the movement and to the intensity of expression—in short, to the context. Short trills have few repercussions, and because of the brevity of these trills, initial dwellings or afterbeats are rare. Sometimes, especially in those trills approached from above, the short trill is really a half trill starting with the main note.

Consecutive trills are unusual before 1700—'One hardly approves two trills together,' says Muffat. In some of the more elaborate trills specific signs are used for those which have initial dwellings or introductory figures and/or afterbeats. The violin trill in thirds (double-stop trill), however, is written out. A particularly interesting example of a trill and its realization

Ex. 109

2 For more detailed information, see Arnold Dolmetsch, op. cit.; Edward Dannreuther, *Musical Ornamentation*, 2 vols., London, 1893–5; *Grove's Dictionary*, 5th ed.; and Willi Apel, *Harvard Dictionary of Music*. See also Putnam Aldrich, *The Principal Agréments of the 17th and 18th Centuries*, Harvard Ph.D. dissertation, 1942, the most elaborate and best study of ornamentation. Unfortunately, it is still unpublished.

occurs in Georg Muffat (Ex. 109c). In this example, as Muffat explains, the upper note e″ of the trill is connected more smoothly to the preceding c″ if d″ (marked ★) is included as a passing note.

The true mordent starts with the written note, uses the semitone or tone below, and ends on the written note. Muffat, who summarizes French practice, is the most complete source of information about violin ornamentation at this time. He calls the mordent a *pincement* or *tremblement coupé* (signs: ✳, ✣), and says it is 'performed very short, often being content with a single repercussion' (Ex. 110a). The Italian word *mordente* means 'bite'—a good description of the effect. A typical English term for the mordent is 'beat'. The French also use the word *pincé*.[3]

Muffat's ornaments include those shown in Ex. 110b–e with their signs and execution. Ex. 110b is a short appoggiatura on the beat (called *accentuation*). It is worth noting that the appoggiatura, while frequently written-out in music before 1700, is seldom indicated by the grace note that is common in the eighteenth century. Ex. 110c is called the *port de voix*; Ex. 110d, the slide (*exclamation*); and Ex. 110e, the turn (*involution*), also called by others *cadence double*. Note that these ornaments start on the beat, not before it, as is usual today. In Ex. 110e, a short rest, probably inspired by a desire for better articulation, precedes the actual turn.

Ex. 110

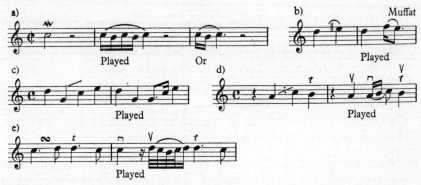

The vibrato

This 'ornament', which has already had a long history among the lutanists and violists, is used also by violinists, but it is rarely indicated by a sign. Occasionally (Ex. 111) the German violinists used the sign *m* in the music. Merck gives this sign for vibrato in his treatise of 1695, and he instructs the player to press the fingers of the left hand strongly on the string while the hand moves. Presumably the violin vibrato is used most commonly on long

---

[3] The mordent should not be confused with the *battement* (G.: *Zusammenschlag*). See p. 455 and Ex. 227.

notes in combination with the *messa di voce* (see p. 255 above). However, viol and lute players apparently indulged in more elaborate usage, using two types of vibrato: the true vibrato with one finger and the 'close shake' with two. In the latter type, one finger is pressed firmly on the fret, and a second finger makes a rapid beating or shaking very close to the pressed-down first finger (hence the name 'close shake'). Actually this type of vibrato is not a

Ex. 111

true vibrato at all. It is really a species of trill, the repercussions of the upper note being considerably less than a semitone higher than the main (written) note, but it has not the feature of the true vibrato, namely, undulations of pitch both above *and* below the written note. The 'close shake' type of vibrato is described by Rousseau[4] as a *batement* or a two-finger vibrato. He adds that 'it is used on all notes long enough to permit it, and it must last as long as the note'—thus advocating a species of continuous 'vibrato'. Marin Marais also mentions these two species of vibrato for the viol; and Mace, who calls the lute vibrato the 'Sting', says it is not Modish 'in These Days' (implying that it was 'Modish' formerly?):

> 'yet, for some sorts of Humours, very Excellent; And is Thus done, (upon a Long Note, and a Single String) first strike your Note, and so soon as It is struck, hold your Finger (but not too Hard) stopt upon the Place, letting your thumb loose and wave your Hand (exactly) downwards, and upwards, several Times, from the Nut, to the Bridge; by which Motion, your Finger will draw, or stretch the String a little upwards, and downwards, so as to make the Sound seem to Swell with pritty unexpected Humour, and gives much Contentment . . .'[5]

Mace's remark about the 'Swell' is not casual. From the above context it seems reasonable that 'swell' refers to nuance as a natural accompaniment to the vibrato. In any case, the nuanced vibrato was later recommended for violinists both by Leopold Mozart and Geminiani.

Improvisation

Improvisation, especially in the sense of ornamental *passaggi* (passage work) to slow movements, made good sense as long as the performer was the composer or was blessed with musical taste and restraint. Lully, whose dictatorial powers over French music were legendary and who regarded the musical taste of no one higher than his own, banished these improvisations

---

[4] Rousseau, op. cit., pp. 100–1.   [5] Mace, op. cit., p. 109.

from the music he controlled. The great tradition of improvisation in the late seventeenth century was English and Italian, not French. Simpson's *The Division-Viol* and its imitator, Playford's *The Division-Violin*, are monuments to the variation and to improvised formulas used in this and similar connexions. In Italy the practice must have been so common that it was taken for granted. Corelli's direction *Arcate sostenute e come sta* (see p. 256), which forbids adding ornaments with the phrase *come sta*, occurs only once in his entire works (Op. 6, No. 8), and hence this prohibition must be regarded as something exceptional to common practice.[6] These improvised passages were rarely written-out—a natural result where the performer normally improvised according to temperament and ability. When Bach wrote out the elaborate ornamentation and *passaggi* in the slow movement of his *Italian Concerto* for harpsichord, he did something quite exceptional, even for the early eighteenth century. Similarly, the 'Graces' printed in Roger's Amsterdam edition of Corelli's solo sonatas of Op. 5 are unusual, not because they were not played that way in actual performance, but because they were seldom written out (Ex. 112). Apparently, such ornamental additions were usual on the repeats of the slow movement, often being played the first time according to the written-note version. The cadenza—'un chant de caprice'—was essentially an elaboration of the practice of ornamenting cadences, and such cadenzas can be seen in written-out form in Corelli (see Ex. 63).[7]

Ex. 112

Corelli (Op. 5, No. 1)

Corelli's "graces"

Corelli original

Basso continuo

[6] From time to time composers from the seventeenth century onwards registered protests about their pieces not being played as written, but apparently they accepted improvisation as a matter of course if done with good taste and judgement. In Bononcini's preface to his Op. 6 (1672) he complains that performers 'wish, with their ill-ordered and indiscreet caprices of bow or voice, to alter and deform the compositions (however carefully made) so that the authors have become obliged to ask these singers and players to sing and play things simply as they are written'. He then continues, 'This does not include certain graces, which . . . when well employed ornament and add beauty to the compositions.' See William Klenz, *Bononcini*, op. cit., p. 34.

[7] For a more elaborate 'cadence-caprice' (cadenza) for violin in a sonata of Weichlein (Innsbruck, 1695), see Marc Pincherle, *Feuillets d'Histoire du violon*, Paris, 1927, pp. 128ff. For the sound of Ex. 112, cf. our recording.

Furthermore, whereas Corelli ornamented only the slow movements of his church 'solo' sonatas (Op. 5, Nos. 1–6), his pupils and his pupils' pupils in the eighteenth century ornamented the fast movements and the dances of his chamber sonatas as well (cf. p. 222). Ex. 113 affords an opportunity to compare the unadorned Corelli line with its ornamented versions by Geminiani and Dubourg. It is obvious that as a class these improvised ornaments must have been played freely in the true spirit of improvisation; and in the written-out versions of these improvisations there is often no real attempt to make the notation mathematically exact as to time values in every case. Today the only modern vestigial counterpart of these improvised elaborations occurs in jazz.

Ex. 113

Dynamics (for the early seventeenth century, see pp. 178ff.)

Loudness and softness and especially the gradations between were indispensable devices of expression. In the mind of the seventeenth-century musician, dynamics were closely related to descriptive effect or especially to the expression of a particular *Affetto* (= Affect = emotional state). Simpson says, 'We play Loud or Soft, according to our fancy, or the humour of the Musick. Again, this Loud or Soft is sometimes express'd in one and the same Note, as when we make it Soft at the beginning, and then (as it were) swell or grow louder towards the middle or ending.' When the long *crescendo* appears for the first time as a written direction in a seventeenth-century score, it serves the purposes of description (see p. 292 below).

Most scores before 1700 are limited to terms that indicate a specific level of loud or soft: *forte* (f), *fortissimo* (ff), *mezzo piano* (mp), *piano* (p), *più piano* (= the modern pp), and *pianissimo* (= the modern ppp). These indications suggest terraces of sound ('terraced dynamics') such as the 'echo' effect in which a passage is literally repeated more softly as in an echo. The echo is one of the musical effects specifically indicated by *piano* following a *forte*.

The extent and use of graded dynamics (i.e. *crescendo* and *diminuendo*) in the seventeenth century are not clearly understood today. Indications of *crescendo* and *diminuendo* appeared with relative rarity in printed music of the seventeenth century. Nevertheless, such graded dynamics were often used in actual performance. The short *crescendo-diminuendo* effect (*messa di voce*), generally of a measure or less, was traditional on long notes combined with vibrato, and Simpson speaks of swelling or growing louder toward the middle and ending in 'one and the same Note'. (For Corelli and North in this connexion, see pp. 254–5.) The French composer Toinon explains (1699) about 'swelling the sound' (*enfler le son*)—unusual information from the French—in these words: 'To swell the sound is to increase it little by little, and then to diminish it proportionately, which is ordinarily done on long notes'.[8] Sometimes *diminuendo* was an unwritten effect understood in relation to harmony. North speaks of discords being followed more softly by their resolutions.[9]

Under certain conditions the indication f—p (*not* fp) meant a short *diminuendo* of a measure or less, and the long *diminuendo* is indicated by f—p—pp, an effect that occurs on the last page of Corelli's 'Christmas' Concerto (Op. 6, No. 8) and in Walther's *Hortulus Chelicus* (pp. 78–9). In both Corelli and Walther this effect occurs twice consecutively, and the context suggests that each of these means a long *diminuendo*. This interpretation is consistent with an account of Roman concert life related by Scipione Maffei, a contemporary:

> 'One of the principal sources from which the skillful in this art [of music] derive the secret of especially delighting those who listen is the piano and forte (*fortezzo*) be it in subjects (*proposte*) and answers (*risposte*), or be it when with artful degree the tone (*voce*) is diminished little by little, and then resumed [suddenly] in a loud manner; and this artifice is used frequently, and with marvelous effect, in the great *concerti* at Rome.'[10]

[8] Quoted in La Laurencie, op. cit., Vol. I, p. 42.
[9] *Roger North on Music*, op. cit., pp. 218–19.
[10] Scipione Maffei, 'Nuova Invenzione d'un Gravecembalo,' an article in *Giornale dei Letterati d'Italia*, tom. v, p. 144, Venice, 1711. For the Italian text and a more literary, but less accurate, translation, see Rosamund E. M. Harding, *Origins of Musical Time and Expression*, London, 1938, p. 94.

'The great *concerti* at Rome' can only refer to the concertos of Corelli, and the gradual *diminuendo* 'little by little' and then resuming in a 'loud manner' are exactly the effects specified by Corelli on the last page of his 'Christmas' Concerto.[11] According to Beckmann, Westhoff requires the same effect of *diminuendo* but on a smaller scale in his sonatas of 1694: p—pp—ppp. Strangely enough, the *diminuendo* seems to be commoner than the *crescendo*. An exceptional use of both occurs in the course of Matthew Locke's incidental music (strings) to *The Tempest* (1672). An indication on the score says 'louder by degrees', and the 'tempest' gathers intensity for nearly nine measures of *crescendo*. The climax of the tempest is marked 'violent' in the score, and the end of this piece is marked 'soft and slow by degrees'. These directions are most unusual in seventeenth-century scores, and are apparently the first specific written-out indication of a long *crescendo* and a long *diminuendo*.[12]

Rhythm and tempo

The correct tempo is always vital to the effect of a piece of music, but correctness is often relative to actual performing conditions, since the tempo may be affected by external factors such as the size of the hall, its furnishings, and its acoustical properties. Performers themselves often have marked convictions about the tempo proper to the character of the music itself, especially if it is in an idiom the players know and understand. In older or unfamiliar music, the proper tempo is more problematical. The correct tempo of a *tripla* section in a piece of early seventeenth-century music (cf. pp. 180ff.) would be almost impossible for a modern musician to divine without special information; and the notion that a seventeenth-century saraband should occasionally be played fast is contrary to all current folklore of music. Nevertheless, a number of sarabands of this time are marked 'fast' in the music (others being marked 'slow'); and Furetière, a contemporary theorist, writes concerning the saraband: 'The violins play a *sarabande* very fast (*fort gaye*) . . . one ordinarily dances it to the sound of the guitar or the castanets and it has a gay and amorous movement.'[13] The fact is, of course, that the saraband was originally a fast dance and got progressively slower.

---

[11] This *diminuendo* would not be applicable in cases where the literal repetition of music 'in echo' was involved. For example, in Purcell's *Fairy Queen* (*The Works of Henry Purcell*, op. cit., Vol. XII, p. 43), an instrumental interlude labelled 'Echo' has a number of indications 'Loud—Soft—Softer', which clearly mean a 'terraced' echo in this context.

[12] The music is printed in Ernst H. Meyer, *English Chamber Music*, op. cit., pp. 237–9. For further details on dynamics, see Rosamund E. M. Harding (as in note 10).

[13] Antoine Furetière, *Dictionnaire universel, contenant généralement tout les mots français tant vieux que modernes*, 2nd ed., The Hague and Rotterdam, 1701. See also Robert Stevenson, 'The Sarabande' in *Inter-American Music Bulletin*, Pan-American Union, Washington, July 1962. For the earliest known reference to the saraband (1569), see

Muffat recognized the fundamental problem of determining the inherent tempo, and his general remarks in this context are to the point: 'In determining the different tempi, three things are essential: 1. to be able to recognize the true [inherent] tempo of each piece; 2. having recognized this, to maintain it as long as one plays the same piece, always the same without ritarding or speeding up; and 3. to alter and compensate (*recompenser*) the value of certain notes for greater beauty.'[14] (Cf. *notes inégales*, below.) In his *Auserlesene Instrumental-Music* (1701), Muffat says that the Italians go much slower in slow tempo and much faster in fast tempo 'than we [i.e. the Germans] do'.[15]

Muffat elaborates on his first point above by saying that signatures and a knowledge of dances are helpful in determining the true tempo. About 1700 the typical duple signatures and their usual tempi are these:

C   slow to moderate.

₵   (alla breve), faster or twice as fast.

𝄵   brisk.

2   somewhat slower than ₵. Muffat says that in this tempo the notes have nearly the same value as the Italian presto C in four-time.

Signatures in triple time:

3/2   grave ('restrained').

3   slow ('slow triple').

6/4   'fast for Jiggs [gigues] and Paspies' [passepieds, a fast species of minuet].

3/4   'gayer' than 3/2.

In Italy 6/8 and 12/8 are associated with the fast gigue.

By 1700 these signatures are real time signatures—less frequently proportional signs. Nevertheless, vestiges of the old mensural, proportional system (see pp. 181ff.) are not uncommon.[16] The following signatures occur occasionally in Corelli's works: C 3/4, C 3/8, C 3/2, C 12/8, C 2/4, C 9/8, and C 6/8. Corelli, in short, is still using the proportions. In music with the 'signature' C 12/8, for instance, he sometimes inserts 8/12 (or 8), meaning to play the eight eighth-notes in the same time as the preceding twelve.[17] In C 3/4 Corelli occasionally uses the 9/6 proportion for triplet divisions. Sometimes he uses two proportional signatures simultaneously, for example

---

Robert Stevenson in a communication to the *Journal of the American Musicological Society*, Spring, 1963, pp. 110–12.

[14] *Florilegium Secundum*, op. cit., p. 47.

[15] See Strunk, op. cit., p. 451.

[16] As implied by the above, there is a loose relationship between signature and tempo in this period, but beware of the dogmas of a rigid system as in Fritz Rothschild, *The lost Tradition in Music: Rhythm and Tempo in J. S. Bach's Time*, London, 1953.

[17] See Ex. 123 below, found in *Les Oeuvres de Arcangelo Corelli*, ed. by Joachim and Chrysander, London [1891], Vol. II, p. 177.

C 6/8 in an upper part and C 2/4 in the basso continuo (for an example of three different time signatures in G. B. Vitali, see Ex. 61 above).

A particularly interesting example of proportions occurs in Playford's *The Division-Violin*. The second piece in this collection uses the same ground-bass throughout, and the proportional signatures must then be geared to the time of the ground-bass, since it is repeated over and over again. The piece in question begins *alla breve*, using four quarters or the equivalent to a measure. A later variation in ₵ 3 (= 12/8) must represent a speeding up of the eighth-note, since there are twelve where the initial variation had eight. Within individual variations a process of slowing down is effected by similar proportions: No. 7 starts ₵ 9/4 and changes in its course to 6/4 and 3/2.

By 1700 tempo markings are gradually making the old proportions and their signatures obsolete. There are naturally more tempo markings than before. *Andante*, previously not indicated because it was the normal speed, now appears occasionally as a term.[18] The number and subtlety of terms meaning fast or slow have increased, and still other terms are added: *più allegro, più adagio*, and even *adagissimo*.[19] Prior to the eighteenth-century influx of Italian terms in England, Purcell uses 'Quick', 'Brisk', and 'Slow' in his viol Fantasias of 1680. 'Drag' is used by Mace in a context that must imply slow, not *ritardando*. If there were no recognized terms for increasing and decreasing the speed, these effects were certainly known and practised. Frescobaldi was no stranger to fluctuating tempos in the early seventeenth century, and, since Muffat assails the practice of speeding up and slowing down, these vices (or virtues) must have been much in vogue in the late seventeenth century as well.[20]

Muffat also says that time was beaten with the foot, and such noisy practices seem to have been a regular part of the musical scene, at least in France. In the French opera, time was beaten audibly by thumping up and down with a large stick. Lully, carrying this method into the performance of a *Te Deum* (1687) in honour of the King, wounded himself so severely when he mistook his foot for the floor that he died from the resulting complications.

Alterations of rhythm

In the seventeenth and eighteenth centuries (possibly earlier), conventional alterations were made in the rhythm of certain figures, sometimes for expressive reasons, sometimes to correct an imperfect notation. This remark applies to particular kinds of dotted-note figures and to certain running passages in equal-note values.

[18] In Corelli's works, the term *andante* occurs in Op. 3, Sonata 5, and in Op. 6, Concertos 2, 7, 10, and 11.
[19] *Adagissimo* occurs in Walther's *Hortulus Chelicus*, p. 105.
[20] Muffat, *Florilegium Secundum*, op. cit., p. 47.

Lengthening of dotted figures

Writing in 1752, Quantz says: 'Eighths, sixteenths, and thirty-seconds with dots do not follow the general rule on account of the vivacity which they must express.'[21] Quantz explains, and his examples show, that the dotted notes are elongated so that in dotted eighths and sixteenths the following short note is a sixty-fourth note in both cases, thus elongating the dotted eighth to a triply (*sic*) dotted eighth, and the dotted sixteenth to a doubly dotted sixteenth. Only the dotted thirty-second remains as written (for examples and a fuller discussion, see pp. 478ff.). For purposes of added articulation, all or part of the dot may be performed as a rest. Quantz also applies the lengthening-shortening in reverse, so that (for example) in Lombard figures (♪♩) the short note is shortened and the dotted note correspondingly lengthened. In a later chapter[22] he says: 'When thirty-second notes follow a long note and a short rest, the thirty-seconds are always played very quickly, either in Adagio or Allegro.' (Ex. 114.) None of Quantz's remarks apply to dotted halves or quarters. (For an occasional use of doubly dotted quarters, see p. 479, below.)

Quantz

Ex. 114

How widely was this alteration practised in the seventeenth century, long before Quantz? The double (or triple) dotting was appropriate to 'vivacity', to short note values, and to music of a pronounced emphasis and swing. As such, one would relate double dotting to certain types of dance music and to the emphatic rhythms of Lully's majestic French Overture. On the whole, double dotting is probably more applicable to French than to Italian music at this time, but it is curious that Muffat, who discusses Lully's practices in detail, does not mention the lengthening of dotted notes by double dotting—a custom that would affect every French Overture and a number of dances, the daily bread of the Lullists.

As a matter of fact, the lengthening of dotted notes to doubly dotted notes seems to have been little mentioned in theory books before Quantz, and we can only guess how widespread its use was in the seventeenth century. The only evidence specifically applicable to such cases in the late seventeenth century occurs in an obscure and curious set of 'Rules for Gracing on the Flute' (*c.* 1700), which contains this direction: 'Where there is a Prickt Crotchet quaver & Crotchet [= ♩. ♪♩] stay Long upon ye

---

[21] Quantz, ch. 5, para. 21.　　　[22] Ch. XVII, sec. 2, para. 16.

Prickt Crotchet.'[23] This might be taken as equivalent to double dotting. At any rate there is considerable documentary evidence to prove that the practice of double dotting continued to flourish long after its description by Quantz. Although the double dot is apparently specifically described for the first time by Quantz, Leopold Mozart is the first (1756) to use it in regular notation.[24]

Alteration of dotted and other figures in the context of triplets

In music that uses mixed time signatures the meaning of the notation is by no means clear in all respects. A number of gigues, for instance, use 6/8 or 12/8 in one or several parts and 2/4 or 4/4 in another. Ex. 115a and Ex. 115b raise the issue of playing the notes as written or altering the bass to the rhythms of 6/8 as shown below the staff.

Ex. 115

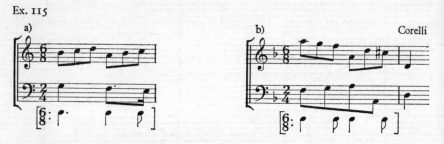

Similar complications may occur within a single part or in a piece whose voice parts all use the same time signature. The last movement of Bach's Fifth 'Brandenburg' Concerto is written in 2/4 (Ex. 116a), the first measure using dotted figures, and the second measure, triplets. Should the first measure be performed as written or as shown in Ex. 116b? In Bach's C-minor

Ex. 116

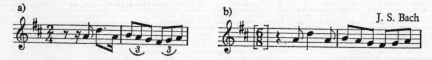

[23] See *The Galpin Society Journal*, Vol. XII, 1959, p. 93. Max Kuhn in his *Die Verzierungs-Kunst* (Leipzig, 1902), p. 79, gives an example from Bovicelli's *Regole, Passaggi di Musica* (1594) in which he says two equally written eighths are to be performed as a doubly dotted eighth followed by a thirty-second. Strictly speaking, Kuhn is in error. The Bovicelli example shows a dotted, not a doubly dotted, note. Nevertheless in his text (p. 11) Bovicelli speaks in a way that could be interpreted to support Kuhn's example of doubly dotted eighth. Bovicelli, in explaining the performance of equally written eighths, says: 'Note that the more one holds the first note and makes the second more rapid, thus is there more grace (*gratia*) in the voice [part].'

[24] For these and similar questions, see Newman W. Powell, *Rhythmic Freedom in the Performance of French Music from 1650 to 1735*, Ph.D. dissertation, Stanford University, 1959, available through University Microfilms, Inc., Ann Arbor, Michigan.

Sonata for Violin and Harpsichord, the *Adagio* movement (in E flat major) begins as shown in Ex. 117. Should the violin part be played as written or should the dotted figure be assimilated to the triplet rhythm of the accompaniment?

Ex. 117

J. S. Bach

The answers to these questions are even more difficult to give than usual because two eminent eighteenth-century theorists, Quantz (1752) and C. P. E. Bach (1753) give exactly opposite opinions. Quantz wants the dotted figure played doubly dotted. With respect to Ex. 118a, he says: 'This rule [of double dotting] must likewise be observed when there are triplets in one part and dotted notes against them in another part. Hence the short note after the dot must not be played with the third note of the triplet but directly after it, otherwise it would sound as though it were in 6/8 or 12/8 time . . . [and] thus the expression of the passage would not be brilliant and splendid but very lame and simple.'[25] Quantz, incidentally, says nothing about two equal eighths (♪♪) being transformed into ♩ ₃ ♪ in performance (cf. Ex. 115b). C. P. E. Bach explains a similar example (Ex. 118b and Ex. 118c), but his explanation is quite different: 'With the advent of an increased use of triplets in common of 4/4 time, as well as in 2/4 and 3/4, many pieces have appeared which might be more conveniently written in 12/8, 9/8 or 6/8. The performance of other lengths against these notes is [also] shown.'[26] In his accompanying example C. P. E. Bach spaces the notes under each other as shown in our Ex. 118b and Ex. 118c, implying that ♩.♪ and ♪♪ in 2/4 may both equal ♩ ♪ in 6/8. However, his statement is not as mandatory, dogmatic, or specific as we have been led to believe, even for the

Ex. 118

a)
Quantz

b)

c) C. P. E. Bach

[25] *Versuch*, op. cit., ch. 5, para. 22.
[26] *Essay on the True Art of Playing Keyboard Instruments* by Carl Philipp Emmanuel Bach, translated and edited by William J. Mitchell, New York, 1949, p. 160.

H.V.P.–X

keyboard, much less ensemble music. Bach's text could also be interpreted to mean that this notational practice was of relatively recent origin. Dolmetsch, whose pioneering work has been of such consequence for the music of this period, is strangely inconsistent in this matter. He makes much of the point that Quantz's treatise applies properly to the music of J. S. Bach and earlier composers, while C. P. E. Bach's work deals more with his own practice and that of a succeeding generation. Thereupon, Dolmetsch proceeds to settle the matter of dotted figures in favour of the method advocated by C. P. E. Bach without even mentioning Quantz's strong statement to the contrary.[27]

A large number of performers today, perhaps swayed by Dolmetsch, have adopted C. P. E. Bach's solution, thereby making the music and their performance simpler, but less 'brilliant and splendid'. In a recent article Eta Harich-Schneider (herself a harpsichordist) has made an elaborate study of this question.[28] For music before 1750, Harich-Schneider believes that dotted figures in the context of triplets were generally meant to be played as written. In her view C. P. E. Bach's remarks apply to the changing style of his own time and to the following generations whose leader and spokesman he became. As a broad statement, Harich-Schneider's findings have something to be said for them, and, in any case, they are a refreshing antidote to the prevailing view based on the C. P. E. Bach passage just quoted and applied retroactively to earlier music, including that of the seventeenth century. Nevertheless, there are a number of instances where dotted and other figures (especially ♫ and ♪.♪) in the context of triplets must have been assimilated to 6/8 or 12/8 time *a la* C. P. E. Bach. In short ♪.♪ (or ♫) is sometimes a notational device used to indicate ♩₃♪. On the other hand, ♪.♪ and ♫ may mean what they say in the context of triplets, and the problem is to discover which notation is applicable. Thurston Dart's rule[29] *'assimilate all dotted rhythms to the dominant rhythm of the movement'* is a convenient rule of thumb, but it is often difficult to apply in practice. The 'dominant rhythm' is not always easy to determine (cf. Ex. 117), nor does this rule cover the case of triplets against two equal eighths.

For string music of the late seventeenth century, our main concern at this point, Corelli furnishes us with a number of interesting examples of this rhythmic problem. A good example of assimilation is Ex. 119a. In this music

[27] See Arnold Dolmetsch, op. cit., ch. III.

[28] 'Über die Angleichung nachschlagender Sechzehntel an Triolen' in *Die Musik Forschung*, January–March 1959, pp. 35–59. For a more conventional view, see Erwin R. Jacobi's rebuttal of Harich-Schneider's article in the same journal, July–September, 1960, pp. 268–81. The whole question needs further and more comprehensive investigation than either of these authors (particularly Jacobi) have brought to the subject. See the Collins dissertation cited below on p. 484, note 34.

[29] Thurston Dart, *The Interpretation of Music*, London, 1954, p. 89.

it is inconceivable that the rhythmic imitation, starting between the solo violin and the bass at the end of measure one, is not carried out in note values of the same length; and therefore the true rhythm of the bass is 12/8, being performed as shown below the staff. In Corelli's works, pieces are written in mixed signatures (cf. Ex. 119a) when one of the parts, usually the bass, has little or no triplet motion. (On the other hand, when triplet movement occurs in all parts, Corelli usually notates every part in 12/8 or 6/8 time.) In such cases as Ex. 119a, Corelli uses 4/4 or 2/4, setting the part in question to quarters without using dots and without using as many rests—a convenience in writing and a saving in engraving costs. In theory at least the performer then alters the rhythm mentally to 12/8 or 6/8, thinking of the quarters as dotted, lengthening the first of the two equally written eighths where they occur, and inserting the extra eighth rests.[30] Another striking example (Ex. 119b) occurs in Corelli's *Concerto Grosso* No. 3, last movement. The *concertino* is written in 12/8 and the *ripieno* in 4/4 (by writing the numerous parts in this way the engraving costs saved in the case of the concerto would be still greater than in the case of the sonata given in Ex. 119a). In Ex. 119b, where the notes of the *concertino* are exactly doubled by the corresponding *ripieno* part, it is difficult to believe that the of the ripieno part

Ex. 119

---

[30] A somewhat ambiguous remark occurs in Brossard's *Dictionary* (Paris, 1703; English translation by Grassineau, 1740): 'The Italians most often mark the Gigue in 6/8 or 12/8 for the violins, and sometimes the bass with C or 4/4. In this case one plays the bass as if it were *pointée* [dotted].' Does this mean 'dotted' in the sense of the bass in Ex. 119a being thought of as dotted (as above)? Or does *pointée* have some connotation of *notes inegales*? (See below.) It probably means the former. The passage just cited occurs only in Brossard's first edition (1703; article '*Giga*'), not in the second edition (1705) nor in the English translation (1740).

were not played as ♩₃♪ to match the *concertino*, the *ripieno* part really being in 12/8 and the quarters being regarded mentally by the player as dotted quarters.

The dotted-eighth figure (♪⁀♪) is used against triplets only *once* in the entire works of Corelli (Ex. 120). In this particular example the prevailing rhythm is triplet, and assimilation of the dotted figure to ♩₃♪ is strongly suggested here. Ex. 120 is, in fact, a good example of a convention of notation that was widely practised in similar situations well into the eighteenth century. For instance, in the music of J. S. Bach one invariably finds ♪⁀♪ , *not* ♩₃♪ in a context of triplets (♪♪♪₃) in 2/4, 4/4, or (less often) 3/4 time. (Of course, the notation ♩ ♪ is usual in 6/8, 12/8, or 9/8 time.) If, then, in prevailing triplet divisions in 2/4, 4/4, or 3/4 time, we frequently find such rhythmic patterns as 2/4: ♪♪♩₃ ♪⁀♪ but not 2/4: ♪♪♩₃ ♩₃♪ the implication in these special cases is that ♪⁀♪ = ♩₃♪. Similarly, ♫♪ = ♪₃♩. However, this convention clearly applies only when the dotted-eighth figure just mentioned is the only one that is duply divided in the context of triplet divisions.

Corelli, Op. 4, No. 4

Ex. 120

In Corelli's music, mixed time signatures, such as 4/4 and 12/8, seem to be used for reasons of simplicity and saving in engraving costs (or, quite probably, because they were part of a lingering tradition of notation from the past). However, there are instances in other composers of the late seventeenth century where different time-signatures reflect a polyrhythm. Ex. 61, taken from G. B. Vitali, is a case in point, the duple division of the upper part being played as written against the triplet division of the second part. (Cf. p. 219 above.)

Apart from mixed time signatures, there are also certain musical situations where it seems inevitable that dotted or other duple figures in the context of triplets were really intended to be played as written, not assimilated. At the beginning of Ex. 121, taken from Bach's *St. John Passion*, both parts are in duple rhythm, the bass using the dotted figure. At the point where the melody part changes to triplets, it would not make musical sense to alter the constant and prevailing dotted figure in the bass to ♪₃♪, especially since the dotted figure in the bass is obviously vital to the musical depiction of the text ('scourged'). In general, the sudden appearance of triplet figures in an established context of dotted figures is not a sign of assimilation of the dotted figures to triplet rhythm, retroactively. In Corelli's music, most of the instances involving this kind of ambiguity occur in gigues, and normally they are written in 6/8 or 12/8 (with or without a part in duple time). In one case, however, Corelli writes two parts of a gigue in 4/4, and *both* parts have duple divisions as well as triplets (opening of gigue in Ex. 122). The implication is that Corelli wanted two notes played equally

Ex. 121

Ex. 122

Ex. 123

in the time of three equal notes, a true polyrhythm. Similar cases occur in Muffat.[31] Sometimes the contrast between triple and duple time is indicated in the same voice part by means of the old proportions. A case in point is Ex. 123, taken from Corelli's Op. 3, Sonata 10, last movement. The prevailing 12/8 is interrupted by '8', which means that eight notes are to be played

[31] See Harich-Schneider, op. cit., p. 43.

in the time of the previous twelve. Four basic beats are common to both measures. It would be a waste of time to indicate the '8' proportion in measure 2 (in the context of the 12/8 measures of measure 1 and measure 3) if measure 2 were to be played in the 12/8 rhythm shown below the staff. Hence measure 2 should be played as written.

Proportions belong to an old tradition, and they continue for some time, still appearing occasionally in eighteenth-century music. The emphasis on rhythmic differences of the parts of the ensemble and the general effect of the music as a whole were undoubtedly basic to Quantz's instructions to play the dotted figures as written, not as assimilated to triplets; and whenever the music calls for something 'brilliant and splendid'—to use Quantz's words—we will be well advised to consider his directions, no matter what the context.

Unfortunately it is impossible to formulate a simple rule that will serve as an infallible guide to the performance of the rhythms written in the ways mentioned above. It is evident from the examples just cited that the dotted-eighth figure and also the equally written eighths were sometimes played as written, and sometimes both were assimilated to a prevailing triplet rhythm. Each case must be decided on the musical merits of the situation. The following observations regarding seventeenth-century music are offered for what they may be worth:

1. In a single part in 2/4, 4/4, or 3/4 time, dotted-eighth figures, provided they are the only duple divisions occurring in the context of triplets, may be, and often should be, played as ♩₃♪ (Ex. 120; but cf. Quantz on Ex. 118a).

2. In mixed time signatures (such as 12/8 or 6/8 in one part and 4/4 or 2/4 in another), the duple divisions (♫♬, ♫) *may* be assimilated as ♩₃♪ to a prevailing triplet rhythm. The context will generally show whether to assimilate or not (cf. Ex. 119b).

3. Triplet rhythm, introduced into passages of already dominant duple division (including dotted figures), does not generally influence the dotted and other duple figures to triplet rhythm retroactively (Ex. 121).

4. Where a number of duple divisions in a single part (such as ♫ , ♫♬, ♫♫, ♫♫♫) occur in the context of triplets or against triplets in another part, assimilation of the duple figures to triple rhythm is unlikely. That is, the polyrhythm suggested by the notation generally prevails (Ex. 61). In these cases, perhaps the dotted figures may be made more effective in the polyrhythm by lengthening the dot slightly.

5. A double signature (e.g. 3/4, 9/8) in the same part may (or may not) imply that measures which are properly in 3/4 use the dotted figure as written and that in measures properly in 9/8 the triplet figure prevails.

Notes inégales

Under certain conditions, especially in French music, progressions of notes *written* equally were *played* unequally, hence the term *notes inégales*. The normally stressed note was elongated, sometimes barely so, sometimes actually dotting the note (e.g. ♪), called *pointer* by the French. This practice was a natural consequence of the French attempt to regulate and systematize the exuberance of early seventeenth-century music, which altered written notes at will, especially in pieces of improvisatory character as in preludes and toccatas. The French *pointer* is described in French sources of the late seventeenth century (Rousseau, Marais, Loulié, Muffat); and the rules given in these works are the basis of an elaborate literature and practice in the eighteenth century, including German sources, notably Quantz, whose style and practice often represent an eclectic point of view. The French *notes inégales* may be considered a vestige of the old spirit of improvisation, and it is significant that a number of references to *notes inégales* appear at the same time that Lully was forbidding improvisation. However, isolated references to this practice occur in the sixteenth century, also in French sources.[32] The Italians continued to improvise, elaborating the bare bones of their slow movements with flights of fancy; and into these improvisations all sorts of rhythmic alterations could be introduced *ad libitum*. There is little evidence of 'unequal notes' in Italy after 1650.[33] Apart from improvisation, the Italian scores were meant to be played rhythmically much as written. In his *L'Art de toucher le clavecin* (1716), François Couperin explains the *notes inégales*, and in the course of his explanation he says, 'We write a thing differently from the way we play it . . . the Italians, on the contrary, write their music in the true time values which they intend.'

Muffat, the chief apologist for the Lully style, is quite specific about the practice of 'unequal notes', and it is suggestive that he introduces his comments and rules directly after he has admonished his readers at some length on the necessary virtue of maintaining strict time. Quantz, who gives the most elaborate of all rules, does so after similar remarks in a like context.[34]

---

[32] See Loys Bourgeois, *Le Droict Chemin de musique*, Geneva, 1550, ch. 10.
[33] Prior to that time there are good examples of this practice in Italy. Cf. Bovicelli in note 23, p. 296, above.
[34] The most thorough-going exposition in favour of this type of rhythmic alteration is found in Sol Babitz, 'A Problem of Rhythm in Baroque Music' in *The Musical Quarterly*, October 1952. In Babitz's view, rhythmic alteration had much wider currency than implied above. For a fine summary of French practice, see Eugène Borrel, *L'Interprétation de la Musique Française*, Paris, 1934, pp. 150ff. See also Borrel's earlier article 'Les Notes Inégales dans l'ancienne Musique Française' in *Revue de Musicologie*, November 1931. See also John Fesperman, 'Rhythmic Alteration in Eighteenth-Century French Keyboard Music' in *Organ Institute Quarterly*, Vol. 9, Nos. 1 and 2 (Spring and Summer, 1961).

What Muffat actually says is this:

'The shorter (*diminuantes*) notes of the first order, such as sixteenths
in four-time, the eighths in two-time or *alla breve*, and those notes which
go twice as fast as the basic beat in triple time of somewhat gay
character and in the "proportions" [6/8?, 12/8?]—such notes being put
one after the other are not played as if one were equal to the other, as
they are marked, for that would be something sleepy, rough, and flat,
but they are changed in the French style by adding a dot to each of the
odd-numbered notes. Such notes becoming longer render the following
note shorter by as much.'[35]

Then Muffat gives examples of which Ex. 124 is typical.

The above passage from Muffat makes it clear that the note values which
may be altered to *notes inégales* should be a half to a quarter of the value of the
basic beat (cf. also Loulié, below, on this point). In addition, the cited
examples of 'unequal notes' in Muffat consist of passages that are principally
in stepwise (conjunct) motion. Apparently, conjunct motion is one of the
requisites of passages to which the *notes inégales* are applicable. Couperin says

Ex. 124

as much (1716): 'We dot (*pointer*) several consecutive eights in conjunct
motion (*degrés-conjoints*) and yet we write them as equal. Our custom
[probably referring to Lully] has enslaved us, and we hold fast to it.' Neither
Muffat nor Couperin speak of 'short-long' inequality. However, Couperin
speaks of the performance of '*coulés*' (Ex. 125) 'whose dots marking the

Ex. 125

second note of each quarter [group] ought to be more stressed (*appuyée*)'. If
by *appuyée* Couperin means 'prolonged', as he probably does in connexion
with harpsichord playing, he is speaking of 'short-long' in this case. However, Couperin uses this sign only in Books I and II of his harpsichord pieces,
not elsewhere in his instrumental music. In his chamber music, the term
coulé-pointé appears to describe inequality.

---

[35] *Florilegium Secundum,* op. cit., p. 48. See also Muffat's comments on the same subject
in his *Florilegium Primum,* where he implies that *notes inégales* are not used in Italian
practice (cf. Couperin, above). For this, see Strunk, op. cit., p. 444.

Short-long inequality, however, is made explicit by Loulié (1696) in a treatise which is the clearest and most complete seventeenth-century source concerning *notes inégales*.[36] He speaks of the short-long ratio somewhat as an afterthought, and, from this and other sources, one deduces that the long-short inequality was much more common than short-long. Loulié also defines *détacher, lourer, piquer*, and *pointer*. This is what he says:

'In any time-signature but especially in triple meter, the half beats [e.g., an eighth in 3/4] are performed in two different ways although they are written the same.

   1. Sometimes they are performed equally. This way is called *detaching (détacher) the notes*. One employs this way in melodies the tones of which proceed by skips, *and in every kind of foreign music one never dots a half-beat unless it is marked*. [Italics in the original.]

   2. Sometimes one makes the first half-beats a little longer [than written]. This way of playing is called *Lourer*. One uses it in melodies the tones of which proceed by stepwise motion (*Degrez non interrompus*) . . .

   There is still a third way in which one makes the first half-beat much longer than the second but [in this case] the first half-beat ought to have a dot. One calls this third way *Piquer* or *Pointer*. See [further] in Part III.'

In Part III, we find this (p. 71):

'In Part II, while speaking of the signatures for triple meter, one had forgotten to say that the first half-beats may be played in still a fourth way in which the first is shorter than the second, thus.' (See our Ex. 126.)

 Ex. 126

Earlier Loulié speaks about rhythmic alteration in a more general way, as follows:

'In any time signature the first and the third quarter of each beat are longer than the second and the fourth quarter although they are written as equal. (p. 35.)

---

[36] Etienne Loulié, *Elements ou principes de musique mis dans un nouvel ordre*, Amsterdam, 1698; original edition, Paris, 1696, with one difference in title: '*Elemens* . . .' The quotations are from the Amsterdam edition, pp. 38-39, p. 71, p. 35, and p. 41.

Note that 4/8 is beaten in two, two eighths to each beat for greater convenience, but all the eighths are equal, as opposed to 2/4 where the first and the third eighths are longer than the second and the fourth [eighths].' (p. 41.)

The codification of rules of 'unequal notes' also included exceptions, which later in Quantz became as elaborate as the rules themselves (cf. pp. 473–5). One important exception is already mentioned by Marin Marais in Book II of his *Pièces de Violes* (1701). Marais says that staccato dots over eighth-notes in triple time mean that these notes are to be played 'equal', not 'dotted as usual'. By dotted, Marais means *prolonged* in this connexion.

There is also one seventeenth-century German source that refers to 'unequal notes'. Printz says in his vocal treatise of 1678:

'Before we close this chapter, I first call to mind that all running figures can be checked by adding a dot to those notes intrinsically long (which would be numbered with uneven numbers) and the subtraction from the notes following: ♪ ♪♪ ♪'[37]

Printz's comment is especially interesting because it is added almost as an afterthought, apparently as advice to dot the notes in passagework to prevent their running away.

The use of the 'unequal notes' calls for considerable taste and judgement. These rhythmic alterations are not subject to a rigid and doctrinaire application—or they ought not to be. As Borrel says, each case ought to be looked at on its own merits, avoiding applying *notes inégales* indiscriminately like an automobile driver stopping at a red light. The notion of taste, Borrel continues, 'was for the times the supreme and infallible judge of all aesthetic laws'.[38] Is this not true today?

Summary

In the late seventeenth century the most conspicuous developments in violin playing were the emergence of national schools in sharper focus and the rise of virtuosity, especially among the Germans. National differences in music appear as counterparts of the cultural and political differences of nations at the time, and virtuosity is a natural result where individualism and experiment are encouraged and where gifted artists are given a free hand. The national style of the French was identified with the conservative technique of dance music; the Italian and especially the German style was allied to the progressive and sometimes virtuoso technique required in the sonata, concerto, and certain forms of the variation.

By and large the Italians were still the most important nation in all

[37] W. C. Printz, *Musica Modulatoris Vocalis*, op. cit., p. 56.
[38] Eugène Borrel, 'A propos des Notes Inégales' in *Revue de Musicologie*, July 1958, pp. 87–88.

aspects of the violin. The great makers improved the models of their pre-decessors; and, patently, Nicola Amati's 'grand' model and Stradivari's 'long' model violins were inspired by the new musical demands of the sonata and concerto players. Simultaneously a great violin maker, the Austrian Jacob Stainer, appears for the first time in a country other than Italy—a significant indication of the new importance of German violin music and technique. Nevertheless, Stainer is still linked to Italy, his violins being modelled on those of Nicola Amati. Other countries produced no great makers. In these countries, native violinists purchased Italian instruments when they could, and, for the most part, native schools of violin making copied Italian models. The Talbot manuscript, to which we are indebted for a number of details about the seventeenth-century violin, shows that a typical model in England at the end of the century was the 'grand' model Amati. The details of construction of the violin, stringing, pitch, and tension, indicate a greater volume of sound and more brilliant effect among the Italians and Germans than among the French.

The development of the bow indicates similar improvements and national differences. In general, the bow was lengthened and strengthened, a distinct bow head appeared, and a movable frog adjusted by a screw was used to tighten the best bows. The French bow, used primarily for the short, rhyth-mic strokes of dance music, was shorter than that of the Italians. The bow was still completely unstandardized as to weight, balance, and length, some bows being very short and a few even longer than the modern bow. How-ever, the best bows, like the 'Stradivari' bow, were beautifully made of excellent wood, and were worthy of the finest violins of the time. Above all, these bows were completely suited to the performance of the music that called them into being.

From a musical point of view Italy also dominated the world of the violin. For the first time a composer of first-rate importance devoted himself to violin music. In Corelli the violin found its first great champion, a violinist and composer who was able to consolidate the technical and musical gains of a century. His compositions, which combined musical values and technical interest in equal measure, impressed violinists of the seventeenth and eighteenth century in the same degree as Bach's preludes and fugues inspired pianists in the nineteenth century. This praise of Corelli does not imply disdain for many other composers of the time, including the whole Bologna School and G. B. Vitali, its most important representative. The Italian style combined a new interest in the cantabile with the development of running figures and double stops. The chief instrumental forms were the variation and the sonata. After 1650 the latter clearly separated into the church sonata and the chamber sonata (the last-mentioned consisted mainly of dances). The slow movements of the church sonata were often decorated with improvised 'graces'. The instrumental concerto dates from the last years of the century.

The Germans developed certain special aspects of technique to a new peak of virtuosity. Their interest in the upper register of the violin, in elaborate double stops, and in the *scordatura* produced results that were considerably above the level of the Italians from a purely technical point of view. Indeed, Walther could be described as the Paganini of the seventeenth century. Biber, another leading German, was, if anything, more significant musically, and both he and Walther took considerable interest in descriptive music in whose composition certain technical devices flourished and perhaps originated.

The newer uses of the violin did not eradicate its traditional role and value in accompanying vocal music, music for the theatre (including the opera), and playing for dancing, feasts, and court ceremonials. But, naturally, this traditional music required only a simple technique of no great challenge either to composer or player. Playing for dancing, probably the oldest function of the violin, was a common occupation of violinists in all countries, but it was the chief one in France; and the formation of a distinct dance style became synonymous with the French style of violin music and playing under Lully at the court of Louis XIV. The technical demands of this style were relatively slight, but the bowing discipline involved in it became highly stylized and even sophisticated. This was the style practised by the celebrated *24 Violons du Roy* and especially by *Les Petits Violons*.

It was also the style that dominated the English Court musicians directly after the Restoration of Charles II, who, aping the French Court where he had spent his exile, created a band of *24 Violins of the King* and a smaller band for the 'private music'. At the same time, a more progressive style emerged in England from a marriage of the violinists and violists, and violin parts occur from time to time in the brilliantly expiring literature of the viol fancy —for example, in those of John Jenkins. The Italian sonata gradually became known in England; and inspired by this example, Purcell wrote two sets of trio sonatas in 'just imitation of the most fam'd Italian masters'. A number of foreign violinists invaded England, the two best known being Baltzar and Matteis, who introduced the German and Italian styles of violin playing to England.

The divergence of styles along national lines produced a theoretical literature to define and explain them. Sometimes polemical, this literature might be considered a prelude to the musical wars of the eighteenth century. National differences frequently meant the differences between progressive and conservative, the perennial clash of the new and the old; and this, too, was reflected in the theorists. A related aspect concerned the gradual demise of the viol and its music before the onrush of the violin. Characteristically, the viol maintained its pride of place longest in France—indeed, it enjoyed a renaissance at the end of the seventeenth century. In Italy, by way of contrast, the ever-increasing success of the violin had engulfed the viol a half century earlier. The voices of the sad and angry men among the theorists like Mace, who cried out against the violin, were seeking to sustain or regain an era that was passing rapidly into history.

A sign of the times was the adoption of the violin by amateur violinists, who gradually abandoned the viol. This transference of allegiance resulted in an improvement of the social position of the violin and also in a rash of do-it-yourself violin methods for amateurs in England and Germany. These treatises reflect the audience for whom they were written and in no way mirror the technical equipment needed by professional violinists in Italy and Germany.

The advanced methods of the Italians and Germans are not described in treatises, and they can be deduced partly from the demands of the music and partly by carrying back eighteenth-century methods described in later works for similar musical situations. National styles are reflected in the manner of holding the violin and bow. The best Italian and German players held the violin at the neck and the bow with the Italian grip. The French probably held the violin somewhat lower and the bow with the French grip. The problem of holding the violin was related to the demands of shifting, especially downward shifting. Obviously, the Germans, like Biber and Walther, who were shifting downward from as high as the seventh position had to find a more secure method of holding the violin than the French who were playing mainly in first position without shifts. The same remarks apply generally to matters involving the left hand, including multiple stops, extension of the fingers, and the occasional use of vibrato.

The advances in bow design and the firmness of the bow grip are related to new demands on the right hand. The bow has become 'the soul' of the instrument. The management of the long stroke, its relation to tone and dynamic variety, the new cantabile, and the great variety of bow strokes are all manifestations of the importance of bowing in the late seventeenth century. The old Rule of Down-Bow is interpreted in new and more complicated ways among the French to suit the particular requirements of individual dances; and an even greater variety of strokes, required in the sonata and descriptive music, appear in Italian and German music. These varieties of bowing include basic non-legato, staccato, and legato (slurred) strokes in addition to such others as slurred staccato, slurred *tremolo, ondulé,* and the *bariolage.* The bowing of multiple stops poses a number of questions that cannot be fully answered. There are still substantial uncertainties about the performance of individual triple and quadruple stops and the implication of the notation with respect to duration and phrasing. Among special effects, the *pizzicato* became more clearly defined, but other devices like the *col legno* seem to be momentarily in limbo.

The general musical problems which faced the violinist include the realization of ornaments. Ornaments are now more frequently reduced to signs, less often written out, as they were previously. The new signs appear earliest and most often in France. In the degree that ornaments are specifically notated by signs, improvisation tends to wane. Characteristically Italy and, to a lesser extent, England were the countries where improvisation still flourished, not France. Among the most important unwritten ornaments was the vibrato which was used as a device of expression, ordinarily in connexion with long notes and combined with a nuanced tone.

Nuances were characteristic of the dynamics of the violin, but they were still a part of the unwritten tradition that surrounded music. Relatively few marks of louds or softs are found in the scores, but we know from other sources that *crescendo* and *diminuendo* were used widely in melodic instruments for purposes of expression.

The old problems of determining the correct rhythm and tempo, explained in connexion with our discussion of the early seventeenth century, have lessened in certain respects. The proportional system is dying, and in its place there are now far more tempo markings than previously. The problems of alteration of rhythm are, however, very considerable. These include lengthening of dotted figures, the assimilation of dotted and other figures to triplet rhythms, and the 'unequal' playing of notes written as equal. To recognize the notation and the context which permits or demands these rhythmic alterations requires special knowledge, study, and judgement.

The quest for greater power must have continued during the late seventeenth century as experiments in violin construction and the lengthening and strengthening of the bow suggest. The music written for the violin and the expansion of technique that it implies must have created new sonorities, notably the brilliant soprano of the highest register and the dark contralto of the lowest string. Musicians of the late seventeenth century also began to exploit the colour contrast of strings by means of the *scordatura* and by various special types of bowings like the *bariolage*. As explained above, there were considerable national differences in brilliance and sonority.

The violin itself was developed and its power increased by the genius of great craftsmen, but the credit for the development of the inherent tonal and colour resources of the instrument belongs to the musical and technical imagination of composers and violinists. For the violin the late seventeenth century was an important period *per se*; it was then that violin music and violin technique reached their first maturity. In the larger sweep of history, however, the late seventeenth century was more than this. It laid the groundwork for the achievements of the eighteenth century, truly called 'the century of the violin'.

PART FOUR

The Culmination of the Early History of Violin Playing 1700-1761

'The Intention of Musick is not only to please the Ear, but to express Sentiments, strike the Imagination, affect the Mind, and command the Passions.'

GEMINIANI,
The Art of Playing on the Violin, 1751, p. 1

'The good effect of a piece of music depends almost as much on the performer as on the composer himself.'

QUANTZ,
Versuch, 1752, Ch. XI, para. 5

The Culmination of the Early History of Violin Playing, 1700-1761

IN these two quotations Geminiani and Quantz have expressed the central aims of early eighteenth-century musicians—indeed, of all musicians—to 'affect the mind and command the passions' through music whose effect is perfectly realized by the performer. If such ideals have ever been attained, the early eighteenth century came near to doing so. In violin music, in particular, the sonata and the new concerto 'affected the Mind and commanded the Passions'; and they flourished with an extraordinary vigour, accompanied by corresponding technical advances, capable of achieving a 'good effect'. The names of great violinists and great composers were legion. Most composers were also performers; and sometimes, as in Vivaldi's case, a great composer was an equally great violinist. There has hardly been a time before or since that could boast of such talents in violin music and its performance as Bach, Vivaldi, Locatelli, Veracini, Geminiani, Leclair, and Tartini; or for making violins as Stradivari and Joseph (del Gesù) Guarneri. Under this perfect trinity of composer, maker, and player, violin music and technique reached a high point of development.

The eighteenth century was truly the century of the violin, but the musical and technical development of the instrument differed in the two halves of the century. Before 1750 the final years of the Baroque era witnessed a culmination of the early history of violin playing in terms of the violin of the time and the 'old' bow. A new virtuosity of both left and right hand was an aspect of this culmination—a fact little appreciated today, but one which will be amplified in detail in later chapters.

After 1750 the different ideals of the Rococo and particularly the Classic period at the end of the eighteenth century prompted an expansion of some aspects of the old technique and a change in others, creating a different technique adapted to new musical aims. The most striking outward manifestation of these changes was the Tourte (modern) bow (see Plate 28), perfected about 1780, which made possible a better realization of the new cantabile, more power to compete with the larger orchestras in concertos, and other musical demands related especially to the types of bow strokes. Tourte standardized the bow and brought to its manufacture a craftsmanship comparable to that of Stradivari. With small changes of details, the model that Tourte perfected has persisted to the present day. At the same time certain musical features of earlier music were less perfectly achieved by the modern bow than by the bow for which the old music was intended, a point frequently, and sometimes conveniently, overlooked.

Such oversights are unfortunate and misleading, and consequently a clear view of the whole history of violin playing has sometimes been obscured by ignorance and faulty perspective. Alberto Bachmann is a case in point when he says:

'When we consider the time which has elapsed from the creation of the violin, properly speaking, to the appearance of Paganini, it must be admitted that the evolution of progress was slow up to the moment when the tremendous genius of the great Italian illumined the firmament of art by the deploy of his magic powers.'[1]

Such a statement cannot be taken seriously today. The achievements of Vivaldi and Locatelli—to select two—show that the 'evolution of progress' in the technique and idiom of the violin was remarkably rapid, and Paganini's 'deploy of magic powers' would have been impossible without theirs a century earlier.

Bachmann's implied analogy between the 'evolution of progress' in art and Darwin's biological theory of evolution is worth a brief digression to correct the perspective. The whole history of art (including the history of violin making, violin music, and violin playing) can be examined profitably in terms of Darwinian theory only if one fundamental point is kept in mind: namely that the evolution of particular forms and styles continues only so long as the aesthetic aims that nourish them prevail. The history of art is the history of a succession of artistic ideas, ideals, and beliefs; and the life span of the forms and styles involved is measured by the degree of success attending the artist's aims. The tenets of the Vivaldi concertos are quite different from those of Mozart, Beethoven, or Paganini; and to trace the evolution of one from the other is rewarding only in so far as the different artistic aims are understood. Above all, the evolutionary theory of progress is faulty when confused or identified with value judgements. According to one evolutionary interpretation, art evolves in a continuous line to the perfection of the present. If this is so, the world of art today must be the best of all possible worlds—a conclusion that is palpable nonsense.

In the history of any art, forms and styles die out and become obsolete, but not necessarily in the biological sense or for the same reason obtaining among the biological species. Musical forms, for example, change when tastes change; and while it is true that an inherent weakness may obliterate a musical species just as it does a biological species, the obsolescence of a musical form comes about more often as a result of changing taste, when it ceases to have validity for the composers of a new era. Unlike the biological species, an 'obsolete' art form continues as a residuum of art history; and this form, embodied in the individual masterpiece, is always alive to a public, past or present, that perceives its value. The true criterion of an art work is the success with which the artist realizes the aims that have validity for him

[1] Alberto Bachmann, *Encyclopedia of the Violin*, New York, 1925, p. 188.
H.V.P.–Y

and his public; and the continuing life of an individual work of art is determined by the intellectual and emotional values it has for the public over long periods of time.

The evolutionary theory of art breaks down unless the factor of changing taste is considered fundamental to the process of survival and the natural selection of species. This uncomfortable and inconvenient fact makes it extraordinarily difficult to perceive and describe the evolution of any art and its state of 'progress' at any point in history. In the history and evolution of violin playing, this is why the complex interaction of composer, performer, and maker must be viewed against the diverse musical conditions and changing tastes that influenced violin music and violin playing and of which they were an inseparable and organic part.

In the early eighteenth century the progress of violin music, technique, instrument, and bow may be discussed as a direct evolution from the seventeenth century, because the aims of the early eighteenth century were similar to those of the age that immediately preceded it. The same forms and styles continued and increased in popularity, and consequently the demand for the violin intensified as seventeenth-century forms of chamber music, notably the sonata, became more widespread. Much that was tentative and experimental came to flower in the early eighteenth century. The new concerto, developing on principles already inherent in the seventeenth century, elaborated the technical idiom of the violin, and it dictated certain changes in the violin and bow to meet the new demands. The international vogue of the opera, particularly strong in Italy and France, increased the need for violins and violinists to maintain the opera orchestra, the backbone of which was the stringed instruments. The violin was also used in increasing numbers in the forms of sacred and secular vocal music.

The musical prestige of Italy was never higher than in the early eighteenth century. This was predominantly true with respect to the opera and the world of the violin, particularly violin making. In Cremona, Antonio Stradivari and Joseph Guarneri (del Gesù) were making the great instruments on which their fame as the greatest makers of the violin rests today. In their own time, however, the reputation of these makers was challenged and sometimes surpassed by Nicola Amati, their older colleague in Cremona, and by Jacob Stainer at Absam in Tyrol (see p. 195). The struggle between the arched model of Amati and Stainer and the flat model of Stradivari and Guarneri was not clearly resolved in favour of the latter until Viotti introduced Stradivari's violins to Paris about 1775 and until Paganini spread the fame of his Guarneri violin throughout Europe in the early nineteenth century. During the lifetime of Stradivari, the manufacture of fine violins became more widespread throughout Italy and Europe as musical demands dictated. The famous opera at Naples, the new concertos at Venice (Vivaldi), the music-loving public in Rome, all required expert luthiers to make and repair instruments, and a similar situation existed in Europe as a whole. A great demand for cheaper instruments among ordinary players led to a flourishing mass production in the schools of Mirecourt, Markneukirchen, and Mittenwald.

As the century wore on the leadership of Cremona declined in Italy—that of Brescia had already done so (see ch. 9)—and by 1800 Italian makers enjoyed far less prestige than their colleagues prior to 1750. New technical and musical advances in France were responsible for displacing Italy from the leadership it formerly enjoyed, and for the first time a great violin maker, Nicholas Lupot, appeared in France. The modern bow was also perfected in France in the late eighteenth century. It is significant of the changing times that Viotti, an Italian who came to Paris about the same time, nurtured the French school of Baillot, Rode, and Kreutzer, a school that exerted a most important influence on violin technique in the nineteenth century. Paganini, the last of the great Italian violinists, was the star and symbol of nineteenth-century violin virtuosity, but the true teacher of the nineteenth-century violinist was Baillot, a Frenchman. The contemporary figure comparable to the great Italian violin makers of the eighteenth century was Jean-Baptiste Vuillaume (1798–1875), also a Frenchman. However, all this belongs to a later time.

In the early eighteenth century the most strongly contrasted national styles were Italian and French, just as they were in the seventeenth century. The Italian style of composing and playing was based on the cantabile of the voice and the brilliance of figuration. Included also were multiple stops and various other special effects. The typical forms of the *avant-garde* were the sonata and the concerto, and the mode of playing was expressive and dramatic, especially in the solo concerto. Nuance, vibrato, and *tempo rubato* were devices typical of the Italians.

From the seventeenth century the French inherited a strong and nearly exclusive interest in dance music and a technique appropriate to its performance. After the first quarter of the eighteenth century, however, French violinists, a number of whom had been trained in Italy, adopted the forms and, to a considerable extent, the technique of the Italians. Leclair is a good example. The sonata and concerto were introduced into France, and the technique of the French underwent a change necessary to cope with the musical changes. The manner of performance became more expressive, notably in the use of nuance. Not surprisingly, the social position of the violin improved in France once the violin ceased to be the primary concern of the professional dance musician. As a contemporary journal notes, 'The violin has been ennobled in our time; it is no longer shameful for honest men to cultivate it'.[2]

[2] *Mercure*, June 1738. Quoted in La Laurencie, *L'École française*, Vol. III, p. 12.

After the introduction of the Italian style, the progress of the violin in France was rapid, and the technical leadership passed from Italy to France in the late eighteenth century. Milestones in this change were L'Abbé le fils's treatise of 1761 (see p. 359), and, as mentioned above, the perfecting of the bow by Tourte as well as the first appearance of a great French violin maker in the person of Nicholas Lupot.

The German school leaned heavily on the Italians for inspiration, and the commanding position of the Germans as leaders in the school of virtuosity at the end of the seventeenth century was again pre-empted by the Italians. It is true that some of the greatest and most difficult works for the violin emanated from J. S. Bach, but nevertheless composing for the violin was not one of his main interests. It is significant that Bach turned to the Italians for the models of his concertos, notably to Vivaldi, some of whose pieces he transcribed. It is also typical that Leopold Mozart's *Violinschule* incorporates a number of technical ideas derived from Tartini's *Traité des Agrémens* (see p. 361). The Germans still continued to be interested in multiple stops.

By the early eighteenth century, England had virtually become a musical province of Italy, a country that flooded Europe with musicians, particularly opera singers and violinists. As a result, the English school of violin playing was essentially Italian, and the first important treatise of violin playing in the eighteenth century was published in English in London by Geminiani, an Italian by birth and a pupil of Corelli, but one who spent most of his life in England.

CHAPTER FOURTEEN

The Violin and Bow of the Early Eighteenth Century

ANTONIO STRADIVARI, whose early works and experiments have already been described (p. 197), continued to make violins steadily until the end of his long life (1737), a career uniquely distinguished by its productivity and consistent output of extraordinary instruments. Having abandoned his 'long' model violin about 1700, Stradivari produced shortly afterwards a 'classical' model which embodied the tonal and acoustical principles that served him to the end of his life.[1] The earliest celebrated example of this model was the 'Betts' violin of 1704 (Plate 33a), with which Stradivari enters his so-called 'golden' period. Among the great violins of this time were the 'Alard' of 1715, the 'Messie' of 1716,[2] and the 'Rode' of 1722, the last of the ornamented violins. While Stradivari continued his experiments to the end of his life, this classical flat model created a standard that has prevailed to the present. The significance of Stradivari lies partly in establishing and perfecting a model more influential than any other in history, and partly in the extraordinary perfection of his instruments. The latter combined the highest standards and beauty of craftsmanship, wood, and varnish with exceptional tonal properties, ease of playing, and carrying power. Stradivari enjoyed an immense fame in his lifetime, although (as has already been pointed out) he shared the highest esteem with others. A contemporary wrote:

'The best violins are those of Antonio Stratifario [sic] in Cremona . . ., also those of Jacob Stainer in Absam . . ., and these [violins] will overpower a whole musical choir. However, since these are very costly, one must content oneself meanwhile with German instruments [the author being a German] such as those of Hoffmann in Leipzig, Hasert in Eisenach, and Ruppert in Erfurt of which many are also agreeable and sufficiently powerful.'[3]

[1] See Hill, Stradivari, p. 152.
[2] Still in mint condition, the 'Messie' is preserved in the Ashmolean Museum at Oxford.
[3] J. P. Eisel, Musicus Autodidaktos, Erfurt, 1738, p. 30.

The tradition of Stradivari was continued in the eighteenth century by his sons, Omobono and Francesco, by Carlo Bergonzi, G. B. Guadagnini, and by many others who, in one way or another, were influenced by his example from then to the present.

In contrast to Stradivari, Joseph (del Gesù) Guarneri (1698–1744) was one of a celebrated family of makers, the fifth and last of its members.[4] The earliest was Andrea Guarneri (*c.* 1626–98), the pupil of Nicola Amati and the fellow worker of Stradivari in the latter's early years. Andrea had two violin-making sons: Pietro Giovanni (1655–1720), commonly called 'Peter of Mantua', from the city where he worked; and Giuseppe (Joseph) G. B. Guarneri (1666–1739/40). The latter was also the father of two violin makers: Pietro (1695–1762) and Bartolomeo Giuseppe, known as Joseph del Gesù. Joseph, the father, is known as 'Joseph, the son of Andrew' (Filius Andreae), to distinguish him from his more famous son, Joseph del Gesù. Peter, the brother of del Gesù, was called 'Peter of Venice' to distinguish him from his uncle in Mantua.[5]

The best of these five Guarneri were Peter of Mantua and Joseph del Gesù, both of whom were players as well as great craftsmen. The greatest maker of them all was undoubtedly del Gesù. In his own time he enjoyed a lesser reputation than Stradivari. Pugnani was the first important violinist to use del Gesù's violins, and, as explained above, the reputation enjoyed by del Gesù today dates from the time of Paganini. The great reputation of Stradivari's violins dates earlier, from Viotti's time (see p. 314). Del Gesù's life was far shorter than Stradivari's and he made about two hundred violins (no violas or cellos)—a mere fraction of Stradivari's output. The violins of del Gesù were probably inspired partly by the Brescian model of Maggini (see p. 108), and partly by Stradivari, but his work is less elegant and more variable than the latter's (cf. Plate 33b). A number of his violins also show signs of haste, perhaps due to the alleged irregularity of his life. His usual model was flat and on the small side. However, its bold outline often makes the violin appear larger than it actually is. Del Gesù was an isolated genius; he had no pupils and no real followers.

Among a host of violin makers in Italy and other European countries the Stainer-Amati influence remained strong throughout the eighteenth century. This was true of a number of makers in Rome, Venice, Florence, Genoa, Mantua, and Naples. It was generally true in England, Germany, France, and Holland. In England, in particular, violin makers were almost com-

---

[4] The added phrase del Gesù (of the Jesus), applied to Joseph about 1726, originated in his labels, which have the three letters I.H.S. surmounted by a cross. I.H.S. stood for a contraction of the Greek word for Jesus, hence del Gesù.

[5] For the Guarneri family, see W. H., A. F., and A. E. Hill, *The Violin-Makers of the Guarneri Family* (1627-1762), London, 1931.

pletely 'Stainerized', the main exception being Daniel Parker, who followed the model of Stradivari.

Although it is impractical to describe the merits and influences of all the well-known makers of the early eighteenth century, it is appropriate to enumerate the best known and the cities in which they worked (those already mentioned will not be repeated here). In Mantua, for example, were members of the Grancino and Testore families, Camillo Camilli, and Tommasso Balestrieri. In Bologna the best-known name at this time was Giovanni Tononi; in Venice, Santo Seraphin, Matteo Gofriller, and Domenico Montagnana; in Rome, David Tecchler and Michael Platner; in Naples, the Gagliano family, of whom the best was probably Gennaro; in Florence, Lorenzo and Tommasso Carcassi; in Treviso, Pietro and Antonio dalla Costa; and in Piacenza, Lorenzo and J. B. Guadagnini. The latter also worked in Turin and Parma.[6]

With the death of Joseph Guarneri (del Gesù) in 1744 and that of Carlo Bergonzi in 1747, the greatest glory of Cremona was over. The death of Peter Guarneri of Venice in 1762 marked the end of the great Venetian makers and a general decline of violin making in Italy. No longer were the commissions so rich, cheaper violins were being made in Italy, and violin makers became more active and proficient in other countries.

These countries, however, were not yet noteworthy for the number of distinguished makers. In Germany the best were members of the ubiquitous Klotz (Kloz) family in Mittenwald, notably Matthias I (1656–1743) and his son, Sebastian I. In Paris the names of Claude Pierray (1698–1726) and his pupil Louis Guersan (c. 1713– after 1781) may be singled out. In England the most distinguished luthier was Barak Norman. Daniel Parker, already mentioned as a follower of Stradivari, lived in London between 1700 and 1740. To these may be added Peter Walmsley and his pupil, Joseph (II) Hill (1715–84) of London, one of the first of the famous Hill family.

Details of the violin and its fittings

The violin itself, as already explained, was generally made either in the arched model of Stainer and Amati or the flat model of Stradivari and Guarneri, the length of the body averaging fourteen inches. The tension on the strings, vertically and horizontally, was less than that obtaining today, but, as far as we know, there was little increase in this respect from the late seventeenth to the early eighteenth century. Indeed, many, if not most, of the details of the violin itself in the first part of the eighteenth century were substantially the same as those in vogue fifty years earlier (cf. ch. 9). In particular, the neck still emerged straight from the body, as it had earlier. Similarly, compared to the modern neck, the old neck was generally shorter

[6] See E. N. Doring, *The Guadagnini Family of Violin Makers*, Chicago, 1949.

(quarter-inch to half-inch) and, as a consequence of nailing rather than modern mortising to the body (see p. 197), the neck of these instruments was somewhat fatter and rounder at its base where it joined the body of the violin. Plate 34 shows the three rough-headed nails in the top block of the 'Betts' Stradivari violin. It also shows the position of four of the six blocks, the two at the right corners not being shown. Another feature is the linings of the ribs. Note the particular care with which Stradivari fitted the lining of the middle bout to the corner blocks. (For the bass-bar, see p. 321.)

Because the eighteenth-century violin had a slightly shorter neck than it does now, the length of the string from nut to bridge (the 'string stop') was also a bit less than on the modern violin.[7] The fingerboard was not parallel to the straight neck, but was elevated, as needed, by a wedge in order to clear the arch of the belly and conform to the height of the bridge (cf. Plate 6). The fingerboard was somewhat wider at the pegbox end and somewhat narrower at the bridge end than the modern counterpart. The length of the fingerboard was determined by the range of violin music at that time. Before 1750 violin music rarely exceeded the seventh position, and therefore the fingerboard was normally not more than eight or eight and a half inches long, roughly two or two and a half inches shorter than it is now (cf. Plates 6 and 26)—that is, long enough to permit the violinist to play through the seventh position and stay on the fingerboard.

The design of the bridge began to approach the modern form. Some of Stradivari's bridges have been preserved, and that of the 'Tuscan' viola is very close to the design of the modern bridge, substituting a bar in the lower part for the older arch (see Plate 27 and p. 202, including note 16). However, compared with the modern bridge, this bridge of Stradivari is still somewhat more open in design and it is a little lower, conforming to lower tensions.[8] Little can or need be added to our previous account of the bridge (p. 202). The same variety obtains. If a generality is possible, the bridge of the early eighteenth century was slightly lower, thicker, and flatter than the modern bridge.

---

[7] In Peter Prelleur's The Modern Musick-Master (London, 1731) the fingering chart found in Part V ('The Art of Playing on the Violin') shows the exact length of string from nut to bridge. It measures twelve and a half inches, a half-inch less than is usual today. See also p. 200 n. 12.

[8] Sol Babitz has experimented with reconstructed bridges based on the Stradivari model, which he believes improves the tone quality vis-à-vis the modern bridge. According to Babitz, when the Strad-model bridge was made thicker than the modern bridge, it increased the tone; and when thinner, the tone was less. This opinion, however, is in conflict with Leopold Mozart's, cited below (p. 322). For a collection of old pegs, mutes, bridges, tailpieces, templates, and end buttons, see Kenneth Skeaping, 'The Karl Schreinzer Collection of Violin Fittings' in Music Libraries and Instruments (Hinrichsen's Eleventh Music Book, London, 1961), p. 251 (plates begin after p. 160).

Since the horizontal and vertical tensions on the instrument were less than they are now, the old bass-bar was somewhat shorter and slighter. For the same reason the sound post used in early eighteenth-century violins was also somewhat thinner than the modern type, although probably somewhat thicker than the 'goosequill' diameter reported by Talbot between 1685 and 1701 (see p. 201 above). On the whole, it is unlikely that either the sound post or the bass-bar changed very much between 1700 and 1750. That is to say, at both times they were slighter than modern ones (cf. Plate 34, showing a modern bass-bar and that of the 'Betts' Strad). However, there was the typical variety in these fittings suited to different instruments and situations. The normal bass-bar, for instance, was about nine and a half inches long (compared to the average of ten and a half today), but an early violin (1621) of A. & H. Amati had a bass-bar longer than any Stradivari and even longer (ten and five-eighths inches), though slighter, than the modern bass-bar. Similarly, the 'Messie' Strad (1716) had one of the largest bass-bars of its time. It was a half-inch longer and slightly deeper than the average. All these bass-bars, however, were narrower and shallower than the modern bass-bar. By way of comparison:[9]

	Length (in.)	Width (in.)	Depth in centre (in.)
Modern violin	$10\frac{1}{2}$	$\frac{1}{4}$	$\frac{7}{16}$
Average, 1650–1750	$9\frac{1}{2}$	$\frac{3}{16}$	$\frac{1}{4}$
'Messie' Strad	10	$\frac{3}{16}$	$\frac{5}{16}$

The strings were still gut. However, the lowest (G) was frequently wound with silver, a notable change compared to the seventeenth century and reflecting the greater use of the G string and the necessity of an improved resonance and response. Brossard speaks of a G string 'entirely wound with silver' in his manuscript treatise (*c.* 1712), and he says that it is not as thick as a G string made simply of gut. Others who mention the silver-wound G string are Majer in 1732, Quantz in 1752, and Löhlein in 1774.[10] Brossard also furnishes the extraordinary information that the D string is 'at present almost always partially wound with silver', and, as in the case of the G string, a string so wound is thinner than its counterpart made simply of gut.[11] In line with lesser tension, the strings were probably

[9] For these figures, see Hill, *Stradivari*, p. 190. The bass bar of the 'Messie' Strad was removed by Vuillaume in the nineteenth century. Later it was recovered by the Hills of London and placed with the 'Messie' Strad in the Ashmolean Museum at Oxford, where it is today.
[10] See J. F. B. C. Majer, *Museum Musicum*, 1732, p. 75; Quantz, *Versuch*, ch. XVII, sec. 2, para. 28; and G. Löhlein, *Anweisung zum Violinspielen*, Leipzig, 1774, p. 9.
[11] Sébastien de Brossard, *Fragments d'une méthode de violon*, MS. in the *Bibliothèque Nationale*, Paris, *c.* 1712, p. 12.

thinner than they are today (cf. p. 203), but, again, the thickness varied considerably according to the requirements of different players and according to the varying pitches of different countries and even cities. Quantz and Leopold Mozart both note that stringing is related to individual require- ments. According to the latter, thicker strings are more effective for flat pitch and large-model violins, while thin strings are better for sharp pitch and small models.[12] Leopold Mozart recommends a strong stringing to achieve his ideal of a strong, manly tone.

Eighteenth-century musicians were well aware of metal strings, and they must have used gut strings for the upper three strings of the violin because they preferred them (cf. p. 203 for the same situation in the seventeenth century). In the early eighteenth century Grassineau mentions wires of various metals used in connexion with musical instruments. He gives sizes ranging from one twentieth of an inch to one hundredth of an inch, and he says that the tonal strength of various metals is greatest with gold and successively less with silver, brass, and steel (iron).[13]

The 'tuner' for the steel E string, so common today, was not used earlier, since it was not necessary or suitable for use with the gut E string. The latter was not displaced by the steel E string until the early twentieth century.

The mute (*sordino*) was in fairly common use in the eighteenth century. Leopold Mozart says that mutes 'are made of wood, lead, tin, steel, or brass'; and he warns the player to avoid the open string when using the mute, since the latter makes the open string sound too shrill compared to the tone of the stopped string.[14] Quantz lists the same material for mutes, adding that steel is the best. Like Leopold Mozart, he cautions the violinist to avoid open strings; and he further advises not to play with maximum strength in muted slow movements.[15]

Leopold Mozart's comments on the violin in general are remarkably enlightened and enlightening. He wishes to standardize the violin, and in his book he pleads with mathematicians to help in the necessary research.[16] He speaks of the necessity of adjusting the violin properly to achieve the best tone. He notes the close relationship in this respect between strings, bridge, and sound post, stressing particularly the importance of adjusting the latter properly. The type of bridge and its position on the violin affect tone greatly, he says; and if the tone is too piercing or shrill, it can be muted

[12] Leopold Mozart, *Versuch*, Introduction, sec. 1, para. 7. See English translation, p. 16.

[13] James Grassineau, *A Musical Dictionary*, London, 1740, article 'wire'. This work is a translation, with additions, from the French dictionary of Sébastien de Brossard, 1703.

[14] Leopold Mozart, ch. 1, sec. 3, under *Con Sordini*. See English translation, p. 52.

[15] Quantz, ch. XVII, sec. 2, para. 29. For the use of the mute in the seventeenth century, see our Index.

[16] Leopold Mozart, Introduction, sec. 1, para. 6. See the English translation, p. 15.

by using 'a low, broad, and rather thick bridge which has been but very slightly cut away underneath'. If the tone is too weak, use a thin, not too broad bridge, and as high as possible, 'greatly carved away both underneath and in the centre'.[17]

Other members of the violin family. Terminology

While violin making was enjoying one of its greatest periods in the early eighteenth century, the making of violas had practically died out. The models were smaller than a century earlier, and they were in less demand because they were less used in the prevailing forms of chamber music, not being used at all in the 'solo' and trio sonata. In short, there were sufficient violas already in existence to satisfy existing demand. The cello underwent a reform by Stradivari, who standardized the model on a somewhat smaller pattern.

The terminology, tuning, and sometimes tonal strength of members of the violin family are still the cause of some confusion:

1. *violino piccolo*: a small violin. In the seventeenth century this instrument was tuned upward in fifths from c′, that is, a fourth higher than the usual violin. The same tuning is repeated in the early eighteenth century in Walther's *Musikalisches Lexikon* (1732). On the other hand, J. S. Bach, a contemporary of Walther's, used a tuning a minor third above the usual violin, tuning the *violino piccolo* to b flat in Cantata *Wachet Auf* (No. 140) and in the First 'Brandenburg' Concerto.

2. *violino scordato*: a violin with *scordatura* tuning.

3. the *viola*. If Quantz is a sound criterion (see ch. 19 on instrumentation), the tonal strength of the viola relative to the violin must have been greater than the corresponding situation today, since the number of violins recommended to balance the violas in the ensemble was four to one, greater than is usual now. However, the proportion may also have been dictated by the desire to have a brilliant and prominent top part and weak middle parts.

In the early eighteenth century there were as many as four distinct viola parts, all tuned to the same pitch (upward from c). Three viola parts all of the same pitch—'the parts of the middle'—were mentioned earlier by Mersenne (1636; see p. 117). After 1700 these three parts became four on occasions. The viola was equated with the *viola da brazzo* (*braz*). Brossard's *Dictionnaire* (1703) gives:

Braz. 1 = *Haute contre* = alto viola = viola I (C clef first line).

Braz. 2 = *Taille* = tenor viola = viola II (C clef second line).

Braz. 3 = *Quinte de violon* = viola III (C clef third line).

Viola IV (says Brossard) is not used in France, but in foreign works (C clef fourth line).

[17] Leopold Mozart, Introduction, sec. 1, para. 7. English translation, p. 16.

4. *violetta*: either a *dessus de viole* (treble viol) or a viola—either viola I or viola II (C clef third or fourth line). (For *violetti c.* 1770 as tenors, see p. 26 above.)

5. *violetta marina*: a viola with sympathetic strings used by Handel in his operas *Orlando* and *Sosarme*. The instrument was invented by Castrucci, the leader of his opera orchestra.[18]

6. *Fagott-Geige*: a viola, with the tuning and range of a cello, but played on the arm. It required stronger strings than the normal viola.[19]

7. *violoncello* (cello), *basse de violon*. The normal bass of the family, tuned to C or BB flat.

8. *violone*: the double bass of the family; more properly the double bass of the viol family. Brossard gives *basse de violon* or double bass. Walther (1732) gives the same definition, but his tuning is that of a six-stringed viol tuned upward from GG.

The bow

The early history of the violin bow needs to be rewritten. The specimens described and illustrated in available accounts are often singularly deceptive, being represented as shorter and clumsier than those shown in paintings or those still extant in museums and elsewhere. A classic example is a sequence of illustrations of bows purporting to show the orderly evolution of the bow from Mersenne (1636) through Corelli (1700) and Tartini (1740) to Viotti (*c.* 1780), published first in Fétis's *Antonio Stradivari* (Paris, 1856), and reproduced in various subsequent accounts including (lamentably) the article 'Bogen' in *Die Musik in Geschichte und Gegenwart* (1952). The bows represented in this sequence have little relation to reality, and their source is not documented (cf. Plate 35). What, for example, do we know specifically of the Corelli bow about 1700? Very little. We may imagine that it was similar to the Italian bow of the time—quite probably similar in appearance and length to the 'Stradivari' bow (Plate 28), resembling, no doubt, a shorter version of the bows used by Veracini and Geminiani (cf. Plates 30 and 36). The only known representation of Tartini's bow is that shown in the Calcinotto portrait (*c.* 1760?), which shows a straight stick of moderate length with a pike's head approaching the height and curvature of the hatchet head.[20] The nut is apparently tightened by a screw mechanism; at least, a typical screw cap of the time is clearly visible.

[18] See Burney, *General History*, reprint, Vol. II, p. 698, note.
[19] See J. F. B. C. Majer, *Museum Musicum*, 1732, p. 80. Earlier (1695), Merck's *Compendium* (ch. 8, p. C3 verso) includes a similar reference, speaking of the use of the viola as a bass: 'And if one uses three gut strings overspun with copper or Lyonnais wire, the instrument sounds like a bassoon (Fagott), [and] the tuning is then thus but only three stringed (e, A, D), and the [instrument] is also bowed like the Alto or Violette' (i.e. bowed on the arm).
[20] Reproduced in Erwin Jacobi's edition of Tartini's *Traité des Agrémens*; see p. 362, below.

Historians of the bow have shown a lamentable tendency to oversimplify and to select facts that fit prevalent theories. Henry Saint George is correct when he says with refreshing candour:

'To a casual reader like myself the mass of conflicting details found in examining ancient bows and the record of their use is extremely disconcerting. The practised scientist, however, surveys such things with calmness, for his trained eye immediately selects those details that support the theories he wishes to promulgate and the rest are quietly consigned to oblivion. In this way the most charmingly satisfactory results are obtained.'[21]

As Saint George says, the early bows varied greatly, the best among them being 'marvels of workmanship . . . exquisite works of art upon which no pains have been spared'. He also complains that in Fétis none of the illustrations of bows shown prior to Tourte have a concave arch (*cambre*), yet such bows actually appear before 1750. The history of the bow is a tangled skein, and we must be prepared to accept the variety and inconsistency of the actual facts, not merely those that fit preconceived theories.

The bow, the 'soul' of the instrument, is still completely unstandardized. There is a general distinction between the long bow used for the sonata and the short bow used for dance music. This distinction explains Raguenet's remark in his *Parallèle des Italiens et des Français* (1702) that the Italians use much longer bows than the French, the Italians being interested in the sonata and the French in the dance. However, this remark is not applicable to the new school of French composers and players of the sonata that emerges after 1720.

In the early eighteenth century the bow continues to evolve more rapidly than the violin itself. The bow stick tends to lengthen and to straighten; and a few bows already anticipate the concave arch of the modern bow stick, as we have just explained. Hawkins, commenting on Raguenet (just mentioned), says in 1776:

'The bow of the violin has been gradually increasing in length for the last seventy years; it is now about twenty-eight inches [over-all length]. In the year 1720, a bow of twenty-four inches was, on account of its length, called a Sonata bow; the common bow was shorter; and by the account given above [Raguenet's] the French bow must have been shorter still.[22]

21 Henry Saint George, *The Bow*, London, 1896, 2nd ed., 1909. The quotation is from the 1909 edition, p. 24.
22 Sir John Hawkins, *A General History of Music*; for the quotation, see the reprint of 1875, Vol. II, p. 782, note.

The bow shown in Veracini's Op. 2 of 1744 (cf. Plate 30) has approximately twenty-eight inches of playing hair (if the bow is properly scaled to the violin), appreciably longer than the standard modern bow. The bow held by the violinist in the French edition (1752) of Geminiani's *The Art of Playing on the Violin*, has playing hair that measures between twenty-five and twenty-six inches, about the same as the modern bow (Plate 36). Both of these bows have straight bow sticks, and are elegant in appearance. The 'Stradivari' bow (described in ch. 9, see p. 207) is about twenty-eight inches over-all length, having about twenty-four of playing hair. The French bow is also straight, but it is somewhat shorter (as Hawkins says) than the Italian bow (cf. Plate 31). About 1750 or a little afterwards Tourte, the father, produced some bows longer than the standardized model of his famous son, François.

About the same time, although the prevailing bow stick is straight, some bows are slightly concave, and the pike's head, characteristic of the bow about 1700, is gradually changing to the modern head of the later eighteenth century. Saint George (cf. note 21) points out that some bows with pike's head already have a slight concave arch to the bow stick. This tendency in bow making, if it was a tendency before 1750, must have given an impetus to the creation of the modern type of head in order to separate the hair farther from the stick at the point. Obviously the old pike's head was incompatible with a greater concave arch to the bow, since the pike's head did not permit much separation of the hair and the bow stick at the point and since the concave arch tended to lessen this separation still further. Whether the modern head or the concave bow stick came first, we cannot say. They were two aspects of the same thing, like the chicken and the egg; and, organically speaking, the presence of one eventually implied the presence of the other.

The common German bow, alone among violin bows of this time, had an outward curve, sometimes pronounced, but not sufficient to sustain three-part chords and especially those in four parts, as is often claimed. Good examples of the German bows of the eighteenth century are those shown in Weigel (our Plate 37) and later, in Leopold Mozart (cf. Plate 39b: the bows in the latter are clumsily drawn, however) and in Löhlein (1774). The bows shown in the frontispiece to Walther's *Musikalisches Lexikon* are crude by any standard. No bow that belonged to J. S. Bach is known to exist. In the inventory of his property made at his death, no bow is mentioned, although several violins, including one by Stainer (see p. 195), are explicitly listed and appraised as to their value.

In addition to length and curvature, one should remark on the weight of the bow, balance, and methods of tightening the hair. Contrary to a current opinion, the extant bows of the early eighteenth century are lighter, not heavier, than the modern bow. To judge by the numerous examples of fluted bows of this period, the ideal was lightness combined with strength. The most typical wood was snakewood, but Pernambuco wood (a superior variety brazil-wood), invariably employed in any good modern bow, was known and used in a few of the best 'old' bows, including the 'Stradivari' bow (cf. p. 207). Because of the light head, the balance of these old bows was generally at a point nearer the frog (nut) than in the modern bow. Consequently, the upper part of the old bow had less weight and less momentum, and the strokes in the upper half are more naturally and clearly articulated (see p. 207). The screw to regulate the tension of the hair became common well before 1750, having already been used in some bows at the end of the seventeenth century (see p. 209). Sometimes the nuts of these bows are extraordinarily ornamented, as in the 'Stradivari' bow (cf. Plate 28b).

By the middle of the eighteenth century the future direction of bow making could be predicted in its general outlines, and these changes were related to musical changes, as suggested above (p. 312). François Tourte played the role of many a genius before and after him: he compounded all the experiments of his immediate predecessors into a bow of perfect design and perfect workmanship that proved to be the ideal and standard for all future bow makers; and his example turned out to be even more decisive than the 'Betts' model Stradivari violin that did so much to establish the classical model of the violin.

Among those who had a hand in the development of the bow between 1750 and 1780 (cf. Plate 38) were François Tourte's father (*Tourte père*), his brother (*Tourte l'aîné*), the violinist Wilhelm Cramer (1745–99), and John Dodd (1752–1839), the great English bow maker, contemporary with François Tourte, who is thought to have arrived at a similar solution independently of Tourte about the same time (cf. Saint George as in note 21). The great violinist Viotti is also said to have collaborated with François Tourte in producing the modern bow; and this is one of those unproved bits of standard hearsay that is worth repeating only because makers have always been influenced by outstanding players.

What did Tourte actually do? Apart from the perfection of his craftsmanship, which cannot be explained, he standardized the total length of the violin bow at approximately twenty-nine and a half inches (twenty-five and a half of playing hair)—the viola and cello bows being a bit shorter. The concave curve (*cambre*) of the bow stick became the basic design in combination with a modern head of great beauty and delicacy (Plate 28). Tourte achieved the *cambre*, not by cutting to this curve (as others did), but by a laborious process of heating the straight bow stick and bending to the desired *cambre*. Tourte also fixed on Pernambuco wood as the ideal material for combined strength and elasticity, and the bow tapered gradually toward the point in a way that pleased the eye, the player, and even the mathematician.[23] The new design of the modern bow head, being higher, more massive, and (consequently) heavier than the earlier pike's head model, disturbed the balance of the bow. To restore it, Tourte loaded the nut with metal inlays (cf. Plate 28b). Even so, the balance point of the Tourte bow is farther up toward the point (nineteen to twenty centimetres from the frog) than that of the typical 'old' bow with its light head. Tourte also widened the ribbon of hair, and to make it lie perfectly and uniformly flat while playing, he fixed the hair at the frog with a ferrule. He was also probably the one first to affix a plate of mother of pearl extending from the ferrule along the base of the frog, thus concealing the hair fastening. Finally, a number of his bows have special materials of extraordinary beauty. The nuts themselves were sometimes made of ivory or tortoise-shell; and sometimes the plate at the tip of the bow, the screw cap, and the metal windings under the player's fingers were made of silver or gold. Tourte's bows, works of art in themselves, were so perfectly adapted to the music of his and subsequent times that the Tourte bow is a synonym for the modern bow, and has been for nearly two hundred years. His bows were universally imitated as the perfect model. They have never been surpassed.

Before 1750 bow makers remained anonymous, and bow making was not the speciality it became after the middle of the century.[24] John Dodd was among the first to sign his bows; but, true to the old tradition, Tourte never did, although he was recognized as the Stradivari of the bow in his own lifetime. A number of violin makers before 1750 must also have made bows, although we cannot often identify them. However, Peter Guarneri of Mantua and Stradivari were certainly among them. At the death of the former in 1720 an inventory of his property mentions 'sixteen violin (*da violino*) bows of snakewood (*di serpentino*), some finished, some partly finished'.[25] According to the Hills, a bow was found with the Stradivari violins belonging to the Spanish King.[26] This bow may or may not have been made by Stradivari. However, in the remnants that came from Stradivari's workshop there were drawings for making bows, including designs for nuts and heads, all appropriate to the usual type of bow of this period. Moreover, there exists an interesting letter written by Paolo Stradivari, the maker's

---

[23] Vuillaume showed that when the bow was unstrung this taper could be expressed mathematically in terms of a 'logarithmic curve of which the ordinates increase in arithmetical progression, while the abscissas increase in geometrical progression'. See F. J. Fétis, *Notice of Anthony Stradivari*, translated by John Bishop, London, 1864, p. 124.

[24] A *viola da gamba* bow by Peter Walmsley (working about 1720–44) is a rare exception, being stamped WAMSLEY on its ivory frog. This bow is in the Ashmolean Museum, Oxford.

[25] See Hill, *Guarneri Family*, p.42.   [26] See Hill, *Stradivari*, p. 208.

son, to M. A. Briatta, the agent of Count Cozio de Salabue, the famous collector of Stradivari instruments. In this letter, dated Cremona, June 4, 1775, Paolo speaks of two bows of snakewood 'which I have'. Since Stradivari's son was talking about selling other things of his father's in the context of this letter, it is a fair assumption that these two bows were made by Antonio Stradivari.[27] If the bow attributed to Stradivari and now in the Ansley Salz Collection of the University of California (Plate 28) is any criterion, Stradivari took the same pains with his bows as with his violins and their fittings. The Hills remark of Stradivari:

'Painstaking, thorough and careful to the smallest detail, we see him specially designing everything—even to bridge, pegs and tailpiece— for a given instrument, and then further embellishing these fittings with painted or inlaid designs. . . . Nothing apparently was too unimportant for his attention.'[28]

Even without positive evidence that Stradivari made bows, it is a reasonable inference that a man 'careful to the smallest detail' would insist himself on creating the bow, the principal means through which his violins were able to sound to best advantage and attain their greatest technical potential.

Summary

The eighteenth century was a most important period in the history of the violin and bow. Stradivari established the classical flat model of the violin in the opening years of the century, and this model, together with that of other great makers like Joseph del Gesù Guarneri gradually superseded the arched model of the Amatis and Stainer. In the fittings of the violin the bridge approaches the form of the modern design, the fingerboard lengthens to accommodate the higher positions in playing, and the lowest (G) string is wound with silver to increase the resonance and response of this string. The use of the mute is extended from ensemble to solo playing.

The bow enjoyed a still greater development. In the first part of the century it remained unstandardized as to length and design. Nevertheless, it tended to lengthen and straighten, and in some cases a few bows assumed a concave shape before 1750. Although the bow of a village fiddler might well have been a clumsy object, many of these 'old' bows were extremely elegant, and the flutings of the stick gave the bow distinction and lightness without decreasing its strength. The pike's head of these bows began to evolve into the modern head of the Tourte bow, and the screw mechanism, used today

---

[27] For this correspondence, see (among others), E. N. Doring, *The Guadagnini Family*, pp. 203–4.
[28] Hill, *Stradivari*, p. 207.

H.V.P.–Z

to tighten the hair, became common. Indeed, by 1750 the direction of the modern bow, which in its main essentials was perfected about 1780, was already forecast in certain bows of Tourte, the father, and his contemporaries.

If bow makers before 1750, who doubtless included Stradivari, remained anonymous, it was not from a sense of false modesty, but simply because they considered the bow an indispensable part of the violin, just as much as the pegs, fingerboard, or tailpiece; and the bow was made to fit the instrument in the same manner. There is no reason to think that bows were executed with less care than the instrument itself. The notion that Stradivari would have tolerated a clumsy bow is as preposterous as the idea that he would have tolerated a clumsy violin.

Such were the violins and bows of the early eighteenth century. Through the medium of these remarkable creations was heard for the first time the equally remarkable music, about to be described, of an era that called both into being.

CHAPTER FIFTEEN

⟨∿∿⟩

The Violin Music of the
Early Eighteenth Century

IN the eighteenth century the ever-increasing popularity of the violin and its music was not without opposition from lovers of the viols and vocal music, who were generally champions of the good old times and who saw their favourites encroached upon by the upstart violin. Hubert Le Blanc (1740) lamented the 'enterprises of the violin and the pretensions of the cello'; and as late as 1760 Hawkins voiced his opposition to the violin and his predilection for vocal music, particularly of earlier times:

> 'Music was in its greatest perfection in Europe from about the middle of the sixteenth to the beginning of the seventeenth century, when, with a variety of treble instrument [the violin], a vicious taste was introduced, and vocal harmony received its mortal wound.'[1]

If vocal music received its mortal wound at the hands of the violin in the seventeenth century, it suffered a true *coup de grâce* in the eighteenth. The normal technical progress, expected of any instrument in the course of time, was vastly accelerated in the eighteenth century by the advent of the violin concerto, which offered extraordinary attractions to composer and player alike, and received corresponding attention from them.

In the same way that the history of the sonata is bound up with the violin in the seventeenth century, the early history of the instrumental concerto is linked to the history of violin playing in the eighteenth; and, if only for this reason, the origin and progress of the concerto must be described briefly.[2]

---

[1] For Hubert Le Blanc, see his *Défénse de la basse de la viole contre les entréprises du violon et les prétentions du violoncel*, Amsterdam, 1740. For Hawkins, see Robert Stevenson's review of Percy A. Scholes, *The Life and Activities of Sir John Hawkins*, Oxford, 1953, in *The Journal of the American Musicological Society*, Spring 1954, p. 83.

[2] On the other hand, it hardly seems necessary to point out again that the violin was used extensively in the eighteenth-century opera, in church music, and in the other forms of vocal music. The following description of 'violin' music will be limited to music primarily for the violin. For information on the orchestra used in operas, motets, and concertos, see E. Borrel, *L'Interpretation*, pp. 40ff.

The early concerto was developed by and for violinists accompanied by a string orchestra. There are few instrumental concertos before the end of the seventeenth century, one being a piece by J. H. Schmeltzer for solo violin, accompanied by string orchestra in fairly advanced style, written as early as 1664.[3] The first true instrumental concertos date from the last years of the seventeenth century in the works of Corelli, Torelli, and Albinoni. These beginnings were continued and amplified in the eighteenth century by Vivaldi, the most important composer of concertos in the early eighteenth century, and, among others, by Locatelli, Bach, Leclair, and Tartini.

The essential principles embodied in the violin concerto had been used in vocal music for some time. In its original meaning, the term *concerto* (also: *concertare, concertato*) meant simply an ensemble of instruments and/or voices. About 1600 *concerto* came to have the additional meaning of opposition or contrast, in the sense of one choir opposed to another, or, more particularly, of a soloist or soloists striving against an ensemble of voices and/or instruments (cf. p. 132, note 9). In this new sense of opposition or contrast, the concerto appeared frequently in ensemble music for voices and instruments in the early seventeenth century—for instance, in Monteverdi's music—but not until the end of the century was the new concerto principle applied to the purely instrumental ensemble. The first of these ensembles was the *concerto grosso*. In this species of concerto a group of soloists, called the *concertino* and generally composed of two solo violins and solo cello, was opposed to the 'orchestra', also called the *ripieno*, which consisted of a string orchestra in the four parts of violin I and II, viola, and bass. In its forms, textures, and order of movements, the *concerto grosso* betrayed its origins from the trio sonata. In effect, the latter formed the *concertino*, which was amplified orchestrally by the addition of the *ripieno*. The contrast principle of the concerto consisted in opposing the soloists to the mass of the orchestra. The order and number of movements was also that of the trio sonata: four or more, usually in the order of slow, fast (often fugal), slow, fast. Corelli's *concerti grossi* (Op. 6) were among the first examples of this type, later examples being those by Vivaldi, Bach, and Handel, among others.

Formally speaking, it was a relatively short step from Corelli's trios to his *concerti grossi*. But the step of introducing soloists into a mass of players was a much longer one, and it had much greater consequences with respect to tone, technique, and the instruments and bows themselves. In short, the true innovation of the first instrumental concertos, which were *concerti grossi*, was not in the formal structure of the music but rather in the new

[3] An excerpt is printed in G. Beckmann, *Das Violinspiel*, Anhang, No. 18. For further material on the concerto, see Arnold Schering, *Geschichte des Instrumentalkonzerts*, Leipzig, 1905; Abraham Veinus, *The Concerto*, London, 1948; and Arthur Hutchins, *The Baroque Concerto*, London, 1961.

relationship of the soloists to the other players. In the case of the solo concerto, about to be discussed, the contrasts in this relationship were intensified, and a new form was produced.

Shortly after the advent of the *concerto grosso*, the solo concerto appeared, first in the works of Albinoni and Torelli, and later, in far more varied and developed forms, in Vivaldi (see p. 342 below). The solo concerto embodied a more thorough-going application of the contrast principle, since the playing of a single virtuoso and the individual *timbre* of one instrument in the solo concerto afforded an opportunity for a more striking contrast to the orchestral mass of sound and tone colour than obtained in the *concerto grosso*. There were several natural results stemming from the appearance of the solo concerto. For one thing, the single virtuoso needed a violin of distinctive tone and greater power to compete on equal terms with the orchestra—even with the relatively small string orchestra of the time—and to produce the greatest possible contrast to the massed and more homogeneous tone of the orchestra. These needs and developments explain Stradivari's experiments with the 'long' model violin to achieve distinctive tone and especially increased power (cf. p. 198). Similarly, the bow was developed to produce more subtle and varied effects (cf. pp. 325ff.).

The solo concerto also furnished an incentive to the composer and the virtuoso violinist to develop a new and more advanced idiom of the violin and the technique to realize it. In this respect the solo concerto and the solo sonata, featuring the single virtuoso, were more important in the development of violin playing and virtuosity in the early eighteenth century than the *concerto grosso* with its several soloists. Finally, the contrast principle was still further emphasized in the solo concerto by assigning to the soloist thematic material or virtuoso figuration often quite different from that of the orchestra. From a technical point of view, this differentiation permits the soloists to display a technique far superior to that of the orchestral player. In the *concerto grosso* the contrast between soloists and orchestra is not nearly as pronounced, with respect to thematic materials or the technical capabilities of the players, as it is in the solo concerto.

The sharp juxtaposition of the soloist and the orchestra created a new and distinctive form, known today as the *ritornello* form, especially characteristic of the first (fast) movement. In the *concerto grosso* the contrast is achieved mainly by the opposition of unequal masses of tone and the juxtaposition of loud and soft, the formal principle being that derived from the trio sonata. In the solo concerto the manner of producing contrast extends also to the thematic materials, thereby producing a new structure, the *ritornello* form, in which the orchestra and soloists are conspicuously opposed. Typically, the orchestra begins alone with an opening statement called the *ritornello*, followed by the soloist prominently featured and lightly accompanied by the orchestra. The term *ritornello* refers to a 'little return' or recurring section. Considered as a whole, the *ritornello* form is essentially a scheme of recurring *tutti* (i.e. orchestral) statements, alternating and contrasting with the following statements of the soloists. Thematically, the solo entries may repeat, or be related to, the *tutti* statements; or they may be entirely new, by way of complete 'opposition'. The thematic material of the recurring *ritornelli* is generally the same or related to the opening *ritornello*, although the recurring statements are often fragmentary statements of the opening. A typical *ritornello* form as developed by Vivaldi is shown by the following letter scheme (R = *ritornello* or orchestral *tutti*; S = solo statement), summarized as 5R—4S:

$$R^1—S^1—R^2—S^2—R^3—S^3—R^4—S^4—R^5$$

The first *ritornello* and the first solo are in the tonic key of the piece, the next statements modulate to closely related keys such as the dominant or relative major, and the final statement(s) return to the tonic.

A distinctive feature of the solo concerto is the cadenza, in which the soloist indulges in a flight of fancy or caprice (hence such optional terms as *fantasia* and *capriccio*), usually improvised. The beginning of the cadenza is indicated by the fermata (⌒), at which point the orchestra generally falls silent, awaiting in a mixture of admiration, awe, and boredom the soloist's display of technical virtuosity, one of the normal ingredients of the cadenza. In the early eighteenth century the cadenza was generally a more or less elaborate amplification of the cadence as the name implies, and consisted as a rule of arpeggios, virtuoso figuration, special effects, such as the *bariolage*, and so on (cf. Ex. 235 and Ex. 236). Musically there are few attempts to relate the material of the cadenza to the thematic substance already heard in the body of the movement. The idea of the cadenza being musically integrated to what has preceded is not prevalent in the theoretical literature until the middle of the eighteenth century, Quantz being among the first to note that cadenzas should be constructed of the main ideas of the piece.[4] The cadenza may occur at any cadence point in any of the movements. The favoured position, however, is the end of the first movement as it is in the later 'Classic' concerto of composers like Mozart. Sometimes, even in the early eighteenth century, the cadenza is written out by the composer—Bach and Vivaldi are examples (cf. Ex. 235)—who, in any case, often wrote the concertos for their own use as performers; sometimes the cadenza is lightly accompanied, if only by a pedal tone in the basses of the orchestra.[5]

The term *caprice* (*capriccio*) may be used interchangeably with cadenza, as

---

[4] Quantz, *Versuch*, ch. XV, para. 8.

[5] For a similar 'cadenza' in a sonata of Corelli, see Ex. 63. For further material on the cadenza, see the books cited in note 3 above. Quantz devotes an entire chapter (XV) to the cadenza. For a special study, see H. Knödt, 'Zur Entwicklungsgeschichte der

it often is in Tartini; or it may mean a semi-independent form (Locatelli), or even a separate form in the sense of the old *capriccio*.[6]

The solo concerto invariably has three movements: fast, slow, fast, in the manner of the Italian operatic overture. The textures are primarily harmonic in contrast to the frequent polyphony found in the *concerto grosso*. The middle (slow) movement generally has the character of an aria or an interlude between the first and last movements.

There is still a third type of concerto, sometimes called 'orchestral' concerto. This species harks back to the old and original principle of the concerto as an ensemble *without* soloists. It is a pure ensemble concerto, and, as a rule, it has the number and order of movements characteristic of the sonata. The second movement, for instance, is often a fugal allegro.[7]

The concerto is better regarded in terms of its essential principles than as a stereotyped formal mould. The immense number of concerto types in Vivaldi is perfectly comprehensible in terms of the two main concerto-principles of (1) ensemble on the one hand, and (2) opposition of soloist(s) and orchestra on the other. In no other way can the bewildering variety and mixtures of formal procedures and order of movements be understood. The chief formal expression of these two principles is relatively clear: the *concerto grosso*, the solo concerto, and the ensemble (orchestral) concerto. However, there are many intermediate types which mix distinctive features of these three principal types. Vivaldi, for example, writes the first part of a Concerto in G minor (Pincherle Catalogue No. 407; see p. 342, note 18) as an ensemble concerto without soloists, beginning with a slow movement and following it with a fugal allegro. Then he continues with two additional movements featuring a soloist in the style of the solo concerto. This example is only one of a number of possibilities of mixed types, including concertos for two, three, or four violin soloists, treated in the style of the solo concerto, not in that of the *concerto grosso*.

While the essays in the instrumental concerto in the first years of the eighteenth century were predominantly for violin *soli* accompanied by string orchestra, this situation changed in the succeeding decades when more and more concertos were written for instruments other than the violin, and when the orchestra was composed of strings and wind, not solely of the

---

Kadenzen in Instrumentalkonzert' in *Sammelbände der Internationalen Musikgesellschaft*, XV (1913–14), pp. 375–419. See also 'A. Schering, 'Die freie Kadenz in Instrumental-konzert des 18. Jahrhunderts' in *Kongress der Internationalen Musikgesellschaft*, Basel, 1906.

[6] See, among others, the twelve *caprices* included in Guillemain's Op. 18 (1762). For the Locatelli *caprices* and further distinctions of terminology, see ch. 20.

[7] The eighteenth-century form called *sinfonia* is sometimes a solo concerto and some-times the ensemble (orchestral) concerto just described. Therefore, the term *sinfonia-concerto*, proposed by Schering (as per note 3, above) to describe the ensemble (orchestral) concerto, is imprecise and confusing.

former. About half of Vivaldi's concertos, numbering over four hundred, are for violin soloist(s), the rest involving other stringed or wind instruments. The Bach 'Brandenburg' concertos are examples of the use of the concerto principles with mixtures of the three principal formal types of concerto. These particular pieces use a variety of wind, stringed, and keyboard instruments both in the orchestra and as soloists.

The concerto has been described at length because it was intimately connected with the development of violin playing and with new idioms characteristic of violin style in the early eighteenth century. Besides, the concerto was a new form, using principles applied for the first time to purely instrumental music. The old forms, already described in the previous chapters, continued, but with changes occasioned by new needs. The trio and 'solo' sonata accompanied by keyboard (see p. 213) proceeded along paths laid out in the seventeenth century. At the same time, there were new developments. The sonata tended to mix the elements of its 'church' and 'chamber' varieties, and there was at least one new type, the sonata with violin solo and written-out part for harpsichord. Bach's six sonatas for violin and harpsichord are examples of this species. They are essentially trio sonatas in which the first violin part of the old trio sonata is assigned to the violin solo and the second violin part of the trio sonata is given to the right hand of the harpsichordist. The accompaniment is then played by the left hand, the right hand also participating at need. In France, Mondonville's *Pièces de Clavecin En Sonates, Avec Accompagnement de Violon* (Op. 3, c. 1734) are primarily harpsichord sonatas with an *obbligato* violin part, anticipating the sonatas of this kind in the later eighteenth century. One of these Mondonville sonatas is actually a concerto in form.

The highly specialized and relatively rare sonata *senza basso*, the true 'solo' sonata without accompanying keyboard, is developed to a high point in the early eighteenth century, notably in the six unaccompanied sonatas (properly three sonatas and three partitas) of J. S. Bach.[8] This species, found more often in Germany, also appears for the first time in Sweden and France, respectively in J. H. Roman's six *Assaggi* (1730-40) and Louis-Gabriel Guillemain's *Amusements pour le Violon seul* (Op. 18, 1762).[9]

The variation continued to be a favourite form, and it was often treated as an art of bowing, as it had been in Corelli's *La Follia* (see p. 222). Classic examples of the variation are Bach's *Chaconne* from the D minor unaccom-

---

[8] The partitas are basically suites of dances. In the Bach autograph the word is spelled 'Partia', presumably an old spelling of partita.

[9] There is a modern edition of the Roman pieces: *Assaggi à Violino Solo* edited by Ingmar Bengtsson and Lars Frydén in *Monumenta Musicae Svecicae* I, Stockholm, 1958. Other examples of the unaccompanied violin sonata are those by Lonati (facsimile of the opening in Pincherle's *Les Violinistes*, p. 41); Geminiani (in B flat; editions by Studeny and Betti), and Pisendel (*Hortus Musicus*, No. 91), the pupil of Vivaldi.

panied Partita and especially the fifty (originally thirty-eight) variations of
Tartini bearing the significant title *L'Arte del arco*, on a theme drawn from
Corelli. An example of the *air varié*, a favourite form of the eighteenth-
century French school, may be found in L'Abbé le fils's collection, *Jolis airs
ajustés et variés pour un violon seul* (Op. 7, 1763).

The programme element entered violin music in the seventeenth century
(see p. 225), and the same element persisted in the purely instrumental
forms of the early eighteenth century. In certain Vivaldi concertos musical
description is so fundamental to the mood and intent of the music that
Vivaldi practically established the 'programme' concerto as a special type.
The first four concertos of his Op. 8, entitled *Il Cimento dell' Armonia e dell'
Inventione* (The Contest of Harmony and Invention), are descriptive of the
four seasons, each concerto being prefaced by a poem describing successively
spring, summer, autumn, and winter. These texts afford Vivaldi many
opportunities for musical illustrations, and at the appropriate place in the
score he prints the phrase of text which the music illustrates. In the 'Spring'
Concerto (Op. 8, No. 1), the music portrays with naïve reality such phrases
as 'the barking dog', 'the storm', and 'the drunkard'.

Vivaldi also uses terms that suggest descriptive effects related to other
instruments. Three concertos are written 'per violino in Tromba', and
Vivaldi uses brilliant sonorities and chains of thirds, obviously in the style of
the trumpet. A more esoteric direction, 'Violini in Tromba Marina', refers to
effects associated with the *tromba marina*, such as natural harmonics or
perhaps a characteristic buzzing.[10]

In France, a favourite form that permits descriptive effects is the *chasse*
(hunt). Sometimes the programme concerto is more concerned with the
'expression of feeling than of painting'—to use a famous phrase of Beethoven.
A case in point is Locatelli's *Il pianto d'Arianna* (Ariadne's Lament), the last
of *VI Concerti a quattro* (Op. 8, 1741).

Programme music and descriptive effects are part of an eighteenth-
century aesthetic doctrine which glorified nature and which would have
music mean or portray something (cf. p. 490, ch. 21). Geminiani complained
about the obvious and naïve forms of descriptive music in these words:

'As the imitating the Cock, Cuckoo, Owl, and other Birds; or the
Drum, French Horn, Tromba-Marina, and the like . . . rather belong
to the Professors of Legerdemain and Posture-masters than to the Art
of Musick, the Lovers of that Art are not to expect anything of that
Sort in this Book.'[11]

[10] See Pincherle, *Vivaldi*, pp. 94 and 126.
[11] In the Preface to his *The Art of Playing on the Violin* (1751). This preface was omitted
in the French translation (Paris, 1752?)—a significant omission in view of the fact
that France was a stronghold of musical description at that time.

The more subtle forms of description are intellectualized into a doctrine or system of 'Affects'. These *affetti*, roughly moods or emotional states, are portrayed by set rhythms, melodic formulas, and sometimes by particular keys[12] appropriate to the emotional state concerned; and these rhythms and melodic formulas often persist through whole sections in conformity with the prevailing 'affection'. Music, being related to moods and sometimes to words, is often compared to rhetoric or oratory.[13] Geminiani says that Example XIII of his violin treatise should be 'executed in such a Manner as to resemble an affecting Discourse'; and concerning 'Piano and Forte' he is more explicit: 'As all good Musick should be composed in Imitation of a Discourse, these two ornaments are designed to produce the same Effect that an Orator does by raising and falling his voice.'

The development of the violin idiom

Like Baroque music as a whole, violin music of the early eighteenth century represents the expansion of an idiom developed in the seventeenth century. By 1700 a virtuoso technical level had been achieved in Germany and, to a lesser extent, in Italy. In the course of the eighteenth century this advanced idiom spread to other countries, and was developed still further by the violin virtuosi of the time, particularly by the Italians through the concerto. Between 1700 and 1750 the range demanded of the violin became larger, the usual limits for good players being from the open G string through the note a''' (seventh position on the E string); and this is the range found in the treatises of Leopold Mozart and Geminiani in mid-eighteenth century. The increased use of the lowest string is probably related to the introduction of a wound G string for the violin (see p. 321). The high positions were used occasionally on the lower three strings for figurations across the strings, arpeggios, and double stops; but on these lower three strings the fourth position was a more usual limit. In exceptional cases the seventh position was exceeded on the highest string. Locatelli's *caprices* in the concertos of his *L'Arte del violino* (see p. 466) contain notable examples, the fourteenth position being required in the *caprices* of Concerto XI. Indeed, in the flights of fancy of these *caprices*, Locatelli reaches a point of virtuosity unsurpassed until Paganini's time, nearly a century later. While Locatelli's *caprices* covered the whole range of the violin, still other Italian virtuosi were famous, or notorious, for music that specialized in the upper strings and neglected the lower. Quantz complained that 'much of the time' the Italians 'rob the instrument of its gravity and charm, which the thick [lower] strings are capable of effecting'.[14] This complaint, however,

---

[12] Cf. Quantz, ch. XIV, para. 6.   [13] See Quantz, ch. XI, para. 1.
[14] Quantz, ch. XVIII, para. 61. Apparently, the Italians were not the only ones. North speaks of players using 'the hypersuperior octave which they call high notes, and

cannot be directed at Vivaldi (or, as we have just mentioned, Locatelli), who uses all the strings with admirable impartiality and effectiveness.

The violin music of the time shows that the art of fingering and shifting had advanced. A particular feature involved extensions and contractions of the hand (cf. Ex. 144 and p. 381). Fingerings of this type may be deduced from certain passages in the music and from a few specific fingerings furnished by composers themselves. In the seventeenth century such extensions had been used in a relatively modest way, requiring an additional tone or semitone. By 1750 some composers were demanding the stretch of a third, fourth, or even a fifth beyond the normal limits of the hand—that is, the interval of a tenth, eleventh, or twelfth on two adjacent strings (Ex. 146 and Ex. 147). Hardly more is required by Paganini in his *caprices*. These extensions are utilized to enlarge the sonorous possibilities of the violin and also the repertory of double stops, especially tenths (Ex. 145). Indeed, the whole vocabulary of multiple stops had enlarged and increased; and double, triple, and quadruple stops are used in ingenious and bewildering variety, as a glance at the Bach solo sonatas will reveal. While these works of Bach represent a continuity of the German tradition of multiple stops, there are numerous stops of like character to be found in Italian music as well as in the French school that imitated it. Besides, there are certain novelties in fingering. One of the most interesting is Geminiani's fingering of the chromatic scale in which each semitone is fingered without sliding (fingered chromatics)—generally considered a modern invention (Ex. 131c). Mondonville uses the natural harmonics complete in his *Les sons harmoniques* (*c.* 1738; cf. Ex. 152), and less than twenty-five years later (1761) L'Abbé le fils gives all the natural and *artificial* harmonics, including a minuet to be played entirely in a combination of both (Ex. 154; cf. our recording). It is also in the early eighteenth century that the mute begins to appear in solo pieces (Vivaldi), having already been used in the ensemble music of the seventeenth century (see p. 278).

Guillemain

Ex. 127

Violin figurations in the music show a greater use of the lowest string (including the open G), octave and other large leaps, and even the three-octave leap (Ex. 127). Ex. 128 shows broken octaves in Locatelli's Concerto XI, proceeding upward to the eleventh position; Ex. 129 shows figuration in tenths also from Locatelli. Tartini's thirty-fifth variation in his *L'Arte del*

---

with which is commonly joyned the arpeggio'. He says also that the 'use of double notes is too much affected' (*North on Music* [*c.* 1726], pp. 234–5). North is also against too many swift divisions (p. 235) so enjoyed by the players.

arco is devoted to a systematic study in octave leaps. A special type of figuration, also seen occasionally in the seventeenth century (cf. Ex. 72, last measure), is a pedal-tone figuration in which one tone is constantly reiterated as a pedal, and the figuration swirls about above or below it (Ex. 129). The pedal is often an open string, including the open G string. (For the sound of Ex. 129, cf. our recording.)

Ex. 128

Ex. 129

The scores of the early eighteenth century are marked much more explicitly than those of their predecessors. Slurs and the various signs for articulation, such as staccato dots and strokes, are far more frequent; and, as a consequence, one can be certain that the varied and complex bowings which result, including mixed and syncopated bowings, are clearly intended by the composer. (For extended discussion of bowings, see ch. 18.) Previously—and this is still true to a moderate extent in the eighteenth century—bowings were inserted by the player according to current conventions, which today belong to the category of lost traditions and which make the interpretations of much older music so enigmatic.

In matters of expression the scores are also more specific in the early eighteenth century. Vibrato is occasionally indicated by a sign, as it had been at times in the seventeenth century (see p. 287). Signs for different degrees of loud and soft had been known in the seventeenth century, but not those for *crescendo* and *diminuendo*. Shortly after 1700 *crescendo* is indicated by ◀━ and *diminuendo* by ━▶; and these filled-in versions of modern nuance signs occur first in sonatas published in Paris (1712) by Piani, a Venetian violinist and composer. Later Veracini and Geminiani used the same signs in their music (see p. 486). However, the application of nuances is often understood rather than written out. The *messa di voce*, for instance, is traditionally applied to long notes without specific indications.

Many of the ornaments, even compound and complex versions, are also indicated by signs, including those which stand for the trill with special prefixes and/or terminal notes (see p. 450). The appoggiatura is expressed with 'little notes', and sometimes has special rhythmic and dynamic connotations for the player (see p. 455). The trill becomes increasingly elaborate, being played at a variety of speeds to suit musical context. For the virtuoso, the repertory of trills includes the double trills in thirds and even sixths, consecutive trills (frowned on in the seventeenth century), trills reached by sudden leaps, and trills on syncopated beats or parts of beats. Even the esoteric octave-trill occurs in the French school (see p. 453). All this, naturally, belongs rather to the *avant-garde* violinist, not to the average player or to amateur tradition. Ornaments in general are inserted, and improvisations added, in the manner already explained (ch. 13). Particularly interesting examples in the eighteenth century are the Dubourg ornamentation to certain of the sonatas of Corelli (see p. 222), Geminiani's own ornamental additions of 1739 to his Op. 1 (originally published in 1716; cf. Ex. 234), and the ornamental formulas emanating from Tartini's 'School of Nations' at Padua (cf. Ex. 233). The ornaments characteristic of Tartini and his school are incorporated in his *Traité des Agrémens* (see p. 361) and in his *L'Arte del arco*.

Last but not least, the violin continued to sing in broad cantabile, especially in the slow movements which often resembled operatic arias, and Vivaldi even introduces the cantabile into fast movements (see p. 343). The violin's power of rivalling the human voice is one of its greatest assets, a fact which must not be taken for granted or lost sight of in the excitement of virtuoso figurations, bowings, and special effects. Evidently, a notion of this kind moved Galliard to exclaim, 'a little less *Fiddling* with the *Voice*, and a little more *Singing* with the *Instrument*, would be of great Service to Both'.[15]

Contributions of individual countries to violin music

Before 1750 Italy dominated the world of music, and her principal export to foreign countries was musicians, especially opera singers and violinists. However, by the middle of the century France began to emerge as a formidable rival to Italy in the opera, in violin music, and the manner of performing it. An important factor in violin music was that a number of distinguished composers were also practising violinists and sometimes virtuosi.

Italy

About 1700 the leading Italian composer-violinist was Corelli, and his music summarized the violin idiom of the seventeenth century. Even his *concerti grossi* (Op. 6), published for the first time in 1714 a year after his death, were probably composed in large part in the seventeenth century, some at least by 1682. The musical impact of Corelli was strong in the eighteenth century by virtue of the numerous editions of his music and

[15] J. E. Galliard in the introduction (p. xii) to his translation of Tosi's *Observations* (1743).

through the office of his pupils, who amplified his rather modest technical demands and who influenced violin playing throughout Europe. Among them were Geminiani, Locatelli, the French violinist Jean-Baptiste Anet, and G. B. Somis (1686-1763), famous for his incomparable fullness of bowing. Somis, through his school at Turin, influenced Giardini, Pugnani, and the new sonata school of French players and composers, including Guignon, Chabran, and especially Leclair.

Corelli composed no solo concertos. The earliest examples in this genre were by Tomaso Albinoni (1671-1750) in Venice and Giuseppe Torelli (1658-1709) in Bologna.[16] Albinoni's Op. 2 (1700), entitled *Sinfonie e Concerti*, distinguish the two types: his *concerti* are incipient solo concertos; and his *sinfonie* are ensemble concertos. The first six *concerti* of Torelli's Op. 8 (1709) are *concerti grossi*, the last six are solo concertos. Almost all these concertos of Torelli have three movements in the order fast, slow, fast; and the slow movements have a distinctive tempo arrangement in themselves: slow, fast, slow.[17]

Although the virtuoso concerto was developed by Locatelli and although he contributed a new sonority to the *concerto grosso* (see p. 446), the most important influence on violin technique and the concerto form was doubtless wielded by Antonio Vivaldi (*c.* 1675-1741). Vivaldi lived and worked in Venice, a city of immense musical importance to the opera, instrumental music, schools of music, and publishing.[18] His significance in the development of the concerto has already been discussed (pp. 333ff.), and he influenced all subsequent composition of this sort. Bach transcribed certain of the concertos of Vivaldi's Op. 3, and he obviously used Vivaldi as a model for his original concertos, including the *Italian Concerto* for harpsichord. Vivaldi continued to develop the figuration and idiom of the violin throughout his life, and a steady progress in these respects, in sonority, and in the

[16] For Albinoni, see R. Giazotto, *Tomaso Albinoni*, Milan, 1945. For Torelli, see Franz Giegling, *Giuseppe Torelli*, Kassel, 1949.

[17] There are three short movements of Torelli, set for two violins and *basso continuo*, bearing the mysterious title *Perfidia* and displaying a certain interest in virtuosity. The curious term *perfidia* seems to have been little used; and its fate is to be buried in the obscurity of learned footnotes such as this. For the record, *perfidia* is defined (in part) in Brossard's *Dictionnaire de musique* (1703) as follows: 'In music the term signifies a [species of] ostentation, an effect which consists in always doing the same thing, always following the same design, or continuing the same movement, the same melody, the same passage, the same figuration, etc.'

[18] For Vivaldi's life and instrumental music, see Marc Pincherle, *Antonio Vivaldi et la musique instrumentale*, Paris, 1948. Vol. II of this work is a catalogue of the instrumental music. The present catalogue numbers used to identify the works of Vivaldi are at chaotic variance with each other. The currently appearing complete edition of Vivaldi, admirable in many ways, has done little to rectify this situation. For details of the performance of Vivaldi's music, see W. Kolneder, *Aufführungspraxis bei Vivaldi*, Leipzig, 1955.

cantabile of his melodies may be observed in each succeeding set of concertos.[19] Quantz implies (ch. XV) that the cadenza itself (in the sense of the
improvised cadenza after the fermata) originated with Vivaldi (but cf.
p. 461).

To Vivaldi the concerto, particularly the solo concerto, must have
presented all the potentiality of a musical drama in which the solo and
orchestra were the *dramatis personae* and their conflict, the chief element.
Vivaldi originates a powerful style suited to this dramatic conception.
Driving rhythms, insistently repeated notes, powerfully conceived subjects,
unison passages, and large leaps of an octave or more, all constitute one side
of his style. In this he never neglects the colour contrast of different registers
of the violin, and he employs various species of figuration and idioms of
expression throughout the whole range of the instrument. Contrasted to his
dramatic style are expressive chromatics and the remarkable lyrical melodies
suited to the cantabile nature of the violin. A number of the slow movements
resemble operatic arias, and were obviously inspired by them. The 'singing
allegro', so characteristic of Wolfgang Mozart, is anticipated by Vivaldi.[20]
Vivaldi's harmony is sometimes extraordinary, but his interest in the
counterpoint of inside voices (and consequently the variety and rhythm of
the ensemble) is generally less than Bach's. A comparison of the original
Vivaldi concertos with their Bach transcriptions is instructive in this regard.
Bach generally retains Vivaldi's melodies, but at the same time he amplifies
and animates the inside voices, so that the harmonic variety is considerably
greater, and the rhythm more interesting, than the original.

F. M. Veracini (1690–1750) and Giuseppe Tartini (1692–1770) were two
other figures of importance and significance, particularly the latter. (For
Geminiani, see p. 350.) Veracini's best-known work is his *Sonate accademiche à
violino solo* (Op. 2, London, 1744), which includes a beautiful picture of him
playing the violin (Plate 30). Specific signs for *crescendo* and *decrescendo*,
explained in his valuable preface, are marked in the music (cf. Ex. 244 and
p. 486). These nuance signs are similar in appearance to those of Piani
(p. 486). Veracini is a less important composer than Tartini, but both of
them were regarded as the greatest violinists of their own time. According
to Burney, Tartini was humble and timid, but Veracini was vainglorious,
boasting that there was but one God and one Veracini.[21] There are also
concertos of Veracini, still in manuscript, and arrangements, also in manuscript, of Corelli's twelve solo sonatas.[22]

Tartini, whose style was influenced by Veracini, was something of a

[19] Compare, for example, the music of Op. 3 (*c.* 1712), Op. 8 (*c.* 1725), and Op. 9 (1728).
[20] For example, in Op. 3, No. 8, last movement (violin II).
[21] Charles Burney, *A General History*, 1776. See the reprint, Vol. II, p. 450.
[22] According to William S. Newman, *The Sonata in the Baroque Era*, p. 186.

transitional figure between the Baroque and the Classic periods, and his style shared characteristics of both. In any case, he is the most important figure in the violin concerto between Vivaldi and Viotti. Large numbers of his solo sonatas and concertos remain in manuscript, although some of his sonatas were published in his own lifetime (Op. 1, 1732; Op. 2, 1743). Through his 'School of Nations', founded at Padua in 1728, Tartini exerted an influence on violin playing comparable to Corelli's before him. Among his pupils (whose significant work takes place after the chronological limits of this book) were Pietro Nardini (1722–93), Pasquale Bini, Paolo Alberghi, and many others.[23] Manifestations of Tartini's teaching are the *Traité des Agrémens* and the *Letter* (1760) to his pupil, Maddalena Lombardini, later Madame Sirmen (see p. 361). Other important works are his *L'Arte del arco* (see p. 361) and the 'Devil's Trill' Sonata, the trill of which is quoted by Leopold Mozart.[24] In his sonatas, Tartini often uses a rather unusual order of movement: slow, fast, faster. (For his combination tones, see p. 385; for improvisation, see p. 461.)

France

In the early eighteenth century French violin music awoke from the dance reverie that had previously entranced and restricted it. The halting French essays in the violin sonata at the end of the seventeenth century (see p. 227) were followed by pieces of genuine vitality and interest in the early eighteenth century when composers and violinists of the stature of Couperin, Leclair, Mondonville, and Guillemain became interested in Italian violin technique and began composing after the manner of the Italian sonata and

[23] The most celebrated collections of Tartini MSS. are at Padua, Paris, and Marburg. Another important, but little known, collection is at the University of California (Berkeley), which in 1958 acquired an important manuscript collection mostly of violin sonatas and concertos of Tartini and members of his school. This collection comprises more than a thousand works for string ensemble, dating roughly between 1750 and 1800. Some eighty composers are represented, twenty of them unknown to Eitner. This collection is probably second in importance only to those in Padua and Paris in the extent and interest of its Tartini manuscripts. A special feature is the large number of anonymous works, some three hundred pages of which are devoted collectively to cadenzas (a dozen pages or so) and melodic embellishments à la the Corelli 'graces'. Also included in this collection is a copy of the hitherto unknown Italian MS. of Tartini's *Traité des Agrémens* (see p. 361). See Vincent Duckles and Minnie Elmer, *Thematic Catalog of a Manuscript Collection of Eighteenth-Century Italian Instrumental Music*, Berkeley, 1963.

[24] *Violinschule*, end of ch. 10. The complete sonata was published for the first time in J. B. Cartier, *L'Art du Violon*, Paris, 1798. For Tartini's concertos, see M. Dounias, *Die Violinkonzerte Giuseppe Tartinis*, Munich, 1935. For Tartini's life and works, see Antonio Capri, *Giuseppe Tartini*, Milan, 1945. For a splendid study of the sonatas and an up-to-date catalogue of the sonatas, see Paul Brainard, *Die Violinsonaten Giuseppe Tartinis*, unpublished Ph.D. dissertation, Göttingen, 1959. See also by the same author, 'Tartini and the Sonata for unaccompanied Violin', in the *Journal of the American Musicological Society*, Fall 1961.

concerto. After 1720, a freshness and experimental daring, markedly absent during the preceding century, appeared in French violin music. The natural harmonics used in the violin music of Mondonville, the 'artificial' harmonics in the treatise of L'Abbé le fils (1761), and the extraordinary music of Leclair and Guillemain are all prophetic of the swiftly advancing technical capacity of the French violin school.[25] By the end of the eighteenth century the leading violin school was French, not Italian; and the French maintained their position of leadership throughout the nineteenth century.

In the early eighteenth century an end to the dominance and restrictions of dance music among the French was insured by the increasing number of Italian violinists in Paris and by the new group of Italian-trained French violinists. Many of these Italian and French violinists were also composers of ability. Among the Italians were Antonio Piani (called Desplanes), a Venetian; and the Neapolitan, Michel Mascitti (1664–1760), a pupil of Corelli. The Italian-trained French included Jean-Baptiste Anet (1661–1755), also Corelli's pupil; and Jean-Baptiste Senaillié (*c.* 1687–1730), a pupil of Anet and Piani. François Couperin ('le grand') showed and acknowledged the Italian influence of Corelli in his trio sonata entitled *Le Parnasse, ou L'Apothéose de Corelli* (1724).

The greatest as well as the most fascinating of the French was Leclair, a pupil of Somis, himself the pupil of Corelli. Leclair brought a new virtuosity, including multiple stops, to France in his numerous works for violin—among them, solo sonatas, trio sonatas, violin duets, and concertos. His Chaconne, the last movement of Op. 5, No. 4, is a veritable art of bowing. As Pincherle says, 'if they [the sonatas] neglect some new effects in which modern technique prides itself, it is not that Leclair was incapable of realizing them, but only that he had not thought of them'.[26]

At first the French violin sonata and concerto imitated the Italians, but in Leclair and his followers an unmistakable French flavour persisted although the external model was Italian. Movements of French derivation, such as the *chasse*, were incorporated in the sonata. The first French concertos by a French composer were published by Jacques Aubert (Op. 17, 1735), inevitably influenced by Vivaldi. The French distinguished between the terms *concert* and *concerto*. The former designated merely an ensemble piece, and this explains why a trio sonata can be described by the term *concert* (e.g. Couperin's *Concerts Royaux*). The term *concerto* was used in France to describe the true concerto based on Italian models.

[25] See Lionel de La Laurencie, *L'Ecole française de violon de Lully à Viotti*, 3 vols., Paris, 1922–4.
[26] Marc Pincherle in the *Bulletin français de la Société Internationale de Musique*, October 1911, p. 27. For a complete study of Leclair, see the same author's *Jean-Marie Leclair*, Paris, 1952. For other technical aspects of Leclair, see the Index. See also, E. Appia, 'The Violin Sonatas of Leclair', *The Score*, June 1950.

It goes without saying that the French continued to compose dance music. The French dances were the models for Europe, and the literature of *allemandes, sarabandes, courantes, gigues, minuets,* and so on, was very large. Some of these had special characteristics, such as the *courante* with its alternating 6/4 and 3/2 time, resulting in the old *hemiola* effect (see p. 185). Similarly in the *passepied,* a kind of fast *minuet,* the usual 3/8 time may be varied by introducing a measure of 3/4. In effect, the latter is two measures of 3/8 with the third and fourth eighth-note tied together—again, the *hemiola* effect.

Dance musicians in France were a vested interest to whom the concerto and sonata players were something like modern beatniks and a challenge to their status and security. The old *24 Violons du Roi* and the Musicians' Guild (*Confrérie de St. Julien*) were jealous of their prerogatives and standing as traditional dance musicians, and they sometimes succeeded in harrassing and restricting those who represented foreign influences inimical to their position. Anet and Leclair, both strongly 'tainted' by the Italian sonata influence, suffered at their hands.[27]

Other French violinist-composers were Sébastien de Brossard, J.-F. Rebel (1666-1747), François Duval (*c.* 1673-1728), and Elisabeth-Claude Jacquet de la Guerre (1664-1729). These composers were among the first of the native French to write sonatas, and Duval was one of the first who played, or was able to play, the solo sonatas of Corelli. Thus, he was one of the first of the French to master the style of playing in double (multiple) stops. La Guerre composed not only the usual type of sonatas, but also duets for two violins unaccompanied, a species cultivated by Leclair as well.[28]

Mondonville, Guillemain, and Guignon were more important figures (with the exception of Leclair) than those just mentioned. J-J. C. de Mondonville (1711-72) was an experimenter and innovator. Within the conventional framework of the solo sonata with figured bass, he experimented with harmonics in his *Les sons harmoniques* (Op. 4, *c.* 1738). In these sonatas Mondonville exploits the natural harmonics, and the fascinating preface of this work explains the origin and reasons for their use (see p. 384 below). Mondonville is also an innovator in the form itself, especially in the relation of the solo violin to the keyboard accompaniment. In the typical solo sonata, the solo violin is accompanied by the *basso continuo* from which the harmonic foundation is supplied by the keyboard. With Mondonville and others a new type of sonata appears in which the interest is shared between the solo violin and keyboard or in which the dominant roles are reversed. Sonatas of the latter type are essentially for harpsichord with violin accompaniment, as in

---

[27] See Van der Straeten, *The History of the Violin*, Vol. I, p. 79. For details, see L. Grillet, *Les Ancêtres du Violon.*

[28] For further details on all these composers, see La Laurencie, *L'École française.*

Mondonville's *Pièces de Clavecin En Sonates, Avec Accompagnement de Violon* (Op. 3, *c.* 1734). This species of harpsichord piece with optional violin part was not original with Mondonville. More than twenty-five years earlier (1707) La Guerre published *Sonates Pour le Violon et Pour le Clavecin*. The sonatas 'Pour le Clavecin' are 'harpsichord pieces which could be played on the violin'.[29] These sonatas are set out on two staves; if the violin is at hand, it plays the upper staff, and the harpsichord reverts to the role of accompaniment. Still earlier, Dieupart wrote six harpsichord sonatas (*c.* 1700), adding an optional violin part. Procedures of this kind did not stop with the later sonatas of Mondonville. In 1745 Guillemain published his Op. 13 as *Pièces De Clavecin en Sonates*, 'to which he added a violin accompaniment to conform to present-day taste'. This was not his original intention, he says, as he has 'often noticed that the violin covered [the harpsichord] too much, which prevents one from hearing the true subject'.[30] This species of sonata survived its own time, and was, if anything, the dominant type in the early years of the following Classic period. It is a prominent scheme even in the early Mozart sonatas for violin and piano.

Between 1735 and 1750 Louis-Gabriel Guillemain (1705–70) and J. P. Guignon (1702–74) brought a new lustre to the French violin school. Guignon, the last 'King of the Violins', was a pupil of Somis. Guillemain, a virtually unknown composer today, wrote some extraordinary music.[31] To judge by the few available pieces, Guillemain's music has great interest as such, and the technical demands involved are on a level with those required by Leclair. Indeed, perhaps Guillemain surpasses Leclair in bowing requirements. (For Guillemain's unaccompanied violin sonatas, see p. 336; see also Ex. 127 above.)

Tremais (first name unknown) is a mysterious figure who specialized in the *outré* technical devices of violinists. He wrote for the *scordatura* violin (*violon discordée*), he calls for passages consisting of notes alternately bowed and plucked, and he requires elaborate multiple stops. Extensions of the hand, registers as high as the twelfth position, and even the octave trill are not beyond his imagination.[32] In part, Tremais represents influences of the newer Italian school, having been a Tartini pupil.

In his treatise L'Abbé le fils includes a considerable amount of music which combines features of the French and the Italian styles. To the former category belong dances (like the minuet), *Air, Rondeau, Chasse*, and particularly

[29] See La Laurencie, *L'Ecole française*, Vol. I, p. 122, note 1.
[30] See C. L. Girdlestone, *Rameau*, London, 1959, p. 42.
[31] Few of his pieces are published. There are three in Cartier's *L'Art du Violon*: pp. 124, 176, and 266.
[32] In Op. I, Sonata 9 (1736). However, Corrette was the first to use the scordatura in France (1738) in his 'Concerto for Violin alone'. See La Laurencie, *L'École française*, Vol. III, p. 19.

two lengthy suites of 'Opera Airs' (which include dances) in the form of duos for two violins, presumably for teacher and pupil. To the Italian style belong the various lessons in 'the manner of sonatas'. The variation form is represented by a 'Suite de jolis Airs' for violin alone. The pieces in his treatise are representative of the variety and styles of his violin music independent of the treatise.[33]

Finally, the *Concert Spirituel*, the first public concerts in France, founded by A. Philidor in 1725, undoubtedly helped advance the cause of French instrumental music at the time. These concerts were held on holy days (mainly in Lent), when the opera was suspended; and they continued each year up to the time of the French Revolution (1791). At first only sacred vocal works were performed, but later secular works were admitted, including 'symphonies' and concertos.

Germany

The advanced technique of the Germans at the end of the seventeenth century was absorbed into the main stream of the Italian tradition in the early eighteenth century. The Germans fell under the violinistic spell of the Italians, who, with violinist-composers like Vivaldi and Locatelli, again assumed the leadership in the technique and music of the violin. To the great German composers of the time violin music was essentially a side line. On the other hand, to Vivaldi and Locatelli it was a central fact of existence, and they pioneered in the formal development of the concerto. As a natural result, they also advanced the technique of violin playing. However, the violin sonatas and concertos of J. S. Bach, while small in quantity and hardly central to his main activities as a church musician, must be regarded as towering works by any musical or technical standard. The six unaccompanied sonatas—in reality, three sonatas and three partitas (i.e. suites of dances)—are, like *Hamlet*, full of the greatest beauties and bewildering enigmas of interpretation. From a technical point of view these enigmas revolve primarily about the bowings in Bach's own autograph(s), which are generally disregarded today as 'impractical',[34] and about the great difficulties posed by the polyphony of the multiple stops. (For the technical details involved, see ch. 19.)

In the evolution of violin music these sonatas represent an extraordinary

---

[33] For a list, see La Laurencie, op. cit., Vol. III, pp. 220-1. For the technical features of this music, see L'Abbé le fils in our Index.

[34] Consequently, there are numerous 'practical' editions of the 'sonatas' in which scarcely a vestige of the original Bach bowings survive. The edition of Joachim and Moser is exceptional in that it gives the text in a 'practical' version and also, underneath, the original Bach bowings. Even so, the latter should be checked for errors against the autographs, one of which is published in facsimile by Bärenreiter-Verlag (Kassel and Basel, 1950). For the other autographs, see Wolfgang Schmieder, *Bach-Werke-Verzeichnis*, Leipzig, 1950.

blending of the German and Italian tradition of the past. The heritage of the Italians is largely external, the sonatas proper resembling the Italian church sonata (*sonata da chiesa*) and the partitas, the Italian chamber sonata (*sonata da camera*). But only a German, or, more accurately, only Bach, could have made of the second movements of the church sonata such monumental fugal structures, especially in the C major sonata, continually expanding and growing in accumulative interest. The astonishing polyphony of these works is also essentially German, requiring the most enormous technical and musical concentration from the violinist, who must call up every resource, not only of his technique, but of his mind and spirit. The multiple stops of the polyphony are a continuation of the German violin tradition of an earlier generation, notably of Biber and Walther; and this is true, as well, of certain specific movements like the *Chaconne* in the D minor *Partita*, a variation of gigantic conception. In other respects, Bach abandons the favourite preoccupations of his German forebears. He shows no interest in the violin *scordatura* that so fascinated Biber, nor is there any of that descriptive music that ranged from cuckoo-calls in Walther to 'Christ's Prayer on the Mount of Olives' in Biber's 'Biblical' Sonatas.

Bach's other works for violin are in the Italian tradition. His six sonatas for violin and *obbligato* harpsichord are really Italian trio sonatas in design, the right hand of the keyboard player taking one solo part and the left hand furnishing the harmony, or sometimes, additional polyphony. Genius, however, transcends its models, and so it is with Bach. Like Mondonville and others in France (see p. 346), Bach creates a new relationship between the violin and keyboard, and they become partners, while the Italians continue to favour the solo sonata with *basso continuo*, in which the keyboard remains in a subordinate position.

Bach likewise transcends his Italian models in the concerto form. At the same time, he offers Vivaldi the sincerest form of flattery by imitating him and by arranging some of his concertos for various mediums. Bach's surviving violin concertos—two for solo violin and one for two violins—betray the inspiration of their Italian origin in the use of three movements and the *ritornello* form within the fast movements. Yet Bach was as incapable of mere imitation here as in anything else, and in the violin concertos he fragments and intermixes elements of the *tutti* (*ritornello*) and solo; and the harmonic and contrapuntal interweavings of the parts are generally more interesting and vivid than the Vivaldi counterparts. The six 'Brandenburg' concertos, Bach's particular and unique brand of *concerti grossi*, are not limited to strings, but use a varied instrumentation from concerto to concerto, including (collectively speaking) wind instruments and a solo harpsichord, which, in the fifth concerto, has a written-out cadenza of great length and difficulty. (For Handel, see p. 351.)

Two important German centres for violin music were Dresden and the court of Frederick the Great at Potsdam. At the latter were the Graun brothers and J. J. Quantz, the noted flute virtuoso and theorist, who had also studied the violin and understood it thoroughly.[35] At Dresden the presence of Veracini (from 1717 to 1722) gave an impetus to violin playing, and in this city were also J. D. Heinichen (1683–1729), J. G. Pisendel (1687–1755), the pupil of Vivaldi, and, for a time, Franz Benda (1709–86), a pupil of J. G. Graun and later in the employ of Frederick the Great for forty years at Potsdam.[36]

The Mannheim School of composers, centring around the Court orchestra, contributed able violinists, among them J. W. A. Stamitz (1717–57) and his son, Karl Stamitz (1745–1801). However, the success of this school belongs rather to the later eighteenth century and the early Classic period. It was after 1750 that the discipline of this orchestra and its effects of continuous *crescendo* became so famous throughout Europe.

England

There were many Italian violinists in eighteenth-century England, the haven and paradise of foreign musicians. This musical invasion was a simple instance of the workings of the law of supply and demand. England, in short, developed a voracious appetite for music and possessed the means to satisfy it. A natural complement to musical demand was an increase in music publishing (e.g. John Walsh), and London played a very active role in publishing violin music and violin treatises (the latter mostly for amateurs; see p. 358).

The most important of these foreign violinists was undoubtedly Francesco Geminiani (1687–1762). He came to England in 1714 (1715?), shortly after the death of Corelli (1713), and never returned to his native Italy. In his first years in London he enjoyed a considerable success as a virtuoso— playing before King George I with none other than Handel as accompanist (1715). His later prestige, which was immense, emanated rather from his success as a composer, teacher, and especially theorist. Among his writings, the most successful, and the one by which he is best known today, was *The Art of Playing on the Violin*, published in 1751, the first violin treatise which is addressed to professional violinists and reflects their practices.[37]

---

[35] As a young man Quantz studied the violin with Biber, Walther, and Albicastro, according to his autobiography in F. W. Marpurg, *Historisch-kritische Beyträge zur Aufnahme der Musik*, 5 vols., Berlin, 1754–78, Vol. I (1754–5), 3tes Stück, p. 201.

[36] For a violin concerto of Pisendel and another of G. P. Telemann, see *Denkmäler Deutscher Tonkunst*, Vols. 29–30, entitled 'Instrumentalkonzerte Deutscher Meister'. Telemann was an enormously prolific composer, but his violin music is not particularly significant in the history of violin playing.

[37] A facsimile edition with an introduction by David D. Boyden was published by Oxford University Press in 1952. A good account of Geminiani's life and works is still lacking. A full-scale study of Geminiani was projected by Adolfo Betti, but it

Geminiani composed a number of solo sonatas, trio sonatas, and *concerti grossi*, but no solo concertos. The instrumentation of certain of the *concerti grossi* is arranged with an ear to an increased sonority in the *concertino*, a viola being added to the two violins and cello that comprised the grouping usual in Corelli; and, by way of compensation, the viola part is deleted in the *ripieno*. (In the concertos of Locatelli, another Corelli pupil, the *concertino* is sometimes augmented to five solo parts by adding a second viola.) Geminiani's music has remained virtually unknown to the public at large, which consequently has been unable to appreciate his solid virtues in harmony, rhapsodic freedom in rhythm and form, and a highly expressive manner of performance. If not a genius, Geminiani was more than a composer of talent; and it is unjust that his music has been neglected, and his reputation obscured, by the greater gifts and more accessible works of Vivaldi. However, Geminiani's reputation as a teacher was illustrious in his own time, and, like Corelli, he influenced a circle of pupils that included Matthew Dubourg, Charles Avison (his chief apologist), Michael Festing, and a number of influential persons in musical and social life, among them the Earl of Essex, the Duchess of Burlington, and the well-known publisher, Robert Bremner (see p. 255).

Like Geminiani, Handel came to England early in his life and settled there. Unlike Geminiani, Handel was primarily an organist and harpsichordist rather than a violinist; and, as a composer, his central concern was the opera and oratorio. Nevertheless, Handel had been a violinist of sorts, and his works for the instrument include pieces of great imagination and verve. The accompanied solo sonatas for violin and the *concerti grossi*, especially the 'Grand Concertos' of Op. 6, are based on Italian models. But Handel never permitted his models in violin music or anything else to inhibit the flow of his ideas, to dictate the limits of the form, or to determine the order or number of movements. If Handel's violin music recalls the sonorities and forms of the Italians, the musical force which animates them is Handel's alone—a remark applicable with equal justice to Bach, among other great composers. Unlike Vivaldi, Handel did not push ahead into new technical or formal territories; and significantly, Handel wrote no solo violin concertos, the vehicle *par excellence* for the technical, the formal, and the experimental in violin music of the early eighteenth century.

Other foreign violinists of note in England were Pietro Castrucci (1679–1752), the leader of Handel's opera orchestra, F. M. Veracini (who arrived

---

was never completed. However, Betti published a short monograph of some twenty pages entitled *La Vita e L'Arte di Francesco Geminiani* (Lucca, 1933). The most thorough discussion of Geminiani's music is contained in Marion E. McArtor, *Francesco Geminiani, Composer and Theorist,* an unpublished Ph.D. dissertation, University of Michigan, Ann Arbor, 1951.

for a three-year visit to England in 1714, the same year as Geminiani), and Attilio Ariosti (1666-?), a string player and a rival of Handel as an opera composer. Ariosti enjoys the unique distinction of writing pieces for violinists which are not for the violin! That is to say, his six 'Lessons' for viola d'amore (*c.* 1728) were written so that violinists could play them directly on the viola d'amore by means of a tablature-like notation, specially invented by Ariosti for this purpose. This notation specified automatically and exactly the fingering and hand position of every note, and consequently it has a special interest in the history of violin playing.[38]

Native English composers of the time include J. C. Pepusch (1667-1752); William Boyce (*c.* 1710-79), whose twelve sonatas for two violins and *continuo* have been strangely neglected; T. A. Arne (1710-78); and William Corbett (d. 1748). Public concerts in London, begun in the seventeenth century (see p. 231), were continued in the eighteenth. In particular, Thomas Britton (1644-1714), the 'Musicall Small-Coal Man', established weekly concerts and a species of club for the practice of music (1678). These concerts continued until his death, and featured many famous performers, including Handel. Some idea of the extent of the music played at these concerts may be gained by examining the inventory of his books, music, and instruments made at his death.[39]

Other Countries

Even in the early eighteenth century we still know little about the progress of the violin and its technique in countries other than those already mentioned. We simply hear bits and snatches about violins and violinists now and then. In Sweden, for instance, the chief figure was J. H. Roman (1694-1758), whose violin *Assaggi* have already been noted.[40] In Holland, Pietro Locatelli settled in Amsterdam and became the most celebrated violin virtuoso and composer for that instrument in the country. Dutch publishers were also renowned for their publications of music, and Amsterdam in particular was the centre of a flourishing industry that produced numerous editions of violin music, including that of Corelli, Vivaldi, and Locatelli, among others. In Switzerland the isolated figure of Henrico Albicastro appeared, some of whose concertos have recently been published through the initiative of the Swiss Musicological Society.[41]

A tantalizing glimpse of Polish 'fiddle' [violin?] music of the early

[38] See David D. Boyden, 'Ariosti's Lessons for Viola d'amore' in *The Musical Quarterly*, October 1946.

[39] For this, see Hawkins, *A General History*, reprint (1875), Vol. II, pp. 792-3.

[40] See p. 336 above. For a study of Roman, see Ingmar Bengtsson, *J. H. Roman och hans Instrumentalmusik*, Uppsala, 1955.

[41] Henricus Albicastro, *Zwölf Concerti A 4, Op. 7* [1700-1705], edited by Max Zulauf, Basel, 1955.

eighteenth century is to be found in Telemann's autobiography (1740), as follows:

'I had an opportunity in upper Silesia as well as in Cracow of getting to know Polish music in all its barbaric beauty. One would hardly believe what wonderfully bright ideas such pipers and fiddlers are apt to get when they improvise, ideas that would suffice for an entire lifetime. There is in this music a great deal of merit provided it is treated right. I have myself written in this manner several large concertos and trios that I clad in Italian clothes with alternating Adagi and Allegri.'[42]

That Spain had a tradition of violin playing in the eighteenth century is shown by two publications. The first of these, *A posento Anti-Critico*, a work published in Salamanca in 1726, was written by Don Juan Francisco de Corominas, 'Musician and first violin at the University at Salamanca', who undertakes a defence of modern music and the use of violins in places of worship. The author says that in the hands of a good player the violin sings like a sweet flute, and he exclaims, 'How can you endure wind instruments, such as the oboe, clarianet [*sic*], small flutes, clarion, and howls of the cornett if a violin annoys you?' He speaks of Corelli and others, and this implies a knowledge of European violinists of the time and the gradual establishment of the violin in Spain.

A more significant publication was José (Joseph) Herrando's violin treatise in 1756, in the preface of which the author says that he received lessons from Corelli.[43] Herrando's book was the first of its kind in Spanish, and its appearance indicates a need for advanced instruction on the part of a substantial number of violinists to justify the labour and expense involved in publication. (For further details of this treatise, see p. 362.) The books of Don Juan Francisco and Herrando point to the increased use of the violin in Spain, a knowledge of European violinists, and especially a reliance on the Italian tradition of Corelli. This situation was quite natural, considering Spain's close ties with Italy, a substantial part of which it governed in the

---

[42] See Johann Mattheson, *Grundlage einer Ehren-Pforte*, Hamburg, 1740, new edition by M. Schneider, 1910, p. 360. According to Dragan Plamenac (*Notes*, March 1962, p. 233), Prof. Zdzislaw Szulc of Poznań published (1953) a valuable 'Dictionary of Polish Violin-Makers' (*Słownik lutników polskich*). This has not been accessible to me. For Czech violinists, see M. Pincherle, 'Les Violinistes Tchécoslovaques' in *Feuillets d'histoire du violon*, Paris, 1927.

[43] José Herrando, *Arte y puntual Explicación del modo di Tocar el Violin*, first published in Paris in 1756 (not 1757 as stated in W. S. Newman, *The Sonata in the Classic Era*, Chapel Hill, 1963, p. 287). The entry of Herrando's treatise into Spain was authorized in a 'privilege' dated 26 February 1757, the date of its Spanish publication being 8 March 1757. 'Another' work of Herrando is sometimes cited under the title *Libro nuevo de Musica: Arte para aprender a tocar el Violin*, dated 8 March 1757. This is simply Herrando's 1756 treatise with a garbled title and the date of Spanish publication. For this information, I am indebted to M. Marc Pincherle of Paris.

eighteenth century, and its many international connexions with other parts of Europe. Unfortunately, we do not know any violin music that is specifically of Spanish origin.

Publication, performance, and patronage

Prior to 1750 the production and consumption of music was basically a matter of private patronage, controlled by the Court, the nobility, and the clergy. Musicians depended for their livelihood on the patron; and if regularly employed in a royal or aristocratic household, the musician was essentially a servant who wore livery and who required permission of his master to change his employment. In 1717, for instance, Bach was imprisoned for nearly a month by the Duke of Weimar because he demanded his release in a manner displeasing to that petty prince.

Musicians' guilds did not have the social force or bargaining power of unions today. The guilds regulated the internal affairs of their membership, set standards for entrance into the guild, and, to some extent, dictated the conditions and terms of payment for individual engagements. But all this was dependent on the pleasure of the monarch. In seventeenth-century France the 'King of the Violins' enjoyed less real authority over violinists than did Lully, the true musical dictator of France, whose authority emanated from Louis XIV.

Most concert life was dominated and organized by the private patron. However, in the late seventeenth century public concerts on a small scale began in England (see p. 231), and continued there in the eighteenth century. In France the public concert began with the *Concert Spirituel* in 1725 (see p. 348). In Germany a species of concert took place in the guise of private societies, such as the *Collegium Musicum*, but these were not really public concerts in our sense. Throughout Europe, music in church constituted a kind of semi-public concert. Opera, too, was open to the public in certain cities, notably in Venice. Basically, however, opera was the affair of the nobility and particularly of the Court; and the opera often served the purpose of glorifying the monarch, a classic case being Louis XIV and the Lully opera in France. The real public concert dates from the rise of the middle class in the nineteenth century after the French Revolution. Before this there was very little 'box office', and entry to a concert was by invitation or membership.

The publication of music was ostensibly a commercial enterprise on the part of the individual publisher and composer. In reality, the patron entered into the arrangement through the dedication, traditionally flowery and flattering, if not obsequious. The dedications of Geminiani's music are addressed to powerful personages in the English Court, among them Baron Kielmannsegge, the Duchess of Marlborough, the Duchess of Burlington, and the Countess of Orrery. By custom, the patron responded to this flattery with some appropriate reward; and this may have been the only return received by the composer. Copyright laws were practically non-existent, and composers had virtually no protection against those publishers who wished, as they frequently did, to pirate an author's work. According to Hawkins, Geminiani got the better of the publisher John Walsh, who threatened to pirate Geminiani's Op. 2 outright. Geminiani, however, took the matter to the law courts, and succeeded in getting redress. But such cases were most exceptional, and Geminiani was certainly one of the few ever to get the better of John Walsh.

How did musicians live? They might be employed as household musicians by an individual patron; they might be attached to a church or a court; or they might be employed as town musicians. The latter species of livelihood was often considered preferable to the more ephemeral existence at the whim of private or Royal patronage. A musician might also engage in private teaching and, with luck, he might number among his pupils a rich and generous patron. He might derive some income from composition, as explained, and he might be employed as a performer. Naturally, the income and benefits accruing to individual performers varied greatly. The famous virtuosi, especially Italian singers, received staggering sums, but the wages paid to ordinary musicians who played in orchestras were not high. Sometimes musicians organized 'academies' (essentially benefit concerts) for themselves.

For most musicians their profession was a relatively precarious affair, and for most of them their livelihood depended on patronage in one form or another. This situation existed to the end of the eighteenth century. Haydn lived a fairly prosperous life under the patronage system—but he was still a liveried, if highly valued, servant. Mozart was one of its major victims, and even Beethoven lived in its vanishing shadow.[44]

[44] For a more elaborate account, see Manfred F. Bukofzer, *Music in the Baroque Era*, New York, 1947, ch. 12.

‿⁀∾⁀‿

CHAPTER SIXTEEN

The Technique of the Violin, 1700-61 (I): The Treatises. Holding the Violin and Bow. The Left Hand

ECHNIQUE is the indispensable means of transmitting the musical intentions of the composer to the listener. As Quantz rightly says, 'The good effect of a piece of music depends almost as much on the performer as on the composer himself'. This is a general and simplified statement of the vital role of the performer in realizing the intentions of the composer. Broadly considered, a performer's technique embraces far more than the mere mechanics of the instrument; to the latter must be added an understanding of contemporary notions of good taste, rhythm, dynamics, and expression.

In the early eighteenth century, as in still earlier times, the freedom allowed to an executant was much greater than it is today. The role of individual taste and judgement is continually stressed in contemporary accounts—one reason why the scores were less explicitly marked then than they are now. The performer was regarded as a person worthy of artistic opportunities commensurate with his responsibilities as a creator complementary to the composer. Besides, since many pieces were written for the composer's own use as a performer, there was relatively little need for performing signs. At any rate, every educated musician of the eighteenth century was well aware of the conventions of his time, many of which no longer exist today; and within these conventions and limitations it was taken for granted that the performer had the necessary judgement required for the proper exercise of the freedom he enjoyed as an artist. For us, a knowledge of these conventions is crucial, and this explains the true importance of the methods and treatises of the time, which hint at, even if they do not always fully explain, typical attitudes toward expression, dynamics, phrasing, articulation, and purely technical questions of the voice and instruments. To realize the intention of the composer—often expressed in the score with a minimum of performing signs—the modern musician must study the old treatises to understand the spirit of an earlier time and the conventions within which the responsible performer felt free to exercise his liberties.

Violin treatises, 1700-61

There is a marked discrepancy in the technical level of treatises for the instruction of amateurs and those for advanced players. This situation is a natural reflection of the corresponding gulf between the amateur and the professional violinist in the early eighteenth century. The virtuosi of the time would be regarded with great respect by the leading violinists today, but the amateur player of the eighteenth century, and even those in most orchestras, possessed a fairly elementary technique, far below the general level of the average player now.

The instruction of virtuosi was, and (for the most part) still is, the responsibility of an individual master; and the pupil-master relationship was central to advanced instruction. For the first time, however, treatises devoted to the instruction of advanced players appeared about 1750. These were intended to be used with a teacher, and they had the effect of helping both the teacher and the pupil, making instruction more uniform, and introducing ideas of the best current practice in Italy and Germany to a far wider circle than had been possible previously. The first of these advanced methods was Geminiani's *The Art of Playing on the Violin*, published in London in 1751.[1] Five years later the most influential of all eighteenth-century violin methods appeared: Leopold Mozart's *Versuch einer gründlichen Violinschule*, published in Augsburg in 1756.[2] By his own account, Mozart was inspired by the complaint of Marpurg (1754) that there was no guide to violin playing, and he believed that his was the first violin method. Either Mozart did not know or he thought little of the German, English, or French treatises that had preceded him in the eighteenth century (for seventeenth-century treatises, see p. 244). At the time his *Violinschule* was first published, Mozart apparently had not read Geminiani's treatise, but in the second edition of

---

[1] There is no substance to the claim that this work dates from 1731 or 1740. See the introduction to the facsimile edition, referred to on p. 350, note 37. See also the author's articles mentioned on p. 246, note 4. A French translation of Geminiani's treatise came out in 1752 (?).

[2] Facsimile of the first edition, edited by B. Paumgartner, Vienna, 1922; facsimile of the third edition (1787), edited by H. J. Moser, Leipzig, 1956. Translated into English as *A Treatise on the Fundamental Principles of Violin Playing* by Editha Knocker, Oxford University Press, London, 1948; second (corrected) edition, 1951.

1769–70, he included the so-called 'Geminiani' grip (see Ex. 130). Mozart's treatise must have met a demand, because the first edition was exhausted about 1764, and it achieved four German editions by 1800. There were also editions in Dutch (1766) and French (*c.* 1770).

To Leopold Mozart the extensive instruction on violin playing contained in Quantz's treatise, published four years earlier (1752), obviously did not constitute a violin method. The reasons undoubtedly were that Quantz directed his remarks almost entirely to orchestral players and he was more interested in the right hand (bowing) than the left. However, although Quantz's section on the violin is not systematic or complete, what he has to say is valuable, as we shall see in the quotations in later chapters.

Geminiani and Leopold Mozart exerted a very considerable influence through their treatises, and their works were widely imitated. After Geminiani's death, a simplified version of his treatise was published by one Stephen Philpot; an abbreviated version appeared in the United States;[3] and numerous English publishers paid Geminiani the dubious compliment of using his name on posthumous publications, very little of whose contents was his (see below). In the case of Leopold Mozart, later German theorists were inspired by his example, but the results were works of a much simpler technical level. G. S. Löhlein, for example, justifies his book, *Anweisung zum Violinspielen* (Leipzig, 1774) on the grounds that both Quantz and Leopold Mozart lack simple instruction for real beginners and that both works are very expensive.

By way of contrast to the professionally slanted instruction of Geminiani and Leopold Mozart, the tradition of 'self-instructors' for the violin began in the late seventeenth century (see pp. 244ff.), and it continued to flourish in the eighteenth century. At least thirty works devoted to amateur violin instruction were printed in England alone between 1658 and 1731, and these works were apparently read in other countries.[4] In the latter year one of the most important was published: Peter Prelleur's *The Modern Musick-Master* (London, 1731; some copies are dated 1730), a publication which contained six tutors, one for the voice and five others for the most usual instruments. Part V was entitled *The Art of Playing on the Violin*; and because this title and

---

[3] Stephen Philpot, *An Introduction to the art of playing on the violin*, London 1767 (?). Philpot was a pupil of Festing, the pupil of Geminiani. In 1769, an abbreviated version of Geminiani's 1751 work appeared under the title *An Abstract of Geminiani's Art of Playing on the Violin*, printed by John Boyles (Boston, Mass.).

[4] For a list of these works, see the articles mentioned above on p. 246, note 4. A copy of *The Self-Instructor on the Violin* (1695) found its way to the library of the *Liceo musicale* in Bologna. A copy of another of these amateur treatises, John Lenton's *The Useful Instructor on the Violin* (1702), was owned at one time by the Swedish violinist J. H. Roman (1694–1758), but by 1955 it had disappeared (see I. Bengtsson, *J. H. Roman*, Uppsala, 1955, p. 66).

that of Geminiani's 1751 work were identical, a legend, born of a casual surmise by Heron-Allen in the nineteenth century, has grown up that Geminiani was the anonymous author of Prelleur Part V. This legend has no foundation in fact. Actually, Prelleur Part V was pirated from an anonymous work, charmingly entitled *Nolens Volens or you shall learn to Play on the Violin whether you will or no* (London, 1695), which Geminiani, baptized (and probably born) in 1687 in Lucca, could not possibly have written. (For *Nolens Volens*, see pp. 245-6 above.) In any case, Prelleur's and Geminiani's works are entirely different in language and content, Prelleur's being completely elementary.[5] Prelleur continued in print for a number of years, and similar works were issued frequently by publishers anxious to take advantage of a good thing. After Geminiani's death in 1762, a large number of 'Geminiani' treatises appeared and continued to appear at least until 1800. None of these was written by Geminiani, the contents being nine-tenths Prelleur Part V (or very similar material) plus the table of ornaments from Geminiani's 1751 work.

In France similar books of amateur violin instruction were printed. The modest tutors by Brossard, Montéclair, and Dupont appeared in the first quarter of the eighteenth century.[6] A work of a far more advanced character was Corrette's *L'École d'Orphée*, published in Paris in 1738. This method reflects the notable advance in violin playing in France after the advent of the Italian sonata. Corrette reports on both French and Italian styles of playing, both being prevalent in France in his time. He recommends holding the violin under the chin in the Italian style, and he mentions both the Italian bow grip, used by the new French sonata players, and also the old French (thumb-under-hair) grip of the traditional dance violinists. Corrette also associates first-position playing with the French style, and positions as high as the seventh are described as part of Italian practice. Over forty years later (1782) Corrette wrote another violin treatise, and the changes are significant. The old French grip, for instance, is no longer mentioned. The advanced technique of the French had made the old bow grip completely obsolete by 1782. Corrette's work of 1738 is the most advanced treatise for the violin to appear in France before that of L'Abbé le fils in 1761.

The latter, entitled *Principes du violon*, is a work of great interest in its own

[5] Prelleur was probably inspired by an earlier compendium *The Compleat Musick-Master* (London, 1704; 2nd ed., 1707, 3rd ed., 1722). This work also had several parts devoted to various instruments and the voice. A comparison of its content and that of Prelleur furnishes striking evidence of the waning popularity of the viol. *The Compleat Musick-Master* devotes one 'book' to violin instruction, but three books to the viols: one each to bass, treble, and tenor. Prelleur, a generation later, has no instruction for the viols at all.

[6] M. Montéclair, *Méthode facile pour aprendre* [sic] *à joüer du violon*, Paris [1711–12]; Pierre Dupont, *Principes de Violon*, Paris, 1718. For Brossard's manuscript 'fragment', see p. 321, note 11.

right; it also serves to emphasize the new technical ability of the French.[7] After its publication, the French gradually assumed leadership in violin playing, and the pre-eminence of the Italian school receded in proportion. L'Abbé le fils (1727–1803) goes a step beyond Mondonville and Leclair, whose pupil he became in 1740. L'Abbé includes not only all the natural harmonics found in Mondonville, but also all the artificial ('two-fingered') harmonics as well, the extent and variety of which were not exceeded until Paganini's time. (For a minuet of L'Abbé's, entirely in harmonics, see Ex. 154.) Among other reasons, L'Abbé's treatise is distinguished by its use of extensions, occasional high positions (up to the tenth), its double stops (the first French treatise to deal with them), and numerous types of bow strokes. His is also the first violin tutor to recommend holding the violin with the chin at the left side of the tailpiece as is done today (for further details, see p. 369, note 15). It is also symptomatic of the absorption of Italian style into French practice that L'Abbé described the Italian, not the French bow grip, and that he includes pieces in the style of 'sonatas'. If L'Abbé has nothing to say about the expressive device of the vibrato, he nevertheless tells us where to use *crescendo* and *diminuendo*, and he distinguishes sustained bow strokes from those accompanied by dynamic nuance.

In Germany the level of 'instructors' for the amateur violinist was a shade higher than elsewhere but, none the less, they are imitative and unenterprising. J. F. B. C. Majer's *Museum Musicum* (1732) contains a section on the violin drawn almost entirely from Falck's treatise of 1688, nearly a half-century earlier. J. P. Eisel's *Musicus Autodidaktos* (1738), whose title, 'Musician Self-Taught', is typical, discusses the violin, among other instruments, and contains information similar to self-instructors in general, together with a few statements of exceptional interest (for his remark on Stradivari and Stainer, see p. 317). Quantz's famous flute treatise of 1752 is actually an omnibus of eighteenth-century information. Considerable attention is devoted to stringed instruments, and his section on the violin (ch. XVII, sec. 2) is particularly instructive about bowing and the training of orchestral players. In 1754 there appeared the anonymous *Rudimenta Panduristae*, actually written by the Viennese composer, G. C. Wagenseil, published in Augsburg by J. J. Lotter, also the publisher of Leopold Mozart's *Violinschule* two years later. Mozart had heard of this work about 1755, but he had not seen it before his own work appeared.

The only Italian treatise known in the early eighteenth century is Carlo Tessarini's *Grammatica di musica* (Rome, 1741?), a work which indicates the second, third, and seventh position on the fingerboard, but is sketchy in

---

[7] L'Abbé le fils [J.-B. Saint-Sevin], *Principes du violon*, Paris, 1761. A facsimile reprint with an introduction by Aristide Wirsta was published in Paris in 1961.

information.[8] Geminiani's 1751 treatise is a better clue to the advanced practices of the Italian school continuing from Corelli, his teacher. However, Geminiani's work was first published in English and in England; and while there were French and German translations (see p. 357, note 1), there was none in Italian.

Strangely, the Italians published very little concerning violin instruction during the period of their greatest influence. The reasons were compounded, no doubt, of the old attitude of master-pupil relationship and a jealous guarding of instruction as trade secrets. Veracini and Tartini, two of the most famous masters of the violin, are interesting examples. A theoretical treatise of Veracini, said to be in the *Conservatorio Cherubini* in Florence, is mostly about singers and gossip but contains nothing about the violin.[9] Tartini is the author of two works which treat the violin in one way or another: his 'Letter', dated 1760, to his pupil, Maddalena Lombardini; and his treatise on ornaments printed for the first time in French (1771), as *Traité des Agrémens*, a year after his death. His *L'Arte del arco* (The Art of Bowing) is a series of variations on a theme of Corelli, and while it is instructive *per se*, it has no explanatory text.

The 'Letter' is not a treatise on violin playing but a survey of several important and basic points in one sweeping lesson, dashed off by Tartini to his pupil in the form of a letter. It is an important document, but only treats a fragment of the subject.[10]

What information we have about Tartini's methods of teaching the violin may be supplemented by his detailed treatise on ornaments, just mentioned. This treatise was intended as a guide for playing and singing, presumably the embodiment of his teaching and practice in the 'School of Nations', a school for violinists, founded by Tartini in Padua in 1728. This work was prepared for his pupils, circulated in manuscript and, as explained above, never published in Italy. The Italian manuscript version must have been in existence by about 1750, since Leopold Mozart incorporated parts of it into his *Violinschule* of 1756. Actually Tartini's treatise may have originated at any time between 1728 and *c.* 1754.[11]

---

[8] According to Eitner, *Quellenlexikon*, this work is Tessarini's Op. 1. No place, publisher, or date is given on the title-page, but the dedication is dated 'Roma, li 20/2 1741'. This work was translated into English as *A Musical Grammar*, Edinburgh [176–?].

[9] If this work is in the above-named *Conservatorio*, it is not in the catalogue of that institution. The above information about its contents is taken from Edward Allam's article, 'Allessandro Stradella' in *Proceedings of the Royal Musical Association*, 1953–4.

[10] The 'Letter' was published in an English translation by Charles Burney (1771), together with the original Italian text. The Burney version, with English and Italian text, plus French and German translations may be found in Erwin Jacobi's edition of the *Traité* (see note 11 below).

[11] The original Italian manuscript, long given up for lost, has recently been discovered in two independent copies, one now in Berkeley and the other in Venice. For the

For the first time a violin tutor appeared in Spanish. Herrando's *Arte y puntual explicación* was published in Paris in 1756 (see p. 353, note 43), the same year as Leopold Mozart's *Versuch*. This treatise has no special Spanish flavour, being based on the Italian tradition of violin playing. It belongs to the advanced works of the time, to be compared with Geminiani's, not with the self-instructors. Herrando describes himself as the 'first violin of the Spanish Royal Chapel', and in the dedication of his treatise, dated 21 April 1756, he says he received lessons from Corelli. This explains the Italian derivation of his work. Herrando's tutor has a curious relationship to the French edition (1752?) of Geminiani's treatise. The latter contains a splendid picture of a violinist in playing position. Herrando's work contains the same picture, identical to the smallest detail, except that the head of the player is different. How or why this came about is a mystery. However, since both works were printed in Paris, the same engraver may have been responsible.

As usual, even the most advanced methods lag behind the practices of the best players, and one searches in vain for instructions concerning certain difficulties inherent in some of the music of the time, such as the mechanics of shifting or detailed information about the performance of multiple stops. From this one may conclude that there was no uniformity in such matters or that they were left to the player's discretion. Leopold Mozart says in his preface that he has 'laid the foundation of good style. . . . This alone was my intention. Had I wished to deal with all the rest, this book would have been twice the length. . . .' Similarly, at the end of his book, he says, 'There is still more that I could have said for the benefit of our worthy platform artists.' These statements imply that the detailed mechanics of a 'good style' were often left to the individual player. Mozart's half-promise that the

---

Berkeley MS., see David D. Boyden, 'The Missing Italian Manuscript of Tartini's *Traité des Agrémens*' in *The Musical Quarterly*, July 1960; for the Venice MS., see Erwin R. Jacobi, 'G. F. Nicolai's Manuscript of Tartini's *Regole per ben suonar il Violino*' in the same journal, April 1961. For a modern publication, containing the treatise in its French (printed) version, modern translations into German and English, and a facsimile of the Italian (Venice) manuscript, see 'Giuseppe Tartini, *Traité des Agréments de la Musique*, edited by Erwin R. Jacobi; Celle and New York, 1961. In the preface to his edition, Jacobi says, 'the date of origin [of Tartini's treatise] can be assumed to be between 1752 and 1756'. This is merely an assumption, and Jacobi offers no convincing evidence for such exact dating. The manuscript treatise could have come into existence at any time between Tartini's founding of the 'School of Nations' (1728) and *c*. 1754, when Mozart began to write his *Violinschule*. It is probable, however, that the date was nearer the latter than the former, since Tartini recommends practices, such as the tonic six-four chord preparation of the cadenzas, that are relatively late in their development. The 'Bowing Rules' found only in the Venice MS. (not in the French print or in the Berkeley MS.) are quite likely by Nicolai and not by Tartini. For a critical commentary and the first English translation of the *Traité*, see the edition of Sol Babitz (Carl Fischer, New York, 1958).

Violinschule would be followed by another book, devoted to still more advanced practices, was never fulfilled.

As a whole the treatises demonstrate not only very different levels of instruction but also different kinds of bias. Quantz, for instance, is most interested in problems of bowing. Both Quantz and Mozart have a good deal to say about the training of the professional orchestral player. They obviously sympathize with the trials and humble position of the latter, and they hold the good ones in high esteem. Quantz implies that the average orchestral player was not very accomplished, but he points out the importance of orchestral training before playing solos.[12] Mozart makes a similar remark, and he says that few soloists read well, by implication blaming this on their lack of previous training and experience in the orchestra.

The treatises of Geminiani, Mozart, or L'Abbé le fils could be used to instruct advanced players. To Mozart 'good style' apparently meant the basic technical training, and 'musical good taste' he considered essential to all players whether beginners, advanced players, orchestral players, or soloists. The extent of Mozart's treatise far exceeds that of any previous book. As a detailed, complete, and systematic treatment of violin playing, it is truly new and significant. Earlier works, including Geminiani's—which has nine pages of text, twenty-four long examples, and twelve complete compositions—devote themselves primarily to a concise *exposé* of the principles and include a number of complete examples and compositions through which the pupil and teacher could work out these principles. Mozart's *Violinschule* (1st ed.) consists of two hundred and sixty-four pages of text, and almost every technical point is immediately followed by a short example. Longer examples are not lacking, but there are no complete compositions as in Geminiani. L'Abbé le fils's treatise was published five years after Leopold Mozart's, but his scheme of presentation and instruction resembles Geminiani's far more than it does Mozart's. Probably L'Abbé knew Geminiani's treatise through the French edition of 1752 (?). Mozart's work was not translated into French until *c.* 1770.

Mozart's attitude toward teaching and toward his pupils is also far more personal than that found in earlier works. He displays a toughness of mind, strict to the point of being a martinet. Nevertheless, he is always sympathetic to the problems of learning a difficult instrument. The pupil must be tested constantly, and nothing new must be undertaken before mastering the old. 'Here are the pieces for practice,' he says (p. 88, translation). 'The more distasteful they are the more I am pleased, for that is what I intended to make them.' He forces the pupil to read at sight, and he will not permit those of 'merry temperaments' to study only fast pieces, which they naturally take too fast (p. 34).

[12] Quantz, ch. XI, para. 8.

Although Mozart does not believe in coddling his students, their interests are always close to his heart. He provides encouragement for the disheartened pupil, and brings teacher and student closer together through duets in which the parts can be alternated. Throughout his book, Mozart shows his solicitude again and again for the beginning violinist, and the book itself is arranged according to its order of difficulty. Tone production, for example, is deferred to chapter 5 to permit the beginner first to accustom himself to holding the instrument, to the bow grip, and to fingering. Geminiani displays a similar attitude when he postpones discussing bowing until the student has learned the rudiments.

By the 1750s the treatises are beginning to reflect the signs of the times, musically and violinistically. They are inevitably based on the technique inherited from the past. At the same time, their interest in the world about them is manifest. The attention to elaborate ornamentation in the treatises of Quantz, Geminiani, Leopold Mozart, and Tartini is characteristic of Rococo music about and after 1750. The cantabile melodies of the time require special attention to the tone of the violin in general and to the tone colour or each individual string in particular. In certain melodies uniformity of the tone colour of a single string may be preferred to the contrasted colours of several; and this uniformity may be achieved by using the higher positions on a single string even though it entails more difficulty. In short, the tonal results are worth the necessary technical effort (see p. 376 and Ex. 134).

The treatises as prototypes

The treatises of Geminiani, Leopold Mozart, and L'Abbé le fils appeared in the decade between 1751 and 1761, and together they summarize the times, suggesting prototypes of violin playing in Italy, Germany, and France. Geminiani's treatise is based on the long-established tradition and teaching of the classical school of violin playing that had dominated Italy and Europe for two centuries. The instruction of this treatise is fundamental to the technical education of the post-Corelli generation, the most brilliant representatives of which were Locatelli, Veracini, and Geminiani himself (cf. Plates 30 and 36). The details of the technique and expression of this and other schools are amplified in the sections and chapters to follow.

Mozart's work is methodical, eclectic, and thorough—typically German in this respect—and it represents a new attitude toward teaching. It is more than half Italian in inspiration, and it is no accident that part of Tartini's *Traité* is incorporated in it. The technical instruction in Mozart's treatise is undoubtedly basic to German violinists like the Graun brothers, Pisendel, Johann and Karl Stamitz, Franz Benda, and the following generation, including Wolfgang Mozart, who was an accomplished violinist. The German polyphonic tradition, developed in the late seventeenth century, has its most notable continuation in J. S. Bach and, to some extent, Bruhns, but it is a sign of the times that by 1756 Leopold Mozart no longer emphasizes polyphonic playing above other technical features. The same is true of Quantz. In this connexion, we must keep in mind that there was also a well-developed tradition of multiple stops among the Italians. (For a German violinist of the time, see Plate 37, and, better, Plate 39b.)

The treatise of L'Abbé le fils amalgamates the old French dance tradition, the 'new' Italian sonata tradition, and a progressive, rather daring, attitude towards innovation. The Italian tradition in France is embodied in violinist-composers like Anet and Leclair, and the more advanced features of violin playing in Mondonville, Guignon, Guillemain, and Tremais. The treatise of L'Abbé le fils, in fact, marks the beginning of the leadership of the French school during the following century, and it forecasts the shape of things to come by its advanced precepts on at least two points: it advocates something approaching the modern way of holding the violin (see p. 369, note 15); and it sets out all the harmonics, both natural and artificial. By way of contrast, both Mozart and Geminiani are using traditional ways of holding the violin; and while Mozart mentions harmonics only to disapprove of them, Geminiani mentions them not at all. (For a French violinist of the time, see Plate 31.)

There is still another tradition of violin playing which we must not forget, one that cuts across national lines. It is that of the amateur, and for him publishers of the time, especially in England and Germany, printed many a do-it-yourself treatise. These treatises, based on the simplest rudiments, were derived from earlier models in the seventeenth century, and it is significant that a violin treatise of this sort, *Nolens Volens*, published in London in 1695, could be kept in print, in one form or another, practically unchanged for a century (see p. 359). The phenomenon of the amateur violinist is of no importance in the technical advance of the violin in the eighteenth century, but the increasing number of amateur violinists—literally, 'lovers' of the violin—has an important effect in raising the social status of the violin to a position it had not enjoyed when solely in the hands of professionals. Moreover, it is important to recognize that the amateur violin treatise existed in far greater numbers than the treatise for professionals, and it appeared earlier. Only when the facts above are appreciated, can we gauge the level of violin playing properly and relate the information of the amateur treatise to it. The gap between the technique of the amateur and that of the professional was a large one, reflecting two different worlds.

By 1750 the technique of good violinists was a very respectable affair. It was solidly based on the foundation laid by earlier violinists, but it combined a comparatively greater technique of the left hand with greater powers of expression of the right. To a large variety of bow strokes these violinists applied an equal variety of dynamic nuances. The technical advances in question are mirrored in the treatises of Leopold Mozart, Geminiani, and L'Abbé le fils, which suggest a subtlety of playing, bowing, and special effects hitherto unknown; and while their works reflect the past, they also predict the future.

How the violin was played

Paradoxically, we know both too few and too many details of violin playing in this period: too few, because a number of questions about performing the music cannot be answered with any degree of assurance; too many, because there is sometimes a bewildering variety of answers. Such copious information suggests that there is not one but a variety of eighteenth-century styles. Indeed, these different styles correspond loosely to the difference between national styles and sometimes to the differences between professional and amateur players. While each national style has a certain consistency in itself, it is not definable in rigid terms, and for this reason, among others, there is no such thing as one definitive and authentic performance of a piece of eighteenth-century music to the exclusion of all other performances. In the eighteenth century and earlier, this variety of 'authenticity' (so to speak) is consistent with the freedom of the performing artist already described (p. 356). However, it is true that eighteenth-century styles, whether few or many, fall within certain boundaries. The following pages are devoted to a description of what these boundaries were in the eyes of composers, violinists, and theorists of the early eighteenth century.

Conventions of notation

In the first place, certain conventions of notation must be understood before approaching a score of the time:

1. Accidentals are not valid throughout a whole measure, as they are today, but affect only the note which follows the accidental in question. There is one exception to the rule: in a series of consecutive repeated notes of the same pitch, an accidental placed before the first of the series affects them all and need not be repeated. Similarly, if the series of repeated notes crosses the bar-line into a new measure, the repeated note (or notes) in the new measure is still affected by the original accidental, and no new accidental is required. In modern practice, the accidental would be repeated at the start of a new measure in a comparable situation.

The natural sign (♮) is not commonly used until the eighteenth century, and an old practice, inherited from earlier times, still persists: a sharp is frequently used to cancel a flat, whether the flat is inserted in the course of a piece or is in force from the signature. In the same manner, a flat before a sharp cancels the sharp, and has the force of a natural sign. The sign for a double sharp (✕) also makes its appearance at this time. However, a double sharp can also be indicated by *two* sharps or by a sharp preceding a note already sharped from the key signature—a matter of some confusion. The double flat may be indicated by flatting a note already flatted from the key signature or by the sign used now (♭♭).

2. The *custos* (E: *guide* or *direct*; Sp: *guiones* [Herrando]) is a little checkmark resembling a 'w' placed on a line or space of the staff at the end of a line of music to indicate to the player what the first note of the following line will be. Thus: ═══ᵥᵥ This convenient aid to sight reading was used as early as plainsong notation and continued up to the nineteenth century.

3. The *fermata* (⌒) or *corona* (F: *point d'orgue*) indicated a pause in general or a *cadenza* in particular.

4. *Scordatura* signatures are indicated in the same way and have the same effect as those in the seventeenth century (p. 250; see also p. 444 below).

5. G clef, second line, is the normal clef for violin music except in France, where G clef, first line, is used up to about 1725 as an inheritance from the past and possibly as a symbol of resistance to Italian influence.

6. When a number of figures of the same kind follow each other and only the first figure has particular markings (e.g. a slur, staccato marks, and so on), the remaining figures of the same kind are played in the same manner as the first group.[13]

7. In special cases, as in certain pieces of Vivaldi, violins are sometimes used to play the *bass* of the ensemble and are then called *bassetschen*. In this situation the violin parts are generally written in the F clef of the bass instruments, and the parts are transposed at sight an octave higher by the player.[14]

8. In some music (e.g. Locatelli, L'Abbé le fils) a sign (8ª) is used above and a wavy line (----------) *below* the staff to indicate that the notes are to be played an octave above the written notes. Today these wavy lines with an 8ᵛᵃ sign are generally both placed *above* the staff.

9. ♩. ♫♫ may commonly stand for ♩ ♫♫

Holding the violin. Tuning the violin. Intonation systems

The methods of holding the violin are extremely varied, and they include those derived from the seventeenth century (cf. pp. 152 and 247) as well as new grips which approximate modern methods. The violin is held by the left hand between the thumb and first finger but without allowing the neck to sink into the hollow between them, and the instrument is braced or held

[13] Cf. Quantz, ch. XVII, sec. 3, para. 5.
[14] See Walter Kolneder, *Aufführungspraxis bei Vivaldi*, pp. 99ff. The term is Quantz's (ch. XVII, sec. 2, para 34).

against the body of the player in one of several ways. The old breast position is still in vogue with dance violinists and for easy music which stays mainly in first position (cf. Plate 22). However, most of the 'new' music of the eighteenth century required a firmer support furnished by one of two additional types of grips: (1) at the collarbone or braced against the neck without chin support; (2) secured under the chin or jawbone. The first of these is best illustrated by the well-known picture of Veracini (Plate 30; cf. also the French violinist in Plate 31). However, one wonders whether Veracini posed for this picture in the spirit of vanity for which he was celebrated. Was this actually and habitually the true playing position of Veracini, one of the two 'best violinists' of the time? Or did he brace his violin under the chin, at least when descending from the higher to the lower positions? The latter possibility is suggested by an impressive amount of evidence that chin support was becoming general among violinists, even among amateurs (see below). Geminiani, however, appears to use the collarbone position without chin support—'The Violin must be rested just below the Collarbone', he says—but the frontispiece (Plate 36) of his French edition, which uses the same text just cited, shows a violinist bracing the violin against the neck and securing it with the jawbone held in the centre of the violin over the tailpiece, or a bit to the right of it. The German edition of Geminiani's treatise (1782) says explicitly that the violin must be held 'between the collarbone and the jawbone' (*zwischen dem Schlusselbein und dem Kinnbacken*) and that the chin comes 'at the right and not at the left side of the string-holder'. In view of Geminiani's own fingerings, which involve relatively large shifts of the hand downward, the picture in the French edition may well represent his actual practice.

In the other grip, the violin is secured under the chin or jawbone, usually to the right of the tailpiece, a method described by various authors in the early eighteenth century, including those concerned with relatively simple instruction. For example, Montéclair says (1711–12): 'To hold the violin securely so that it will not move, one must press the button that holds the strings well against the neck under the left cheek.' This language is somewhat ambiguous, but it certainly implies that the violin is held securely *by* the left 'cheek'. Corrette (1738) instructs the player to secure the violin with chin support while shifting to give every liberty to the left hand, especially when returning to the 'ordinary' position. Robert Crome's *Fiddle, New Modell'd* (174–?) says to rest the violin 'on your left Breast, the best way is to stay it with your Chin, that it may remain steady'. By 'left Breast', Crome must mean 'left shoulder'. In 1756 Herrando says: 'The stringholder must come under the chin, being secured by it, the face turned a bit toward the right hand'; and this is an accurate description of the accompanying picture, which in all *playing* details is identical with that of Geminiani's French edition. Leopold Mozart's statement is the clearest and most explicit of all. 'There are mainly two ways of holding the violin,' he says: unsecured shoulder position and that steadied by the chin. He strongly recommends the latter. Mozart illustrates both positions. He remarks that the former (Plate 39a) looks well, but is 'somewhat difficult and inconvenient for the players as, during quick movements of the hand in the high positions, the violin has no support and must necessarily fall unless by long practice the advantage of being able to hold it between thumb and index-finger has been acquired' (cf. also our Fig. 5). The other position (Plate 39b), says Mozart, is 'the comfortable position', and in this the violin is placed against the neck, and the right side of the instrument comes under the chin, 'whereby the violin remains unmoved in its place even during the strongest movements of the ascending and descending hand'.

In effect, Mozart rejects the old breast position by not even mentioning it; and, in view of the advancing technique with its demands of the seventh position (and even higher) for good players, his recommendation of the firm chin-braced position is logical and reasonable. L'Abbé le fils (1761) goes a step beyond Mozart, recommending a chin-braced grip not on the right but on the *left* side of the string-holder—in principle, the method used today. Still, these chin-braced grips were not as steady as that used now. For one thing, there was as yet no chin rest, which was invented by Spohr about 1820.[15]

In both these grips the E string side of the violin is turned somewhat downward so that the bow arm will not have to be raised too high to reach the lowest string. Geminiani instructs the player to turn 'the right-hand side of the Violin a little downwards, so that there may be no Necessity of raising the Bow very high, when the fourth string is to be struck'. In pictures of the time the violin is usually held with the scroll somewhat lower than the tailpiece (cf. Geminiani and Corrette in Plates 36 and 31, respectively), but the language of the treatises suggests that the ideal was holding the instrument nearly horizontal. To quote Geminiani again: 'Observe also, that the Head of the Violin must be nearly Horizontal with that Part which rests against the Breast, that the Hand may be shifted with Facility and without any Danger of dropping the Instrument.'

Geminiani says that the correct position of the left hand is determined by holding down the four strings simultaneously with the fingering shown in

---

[15] L'Abbé le fils must be describing a chin-braced grip although he does not actually say so: 'Le violon doit être posé sur la clavicule de façon que le menton se trouve du côté de la quatrième corde . . .' ('The violin ought to be placed on the collar-bone, so that the chin is on the side of the fourth [G] string.') However, what L'Abbé says would not make much sense unless the instrument were braced by the chin, inasmuch as an unbraced violin at the left side of the string-holder would tend to slide away from the player. This is probably why grips braced by the neck but without chin support are held over the string-holder or at the right of it (cf. Plate 31).

Ex. 130. This position, known as the 'Geminiani' grip, was an ingenious solution to the correct hand position for each individual player, and it became a standard article of instruction for years afterwards. The position of the left elbow is obviously related to the position of the left hand and, to some extent, is determined by it. The left thumb and elbow are the key to playing in the high positions. It is obvious that to play in them without too much commotion and to equalize the hand in all fingers and on all strings, the elbow must be well under the instrument. This anatomical fact is reflected in the position of the left thumb. Geminiani says that the thumb must always 'remain farther back than the forefinger' until with the higher

Geminiani

Ex. 130

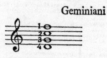

positions 'it remains almost hid under the neck of the violin'. As the higher and higher positions are attained, the left elbow is drawn successively farther in toward the body of the player and under the violin. In normal (first) position, says Mozart, the thumb must not project 'too far over the fingerboard, for otherwise it would hamper the player and rob the G string of its tone'.[16] The fingers of the left hand are curved, pressed down firmly, and kept in a given position until they must be lifted for other notes.

The violin is normally tuned in fifths upward from 'g', as it is today and as it was from its origins in the sixteenth century. This normal tuning was called *accordatura* (the general term for tuning), and exceptions to it were called *scordatura* (mistuning).[17] The second string (a') is usually tuned first, although the d' string is sometimes preferred. The variety of pitch is still a great problem, and Quantz complains that this variety is very bad, calling for a uniform standard of pitch.[18]

Another problem is the variety of intonation systems in vogue (see pp. 185-6). When accompanying other instruments, particularly those with fixed pitch, such as keyboards and wind instruments, the violin had to accommodate itself to their intonation systems. To what extent, or when, the violin played in the meantone temperament (common to keyboard instruments), in equal temperament, or in a species of just intonation is a

[16] Mozart, ch. 2, para. 4. English translation, p. 57.
[17] In the eighteenth century the common German term for *scordatura* was *Verstimmung* (modern term: *Umstimmung*). Corrette uses the phrase '*Pièces à cordes ravallées*'—referring to the original practice of 'lowering' the lowest string(s). There are various examples of *scordatura* pieces in the early eighteenth century: in Vivaldi, for instance, Op. 9, Nos. 6 and 12; Op. 28, No. 3 (Pincherle No. 368, found in the complete edition, Vol. 136). For a general survey of the *scordatura*, see the article of this name in *MGG*.
[18] Quantz, ch. XVII, sec. 6, para. 6.

moot question.[19] However, contrary to modern practice, a sharped note was often considered lower in pitch than the flatted form of the note a tone higher: for example, G sharp was often played lower than A flat, as fingerboards in violin treatises of the early eighteenth century show (see note 19). This situation changed about 1800, when violin treatises began to show G sharp higher than A flat (e.g., in Campagnoli's violin method)—a practice that is general today.

Holding the bow

The manner of holding the bow is obviously related to the manner of holding the violin. Whether the violin is held under the chin, at the right, centre, or left side of the tailpiece, or whether the scroll is level or below that of the tailpiece, all affect the right arm, and vice versa. That the right elbow must not be held too high—that is, too far away from the body—is implicit in the frequent admonition to tilt the violin down at the E string side to prevent the bow arm being raised high to play on the G string. On the whole, the elbow seems to have been held freely and unconstrained, not as close to the body as in nineteenth-century practice, nor as far from the body as in modern playing. Herrando says the elbow is 'separated from the body about the distance from the tip of the thumb to the tip of the forefinger when the two are stretched out as far away from each other as possible'.[20]

The methods of gripping the bow prevalent in the early eighteenth century are still those inherited from the late seventeenth century. As we have seen (cf. p. 248) in the old French grip, the thumb is placed under the hair, three fingers are on the bow stick, the little finger is sometimes braced on the player's side of the stick, and the hand grips the bow stick at the frog. In the Italian grip, the bow stick is grasped by the four fingers and by the thumb, which is inserted between the stick and the hair. The hand often grips the stick well above the frog. In his *L'École d'Orphée*, Corrette illustrates the French grip (Plate 31), and he describes both the French and Italian grips in this interesting passage:

'The Italians hold the bow at three quarters [of its length], putting the four fingers at letter A [Fig. 6] and the thumb underneath at B; and the French hold it at the side of the frog (*hausse*), putting the first, second, and third finger above the wood at CDE, the thumb underneath the hair F and the small finger at the side of the bowstick at G. These two ways of holding the bow are equally good, depending on the master who teaches. The eighths and sixteenths are played at the end of the bow at HJ.'

[19] See David D. Boyden, 'Prelleur, Geminiani, and Just Intonation' in *The Journal of the American Musicological Society*, Fall 1951; also, Murray Barbour, 'Violin Intonation in the 18th Century' in the same journal, Fall 1952.

[20] Herrando, *Arte y puntual explicación* (1756), p. 2. Cf. p. 362 above.

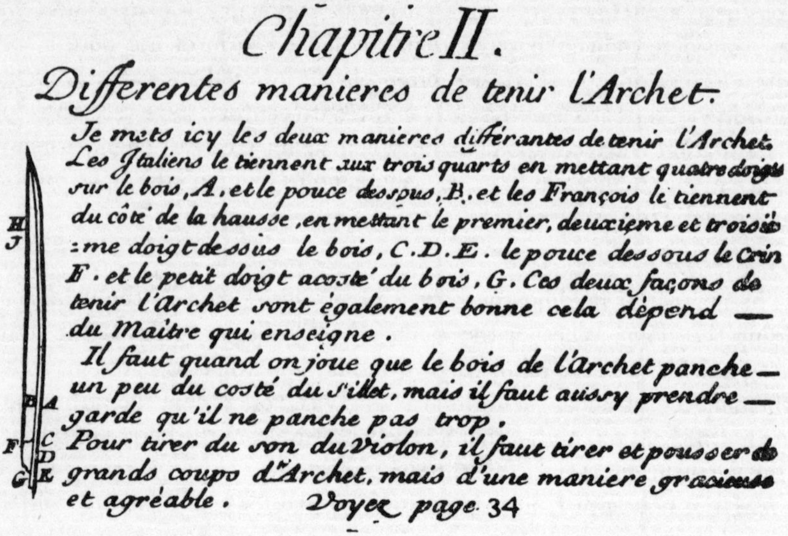

Chapitre II.

Differentes manieres de tenir l'Archet.

Je mets icy les deux manieres differantes de tenir l'Archet.
Les Jtaliens le tiennent aux trois quarts en mettant quatre doigts
sur le bois, A. et le pouce dessous, B. et les François le tiennent
du côté de la hausse, en mettant le premier, deuxieme et troisié
= me doigt dessus le bois, C. D. E. le pouce dessous le Crin
F. et le petit doigt acosté du bois, G. Ces deux façons de
tenir l'Archet sont également bonne cela dépend —
du Maitre qui enseigne.
Il faut quand on joue que le bois de l'archet panche —
un peu du costé du Sillet, mais il faut aussy prendre —
garde qu'il ne panche pas trop.
Pour tirer du son du Violon, il faut tirer et pousser de
grands coups d'Archet, mais d'une maniere gracieuse
et agréable.   Voyez page 34

Fig. 6. Bow and bow grip explained. From Corrette's 'L'École d'Orphée' (1738).

From this quotation it is clear that the French grip is still common in France in the early eighteenth century. However, it was obsolete after 1750, and only the Italian grip is described in Corrette's 1782 violin treatise. Nor is the French grip mentioned by L'Abbé le fils in 1761. The old French grip, suitable primarily for dance music, gradually became obsolete in France after the advent of the French *sonatistes* about 1720. Nevertheless, even in Italy, the French grip, while long since discarded by good players, must still have been practised, probably for dance music, well into the eighteenth century. At any rate, a painting of Gasparo Diziani (1689–1767), entitled 'The Ecstasy of St. Francis', shows a player using this grip.

The position of the first finger and that of the thumb vary in their relation to each other and to the bow stick. The latter is often grasped well above the nut (see the quotation from Corrette, above), from one to three inches higher than in modern practice, in which the hand is at the nut. However, this is a highly individual matter, depending on the length of bow, its balance, and the effect to be achieved. In general, grasping the bow several inches above the frog—presumably to achieve a better balance in an unstandardized bow—must have meant somewhat less power. Significantly, Leopold Mozart speaks constantly of virile tone, and he holds his bow at the frog.[21] (For the bow stroke itself, see p. 392, below.)

[21] In describing the holding of the bow, treatises of the time have nothing to say about 'pronation' or 'supination', those terms so dear to modern theorists. The treatises sometimes speak of the bow arm being close to the body or away from it, but there is no mention of the degree of wrist turn-in toward the body.

The bow is chiefly controlled by the index finger, the pressure sometimes being exerted between the first and second joint, sometimes in the middle of the second joint (L'Abbé le fils), or even between the second and third joint, as in Mozart's preferred bow grip (Fig. 7), a surprisingly modern one. From the latter grip, a more virile tone, toward which Mozart appears to aim

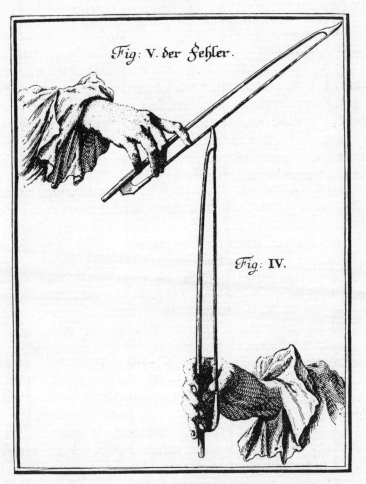

Fig. 7. *Bow grips from Leopold Mozart's 'Violinschule'. Fig. V shows the faulty grip ('der Fehler').*

throughout, can be obtained. Mozart's hand is also shown at the frog—not well above it, as in the picture of the player in the French edition of Geminiani's treatise (Plate 36)—and the little finger rests on the stick, apparently to be used as needed for additional control. L'Abbé le fils directs the player to place his little finger on the part of the bow stick fastened to the frog; and this seems to say that the hand is at the frog, not an inch or so above it. L'Abbé le fils also aims at greater power by separating the index finger slightly from the others. In his grip, the thumb is opposite the middle finger, and the thumb sustains all the weight of the bow. The bow stick is not placed perpendicularly above the hair but leans slightly in the direction of the fingerboard.

The left hand. Fingering

According to Quantz, the left hand should be equated in strength to the right; and the numerous details in his and other treatises show that ample attention was being paid to both.[22] The left hand was trained by a profusion of scales given in diatonic, chromatic, and mixed forms, systematically embracing the seven positions in advanced works like Geminiani and Leopold Mozart. The G major scale soon became a favourite;[23] and notions about efficient fingering are expressed from time to time in the treatises. L'Abbé le fils gives 'the general rule not to raise the fingers without good cause'—which seems to mean keeping the fingers on the string, raising the individual finger only when it is to play. This rule is in general practice today.

The use of open string is increasingly restricted, especially in melodies, to avoid the difference in *timbre* between open and stopped strings.[24] Roger North (*c.* 1726) links greater use of the stopped string to increased attention to beauty of tone in violin playing, and he recommends 'sounding all the notes under the touch [i.e. stopped], and none with the strings open; for those are an harder sound than when stopp'd and not always in tune . . .'[25] The first-position alternative to open string is fourth finger, and Quantz's emphasis on the use of this finger is a sign of the times. L'Abbé le fils also makes considerable use of the fourth finger, even in trills, including the double-stop trill (see below, p. 452). However, wherever possible Quantz avoids the difficulty of using the fourth finger in trills by shifting to another position. The surprising number of fingerings involving 4-4 in double stops or figuration may possibly be explained on the grounds that the fingerboard was flatter. In any case, this fingering would involve a strong and accurate stopping for good intonation. Open string, however, still persists in certain

---

[22] See Quantz, ch. XVII, sec. 2, para. 32.

[23] For systematic scale studies in various forms, see Geminiani's *The Art of Playing on the Violin*, Ex. I–VII.

[24] Open string is generally indicated by 'o' or by 'a' (France). The fingerings used are 1 (index finger), 2, 3, and 4. The thumb has no figure, and when (as occasionally happens) the thumb is needed to stop a string, the word for it is written out (cf. 'pouce' in Ex. 133a). By way of comparison, piano fingering labels the thumb as 1, and the other fingers 2–5.

[25] *Roger North on Music*, p. 234.

scale passages, figurations, and double stops; and it is used to facilitate shifting.[26]

Chromatic scales are generally fingered by sliding the finger a half-step upward for sharps or a half-step downward for flats. Leopold Mozart recognizes a difference in fingering chromatic scales in sharps and those in flats (Ex. 131a and b). Sliding the finger is usual in chromatic scales, but Quantz occasionally, and Geminiani systematically, advocate a species of chromatic fingering involving a finger to each chromatic note (Ex. 131c)—a fingering

Ex. 131

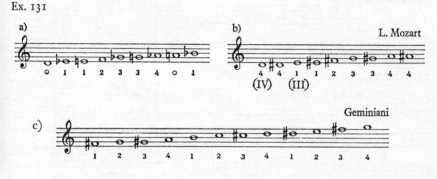

so revolutionary and ahead of its time that it had to be rediscovered in the twentieth century. In advocating this fingering and in discarding the sliding variety for chromatic scales, Geminiani says: 'Two Notes cannot be stopped successively with the same Finger without Difficulty, especially in quick Time.' Other reasons, such as a desire to avoid *portamento* slides and to achieve more legato connexions (cf. p. 380 below), may have prompted this variety of chromatic fingering. In any case, Geminiani characterizes the sliding fingering in chromatic scales as 'extreamly faulty'.

There is no evidence that the natural harmonic of an octave above the open string, so common today, was employed then as a substitute for the fourth finger in fourth position. Harmonics are not commonly found in this period, and Leopold Mozart rejects them altogether, except for pieces *entirely* in harmonics. Originally Mondonville used harmonics in first position to simplify fingering and to avoid shifting (see p. 384).

There are various special fingerings, including the use of the thumb and a fingering that Mozart calls *Überlegung* (overlapping).[27] This fingering is used on diminished fifths (or the like), whether as a double stop or as successive notes (Ex. 132). The thumb is required occasionally to perform multiple

---

[26] Many fingerings are given in the violin methods of the time. Occasionally fingerings are also indicated in the music itself: for instance, Geminiani, Op. 1, revisions of 1739; and Ariosti's Lessons for viola d'amore (see p. 352).

[27] In L'Abbé le fils, the comparable term is *croiser*. Other special fingerings will be discussed under shifting and extensions.

stops in which one has, so to speak, run out of fingers—the first finger being required both on the lowest and on a higher string. In this case the thumb plays the lowest note, as in Exx. 133a and b.[28]

Positions, shifting, and the fingerings involved

With his usual succinctness, Leopold Mozart gives three reasons for the use of the positions: necessity, convenience, and elegance.[29] Mozart's first reason was obviously the original one, since positions were necessary to extend the range upward. As violin music and playing became more complex, positions also had to be used in certain double stops which were otherwise impossible. This was true also of certain figurations across the strings, which were sometimes possible to play without the positions, but which were made far easier and more convenient with them. Mozart's categories of convenience and elegance cannot always be distinguished. In preference to the open string, the stopped note of an upper position was sometimes used for reasons of uniformity of colour, and sometimes for convenience's sake. Shifting to an upper position was also a convenient alternative to the weak fourth finger on certain trills, a procedure recommended by Quantz.[30] The higher positions are sometimes used to maintain an 'elegant' uniformity of tone colour on a single string rather than the contrast of several in the lower positions. With respect to the passage shown in Ex. 134, Mozart says 'from the fourth measure on, the whole passage is played on one string, and by the

Ex. 134

---

[28] See also Leclair, Op. I, No. 8, p. 77, where 'le pouce' is marked for an arpeggio passage.
[29] Mozart, ch. 8, sec. 1, para. 2. English translation, p. 132.
[30] Quantz, ch. XVII, sec. 2, para. 33.

equality of the sound, an agreeable performance is assured'. (For the sound of Ex. 134, cf. our recording.)

The normal limit for good players was the seventh position on the highest string—third position was more usual for 'learners'[31]—and perhaps third or fourth position on the lower three strings. These limits were occasionally exceeded, especially in double stops. Mozart says that the player must 'know how to use the positions on all four strings', and he implies that all seven positions are to be played on all four strings.[32] Geminiani advocates seven playing positions in his text and musical examples; and the examples illustrating double stops (XXII–XXIII) require the use of the seven positions ('orders') on *all four* strings. In his compositions, Geminiani is somewhat more conservative. L'Abbé le fils also gives seven positions in his systematic exercises; and in the compositions in his treatise he occasionally goes even higher to the ninth or tenth positions (i.e. to d''''').[33] That Vivaldi used the highest range of the instrument is suggested not only by his music but also by an account of a contemporary, Johann Friedrich Uffenbach, who reported having heard Vivaldi play at the San Angelo Opera House in Venice in 1715:

'Vivaldi himself played a *solo accompagnato* admirably and added a fantasy [cadenza] which amazed me. His fingers almost touched the bridge, so that there was hardly any room left for the bow. He played a fugue on all four strings with such speed that everybody was startled. But I could not say that I really enjoyed this performance, as it seemed too artificial to me.'[34]

The second position ('half shift') begins to assume greater importance, and considerable use is made of it. According to Burney, Geminiani claimed its invention, and although his fingering shows copious use of second position, his claim cannot be considered very seriously in view of its prior appearance in the music and treatises of the seventeenth century.[35] L'Abbé le

[31] 'Learners' and amateurs normally stayed in the lower positions, and any use of the higher positions was generally limited to extending the range on the highest (E) string. Thus Brossard's manuscript treatise (*c.* 1712) gives the first position as normal, but shows also a fingering on the highest string for the fifth and sixth position, remarking that this fingering is used when 'transposing or displacing the hand [shifting] which rarely happens'.

[32] Mozart, ch. 8, sec. 1, para. 6. English translation, p. 133.

[33] The modern second position is called 'first position' by L'Abbé le fils. Thus his sixth position would be called 'seventh' now.

[34] See Uffenbach's *Diary*, edited by Dr. E. Preussner, Salzburg. Quoted by Paul Nettl in 'Musical Life in the Venice of Casanova', *The Music Journal*, October 1955, p. 43.

[35] See Burney, *General History* (reprint), Vol. II, p. 445, note: 'Geminiani used to claim the invention of the half-shift on the violin, and he probably first brought it to England; but the Italians ascribed it to Vivaldi; and others to the older Mateis [*sic*], who came hither in King William's time.' See also, Hawkins, *General History* (reprint), Vol. II, p. 902, note.

fils also makes generous use of second position, and Tartini, in his 'Letter' to Maddalena Lombardini (1760) recommends playing whole pieces in second position. Mozart notes, however, that 'many passages which seem to fit the half position [= modern second position] perfectly can and must often be played in the whole position [modern third position]'. Mozart's 'compound' or 'mixed' position is 'that manner of playing when now the whole and now the half position is used'.[36]

What is known today as 'half' position is not rare in the music or treatises of the eighteenth century, but only L'Abbé le fils has a designation for it. His abbreviation 'R' means 'reculer la main contre le sillet' (move the hand back against the nut [of the fingerboard]), and he illustrates its use with the passage shown in Ex. 135. Much later, Bornet *l'aîné* (*c.* 1807) calls this 'demi-position ou celle du sillet'.

Ex. 135

Terminology

Eighteenth-century terms denoting position or shifting from one position to another are as follows:

1. In France: *ordre* or *position* means 'position'; but, as has already been pointed out, 'first position' in French was often the modern second position, and so on through all the positions. In Corrette *demancher* means to shift. In L'Abbé le fils 'D' means a shift downward ('*descendre la main*'), and he uses the verb '*monter*' (but no abbreviation of it) for an upward shift.

2. In Germany: *halb Applicatur* (half application or position) meant either second position, or collectively, the second, fourth, and sixth positions. *Ganz Applicatur* (whole application or position) meant either third position, or collectively, the third, fifth, and seventh positions. Later, Hiller (*Anweisung*, 1792) uses the explicit phrase *dritte Lage* (third position). In Leopold Mozart, *aufsetzen* means to shift.

3. In England: today's first position was called 'natural position'; *half shift* meant the modern second position; *whole* or *full shift*, third position; *double shift*, sixth position; *last shift*, seventh position. Geminiani, writing in English, but steeped in French and Italian terminology, describes positions collectively as 'orders' (cf. the French). In his Example XV he writes *Trasp^ne* (*trasposizione*), and the text speaks of the 'succeeding Order, upon which the Hand is to be transposed'. This implies that his *transposition* is roughly equivalent to 'shifting' to a new position. The word *transport(s)* is used by others in the same sense.

---

[36] For the first quotation, see Mozart, ch. 8, sec. 2, para. 12; for the second, ch. 8, sec. 3, para. 1. English translation, pp. 145 and 147, respectively.

4. In Italy: the word *manico* (neck, fingerboard) was central to the terminology of positions. Quantz uses the Italian phrase *mezzo manico* to describe positions or shifting in general. In Tessarini (1741), *Trasporto dalla mano* has the same meaning as the comparable term in Geminiani. *Portamento* = position, *prima portamento* = second position, and so on. Tartini speaks of first position as the 'natural position' (*luogo naturale*); *mezza smanicatura*, second position; *seconda smanicatura*, third position; and *terza smanicatura*, fourth position.

Shifting

None of the treatises discusses the actual mechanics of shifting, but numerous fingerings are given, and Leopold Mozart offers sound advice about the best places to shift, especially downward: by taking advantage of open strings, by using similar fingerings on similar passages, by changing the hand position on a repeated note, and after a dotted figure (Ex. 136). With respect to the latter, Mozart says, 'the descent can be made very conveniently. At the dot the bow is lifted, during which the hand is moved and the note F taken in the natural position'.[37] Mozart also advises the player to look ahead so that positions can be worked out economically, to avoid all unnecessary backward and forward movements of the hand (para. 14), and consequently to remain in a position as long as is necessary.

Ex. 136

The variety of fingering shows that there is no clear standard of fingering for shifts in *diatonic* scales. Geminiani gives the following varieties in Example V from *The Art of Playing on the Violin*:

123—1234;   1234—234;   12—12—123;   123—1234;
123—234;   1234—1234;   123—23—234;   1234—34—34

These fingerings seem to imply that Geminiani favours larger shifts to reduce the number of shifts required. He gives a specific shifting exercise to train the hand in shifting a third up and down (Ex. 137). Mozart and L'Abbé

Ex. 137

[37] Mozart. ch. 8, sec. 1, paras. 16–19. The quotation comes from para. 19. English translation, pp. 138–9.

le fils are more inclined to smaller shifts, such as 23—23, or 12—12. Ex. 138 (taken from Sonata 3 of the 1739 revisions of Geminiani's Op. 1) shows three forms of shifting: the first involves shifting down a position (seventh to sixth) on a repeated note; the second, a direct downward shift of a fourth from sixth to third position (not difficult with the old neck); and the third, what is evidently a contraction of the hand in order to shift from third to first position (more difficult). These fingerings, involving movements of the

Ex. 138

hand downward, imply that the violinist had a secure grasp on the instrument, arguing for a violin anchored by chin support. Where shifting is involved in making sequential patterns, the same sequence of fingers is used, and the degree of shift depends on the interval involved in the sequence.

In double stops involving suspensions downward, the sliding finger is often used to pass by step from one position to another, frequently requiring

Ex. 139

a finger extension (Ex. 139). A related type of fingering is that involving the change of a finger during a single or a tied note. Geminiani is a specialist in this type of procedure (Ex. 140), and such fingerings, which obviously aim at a greater legato, have a counterpart in the more legato fingerings used in

Ex. 140

keyboard music.[38] A special type of fingering is the repeated note under slur, involving a shift to articulate the repeated note, as shown in the passage in Ex. 141, taken from Vivaldi.

Portamento in shifting (in the sense of a perceptible slide) was apparently

---

[38] Cf. Couperin, *L'Art de toucher le clavecin* (1717); and the preface to Gottlieb Muffat, *Componimenti Musicali*, Vienna, 1726.

not the rule, but it seems to have occurred occasionally. In discussing Geminiani's unconventional chromatic fingerings, Burney[39] says:

> 'Geminiani, however, was certainly mistaken in laying it down as a rule that "no two notes on the same string, in shifting, should be played with the same finger"; as beautiful expressions and effects are produced by great players in shifting, suddenly from a low note to a high, with the same finger on the same string.'[39]

Ex. 141

This passage implies that in Burney's time (1776) and perhaps earlier, 'great players' sometimes indulged in *portamento* slides, while, at the same time, Geminiani set his face against this practice. Leopold Mozart gives the passages shown in Exx. 142a and b as part of a cadenza passage to play at the

Ex. 142

close of an *adagio*. The 3–3 fingering to shift from third to first position (and first to third) implies a species of *portamento*. Ex. 143 shows an instance of a deliberate *portamento* in double stops, found in the treatise of L'Abbé le fils (D = shift downward).

Ex. 143

Extensions and contractions

On a single string of the violin, the hand normally spans the interval of a perfect fourth. When the hand is in first position, the open note plus this interval gives a normal range of a perfect fifth on each string; and the first-position range of the violin extends from the open G of the lowest string to b″, a fifth above the highest (E) string. Very early in the history of violin playing this range was extended a semitone upward by an extension of the little finger to c‴ on the E string. Later, semitone extensions of a similar kind were used on the lower strings to reach the notes d′ sharp, a′ sharp, and e″ sharp, particularly in scales using signatures of four or more sharps. These

[39] Burney, *General History* (reprint), Vol. II, p. 992, note 'n'.

extensions on a single string were very useful in extending the range and in adding to the compass of any given position. Two examples from Leopold Mozart illustrate eighteenth-century practice. Ex. 144a shows a semitone extension used to embrace a given figure without shifting. Ex. 144b embodies a greater extension for the player 'who has a large fist', increasing the usual span of a fourth to a major sixth. In the latter example the extension principle is applied accumulatively, so to speak, to the stretch between individual fingers.

Ex. 144

L. Mozart

L'Abbé le fils marks his extensions explicitly with the letter 'e', and he has this to say by way of explanation:

'The letter "e" above or beside a figure signifies *Extension*, that is to say that it is necessary to extend or draw back the finger, which is indicated by the figure, without shifting the hand or any other finger save that which is concerned [in the extension].'

The extensions discussed so far apply to a single string, but a similar procedure can be used to advantage in multiple stops or figurations involving two or more strings. On two adjacent strings, the normal range encompassed by fingers 1–4 is an octave, but through extensions the range may be enlarged to a ninth, tenth, eleventh, or even a twelfth or more. However, a twelfth is apparently the limit of the early eighteenth century. It is immaterial to the left hand whether these extensions are used to play double stops or figuration involving two adjacent strings, as in the tenths shown in Ex. 145. Obviously, extensions of this character enlarge the range and

Ex. 145

Locatelli

segue

L. Mozart

Ex. 146

increase the number of double stops, and the same principles and observations apply to multiple stops, arpeggios, and figurations involving three or four strings. A few examples will illustrate the point. In Ex. 146 Mozart anchors the fourth finger on a high note, and the first finger is extended backward until the major tenth, a third greater than the normal span, is reached. Vivaldi calls for the very large extension of the twelfth in the 'anchored-note' figuration shown in Ex. 147. (For the sound of Ex. 147, cf. our recording.) In reverse fashion, the first finger can be anchored and the extension take place upward, as in Ex. 148 from L'Abbé le fils. Note the 'e4,' which means extended fourth finger. Another favourite device of extension is the stopped unison, involving the stretch of a whole tone to the adjacent lower string (Ex. 149).

Ex. 147

Ex. 148

Ex. 149

In modern technique, extensions are often used to avoid formal shifts—in effect, to obliterate set positions and the distinctions between them. This sort of thing was already understood in the eighteenth century, and L'Abbé le fils (among others) is a good example of it in theory and practice. In discussing extensions he says: 'Sometimes it is necessary to displace the other fingers immediately after the extension; [and] in this case, the extension is not marked, in order to make less noticeable the change of position.' In other words, extensions permit a shift without a shift, but this backdoor method is not to be called to anyone's attention! This method is equally effective shifting up or down. The passage given in Ex. 150 shows how L'Abbé le fils effects a downward movement from third to first position by extensions and without actual shifts.

L'Abbé le fils

Ex. 150

Contractions of the hand are the reverse of extensions, narrowing rather than enlarging the normal span of the hand. The chromatic fingering of

Geminiani embodies this principle (Ex. 131c). Geminiani seems to have taken a special interest in contractions. One of his characteristic fingerings for downward shifts (1–4; see Ex. 138) implies a hand contraction followed by a rapid return to normal hand position, rather than a quick shift downward through a comparatively large interval. The hand is also somewhat contracted, especially in double and triple stops in certain examples of modern 'half position'. Geminiani's principle of a separate finger for each semitone is carried to a logical conclusion in Ex. 151a, where he gives the fingering 2–4 for the interval of a whole tone, thus allowing a separate finger for the missing semitone. Ex. 151b, also from Geminiani, calls for a further hand contraction, but this procedure has no obvious justification or need since no shift is involved.[40]

Ex. 151

Harmonics. Combination tones

Before 1750 only natural harmonics were used, and these only sparingly. The first extensive use of natural harmonics in violin music occurs in Mondonville *Les Sons Harmoniques* (Op. 4, *c.* 1738). In the preface to this work Mondonville lists all the natural harmonics that are theoretically possible, and he says that he introduced harmonics primarily to permit violinists, not secure in their 'transpositions' (shifting), to take certain notes by harmonics without shifting the hand. In his music, therefore, he has alternate methods of notating high notes by positions of the hand on either a low or high string (Ex. 152a; the lower trill sign indicates the harmonic). Inspired by the possibilities, Mondonville soon proceeded to exploit harmonics for their own sake in double stops (Ex. 152b) or to produce sudden changes of register so that a number of his harmonics constitute special effects, no longer related to the idea of simplifying performance.[41]

Ex. 152

40 However, this example is not isolated in Geminiani's works. See, for instance, *The Art of Playing on the Violin*, Ex. IV, line 3; or Ex. VI, line 1. For L'Abbé le fils's contracted fingering of trills in thirds, see p. 452.

41 For an additional use of these harmonics, see a piece of Chabran (*c.* 1750), in J. B. Cartier, *L'Art du Violon*, Paris, 1798, pp. 94–95.

About twenty-five years after Mondonville, L'Abbé le fils sets forth all the natural ('one-fingered') harmonics and also all the artificial ('two-fingered') harmonics in common use today. In the 'two-fingered' harmonics the first finger acts in effect as the nut of the fingerboard, and the second finger produces the harmonic by stopping the string lightly at the point indicated. In Ex. 153a the firmly stopped finger which presses down e' on the D string acts in effect to give a new open string sounding e', and then the lightly touched a', a fourth above, gives the harmonic, sounding e''', two octaves above the fundamental e'. When the lightly touched note is a major third, rather than a perfect fourth, above the first finger, the harmonic sounds two octaves and a major third above the fundamental (Ex. 153b).

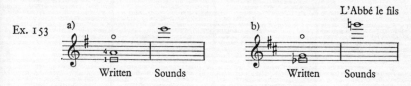

Ex. 153

By mixing natural and artificial harmonics, L'Abbé produces complete scales, both diatonic and chromatic, in harmonics. Even trills and whole pieces in harmonics are not beyond him. The minuet, shown in facsimile in Ex. 154, is composed entirely in harmonics of both kinds. There are two trills in harmonics, indicated by +, one being in the next-to-last measure. When both notes of a 'double stop' are black with the harmonic sign (o) above *and* below, it is a double stop, as indicated, in *natural* harmonics. The 'D' in line three indicates a downward shift (cf. p. 378; for the sound of Ex. 154, cf. our recording).

Ex. 154

Tartini discovered, or perhaps co-discovered, the phenomenon of 'differential' (or 'combination') tones, called by him 'third tones'.[42] In Ex. 155, when the two upper notes are played as a double stop firmly and exactly in

---

[42] See Tartini, *Trattato di musica*, Padova, 1754. The phenomenon was mentioned earlier by G. A. Sorge (1745).

tune, the differential tone, shown in black below, will be faintly but distinctly heard. Leopold Mozart, from whom this example is cited, and who doubtless copied Tartini, devoted a whole section to these tones, which were used by these two musicians to check the purity of the intonation of double stops. Both Tartini and Mozart sometimes heard the differential tones in the wrong octave (in Ex. 155, the blackened differential tone should be an octave lower), and the differential tone for the interval of the minor sixth is given incorrectly by both. In the nineteenth century Helmholtz formulated the correct scientific relationship of the differential tone to its generating tones: namely, the frequency (pitch) of the 'third tone' is the difference of the frequencies of the two generating tones.

Ex. 155

L. Mozart

The vibrato

In modern violin playing the vibrato is considered as an organic part of left-hand technique. In all early playing, including the eighteenth century, the vibrato was considered as an ornament to be applied occasionally and for specific effects of expression. However, because something approaching the continuous vibrato appears for the first time in the early eighteenth century, the vibrato is included here as a part of the technique of the left hand, which, after all, produces it.

In his treatise of 1751, Geminiani describes the vibrato as a 'close shake' or 'tremolo', including what is essentially a continuous vibrato. He says:

'To perform it, you must press the Finger strongly upon the String of the Instrument, and move the Wrist in and out slowly and equally, when it is long continued swelling the Sound by Degrees, drawing the Bow nearer to the Bridge, and ending it very strong it may express Majesty, Dignity, etc. But making it shorter, lower and softer, it may denote Affliction, Fear, etc., and when it is made on short Notes, it only contributes to make their Sound more agreeable *and for this Reason it should be made use of as often as possible.*' [Italics added.]

Geminiani had already described the vibrato in his earlier *Rules for Playing in True Taste* (Op. VIII), where he distinguishes between the violin vibrato, 'which may be made on any Note whatsoever' (i.e. essentially a continuous vibrato) and the flute vibrato, which 'must only be made on long Notes' (i.e. a vibrato only as a specific ornament). Continuous vibrato, however, found little favour with others like Leopold Mozart, who recommends that the vibrato be restricted to a closing note or any sustained tone. However,

Mozart acknowledges the presence of continuous vibrato among some players by noting: 'Performers there are who tremble consistently on each note as if they had the palsy'.[43]

The vibrato probably embodied a somewhat smaller movement of the hand than it does today. Mozart says, 'the finger is pressed strongly down on the string, and one makes a small movement with the whole hand'.[44] Here again nothing is said about the actual mechanics of the vibrato. From the quotations above, one may conclude that the vibrato was executed with the finger and wrist, but not with the arm, and that it was somewhat narrower than the modern vibrato.

Within this limitation, however, the vibrato could be slow, increasing, or rapid in oscillation. Tartini is explicit about this matter in his *Traité*, and so is Leopold Mozart, who copied him. If the signs given in Leopold Mozart are a proper criterion, the rapid vibrato was twice as fast as the slow variety. From Geminiani's description quoted above, one infers that these different speeds were related to tempi and to the emotional effect desired. According to Tartini, 'the vibrato is impressed on the finger with the force of the wrist, without the finger leaving the string, despite its being lifted slightly'. The last phrase refers to an after-pressure of the finger to emphasize the pulse of the meter. With respect to Ex. 156 Tartini says: 'This should always be

Ex. 156

equal and performed so exactly in time that the strength [i.e. finger pressure] of the vibrato occurs on the second of the two slurred notes marked with a 2 and the weak [lessened finger pressure] on the first marked with a 1.' Tartini also makes allowance for the vibrato in double stops, and he uses the same 'after-pressure' just mentioned. Leopold Mozart's section on vibrato embodies the essence of Tartini's, although it is somewhat elaborated in language and, on the whole, is somewhat clearer and more specific. These examples and instructions of Tartini and Mozart would seem to indicate that the eighteenth-century vibrato, even with its varying speeds, was on the whole somewhat slower than it is today, and that it was regarded as strictly measured with pulsations emphasizing the strong beats or parts of

43 Mozart, ch. 11, para. 3. English translation, p. 203.
44 Mozart, ch. 11, para. 2. English translation, p. 203.

beats.[45] On the other hand, this strictly measured vibrato may well have been a teaching device to introduce beginners to the vibrato. The measured feature could hardly have been preserved in a vibrato increasing in speed. It is also noticeable that Geminiani says nothing about the measured vibrato, and the very idea of measure is somewhat contrary to the emotional character of the vibrato stressed by Geminiani.

In the tradition of the past, dynamic nuance ('swelling the sound') frequently accompanied the vibrato, especially in its application to long notes. Geminiani says that 'all long notes' should be played soft, swelled to the middle, and decreased; and if this instruction is combined with the remark that vibrato is to be used as often as possible, Geminiani must have combined vibrato and dynamic nuance most of the time. In addition, he gives the vibrato sign combined with the nuance sign over a long note in his first 'Compos.[ne]' in *The Art of Playing on the Violin*; and in his text, describing the performance of the vibrato, he speaks of 'swelling the sound by Degrees' (he does not, however, say it is 'swelled' and then diminished).

Leopold Mozart is more explicit.[46] In describing his first 'division', devoted to enabling one 'to sustain a long note in Adagio purely and delicately', he instructs the player to begin softly, to increase strongly to the middle of the bow and to end softly (i.e. the *messa di voce*).[47] Mozart then continues in a passage which, taken with the above, shows the combination of long notes, nuance, and vibrato:

> 'In this first division in particular, as also in the following, the finger of the left hand should make a small slow movement which must not be sideways but forward and backward. That is, the finger must move forward towards the bridge and backward again towards the scroll: in soft tones quite slowly, but in loud rather faster.'

Mozart's information on the vibrato is the most detailed of all theorists in the eighteenth century in every respect: he explains the vibrato in its dynamic context, he tells us at the same time about its speeds, and he specifies the relation of the right hand and the left hand to its performance.

L'Abbé le fils and Tartini are conspicuously different in their treatment of this matter. L'Abbé does not mention the vibrato at all, but he places an

---

[45] For a special type of vibrato-trill, unique to Tartini, see p. 453 below. Incidentally, it is rather surprising that no vibrato is mentioned by Abbé le fils, who is so forward-looking in certain respects.

[46] Leopold Mozart, ch. 5, paras. 4–5. English translation, pp. 97–98.

[47] He also says that in soft playing the fingers of the left hand should be relaxed on the fingerboard and that in loud playing they should be pressed down strongly. This information is unusual. In the general tradition of the past, Mozart says, too, that in soft playing the bow is placed a little farther from the bridge, but in loud playing nearer to it.

emphasis on 'enfler et diminuer le son' (swelling and diminishing the sound = the *messa di voce*), he has explicit signs for this effect ($\Longleftarrow \Longrightarrow$), and he uses the 'swelling' and 'diminishing' copiously in his music. Tartini describes the vibrato (as above) in detail. He also gives the *messa di voce*, but he prohibits it in connexion with vibrato in the following words:

'This ornament [the vibrato] is entirely excluded from the *messa di voce* in which one ought to imitate perfectly not only the human voice but the very nature itself of perfect intonation to a mathematical point, that is to say, that the intonation of the note in the *messa di voce* ought not to be altered at all as it would be in the vibrato or undulation of the voice, in which the intonation [pitch] is never at a fixed point but is slightly higher or lower [than notated pitch], although imperceptibly.'[48]

Tartini's attitude on this point is hard to understand. He forbids a practice that had enjoyed a long usage in vocal instruction, and his directions are contrary to those of Mozart and Geminiani. The latter, at least, may be presumed to represent the Italian tradition from Corelli onward.

Finally, our discussion of the vibrato would not be complete without issuing a *caveat emptor*. The vibrato was a well-known device and had been for years. But, with certain exceptions like Geminiani, it was generally restricted to certain contexts as an ornament. It was also primarily the property of advanced players and soloists. It is unlikely that orchestral players used it at all.

Terminology of the vibrato

The usual names for vibrato during this period are *tremolo*, *Bebung* (sometimes *Schwebung*),[49] and *tremblement* or *tremblement serré*. *Tremblement* also means trill, but the context usually clarifies the meaning. References to

---

[48] This passage, difficult enough to understand in the original, is incomprehensible in the French translation, where the key word, *messa di voce*, was translated as *demi sons*, obviously because the French translator, Denis, mistook *messa di voce* for *mezzo voce* (half voice), a reasonable equivalent of which would be *demi sons* in French. To compound the confusion, the French term has, until now, invariably been mistranslated into English as 'semitones' (the proper word for semitones in French is *demi-tons*) by a number of persons who should know better, including the author of this book. However, until the original Italian version was discovered in 1958 (see p. 344, note 23), only the French version was available, and no rendering of the French term *demi sons* made any sense. It is unfortunate that the new edition of Tartini's *Traité* (see p. 362) perpetuates the 'semitone' nonsense. Erwin Jacobi, the editor of that edition, suggests that *demi sons* was used for *messa di voce* because the latter 'was a singing style unknown in France'. This is not so. L'Abbé le fils's treatise, published ten years before the French translation (1771), makes copious use of the *messa di voce*, as we have just seen. The simple fact is that the French translator made a bad mistake.

[49] See Ignaz Kurzinger's *Getreuer Unterricht*, Augsburg, 1763.

vibrato are rare in French sources until the time of Corrette's second treatise on violin playing (1782), where it is mentioned under the name of *balancement*. Geminiani uses the phrase *close shake* as well as *tremolo*, the conventional Italian term. Geminiani's sign for the tremolo (ᰃ) is close to the usual trill sign, but he distinguishes the vibrato from the trill by using 'tr' for the simple trill. Other and less usual terms for the vibrato appear from time to time—for instance, *flatté* (Bailleux, 1798), and *ondeggiando* (Löhlein, 1774). Finally, Tartini's *Traité* uses *ondulation* as a synonym for *tremblement*, the latter term being a translation of the Italian term *tremolo* = vibrato.

CHAPTER SEVENTEEN

The Technique of the Violin, 1700-61 (II): The Right Hand. The Bow Stroke and Bow Change. The Rule of Down-Bow

I N the eighteenth century, as always, the musical effectiveness of the violinist depended on the skilful co-ordination of the right and left hand, each of which played a distinct role, but a role that was complementary to the other. The left hand was responsible for fingering and for certain means of attaining expression and colour, notably vibrato, ornaments, harmonics, and the tone colours of different strings in their different hand positions. The right hand was responsible for producing the tone in general and for giving it an expressive eloquence through the variety of bow strokes, through the dynamic nuances applied to them, and through such special effects as *pizzicato* and *sul ponticello*. While these are the general responsibilities of the right and left hand in all periods of violin playing, a difference of degree or emphasis distinguishes one period from another. Compared to modern custom, for instance, the eighteenth-century violinist used a less intense vibrato, he used it less frequently, and he practised a bow stroke that was less sustained but more articulated and nuanced.

By the late seventeenth century the bow was already known as the 'soul' of the instrument (see p. 253), and the importance of the bow's function was perceived in principle if not fully realized in fact. In the eighteenth century the same sentiments prevailed—'One can call the bow the soul of the instrument it touches', says L'Abbé le fils. At the same time, the repertory of bow strokes was expanded as never before, and many shades of dynamic nuance were added to the individual slurred and articulated bow strokes. These developments went hand in hand with the development of the bow itself (see pp. 324ff.), a bow which evolved from the musical demands of the time and for which it was eminently suited. The different types of bows reflect the different types of music and their function, being especially contrasted in France and Italy. However, after *c.* 1720 France began to emulate and learn from the Italian style (cf. p. 345).

Hubert le Blanc's account (1740) of the rivalry of the viol and violin (see below, note 5) is especially illuminating in this context of contrasting, changing, and merging styles. Of the violin, which he calls derisively 'Sultan Violin, an abortion, a pigmy', Le Blanc says:

> 'Playing in the new manner, he [the violin] made himself admired as he had not done in the time of Lully where the bow strokes were chopped out, and the axe blow marked each measure. . . . Here [in the new style] one disentangled neither the *tiré* [down-bow] nor the *poussé* [up-bow]. A continuous sound is heard [showing] that one was master of crescendo or diminuendo (*enfler ou diminuer*) like the voice.

The 'new manner', in other words, is closer to the Italian style. But there is still a difference between the French style and the passionate, nuanced, and more varied Italian style. One can read this between the lines in another passage from Le Blanc:

> 'If one of the most beautiful things to hear was an adagio of Corelly played à la Geminiani . . . , [then] one would be forced to agree that no man in the world has ever played the sonatas of M. Michel [Mascitti] with as great taste, as pure, as correct, as Forcroi le Père.'

Hubert le Blanc also notes a far greater variety of bow strokes among viol players, and his words are equally true of violinists: the work of the right hand (he says) consists of the 'modern bow strokes which reproduce and multiply expression in the way the rays of the sun are reflected . . . the old bow strokes have the effect of a simple candle without reflection'.

The bow stroke

After the player learned to hold the bow (see p. 371), he then had to be taught how to draw it across the strings properly to produce a beautiful tone. With this in mind, the treatises instruct the player to keep the bow stick parallel to the bridge, the hair flush to the strings, and the bow stick slightly inclined toward the violin neck. The string is bowed near the bridge for loud tone and when the upper or thin strings are involved. The bow moves away from the bridge in proportion as the tone becomes softer and as the lower or thicker strings are used.

The actual beginning of the stroke calls for some comment. The problem of starting the stroke is mentioned for the first time by Leopold Mozart and shortly afterwards by Tartini:

'Every tone [says Mozart], even the strongest attack, has a small, even if barely audible, softness at the beginning of the stroke; for it would otherwise be no tone but only an unpleasant and unintelligible noise. This same softness must be heard also at the end of each tone. Hence one must know how to divide the bow into weakness and strength, and therefore how by means of pressure and relaxation, to produce the notes so that they are beautiful and moving.'[1]

Then Mozart explains his 'Divisions', which show the application of dynamic nuance to the bow stroke. Tartini's description is similar to Mozart's:

'The first study ought to be the leaning (*appoggio*) of the bow on the string just lightly enough so that the beginning of the sound that emerges shall be like a breath and not like a blow on the strings. This is achieved by [initial] lightness of pressure, followed immediately (*subito*) by the bow stroke which may be reinforced as much as one wishes, because after the light leaning there is no further danger of harshness or crudeness.'[2]

From these descriptions, Sol Babitz has postulated a theory that the basic bow stroke of the eighteenth century was a *crescendo-diminuendo stroke*, resembling the *messa di voce* ($\longleftarrow \Longrightarrow$), and he interprets Mozart's four Divisions as species of this nuanced stroke.[3] Mozart's 'small softness' comes at the beginning of the bow stroke and at its end—presumably at the bow change—and this may be so small as to be 'barely audible'. Tartini speaks of the brief initial 'leaning', but he does not mention the 'small softness' in connexion with the end of the stroke. What Mozart and Tartini seem to be saying is that there is a small initial 'give' to the old bow which has to be taken up before a good tone can emerge; and this remark is perfectly consistent with the character of the old bow. The same 'give' also occurs in the modern bow, but it is much less because the concave construction of the modern bow stick does not permit it; and this fact, combined with a modern

[1] Leopold Mozart, ch. 5, para. 3. English translation, p. 97.
[2] Tartini, *Lettera* (1760); translated by Charles Burney, London, 1779. In the above passage Burney unfortunately mistranslated *subito* as 'gradually' instead of 'suddenly' or 'immediately'. The new edition of Tartini's *Traité* (see p. 362) has reprinted Burney's translation without rectifying or commenting on this error.
[3] Sol Babitz, 'Differences between 18th-century and modern Violin Bowing' in *The Score*, March 1957 (also available through the American String Teachers' Association, School of Music, University of Illinois, Urbana, Ill.). The same theory is implicit or developed in various articles by Babitz in *The International Musician*, the organ of the American Federation of Musicians.

H.V.P.–DD

technique that cultivates the smoothest possible initial attack and bow change, makes this 'small softness' practically imperceptible to the ear in modern playing. However, acoustical experiments and measurements show that even the most skilful modern attack or bow change cannot be accomplished without some 'small softness', even if practically inaudible.

As a matter of fact, the small softness involved in Mozart's bow change must sometimes have been all but unnoticeable. Mozart discusses the bow change in these words:

'Now if a string be bowed again and again, and is therefore pushed each time from the old vibration into either similar or slower or quicker movement according to the strokes following each other, the stroke must necessarily be started gently with a certain moderation and played in such a way that *even the strongest stroke brings the already vibrating string quite imperceptibly from one movement into another and different movement. This is what I would have you understand by that softness of which something has already been said in paragraph 3.*' (Italics added.)[4]

It is true that the modern *martelé* stroke begins with a bite that resembles a small explosion of tone, and, far from starting with a small softness, the tone appears to begin *ex abrupto*. Since this stroke was not known in the early eighteenth century, it is sufficient to remark that the difference between the initial attack of the *normal* bow stroke today and that of the early eighteenth century is essentially one of small degree at its beginning and at the bow change. If the bow stroke is defined to include the movement of the bow from the time it starts in one direction until the direction is changed, Babitz's term *crescendo-diminuendo stroke* is applicable only to a stroke of the shortest duration—in fact, one that consists mainly of beginning and end. A number of strokes, however, consist of a discernible beginning, body (or middle), and end. It is what happens to the body that determines the nuanced character of a stroke of any length; and Mozart describes the total character of the stroke, which includes the body as well as the beginning and end, in his four dynamic Divisions. These are distinguished by four types of nuances: (1) *messa di voce*, (2) *diminuendo*, (3) *crescendo*, and (4) double *messa di voce*. In addition, he mentions, almost as an afterthought, an evenly sustained bow stroke.

As just explained, the difference between the normal modern stroke and the eighteenth-century stroke is that the latter has a brief softness and hence a slight *crescendo* at its beginning, and, similarly, a light *diminuendo* at its end; while, by way of contrast, the comparable modern stroke has these in practically imperceptible degree. In rapid passages this means that in the

---

[4] Leopold Mozart, ch. 5, para. 10. English translation, p. 99.

eighteenth century the notes would have been more clearly separated and articulated than today—what amounts to a non-legato stroke (described earlier; see p. 263). Where the bow stroke has more duration, the differences become even more noticeable because the body of the eighteenth-century tone is generally nuanced in the manner of the four Divisions (the even *sostenuto* being somewhat exceptional), while in modern violin playing the body of tone is normally sustained at the same dynamic level, being nuanced only when called for by a specific direction.

In all this one should distinguish what the old bow actually did and what it is capable of doing. An expert player today can produce a tone and make a bow change about as imperceptibly with the old bow as with the modern bow. Presumably this is so because modern technique makes more use of the fingers in producing the initial stroke and the bow change. The difference here is one of technique.

With this in mind, it is significant that Mozart and Tartini describe the 'small softness' at the beginning of the stroke as if it were physically unavoidable, not aesthetically desirable. To the latter category belong the Divisions, which in reality determine the expressive character of the bow stroke, considered *in toto*. These four types of nuanced strokes are applied to single bow strokes in order to achieve purity of tone and as they are appropriate in the context of different kinds of music and tempi:

1. *Division 1* ($\Longleftrightarrow$) is the bow stroke to which the old *messa di voce* is applied—that is, swelling to the middle of the stroke and decreasing to its end. This Division, like all of them, is to be practised both down-bow and up-bow, and in this particular Division the bow is to be held back as much as possible 'to sustain a long note in Adagio purely and delicately'. In other words, this is the stroke, nuanced with the *messa di voce*, used traditionally throughout the seventeenth century on long notes, especially in slow movements.[5] Division 1 is also accompanied by the vibrato, slow in the soft part and faster in the loud.

Division 1 is a photographic enlargement, so to speak, of the pattern suggested by Mozart's 'small softness' at the beginning and end of the bow stroke; and it is not surprising that Babitz considered this to be the fundamental Division or that he made the others subordinate to it. But observe

---

[5] The holding of a long note must have been the subject of long attention, admiration, and struggle to perfect. Hubert le Blanc (*Défense de la basse de viole contre les entreprises du violon*, Amsterdam, 1740) says that the violinist Somis 'displayed the majesty of the most beautiful bow stroke in Europe' and that he achieved a great victory (*grand oeuvre*) on the violin, 'the holding of a whole note. A single down-bow lasts so long that one is made breathless thinking of it.' The original French version of Le Blanc is reprinted in the following issues of *La Revue Musicale* (Paris): November and December 1927; January, February, March, and June 1928. The above quotation is found in the March 1928 issue, p. 139.

that Division 1 is specifically related to slow movement and long notes. Significantly, Mozart gives a different type of nuance for fast movements, as in Division 2.

2. *Division 2* (⟩) is a bow stroke to which diminuendo is applied: it begins strongly, diminishes gradually, and finishes softly. It is to be practised down-bow and up-bow, like all the Divisions. Mozart says that this Division is 'used more in cases of shortly sustained tone in quick tempo than in slow pieces'. Even though this Division begins strongly, one assumes that a barely audible softness marks the actual beginning of the stroke. Nevertheless, it can hardly be confused with Division 1 or classified as subordinate to it.

3. *Division 3* (⟨) is a crescendo stroke: it begins softly and increases the tone to the end, finishing with strength. In discussing this Division, Mozart makes the important observation that in playing softly the bow is drawn slowly, but when the volume is increased, the bow is drawn faster, and 'in the final loud tone, very quickly'. This is the first time that any violin treatise speaks of the speed of the bow stroke being used to increase volume (see further on this point, p. 399). Mozart's predecessors and contemporaries speak only of the pressure of the finger, usually the index finger, in this connexion.

4. *Division 4* alternates crescendo and diminuendo (⟨⟩⟨⟩)—in effect, two successive *messe di voce*. Even more of these 'swellings' may be performed in one bow stroke, says Mozart.

From these Divisions one learns 'to apply strength and weakness in all parts of the bow'. Then Mozart adds: 'Besides this, a very useful experiment may be made. Namely, to endeavour to produce a perfectly even tone with a slow stroke.' From this it appears that Mozart's *sostenuto* was relatively exceptional, and that the nuanced stroke was the normal order of things. This is entirely consistent with the nuanced bowings preferred by Geminiani and Quantz.

The information in L'Abbé le fils also conforms in principle to Mozart's four Divisions and the 'very useful experiment' in sustained tone. According to L'Abbé le fils, the bow serves to give 'expression to the tones, to spin them out, to swell them, and to diminish them' (*L'expression aux sons, à les filer, à les enfler, et à les diminuer*). He adds: 'To spin out a tone means to sustain it for a certain duration with the same degree of force' (*Filer un son, c'est le soutenir un certain tems au même degré de force*).

Thus L'Abbé le fils has a clear terminology to distinguish an evenly sustained tone (*filer*) from nuanced tone. Nuance is indicated not only by terms but by signs: *crescendo* by *enfler* and *diminuendo* by *diminuer*, and he gives the sign ⟨⟩ 'pour Enfler et Diminuer les Sons' (i.e. the *messa di voce*). In other parts of the treatise he gives the signs separately for crescendo (⟨)

and diminuendo (⊏⊃⃗). These signs are descendants of the blacked-in forms of the early eighteenth century (◄▬ ▬►) and they are very close to the modern versions (⊏⃗ ⊐⃗).[6]

Mozart's Divisions are applied to a bow stroke which had a barely perceptible softness at its beginning and at the bow change; and while the first Division (◄⊏⊃►) may be viewed as an elaboration of this phenomenon, the Divisions as a whole were not uniquely related to the 'small softness', but had the larger purpose of cultivating purity of tone, variety of expression, and mastery of the bow in all its parts. The truth of this assertion is underlined by Campagnoli's treatment of the four Divisions some forty years later.[7] By this time the Tourte bow was in common use, and it is significant that Campagnoli says nothing at all about the 'small softness' at the beginning or end of the stroke. Nevertheless, he uses Mozart's words[8] almost *verbatim* to describe the four Divisions. This shows that the Divisions were not uniquely associated with the old bow or with its bow stroke, but were dynamic shadings, considered as an indispensable and organic resource of tone and expression, and as a means to the mastery of the bow.[9]

How the bow stroke was made. The bow change. Power and tone

Through the first half of the eighteenth century the bow stroke began with the wrist, and only the wrist and lower arm were used for the shorter strokes. In longer strokes the upper arm and a little of the shoulder were used. Geminiani's description is clear and vivid:

'The Motion is to proceed from the Joints of the Wrist and Elbow in playing quick Notes, and very little or not at all from the Joint of the

[6] L'Abbé's clear distinction between evenly sustained tone (*filer*) and nuanced tone (*enfler, diminuer*) no longer exists. Today *filer* may mean either sustained tone or tone nuanced with the *messa di voce*. This confusion was introduced no later than 1803, when the official violin method of the newly founded French Conservatory was published (*Méthode de Violon* by Baillot, Rode, and Kreutzer). In this work, the authors distinguish (pp. 135-6) between *sons soutenus* (evenly sustained sounds), crescendo (*sons enfles*, indicated by ⊏⃗), *diminuendo* (indicated by ⊐⃗), and the *messa di voce* (*sons filés*, indicated by ◄⊏⊃►). For an account of evenly sustained vs. nuanced bowings in the late seventeenth century, see pp. 254ff., above. For an earlier use of *enfler = crescendo*, see p. 291. For other dynamic effects in L'Abbé le fils, see p. 489 below.

[7] Bartolomeo Campagnoli, *Metodo per violino*, Op. 21 (Milano?), 1797. Translated into English by John Bishop as *A New and Progressive Method*, London, 1856. There were also French and German translations. For the four Divisions, see the English translation, Part I, para. 41.

[8] Or perhaps Tartini's, from whom Mozart took so much. Campagnoli was the pupil of Nardini, the favourite pupil of Tartini.

[9] In the nineteenth century the Divisions of the bow came to mean something else: the physical divisions of the bow into parts (upper third, lower third, and so on) for technical analysis of bowing technique. The application of nuance was considered a separate problem.

Shoulder; but in playing long Notes, where the Bow is drawn from one End of it to the other, the Joint of the Shoulder is also a little employed. . . . The best Performers are least sparing of their Bow; and make Use of the whole of it, from the Point to that Part of it under, and even beyond, their Fingers.'[10]

This passage implies a bow grip held well above the nut. Geminiani continues with a good account of the bow change and the function of the wrist in it:

'In an Upbow the Hand is bent a little downward from the joint of the Wrist, when the Nut of the Bow approaches the Strings, and the Wrist is immediately streightned [*sic*], or the Hand rather a little bent back or upward, as soon as the Bow is began [*sic*] to be drawn down again.'

From such explicit descriptions, it is difficult to believe that the fingers were not called into play. Nevertheless, L'Abbé le fils is the first one to mention specifically the role of the fingers in the bow stroke and bow change; and the lack of attention paid to this point is one thing that distinguishes earlier treatises from those in the late eighteenth century and thereafter. L'Abbé le fils says:

'The bow should be held firmly, but without stiffening the fingers. On the contrary, all the joints of the fingers should be very flexible (*libres*) so that the fingers will make, quite naturally, imperceptible movements which will contribute much to the beauty of the sound. The wrist should also be very flexible [and] it should guide the bow at right-angles (*conduire L'Archet droit*) and direct it always over the sound hole of the violin. The forearm should function by following the wrist in all the movements. The arm as a whole should be used only when one employs the bow from one end to the other. The elbow should always be separated (*détaché*) from the body.'

The various passages quoted above make abundantly clear that the whole bow was used on occasions and that the best players were 'least sparing' of their bow.[11] But, of course, the whole bow is used mainly in slow time and for long notes. It is clear that rapid notes are played mainly in the upper part of the bow and with a short length of bow. In his 'Letter', Tartini recommends playing sixteenth-note passages at the point of the bow, between the point and the middle, and at the middle. He makes no mention of using the

[10] Geminiani, *The Art of Playing on the Violin*, p. 2.
[11] Even amateur players are being guided toward the long stroke (i.e. the whole arm) as an ideal. J. P. Eisel, in his treatise for the 'self-taught musician' (*Musicus Autodidaktos*, 1738, p. 30), speaks of 'an untiring Arm which guides a gallant (*wackern*) long stroke: for the short strokes are traditional and peculiar to tavern fiddlers'.

lower part of the bow. In longer notes, as in slow movements or cantabile passages, the whole bow is used. The balance of the old bow was lower down toward the frog (see p. 327), and the comparative lightness of the bow in its upper half made a clearly articulated stroke quite easy and natural, well suited to the performance of rapid notes. Below the middle the bow was heavier and less manageable, and hence was less suited to executing rapid passages with clarity and dispatch. On the other hand, the comparative heaviness of the lower part of the bow made it suitable for loud passages. Quantz makes this point:

'The fortissimo, or the greatest strength of tone can be practised most fittingly with the lowest part of the bow and somewhat near the bridge; but the pianissimo, or the weakest tone, with the point and somewhat separated from the bridge.'[12]

Quantz comments on the numerous gradations between these dynamic extremes, and the implication is that the bowing was adjusted accordingly with respect to the part of the bow used and its position relative to the bridge.

Power and tone are controlled by the index finger as a rule. Geminiani says specifically that the whole weight of the hand must not be used. Mozart calls for a loud, manly tone from the beginning of instruction, and (as has already been pointed out) his grip was eminently suited to a strong tone. Mozart's index finger is also the central factor in power. However, Mozart also uses a more rapid bow stroke to increase volume, and vice versa. In modern violin playing the speed of the bow stroke is a chief factor in the volume of tone produced, but among eighteenth-century treatises Mozart's is almost alone in mentioning bow speed. Nevertheless, it is quite possible that the speed of the bow relative to volume was more unmentioned than unexploited. Moreover, certain statements may imply the use of bow speed for control of volume. When Geminiani says 'the best performers are least sparing of their bow', he may well be hinting at the bow speed as well as a long bow stroke.

In musical terms the bow stroke of the early eighteenth century produced what was, by modern standards, a relatively light, clearly articulated tone; and the normal nuanced style of the full bow stroke was far more expressive than the modern counterpart. A kind of non-legato stroke must have resulted from the rapid wrist articulation of fast notes, approaching the modern *spiccato* in effect, but attained without actually leaving the string. There is no evidence of the modern *serré* stroke or the *martelé*, and these strokes are out of place in Baroque music, much as chromium would be in the furnishings of an eighteenth-century coach-and-six.

---

[12] Quantz, ch. XVII, sec. 7, para. 20. Note, however, that practically all eighteenth-century violinists in pictures are shown playing above the middle of the bow.

Bow strokes in general. The Rule of Down-Bow

To the violinist the bow is the essential means of expression—what breath is to the singer or the tongue is to the orator. The bow is responsible for the production of the sound and the form it takes. Whether the sound is long or short, loud or soft, heard as individual notes or in groups, detached or sustained—all are the responsibilities of the bow. The left hand is the indispensable handmaid of the bow, but its expressive role is limited primarily to the vibrato. On the other hand, the expressive powers of the bow in the hand of a virtuoso are practically infinite within the limitations of volume and tone colour of the instrument.

This inherent potential explains the fascination that the subject of bowing exerted on many writers such as Quantz; and, among composers, it makes clear why the variation was a natural vehicle for developing many varieties of bowing. Tartini's *L'Arte del arco* is a case in point, and so, on a more modest scale, are numerous variants set to short passages in Leopold Mozart and Geminiani, among others. In his Example XVI from *The Art of Playing on the Violin*, Geminiani shows in how many ways one may play two, three, four, five, and six notes—the latter being set in some sixty-two ways. To Example XVI Geminiani adds this comment:

> 'The Learner should be indefatigable in practising this Example till he has made himself a perfect Master of the Art of Bowing. For it is to be held as a certain Principle that he who does not possess, in a perfect Degree, the Art of Bowing, will never be able to render the Melody agreeable nor arrive at a Facility in the Execution.'

The phrase 'The Art of Bowing' became a significant slogan in the eighteenth century.

The use and selection of different bowings were determined by the kind of thing to be expressed. Quantz remarks on the totally different impression that different bowings of the same passage make. Mozart puts the case eloquently:

> 'The bowing gives life to the notes; . . . it produces now a modest, now an impertinent, now a serious or playful tone; now coaxing, or grave and sublime; now a sad or merry melody; and is therefore the medium by the reasonable use of which we are able to rouse in the hearers the aforesaid affects [i.e. emotional states].'[13]

The intimate relationship of bowing to expression explains why some bowings are preferred to others in certain periods, and why still others die out and become obsolete.

The principles of ordering the bow strokes, developed by the Italians and

[13] Mozart, ch. 7, sec. 1, para. 1. English translation, page 114.

the French in the seventeenth century (see pp. 256ff.), were focused in the Rule of Down-Bow, which continued to be the chief guide in the eighteenth century. The main consideration which dictated this Rule was simple enough: stress was equated with down-bow. Hence the down-bow was normally used for the first of each measure (Ex. 77a). The Rule was also applied to accented parts of single beats when the tempo permitted (Ex. 77b), and, as a logical complement, up-bow was used on unaccented notes and unaccented parts of beats (Ex. 77c). In actual practice, there were numerous complications, modifications, and exceptions, depending on the context of duple or triple time, fast or slow tempo, and the manner of expression (cf. pp. 258ff.).

Since bowing possibilities were greater in the eighteenth century than before, opinions were more numerous concerning the application of various bowings to the central Rule of Down-Bow. The books of instruction for advanced players, which appeared for the first time about 1750, were rich in such detail. The elementary tutors were confused by this diversity, deciding with difficulty between various methods of bowing advocated by skilful players seeking to amplify their technique and range of expression.

In the eighteenth century the Rule of Down-Bow is stated concisely by Leopold Mozart: 'Except when the measure begins with a rest, the first note of every measure is played down-bow, even if [by so doing] two down-bows come together' (cf. Ex. 81a). Mozart basically follows this Rule, as do many others. But there are signs of revolt against this rational but restrictive discipline, which was first systematized by Lully for his dance musicians (cf. pp. 260–2) and prevailed for a long time in eighteenth-century France. Geminiani instructs his pupils to perform the scales in Example VIII of *The Art of Playing* alternatively with down-bows and up-bows, 'taking Care not to follow that wretched Rule of drawing the Bow down at the first Note of every Bar'. Geminiani's attitude may be viewed either as the revolt of the individual artist against the *status quo* of convention or as part of the larger struggle between Italian and French music in the eighteenth century.

All the problems attendant on putting the Rule of Down-Bow into practice were considered in the seventeenth century, and the same questions continue to occupy the eighteenth century: bowing in duple and triple time, what to do with an odd number of notes (three, five, seven, and so on) in a measure, differences of bowing in fast and slow time, the effect of rests, when to use two consecutive down-bows or up-bows, and how to play them. Since all these points have been discussed and illustrated in earlier chapters (cf. p. 157 and p. 256), they need not be repeated in detail here. However, two instances of Leopold Mozart's application of the Rule of Down-Bow are instructive. He deals with triple time in a broad musical way, relating it to the Rule and to its musical context:

'When in triple time only quarter-notes occur, two notes of the three must [according to the Rule of Down-Bow] always be taken together in one stroke. . . . Now the question is, whether the first or last two notes should be slurred or detached? Both depend on the cantilena of the piece and on the good taste and sound judgement of the performer, if the composer has forgotten to mark the slurs, or has himself not understood how to do so. Still, the following rule can serve to some extent: Notes at close intervals should usually be slurred, but notes far apart should be played with separate strokes and in particular should be arranged to give a pleasant variety.'[14]

In the second instance, Mozart gives consecutive up-bows after rests, a bowing that is usual today and that is a consistent extension of the Rule of Down-Bow (Ex. 157).

Ex. 157

L. Mozart

The main developments in the eighteenth century were concerned with more varied applications of the Rule and certain modifications of it. The insistence on down-bow at the beginning of every measure was modified, even by the orthodox; and there were others, like Geminiani, who rejected the Rule completely. L'Abbé le fils does not even mention the Rule as such, although many of his bowed examples are broadly consistent with it, including the old *craquer* bowing (see p. 260 and p. 421). L'Abbé also allows for down-bow every other measure (as in Ex. 158) and his bowing is apparently affected, as regards the length of the stroke, by a consideration of the *notes inégales* (see ch. 21 and Ex. 239b). In Ex. 158, taken from Leopold Mozart, down-bow comes on the first note of every other measure, not every measure, of triple time; and in Ex. 81e (see p. 261), the same principle of alternate down-bow and up-bow is applied to a gigue. The latter example comes from the seventeenth century, but examples similar to it can be found in Quantz, who, moreover, stresses the point that a good effect from such passages depends on the down-bow and up-bow being equally weighted.[15]

Ex. 158

L. Mozart

---

[14] Mozart, ch. 4, paras. 28–29. English translation, p. 83.
[15] Quantz advises the player to practise figures such as Ex. 81e so that the sound of down-bow will be equated with the sound of up-bow, but he admits that in especially sharply separated notes, down-bow has an advantage over up-bow (see his ch. XVII, sec. 2, para. 11).

Tempo also exerts a powerful and modifying force on the bowing. In rapid time, for instance, the use of slurs is much more common (cf. Ex. 77b: the bowing in slow time is indicated above, and that for fast time below, the example). In such patterns as those in Ex. 159a, played at *presto*, the dotted figure is taken in one up-bow, the 'bow is lifted at the dot and the first note perceptibly separated from the last—the latter being deferred till the last moment'. When the figure is reversed (Ex. 159b), it is simply slurred without separation.[16] In short, although the Rule of Down-Bow was modified, it remained a guiding force in the eighteenth century. Its spirit still persists today.

Ex. 159

Terminology and signs

The signs and terms for down-bow and up-bow in the early eighteenth century are numerous and varied. The most usual follow. For the first time we have Spanish terms (from Herrando, 1756).

	Down-bow	Up-bow
England:	d	u
France:	t (*tiré*)	p (*poussé*)
Germany:	*Herabstrich or Abstrich*	*Hinaufstrich or Aufstrich*
Italy:	g (*giù*)	s (*su*)
Spain:	O	A

To this should be added certain comments:

1. In France, p (*poussé* = up-bow) should not be confused with p (*piano* = soft). In French music, soft is commonly indicated by d (*doux*).

2. In Germany, Wagenseil's *Rudimenta Panduristae* (1754) uses strokes under the lines or notes to mean down-bow; strokes over the lines or notes to mean up-bow.

3. In Italy, Veracini's Op. 2 (1744) uses the following signs and terms: ⌐ = *arcata in giù* = down-bow; ⌐ = *arcata in su* = up-bow.

---

[16] For these examples and the quotation, see Mozart, ch. 4, paras. 11 and 12. English translation, pp. 76–77.

CHAPTER EIGHTEEN

⟨∾∾⟩

The Technique of the Violin, 1700-61 (III): Bow Strokes and Their Execution

OWING indications, such as slurs and staccato marks, appear with increasing frequency in the early eighteenth century. When these marks are totally absent or very sparsely furnished it is not necessarily safe to assume that the score in question represents the composer's intentions or that the music is then performed simply with individual bow strokes alternately down and up. As Leopold Mozart says (see p. 402 above), the bowing depends 'on the good taste and sound judgement of the performer, *if the composer has forgotten to mark the slurs, or has himself not understood how to do so*'. (Italics added.) In such situations a knowledge of the Rule of Down-Bow and its numerous applications is very helpful as a guide to the insertion of bowings in various musical contexts. On the other hand, the bowings indicated by a composer should be set aside only after the most careful scrutiny and consideration. Bach's bowings to the unaccompanied violin sonatas, generally disregarded by modern violinists as 'impractical', should be studied carefully and adhered to as far as possible. To quote Leopold Mozart again: variations of bowings are 'usually indicated by a sensible composer and must be observed exactly'.[1]

A confusing situation sometimes arises when similar or even identical passages in the same piece are bowed in different ways by the composer. To a layman or even to editors, such bowings may appear to be errors or at least inconsistencies. But this is not necessarily so to the player, since the context may require a change either musically or technically. It may be, too, that different bowings of the same passage are given merely for variety's sake.

An important key to the type of bowing and, if need be, to the insertion of bowings, is the character of the music itself. This point is increasingly

---

[1] Leopold Mozart, ch. 6, para. 3. English translation, p. 104.

stressed in the eighteenth century. Both Mozart and Quantz have a good deal to say about this. The former remarks, 'Merry and playful passages must be played with light, short, and lifted strokes, happily and rapidly; just as in slow, sad pieces one performs them with long strokes of the bow, simply and tenderly.'[2] Quantz takes account of the different bowings in French and Italian style, in cheerful and sad pieces, and in different kinds of dances. He tells the violinist to moderate his bow stroke in sad pieces, not moving the bow with violence or with too great a speed.[3] In accompanying lively pieces, he says, the short articulated French stroke is better than the longer drawn-out stroke of the Italians. Sixteenths in *allegretto* and eighths in *allegro* are best performed with a short bow stroke made with the wrist, not with the whole arm; and the strokes are more separated than drawn out (*mehr tockiret als gezogen*).[4] French dance music must frequently be played seriously with a heavy, but short and sharp, bowing; and the bow strokes are more lifted (*abgesetzen*) than slurred.[5] Quantz gives particulars of many of the French dances and the bow strokes appropriate to them. For example, the *Bourrée* and the *Gigue* are both played with short, light bow strokes. The *Canarie*, although similar in tempo to the *Gigue*, uses short, sharp bow strokes to bring out its dotted-note style.[6]

Finally, Tartini (or some of his pupils) distinguishes an instrumental style (*sonabile*) from that which is vocally inspired (*cantabile*). In the latter the melody moves by step and should be performed legato; in the former the melody moves by leaps and should be played in a detached manner.[7]

The individual bow stroke

Individual bow strokes were used at all tempi for notes of various duration and with different degrees of articulation and nuance. The normal bow stroke was a non-legato stroke (see p. 395); and to it, depending on its length, tempo, and musical context, various nuances were applied. Geminiani deals with nuance, as applied to bowing, in Example XX of *The Art of Playing on*

---

[2] Mozart, ch. 12, para. 18. English translation, p. 223.
[3] Quantz, ch. XVII, sec. 3, para. 9.
[4] Quantz, ch. XVII, sec. 2, para. 26.
[5] Quantz, ch. XVII, sec. 7, para. 56.
[6] Quantz, ch. XVII, sec. 7, para. 58. See also Barbara Seagrave, as per p. 262, note 9.
[7] See the 'Rules for Bowing' (*Regole per le Arcate*) printed in Erwin Jacobi's edition of Tartini's *Traité des Agrémens* (see p. 362). Whether these rules are by Tartini or his pupil Nicolai is immaterial to this context. It is unfortunate, however, that the English translation of the 'Rules' renders the Italian term *sonabile* as 'allegro music', an inaccurate and meaningless phrase. Since the sixteenth century, *cantare* and *sonare* were used to distinguish vocal and instrumental music, respectively; and hence *sonabile* = instrumental. Moreover, if *sonabile* is translated as 'allegro music', it is very difficult to distinguish fast from slow instrumental style. Yet there are numerous examples of slow movements in instrumental style (e.g. *Largo e staccato*), which the 'Rules' characterize as disjunct style.

the Violin. In the section devoted to individual bow strokes he labels as 'good' those nuanced (━━) half-notes, quarters, and eighths that occur in *adagio* or *andante*, but the same played with 'plain' (non-legato) strokes are labelled as 'mediocre' or 'bad'. In *allegro* or *presto* the same situation obtains with respect to individual half- and quarter-notes: they are good if nuanced, but mediocre if played 'plain'. At this tempo individual sixteenths played with 'plain' strokes are called 'good', presumably because the notes are too fast to be nuanced; but 'plain' eighths are called 'very bad'. The 'good' eighths are bowed with staccato strokes.

After Geminiani, both Mozart and L'Abbé le fils deal with the application of nuance to bow strokes, individual and otherwise. Mozart's Divisions (p. 395) and L'Abbé le fils's *enflé* and *diminué* (p. 396) are examples. A special effect, prophetic of the future, is used by L'Abbé. He applies a continuous *crescendo* to a passage of fourteen ascending thirty-second notes, whether bowed with individual strokes or played with one bow stroke under a slur from the beginning to end.

The variety of rapid passagework played with individual strokes increased. Tartini illustrates this point when, in his famous 'Letter', he gives a passage in sixteenth-notes 'to acquire a greater facility of executing swift passages in a light and neat manner', and his illustration (Ex. 160) requires the violinist to skip strings systematically in a type of bowing called *brisure* by the French (see below).

Tartini

Ex. 160

Broken chord passages or arpeggios are sometimes played with individual strokes and sometimes slurred; and these different manners of bowing are distinguished later by terms. J. J. Rousseau defines a *batterie* as a continuous arpeggio with all the notes detached, not slurred as in an arpeggio.[8] Sometimes a *modèle de la batterie* is shown for passages written out in chord form.[9] Among modern writers, Pincherle defines a *batterie* as a formula that comprises repetitions either of a note or of a design. He distinguishes *brisure* as a type of *batterie* where the bow plays on two non-adjacent strings (cf. Ex. 160).[10]

[8] J. J. Rousseau, *Dictionnaire de musique*, Paris, 1768, article 'Batterie'. François Couperin (*L'Art de toucher le clavecin*, Paris, 1716) says that 'batteries' or 'arpègemens' had their origin in the 'sonades' (i.e. the Italian sonatas).
[9] See, for instance, Michel Corrette, *L'Art de se perfectionner dans le violon*, Paris, 1782, pp. 35, 43, and 46. For models of arpeggios (slurred), see p. 439 below.
[10] See Pincherle's article referred to on p. 227, note 18. *Brisure* is similarly defined by La Laurencie, *L'École française*, Vol. I, p. 328.

Slurred bowings

In simple slurred bowings the principal difficulty involved is the number of notes to be taken in one bow stroke and the ordering of the down-bow and up-bow. The latter follow the principles of the Rule of Down-Bow. As in the seventeenth century, it is customary to emphasize and prolong slightly the beginning note of the slurred group. The number of notes now included under one slur is often greater than formerly, although the German virtuosi at the end of the seventeenth century had included a large number under a single slur in isolated cases. When in 1731 the violinist Castrucci, 'first violin of the opera [of Handel]', boasted that he took 'twenty-four notes in one bow',[11] it was not that this feat had not been done before, but that it was remarkable for the general average of violinists. (For the meaning of *tenue* and *liaison*, see p. 265, note 17). By 1761, however, L'Abbé le fils was occasionally putting as many as thirty-six notes under one slur.[12]

The special types of slurred bowings introduced in the seventeenth century continued and were sometimes elaborated in the early eighteenth. These included syncopated bowings, *ondeggiando*, *bariolage*, and repeated notes (*tremolo*) slurred and unslurred (for these terms, see p. 265). Slurred *tremolo* is found in Bach and Handel, for instance (see p. 422). The use of the *bariolage* is extended in the early eighteenth century. This type of bowing may be played either as a slurred bowing or one in which the notes are played with individual bow strokes. Vivaldi introduces the *bariolage* on the two lower strings (Ex. 161a) without slurs. Locatelli's *Caprice* to the last

Ex. 161 (a   Vivaldi

(b   L'Abbé de fils

movement of Concerto I, Op. 3, opens with a slurred *bariolage* on the D and G strings. L'Abbé le fils calls for a slurred *bariolage* (Ex. 161b) that acts like a soprano pedal in the figuration. Bach writes a remarkable unslurred *bariolage* in the Prelude to his Third Partita for unaccompanied violin, which requires the use of three rather than two strings.

The combination of types of individual notes and slurred groups leads to many varieties of 'mixed' bowings, which are also conventionally combined with nuance (as in Geminiani's Ex. XX from *The Art of Playing on the Violin*).

---

[11] See Burney, *General History* (reprint), Vol. II, p. 770, note 'm'.
[12] L'Abbé le fils, *Principes*, p. 79.

These mixed bowings, however, depend also on the use of various types of staccato, which should be discussed first.

The violin staccato in the early eighteenth century

The term *staccato* is subject to various shades of meaning and styles of execution. Staccato means different things to the pianist and the violinist; and to the violinist in the eighteenth century the term conveyed something quite different than it does now. The modern violin staccato means a series of *martelé* (hammered) strokes taken in one bow stroke. The bow stays on the string, and consists of a series of biting attacks and releases. These strokes cannot be played much above moderate speed. In modern violin playing a stroke may also be played detached, keeping the bow on the string between strokes (no *martelé*). If the notes are not too fast, they may be played off the string by a controlled 'thrown' stroke involving the wrist and fingers. Rapid individual strokes are frequently played detached by means of a bow stroke which is due to a natural bounce of the bow from the elasticity of the bow stick. This is done in the middle (sometimes above the middle) of the bow and is called *spiccato* or *sautillé*, the latter occasionally being distinguished in certain technical respects.[13]

In the eighteenth century the term *staccato* indicated a separation between notes. This was its general meaning for all music, and in this general meaning *staccato* or *stoccato* was generally synonymous with *spiccato*, *détaché*, *piqué*, and *pointé* (the last two could also refer to dotted notes in the sense of a dotted eighth). In 1703 Brossard's *Dictionary* defines the term as follows:

> '*Staccato* or *Stoccato* means almost the same thing as spiccato. That is to say that all stringed instruments should make such strokes dry without dragging (*traîner*) and well detached or separated from each other —almost what we call in French *Picqué* or *Pointé*.'

Brossard exerted great influence on the terminology of the eighteenth century, especially on younger lexicographers and theorists in England, France and Germany. James Grassineau, who used Brossard for the basis of

---

[13] There is almost as much confusion today with respect to terms for bow strokes and particularly their notation as there was in the eighteenth century and earlier. On the whole, modern terms are somewhat clearer than modern notation. The meanings of the terms given above are relatively clear as far as they go—some commonly used bow strokes, such as the 'thrown stroke' just mentioned, have no generally accepted names. On the other hand, the notation is often ambiguous. A common notation for individual *martelé* strokes is the dot (·) over a note, and, reasonably enough, dots over notes under slurs are used to indicate the modern staccato (slurred *martelé*). Nevertheless, wedge-shaped signs (▼) or tear-drop shapes (♦) are sometimes used to mean the same thing. Today, however, these wedges or tear-drop shapes are more commonly used than dots to indicate spiccato or *sautillé*. Often the distinction has to be made either by the specific term or by context.

his *A Musical Dictionary* (1740), gives the same definition.[14] Corrette says (1738): 'Staccato or spiccato ought to be played dryly without dragging and very detached'—strangely reminiscent of Brossard; and the Germans such as Majer (1732) and J. G. Walther give similar definitions. Walther gives an additional term, *Punctus percutiens* (lat.), which, he says,

> 'means the kind of dot that in both vocal and instrumental pieces is set over or under the notes to indicate that such notes should be separated (*abgestossen*). If slurs stand over or under dots in instrumental pieces, they must be executed in one bow stroke.'[15]

Roger North uses the picturesque phrase 'Stoccata or Stabb', and he says 'old Sigr. Nichola Matteis used this manner to set off a rage'.[16] L'Abbé le fils's term is *détaché*, and he notates staccato passages with strokes (ı) above or below the notes concerned. The same notation is used by Rameau in his harpsichord pieces (1731, 1736), but he calls the notation *son coupé*. In Italian the word *puntato* (dotted) is sometimes used to describe the staccato style in the sense of notes with dots above or below them. It is also used at times to describe 'dotted' notes such as dotted eighths.

Sometimes whole movements are indicated as 'staccato' to save writing out the signs throughout a whole section that is to be played staccato. In Veracini's Op. 2 several slow movements contrast staccato sections (marked *Largo e staccato*) with alternating ones specifically marked *cantabile*. In Sonata VIII, movement 2, the beginning section is marked *Ritornello Largo e Staccato*, the following section being labelled *cantabile*. Thereupon the *Ritornello* returns, and the staccato strokes are put over individual notes. Another *cantabile* section continues the movement, which concludes with a section in slurred staccato (marked with strokes under slurs). Similar indications could be duplicated many times in the music of the eighteenth century, and they are not limited to *Largo* movements. In his *Acis and Galatea*, for instance, Handel uses the terms *Allegro e Staccato* and *Andante e Staccato*.

The general effect of the eighteenth-century staccato is a detaching or noticeable degree of articulation.[17] At moderate tempo the staccato applied to quarter-notes normally results in dividing the written note half into sound and half into rest. It also results in some feeling of accent. The manner

---

[14] Grassineau gives another and novel term, which he takes from Brossard: *Tronco per grazia* (*coup de grâce*). Grassineau defines this term as 'a small silence between each sound; which has a very good effect in expressions of grief, to make sighs, and also in expressions of wonder and surprise, etc.'

[15] This last sentence constitutes a definition of our 'slurred staccato', discussed below.

[16] *Roger North on Music*, p. 168.

[17] On the subject of articulation in general, see Hermann Keller, *Phrasierung und Artikulation*, Kassel, 1955. On the meaning of staccato signs in Wolfgang Mozart, see the same author's *Die Bedeutung der Zeichen Keil, Strich und Punkt bei Mozart*, Kassel, 1957.

of performing the staccato differs at different tempi. As Quantz says, 'in adagio, the staccato is not as short as in allegro, otherwise the adagio would sound too dry and thin'.

The various terms for staccato, given above, are all used for music in general. To some extent the same may be said for the signs which indicate degrees of staccato. However, the three principal signs involved were more closely connected with violin playing than the performance of other types of music: the dot (·), the stroke (ı), and the wedge (▼). Tear-drop shapes are not common at this time. A hard and fast distinction between these signs simply cannot be drawn, because it often does not exist, these signs sometimes being used interchangeably by printers. If any generality is valid at all, it is that strokes are more commonly used than dots to indicate staccato. Some scores, however, especially French ones, use the dot where it would be more usual to write the stroke. The stroke and wedge are even more closely identified, and no distinction between them, as regards execution, is possible. The situation is different when dots and strokes (or wedges) occur in the same score, the staccato stroke (or wedge) then generally meaning a greater degree of articulation.[18]

By the eighteenth century it had become customary to indicate a staccato style by terms or by the signs just mentioned, as Quantz specifically says (see below). But not always. Apparently there were certain well-understood conventions according to which a detached style was understood and played without specific directions. 'In quick pieces', says Leopold Mozart of Ex. 162,

L. Mozart

Ex. 162

'the bow is lifted at each dot: therefore each note is separated from the other and performed in springing style.'[19] In discussing the performance of the *Entrée, Loure,* and *Courante,* Quantz remarks, 'the bow is lifted at every quarter-note whether there is a dot [staccato dot] or not'.[20] Quantz also points to special cases where a note is shortened. He gives the general rule that where an appoggiatura is preceded by the same note, the latter is shortened.[21] His example is shown in our Ex. 163. Quantz also distinguishes

---

[18] Since specific signs are used for the staccato, it is clear that the normal stroke was not staccato, although, as explained above, the normal bow stroke was probably a more articulated (non-legato) stroke than is usual in modern playing. For these reasons there is no justification for modern performances which make all the notes detached, especially in playing the *basso continuo.* This practice, which is widespread, is neither aesthetically convincing nor historically correct.

[19] Leopold Mozart, ch. I, sec. 3, para. 10. English translation, p. 41.

[20] Quantz, ch. XVII, sec. 7, para. 58.

[21] Quantz gives this rule on three separate occasions: ch. XII, para. 15; ch. VI, sec. 1, para. 8; and especially ch. XVII, sec. 2, para. 8.

between quarters and eighths with respect to maintaining written-note
values in the context of rapid notes or rapid tempo:

'In allegro assai, where thirty-seconds are the fastest notes, the eighths
must usually be played short [*kurz gestossen*] by means of the tongue
[he is discussing the flute in this connexion], but the quarters on the
other hand are to be played cantabile and sustained.'[22]

Ex. 163

The performance of the individual (unslurred) staccato note

In the eighteenth century there are various ways of executing the
different forms of the violin staccato. To understand the whole range of
detached strokes, we must begin with the normal individual bow stroke of
the time, as compared to that in vogue today. To review: the normal bow
stroke of today is basically a legato stroke in which the single stroke is bound
to the following stroke by a bow change effected as smoothly as possible.
For this kind of stroke the remarkably inappropriate term *détaché* is general
at the present time. A true detached stroke is rarely called *détaché* nowadays,
and the old and original meaning of 'detached' survives only in the sense
that single notes are played detached as single notes and not played as
slurred groups. Compared to the legato individual stroke used today, the
normal eighteenth-century stroke was already a non-legato, that is to say,
somewhat detached by modern standards, and the slight 'give' at the beginning and end of this stroke (if played rapidly) is close to the sound of our
spiccato now. (For the sound of the non-legato stroke and the different
staccatos, cf. our recording.)

When a degree of articulation greater than this non-legato was desired,
eighteenth-century composers used a staccato sign. In slow tempo or for
notes of any duration, individual notes marked *staccato* were performed with
'lifted' (controlled) bow. At faster tempi the bow remained on the string,
although the *effect* may have been that of a slight bounce, as in today's
spiccato. German terminology of the eighteenth century is particularly
interesting in the use of terms reflecting these distinctions. The most
general and all-embracing term for detaching is *staccato*. If a detached stroke,
without lifted bow, is to be indicated, the terms *gestossen* (or *abgestossen*),
tockiret, or *abgesondert* are usual. In explaining Ex. 164, where staccato strokes
(1) are written over individual notes, Leopold Mozart uses the terms *recht*

22 Quantz, ch. XII, para. 22. For a distinction between legato and staccato styles in the
organ music of Bach's time, see Philipp Spitta, *The Life of Bach*, English translation,
3 vols., London, 1899, Vol. II, p. 301.

abgestossen and *abgesondert* to indicate separation. He says nothing about lifted bow, as he does later in other contexts. In his definitions of 'stoccato or staccato', he uses the term *gestossen*, and says the notes are 'to be well separated (*absondern*) with short strokes and without dragging the bow'.[23] There is no mention of 'lifting'.

Ex. 164

For the 'lifted' (off-string) stroke—apparently controlled by the fingers and wrist rather than bounced—Quantz's term is *Absetzen* (*abgesetzet*; *etwas abgesetzet*).[24] Mozart uses *Aufheben* or *Erheben* interchangeably to mean the same thing.

Quantz is especially illuminating on the question of staccato. He uses *staccato* and *abgestossen* (*gestossen*) in the general sense of separated or 'pushed'. Under certain conditions, he uses *staccato*—but not *abgestossen* (*gestossen*)—in the particular sense of 'lifted' bow. As just mentioned, his specific term for the latter is *Absetzung*. Quantz's description, although wordy, should be quoted in full:

'If a piece is labelled staccato, the notes must all be played short and with lifted (*abgesetzet*) bow [for exception made by Quantz, see below]. But since, at the present time, one is seldom accustomed to set a piece with the same kind of notes throughout but rather with a mixture [of different kinds] of notes, the little strokes are written over those notes which require the staccato.

In such notes one must proceed according to the tempo, whether the piece is played very slow or very fast, for the notes in an adagio are not separated (*abstossen*) as shortly as they are in allegro; otherwise those in adagio would sound too dry and thin (*mager*). The general rule which one can give is this: when little strokes stand over notes, these notes must sound half as long as they are worth. But if a little stroke stands over a note after which some notes of smaller worth follow, the note is not only to be played half as short [as it is written] but it is also at the same time to be accented with bow-pressure [approaching the *martelé* or Mozart's 'Division II'?].

Thus eighths are made out of quarters, and sixteenths out of eighths [i.e. a stroke over a quarter-note makes its sound equivalent to an eighth, etc.].

[23] Mozart, ch. 1, sec. 3, para. 20, and under 'Technical Terms'. English translation, pp. 47 and 51.
[24] Quantz, ch. XVII, sec. 2, para. 27; and elsewhere.

As noted above, the bow must be somewhat lifted (*etwas abgesetzet*) from the string in the case of notes over which there are strokes. By this I mean only in the case of such notes as the time permits. Thus in allegro the eighths and in allegretto the sixteenths are excluded if many of them follow one another: for these must be played with quite a short bow stroke, but the bow is never lifted (*abgesetzet*) or separated (*entfernet*) from the string. For if one always lifted (*Aufheben*) the bow as far as is required for the so-called *Absetzen*, there would not be time enough to return the bow [to the string], and this way of playing would make the notes sound as if they were hacked or whipped.

In an adagio the notes which furnish the movement under the con-certato [solo] voice can be regarded as half-staccato, even if no little strokes stand over them, and consequently a small silence can be observed between each note.

If dots (*Puncte*) stand over notes, they must be touched boldly (*tockiret*)[25] or pushed (*gestossen*) but not lifted (*abgesetzet*). If over the dots there is a slur, the notes included must be taken in one bow stroke and marked with [bow] pressure.'[26]

Quantz notes that lifted bow in eighths in allegro would be too fast. But this is the *one* time that Geminiani claims the staccato is 'good'. Since Geminiani says that in the staccato 'the Bow is taken off the Strings at every Note', one would think, with Quantz (see p. 412), that his eighths in allegro would sound 'hacked or whipped'. Perhaps Quantz's allegro was faster than Geminiani's, or perhaps Geminiani—a soloist as opposed to Quantz's orchestral players—was able to play these eighths in a way that was not 'hacked or whipped'. Geminiani's attitude is not at all clear. Whereas Quantz allows staccato in both fast and slow tempi, and, where the time permits, will have the staccato executed with lifted bow, Geminiani tolerates no staccato whatever in adagio or andante. At this tempo he labels staccato quarters, eighths, and sixteenths as 'bad' (*cattivo*) or 'to be used under special circumstances' (*particolare*). In allegro or presto Geminiani labels sixteenths 'bad', but the identical passage with plain bow 'on the string' he labels 'good'. He calls staccato eighths 'good' in allegro (Ex. 165a),

---

25 *Tockieren* means literally 'to paint with a few bold touches of the brush' (Muret-Sanders).

26 Quantz, ch. XVII, sec. 2, para. 27. Quantz uses the word *abgesetzet* in his chapter 'On good Performance in Singing and Playing generally' (ch. XI, para. 11). He says, 'The sustained and "flattering" notes must be played legato; but the gay and skipping notes must be "lifted" (*abgesetzet*) and separated from one another.' In this section, describing playing in general, the word *abgesetzet* cannot mean 'lifted bow' in the case of the voice and all the instruments; and hence its general meaning is simply *staccato* in this connexion. However, in its context of string music, there is no doubt that it means to play staccato by means of 'lifted' bow.

while the eighths mixed in with a slur are called 'better' (Ex. 165b). He gives no series of staccato quarters at this tempo, but the mixed bowing in Ex. 166 he considers 'best' (*ottimo*).

Ex. 165

a) "Buono"

Geminiani

b) "Meglio"

Ex. 166

Geminiani

"Ottimo"

The individual bow strokes, then, include a normal ('on-string') non-legato stroke[27] plus a staccato stroke, either on the string or a controlled 'lifted' stroke, off or somewhat off the string. According to Quantz (above), the staccato stroke (ꟷ) over a note meant a lifted bow when the tempo permitted. The staccato dot (·) meant that a detached bow stroke remained on the string.

It is possible, but not clearly established, that still another bow stroke, in which the bow actually bounced (as in the modern *sautillé* or spiccato), was included in the general notion of staccato. In his sonatas of 1712, Piani expressly uses the French term *sautillé*, which implies bounding bow. He uses dots over series of notes without slurs for '*notes égales articulées et un peu détachées*'. This description is inconclusive in itself, but a special meaning is suggested for '*articulées*' by the distinction in Mondonville's *Les Sons Harmoniques* (*c.* 1738) between *détatché* [sic] and *articulation* (Ex. 167), which

Mondonville

Ex. 167

"détatché" "articulation"
[sic]

clearly implies the difference between a *détaché* bowing and a bounding bow. Elsewhere, however, the term *articulé* frequently appears to mean 'detached' or 'articulated' without implying lifted or bounding bow.[28]

Nevertheless, it seems clear that, in the main, the rapid, individual staccato note was executed by an articulated, but not lifted, bow stroke. Quantz is quite definite on this point (see above), and Tartini suggests the same thing when he explains how to play one of Corelli's *perpetuum mobile*

[27] This is the equivalent of Geminiani's 'plain stroke' on the string. By the time of L'Abbé le fils (1761), it is probable that the 'plain' stroke began to approach the modern legato. In any case, L'Abbé le fils is the first to mention the use of the fingers, which are essential to make the smoothest change from one individual bow stroke to another, as in modern playing.

[28] Leopold Mozart may also be suggesting a bounding stroke with the passage cited above on p. 405. For the implication of *égales* in the passage above, see p. 477.

movements in staccato fashion.[29] In Ex. 168, taken from the 'Letter', Tartini
indicates that the written notes are to be played half as sound and half as rest
(the usual method) with the bow 'distaccato' and 'a little space between one
note and the other'. He says nothing about lifted bow. Similarly, Leopold
Mozart contrasts ways of playing, using the staccato.[30] He does not mention

Ex. 168

lifted bow in connexion with playing individual sixteenths in staccato
(Ex. 169a). Lifted bow is to be used in the slurred staccato (Ex. 169b). In all
this there is no evidence of the modern *martelé*. The eighteenth-century
staccato must have resulted in a species of accent, but not in the special
explosive style of biting pressure and sudden release, characteristic of the
martelé.

Ex. 169

The musical examples and explanatory text which Quantz gives are
particularly instructive. In Ex. 170 each of the repeated notes has an individual bow stroke, and the bow must be taken off the string (*abgesetzet*) after
the syncopated note.[31] As mentioned above, when the appoggiatura is preceded by the same note, the latter is shortened by means of a lifted stroke (cf.

Ex. 170

Ex. 163). When in rapid tempo eighths or sixteenths follow a quarter on the
downbeat (Ex. 171a), the quarter is played down-bow and the bow is lifted
(*abgesetzet*); then the following eighth is played down-bow. In Ex. 171b (no
tempo given), the last of the first three notes that begin the first full

Ex. 171

[29] In his 'Letter'. See Jacobi's edition of the *Traité*, pp. 134–5.
[30] Mozart, ch. 7, sec. 1, paras. 5–7. English translation, pp. 115–16.
[31] Quantz, ch. XVII, sec. 2, para. 8, and *Tabellen* XXII, Fig. 2.

measure must be lifted (*abgesetzet*) a bit to separate it from the downbeat (*Niederschlage*). If two sixteenths follow an eighth (Ex. 171c), the eighth must be accented with the bow and '*abgesetzet*', as if a stroke (ı) stood over the note. In Ex. 172 the execution of the same passage in slow and fast time is contrasted. In slow time (Ex. 172a) Quantz recommends taking all four sixteenths of the first group with one bow, making, however, a small '*Absetzung*' of the bow on the first note. In fast time (Ex. 172b) the four-note group is played as if the first note were marked with a staccato stroke and the following three with a simple slur. Nothing is said about lifted bow in this connexion, and one may assume that an accented detached stroke on the string was intended.[32]

Ex. 172

Slurred staccato

There are numerous instances where two or more notes, each with a dot or stroke, stand under a slur. In this case, the notes are detached in one of several ways, but all the notes under the slur are played in one bow stroke. In this book the general term for this type of staccato is *slurred staccato*. Are there distinctions between the slurred staccato with dots and that with strokes? Do different tempi imply a different execution of the slurred staccato?

Although dots under a slur sometimes mean the same thing as strokes under a slur, certain distinctions may be made between them, just as one may distinguish at times between individual notes with strokes and those with dots (see p. 410). The slurred staccato using dots is more common in andante or adagio, and is generally played on the string, resembling a *portato* (see our Index). Slurred staccato using strokes is more closely identified with fast time, and is often played in 'lifted' style.[33] Quantz's comments on the slurred staccato are to the point:

---

[32] The esoteric term *sticcato pastorale* has nothing to do with the type of staccato explained above. The *sticcato pastorale* is an instrument, apparently a species of xylophone. Eitner (*Quellenlexikon*) lists under James Bremner: 'Instructions for the *Sticcato pastorale* (Strohfidel), London, R. Bremner.' A 'Strohfidel' (strawfiddle) is a xylophone according to Curt Sachs (*History of Instruments*, p. 440). Bremner's treatise must have been published about 1763. In that year R. Bremner, its publisher, established a business in London, and James Bremner, its author, left shortly afterwards for Philadelphia, where he gave lessons to Francis Hopkinson (Bremner was a violinist and harpsichordist).

[33] In his discussion of staccato strokes over individual notes (no slur), Quantz says that they are played staccato with lifted bow 'in so far as the tempo permits'. But this remark is not applicable to the slurred staccato (for which, see below).

'When [simple] slurs are used, the notes should not be *gerücket* or
tockiret [i.e. pushed or touched boldly] as would happen with dots
under slurs [see Ex. 173]. But with strokes under slurs, the notes are
sharply separated in one bow stroke. For there is a distinction to make
between strokes and dots just as there is when the note stands alone
without slurs: namely that the notes with strokes are played lifted,
but those with dots must be played with a short bow stroke and not
lifted (*unterhalten*); the same distinction obtains when slurs stand
over the notes.'[34]

Ex. 173

Quantz says nothing about tempo distinctions, as he does previously
(p. 413), relative to lifted bow and staccato.

Mozart's definitions are similar to Quantz's. The dots under a slur
(Ex. 174a) are separated from each other by a slight pressure of the bow (no
lifting mentioned), 'so that all these notes within the slur must be taken in
one bow stroke but must be entirely separated from each other'. With
respect to the strokes under a slur in Ex. 174b, Mozart continues, 'The first

Ex. 174

note of this example is taken down-bow, but the remaining three notes are
taken with a lifted bow for each note, and are played up-bow with each note
detached from the other by a strong attack (*Abstoss*).'[35] In the whole of
Mozart's treatise staccato dots (as opposed to staccato strokes) occur only
under slurs and then in three places only. To judge by the context, his dots
under slurs probably indicate a *portato*.

Ex. 175

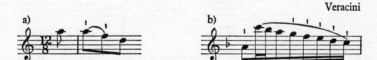

In Veracini's Op. 2 the notation of the slurred staccato is unique. Dots
and strokes stand *outside* the slur, not between it and the notes (Ex. 175a).
There are no slurred staccato groups indicated in the usual way. Ex. 175b is
an unusual instance of a slurred group, partly with and partly without

[34] Quantz, ch. XVII, sec. 2, para. 12.
[35] Leopold Mozart, ch. 1, sec. 3, para. 17. English translation, p. 45.

staccato signs, as indicated in Veracini's (or his printer's) special method. Ex. 175c is still more remarkable. The strokes are above the notes, and the slur below. These unusual methods of notating the slurred staccato do not affect the performance of the slurred staccato, which is the same as that written in the conventional way.

Ex. 175c

Veracini

Leopold Mozart is consistent in directing that slurred staccato with strokes be played with 'lifted' bow; and he gives many examples in duple and triple time in all sorts of groupings from two to twenty-five notes, both down-bow and up-bow.[36] In the triplet figure shown in Ex. 176, the slurred staccato is obtained by 'lifting' (*Erhebung*) the bow. In his section on bowing

Ex. 176

L. Mozart

'even' notes, Mozart gives a considerable variety of slurred staccato groups, six of which are illustrated in Ex. 177 (in this example Mozart's order is not preserved). Each involves lifting of the bow. No. 3, called later the 'drum stroke' by Flesch (and seldom used today), requires the lifted stroke in down-bow as well as in up-bow (cf. our recording). The last note of No. 6 is

Ex. 177

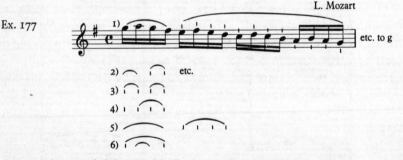

L. Mozart

etc. to g

done with a quick lift. No. 1 calls for special instructions. Just as one learns to slur a whole measure or even two measures all in one bow stroke, says Mozart, one must learn to detach many notes in one stroke. The twelve notes of this slurred staccato are taken up-bow in a quick lift (*geschwinde Erhebung*). In particular, Mozart says:

---

[36] In all Mozart's examples there is only one case of slurred staccato with strokes where lifted bow is not specifically mentioned (cf. ch. 6, para. 11).

'This style of performance will be somewhat difficult to the beginner. A certain restraint (*Mässigung*) of the right hand is necessary to it, and a retarding of the bow. This is more easily shown or discovered by oneself by practice than can be explained with words. The weight of a violin bow contributes much, as does also in no less degree its length or shortness. A heavier and longer bow must be used more lightly and retarded somewhat less; whereas a lighter and shorter bow must be pressed down more and retarded more. Above all, the right hand must be made a little stiff here, but the contracting and relaxing of the same must be regulated according to the weight and length, or the lightness and shortness of the bow. The notes must be played in an even tempo, with even strength, and not over-hurried or, so to speak, swallowed. But in particular you must know how to hold back and guide the bow in such fashion that towards the end of the second bar so much strength remains over, that the crotchet note (G) at the end of the passage in the same stroke can be distinguished by a noticeable accent.'[37]

This clearly implies that the passage is to go on as a slurred staccato for another measure until the open G of the lowest string is reached. In that case, the slurred staccato would consist of twenty-four notes plus the final quarter-note on the open G string. (How is this done? A species of *martelé*? A 'flying staccato'?)

Leopold Mozart's example of bowing in triple time is also extraordinarily interesting. The notes shown in Ex. 178 are bowed in some thirty-four ways,

Ex. 178

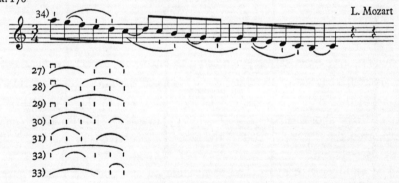

the last eight (Nos. 27–34) all being slurred staccato. The original numbering is retained in our example. The individual staccato strokes in these bowings are to be played short, but no lifting is mentioned. On the other hand, the slurred staccato is taken in one bow and the notes must be

[37] Leopold Mozart, ch. 7, sec. 1, para. 17. Although most of this passage has been quoted earlier (p. 270), we repeat it here, since it is important to our immediate context.

detached by a lift of the bow. Note that Mozart systematically gives both down-bow and up-bow for this lifted stroke. The most advanced and interesting of these bowings is the last (No. 34), which is written out in full in Ex. 178. The other variant bowings, each of which simply repeats the established pattern of its first measure, are given below the example. In No. 34 Mozart writes not only slurred staccatos but also slurs within slurs. The patterns of slurred staccato come out both down-bow and up-bow, and the bowing pattern itself gives a syncopated effect, being composed of four eighths in 3/4 time (cf. our recording).

Ex. 179

Lifted bow is involved in playing certain dotted figures—dotted in the sense of dotted eighth-notes. The dotted note is somewhat elongated as a rule, and the following short note is often written with a staccato stroke and played with lifted bow (Ex. 179). Actually, the lifting may also be done at the 'dot', even though no staccato stroke is given. In Ex. 180, Mozart says

Ex. 180   L. Mozart

the bow is 'always lifted at the second dot'. In Ex. 181 the staccato stroke is given both for the dotted note and the following sixteenth, and Mozart again says 'at the dot the bow is lifted'.

L. Mozart

Ex. 181

Such figures are often very confusing to musicians, especially when only the sixteenth has a staccato sign (♩. ♪).[38] Does the figure just mentioned mean (1) that only the sixteenth is shortened, or (2) that the eighth is actually to be shortened (as in ♪ ♪), or (3) that both eighth and sixteenth are shortened (♪ ♪)? Today, the second alternative is probably the one most often chosen.

The eighteenth century had something to say about similar figures. Quantz, for instance, mentions that the dot of the dotted figure is elongated and the elongation may be produced in part by lifted bow. Quantz is also more specific: in the case of dotted quarters followed by eighths in 3/4 time, used in the *Loure, Sarabande, Courante,* and *Chaconne,* the eighths are played

---

[38] Cf. the reforms proposed by Alfred Pochon, *Le rôle du point en musique,* Lausanne, 1947. For these, see *Grove's Dictionary* (1954), article 'Staccato'.

very short and sharp. The note with the dot is accented and at the dot the bow is lifted. 'One does the same with all dotted notes, time permitting.'[39] A similar situation exists in certain figures where quarters are followed by eighths. In Ex. 182a Mozart says that 'the bow is lifted slightly after the second note [g′]'.[40]

An interesting species of slurred staccato is shown in Ex. 182b. This unusual bowing makes the staccato notes appear even more separated by interspersing rests.

Ex. 182

In a few bowings found in the music, dots are used with slurs in contexts that suggest a species of thrown or *ricochet* bowing. In Ex. 183, Veracini (Op. 2) indicates sextuplets under a slur with staccato dots over each note. Characteristically, the dots are placed outside the slurs. At the tempo given (allegro assai), the articulation could hardly be achieved with a controlled lifting, but would require a thrown or bounded bow. These figures are to be performed both down-bow and up-bow.

Ex. 183

In the French school, the situation concerning slurred staccato is roughly the same, and it shows a continuity with earlier times, although the descriptions are not as detailed as those of Quantz and particularly those of Leopold Mozart. The old *'craquer'* bowing of Muffat (♩♩) is found in Francoeur (1715), indicated as ♪|♪. L'Abbé le fils implies the old *craquer* bowing with his indication: t p p p (t= down-bow and p= up-bow). He also gives a species of notation, which may be regarded as a first cousin (once removed) of the old *craquer* and of Francoeur's above. With respect to the notation of ⌒ and its performance, L'Abbé says:

'The slur indicates that it is necessary to take these two notes with the same bow, and the small stroke, that the bow should be raised after the first note, which one ought to prolong (*nourrir*) in this case; thereupon one pricks (*piqué*) the short note with more or less force, according to the espression one wishes to give to it.'[41]

The above also implies the use of *notes inégales* (see p. 472).

[39] Quantz, ch. XVII, sec. 7, para. 58.
[40] Leopold Mozart, ch. 4, para. 24. English translation, p. 81.
[41] L'Abbé le fils, *Principes*, p. 10.

More elaborate slurred staccatos appear in L'Abbé le fils under the term *Coup d'Archet Articulé*, indicated with dots under slurs (Ex. 184), and he describes this bow stroke as follows:

'When the Notes of a Roulade or some other figure are all slurred two by two, three by three, etc., and when a dot (*Point*) is used over each of these notes, this method of notation is called *Coup d'Archet Articulé*. To perform this bow stroke well, the wrist ought to be very free and ought only to articulate each of these notes with perfect equality, whether in up-bow or down-bow.'[42]

Ex. 184

L'Abbé le fils

Ex. 184 shows only one long slur over dots, but L'Abbé gives other roulades of the same kind slurred by twos and fours. He says nothing about lifted bow in this connexion; in fact, except for the above quotation, he tells us nothing about the actual performance of the staccato, either of the individual or slurred variety.

The slurred tremolo, legato and staccato

The term *tremolo* may mean trill, vibrato, or repeated notes. The latter meaning is all that concerns us here. A group of repeated notes (*tremolo*) may be bowed with individual bow strokes (see p. 405). The group may be indicated as a species of slurred staccato, usually with dots (sometimes strokes) under a slur—in our terminology, *staccato slurred tremolo*. Or the group may be notated by a simple slur (no dots or strokes), called *legato*

Ex. 185

Larghetto   Handel

slurred tremolo. The distinction between staccato and legato slurred *tremolo* is simply one of degree. In the legato species, the composer wishes the separation to be very slight, resembling a slight pulsation, as in Ex. 185, taken from Handel's oratorio *Saul*.[43] In Veracini's Op. 2, the unusual notation

---

[42] L'Abbé le fils, op. cit., p. 54.
[43] *Georg Friedrich Händel's Werke*, 93 vols., 1858–1903, Vol. 13, p. 34. There are numerous other examples, the concluding chorale of Bach's Cantata No. 105 (*Herr, gehe nicht ins Gericht*) being a fine instance. In this chorale, the strings gradually *quiet* down from sixteenth-note motion to triplets, to eighths, and to $\uparrow$ $\downarrow$ (all in legato slurred tremolo) in order to illustrate the text: 'Now I know that thou willst *quiet* all the fears that trouble me.'

(Ex. 186) implies that the eighths begin in legato slurred *tremolo* and become staccato slurred *tremolo* at the sixteenth-notes—that is, they become more markedly separated. The wavy sign over the three eighths of this example was often used earlier for the slurred *tremolo* (see p. 266-8), but at that time there were no clear distinctions between the legato and staccato species. In Ex. 186 the context suggests that the eighth-notes are barely

Ex. 186

separated in the manner of the legato slurred *tremolo* (cf. our recording). Sometimes the wavy sign, meaning *tremolo* (possibly, vibrato?) is simply written over a whole note, as in Handel's oratorio *Israel in Egypt*,[44] and its realization is left to the performer. Ex. 187 shows a rapid *tremolo* indicated by

Ex. 187

dots under slurs. Ex. 188 is not a *tremolo* in the usual sense, although it includes a group of two repeated notes. It is cited here as an interesting example of the old French *craquer* in the 'new' French school, taken from Guillemain's Op. 1 (1734). It differentiates strokes from dots and arranges the figures in such a way that the different species of staccatos are played alternately down-bow and up-bow. The old wavy-line method to indicate slurred *tremolo* is still used by Leclair ( ). In this notation, as already explained, there is no distinction between legato and staccato in articulating the repeated notes.[45]

Ex. 188

How is the *portato* related to the slurred *tremolo*, if at all? The *portato* is not limited to repeated-note groups, and hence it is not a tremolo but rather a species of slurred staccato. *Portato* is normally indicated with dots under slurs, and is generally moderate or slow in speed. Can a *portato* use repeated notes, and hence be classified at times as a staccato slurred *tremolo*? Yes, but

---

[44] *Werke*, Vol. 16, p. 56. The following example (Ex. 187), from Handel's opera *Julius Caesar (Giulio Cesare)* is found in Vol. 68, p. 119.
[45] For Ex. 188, see La Laurencie, *L'École française*, Vol. II, p. 20. For Leclair, see J. B. Cartier, *L'Art du Violon*, pp. 122-3.

the speed would not normally exceed moderato. *Portato* is certainly a simpler and better understood term than staccato slurred *tremolo*, and hence it is preferable where the meaning and context are clear. The *portato* of repeated notes would normally be used in such figures as 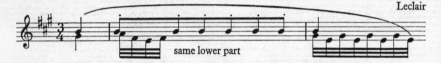 in moderate or slow time, often found in accompaniments.

Mixed bowings

A large number of individual and slurred bowings, legato and staccato, can be mixed in various figures. These are called 'mixed bowings', and we have seen such cases already, for instance, in discussing Geminiani (p. 414). Sometimes different bowings are used simultaneously in double stops. In Ex. 189, Leclair (*c.* 1730) calls for a smooth legato for the thirty-second notes

Ex. 189

played on the lower string, accompanied at the same time by a species of staccato slurred *tremolo* on the upper string, indicated by dots within a long slur. In Ex. 190 Locatelli calls for holding a long note in the lower part, while in the upper part the bow starts legato and finishes with detached notes played on the string—and all of these must be under one slur in order to hold out the whole note below.

Ex. 190

Vivaldi's bowings

Vivaldi's music furnishes a number of interesting and unusual bowings, and it is appropriate to conclude this chapter by singling out for special notice a few bowings and terms of a man who combined one of the most fertile imaginations as a composer with the highest gifts as a violin virtuoso.

Ex. 191

Two instances of bow markings will be sufficient to show Vivaldi's variety and imagination. Ex. 191 is a unique example of the dash in the early eighteenth century and it is original, according to the editor of the complete

edition, currently in progress of publication.[46] In context, this dash appears
to mean a broad detached stroke on the string. A particularly interesting
example of simultaneous use of mixed bowings occurs in Vivaldi's Op. 3,
No. 10: the B minor Concerto for four solo violins (not yet published in the
complete edition). The *Larghetto* begins as shown in Ex. 192, each of the four
violin soloists playing arpeggios with a different type of bowing:

(1) slurred staccato (dots);
(2) three notes slurred plus one unslurred;
(3) individual staccato notes (strokes);
(4) legato slurs by twos.

Ex. 192

There is scarcely another composer of his time who calls for so elaborate an
effect of bowing; and in the variety required and the sonorous imagination
displayed Vivaldi makes one think of Berlioz a century later. In the case of
such a composer as Vivaldi, inspired by his training and inclination as a
virtuoso violinist, it goes without saying that he uses the whole range of
bowings discussed above in a wide variety of ways, including slurred
staccatos of some twenty-four notes (flying staccato?).

[46] By the *Istituto Italiano Antonio Vivaldi*, 1947– , edited by G. F. Malipiero. Ex. 191 is
taken from Vol. 76: Op. 8, No. 1 (the 'Spring' Concerto), third movement, measure
170.

In connexion with his bowing indications, some of Vivaldi's terms need explanation:

1. *Con l'arco attaccato alle corde* (with the bow on the strings): used in connexion with quarter-notes, played forte; presumably a heavily bowed non-legato stroke.

2. *Andante sciolto. Sciolto* appears to mean staccato, generally one note per bow (as in Ex. 192, Violin III). Galeazzi speaks of *note sciolte* in this sense.[47]

3. *Stricciate*, used in connexion with eight repeated thirty-second notes.[48] *Strecciate* [*sic*] means untwist, divide; hence, probably a species of staccato.

4. *Molto forte e strappato. Strappare* = tear off, wrench. Hence, the term probably means very loud and sharply accented.

5. *Largo e spiccato* (Op. IX, No. 9). The movement in question is notated with the wedge-shaped strokes of the staccato. A similar direction: *Largo e staccato.* As noted earlier (p. 409), these terms save writing out the signs through a whole section or movement.

[47] F. Galeazzi, *Elementi teorico-pratici di musica*, 2 vols., Rome, Vol. II, 1796.
[48] See the Vivaldi complete edition, Vol. 9.

༄༅

CHAPTER NINETEEN

The Technique of the Violin, 1700-61 (IV): Multiple Stops. The 'Bach' Bow. Special Effects. Instrumentation and Conducting. The Sound of the Violin

A POLYPHONIC style of playing the violin was developed to a high point by the Germans at the end of the seventeenth century.[1] In the early eighteenth century this style continued in Germany and it flourished in Italy and France as well. The Bach unaccompanied violin sonatas are the zenith of this *genre*, and even for the most gifted musicians these works present great musical and technical difficulties in performance. However, the problems attendant on playing the multiple stops in the Bach sonatas and elsewhere have been compounded, if not exaggerated, by a misunderstanding of the notation and the bow in use at the time.

It is a striking fact that very little is said about the performance of multiple stops in the treatises of the time, even in those of detailed character. Presumably this was so because well-understood conventions made such information redundant, or perhaps because the whole matter was left to the discretion of the individual performer. The latter possibility appears less likely, since Quantz and Mozart, among others, give very precise directions on many matters of considerably less importance. One can only conclude

---

[1] Many of the problems that arise in this connexion have already been discussed earlier (pp. 271 ff.).

that many problems that exist for us now were lesser or non-existent problems then. This in turn may be explained partly by the nature of the old violin and bow and by conventions of the time, both of which are imperfectly understood today. On the other hand, multiple stops did not sound well to everybody in the eighteenth century, and perhaps their performance would not have sounded well to us. Charles Avison, for instance, registers a complaint, as follows:

> 'Even the use of double stops on this instrument [the violin] may, in
> my opinion, be considered as one of the abuses of it; since, in the hands
> of the greatest masters, they only deaden the tone, spoil the expression, and obstruct the execution. In a word, they baffle the performer's
> art, and bring down one good instrument to the state of two indifferent
> ones.'[2]

Double stops

In stops consisting of two notes, the most perplexing problems focus on the questions of whether and where one should insert slurs and break ties. These difficulties, being common to all multiple stops, will be discussed later (see also, p. 441 below). In general, double stops are held out where it is physically possible. As various fingerings show, violinists tried to sustain these double stops even while shifting. In Ex. 193, from Geminiani, the

Ex. 193

notation –3 and –4 implies shifting in the middle of the tied note in order to sustain it. Even in large intervals involving extensions, Leopold Mozart tries to sustain both notes (Ex. 194). The lower notes of Ex. 194 (says Mozart) 'are played throughout in the natural [first] position'.

Ex. 194

[2] Charles Avison, *Essay on Musical Expression*, London, 1752, pp. 96–97. In view of Avison's admiration for Geminiani (whose music has numerous double stops), this criticism is rather strange. Avison was answered by Dr. William Hayes (1753) in *Remarks on Mr. Avison's Essay*. Avison's *Reply to the Author of Remarks* followed later in the same year.

With the development of a more advanced left-hand technique in the eighteenth century, the complications of double stops increased. Large intervals such as tenths became more common, particularly as more and more extensions were used. The stopped unison on the *lower* two strings is found in Geminiani (Ex. 195a) and even consecutively in Aubert (Ex. 195b).

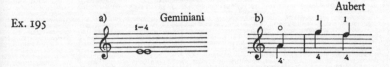

Ex. 195

Leclair is prolific in the use of two strings for trilling, either as double trills in simultaneous thirds or consecutive ones (Ex. 196). Mozart gives the very difficult double-stop trill in sixths (for this and its performance, see Ex. 223 and p. 452), and so does Bach at the end of the first movement of the A minor unaccompanied sonata.

Ex. 196

Triple and quadruple stops. Their notation

Triple and quadruple stops are especially perplexing because the notation of the eighteenth century calls for sustaining them in ways and for lengths that are manifestly impossible today. To the modern performer the notation means what it says, and he approaches any score with this ingrained training and attitude of a lifetime. When Bach writes sustained chords in three and four parts the modern violinist naturally concludes that, while these chords cannot be sustained today, Bach is calling for a style of sustained playing dependent on the 'old' bow. There are two fallacies in this conclusion. One is that Bach expected the music to be played exactly as written; the other is that the old bow could sustain chords in three and especially in four parts.

The fact is that violin notation of early times, especially as to rhythm, was approximate (see p. 272), and the polyphony is written in long note values to show the player the musical progression and to help him distinguish the melodic and harmonic functions of the different voice parts. Even without a special historical knowledge of the conventions of earlier notation, the modern player could easily prove to himself, from the internal evidence of the scores themselves, that the notation of the rhythm must have been approximate. Ex. 197 must imply that the quarters are to be held only as sixteenths; and Bach wrote a number of passages that cannot be held for the specified duration with any bow, old or modern. Sol Babitz has ably demonstrated this point in the case of the Bach sonatas by showing a number of examples which are impossible to play under any condition and in which the written notes must be shortened for one of the following

Ex. 197

reasons:[3] (1) two notes cannot be played simultaneously on the same string (Ex. 198a); (2) nor can they be played simultaneously on two non-adjacent strings (Ex. 198b); (3) a finger that is trilling a note cannot play an untrilled note at the same time (Ex. 198c). Besides, playing the notes in the precise rhythms indicated may involve finger stretches of an 'impossible' kind, not mentioned in any early or modern book on the violin;[4] or following the notated rhythms precisely may require adding and taking away slurs where such changes distort the music and flout the conventions of articulation and phrasing.

Ex. 198

Contrary to general belief, the sustained-note way of writing persisted long after the demise of the old bow—in fact, at least until the time of the original edition of the Paganini *Caprices* (c. 1820?). By Paganini's time the modern (Tourte) bow had long been in general use. Therefore, the sustained type of notation was not exclusively associated with the old bow, and it must have been approximate, the note values not being sustained to their full written value. What the Tourte bow cannot do now it could not do at the time of Paganini.

In spite of clear evidence, certain modern violinists cannot overcome their unshakeable conviction that the score must be performed exactly as written.

[3] Sol Babitz, 'Differences between 18th-century and modern violin bowing' in *The Score*, March 1957, p. 53.
[4] This remark about 'impossible' stretches is not concerned with the thumb. The latter was utilized from time to time in the eighteenth century for special chords and effects not otherwise possible. See Ex. 133a and b and p. 375 above.

Emil Telmányi is a good example. He insists on the inviolability of the Bach autograph on the one hand in order to justify his use of the 'Vega Bach-bow'; and on the other hand, he lists examples that cannot be played as written and require 'negligible changes'.[5] He cannot have it both ways.

The above discussion, which explains that note values were not expected to be played exactly as written, may strike the reader as inconsistent with the view expressed in an earlier chapter that bowing indications should be followed as closely as possible (see p. 404). This apparent inconsistency is simply the inconsistency of the eighteenth century and earlier times. We *know* that the notated rhythmic values could not be strictly observed for the reasons mentioned above; and from the theory books themselves we observe that various interpretations (such as continuous arpeggiation) of the sustained note values in multiple-stop notation were often intended (see Ex. 203). On the other hand, in those cases where bowing marks are indicated in contemporary manuscript and printed scores, we are quite sure they were intended by the composer, as Leopold Mozart says explicitly (see p. 404 above). However, this is not to say that other bowing marks or marks of expression may not have to be inserted. In this sense, the notation of bowing and particularly of expression is an approximation, just as it is in the case of the length of the note values.

The 'Bach' bow

The conviction that the violin must have been able to play sustained chords precisely as written has led to the invention of the so-called 'Bach' bow. This bow, unknown before the twentieth century, is a convex bow of very high arch—as much as four or five inches (or even more) between the hair and the bow stick at the highest point, and it has a mechanical lever worked by the thumb to loosen or tighten the hair at will while playing. When the hair is loose, the violinist can play full chords and sustain them; when the hair is tightened he can play on individual strings (cf. Plate 40a).

The resulting organ-like polyphony has considerable musical fascination, although there is a noticeable loss of brilliance, especially on single strings. The chords also tend to sound louder than individual notes because the overtones are reinforced by the sustained tones. The melodic and harmonic functions of the texture are less clearly differentiated, and of course the violin sounds less like a violin.[6] What has actually happened, however, is remarkably ironic: a modern bow has been invented to play the violin in a way

---

[5] See *The Musical Times*, January 1955. For a reply, see Denis Stevens in the same magazine, February 1955, and Sol Babitz in the issue of May 1955.

[6] There are two complete recordings of the Bach unaccompanied sonatas with the 'Bach' bow, one by Telmányi and another by Rolph Schröder, one of the earliest champions of the 'Bach' bow.

completely foreign to the practice of the early eighteenth century. The proponents of the 'Bach' bow claim either that this is the way the violin sounded in the eighteenth century or—even if it didn't—that this is the way Bach would have preferred the sonatas to sound had he heard them played with the 'Bach' bow. The first claim is an historical and anatomical absurdity, as every serious student of violin playing from Andreas Moser onward has demonstrated,[7] and as we will show presently. We can never know whether Bach would have preferred the 'Bach' bow to the type of bow he actually used. However, it is an historical fact that he never could have heard his sonatas played as they sound today with the modern 'Bach' bow. For one reason or another, the Bach-bowers have instituted a new bow to re-create the Bach sonatas in the musical image of their own time; and the plain fact of history is that the 'Bach' bow has no relation to Bach or anyone else before the twentieth century.

The legend of the 'Bach' bow originated in two articles by Arnold Schering in 1904.[8] The cornerstone of Schering's theory was a passage from Georg Muffat's *Florilegium Secundum* (1698; see p. 257): 'Most of the Germans adopt the Lully bow grip when playing the small and middle-sized violins in that they press the hair with the thumb and lay the other fingers on the back of the bow stick.' Muffat did not illustrate his statement, but his reference to Lully shows that the bow concerned was the typical French bow of the time (cf. Plates 31 and 40b). All these bows have straight sticks. The hair is not curved over the bridge, and it cannot be, because the hair would hit the bow stick.

Relying on the passage from Muffat, Schering and later Albert Schweitzer —who became the most influential proponent of this theory—concluded that with an outwardly curved bow and slack bow hair the sustained chords in the Bach sonatas could be played as written by relaxing the thumb; and *per contra*, that single strings could be played alone by pressing in with the thumb and taking up the slack of the bow.[9] Viewed in a vacuum, Schering's

---

[7] For a summary of the arguments, see David D. Boyden, 'The Violin and its Technique in the 18th Century' in *The Musical Quarterly*, January 1950; or, in somewhat more detail, the same author's 'The Violin and its Technique: New Horizons in Research' in *Bericht über den siebenten Internationalen Musikwissenschaftlichen Kongress Köln 1958*, Kassel, 1959, pp. 29ff. The essence of this information is given below.

[8] Arnold Schering, 'Verschwundene Traditionen des Bachzeitalters' in the 'Bachheft' of the *Neue Zeitschrift für Musik*, September 1904, pp. 675–8; and in an expanded form in the *Bach- Jahrbuch*, October 1904, pp. 104–15. For Schering's modification of his theory, see p. 434 below.

[9] Schweitzer was greatly influenced by the Schering articles mentioned in note 8 above. The historical evidence, which shows clearly the absurdity of Schering's claim, was not available at the time Schweitzer published his book on Bach (1905), which gave wide currency to Schering's theory. Although Schering modified his position in 1920, Schweitzer persisted in his belief in the 'Bach' bow (see Albert Schweitzer,

theory appeared to be a plausible explanation of a very difficult problem. But, quite apart from the fact that the French bow about which Muffat was talking was straight and not curved, Schering made two vital assumptions for which there was no evidence. Neither Muffat nor any other contemporary says anything about slack bow hair or about relaxing the thumb while playing. Nor are these conditions shown in pictures. Muffat pressed the thumb under the bow-hair simply to achieve a firm grip in a simple, rhythmic style of music largely used for dancing. In short, he was merely describing the typical French bow grip of the seventeenth century, which had been used widely by all nationalities still earlier for the performance of dance music. It is also significant that Muffat says nothing whatever about double stops in connexion with this grip, and in the one hundred and sixty-five pages of music accompanying his explanation there is not a single multiple stop of any kind for the violin. Furthermore, not one of the pictures of performing violinists of the time show the bow hair curved over three or four strings, and this would be an absurdity because the hair would hit the straight bow stick, characteristic of both French and Italian bows.

It is true that German bows of the time have a more pronounced arch than typical French and Italian bows, and by using a relatively flat bridge, one might play and sustain three-part, although not four-part, chords (cf. Plate 37). But a flat bridge makes it difficult to play clearly on single strings, and the bridge was not flat but curved. Besides, no German source speaks of relaxing the thumb or of slack bow hair; nor do German pictures of the time show the bow hair arched over the strings, as it should be according to Schering's theory.

Schering also overlooked an historical inconsistency in his theory. The Italian violinists of Bach's time—for instance, Corelli, Geminiani, and Veracini—were writing violin music that used chords in three and occasionally four parts, but they were playing this music with a different bow grip in which the thumb did not press against the bow hair but against the bow stick. The bow stick was straight, and the bridge was arched. In the picture of Veracini playing the violin (Plate 30), relaxed thumb could not have been

---

'A new Bow for unaccompanied Violin Music' in *The Musical Times*, September 1933; see also a delightful report by Joseph Wechsberg on a visit to Schweitzer in *The New Yorker* magazine, November 20, 1954, p. 95). Whether Schweitzer appreciated the overwhelming historical case against the 'Bach' bow or not, he has tacitly admitted the anatomical absurdity of this bow by complaining that the thumb cannot do what Schering claimed it would. Under these circumstances, it is astonishing that Schweitzer welcomed a modern 'Bach' bow to do the things that couldn't be done by the eighteenth-century bow. Since Schweitzer is one of the greatest and most revered men of our or any other time, it is practically impossible to convince the public of the spuriousness of the 'Bach' bow so long as its cause is supported by Schweitzer.

a factor in playing chords, because there was no contact between the thumb and the bow hair, and with this straight bow stick any arching of hair would hit the bow stick.

The fact of the Italian bow and bow grip, and the kind of music in Italy prove that chord playing could not have been uniquely connected with the French bow grip, whether it was used with the French or the German bow. Actually, when the French began seriously to emulate the Italian sonata style about 1720, which included more complex music and chords, they gradually adopted the Italian bow grip and abandoned the old French under-hair grip that was suitable primarily for playing simple dance music. This fact shows that the French bow grip, far from being associated with chord-playing as Schering thought, was actually unsuited to it.

There is also an anatomical difficulty involved in Schering's theory. To play three-part and four-part chords, the greatest control and hence the greatest thumb pressure is necessary. If the thumb is relaxed to play chords, as Schering had to assume, the bow cannot be controlled, and may even fall from the hand.

Considered simply on historical grounds, Schering's theory is untenable for a series of stubborn reasons: (1) There is no evidence of slack bow hair. All evidence points to the contrary and to the fact that the bow hair was not and could not be loosened or tightened while playing. (2) There is no evidence, documentary or pictorial, for relaxed thumb. (3) The old French bow grip, described by Muffat and fundamental to the Bach-bow theory, was used to play simple dance music. There is no evidence that the French bow grip was used, either by the French or the Germans, to play sustained chords in three and four parts; and it is significant that the French abandoned this grip for the Italian grip when more varied and subtle effects, including chords, were desired.

In view of all this, it is not surprising that Schering modified his theory in 1920.[10] But it did not die with his modification. It took a different form in the hands of violinists perplexed by the immense difficulties of performing the Bach unaccompanied sonatas according to the letter of the score. They believed in a literal reading of the score, and they thought that Schering's theory was historical gospel. However, as soon as these violinists tried Schering's theory with any existing bow, either old or modern, the physical difficulties of playing and sustaining three-part and especially four-part chords became painfully evident, and consequently they concluded that the bow must be at fault. Schering has not illustrated the bow of his theory, and

[10] In the *Bach-Jahrbuch*, 1920, p. 57, note, in the course of Andreas Moser's article 'Zu Joh. Seb. Bach's Sonaten und Partiten für Violine allein'. Schering at that time was editor of the *Bach- Jahrbuch*, and he inserted the above-mentioned note modifying his theory, calling Schweitzer's adoption of his theory 'all too optimistic'.

therefore these modern violinists set out to produce a bow to do the things that Schering said it would and that apparently were demanded by Bach's notation.

The result was a bow that had never existed before—in fact, a modern bow, known as the 'Bach' bow—a bow that was absolutely necessary to put into practice a literal performance of Bach's notation according to Schering's theory. By experiment they found that to encompass four strings and to sustain them, the bow had to have a very pronounced arch; and to make the hair tight enough to play on individual strings, the bow required a mechanical contrivance because, as Schweitzer complained with unconscious irony, this could not be done with the thumb alone (cf. note 9 above).

Having examined Muffat, the French and the German bow, and the simple music concerned, one sees that Schering has misapplied the old French bow grip to the difficult polyphonic music of Bach for which it was never intended; and in order to put Schering's enticing theory into practice in this context, modern violinists had to invent a modern 'Bach' bow that is a caricature of the simple French and German bows about which Muffat was speaking. Compare the old French bow with the modern Bach bow side by side (Plates 40a and b). Plate 40b illustrates the kind of bow on which Schering's theory was based; Plate 40a, the kind of bow necessary to put the theory into practice. This comparison is a striking monument to the discrepancy between reality and fantasy in the Bach-bow question.[11]

The 'Bach' bow demonstrates a lamentable confusion between historical truth concerning performance on the one hand and intuitive notions concerning performance on the other. With the modern 'Bach' bow one may perform the sonatas as modern performers think they should sound according to modern technique, on modern instruments, and as modern notions of expression and intuition dictate. The fact remains, however, that the sonatas could not possibly have been played or sounded in this way in Bach's time, and one can justify the use of these 'Bach' bows only on the assumption that Bach should be played in the musical image of the present day.

Multiple stops in actual practice

If three- and four-part chords could not have sounded in the sustained and continuous polyphony beloved by the 'Bach-bowers', how did they sound and how were they performed? The answer is that the chords were rapidly

[11] There have been a number of these 'Bach' bows. The earliest to gain wide attention was that devised by Rolph Schröder about 1930. This bow was enthusiastically endorsed by Schweitzer, and, as explained above, his support has done much to make the Bach-bow theory respectable. Telmányi's 'Vega' bow is of more recent origin. Originally influenced by Schröder, Telmányi had other bows made, one by Arne Hjorth of Copenhagen, and later, the Vega bow he presently uses, by Knud Vestergaard of Viby, Jutland.

broken from bottom to top, sometimes with a dwelling on the lowest note, and, in any case, where the chord was written sustained, the highest note (only) was held. For reasons of resonance, this method seems to have been the preferred way. Contemporary accounts and music also indicate the method of breaking the chord downward, and some such way would have to be used when the sustained melody-note occurred in one of the lower parts of the chord. There is no evidence whatever in the early eighteenth century of the modern practice of chord-breaking where the lower two notes of a four-part chord (for instance) are played just before the beat, the upper two notes then being played on the beat and sustained as a double stop (cf. Ex. 95 and p. 271). In a number of cases the polyphonic passage is simply a sketch of a passage to be played entirely in arpeggios, and on occasion the specific term *arpeggio* is a key to performing the passage in question.

It is something of an error to imagine that full sustained chords must be heard in the manner of an organ to receive the impression of genuine polyphony. For example, it is surprising how clearly the polyphony of the G minor fugue of the first Bach unaccompanied sonata comes out in the lute version which Bach himself arranged. Polyphony on the violin is similar in principle to polyphony on the lute although the sound of the violin does not continue in the lute's evanescent manner. At times Bach himself makes clear that the articulation of a melodic voice in violin music is more important

Ex. 199

than sustained intervals or chords. In Ex. 199, at the points indicated by asterisks, Bach has obviously dropped out the harmony note in both cases so that the motive that resolves the dissonance can be more clearly heard and articulated.

Ex. 200

In the seventeenth century the swift breaking of the single chord is mentioned by various authors, for example, by Christopher Simpson (see p. 275). In the eighteenth century the same tradition continues, and the old method of swiftly breaking the chord from the bottom to the top is again described by Quantz. He gives the music shown in Ex. 200, and says:

'If a rest follows [the chord], the bow must be lifted from the string (*absetzet*) . . . if no rest follows, the bow remains on the highest string.

In both cases the lowest notes, in slow as well as rapid tempo, must not be held but touched swiftly one after the other. . . . And because this chord is used to surprise the ear with an unexpected vehemence, those chords after which rests follow must be played quite short and with the greatest strength of the bow, namely with the lowest part; and when a number follow each other, each must be played down-bow.'[12]

Rousseau's Dictionary appears to admit only arpeggios for chords. The following occurs in his article 'Arpeggio':

'There are some instruments on which one can play full chords only by arpeggiating, such as the violin, the violoncello, and the viol, and all those which one plays with a bow; for the convexity of the bridge prevents the bow from being able to touch on all the strings at once. . . . What one does by necessity on the violin, one practises by choice on the harpsichord'.

Downward breaking of chords for melodic and polyphonic reasons is mentioned, apparently for the first time, by Rameau in his *Avis pour la viole* found in the preface to his *Pièces de clavecin en concerts avec un violon ou une flûte, et une viole ou un deuxième violon*:[13]

'At places where one cannot easily perform two or more notes together, either one arpeggiates them, stopping on that [note] from the side of which the melody continues; or one gives the preference, sometimes to the notes at the top, sometimes those at the bottom, according to the following explanation. . . .'

Ex. 201

Similarly, downward breaking occurs in a *Tombeau* of Leclair (1734). He writes out the passages shown in Ex. 201 without explanation, but none is needed.[14]

There is some evidence that under certain conditions three notes were sustained, at least briefly. In Leclair's Sixth Sonata of Op. 9 (1745), the passage shown in Ex. 202 occurs, and he gives these specific directions:

'To make effective the figure at the beginning of this sonata, one must hear in each chord the note above the first, and hold the three strings

---

[12] Quantz, ch. XVII, sec. 2, para. 18.
[13] Paris, 1741. Printed in Vol. II of the complete edition of Rameau's works (Paris, 1895–1914, 18 vols.).
[14] Leclair, Sonata VI, Op. 5 (Paris, 1734). Reprinted in Cartier, *L'Art du Violon*, Paris, 1798, p. 145. For the sound of Ex. 201, cf. our recording.

under the bow; the small notes indicate a species of continual *tremble-ment* which ought to emerge from the chord and be beaten as swiftly and strongly as possible. The small mark < denotes the two notes that must be beaten against each other.'[15]

Ex. 202

At this tempo the sustaining required of the three strings is not long, since the bow is renewed at every quarter beat. Leopold Mozart has little to say about multiple stops, and it amounts to this: the triple stops 'must be taken together at the same time and in one stroke'.[16]

L'Abbé le fils treats double stops, including trills in thirds, under the heading 'De la double corde',[17] and he gives two-note chords only. In other sections of his treatise, however, he writes occasional triple stops and a few isolated quadruple stops (e.g. p. 37). To judge by the context, all of these three-part and four-part chords present no difficulties, and were performed by a swift breaking of the chord. It is possible that some were performed as arpeggios; and it is striking that, although L'Abbé does not give specific attention in his text to anything except two-part chords, he gives systematic arpeggiation of chords notated as triple and quadruple stops (see p. 440 below). In any case, he gives these instructions about the performance of double stops:

'To play the double stop to perfection, one must observe three essentials:

First, to press equally the two fingers [of the left hand] and to give equal weight to the two strings with the bow. Second, to draw the bow perfectly straight, so that the vibration of the two strings is set in motion equally well.

Third, to raise the bow only in the phrases and figurations which specify the *détaché.*'

Arpeggios

Leopold Mozart seems to distinguish the style of breaking single chords from the style of continuous arpeggios, and this practice of realizing whole progressions in continuous arpeggios must have been widespread, originating perhaps in Italy. François Couperin says that the origins of arpeggios may be found in the [Italian] 'sonades' (see p. 406, note 8, above). Leopold

---

[15] Printed in Cartier, p. 268. For the sound of Ex. 202, cf. our recording.
[16] Leopold Mozart, ch. 8, sec. 3, para. 16.   [17] L'Abbé le fils, pp. 64-65.

Mozart explains this manner of playing as *Arpeggieren* (from *arpeggiare*), the broken chords themselves being called *Arpeggio*: 'The style of performing these broken chords is partly indicated by the composer; partly carried out by the violinist according to his own good taste.' And again, 'As the *Arpeggio* is indicated in the first bar of each example, so must the following notes . . . be continued in the same manner'.[18]

Frequently, there is a 'model' for the arpeggio (as in the Bach *Chaconne*) and in others it is left to the player. Indeed, the word *arpeggio* is not always present in passages that quite probably were meant to be arpeggiated, Bach's first unaccompanied sonata containing a good example.[19] Some of the ways of arpeggiating a chord sequence are suggested by Geminiani's Ex. XXI in his *The Art of Playing on the Violin*, where he gives eighteen ways of arpeggiating the three-measure progression shown in Ex. 203a. The first

Ex. 203

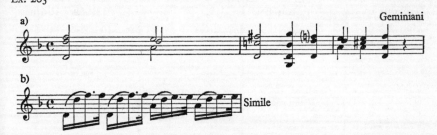

way of arpeggiating is shown in Ex. 203b. All but the last species start with the lower note, probably for the reason of resonance already mentioned. The French violinist François Duval (1673–1728) includes this comment to Sonata VII of his Book V for violin and *basso continuo* (1715): 'This piece can be arpeggiated in different ways; everything in chords of three or four notes

Ex. 204

ought to be arpeggiated'. Then Duval gives models of how to arpeggiate, and these models begin with the *top* note and are arpeggiated downward (Ex. 204). The new and prodigious virtuosity of the French is shown in

[18] Leopold Mozart, ch. 8, sec. 3, paras. 18 and 19.
[19] See the second movement (fugue), m. 35–41. If this passage is played as a continuous arpeggio with gradual *crescendo*, it leads naturally and with a musical climax into the passage beginning at m. 36, which consists of broken-chord passages written out by Bach in sixteenth-notes.

Ex. 205, taken from Guillemain, to be executed in arpeggio fashion, and requiring an extended fifth position of the left hand.[20] L'Abbé le fils sketches out arpeggios and their corresponding notation in triple-stop and quadruple-stop notation. He gives the fingering, and from this we can see that he uses 'all sorts of arpeggios on three strings' and also that he carries the hand at least to the sixth position.[21]

Guillemain

Ex. 205

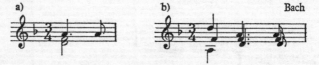

If we follow the directions of eighteenth-century writers concerning the swift breaking of single chords, interesting results are obtained. Some are enlightening and others confusing. Consider the opening of the Bach *Chaconne*. In the autograph this is given as shown in Ex. 206a. Adopting Quantz's method, the chord is played down-bow, breaking the chord upward, d–f–a, dwelling on the top note. The following note 'a' would then be

Ex. 206

played alone, up-bow. That this may indeed have been the way intended by Bach is suggested by the form of notation used in a subsequent statement (variation XXII) where the repeated chord is written out (Ex. 206b). In this case, *both* chords would be broken and both played down-bow. Quantz's method works also for such passages as that shown in Ex. 207, where four

Allegro moderato   Geminiani

Ex. 207

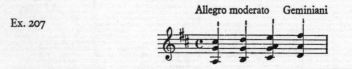

successive chords, marked by staccato signs, are called for by Geminiani (cf. our recording). Here again Quantz's swift breaking of each chord from bottom to top, using successive down-bows, would be quite satisfactory. Quantz's method is particularly appropriate where chords are followed by rests. And there is no difficulty when the highest note of the chord is a melody note which continues as a melody in the top voice, since, according to Quantz's instructions, the top note is held. When there is continuous

---

[20] See La Laurencie, *L'Ecole francaise*, Vol. II, p. 19. For the sound of Ex. 205, cf. our recording.
[21] L'Abbé le fils, *Principes*, pp. 50–51.

melodic interest in a middle voice, Quantz's method sometimes works and sometimes has to be modified. In the dotted figures in Ex. 208a—to return to Bach's *Chaconne*—there is no particular problem, since the dotted notes conventionally imply short rests. Observing this convention would permit the player to break the first chord according to Quantz, to follow the chord by a brief rest at the dot, and to take the sixteenth note in an up-bow. However,

Ex. 208

in Ex. 208b, both upper parts carry the musical interest in two-part counterpoint and, with the exception of the lowest 'a' of the first chord, both parts would presumably be sustained. But if Quantz's method is literally followed here, the first chord would be swiftly arpeggiated, dwelling on the c sharp and then continuing with the double stops. This is inconsistent. The solution here is doubtless to play the 'a' first, then to follow by the held-out interval g-c sharp. A similar situation is that of Ex. 209, beat two. In Ex. 210a,

Ex. 209

the procedure suggested in Ex. 208b can be adopted, then release the top note to emphasize the middle voice, which is the continuing melody part. A possible alternative is to break the chord downward, holding the f sharp and the 'a'. In Ex. 210b the two upper notes must be briefly held, the top note (g) long enough to hear the b flat atainst it in the middle voice.

Ex. 210

Slurring

The problem of adding slurs, breaking ties, and playing chains of suspensions has been discussed in an earlier chapter (see pp. 273ff.). The situation is much the same in the eighteenth century, but the complications are greater and, in certain cases, more puzzling. That double stops did imply the addition of legato slurs on occasions is suggested by certain passages from the theorists. For the music shown in Ex. 211a, Quantz says:[22] 'Those long notes which are mixed among rapid and lively notes must be played with equal strength and sustained'. For Ex. 211b, C. P. E. Bach says:[23] 'Passages in which passing notes or appoggiaturas are struck against a bass are played legato in all tempos even in the absence of a slur.'

Ex. 211

In many fugue subjects and their subsequent answers, the problem of articulating the subject (or answer) in the same manner raises questions of procedure. In Ex. 212, the opening of the first fugue in Corelli's Sonata I from Op. 5 (1700), the subject begins, according to the Rule of Down-Bow,

Ex. 212

with an up-bow. The answer, beginning on the last beat of measure two, should also be played up-bow with individual bow strokes. If, as in the subject, individual bow strokes are to be used in the answer, the tie binding the two 'a's in the upper part must be broken (cf. our recording). A more

Ex. 213

striking example is shown in Ex. 213, the *Caprice* to the Ninth Concerto of Locatelli's Op. 3, marked *allegro*. If individual bow strokes are used in bowing the subject and also at the entrance of the answer, the upper part cannot be

[22] Quantz, ch. XVII, sec. 2, para. 15.
[23] Carl Philipp Emanuel Bach, *Essay on the True Art of Playing Keyboard Instruments* [1753], translated and edited by William J. Mitchell, New York, 1949, p. 155.

held legato with the tie as indicated, unless a rather elaborate *portato* is used in the lower voice.

Sometimes the problem of breaking ties can be avoided by breaking the chord downward, but in certain cases this method gives an unsatisfactory musical result. In Ex. 214a, the dissonance c sharp—b does not sound if the chord is broken downward. The same kind of objection may be made to downward chord-breaking in Ex. 214b.

Ex. 214

The mass of inconsistencies involved in trying to apply one set of instructions to playing all types of multiple stops leads to the conclusion that there was no precise system which applied to all cases. The musical necessity of clear articulation and the clarity of musical progression, including dissonances and their resolution, would seem to take precedence over slurs and ties.[24] These matters must be settled according to context. However, before discarding any slur or tie written by the composer, full weight must be given to the musical factors involved. A case in point is that shown in Ex. 215, taken from the opening *adagio* of Bach's first unaccompanied sonata. Here the elaborate figuration has disguised the fact that Bach is concluding a decorated Phrygian cadence with the trill on f sharp, which concludes the phrase. The new phrase begins on the following 'a' with down-bow. However, most modern editions and concert performances of this passage completely disregard Bach's bowing at this point, customarily slurring the trilled f sharp to the following 'a'. This alteration effectively ruins the Phrygian cadence and obscures the beginning of the new phrase.

Ex. 215

Special effects, including the pizzicato

By 'special effects' we mean some special device or way of playing. The mute is such a device. Although it was known by the early seventeenth century at least, it began to be used in music for soloists only in the early

---

[24] C. P. E. Bach (as in note 23), p. 159, paragraph 25, says, 'The performer may break a long tied note by restriking the key.' And, in a later edition (1787), he adds: 'Occasionally a short tie must be broken in order to clarify the leading of a voice.'

eighteenth century (e.g. by Vivaldi; for its use in ensemble music of the seventeenth century, see p. 278). The usual direction for applying the mute is *con sordino*. This direction is valid only for the movement over which it stands, after which, unless directions to the contrary are given, the mute is removed. This remark applies to such movements as the slow movement of W. A. Mozart's G minor Quintet. The direction *con sordino* does not imply that a movement is invariably soft, as is sometimes said. Many muted movements have *forte* as well as *piano*, specifically marked (cf. the Mozart movement just mentioned).

There are a number of particular ways of playing the violin that come under the category of special effects. Tuning to a *scordatura* is an instance. The problems and peculiarities involved in the *scordatura* have already been explained (see p. 250). There is nothing new in principle. For the first time, however, the French began to write in this style (Corrette, 1738; Tremais, Op. IV, *c.* 1740).

Harmonics constitute another special effect. Before 1750 only natural harmonics were used in violin music, largely among the French (see Mondonville, p. 346). L'Abbé le fils's full complement of artificial harmonies (see p. 385), in addition to the natural variety, is quite exceptional for his time (1761). Leopold Mozart will have nothing to do with harmonics unless used *entirely* throughout a piece. As a matter of fact, Mozart had relatively little sympathy for 'frills'. He says nothing, for instance, about *col legno, sul ponticello*, and *sulla tastiera*; and indeed, effects like these, with which some violinists were already experimenting in the early seventeenth century (see p. 171), are hardly mentioned by the theorists of the early eighteenth century. On the other hand, Mozart, following Tartini's lead, does discuss and illustrate the resultant (combination) tones in connexion with playing double stops in tune (see p. 385).

The most important and widespread special effect was the *pizzicato* (for vibrato, see p. 386). In his 'Technical Terms', Leopold Mozart gives us a clear notion of *pizzicato*.[25] He says the string is plucked with the index finger or with the thumb of the right hand:

> 'The strings must never be plucked from underneath, but always pulled sideways; as otherwise they will strike the fingerboard in the rebound and rattle, and so at once lose their tone. The tip of the thumb must be placed against the saddle at the end of the fingerboard, the strings being plucked with the tip of the index finger, and the thumb only used when whole *chords* are to be taken in one. Many pluck always with the thumb, but the index finger is better for the purpose, because the thumb, by reason of its fleshiness, damps the tone.'

[25] Leopold Mozart, ch. 1, sec. 3, end.

Mozart also gives the term *Col Arco* to signify that the player is to return to bowing after playing *pizzicato*. Quantz's information is very similar to Mozart's. He tells us that most players use the thumb, but that the tip of the index finger is better. He permits the use of the thumb, under certain conditions, to play the lowest note of *pizzicato* chords.[26] Just as in the case of

Ex. 216

a) Allegro
Scordatura
piz. piz. piz. piz.

b) Andantino
Tremais, Op. 4, No. 2
piz. piz.

harmonics, the French show an advanced use of the *pizzicato*. In Tremais's Op. IV (*c.* 1740), for example, a piece already in *scordatura*, the individual *pizzicato* is sometimes alternated with single bowed notes in allegro (Ex. 216a), and sometimes with bowed slurs (Ex. 216b).

Instrumentation and conducting

A number of the facts of instrumentation and 'conducting', described earlier (pp. 278ff.), also obtain in the early eighteenth century, but there are new developments. The typical trio sonata is still issued in four parts, just as it was in Corelli's time, and many *concerti grossi* are published in seven part-books. In concertos this implies that the basic set of parts was intended for soloists in the *concertino* and not more than two players to each of the ripieno parts. In the *concerto grosso*, it is assumed that there were two keyboards, one to accompany the *concertino*, and the other, the *ripieno*. However, since the typical seven-part-books included only one figured cello part, it must have been difficult for the (solo) cellist and *continuo* player to read from the same part. The same thing may be said for the other *continuo* player and double bassist, who also read from the single figured *basso* part. In the solo concerto the number of part books varied, but in most violin concertos the number of part books was relatively small, implying a fairly small orchestra, often simply of strings in four parts.

In any case, different types of *concerti* were seldom distinguished clearly, and the word *concerto* could, and often did, cover them all, including mixed types as well as *concerti* for two, three, and more soloists. Not long after Corelli, the instrumentation of concertos began to depart from his model. Wind instruments were often used with strings (cf. Bach's 'Brandenburg' concertos), and the concertos for one or more soloists followed no defined instrumentation (cf. Vivaldi). Furthermore, the keyboard is often omitted in

[26] Quantz, ch. XVII, sec. 2, para. 31.

solo episodes; Vivaldi and subsequent composers may accompany the soloist lightly with a few players, whose volume and tone are sometimes further reduced by mutes. Again, the relation of parts in the *concertino* and *ripieno* changes. Corelli allotted three parts to the *concertino* and four to the *ripieno*. Muffat sometimes increases the *ripieno* to five parts. Geminiani sometimes has four parts in the *concertino* (and Locatelli, five), while reducing the *ripieno* to three.

At times, the confusion of terminology extends to the part books. For example, 'Alto' and 'Tenore' generally mean Viola I and Viola II, respectively: both are violas, but one uses a higher register than the other. 'Alto' and 'Tenore' are the terms used on the title-page of Albinoni's *Sinfonie e Concerti* (Op. 2, 1700), but the more specific terms 'Alto Viola' and 'Tenor Viola' are used in the part books. This work of Albinoni also includes a part book labelled *Violino de Concerto* to be used with the *Concerti*. This is not a solo part, but the 'violin of the ensemble', that is, violin I of the orchestra. In effect, *Violino Primo* of the *Sinfonie* now becomes the solo violin of the *Concerti*, and another part (the *Violino de Concerto* part) is needed to play violin I in the accompanying orchestra.

By 1752 Quantz is specifying the number of string players in the orchestra ('ripienists'): when one uses four violins (i.e. two each for violins I and II), there should be one viola, one cello, and one medium-sized double bass. For eight violins, one requires two violas, two cellos, a second and larger double bass. For twelve violins, three violas are needed plus four cellos and two basses. A harpsichord is assumed in 'all ensembles large and small'. A second keyboard is suggested when the twelve violins are used (Quantz's remarks concerning the additional wind instruments are not included here). Quantz also gives details of the placement of the instruments.[27]

Quantz makes clear that the orchestra requires a 'leader', but the latter is not a 'conductor' in the modern sense, although he ideally exercises the function of supervising the technical and musical details of performance. Quantz's leader is a performer in the orchestra and is preferably a violinist, the movements of whose bow and violin are, collectively, the baton. The role of the 'conductor' is seldom discussed in any detail in treatises of the time. Quantz's admirable summary of the musical and technical qualities required is a conspicuous exception.[28] The modern (baton-wielding) conductor dates from the first years of the nineteenth century, Spohr and Weber being among the first protagonists.[29]

---

[27] For the above, see Quantz, ch. XVII, sec. 1, para. 16.

[28] See Quantz, ch. XVII, sec. 1, consisting of eighteen paragraphs.

[29] For other ways of conducting, including the keyboard conductor and his relation to the violinist-leader, see Adam Carse, *The History of Orchestration*, London, 1925; and Georg Schünemann, *Geschichte des Dirigierens*, Leipzig, 1913.

The sound of the violin in the early eighteenth century

After 1700 the violin had a greater resource of power and greater variety of tone and expression than previously (cf. pp. 281ff.), partly by reason of changes in the violin and bow, and partly for reasons emanating from a more elaborate technique of playing. A considerable volume of tone was doubtless available to those players who needed it, especially the concerto soloists, who had to fill larger halls and to compete with an orchestra, however small. Concerning the power of violins relative to large halls, Hubert le Blanc (see p. 331 above) makes the point clear when he says that the cello and harpsichord have conspired with the violin to hold concerts (i.e. the 'Concert Spirituel', see p. 348), in large halls, favourable to the violin, but not to the viol. As they had in the past, the Italians sought to produce a greater volume of tone than the French. The French writer Le Cerf de la Viéville says that the Italians 'produce a sound excessively shrill and violent. I am always afraid that the first stroke of the bow will make the violin fly into splinters, they use so much pressure.'[30]

The obvious needs in concert life for larger tone were met by the flat-modelled violins of Stradivari and Guarneri, which carried much better than the high-modelled Amatis and Stainers. (The Stainers, however, were generally stronger in tone than the Amatis.) The longer, stronger bows of the eighteenth century were also aimed at increased volume of tone. Similarly, the technical information from the violin treatises confirms a desire for greater volume. Leopold Mozart speaks of a 'manly' tone as the ideal, and his bow grip is obviously aimed at achieving power. The same thing is true of the bow grip of L'Abbé le fils, who separates his index finger slightly from the other fingers—also aimed at producing a more powerful tone. At the same time the old ideal of a smaller, sweeter tone persisted among those who played chamber music or performed in small rooms, and for them the Amati and Stainer violins were perfection itself. This explains the continuing popularity of these instruments through the eighteenth century.

Changes in the instrument and in the technique of playing must have produced a difference in the sound of the violin. For instance, the addition of a wound G string evened up the sound of the instrument on all strings, and it increased the response and sonority of the lowest string. These new possibilities also encouraged composers to use the lowest string more. The sound of the violin was also affected by the species of continuous vibrato advocated by Geminiani (see p. 386), by the advent of natural and artificial harmonics, especially in the French school, and by the greater use of nuance in general and nuanced bowings in particular, especially among the Italians.

[30] *Comparaison de la musique italienne et de la musique françoise* (1705). For the English translation, see Strunk, *Source Readings*, p. 502.

The brilliance of the highest register and the sonority of multiple stops were other factors.

Actually, of course, there is no such thing as a single characteristic violin sound at any time. Individual players and instruments have their own sound, and styles of playing, individual and national, affect each player and each instrument. Descriptions in contemporary documents are not very helpful in determining the sound of the violin, because there is no way of judging the meaning of their terms. Still, some reports have interest and significance. Eighteenth-century theorists certainly regarded the violin as having a full, strong tone or, as Quantz puts it, 'more penetrating than any of the other instruments most used for accompanying'.[31] Again, Hubert le Blanc speaks of the 'silvery-rounded sound' of the violin, and, at the same time, he remarks on the high degree of tension for which thick strings are essential. But the tension was not yet as great as it became when the commercial concerts of the nineteenth and twentieth centuries required still larger halls. Consequently, even though the eighteenth century produced more powerful violins and bows than hitherto for use in the concerto, the volume of tone must have been somewhat less than that obtaining after 1800, when violins were subjected to still stronger string tensions and played by the more powerful modern bow.

[31] Quantz, ch. XVII, sec. 1, para. 3.

CHAPTER TWENTY

⟨∾≈∾⟩

Specific and Improvised
Ornaments. The Cadenza

B
Y 1700 the conventional ornaments, such as the trill and mordent,
were indicated increasingly by signs. This method was simpler than
writing out the notes; and, if it was less exact, it had other advantages,
including a greater liberty to the performer and a quick distinction between
what was ornamental and what was structural in the music. In certain cases,
as in Tartini's appoggiaturas, the use of grace notes ('small' notes) implied
the addition of a particular kind of nuance as well as slurring the appoggiatura to the following note (cf. p. 455). The specific signs also had the effect
of preventing further ornamentation, as opposed to a part written out in
'big' notes.

The manner of indicating and inserting ornaments varied a good deal.
The customs in France and Italy were markedly at variance in these matters.
In France the intended ornaments were generally indicated by specific signs,
but in Italy signs were used infrequently even when the performer was
expected to insert them according to custom and good judgement. This
remark applies not only to conventional ornaments like trills and mordents
but also to 'arbitrary' (that is, improvised) ornamental figures not capable of
being expressed by specific signs. These improvised figures were sometimes
called 'graces' (cf. the Corelli 'graces' of Op. 5; see p. 222). In the case of
stereotyped ornaments, the performer of Italian music had often to insert
them himself at appropriate places, a typical example being the cadential
trill. The question of where and how often to insert conventional ornaments
cannot be answered exactly, and contemporary treatises often contented
themselves with pointing out, as they had in the past, that the effect of
ornaments is like seasoning in food: if a little is not enough, a lot is too much!
The seasoning, of course, can be added either by the cook (the composer) or
at the table (the performer); and if the French preferred to leave it to the
cook, the Italians were happier to leave it until the table. While all this is
confusing and frustrating to us now, such customs were quite consistent

with the freedom permitted and expected of the performer in earlier times, who was familiar with the types of ornaments and the proper places to use them.

In line with this state of affairs, composers sometimes suggested, usually by means of a small cross (+), the spot where an ornament would be welcome, the specific ornament being left to the artistry and judgement of the performer. The composer is really saying to the performer: 'An ornament would be appropriate here, and I expect you to select (and play beautifully) the one best suited to the situation.' The cross (+) as a general sign for inserting an ornament may be found in French music, in spite of the penchant of the French for more exact notation. L'Abbé le fils uses the cross to specify any and all of four different species of trills, called *cadences* as a class. Mondonville employs the cross in a somewhat different way in Sonata I of Op. 3 (*c.* 1734) as a direction to the violinist to imitate, in parallel situations, the specific ornaments given in the harpsichord part.

Finally, the selection of ornaments is related to the mood to be expressed, to the type of piece, and the tempo. A mordent is good in a lively piece, but it is out of place in a slow one. The long appoggiatura is suited to melancholy. Slow trills are best for sad and slow pieces. And so on.

The trill (common terms and signs: *trillo, tremblement, cadence, t, tr,* ⁓)

Of the specific ornaments, the trill is the most usual and important. When Tartini restricts himself to discussing a single ornament in his 'Letter', it is the trill he selects. In general, the trill starts with the note above the written note, and this auxiliary (or 'upper-auxiliary') note normally belongs to the key obtaining at that point, not being chromatically altered (Ex. 217).

Geminiani

Ex. 217

The note is a half-tone or a whole-tone above the main note, depending on the position of the main note in the scale. In a few cases the trill embraces a minor third (Tartini's *Traité*), but this practice was generally frowned upon.

Just as in the late seventeenth century (cf. p. 286), the basic trill was the upper-accessory trill just described, but this trill could be elaborated by beginning with a kind of prefix such as an appoggiatura (Ex. 218a) or holding of the main note (Ex. 218b); or by ending with 'afterbeats' (G: *Nach-*

Ex. 218

schläge) as in Exx. 219a and b; or by elaborating both beginning and ending (Exx. 218a and b). These compound or composite trills are naturally limited to notes of sufficient duration to accommodate them. Certain types are more

Ex. 219

appropriate to slow time (Ex. 218a) than to fast. A considerable number and variety of these trills are given in the treatises of the time, especially those of Geminiani and Leopold Mozart.

When a long trill is involved, Mozart instructs the violinist to restrain his bow, so that the whole trill can be played without changing bow. With very short trills, especially in rapid time, the trill sometimes begins on the main note, an effect later called *Schneller* by the Germans. When a short trill is

Ex. 220

indicated in a descending melodic line of rapid notes, the main-note trill is obviously the easier solution. L'Abbé le fils gives us an example of a short 'prepared' trill (Ex. 220a). His corresponding upper-accessory trill is shown in Ex. 220b.

Trills may be slow, moderate, or fast. Tartini speaks of these three speeds for trills in his 'Letter' and also in his *Traité*. These speeds are roughly suited to the speed of the movement, and the volume of sound may be increased to match the increasing speed of the trill. In practice, says Tartini, the change from one trilling speed to another is done by gradation, not by 'doubling the velocity all at once'. Mozart gives four speeds suited to the speed and character of the movement: slow, medium, rapid, and accelerating. The latter is mostly used in cadenzas, says Mozart, and is usually accompanied by increasing volume of tone. The speed of the trill also depends on the context and on such considerations as whether the trill occurs on high or low strings. Faster trills are normally associated with high strings, and vice versa. Quantz considered the ordinary speed of a trill to be eight thirty-second notes in the time of M.M. $\downarrow$ = 80.

Uniformity of volume is not particularly desirable in trills, and *crescendo* and *diminuendo* are often applied to the longer ones, as just explained in connexion with Mozart. However, uniformity of tone colour is something else; and to attain it, Mozart, among others, forbids the use of the open string in trilling, although he notes that open string must be used in certain double trills where there is no alternative (see below). However, others like Herrando (1756) still use the open-string fingering for trills.

The seventeenth century did not believe in consecutive trills, but these are used in profusion by 1750. Both Mozart and Tartini use series of them, ascending and descending, and Mozart even uses trills on consecutive semitones. Mozart's consecutive trills are to be played without afterbeats, and he gives alternate fingerings (Ex. 221). The French also use consecutive trills.[1] Another type of trill is the off-beat (syncopated) trill found in Leopold Mozart and especially in Tartini.

Ex. 221

Mozart's discussion of double trills is indicative of the great advance that has occurred. Among other things, he gives double trills in thirds on all strings. L'Abbé le fils gives a double trill of increasing speed with the curiously contracted fingering shown in Ex. 222; and he explains the reasons for this, as follows:

> 'I have noticed in our best masters that the double trills using the first and third fingers are much less beautiful than those using the second and fourth because the stiffness of the open string tends to repulse the first finger, which has less strength because its position is less elevated than the others' (p. 65).

Ex. 222

However, this fingering does not appear to have been adopted by anyone else.

Mozart gives the very difficult trill in sixths (Ex. 223; cf. our recording) which, he says, 'is rarely used and then only in cadenzas as a change and as something special'. In executing this trill 'the first finger must never be lifted, but must be brought across to the D string by means of a movement of the whole hand, with the foremost part only and with a slight sideways movement'. Mozart also quotes the 'Devil's Trill' of Tartini as an example

---

[1] For trills in Leclair, see La Laurencie, *L'École française*, Vol. I, p. 324.

of the *trillo accompagnato* (accompanied trill)—that is, a trill accompanied by another part, resulting in double stops. Tartini's 'Devil's Trill' is a good example of a continuous trill in connexion with double stops and extensions; it also involved shifting the fingers while trilling. The sixth-trill may also be found in J. S. Bach's Second Sonata for unaccompanied violin (*Grave*) and in the works of Guillemain.[2] An occasional octave-trill may be found in music, for example in the Ninth Sonata of Tremais's Op. 1 (1736).

Ex. 223

Several rather *outré* trills may be mentioned. L'Abbé le fils gives a trill in harmonics (Ex. 224; cf. Ex. 154); and Tartini describes a special type of trill that is half trill and half vibrato:

> 'Finally there is a species of trill which can be performed to best advantage by players [of the violin]: the note above . . . is joined to the note below in such a way that the two fingers of the player never entirely leave the string. Consequently, one does not perform this trill by raising the trilling finger but by moving all the hand by a pulsation, and, together with the hand, [moving] the trilling finger in a species of swiftly undulating movements with the force of the pulsation. This sort of trill is legato and not articulated. It makes its best effect in *affettuoso* pieces, its motion is slow, and it works best in semitone trills.'

Ex. 224

The mordent (other terms: *pincé, martellement, battement, beat*)

Like many other ornaments, the mordent has various names and species of execution. Only the most usual will be given here. The typical mordent begins with the main note and alternates this note with the semitone or whole-tone below (Ex. 225). To distinguish trill and mordent, a helpful English dictum dating back to the seventeenth century may be quoted: 'shake [trill] from above and beat [play a mordent] from below'. The mordent is invariably played rapidly. Its very name, from *mordare* = to bite, is indicative of its intent; and it is proper to fast tempi rather than to slow.

---

[2] See Cartier, *L'Art du Violon*, p. 124, line 2. See also the third-trills in the same piece and the relatively easy trill in fifths (line 1).

There is no evidence that it was ever played slowly. As Tartini says, it was for pieces 'gay and vivacious', not for those that are 'grave and melancholy'. The number of repercussions depends on the time available and the speed of the finger. According to Tartini, it consists of two, four, or six notes, depending on the speed of the finger movement. Mozart says it is composed of two, three, or more little notes, which 'quite quickly and quietly . . . grasp at the principal note and vanish at once'. It was used to give stress to the principal note.[3] Mozart gives three types of mordents of which only the first (Ex. 225) would normally be classified as a mordent today. Tartini's information is similar, and Mozart probably adopted his section on the mordents from him.

L. Mozart

Ex. 225

The signs as well as the terms for the mordent vary. Geminiani uses a rather unusual sign (*//*). More common is ✳ . Veracini indicates the mordent by the abbreviation 'Mr'. In connexion with this last sign, Pincherle thinks that the 'm' sign at the opening of Vivaldi's 'Spring' Concerto (Ex. 226) means mordent.[4] This is probable, but it is also possible that it means vibrato. The 'm' sign, meaning vibrato, appears in the seventeenth century (see p. 287), and a similar sign for vibrato is given by Tartini, Leopold Mozart, and Geminiani.

Vivaldi

Ex. 226

[Solo]

There is another species of ornament which resembles the mordent and is often confused with it. This ornament begins with the lower, not the main, note (Ex. 227). Quantz calls this type, as well as the usual mordent, a

L. Mozart

Ex. 227

[3] In his translation of Tartini's *Traité des Agrémens* (see p. 362), Sol Babitz claims that the short mordent of two fast notes before the main one (as in the first group of Ex. 225) is rejected as a violin ornament, but it is characteristic of the keyboard. The statements of Mozart and Tartini refute this claim. The two-note mordent, called a *battement*, also appears in Quantz (Tab. VI, fig. 32). Muffat gives it in connexion with his account of the Lullists in the seventeenth century (see Ex. 110a).

[4] Marc Pincherle, *Vivaldi*, Vol. I, p. 214. The facsimile of the piece in question is reproduced on the plate facing p. 201 in his book.

'battement'. But Mozart distinguishes these types clearly, assigning the name *Zusammenschlag* to the species of ornament in Ex. 227. Prelleur (1731) gives this ornament only under the term *beat*.

The appoggiatura

Eighteenth-century musicians were more conscious of the nature and function of the appoggiatura than those in the seventeenth century. An outward manifestation of this fact is notation by means of the small ('grace') notes. Modern musicians often wonder why appoggiaturas were written as 'small' notes, especially since there appears to be no relation between the indicated length of the grace note and the length of its performance—at least, prior to C. P. E. Bach's *Versuch* (1753). There are several reasons for this small-note notation. One was to show the function of the note as an appoggiatura (an accented and frequently dissonant note). Another was to prevent further ornamentation. The small notes also implied that the appoggiatura must be slurred to its following note of resolution and (generally) played on the same string. Still another reason was that small notes sometimes implied a dynamic interpretation different from the usual (big-note) notation. Tartini explains this quite vividly in his *Traité*. With respect to the following example of a long appoggiatura (Ex. 228), Tartini explains that this 'small' note method is used to distinguish differences of expression. If the passage just cited (he says) were written out in two 'large' notes, as in Ex. 228b,

> 'it would be necessary to play it [the first eighth note] with more force than the second, and it would require a short trill. But as it is only a small note [as in Ex. 228a], the bow or the voice must commence it softly, augmenting the sound by gradation to half of its value and similarly diminishing it as it comes to rest on the large note to which it is joined. This great note requires a short trill which makes it heard with more force.'

Ex. 228

Thus, two different notations indicate *per se* two opposed interpretations concerning the dynamics and the ornaments to be inserted. Although this specific interpretation is unique to Tartini, he is not the only one who uses dynamic effects in connexion with the long appoggiatura. In fact, it is a common interpretation. Geminiani and L'Abbé le fils both apply nuances to appoggiaturas in their treatises.

Appoggiaturas may be treated short in passing, or they may (and more often do) come on the beat and receive an accent. In the latter case they are usually relatively long ('long' appoggiaturas), although short appoggiaturas may also come on the beat. Context is important to the proper performance of the appoggiatura. In the case of descending thirds filled by the 'little' notes, the appoggiaturas are generally played as passing (Ex. 229), as

Ex. 229

recommended by Quantz.[5] In similar situations, however, C. P. E. Bach forbids these passing appoggiaturas, insisting that they must be on the beat.

The general rule of long appoggiaturas is that they are played on the beat and take half the time of the main (following) note. But there are exceptions for various reasons. In the passage shown in Ex. 230, Quantz says that if the

Ex. 230

length of the g′ sharp is halved (as per the usual rule), the basic dissonance of the diminished seventh will be destroyed, and therefore the appoggiatura must be played short. Ex. 231 is another exception, and one that will surprise many performers. According to the rule, Ex. 231a would be played as at (b), but Quantz says that this

> 'would be contrary not only to the intention of the composer, but to the French style of playing, to which these appoggiaturas owe their origin. These little notes belong in the time of the notes preceding them, and hence must not, as in the second example, fall in the time of those that follow them.'[6]

Ex. 231

If the main note is dotted, the preceding appoggiatura takes two-thirds of the time of the main note. In the case of a gigue rhythm, for instance, Ex. 232a is performed as at Ex. 232b. Quantz, whose example this is, also

---

[5] Quantz, ch. VIII, para. 6.   [6] Quantz, ch. XVII, sec. 2, para. 20.

discusses the case of the tie followed by a rest. The main note, in this case, may be pushed ahead into the time of a rest, Ex. 232c being played as shown in Ex. 232d.

Ex. 232

Geminiani prefers a long appoggiatura in general, sometimes as much as three-quarters of the time of the main note, and L'Abbé le fils also requires the same length on occasions. It should be noted that the long appoggiatura was more typical of music about and after 1750 than fifty years earlier. The long appoggiatura was well suited to expressing the 'sighs' of Rococo music.

The turn (often indicated by ∾) is generally a four-note figure, starting with the note above the written note, descending to the main (written) note, then to the note below, and returning to the main note. This ornament is common in keyboard music, but not favoured in violin music. Geminiani mentions it only in connexion with the 'turned shake' (i.e. the trill with afterbeats, as in Ex. 219a), and Leopold Mozart discusses it almost as an afterthought in his chapter on the appoggiatura (ch. 9, para. 26). (For a seventeenth-century turn used in violin music, see p. 287 and Ex. 110e.)

The difficulty with the rules for ornaments, especially the rules for appoggiaturas, is that they are often troublesome to put into practice, and sometimes particular rules are more confusing than helpful. Individual practice varied a good deal (as we see from the treatises), and what works in one composer's music may not work at all in another's. The study of contemporary treatises is helpful in showing the range and variety of individual practice. Unfortunately, this is an extremely detailed subject which we cannot pursue here (but cf. note 2, p. 286). The best advice that can be offered is this: keep the general principles given above in mind, but let common sense and musical instinct be the guide to the solution of individual cases. The eighteenth-century violinist could hardly have done otherwise.

Improvised ornaments

Quantz distinguishes between 'essential' and 'arbitrary' ornaments. By the former term he means the conventional stereotyped ornaments that have just been discussed and that can be indicated by signs. By the latter he means those improvised melodic figures that cannot be reduced to signs. In connexion with these distinctions, Quantz also makes pertinent observations about ornamental usage in French and Italian style. Among the French, he says, the essential ornaments are specifically indicated; in the Italian practice they seldom are, but the Italians insert both the essential and arbitrary ornaments. The latter are not characteristic of the French. The essential ornaments, practised by the French, can be performed without a knowledge of harmony, but this is not so in the case of the arbitrary ornaments of the Italians.[7]

Quantz devotes a considerable amount of space to the proper manner of playing allegros and adagios, the arbitrary alterations of simple intervals, and the playing of cadenzas.[8] At the same time, he counsels moderation: allegro movements permit few arbitrary ornaments, since brilliant passages are already complete in themselves.[9] The same remark applies to a beautiful cantabile melody. Nevertheless, the adagios are the ones that are frequently ornamented, and Quantz devotes a long example (*Tabellen* XVII–XIX) to the ornamentation of a complete adagio movement. In another chapter he gives detailed instructions for the addition of nuances to the same adagio. Usually these alterations are made after the simple form of the melody has been heard. But Quantz does not expect every adagio to be altered.[10] He counsels not to alter a piece that is already beautiful and therefore unimprovable;[11] and he says that it is preferable to play a piece as it is, rather than spoil it with bad or tasteless additions.[12] Leopold Mozart makes similar comments about those who think they must 'befrill' an adagio cantabile and

> 'make out of one note at least a dozen. Such note-murderers expose thereby their bad judgement to the light, and tremble when they have to sustain a long note or play only a few notes singingly, without inserting their usual preposterous and laughable frippery.'[13]

Nevertheless, Mozart's treatment of embellishments shows that, by our standards, he was accustomed to a highly ornamental style. In any case, the phrase *come sta* is still found (just as it was earlier; see p. 289) in slow movements which the composer does not wish altered by arbitrary ornaments.[14]

These ornamental additions, sometimes improvised on the spot, and

---

[7] Quantz, ch. XIV, para. 3.   [8] Quantz, ch. XII–XV inclusive.
[9] Quantz, ch. XII, para. 27.   [10] Quantz, ch. XIV, para. 24.
[11] Quantz, ch. XIII, para. 9.
[12] In a later chapter (XVIII, para. 56–61), Quantz, after extolling the art of singing during the first thirty years of the eighteenth century, says that violinists of midcentury perform quite differently from the singers, implying that violinists are over-interested in florid improvisation and less concerned with the beautiful cantabile of the singing style. In this context, Quantz is critical of Tartini and the later works of Vivaldi.
[13] Leopold Mozart, ch. I, sec. 3: 'Technical Terms', note to *Cantabile*.
[14] See, for instance, Veracini's Op. 2: *Toccata* of Sonata I (Ex. 244); opening *Adagio* of Sonata V; *Passagallo* of Sonata XII.

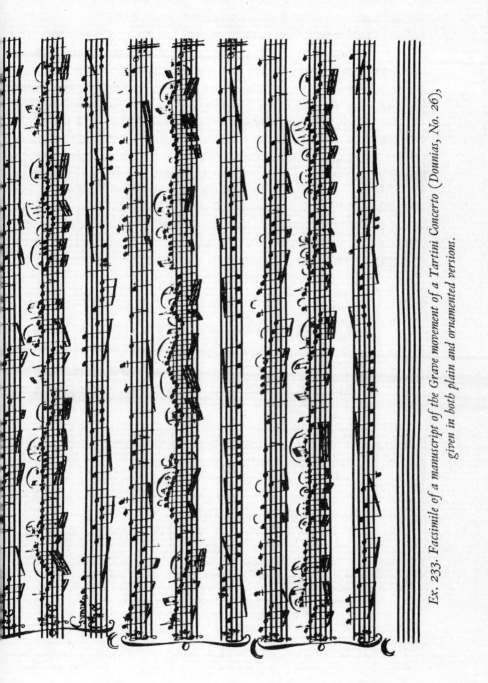

Ex. 233. Facsimile of a manuscript of the Grave movement of a Tartini Concerto (Dounias, No. 26), given in both plain and ornamented versions.

sometimes written out for concert performance, had the purpose of making the line more interesting melodically, more ornamental, and more varied, as in Ex. 233 (Tartini). The interest of the player in the purely technical aspects of some of these figures cannot be denied, and some of the formulas that occur are certainly inspired by violin pyrotechnics. The 'arbitrary' additions vary from simple ornaments to elaborate melodic *fioritura* in the tradition of the complex melodic variation. In the early eighteenth century, the tradition of violin improvisation is essentially Italian, and the extant examples emanate mostly from the Italian school (Geminiani, Tartini), or are Italian-inspired (Quantz, Leopold Mozart).[15] Besides his table of specific ornaments in *The Art of Playing on the Violin*, Geminiani has left examples of his 'arbitrary' additions in his 1739 revisions of Op. 1. In the first five measures of the opening of Sonata VII the original melody is ornamented, but is readily recognizable. However, in the following two measures (Ex. 234a) there are real melodic alterations (Ex. 234b); and while one can recognize a relationship, the ornamental version represents a genuinely new (or 'arbitrary') melodic conception.

Ex. 234   Geminiani

Geminiani, doubtless inspired by the ornamental tradition emanating from Corelli, was himself the originator of a tradition of ornamentation that inspired his pupils, notably Matthew Dubourg (1703–67), who ornamented seven of the sonatas of Corelli, in both fast and slow movements.[16] According to Quantz (ch. XV), the twelve solos of Corelli were ornamented also by N. Matteis, but of these pieces no trace remains.

The Germans were influenced by the Italian tradition. Quantz and

---

[15] The ornamental elaboration of slow movements was not limited to violin music. The fountain-head of improvised ornamentation was the eighteenth-century singer, and the singer's home base was the eighteenth-century opera aria. Improvised ornaments were also common in keyboard music. The slow movement of Bach's *Italian Concerto* is a good example of a written-out ornamental elaboration. See also Handel's ornamental additions to the *Adagio* of his Second Suite (F) for harpsichord, a facsimile of which is printed in Haas, *Aufführungspraxis*, Wildpark-Potsdam, 1931, p. 213. For a general view of improvisation, see Ernest T. Ferand, *Die Improvisation*, Köln, 1956, and H. P. Schmitz, *Die Kunst der Verzierung in 18. Jh.*, Kassell and Basel, 1955.

[16] See p. 222. See also the allegros of Geminiani's Op. III, first published in parts (1733) and later in score (1755) with ornamental additions by Geminiani.

Mozart were probably indebted largely to Tartini for the considerable amount of their information on the subject. There are also certain slow movements of Vivaldi ornamented by his German pupil, the violinist J. G. Pisendel.[17]

Tartini and his school are undoubtedly the great source of improvised ornaments about 1750. His *Traité des Agrémens* (see pp. 361–2) includes considerable material on 'arbitrary' ornaments and also on the cadenza (see below). Cartier's *L'Art du Violon* (1798) is the source of two other examples of Tartini's melodic formulas: (1) his *L'Arte del arco*, consisting of fifty variations on a theme of Corelli (a version of thirty-eight variations appeared earlier in 1758); and (2) inserted at the end, an *Adagio de M*. *Tartini Varié de plusieurs façons différentes*. From this title one cannot say whether the ornamental formulas are by Tartini or whether the *Adagio* is by Tartini and the variations by someone else. Finally, in recently discovered manuscripts of Tartini or his school, there is a large body of music consisting of cadenzas and especially arbitrary melodic ornamentation to the slow movements of concertos and sonatas, Ex. 233 being typical.[18]

The cadenza

The *cadenza* (*caprice, fantasia*; for other terms, see below) is a natural result of ornamenting cadences, and hence the name—*cadenza* meaning 'cadence' in Italian. In instrumental music, such cadential elaborations go back to the sixteenth century.[19] However, the cadenza does not become important to instrumental music until its appearance in the concerto and solo sonata of the late seventeenth century. Quantz assigns the invention of the cadenza to the late seventeenth or early eighteenth century and mentions Vivaldi in this connexion.

It is not always easy to say exactly when an ornamental passage becomes a cadenza. Several of the Corelli solo sonatas (1700) have ornamental passages which are set somewhat apart from the rest of the sonata by the character of the figuration and by the accompaniment of a single bass pedal, labelled *tasto solo*, on the dominant (see Ex. 63, p. 221). Such passages could be classed as cadenzas of a sort, but the true cadenza is generally characterized not only by relatively advanced technical display but also by its isolation as a solo passage near the end of a movement and by its contrast to the orchestra.[20]

---

[17] For examples, see Pincherle, *Vivaldi*, Vol. I, p. 76. See also Robert Haas, *Aufführungspraxis*, p. 204.

[18] These manuscripts are now at the University of California at Berkeley. For further information, see note 23, p. 344, above, and the author's article mentioned on p. 362 above. For an analysis of these ornaments, see Minnie Elmer, 'Tartini's Improvised Ornamentation', unpublished M.A. thesis, University of California, Berkeley, 1962.

[19] See Heinrich Knödt as in note 5, p. 334.   [20] For an early cadenza, see p. 289, note 7.

Quantz says that cadenzas should be constructed of the main ideas of the piece,[21] but this was not generally true in the first years of the eighteenth century where the notion of a cadenza was largely ornamental, consisting of elaborations of the final cadence. Some of these elaborations were also called *fantasia*, and they were, as the term implies, fanciful decorations of the most important cadences. The first cadenzas were fairly short. In concertos of wind instruments, for instance, the cadenza was originally limited in length by the amount of music that could be performed in a single breath by the players.[22]

Our main factual information about the cadenza comes from Quantz (ch. XV), Tartini's *Traité* (which also includes various formulas for the cadenza), and passing references to the cadenza in Leopold Mozart's treatise. Quantz distinguishes the one-voiced and the two-voiced cadenza—the former is not so 'arbitrary' (i.e. it is much freer). Mozart's information shows that he reserved the use of special effects for the cadenza, since it was the province of the virtuoso. His difficult and rarely used sixth-trill (see p. 453) occurs only in the cadenza. Similarly, the accelerating trill, played *crescendo*, is intended primarily for the cadenza. Again, according to Mozart, before beginning the cadenza proper it is customary to sustain a long note either on the tonic or dominant; and on this note a vibrato of increasing speed accompanied by a swell (*messa di voce*) makes a good effect.[23]

In addition to the information in eighteenth-century treatises, one sees that in the music itself cadenzas occur on final or intermediate cadences, and they may be fully written out or indicated merely by a fermata ($\frown$). The fully written-out cadenza may be found in Vivaldi (Ex. 235),[24] Tartini, and Locatelli (see below). The old type of written-out quasi-cadenza (often above the *tasto-solo* bass), observed in the sonatas of Corelli, still persists. The *Adagio* of Locatelli's Sonata VII of Op. 6 (1737) has three elaborate, though short, cadenzas of this character, each time over a *tasto solo*.[25] There are other examples in the music of Leclair, and the *tasto-solo* cadenza is carried over to the concertos of Vivaldi (e.g. Op. 8, No. 8, last movement).

However, the fermata was the traditional and most common way of indicating the position of the cadenza, marking the point at which the soloist was to begin his improvised flight of fancy. Various examples of these

---

[21] Quantz, ch. XV, para. 8.

[22] For this and an interesting account of the early cadenza (and, in particular, the early cadenza in Germany), see Arnold Schering's preface and the music contained in Vol. 29–30 of *Denkmäler der Deutscher Tonkunst*. In this volume, the only violin concertos are by Pisendel and Telemann.

[23] L. Mozart, ch. XI, para. 7.

[24] Ex. 235 is taken from the complete edition of Vivaldi, Vol. 136, pp. 52–53 (Pincherle No. 368). Note that this concerto uses a *scordatura* tuning, the G string being tuned up to b flat. Only excerpts of the whole cadenza are given in Ex. 235.

[25] Printed in Cartier, *L'Art du Violon*, p. 314.

fermatas may be found in the works of Vivaldi and others. In one of Vivaldi's pieces, the fermata comes with the direction *Qui si ferma a piacimento poi segue* (here one pauses ad. lib. [for the solo cadenza] and then resumes).[26] In Locatelli's *caprices*, a fermata is used at the end of individual *caprices* to suggest a short additional improvised flight of fancy around a cadence (see below). Sometimes the fermata indicates a cadenza in pieces that are not concertos, an instance being Geminiani's Example XIII in *The Art of Playing on the Violin*. J. H. Roman also uses the fermata to signify a cadenza in his *Assaggi* for violin alone.[27]

The written-out cadenzas are not long as a rule, generally lasting from a few measures to as many as thirty, the length of Ex. 235. (For a longer Tartini cadenza, see below.) The lengthy Locatelli *caprices* of his Op. 3 constitute a special case (see below). We have no way of knowing the duration of the innumerable unwritten cadenzas, but it is probable that the written-out versions are typical of the improvised and unrecorded variety.

Ex. 235

As an elaboration of a cadence, either intermediate or final, the cadenza of this time normally and naturally begins on the dominant of the key, as in Vivaldi (Ex. 235) and Quantz. The launching of the cadenza from the

---

[26] See Vivaldi, complete edition, Vol. 141, p. 72. For another fermata, see Vol. 146.

[27] See *Assaggio* No. 6, movement 2, measure 18. For these pieces, see p. 336. There are also unpublished cadenza sketches by Roman in the library of the Royal Music Academy in Stockholm.

fermata on the tonic six-four—in which the orchestra draws up and presents arms, as it were—is characteristic of the later Classic concerto, but not before 1750.[28]

Musically, the cadenzas were constructed occasionally of thematic materials heard in the course of the movement (cf. Quantz, note 21 above and Ex. 236). More generally, they consisted of the violinist's, especially the virtuoso's, stock-in-trade: rapid scales, high positions, arpeggios, trills (including double trills), multiple stops, *bariolage*, *brisure*, *pizzicato*, and other special effects. The cadenza generally ended with a trill on the dominant, leading effectively to the return of the orchestra on the tonic. However, as Quantz says, after giving instructions about the cadenza, 'it is impossible to write cadenzas as they must be played . . . to learn how to make good cadenzas you must try to hear many able people'. Then Quantz continues with a passage which is the heart of the matter, explaining as it does the spirit and intent of the cadenza:

> 'The greatest beauty lies in that, as something unexpected, they should astonish the listener in a fresh and striking manner and, at the same time, impel to the highest pitch the agitation of the passions which is sought after. You must not believe, however, that it is possible to accomplish this simply with a multitude of quick passages. The passions can be excited much more quickly with a few simple intervals, skilfully mingled with dissonances, than with a lot of motley figures.'[29]

Terms. The cadenza in Tartini and Locatelli

The fact that the cadenza originated in the practice of ornamenting cadences has contributed additional confusion to terminology. Thus in the early eighteenth century the Italian term *cadenza* may mean a cadence or cadenza proper; and in French, *cadence* may mean cadence, trill, or cadenza proper. The more precise French word for cadenza is *point d'orgue*. To suggest the improvised and fanciful character of the true cadenza, early eighteenth-century writers also used terms like *capriccio*, *caprice*, or *fantasia*. Since these terms had other meanings derived from earlier and quite different forms, the confusion of terminology, especially out of musical context, can easily be imagined.

Quantz recognizes this difficulty in his definition of the cadenza proper, and he makes clear that he is talking about the cadenza (*Cadenz*) as a flight

---

[28] However, Tartini's examples in his *Traité des Agrémens* start the cadenza on one of the notes of the tonic chord, *not* on the dominant. But the written-out cadenzas in Tartini's concertos start on the dominant (see below). For Quantz's use of the dominant, see his ch. XV, para. 1.

[29] Quantz, ch. XV, para. 18.

of fancy, not as a cadence or a trill. In a section entitled '*Cadenze Artifiziali*', Tartini says that this 'flight of fancy' is more a *capriccio* (caprice) than an elaborate cadence or *cadenza*:

> 'This sort of *cadenza* partakes at the present time more of the nature of a *capriccio* than a *cadenza* [i.e. an ornamental cadence] because today every singer and player feels entitled to lengthen it and with such diverse expression that it is surely unreasonable to call it *cadenza*, but better to say *capriccio*, since the *capriccio* can be prolonged at will and can consist of separate parts and of different sentiments and different tempi.'

In other words, the elaborate cadenza has become a matter of 'caprice', having exceeded the boundaries and character of the ornamented cadence.

The implication is that Tartini's capricious *capriccio*, capable of 'different sentiments and different tempi', is longer than the *cadenza* that is an ornamented cadence; and this generally proves true. The *capriccio* is also more frequently written out than the *cadenza*, the latter often being improvised. The longest written-out *capriccio* (so labelled) of Tartini (known to the author) lasts fifty measures and occurs in a cello concerto.[30] On the other hand, the 'cadenzas' at the end of his *Traité* are not more than a couple of lines in length apiece.

Certain of Tartini's *capricci* (so labelled) have exceptional interest in that they are related thematically to the opening ritornello of the piece. A violin concerto in E major relates the opening of the *capriccio* (so labelled) to the

Ex. 236

a) Opening *ritornello*,
Dounias No. 48,
last movement.

b) Tartini's "Capriccio"
(written out)
to the same.
Viola holding

opening of the ritornello (Ex. 236).[31] The *capriccio* of the cello concerto mentioned above relates the *capriccio* to the *last* four measures of the opening ritornello of the movement.

From the musical context of Tartini's own works, it is not easy to make

---

[30] The D major Concerto for cello. The only known surviving copy is the autograph in the *Archiv der Gesellschaft der Musikfreunde* (MS. IX 33952) in Vienna. There is also a *capriccio* in the first movement (a rare occurrence).

[31] Dounias No. 48, in manuscript. I am indebted to Pierluigi Petrobelli for calling this and the cello concerto (note 30) to my attention.

clear distinctions between *cadenza* and *capriccio* beyond the fact that the latter is generally longer and more 'capricious' (however, some *cadenzas* are longer than some *capriccios*). There seems to be no consistent difference in style or technical procedure between them. However, there are two points that should be stressed as regards musical usage in Tartini's concertos:

1. the term *capriccio* is limited to the *last* movement, while the term *cadenza* may be used in any of the movements (why this is so is not clear);

2. sometimes both terms are used in the same piece, in which case the term *cadenza* occurs over a fermata at the end of the *capriccio*.

These two terms are also used together in a similar way in Locatelli's Op. 3, with the difference that Locatelli's *caprices* are pieces of still greater length and are not limited to the last movement. Op. 3 is entitled *L'Arte del Violino: XII Concerti, cioè Violino Solo, con XXIV Capricci ad Libitum* (1733), and each of these twelve concertos has two written-out *caprices*, one for the first movement and one for the last. Toward the end of most of these *caprices* is a fermata followed by the word *cadenza*, indicating at that point a brief improvised elaboration of the cadence. As a rule, the *caprice* is then concluded with a brief written-out section following the fermata-cadenza.

Locatelli's use of a *capriccio* of such length is a *reductio ad absurdum* of Tartini's notion of a *caprice*, quoted above. The fact that these Locatelli *caprices* are marked *ad libitum* and that they are as long as the body of the movement itself—sometimes longer—suggest that they may have been used infrequently, if at all, in performing the concertos. The artistic balance of musical development to virtuoso display would certainly be quite wrong. At any rate, *caprices* of this length in concertos, had no predecessors and no successors. Locatelli's *caprices* are in reality technical studies, species of virtuoso etudes; and after him the lengthy *caprice* for violin alone was treated as an independent form by later composers, including Guillemain (see p. 334-5), Herschel (*c.* 1755?), and, most conspicuously, Paganini.

CHAPTER TWENTY-ONE

❧❀❧

Tempo. Alterations of Rhythm. Dynamics. Expression

'Time is the Soul of Music.'

LEOPOLD MOZART,
Violinschule, ch. 1, sec. 2, para. 1.

B Y the early eighteenth century time signatures had lost much of the tempo connotation they once had (cf. p. 181). Any tempo could be assigned to any note value—in principle, the modern system. As a result, there were more terms for tempo. Leopold Mozart, for instance, gives a large number of terms ranging from *grave* to *prestissimo*,[1] and some of his terms are fairly subtly distinguished. *Largo*, for example, is still slower than *adagio pesante* (which, in turn, is somewhat slower than *adagio*), and should be performed with 'long strokes and much tranquility'. For *grave*, Mozart says: 'Sadly and seriously, and therefore very slowly . . . long, rather heavy and solemn bowing . . . consistent prolonging and maintaining of the various notes.'

Nevertheless, there is still some evidence of the old relationship between tempo and time signatures. Signatures like 3/1 and 3/2 are often associated with slow time, and 6/8 with fast time (but the usual 3/4 may be associated with all types of slow *and* fast). When Grassineau explains in his Dictionary that (for example) an *andante* movement is swifter in triple time than an *andante* movement in common time (C), the implication is that the old proportions still have some effect (see pp. 181ff.). The proportions also operate in the case of *alla breve* (₵), which often means that the same note values are played twice as fast as in 4/4. However, *alla breve* may also mean

---

[1] Mozart, ch. 1, sec. 3, 'Technical Terms'.

faster, not necessarily twice as fast.[2] Grassineau gives C = slow, ₵ = brisk, 𝔡 = very quick. The old proportional division of the notes (cf. p. 181) is also implicit in the persistence of time signatures like C 12/8 or C 3/4; but since these signatures are generally coupled with tempo-terms, they have no practical effect on tempo. C 3/4 may be marked *lento, andante, allegro,* or *presto.*[3]

In the case of such curious terms as *andante allegro* and *andante allegretto* (e.g., in Handel's *Saul*), *andante* apparently has no tempo connotation but means that 'all the notes must be made equal [i.e., avoid *notes inégales*; see p. 472 below] and the sounds well separated'.[4]

It is clear that this system of tempo-terms was not very satisfactory, since these terms did not indicate precisely the correct tempo on which the proper effect of a piece of music so vitally depended. Terms like *allegro, andante,* and so on, no matter how numerous and how subtly distinguished, were completely relative. Besides, the relationship of the terms to each other varied, the general pace of all tempi changed from time to time, and the gap between the fastest and slowest tempi increased. The national differences in this matter added another complication. About 1700 Muffat noted that the Italians played adagios much slower, and allegros much faster, than the Germans (see p. 293). But fifty years later this situation had been reversed, the Germans playing allegros much faster than previously, and the Italians, slower.[5] Quantz notes this shift in Germany. In previous times, he says, *allegro assai, presto, furioso,* and so on, were played at half the speed they are 'today' (i.e. 1752), hardly faster than *allegretto.* 'Many rapid notes in the instrumental pieces of previous German composers appeared much harder and more perilous than they sounded. Today the French have still retained for the most part the manner of moderate speed in lively pieces.'[6]

In view of all this, it is not surprising that such theorists as Muffat (p. 293 above) comment on the problem of recognizing the proper ('inherent')

---

[2] For example, in Bach's Cantata, *Christ lag in Todesbanden* (No. 4), the *alla breve* that concludes the first chorus is certainly faster than the preceding section, but not twice as fast.

[3] A curious device of old notation, called 'white cromes' or *croches blanches,* seems to have no affect on tempo. The white crome is simply played as a quarter note (♪ = ♩) and, similarly, smaller values (♫ = ♪). This notation originated in the fifteenth century in connexion with proportional notation (especially *sesquialtera*) and persisted in a limited way throughout the seventeenth century in pieces with 3/2 signature. It continues still longer in France (e.g. in the works of François Couperin), and the French theorists mention it as late as 1762. See Jane Arger, *Les agréments and le rhythme,* Paris, 1921; and especially Michael Collins, as per note 34 below, p. 71ff. For an eighteenth-century reference, see Brossard, *Dictionnaire* (1703), article 'tripola'.

[4] See Brossard, *Dictionnaire,* article 'Andante'. See also article 'E' ou Ed" which says: '*Allegro ed*' andante. [means] *Gayement & à Nottes égales.*'

[5] See Curt Sachs, *Rhythm and Tempo,* New York, 1953, pp. 322-3.

[6] Quantz, ch. XVII, sec. 7, para. 50, note.

tempo. If this was a difficulty for a composer in his own time, it is doubly difficult for the modern musician, confronted with music several hundred years old whose conventions and aesthetics he may understand imperfectly, if at all. Nevertheless, Leopold Mozart is confident about recognizing the inherent tempo (see below)—but that is for music of his own time.

Obviously, the only sensible way to fix tempo with any accuracy required some time-measure more absolute than terms like *andante* and *allegro*. Gropings toward a solution of this sort were apparent throughout the seventeenth century.[7] Mersenne proposed an impractical pendulum device, and Loulié (1696), a 'chronometer'. Quantz mentions Loulié's device, although apparently he had never seen it. It is clear that musicians were trying to regulate the tempo by the absolute measure of beats per minute. Grassineau proposed to link common time (C) to one beat a second ($\downarrow$ = 60); and Quantz, like many others, sought to relate the tempo to the pulse of the heart. Naturally, he realized that this was no objective measure, and arbitrarily set the pulse at eighty beats to the minute. From this, one can calculate the approximate metronome markings recommended by Quantz. He gives four categories of time. For instance, in 'ordinary common time': allegro assai = $\downarrow$ 160; allegretto = $\downarrow$ 80; adagio cantabile = $\uparrow$ 80; adagio assai = $\uparrow$ 40. In other words, each of Quantz's succeeding tempi is half as fast as the previous one. His dances are given at a surprisingly fast tempo, in line with the faster tempi he notes himself. For instance *bourrée*, $\mathbb{C}$, $\downarrow$ = 160; *gigue*, 6/8, $\downarrow$. = 160; *menuet*, 3/4, $\downarrow$ = 160; and *sarabande*, 3/4, $\downarrow$ = 80. These tempi, applied to certain pieces of Bach, make very rapid playing indeed—in some cases, almost impossibly so.

Perhaps Quantz's markings are intended to be in the nature of rough approximations. In any case, although his tempi, applied to Bach, seem too fast, the chances are that tempi in the time of Bach and Handel were generally sprightly, according to our notions. The tempi of their music were slowed down in the Romantic interpretations of the nineteenth and early twentieth centuries. Today this tendency is being reversed in favour of playing early eighteenth-century music in a lively fashion, probably much closer to the original.[8]

Leopold Mozart places great store by the 'inherent' tempo. 'Every melodious piece', he says, 'has at least one phrase from which one can recognize quite surely what sort of speed the piece demands'.[9] And it is by this ability

[7] For details, including metronome equivalents, see Ralph Kirkpatrick, 'Eighteenth-Century Metronomic Indications' in *Papers of the American Musicological Society*, 1938, privately printed, 1940. See also Curt Sachs, as per note 5 above.

[8] For the question of tempi in Handel oratorios, see J. P. Larsen, 'Tempo Probleme bei Händel dargestellt am "Messias" ' in *Händel-Konferenzbericht*, Leipzig, 1959, pp. 141 ff.

[9] Mozart, ch. 1, sec. 2, para. 7.

to set the true tempo that 'the true worth of a musician can be recognized without fail'. It is to this 'inherent' tempo that Mozart's terms *tempo commodo* and *tempo giusto* refer. 'They tell us that we must play it [the piece] neither too fast nor too slowly, but in a proper, convenient, and natural tempo. We must therefore seek the true pace of such a piece within itself.' Rameau makes a similar comment in the preface to his 'Third' book of harpsichord pieces (*c.* 1728): 'When one has mastered a piece, one grasps its sense unconsciously, and soon one feels its right tempo.'

The view of Mozart and Rameau is a thoroughly musicianly one, even if, in the hindsight of history and experience, it has proved somewhat over-optimistic as regards modern musicians dealing with the unfamiliar music of the past. Nevertheless, seeking 'the true pace' is often the only recourse, and, when an absolute measure of tempo is lacking, the 'inherent' tempo is the soundest rule-of-thumb. In any case, there is really no such thing as one tempo, metronomically speaking, that is absolutely correct under every condition. The varying resonance of halls and many other musical factors enforce a certain flexibility in this matter if one is to achieve the best musical effect.

Tempo rubato

Tempo rubato or 'stolen time' may mean two things: (1) 'broken time', in which the performer deviates from regular time in the course of a piece by speeding up or slowing down the *whole* ensemble at this point or that—an arbitrary *accelerando* or *ritardando*, not marked by the composer; or (2) 'stolen but restored' time, in which the performer maintains strict time in the ensemble, but achieves 'stolen time' in the melody by stealing time from some notes and restoring it to others. The latter species of *tempo rubato* was described later by Chopin in these words: 'The singing hand may deviate, the accompaniment must keep time.' In terms of the keyboard this usually meant that the left hand maintained strict time, and the right hand deviated

Ex. 237

from the tempo in an expressive performance of the melody, now faster, now slower, but always 'restoring' the time to that maintained by the guardian left hand. Couperin's ornament called 'suspension' (Ex. 237a) may be regarded as a species of 'stolen time' in the melody.

Tempo rubato is obviously a device related to expressive or rhapsodic music, and the question is whether the whole ensemble of the piece or only the melody is to be played *tempo rubato*. With the exception of genuinely rhapsodic pieces (such as certain types of toccatas), where keeping the time was secondary to their quasi-improvised and rhapsodic character, 'stolen time' in the eighteenth century seemed to mean 'stolen but restored' time. The eighteenth-century theorists had little patience with the slovenly keeping of time. This attitude is inherent in the treatises of Quantz and Mozart, taken as a whole; and Tosi, in his singing method, says: 'Whosoever does not sing to the utmost Rigour of Time, deserves not the Esteem of the judicious'; and again: 'I cannot sufficiently recommend to a student the exact keeping of Time.'[10] But elsewhere Tosi speaks of 'stolen but restored' time with approval: 'stealing the Time exactly on the true Motion of the Bass'. Later he says: 'Whoever does not know how to steal the Time in Singing does not know how to compose, nor to Accompany himself, and is destitute of the best Taste and greatest Knowledge. The stealing of Time in the *Pathetick* [i.e. expressive] is an honourable Theft in one that sings better than others, *provided he makes a Restitution with Ingenuity*' (italics added); and in a footnote, 'The Bass goes an exactly regular Pace, the other Part retards or anticipates in a singular Manner, for the Sake of Expression, but after That returns to its Exactness, to be guided by the Bass. Experience and Taste must teach it'.[11]

Leopold Mozart's passing reference to *tempo rubato* implies an accompaniment of unyielding tempo in the orchestra and 'stolen but restored' time in the solo part:

'A skilful accompanist must therefore know how to judge a soloist. To a true virtuoso, the accompanist must certainly not yield for he would then spoil the tempo rubato [of the soloist]. What this 'stolen tempo' is, is more easily shown than described.'

Then Mozart goes on to describe the plight of an accompanist to a soloist who steals, but does not restore, the time:

'on the other hand, if the accompanist has to deal with a fancied virtuoso, then he may often, in an Adagio Cantabile, have to hold out many an eighth the length of half a bar, until perchance the latter recovers from his paroxysms; and nothing goes according to time, for he plays after the style of a recitative.'[12]

Leopold Mozart must have taught the 'stolen but restored' variety of *tempo rubato* to his famous son. Twenty-one years after the publication of

---

[10] Pier Francesco Tosi, *Opinioni de' Cantori antichi e moderni*, Bologna, 1723. Translated into English by Galliard as *Observations on the Florid Song*, London, 1743. The above quotations are found in the English translation, pp. 63–64 and p. 99, respectively.

[11] Tosi, English translation, pp. 129 and 156.

[12] Mozart, ch. 12, para. 21, note.

Leopold Mozart's treatise, Wolfgang wrote to his father from Augsburg (1777): 'They are amazed that I always keep time. Nor do they understand that my left hand knows nothing of the tempo rubato in an adagio. [When they play rubato], the left hand gives way.'[13] Geminiani was famous, or notorious, for his *tempo rubato*, but, apart from desiring an expressive performance, he says nothing specific about 'stolen time' in his violin treatise.

The early eighteenth century knew both kinds of *tempo rubato*, but, except for pieces basically rhapsodic in character, it favoured the 'stolen but restored' variety in which a regular tempo was maintained in the ensemble. This preference need not be construed as forbidding a slight *ritardando* at the end of a piece to bring it to a natural close.

Alterations of rhythm

The rhythmic alterations described earlier (pp. 294ff.) persist for a long time in the eighteenth century. In general, the practices are more codified and systematized. These alterations, especially *notes inégales* (cf. p. 303), are French or French inspired. The Italians, according to Couperin, wrote as they intended the music to be played (cf. p. 303 above).

Rhythmic alterations of various kinds should be viewed in the proper context of strict rhythm. Over and over again the treatises of the time insist on maintaining the tempo strictly from beginning to end, even while commenting on specific deviations (cf. Muffat, p. 303). The latter should be regarded as specific licences within a system of fairly strict rhythm. Free rhythms were appropriate, however, to pieces of rhapsodic character. Presumably, elongating some notes beyond their written values (and consequently shortening others) was done for expressive reasons (such as emphasizing the beginning of a phrase), for variety's sake, and perhaps as a species of unwritten ornamentation.

Notes inégales

The French still continue to remark, sometimes rather casually, that certain notes written equally are played unequally (for earlier cases, see p. 303). Couperin treats this matter almost in passing and not very precisely in his harpsichord treatise (cf. p. 303 above). Corrette, however, in his 1738 treatise, is quite explicit about the use of unequal notes in violin music, relative to the type of note values and time signatures, and his information works out in the following way:

[13] Quoted in Curt Sachs, *Rhythm and Tempo*, p. 309. See also Lucian Kamiensky, 'Zum Tempo Rubato' in *Archiv für Musikwissenschaft*, Vol. I (1918–19). Also, *Grove's Dictionary* (1954), Vol. VI, pp. 428–9.

Signature:

2 (as in *rigaudons, branles, gavottes, bourrées*, etc.) ₵, 6/4 3 (as in *menuets, sarabandes, courantes*, etc.)	The second of two eighths is played shorter (i.e. long-short inequality).
C (often in church music and Italian music) 2/4 (common in Italian music, in *vivace, presto*, and in *ariettes*) 3/4, 3/8	Eighths played equally; the second of two sixteenths shorter.
3/2	The second of two quarters is played shorter.

Corrette also mentions 6/8, 9/8, and 12/8 time, and, although inequality is not specifically mentioned by him in connexion with these three signatures, the implication is (at least in 6/8 and 12/8) that the eighths are played equally and the second of two sixteenths shorter. He says nothing of conjunct motion or the inequality short-long—all the above being long-short.

By far the most elaborate account of the 'unequal notes', their uses and exceptions, emanates, not from a French theorist, but from Quantz, a German. In this connexion one must remember that Quantz was an ardent advocate of an international style, and as an eclectic he reports the prevailing practice of unequal notes in France and elsewhere; and he does so in his usual encyclopedic way.[14] The context of Quantz's remarks on unequal notes is important in estimating the conditions and extent of their usage. Just prior to his paragraph on unequal notes, Quantz speaks of performance in general:

'Every note must be expressed in its true worth and in its true time. . . . From lack of knowledge or from atrophied taste they [the performers] often give to the following note something of the time that belongs to the previous one. The held-out and flattering notes must be slurred to one another; but the jolly and skipping notes must be lifted (*abgesetzet*) and separated from one another.'[15]

[14] The enormous influence of French culture on Germany in the eighteenth century can be gauged by the force of the reaction against it by German writers of the *Sturm und Drang* movement at the end of the century. As part of this influence, the French contributed much to German music in one way or another. It is surprising, for example, to find how much Walther's *Musikalisches Lexikon* (1732) owed to the French *Dictionnaire* of Brossard some thirty years earlier (1703). Quantz himself was surrounded by the atmosphere of French culture which thoroughly permeated the court of Frederick the Great, his master at Potsdam.

[15] Quantz, ch. XI, para. 11. The following quotation on unequal notes occupies all of paragraph 12, which was used by Sol Babitz as the basis of his long article on *notes inégales* (see p. 303, note 34).

Having established that 'every note must be expressed in its true worth and its true time', Quantz then continues with a lengthy essay on the unequal notes and their exceptions:

'Herewith I must make a necessary observation, which concerns the length of time each note must be held. One must know how to make a distinction in performance between the principal notes, which one is accustomed to call *anschlagende* [accented = on-beat] notes or, according to the Italians, *good* notes, and between the *durchgehende* [passing = off-beat] which, by some foreigners, are called *bad* notes. Where possible, the principal notes must always be brought out more than the passing notes. As a consequence of this rule, the fastest notes in every piece of moderate tempo or adagio, regardless of the fact that they appear to have the same value, are nevertheless played a little unevenly: so that the accented notes of every figuration, namely, the first, third, fifth, and seventh, are held somewhat longer than the passing notes, namely the second, fourth, sixth, and eighth; but *this holding must not be as much as if a dot stood by the note* [italics added]. By these swift notes I mean: the quarters in 3/2, the eighths in 3/4 and the sixteenths in 3/8, the eighths in *alla breve*, the sixteenths or thirty-seconds in 2/4 or in common time [4/4]. But [this applies] only so long as no figuration of still faster or once again as short notes are mixed together in any meter. For then these last must be performed in the way described above. For example, if one would play the eight sixteenths as shown in letters k, m, and n [Ex. 238] slowly in the same worth, they would not sound so pleasing as if one made the first and third of the four somewhat longer and stronger in tone than the second and fourth.

Ex. 238   k)   m)   Quantz

n)

But from this rule are excepted: first, the fast passages [*passaggi*] in a very fast tempo in which the tempo does not allow them to be performed unequally and where one consequently must make only the first of the four long and strong. Still further are excepted: all fast passages made by the voice, if they ought not otherwise to be slurred: for because every note of this manner of singing passages must be clearly made and marked through a smooth push of the breath and the chest. Therefore, in this case, unevenness has no place. Further is excepted:

the notes over which [staccato] strokes or dots stand or those [passages] in which some come one after the other in one tone [i.e. repeated notes]; furthermore, if a slur stands over more than two notes, namely over 4, 6, or 8; and finally the eighths in gigues. All these notes must be performed equally, that is, one as long as the other.'[16]

While the unequal notes are a distinct phenomenon of the seventeenth and eighteenth centuries, one should keep in mind that playing notes somewhat unequal is a regular, although unsystematized and perhaps unconscious, practice of concert artists in general. The metrically good (accented) notes tend to receive slightly more stress than the unaccented; and the first note of a slurred phrase also tends to be emphasized either by elongation or by being played louder, or by both. Leopold Mozart's remarks can be interpreted in this light. In his treatise, the most detailed work specifically devoted to the violin to the date of its publication, there is hardly anything concerning *notes inégales* as such. In general, he insists on equality of time and the notes. For a passage of thirty-two sixteenths in 4/4 time (which according to Quantz would be played 'unequally'), he says: 'Great pains must be taken with their exact equality, and the first note of each quarter [i.e. the first of each four sixteenths] must be marked with a vigour which inspires the whole performance.' Or again: 'In all these passages and their variations I recommend, as always, evenness of time-measure.'[17] With respect to slurring by twos, Mozart remarks:

'The first of two notes coming together in one stroke is accented more strongly and held slightly longer, while the second is slurred on to it quite quietly and rather late. This style of performance promotes good taste in the playing of the melody and prevents hurrying by means of the afore-mentioned sustaining of the first notes.'[18]

In a later paragraph, he continues:

'The first of two, three, four, or even more notes slurred together, must at all times be stressed more strongly and sustained a little longer; but those following must diminish in tone and be slurred on somewhat later. But this must be carried out with such good judgement that the bar-length is not altered in the smallest degree.'[19]

[16] In a later paragraph (para. 21) Quantz gives as a bad trait of performance: not observing the time nor the notes in their given time value. In ch. XII, para. 5, every note is to be played according to its proper worth, and rushing of passages is prevented by holding out the first note somewhat. The principal notes are held a bit longer than the passing notes. Quantz then refers to the 'unequal notes' described in ch. XI, para. 12, just given.

[17] The first quotation is from ch. 7, sec. 1, para. 2; the second, from ch. 7, sec. 2, para. 2. (For the full quotation of the latter, see p. 479 below.)

[18] Leopold Mozart, ch. 7, sec. 1, para. 3. English translation, p. 115.

[19] Mozart, ch. 7, sec. 2, para. 5. English translation, p. 130.

Four or more slurred notes played in Mozart's way would be contrary to Quantz's system, under which all notes would be equal. What Mozart has to say above is eminently musical, and is what many musicians would do intuitively. Much of Mozart's concern and many of his directions arise from his desire to avoid hurrying. He says that triplets must be played equally, not as if they were two sixteenths followed by an eighth, or an eighth followed by two sixteenths.[20]

The tradition of *notes inégales*, so firmly rooted in French tradition, continues to appear after 1750, largely in French music and treatises. L'Abbé le fils does not mention the phenomenon by name but acknowledges its presence in his bowing exercises, where he implies unequal notes by marking equally written notes with long and short bows, as in Ex. 239a, b, and c (L = long bow-stroke; b = short bow-stroke). Ex. 239c is taken from an exercise labelled *Leçon pour piquer les brèves* (Lesson to 'dot' the short notes). Here the length of the bow strokes clearly enforces the long-short of the *notes inégales*.

L' Abbe le fils

Ex. 239

In his *Dictionnaire de Musique* (1768), Rousseau explains the unequal notes in his article 'Pointer', and he makes it clear that, while the French regularly use them, the Italians do not, unless specifically called for:

'*Pointer*. By means of a dot to make alternately long and short groups of notes naturally equal as, for example, a group of eighths. To "point" them, one adds a dot after the first, making a sixteenth of the second, a dot after the third, then a sixteenth, and so on. In this way, they maintain by twos the same [total] value as before; but this value is distributed unequally between the two eighths in the fashion that the first or the long note takes three-quarters [of the time] and the second or short note the other quarter. To "point" them in performance, one considers them unequal according to the same proportions even when they are notated as equal.

In Italian music, all the eighths are always equal unless they are marked *pointées*. But in French music one makes the eighths exactly equal only in 4/4 time; in all others one always "points" them a little unless they are specifically written *croches égales*.'

[20] Cf. Mozart, ch. 6, para. 2. English translation, p. 103.

The unequal notes persist at least until 1775, when Père Engramelle published his *La Tonotechnie* in Paris. This work, devoted to making the cylinders of music boxes, gives us very precise information on the unequal notes, and defines the long-short ratio, not merely as 3:1 or 3:2, but in more subtle ratios like 7:5.

To summarize: *notes inégales* were used in violin music of the eighteenth century somewhat as follows:

1. Mainly in French music or in music in French style found elsewhere (e.g. Quantz at the Court of Frederick the Great).

2. Basically on note values that are half to a quarter of the basic unit of beat—for example, the quarter in 3/2, the eighth in *alla breve*, the sixteenth in 4/4, 2/4, 3/4, and 3/8.

3. Primarily in running passages of equally written notes which are mainly conjunct. For leaping notes or arpeggios they would be out of place.

4. In patterns of long-short. The treatises of the eighteenth century speak largely of lengthening the first (or metrically accented) of the group, usually by twos. The short-long patterns are much less usual (cf. remarks in Loulié and in Couperin, p. 304–5). The relation of long to short was not precisely determined. French sources often give dotted patterns (relation 3:1), but Quantz says 'not as much as if a dot stood by the note'. Engramelle (above) is one of the few who gives precise relationships.

5. With various exceptions to the conditions mentioned above. The most frequently noted concern the presence of repeated notes or the staccato (indicated either by the term or by dots or strokes), which automatically make the notes equal. Unequal notes are also forbidden in the accompaniment. (For more detailed exceptions, see the quotation from Quantz, above.)[21]

The question of applying the unequal notes in the performance of eighteenth-century music must be settled by the player according to his own inclination and in the context of any given piece. No categorical application of the statements of Quantz and others is necessarily mandatory or even appropriate to any given composer or any particular piece. *Notes inégales* are most suitable to French music in general. But are 'unequal notes' generally applicable to Leclair, whose sonatas are primarily Italian in inspiration? Or to J. S. Bach, who wrote in the tradition of French, Italian, and German music? Would Bach have been more sympathetic to the tradition explained (after his death) by the book of Quantz rather than that found in the specific violin treatises of Leopold Mozart and Geminiani, neither of whom mention

---

[21] For a good summary, see *Inégales* in *Grove's Dictionary* (1954). For the same related to French bowing, see Barbara Seagrave (as per page 262 above), pp. 66ff.

the unequal notes as such.[22] From an historical point of view no one can answer these questions with finality; from an artistic point of view, the answer comes, as it always must, from the intuition and conscience of the individual artist.

Double (or triple) dotting

Under certain conditions, dotted notes in patterns of dotted eighths plus sixteenths (or dotted sixteenths plus thirty-seconds) were elongated to doubly (or triply) dotted notes, the following note being correspondingly shortened. (For a discussion of this practice in the seventeenth century, see p. 295.) Quantz is the first theorist to discuss this matter with more than a passing reference;[23] and he and Leopold Mozart, who also mentions it, show for the first time a notation using double dots.[24] With respect to the music shown in Ex. 240, Quantz plays dotted halves and quarters (Ex. 240a and b) as written, but the dotted eighths and lesser values (Ex. 240c, d, and e) are elongated so that the short note is very short 'because of the liveliness which these notes must express'. In the case of both (c) and (d), the note following the dotted note is to be played as short as at (e)—that is, as a sixty-fourth note, the dotted note then being correspondingly lengthened, 'whether in slow or fast tempo'. At (c) this elongation would require a triply dotted eighth (!), and at (d), a doubly dotted sixteenth. Similarly, Lombard figures ( ) use these rules in reverse, but are often slurred.[25] In all these cases, the obvious intent of Quantz is to play the short note very short rather than to observe mathematical values.

Ex. 240

[22] The nearest Geminiani comes to commenting on unequal notes occurs in a passage which would forbid it: 'If by your Manner of Bowing you lay a particular Stress on the Note at the beginning of every Bar, so as to render it predominant over the rest, you alter and spoil the true Air of the piece.'

[23] It may be that, in earlier times, double dotting was considered an extension of the *notes inégales*: that is, if notes written as equal were played somewhat unequally, notes written as unequal were played still more unequally!

[24] For Quantz's notation of double dots, see his Tab. XXII, fig. 41; for Mozart, see his ch. I, sec. 3, para. 11.

[25] See Quantz, ch. V, paras. 20–21.

A similar procedure occurs when a long note and a rest are followed by a group of thirty-second notes. In this case, the 'thirty-seconds are always played very quickly, either in Adagio or Allegro'. (See Ex. 114 and p. 295; see also Quantz's further remark, below.)

Leopold Mozart accepts double dotting to prevent hurrying and 'to enliven'. His remarks occur after he insists on evenness of time-measure:

'In all passages and their variation I recommend, as always, evenness of time measure (*Zeitmass*). It is only too easy to err in tempo, and nothing is more easy than to hurry in dotted notes if the value of the dot be not held out. It is therefore always better if the note following the dot be played somewhat late. For by means of the notes which are detached by a lift of the bow, the style of performance becomes more enlived [Ex. 241a; all the examples in this connexion have staccato strokes over the short note]. Slurred notes, on the contrary, make the style of performance satisfying, melodious, and pleasant. Not only must the dotted note be prolonged, however, but it must be attacked somewhat strongly, slurring the second decreasingly and quietly on to it.' (Ex. 241b.)[26]

Ex. 241

In another connexion, Leopold Mozart comments: 'There are certain passages in slow pieces where the dot must be held rather longer [than written] if the performance is not to sound too sleepy.'[27]

In all Mozart's examples and in those given so far by Quantz, it is striking that it is the dotted-eighth group and lesser values which are elongated, not the dotted quarter or dotted half. However, toward the end of his book, Quantz deals with the tempo and characteristic manner of performing specific (French) dances, and in this context he requires the elongation of the dotted quarter and the shortening of the eighth. In connexion with the following quotation, Quantz has just been speaking of dances in *alla breve*, which, he says, the French use in 'bourées, entrées, rigaudons, gavottes, rondeaus, etc.':

'In this meter, as well as in three-four time, the eighths which follow the dotted quarters in the Loure, Sarabande, Courante, and Chaconne must not be played with their literal value, but must be executed in a very short and sharp manner. The dotted note is played with emphasis,

[26] Mozart, ch. 7, sec. 2, para. 2. English translation, p. 130.
[27] Mozart, ch. 1, sec. 3, para. 11. English translation, p. 41.

and the bow is lifted during the dot. All dotted notes are treated in the same manner if time allows; and if thirty-seconds or notes of shorter value follow a dot or a rest, they are not played with their literal value, especially in slow pieces, but are executed at the extreme end of the time allotted to them, and with the greatest possible speed, as is frequently the case in Overtures, Entrées, and Furies. One must, however, give every one of these quick notes a separate bow stroke, and one can hardly slur anything.'[28]

As with *notes inégales*, the important question is where to elongate dotted notes and how much. In general, double dotting is used:

1. Where shortening the short notes will enhance the music by 'enlivening' it. Actually, it is the shortening that produces the enlivening effect as much as the elongation of the dotted note. In this connexion, shortening is applied most frequently to notes already short, to patterns of dotted eighths plus sixteenths, or less; sometimes to dotted quarters plus eighths.

2. Where double dotting will prevent hurrying over a dotted note (L. Mozart).

3. In music in French style, especially French dances. In general, double dotting is more suitably applied to the rhythmic effects of dances than to melodies, especially the cantabile of the Italians.

4. In French overtures. On Quantz's evidence (given above) the double dotting would apply to dotted quarter plus eighths in French overtures (Italian overtures were called *sinfonia*). Quantz characterizes the opening of the French overtures as 'grave and majestic';[29] and in explaining how to play in a style of 'majesty' he says: 'The dotted notes must be attacked sharply and must be executed in a lively fashion. The dots are held long and the following notes are made very short.'[30] Therefore, pieces such as the opening section of the overture to Handel's *Messiah* would, if Quantz's instructions are followed, be performed in double-dotted style.[31]

At the same time, in the heady thrill of 'enlivening' this old piece and that, double dotting must be kept to the purpose and the kind of music for which it was intended. It is a means toward a musical end, not an end in itself. And when did this practice actually flourish? In this connexion a number of questions are in order. Why was double dotting hardly mentioned before Quantz if it was such a rhythmic force in performance? Why does not

[28] Quantz, ch. XVII, sec. 7, para. 58.

[29] Quantz, ch. XVIII, para. 42. There is no evidence that double dotting was ever applied to longer note values than dotted quarters.

[30] Quantz, ch. XII, para. 24.

[31] However, there are respected experts today who do not believe that this style ought to be applied to the *Messiah* overture. See the *Report of the Eighth Congress, New York, 1961, International Musicological Society*, Kassel, 1962, Vol. II, pp. 125-6.

Muffat, the chief apologist of the Lully style, mention a practice that would affect practically every one of Lully's overtures? And why does not Geminiani, the contemporary of Quantz, mention it if it had a prominent place in Italian violin music?[32] It is sensible to conclude that where double dotting does not seem to fit the musical mood of a piece or the context of the ensemble of parts, there is no point in applying it. In Bach's D major Fugue of Book I of *The Well Tempered Clavier,* for instance, the dotted eighth figure is better played as written to fit the accompanying thirty-second note figure (cf. Ex. 242).

C. P. E. Bach speaks of elongation of dotted notes in several connexions in his harpsichord treatise, and his remarks are similar to those made by Quantz and Leopold Mozart. In one of his passages, C. P. E. Bach offers eminently sane and sensible advice, applicable to rhythmic alteration and also to musical performance in general:

> 'Because proper exactness is often lacking in the notation of dotted notes, a general rule of performance has been established which, however, suffers many exceptions. According to this rule, the notes which follow the dots are to be played in the most rapid manner; and often they should be. But sometimes notes in other parts, with which these must enter, are so divided that a modification of the rule is required. Again, a suave affect [*sic*], which will not survive the essentially defiant character of dotted notes, obliges the performer slightly to shorten the dotted note. Hence, *if only one kind of execution is adopted as the basic principle of performance, the other kinds will be lost.*' (Italics added.)[33]

Earlier in his book (Mitchell, p. 157), C. P. E. Bach has already mentioned modifications of the practice of shortening the short notes in dotted figures. Of the music shown in Ex. 242, he says it shows 'that occasionally the division must agree with the notated values'. This modification would be applicable to Bach's D major Fugue, mentioned above.

Ex. 242

C. P. E. Bach

To summarize: as far as violin music is concerned and *where double dotting is applicable*:

1. The dotted note is played emphatically.

[32] There are those who explain such mysteries by maintaining that when a thing is especially well known no one bothers to mention it. The possibilities and ramifications of this doctrine of proof *in abstentia* stagger the imagination.
[33] C. P. E. Bach, *Versuch*, Mitchell translation, p. 372.

2. The bow may be stopped (or taken off the string) during all or part of the dot in the interest of better articulation—in effect, a rest.

3. The shortened note after the dot is played very short with a correspondingly short bow stroke. In some cases, the bow may be lifted (cf. Ex. 241a).

4. In Lombard figures, the first note is also shortened, but it is more likely to be slurred to the second.

5. If several notes follow a dotted note (or a relatively long note plus a rest), the several notes are also played rapidly, generally with individual bow strokes (cf. Quantz above).

6. The actual degree of elongation and shortening is not mathematically determined. It depends on context, the tempo, and the desired effect.

Alterations of dotted and other figures in the context of triplets

When such figures as a dotted eighth plus sixteenth occur in the context of triplets (♫♩), either melodically or harmonically, the question arises whether (1) the dotted note is played as written, (2) slightly elongated, or (3) assimilated to the triplet rhythm as ♩ ♪ . In the course of an earlier discussion of this matter (pp. 296ff.), we cited Quantz and C. P. E. Bach, and drew certain conclusions (p. 302). Quantz introduces the question of the dotted figure against triplets directly after his section on double dotting (see above), and he wants the double-dotting rule applied (cf. Ex. 118a); whereas C. P. E. Bach allows for assimilating the dotted-note figure to the triplet (Ex. 118b). The reverse dotted figure (♫) also suffers from the same ambiguity in the context of triplets, and so do equally written eighths, which, according to C. P. E. Bach, may be played as ♩ ♪ (Ex. 118b). Oddly, Quantz does not mention the problem of equally written eighths. In this connexion, C. P. E. Bach says less, and less definite things, than are often attributed to him.

There is no way of reconciling the differences between Quantz and C. P. E. Bach except through the musical context and the application of good taste and sense. As has been shown above, now one and now the other solution must have been used: in Ex. 119a and b, assimilation undoubtedly takes place, but not in Exx. 121, 122, or 123. Harich-Schneider (see p. 298) thought that Quantz's solution was more applicable to music before 1750 and C. P. E. Bach's solution, to music afterwards; but there is no such clear and easy distinction. In J. S. Bach, for example, in 2/4, 4/4, or 3/4 time, one invariably finds figures like ♫♩ ♩. ♪, not ♫♩ ♩ ♪, in the context of triplets (cf. p. 300), and the implication is that ♩. ♪ is a notation device for ♩ ♪ Ex. 116a, the opening of J. S. Bach's Fifth 'Brandenburg' Concerto, is a case in point; and following our Conclusion 1 (p. 302), it would then be assimilated as at Ex. 116b. Nevertheless, this solution would be in direct violation of Quantz's instructions. This movement may be played either way, but it can be played faster and more smoothly if the dotted figures are assimilated to triplet rhythm. Another example is the opening chorus of Bach's Cantata, *Du Hirte Israel* (No. 104). This remarkable piece, in 3/4 with dotted-eighth figures in some of the vocal and instrumental parts and triplets in others, may be performed either way, but the results are quite different. Assimilation is the simplest and smoothest. However, the individual lines come out better when the dotted figures are not assimilated but played doubly dotted, and the effect is much more 'brilliant and splendid', as Quantz remarks (cf. p. 297). In such contexts, double dotting is very effective in bringing out the polyrhythm of the dotted figures against the flowing triplets. Of the three alternatives for performing such notation (as suggested above), there are really two: that recommended by C. P. E. Bach or that by Quantz. Ironically, the least practical is to play the notes strictly as written.

Leopold Mozart does not discuss this question as such, but in the passage shown in Ex. 243, involving dotted figures in the melodic context of triplets, Mozart says that the dot should be lengthened, thus agreeing with Quantz but not with C. P. E. Bach. Note that Mozart gives his example in faster note values than those used by Quantz and C. P. E. Bach, and his example involves a single melodic line only, not two lines in different rhythms.

L. Mozart

Ex. 243

Mozart's example suggests other problems: what happens when dotted figures are mixed in with triplets in melodic lines? And what happens when one figure or the other is the prevailing one? Here Thurston Dart's rule (cf. p. 298) is useful to consider: assimilate all dotted rhythms to the dominant rhythm of the movement. Mozart's example (Ex. 243) would seem to contradict Dart's rule in that the dotted figure is not assimilated to the prevailing triplet; but this example is not long enough to be decisive for a whole piece or to make clear whether the triplet rhythm is the prevailing one. A better example is the *Corrente* (*Courante*) of J. S. Bach's D minor Partita for unaccompanied violin. This piece begins with triplet figures in the first two measures, then introduces dotted-eighth figures in the following two. This is the kind of piece to which Dart's rule may be applied. If it is, the dotted figure becomes ♩₃♪ , and the *Corrente*, marked in 3/4, becomes essentially a piece in 9/8. In this way a fluency is gained; at the same time, a certain variety and piquancy are lost. It is a moot point, rule or no rule, which of these solutions is superior musically.

When dotted rhythms are clearly established first, the later introduction of triplet figures does not necessarily have a retroactive effect. In short, the dotted figures—perhaps best doubly dotted—are continued. A good example of this is the *Allemande* of Bach's B minor Partita for unaccompanied violin. (Cf. also Ex. 121.) This piece illustrates the point made earlier (p. 302) that when several kinds of duple division occur in a single part in the context of triplets, assimilation is unlikely. In the case of the slow movement (in E flat) of J. S. Bach's C minor Sonata for violin and harpsichord (Ex. 117), the assimilation of the dotted figure of the melody to the prevailing triplet, which accompanies, is not out of character.

When triplet rhythm prevails the composer often uses the signature 6/8 or 12/8, and assimilation ceases to be a problem. In these signatures we naturally find ♩♪ not ♩.♫ . In Grassineau's Dictionary, *dodecupla* (12/8) is illustrated by this pattern as the normal rhythmic notation: ♫♩ ♫♩ ♩ ♪♫♩ and this practice conforms to what is found in actual music. Similarly, the pattern ♩ ♪ ♫♩ is normal in 6/8. But if, as seems likely, the same musical effect is meant by the notation ♩. ♩ ♪♩ in 2/4, what is to be gained by the latter notation? Under certain conditions, this notation may have saved time and engraving costs (see p. 299). In any case, it must have been a traditional notation that was well understood.

In all this, it is not possible to decide absolutely on rigid rules of execution, applicable clearly to every case. As C. P. E. Bach says (cf. p. 481 above): 'If only one kind of execution is adopted as the basic principle of performance, the other kinds will be lost'.[34]

Dynamics

The relative scarcity of indications for loud and soft in early eighteenth-century music has led to curious results. Since the existing signs are mainly those for *forte* or *piano*, it supposedly follows that the music should be performed in dynamic 'terraces'—that is, entirely loud, or entirely soft—but

---

[34] A novel approach to the problem of assimilation may be found in Michael Collins's *The Performance of Coloration, Hemiola, and Sesquialtera (1450-1750)*, unpublished Ph.D. dissertation, Stanford, 1963. Collins believes that the triplet figure is often assimilated to the dotted figure, not vice versa as has been generally assumed until now (but cf. Harich-Schneider, as per p. 298, note 28, above). In Collins's view, when assimilation of this sort occurs, the triplet (♫♩) becomes either ♫♩ or ♫♩ The application of Collin's thesis would encounter many musical objections and it would be contrary to Quantz, C. P. E. Bach (as already cited) and also to Leopold Mozart, the most detailed violin treatise of the eighteenth century. The last-mentioned says (ch. 6, para. 2) that a triplet is *not* to be performed as an eighth followed by two sixteenths or as two sixteenths followed by an eighth. On the other hand, Collins admits that dotted figures may be assimilated to triplet rhythm under certain circumstances.

not with the nuances of *crescendo* or *diminuendo* essential to attain the shades in between (called *graded dynamics*).

These notions make little sense artistically, since an abstention from nuance is quite unnatural to a singer or to a player of melodic instruments like the violin. Moreover, there is no historical justification for such ascetic restriction. Even a superficial reading of the treatises of the seventeenth century, and particularly of the eighteenth century, reveals a wide range of louds and softs, including nuances of increasing and decreasing volume in playing instruments and in singing. In short, graded dynamics were used and often expected, though not always expressly indicated. Only in such cases as the harpsichord and the organ were terraced dynamics the rule, and that was so because the instruments themselves had inherent limitations which made them incapable of graded dynamics. Since the seventeenth century at least, these dynamic limitations of the keyboard instruments just mentioned were viewed as restrictions to expression; and the pianoforte was invented by Cristofori early in the eighteenth century to rectify the difficulty. Couperin in his *L'Art de toucher le clavecin* (1716) speaks of certain effects on the harpsichord as substitutes for the crescendo possible on stringed instruments: 'in such cases where stringed instruments would increase their volume of sound, the suspension of the sounds on the harpsichord seems (by a contrary effect) to produce on the ear the result expected and desired' (cf. Ex. 237).

Forte and *piano* are the two opposed and basic effects, those most commonly indicated in printed scores; and they are often used to point out an 'echo' effect to the performer. The number of signs and expressions to indicate loud and soft greatly increased by the middle of the eighteenth century. In Vivaldi, for instance, we have the following expressions to indicate a wide range of dynamic possibilities: *pianissimo, piano molto, piano assai, mezzo p, pp, p, quasi p, mezzo forte, un poco forte, f, f molto, più f, ff*.[35] The increasing usage of dynamic markings is implied by their occasional use even in the *basso continuo*.[36]

Loud and soft in music are comparable to light and shade in painting; and the nuances of *crescendo* and *diminuendo* are similarly comparable to the gradations between them. Where these nuances were possible, musicians took advantage of them, just as the painters did. The truth of this is obvious in treatises of the seventeenth century, where the voice and the violin are concerned (see p. 290). But not until the early eighteenth century are signs for *crescendo* and *diminuendo* specifically used to denote effects already in common usage, and these signs are limited mainly to a note or short phrase. The long *crescendo* or *diminuendo* of a measure or more is a rarity before

[35] According to Walter Kolneder, *Aufführungspraxis bei Vivaldi*, Leipzig, 1955, p. 25.
[36] See Geminiani, *The Art of Playing on the Violin*, Compositions 1, 3, 8, and 10.

1750, and was probably used only in the *messa di voce* (but see Locke's *Tempest*, p. 292). The earliest known example of the short nuance signs is found in Piani's sonatas of 1712, and these signs, like most of those in the early eighteenth century, are the blacked-in versions of the modern signs (cf. Ex. 244a and b).[37] These signs of Piani are the same as Geminiani's—for example, in his 1739 revision of Op. 1 and in his *The Art of Playing on the Violin*—and as Veracini's Op. 2. In the latter Veracini explains his signs in a preface, as follows:

> ◢ means to start loud and decrease;
> ▶ means to start soft and increase;
> ◀ is the combination (*messa di voce*).

Examples of these signs are shown in Ex. 244a and b. Both examples come from slow movements. Ex. 244a is an adagio marked *come sta*, presumably to rule out added ornaments. Instead, the expression depends on the dynamic nuance suggested by the signs. At slow tempo, the type of *diminuendo* nuance of Ex. 244a is somewhat unusual; in fact, the nuance shown in measure 1 is the equivalent of Mozart's Division 2 (see p. 396), which, according to him, is more commonly used in allegro. The *messa di voce* is conventionally applied to long notes, as it is here. An even more expressive example is Ex. 244b. In this *largo* the repeated notes under a slur are emphasized by the pulsating dynamic mark, and the chromatic character of the line itself contributes to the total expression.

Ex. 244

a) *Adagio e come sta*   b) *Largo*   Veracini

In Ex. 244a, the *messa di voce* is explicitly given, and it would have been played in this manner in any case by virtue of a convention concerning long notes going back at least a century. In the treatises of the eighteenth century the convention is reaffirmed by Geminiani when he says: 'In playing all long Notes the Sound should be begun soft, and gradually swelled till the Middle, and from thence gradually softened till the End.' Quantz gives us

---

[37] An example of Piani's music (Op. 1, Sonata 8, *adagio*) and the signs in question may be found in Cartier, *L'Art du Violon*, p. 119. The Piani piece contains the *crescendo* sign and that for the *messa di voce*, but no isolated *diminuendo* sign. (For the short *diminuendo* indicated by f—p, see below.) One of the few examples of the modern (unblackened) nuance signs before 1750 occurs in a piece of D'Auvergne (Op. 2, Sonata 6, 1739), published in Cartier, p. 70. But Cartier was printed in 1798, and the original D'Auvergne may have contained the blackened version. However, Cartier preserves the blackened version for other pieces. By the time of L'Abbé le fils the signs were unblackened.

the same information and adds what is already implicit in Geminiani: namely, that the vibrato (*Bebung*) should also be applied.[38]

Even with the increased use of signs in the scores, many dynamic effects were implied by context and not·specifically written out. The bow stroke itself implies (by modern standards) a 'small softness at the beginning and the end', and, as Quantz says in his chapter on playing adagio movements: 'Every note, whether a quarter, eighth, or sixteenth, must have its piano and forte in itself, as far as the time permits.'[39] The Divisions of Leopold Mozart are evidence of nuanced strokes in relation to particular contexts and tempi (see pp. 395 ff.). Geminiani's preferred bowings contain many nuanced

Ex. 245

examples (Ex. 245), and these bowings would have been used by him as part of a tradition, although not indicated in the score. Various ornaments were played with nuance, Tartini's appoggiatura being an example (see p. 455).

Leopold Mozart is especially rich in suggestions about the application of dynamic nuance to various contexts and types of figures. In playing the dotted figure of Ex. 241b, 'the dot must be joined to the [following] note with a gradual fading away'.[40] With respect to the triplet figures (andante) shown in Ex. 246a, 'the first [note] in the up-bow must be attacked some-

Ex. 246

what more strongly, and the remaining notes, even when you are changing the stroke, must be bound together, so as to let the tone gradually die away'.[41] Chromatic alterations and long notes in the context of short ones are also distinguished by dynamic nuance: 'Notes raised by a sharp or a

---

[38] See Quantz, ch. XIV, para. 10. For the sound of Ex. 244a, cf. our recording.
[39] Quantz, ch. XIV, para. 11.
[40] Mozart, ch. 1, sec. 3, para. 9. English translation, p. 41.
[41] Mozart, ch. 6, para. 13. English translation, p. 110.

natural should always be played rather more strongly, the tone then diminishing again during the course of the melody' (Ex. 246b); and 'it is
customary always to accent half notes strongly when mixed with short notes
and to relax the tone again' (Ex. 246c).[42]

Mozart is not alone in these remarks. Tartini, as already shown, clearly
expects a dynamic interpretation. So does Quantz, who makes a number of
the same points as Mozart, and adds others. Quantz's 'little' notes or grace
notes—for example, the passing appoggiatura and the *Schleifer*—are often
played softer than the main note. Quantz also suggests that the degree of
dissonance should be related to the degree of loudness, and in his Plate XXIV
he shows the degree of loudness he considers appropriate to the consonant or
dissonant chord in question. Quantz also furnishes detailed dynamic directions for playing the examples contained in his Plates (*Tabellen*) IX–XIII and
XVII–XIX, but in these elaborations no precise system can be discerned
beyond the general matters of context and usage already mentioned above.
Some of the dynamic effects, however expressive, appear whimsical and
purely personal to Quantz.

The use of the specially spaced f—p in Exx. 246a, b, and c implies that this
is a way of indicating a *diminuendo* of short duration.[43] This is an important
point, since these markings have quite a different effect, if, as often happens
today, f—p is interpreted as f—*subito piano*, rather than *forte* followed by a
diminuendo to *piano*. f—p as an indication of *diminuendo* (= *decrescendo*) must
have continued for some time. In the autograph of the ten 'famous' string
quartets of W. A. Mozart there are literally hundreds of short 'cresc.' marked
in the score, but only a handful of short 'decresc.'. On the other hand, there
are numerous markings f—p; and the inference is plain that the latter means
decrescendo. Consequently, only under exceptional circumstances is the
marking 'decresc.' necessary for a short *diminuendo* of less than a measure,
f—p being used instead.

Although nuances of a single beat or lasting less than a measure must have
been commonplace, examples of an extended *crescendo* or *diminuendo* lasting more than a measure are rarely found in music before 1750 (but see
p. 292). The old method of indicating the long *diminuendo* by such signs as
f—p—pp continued into the eighteenth century. Already found in Corelli,
this indication occurs later in the music of Vivaldi and Leclair. In a hunting
piece (*chasse*) of Leclair (Op. V, Sonata 9, 1734) there are several interesting
dynamic effects: six measures of *diminuendo* accompanied by *tremolo*, and
an extended *crescendo-diminuendo* indicated by *p, un poco F, piu Forte, Piano,*

---

[42] Both quotations are from Mozart's ch. 12, para. 8; English translation pp. 218–19.
[43] See also similar information in Quantz, ch. XVII, sec. 7, para. 24. Quantz, however,
seems to be speaking more of a *forte* followed by a *subito diminuendo* than the gradual
effect described below.

Pianissimo.[44] Strangely enough, the extended *crescendo* is even rarer than the extended *diminuendo.*[45] Even in Quantz's detailed examples of dynamic nuance, there is no *crescendo* or *diminuendo* lasting more than a measure. On the other hand, the extended *crescendo-diminuendo* was inherent in long notes of a measure or more to which the *messa di voce* was conventionally applied (cf. Ex. 244a). The extended *crescendo* became a trade-mark of the Mannheim Court Orchestra shortly after the middle of the eighteenth century, and, after its introduction by this orchestra, took its place as one of the usual dynamic effects of music. The work of the Mozarts, father and son, points to the change. There are no extended *crescendos* or extended *diminuendos* in Leopold Mozart's treatise; on the other hand, the music of Wolfgang is filled with them.

Dynamic effects, being one of the chief tools of expression, are common in Italian music long before the French used them. Piani, an Italian, introduced specific signs for *crescendo* and *diminuendo* to the Parisians in 1712 (see above, p. 340). But the French theorists did not pay much attention to these new-fangled ways, especially to graded dynamics, until the Italian sonata became acclimatized in France about 1720. In 1738 Corrette makes a note of *crescendo* and *diminuendo* when he says: 'In Sarabandes, Adagios, Largos and other pieces "de gout", the long notes receive a *crescendo* at the end and the final long note at the cadence a *messa di voce.*'

L'Abbé le fils shows the progress of the French in the use of dynamics during the interim of not quite twenty-five years. He gives sufficient signs and terms to make almost any dynamic effect possible, his signs being practically the same as those used now (see pp. 396-7). The long *crescendo*

L'Abbé le fils

Ex. 247

of a full measure or more makes its appearance in L'Abbé le fils; and one long *crescendo* followed by a long *diminuendo* (p. 38) occupies three complete measures (Ex. 247). As in the past, this effect is used in connexion with a long note. L'Abbé also uses *crescendo* to achieve effects of brilliance in

[44] According to La Laurencie, who says 'we have here the first example of *crescendo* and of *decrescendo* in our [French] violin literature' (*L'École française*, Vol. I, p. 324). However, as printed in Cartier (*L'Art du Violon*, pp. 122-3), the direction differs in one respect. Cartier uses *piano Forte* in the measure where La Laurencie reports *piu Forte*. Cartier's version does not make as good sense in context. Presumably, La Laurencie had seen the original, and is correct.

[45] In Geminiani's Composition IX from *The Art of Playing on the Violin*, the direction *p—non tanto—forte*, extending over two measures of a sequence pattern, is doubtless an example of the extended *crescendo*.

H.V.P.–KK

upward scale passages ('roulades'). The passage starts softly, increasing so that the last note is the most brilliant (p. 54). L'Abbé uses dynamics extensively, but it is his only device of 'expression'. He says nothing of vibrato, for instance.

Aesthetics of Expression. The Affetto

The expression and the manner of performing are determined by the all-important *Affetto* (*Affekt*; Effect; Affect)—the eighteenth-century word for the mood, emotion, or passion to be expressed. The *Affetto* was suggested in a general way by such terms as *cantabile, mesto, dolce, vivace*, and the like; and certain tempi, rhythms, keys, intervals, or harmonies were more appropriate to one mood or passion than another. In violin music, the kinds of bow strokes, the dynamics, and the ornaments were closely related to the 'Affect'. Geminiani's remarks on the mordent ('Beat') begin, 'This is proper to express several Passions'; and the expression of these passions, ranging from mirth to horror, depends on the way the mordent is performed. The same latitude may be observed in the manner of performing the vibrato and other devices of expression.

To some musicians and theorists, the *Affetto* could be achieved with the assurance and exactness of a mathematical or chemical formula. In the same way as $2 + 2 = 4$ or as $H_2 + O =$ water, the rational mind of the eighteenth century thought that the rhythmic and melodic ingredients of music could be combined to produce moods of love, fear, hope, and jealousy with infallibility and at will.[46] This doctrine of the *Affetto* preoccupied the German theorists—it is implicit in many of the attitudes of Quantz—but it also found its way into much English writing of the time.

An important complementary notion was the imitation of nature, often held up as an ideal or as a touchstone of excellence. Leopold Mozart says, 'For the purpose of imitation or for the expression and excitation of this or that emotion, figures also are devised, by means of whose characteristics one believes oneself *to come closest to nature*' (italics added).[47]

The French and Italian attitudes toward expression were quite different. The Italians were less rational but more emotional and passionate; they wished to be moved as well as entertained;[48] and they saw no obstacle to achieving direct emotional expression in instrumental music, considered by itself. To the French theorists, however, music existed in relation to something else, and its excellence and powers of expression hardly existed apart

---

[46] See H. Kretzschmar, 'Allgemeines und Besonderes zur Affektenlehre' in *Jahrbuch der Musikbibliothek Peters*, Vols. 18–19 (1911–12).

[47] Mozart, ch. 6, para. 16. English translation, p. 111.

[48] Hubert Le Blanc (1740) says, 'In Italy they exclaim, ha! how moving the music is! and in France, ha! how amusing the music is!'

from concrete representation or function. This French attitude was almost inevitable in a nation so strongly attached to the dance, the theatre, and the ornamental aspects of entertainment. Consequently, French instrumental music, violin music in particular, was an adjunct to the dance and the theatre, the context of which endowed music with meaning through text, gesture, or scenery.

The cult of imitation of nature was especially strong in France; and, in various guises or disguises of imitation, music represented something concrete—in effect, descriptive or programme music (cf. pp. 337–8). The French vogue of the instrumental *chasse*, with its imitation of the sounds of the hunting horns, is a primitive example. In the dedication to his Op. III (*c.* 1734), Mondonville puts the case generally: 'I have tried not to lose sight of the only model worth imitating, I wish to say, beautiful nature'. The close relationship of music to the spoken and written word is obvious in the notion that music is a language, that musical pieces are like an oration, or that a sonata is an ode in music (Brijon).

According to this system of thought, the voice assumes *ipso facto* a superiority to instruments and instrumental music; and by the same token, instrumental music seeks to imitate the cantabile of the voice. According to Pluche, 'the most beautiful melody, when it is only instrumental, becomes almost necessarily cold, then boring, because it expresses nothing'.[49] As late as 1760 D'Alembert says, 'I count as nothing the prodigious quantity of sonatas which we have had from them [the Italians]. All this music, purely instrumental, without design, without object, comes neither from the spirit nor from the soul.'[50] This attitude of the French greatly impeded the progress of instrumental music in France. The Italian violin sonata was a completely incomprehensible mystery to most of the French, as the above quotations show. Not until the time of La Borde is this doctrine clearly on the wane among writers and theorists. 'Let us discard once and for all this famous principle [entreats La Borde], which some would make into an axiom: where there is no imitation, there is no music. . . . The most beautiful concomitant of music is without doubt expression.'[51] La Borde's remark represents a changed attitude already implicit in the introduction and domestication of the Italian sonata by Leclair and others. After 1750, imitation of nature is still a watchword (cf. Rousseau), but it is directed more toward music of simple and immediate expression; and the Italian

---

[49] N. A. Pluche, *Spectacle de la Nature*, Paris, 1732, Vol. 2, pp. 115–16. Quoted in La Laurencie, *L'École française*, Vol. III, pp. 191–2. For an appropriate remark of Fontenelle, see p. 214 above.

[50] Quoted in A. Machabey, *Traité de la critique musicale*, Paris, 1946, p. 172.

[51] J. B. de La Borde, *Essai sur la musique ancienne et moderne*, Paris, 1780, Vol. I, pp. 50–51. Quoted in La Laurencie, op. cit., Vol. III, p. 190.

notion of instrumental music, expressive in itself, gradually seeped into the French psyche.

The Italians had been the fountainhead of expression in European music since the early seventeenth century, as one may see by examining the writings of Caccini and the prefaces of Monteverdi's madrigals, among other documents. The expressive and passionate manner of performing Italian opera is noted by numerous theorists and travellers from its inception well into the eighteenth century. An amusing comparison of Italian and French expression in the opera (and, by extension, in instrumental music) is implied in Rousseau's article 'Genius' in his *Dictionnaire de musique* (1767-8; English translation, *c.* 1770):

> 'Would you then wish to know if any spark of this devouring flame inspires you? Be quick, haste to Naples, listen to the masterpieces of Leo, Durante, Jommelli, and Pergolesi. If your eyes are filled with tears, if you feel your heart palpitate, if gaiety agitates you, if sorrow involves you in transports, take Metastasio and labour; his genius will enflame yours. . . . But if the charms of this grand art leave you calm, if you feel no ravishing transports, if you discover nothing beautiful but what barely pleases, dare you demand what genius is? Vulgar mortal, dare not profane that heavenly appellation. What would it avail to thee to know it? Thou canst not feel it. Compose French music, and peaceably retire.'

In Italian vocal music the text suggests the emotion (*Affetto*) to be represented, and the manner of performance was adjusted accordingly. In Italian instrumental music the abstract patterns of tone, in which the French could see only a vacuum of meaning and the coldness of marble, were merely a skeleton; the expressive manner of performance added the flesh and blood, and made the music live. As La Borde says, 'The most beautiful concomitant of music is without doubt expression', and in actual performance, although not always notated in the scores, the Italians employed a large variety of expressive devices, such as dynamic shading, vibrato, different types of bow strokes, and ornaments, in support of the particular *Affetto*. Vivaldi's music is a good example of variety of expression, and Geminiani's *The Art of Playing on the Violin* is eloquent testimony to expressive performance and how different manners of performance are appropriate to varied musical contexts and 'Affects'. At the same time, the Italians did not rule out the expressive possibilities of concrete verbal association. Vivaldi's descriptive concertos (see p. 337) insert texts into the score; and Geminiani refers to musical performance in terms of language or oratory (cf. p. 338 above).

The systematic doctrine of rhythmic and melodic figures, supporting any particular *Affetto*, was developed by the theorists, but this system applied more to the composer's problem of suggesting the basic *Affetto* in whole sections or even pieces than it did to the expressive nuances of performance. That is to say, rapid and large skips can suggest agitation, and chromatic intervals can suggest sorrow, but these were vastly intensified by the expressive manner of performance implicit in the conventions of the time. In one of the most eloquent passages ever written about performance, Geminiani suggests both points when he refers to the powers of both composer and performer:

'Even in common Speech a Difference of Tone gives the same Word a different Meaning. And with Regard to Musical Performances, Experience has shewn that the Imagination of the Hearer is in general so much at the Disposal of the Master, that by the help of Variations, Movements, Intervals and Modulation he may almost stamp what Impression on the Mind he pleases. . . . I would besides advise, as well the Composer as the Performer, who is ambitious to inspire his Audience, to be first inspired himself; which he cannot fail to be if he chuses a Work of Genius, if he makes himself thoroughly acquainted with all its Beauties; and if while his Imagination is warm and glowing he pours the same exalted Spirit into his own Performance.'[52]

The Italian attitude greatly influenced music throughout Europe. The Germans were apt pupils, and gradually the French followed the Italian lead. The Italian violin sonatas and concertos gained a permanent place in France after *c.* 1720, and the Italian attitude toward expression increasingly permeated French instrumental music. The Italian victory was not complete until the late eighteenth century, as the above quotations show, but the *avant-garde* among French composers of violin music were far ahead of the theorists and aestheticians, and the French school began to assume the leadership after 1750. However, there are earlier examples. François Couperin had shown his attachment to 'feeling' as early as 1716 when his *L'Art de toucher le clavecin* was published. 'All our Airs for the Violin [he says], our pieces for the harpsichord, for the viols, etc. describe and seem to be trying to express some feeling (*sentiment*).'

From all this it is plain that the violin music of the eighteenth century required an expressive performance, especially in Italy. However notated, violin music of this time should not be, and was not intended to be, restricted to simple terraces of dynamics or a literal and uninspired rendition of the bare skeleton of the score. This elastic attitude toward the score and toward expression was especially advantageous to the violin. The Frenchman

[52] Geminiani, *The Art of Playing*, Ex. XVIII, sec. 14.

Brossard commented in 1703 in his Dictionary, 'The violin is characterized as very sparkling and gay, making it proper for the dance. But there are ways of playing it to make it grave and sad, sweet and tender. This is what makes it used so much in all foreign music, whether for the church, chamber, or theatre.'

Significantly, it is under the article 'Expression' that Rousseau has this to say about the violin in his Dictionary: 'There is no instrument from which one obtains a more varied and universal expression than from the violin.' This statement indicates the expressive potential of the violin, and it implies an expressive manner of performance. Above all, Rousseau's words transcend the significance of their immediate context, for they echo the sentiments of violinists, from the humblest to the greatest, over the centuries.

CHAPTER TWENTY-TWO

Practical Hints to Modern Violinists

'It is most certain that all nations and times think their own doings best, and as surely despise the past, whereas in all times and in all manners there was some *suo genere* good.'

ROGER NORTH
Musicall Grammarian (1728).

IN the body of this book I have presented the details of the history of violin playing from its origins to the middle of the 18th century in connexion with the development of the violin, bow, and music concerned. Is this information of more than historical interest? The answer to this question depends very much on the readers of this book and especially on the attitude of individual violinists toward performance. Some violinists say in effect, 'I play the music just as I feel it'—an intuitive approach. Others wish to base their interpretation, as far as possible, on the intentions of the composer, and play accordingly. Naturally, no performer's attitude is ever quite as simple or clear-cut as this, but, nevertheless, these two points of view are basic. They are also fundamentally opposed.

There is not much to be gained by debating the relative virtue of these attitudes, but it does seem advisable for me as the author to explain my own notions in this matter. In the first place, experience in playing and conducting over a long period of time has convinced me that new beauties and effects, which have hitherto escaped the attention, may often be discovered by utilizing the old technique, instruments, and bows. Quite apart from this pragmatic consideration, there is a matter of principle: I cannot myself escape a feeling of responsibility to the past and to the intentions of the composer.

At the same time, other factors must be considered: among them, the difficulty of determining the details of the old tradition, the possible elasticity of the composer's intentions, and the temperament of the individual performing artist. More specifically, the composer creates and, ideally, the performer re-creates, realizing the intentions of the composer. But in music these intentions cannot be exactly expressed, and, in any case, every performance must, in the nature of music, allow for the individuality of the performing artist. For these reasons, there is no such thing as a single authoritative performance of a piece of music to the exclusion of all other performances of the same piece; and this is one of the charms and one of the problems of music.

If, as I believe, the performer has a responsibility to follow the composer's intentions, he has an equal duty to bring to his performance the genuine impress of a musical conviction and temperament. An artist must give each work that he plays the stamp of his own authority, and this can only be based on musical conviction. If some detail of an old performing tradition is not musically convincing to a performer, he would surely be better off playing as an artist than as an archeologist or historian. As far as the composer's intentions are concerned, the truth is that we can never know them exactly unless he is alive to tell us; and this is increasingly true as we proceed backward in time. However, much can be uncovered that gives significant clues to the past, and in the body of this book I have tried to show as many of the details of the performing tradition of violinists from the sixteenth to the eighteenth centuries as can presently be found.

Naturally, I hope that modern violinists will be interested in putting these details to practical use if only for a reason already mentioned: namely, to achieve new effects and to permit new beauties in performance. To help in bridging the old and the new, I think it is worth stressing certain points that may be valuable to modern violinists in the performance of the music with which this book is concerned. In addition, a phonograph record, illustrating the actual sound of the 'old' as compared to the modern violin, is included with this book. The recording was made by the violinist, Alan Loveday, working with me.

The old violin and the old bow

In the first place, there is the matter of the old violin and old bow, as opposed to their modern counterparts, to be considered. The use of the old violin and bow does make a difference in the sound, but it is unlikely that a practising violinist, unless he owns several instruments, can afford to alter his violin to old specifications—a slighter and shorter bass bar, a straighter and shorter neck, lower bridge, and so on. On the other hand, it is relatively easy and inexpensive to procure an old-style bow, to fit a violin with gut strings, and to experiment with a slightly lower pitch.[1]

[1] Old-style bows based on eighteenth-century models can be purchased from (among others) Arnold Dolmetsch Ltd., Haslemere, Surrey, England.

The kind of sound

Whether or not a modern violinist can or will make any changes in violin or bow, he can approximate the old sound and style of the earlier tradition with the modern violin and bow, provided that the kind of sound to be produced is clearly understood. In short, the ingredients of a musical performance are musical and intellectual as well as physical. To be sure, there still remains a stubborn residue of physical difference between the new and old violin, in the sense that the piano cannot sound precisely like the harpsichord; and if the differences between the old violin and bow and their modern counterparts are not as pronounced as the differences between the two keyboard instruments just mentioned, they are of the same order. Among other things, the old violin and the harpsichord produce a clearer, more transparent, and articulated sound than the modern violin and the piano. During the long preparation of this book, numerous experiments were carried out with the old-style violin and bow, using the old technique; and it is from the background of these experiments that the following 'hints' are offered, for what they may be worth, to the violinist today.[2]

What kind of sound did the old violin produce and at what, therefore, should the modern violinist aim? To my way of thinking, the answer is: (1) a more relaxed and less intense sound than is usual today; (2) a sound that is clear and transparent rather than one that is massive, throaty, or luscious; (3) a well-articulated sound that gives a special pulse and vitality in figuration and phrasing; and (4) a nuanced rather than evenly sustained tone as the norm.

These traits of sound are generally characteristic of violin music before 1750, although, obviously, there are degrees of differences from one period to another and between dance music on the one hand and sonatas and concertos on the other. This is not the place to explain these distinctions, which are to be found in the body of the book. (For details, see the Index; for the sound of the old violin, cf. the recording.)

The bow and bowing

Although it is quite possible for a modern violinist to achieve the kind of sound just mentioned, I urge anyone really interested in recapturing the

---

[2] It is only fair to say what my own qualifications are to play the role of practical adviser on interpretation. I was trained from childhood as a pianist, and began the study of the viola at the advanced age of twenty five—too late ever to capture the innate 'feel' of a stringed instrument that comes only from proper training as a child. However, I have played the viola far longer than I care to remember, and I have constantly sought the advice of professional violinists on questions of a technical character. This background, plus considerable experience as a conductor of string orchestras, as a teacher and a scholar, constitute my qualifications.

old sound to experiment with the old-style bow. From observation and experience I know that modern violinists can use the old bow to great advantage, and often to their musical surprise and pleasure, in playing music written before the middle of the eighteenth century. The advantages are particularly marked, and immediately so, in the case of articulation of rapid figuration and repeated notes. What the modern bow can do in this respect the old bow does better and more easily. The old bow produces a natural articulation, especially in the upper third of the bow, that is quite remarkable. I have had the experience of discovering this fact with students playing Vivaldi concertos, in which a clarity of articulation, out of their reach with the modern bow, was immediately possible with the old bow (cf. the Vivaldi excerpt in the recording). Naturally, one must use the old bow with a bowing that is technically advantageous (more of this below) and one must secure a good bow. Having had the opportunity to use (and to supervise others using) genuine early eighteenth-century bows at Berkeley and Oxford, I can say confidently that the beauty and playing properties of these old bows would delight any violinist. With a little practice, the old bow often feels better than a modern bow for certain types of music. (An experienced teacher told me that children often learn to use the old-style bow more readily than the modern bow, and I am not surprised.) Of course, this old-style bow is generally lighter and shorter than the modern Tourte bow, and the balance is different; but the bow is eminently suited to the articulated style that characterizes so much old music. At the same time, I do not underestimate for a moment the magnificent qualities of the modern bow; I simply think that the old bow is better for the music for which it was designed.

This remark brings us to the question of the bow stroke. The ideal of the endless bow and the long bow stroke is quite inappropriate to the typical articulation of music before 1750 (for cantabile playing, see below). With the old bow, one does not try to achieve an immediate pressure on the string, as with the modern bow, but rather to take up first the slight slack ('the small softness' of which Leopold Mozart speaks), then press quickly into the depth of the string, and relax again. The bow stroke is basically a short one, and the resulting sound is a naturally articulated tone. In rapid figuration, a series of these articulated tones resembles a string of pearls, since the sound is nuanced, giving the effect of clear separation of individual tones without the sound of any ceasing completely. To imitate this kind of stroke on the modern bow is quite possible, but to achieve it, the long 'skating' motion of the normal modern *détaché* is not suitable. The articulated type of bow stroke just described is basic in playing pieces like the well-known 'school' concerto of Vivaldi in A minor (Op. 3, No. 6), first and last movement; and this type of stroke will add greatly to the vitality and transparency of the music (the opening of this concerto is played on the recording).

It is important to emphasize that this short bow stroke is not simply hacked out with rests in between, as is commonly done today in imitation of the 'old' style; and nothing is more depressing than *basso continuo* playing done in this disjointed way. The kind of stroke I mean derives its natural articulation from the yielding of the bow, pressure into the string, and yielding again with a short stroke that follows the inclination of the bow itself. This is the kind of stroke that Robert Donington has described so well in relating Arnold Dolmetsch's pioneering efforts years ago: 'Dolmetsch's basic tone on the violin was of a more fiery colouring and a less refined texture than we generally associate with this most versatile of instruments. . . . He played more into the string, and with a more slowly moving bow, than is general nowadays. . . . His cantabile was exquisitely sustained; but the rest of his playing was highly articulated. . . . [His playing] had an intoxicating lightness combined with solid strength and virility. It was at the same time vital and relaxed.'[3] In passing, it should be emphasized that certain strokes used nowadays are not natural to the old style and the old bow: for example, the *serré* bowing and the *martelé*—the latter involving the effect of sforzando.

Since the old bow grip is less tightly held than the modern grip, some experimenting may be required to find the one that works best. It is also useful and illuminating to experiment with the old thumb-under-hair bow grip used in earlier times for dance music (contrary to a popular theory, this grip had nothing whatever to do with double stops). Although completely obsolete today, this bow grip is actually very effective in producing the firmly articulated bow stroke and the rhythmically animated sound best suited to playing the old dances. In this grip, the bow is, as it were, enclosed in the fist, the thumb being placed directly under the hair and pressed into it, as required, to take up any slack. Very little wrist should be used in this bow stroke, and the violinist would be well advised to let this grip play itself, again in short articulated style. If desired, the first and second finger can be spread somewhat for a rather more powerful grip. It was with this bow grip that the old Rule of Down-Bow (see the Index) was developed for purposes of articulation in connexion with specific dances. (In the recording, Ex. 82 is played with this bow grip.)

Off-string strokes with the old bow are generally played as controlled strokes in the lower part of the bow at moderate tempos (this is the eighteenth-century staccato marked with dots or strokes above or below single notes). At rapid tempos, the eighteenth-century staccato was played on the string in the middle of the bow. The resulting sound resembles a

[3] Robert Donington, *The Interpretation of Early Music*, London, 1963, p. 465.

modern spiccato but the bow scarcely leaves the string, if it does so at all. (These strokes are also illustrated in our recording.)

In the case of slow and more melodic music, the same bow stroke is used—that is, it begins again by the yielding pressure—but the bow stroke is naturally longer, and, unlike the typical modern stroke, it is seldom sustained at an even dynamic level. Long notes, for instance, were conventionally played with *crescendo* to the middle of the note and a *diminuendo* to the end; and other effects of nuance were customary, as one may see by examining treatises of the time (e.g., Leopold Mozart's dynamic 'Divisions'; see the Index). This style of music was further animated by the use of vibrato as an ornament (see below), particularly in connexion with long notes. If one plays the opening of Handel's D major Violin Sonata in the dynamic style of the eighteenth century (as in Ex. 244; cf. our recording), adding a vibrato to the first long note on e'', one gets an effect quite different from the usual modern performance (for mixed bowings, see the Index).

Fingering and position

The technical details of fingering are related to the manner of holding the violin. If the instrument is held loosely and without a chin rest, one must use more 'crawling' fingerings, especially in downward shifts (cf. Fig. 5, p. 155). Certain types of fingering and shifting should be avoided. Among them are: (1) open string where the sound of open and stopped string is conspicuously different;[4] (2) portamento slides in shifting; (3) the higher registers of the G String; and (4) the octave harmonic to reach an upper note. However, in melodic passages in which uniform tone colour is desirable, there is no reason why the upper registers of the same string should not be used in preference to the contrast of several in lower positions (cf. Ex. 134 in our recording). On the other hand, playing from one string to another in passagework often gives a variety of colour that is desirable and, of course, sometimes unavoidable.

Altering the modern violin. Reducing tension

There is no denying that the modern violin produces a sound quite different from that of the violin before 1750. The modern instrument is more powerful and under much greater tension. Its wound and steel strings are very good for uniformity of response and for practical considerations of breakage under various conditions of use, temperature, and humidity in different areas an climates. Nevertheless, in the process of developing and

---

[4] Note that on the 'old' violin, under less tension and strung with gut on the upper three strings, the difference between the tone of open string and stopped string is not as noticeable as it is today (cf. the sound of open and stopped strings in Ex. 25 in our recording).

fitting the modern instrument to meet the necessary requirements of modern playing and large concert halls, we have lost some of the mellow and more relaxed tone of the old violin. There is really no way to recapture this quality except to return in whole or in part to old conditions of construction and fitting. On the other hand, it is completely unrealistic for the concert violinist to tamper with his concert violin, and the only obvious alternative is to fit up another instrument on which some of the old conditions can be met.

Short of completely reconstructing the instrument with an old-type bass bar and so on, there are still a number of ways in which a violin can be relieved of some of the tensions to which it is presently subjected. The use of gut for the upper three strings helps, and strings of thinner gauge, where practical, also cut down on the tension. A slightly lower bridge reduces the downward thrust on the table. The design and thickness of the bridge is also a factor. The old bridge was more open in design (cf. Plate 27) and probably a bit thicker and lower than ours today, the result being a somewhat smaller volume of tone. Lowering the tuning by a semitone is another possibility, although this may well create insuperable musical difficulties. Changes of the kind just described are all aimed at a more relaxed and mellower tone.

Reducing tensions in this way has additional advantages of a practical nature. Among other things, a lower tension is easier on a new instrument and helps to prolong the life of an old one. Surely, many valuable violins are being strung today to the maximum limit of tension and are being over-played in order to produce a larger and larger tone. Instruments need relief from this strain. Besides, from a player's point of view, the lower tension means an easier response: the tone emerges more readily, and a true pianissimo is simpler to produce. The quality of easy response can be found in those few old instruments still in original condition. A remarkable Stainer violin of 1668, now in London, has never been opened, having its original bass-bar and its original neck.[5] With a good old bow, the response from this instrument is remarkably swift and easy, and a beautiful pianissimo of true quality is possible on it. It is also interesting that the full power of this violin is within the scope of the old bow to produce, and no greater volume can be produced on it with a modern bow. On the other hand, the modern bow is capable of extracting a greater volume of tone from a violin with full modern fittings than is the old bow.

These remarks add up to saying that we shall gain something important by experimenting with refitting the violin and reducing the tensions on it, especially for the purposes of playing music of the eighteenth century and

[5] This Stainer is the 'old' violin used in our recording, and it is one of those violins on which experiments were conducted while working on this book. (See Pl. 26a and p. 196.)

earlier. Although the volume of sound will be somewhat less, there are important compensations: a mellower, more relaxed sound, and a gain in clarity and ease of response. In addition, the violinist is able to play more softly and with better quality of tone in a true pianissimo.

Holding the violin

Once we become disenchanted with the notion of maximum tension, it is only a step to experiments with less rigid grips on the violin. In general, I think relatively little chin pressure is desirable although I have no doctrinaire attitude in this matter. Doubtless, modern violinists would find it very difficult to play without shoulder support and chin rest, as was invariably done throughout the eighteenth century and before. In the degree that these strong supports are removed, other compensations will have to be made, such as moving the violin so that the chin is directly over the centre of the violin or even at the right side of the tailpiece. Also, the position of the violin at the neck affects the left-hand grip on the violin and the position of the right hand and arm in manipulating the bow.

Other factors, technical and musical, including expression

The use of the vibrato is always a bone of contention. In our context, one must make a fundamental distinction between the modern vibrato, which is basically continuous and organic, and the vibrato before 1750, which is basically occasional and ornamental. In cultivating the old style, the modern player may benefit by trying to play without any vibrato at all for a period of time, concentrating for the moment on the expressive device of the nuanced bowing (see the examples in our recording). Then the vibrato may be added as an ornament to heighten expression at appropriate places. The old vibrato should generally be less intense than the modern variety. The old way of playing the violin was expressive but with this difference: the bowing of the right hand was more expressive in itself than the modern way, but the left hand was less so. To the expressive style of bowing, one adds, according to taste and judgment, the dynamic nuances suitable to a slow cantabile and such improvised ornaments and rhythmic devices as were permitted and expected of performers in earlier times (e.g., *notes inégales*, double dots, and so on; see the Index).

In my pleas for lessening the tensions on the violin and for the use of greater clarity and articulation of tone, I am not advocating an insipid style of playing. Quite the contrary. The articulated bowing gives extraordinary vitality to the individual tone and, when used properly, to phrasing. Moreover, tempos can frequently be more sprightly if the tone is clearly articulated. It cannot be said often enough that dances should be played and should sound like dances with the true rhythmic character of the movement concerned, not merely as exercises in the production of a 'glorious' tone. How often one hears a saraband (for example) played without any vitality or basic movement. Singing a passage generally gives us the key to its proper phrasing; and, in the same way, studying the dances and their steps gives us a true notion of the tempo and the rhythmic inflection necessary for any given dance (for details of some of these, see the Index).

In the extremely complicated matter of double stops, I can only advise consulting the details given in the body of this book. In general, triple and quadruple stops are best arpeggiated swiftly from bottom to top (sometimes the reverse), dwelling on the top (or bottom) note—not, as today, breaking the notes in pairs and holding out one pair (see our recording for examples).

One word about editions: it is surely axiomatic that we must try to discover what the composer really had in mind when he composed the music. The first necessity is a good edition, responsibly and knowledgeably edited. We cannot possibly know, for instance, how Vivaldi expected his music to be phrased unless we have an accurate version of the score. This is only the beginning of a violinist's problems in playing the music, but a reliable edition is an indispensable first step. In this connexion, it is often valuable to consult the original print or manuscript of the music, if available, before proceeding to the actual details of bowing, fingering, and expression, which must, in the last analysis, remain the final responsibility of each player. The easily available facsimile of Bach's autograph of his unaccompanied sonatas and partitas is a case in point, and a comparison of this autograph with the numerous modern editions is an eye-opening experience.

Finally, it seems to me that the ideal of performance in early violin music —as indeed in all music—is not to play faster and louder but with more meaning through expression and phrasing. By analogy to language, it is not the speed or loudness with which an orator speaks that sways his audience, but his expression, his emphasis, his modulation of voice, and his sense of timing and phrasing. How similar considerations affected the technique of violin playing before the middle of the eighteenth century has been the theme of this book, and these matters may be studied in the preceding chapters through the detailed accounts of the leading musicians and violinists over a span of more than two centuries.

Appendix

THE BIRTHDATE OF ANTONIO STRADIVARI

STRADIVARI's birthdate has been the subject of prolonged investigation and controversy. Many of the parish records are incomplete, for the early seventeenth century was a time of plague and war in northern Italy; and no record of the birth of Stradivari has been found either in Cremona itself or in the surrounding towns. The Hills of London, who wrote by far the best book on Stradivari (see the Bibliography), concluded that he was born in 1644, basing their conclusion on some eight labels from instruments of Stradivari's last years on which the maker gives his age as 92 in 1736, 93 in 1737, and so on. The Hills thought the notations of age were in the authentic hand of Stradivari, and these experts were, after all, among the most experienced violin dealers and makers in the world. A large number of Stradivari instruments had passed through their hands, and they knew authentic specimens of Stradivari's handwriting. Consequently, the 1644 birthdate (which has already been proposed by Fétis earlier) was generally accepted. In 1937, however, Renzo Bacchetta on the one hand and, on the other, Carlo Bonetti and associates, working independently, rejected the 1644 date. They claimed that the correct date was 1648 or 1649 on the basis of census returns and on the grounds that the notations of age had been inserted, not by Stradivari, but by Count Cozio di Salabue, a celebrated collector.[1] Count Cozio had purchased a number of Stradivari violins from Paolo Stradivari, the son of the maker. Bacchetta, who stresses the forgery theory, never makes clear what Count Cozio's motive could have been in falsifying labels or whether all eight instruments (including a cello), containing the labels in question, actually passed through Salabue's hands. In his correspondence[2] Count Cozio says he made changes in labels of 1730 and 1731, but he also maintains that the labels of 1736 (age 92) and 1737 (age 93) are in Stradivari's handwriting. Bacchetta reproduces facsimile examples of writing and figures in Count Cozio's handwriting (*Carteggio*, p. 203), but

---

[1] Renzo Bacchetta, *Stradivari non è nato nel 1644*, Cremona, 1937; and Carlo Bonetti, Agostino Cavalcabò, and Ugo Gualazzini, *Antonio Stradivari, Notizie e Documenti*, Cremona, 1937.
[2] Cozio di Salabue, *Carteggio*, trascrizione di Renzo Bacchetta, Milano, 1950.

contrary to Bacchetta's claim, these examples seem to show that the handwriting, especially with respect to the figure '3', is not the same as that of the corresponding figures in the dates of the Stradivari labels. Consequently, the theory of Salabue's forgery cannot be regarded as proved.

Bonetti discusses the documentary evidence at length. This consists of the record of Stradivari's marriage and a number of census returns thereafter. There is no doubt that Stradivari was married in Cremona on 4 July 1667, but the census returns beginning in 1668 are somewhat contradictory. For this reason, these returns were rejected by the Hills as unreliable, particularly since census figures were apparently furnished by the parish priest and not by the persons directly concerned. For example, the census returns of 1668 describe Stradivari as 28, his wife as 26, and his daughter as three months. According to these figures, Stradivari was born in 1640 (or even in 1639). Other census returns from 1669 to 1678 make Stradivari's birthdate variously 1646–48. However, in 1680 Stradivari moved to a new parish (San Matteo), and the census returns of San Matteo for 1681 list Stradivari as 32, making his birthdate 1648 or 1649. His wife is listed as 35 and his daughter as 11. These figures and those of 1668 are ludicrously inconsistent: in the thirteen years from 1668 to 1681, Stradivari has aged only four years, his wife nine, and his daughter eleven. However, Bonetti brings out an important point: from 1681 (really 1680), when Stradivari first moved to San Matteo and his age was given as 32, until 1736, when his age was given as 87, the San Matteo parish records are consistent, producing by subtraction a birthdate of 1648 or 1649. On the other hand, the ages of several of Stradivari's children, whose birthdates are documented, are incorrect in the San Matteo records of 1681, thus casting doubt on their accuracy in general. Moreover, Stradivari's son, Paolo (b. 1708), thought that his father died in 1738 at the age of 94 (i.e. born in 1644), and this is reasonably consistent with the church records (also in San Matteo parish!) of his father's death, which show that Antonio Stradivari died on 18 December 1737 aged 'about 95' (i.e. born about 1642).

There are two other points. The Hills of London put the earliest date of a Stradivari violin 'seen by ourselves' at 1666. It is somewhat more reasonable to find a dated violin of a man aged 22 or 24 (birthdate 1644 or 1642) than an apprentice of 17 (birthdate 1649). This line of reasoning would be more decisive if another violin of 1660, referred to by the Hills (p. 32), could be proved authentic, but the Hills say they 'cannot vouch for this reference'.

Finally, if Stradivari was born in 1648–9, he must have been married at 18 or 19—there being no doubt that he was married in 1667. On the surface of things, this seems very young and economically unlikely for a struggling young apprentice to take on the responsibilities of a family. But there was a special reason. Stradivari married on 4 July and his first child was born less than six months later (21 December 1667). Therefore, a factor more compelling than his age or economic condition may have been the decisive one in an early marriage.[3]

Actually, none of the evidence advanced concerning Stradivari's birthdate is decisive. The parish records of San Matteo from 1681 to 1736, as given by Bonetti, would, if taken by themselves, point consistently to a birthdate of 1648 or 1649. But there is too much other contradictory evidence that cannot be completely explained away,[4] including the early census records, the church records of burial, the opinion of Paolo Stradivari, and the notation on the labels. In short, it is doubtful if the date can ever be definitely established short of the discovery of parish records of his birth.

[3] For an account of the rather lurid past of Francesca Feraboschi Capra, the young widow whom Stradivari married, see, among others, Franz Farga, *Violins and Violinists*, London, 1950, p. 40; original German edition, Zürich, 1940. Farga's account is not documented and should be used with the caution appropriate to fascinating hearsay.

[4] A number of the points raised by Bacchetta and Bonetti in 1937 were considered much earlier by Alfonso Mandelli (*Nuove Indagini su Antonio Stradivari*, Milano, 1903). Mandelli suggested the possibility that Stradivari was born in 1649, raised various objections to this date, and concluded that the 1644 date was more likely.

Bibliography

A. TREATISES

L'Abbé le fils [J.-B. Saint Sevin], *Principes du violon*, Paris, 1761. Facsimile reprint with an introduction by Aristide Wirsta, Paris, 1961.

Martin Agricola, *Musica Instrumentalis Deudsch* [sic], Wittemberg, 1st ed., 1528, rev. ed., 1545.

Anon., *The Compleat Musick-Master*, London, 1704; 2nd ed., 1707; 3rd ed., 1722.

Anon., *Nolens Volens*, London, 1695.

Anon., *The Self Instructor on the Violin*, London, 1695.

Thoinot Arbeau [Jehan Tabourot], *Orchésographie*, Langres, 1589 ('Privilège' dated 1588). Translated by C. W. Beaumont, London, 1925; also by Mary S. Evans, New York, 1948.

Carl Philipp Emmanuel Bach, *Essay on the True Art of Playing Keyboard Instruments* [1753], translated and edited by William J. Mitchell, New York, 1949.

P. Baillot, *L'Art du violon*, Paris, 1834.

P. Baillot, Rode, and Kreutzer, *Méthode de Violon*, Paris, 1803.

Hubert Le Blanc, *Défense de la basse de la viole contre les entréprises du violon et les prétentions du violoncel*, Amsterdam, 1740. Reprint of the original French version in *La Revue Musicale* (Paris): November and December 1927; January, February, March, and June 1928.

Jean Benjamin de La Borde, *Essai sur la musique*, Paris, 1780.

Hercole Bottrigari, *Il Desiderio*, Venice, 1594. Facsimile edition with an introduction by Kathi Meyer, Berlin, 1924.

Sébastien de Brossard, *Dictionnaire de musique*, Paris, 1703.

Sébastien de Brossard, *Fragments d'une methode de violon*, MS. in the *Bibliothèque Nationale*, Paris, c. 1712.

Bartolomeo Campagnoli, *Metodo per violino*, Op. 21 [Milan?], 1797. Translated into English by John Bishop as *A New and Progressive Method*, London, 1856.

J. B. Cartier, *L'Art du Violon*, Paris, 1798.

Salomon de Caus, *Institution Harmonique*, Francfort [sic], 1615.

Domenico Pietro Cerone, *El Melopeo y Maestro*, Naples, 1613.

Scipione Cerreto, *Della prattica musica*, Naples, 1601.

The Compleat Musick-Master, see Anon., above.

G. L. Conforto, *Breve et facile maniera d'essercitarsi . . . a far passaggi*, Rome, 1593 [or 1603].

Michel Corrette, *L'Art de se perfectionner dans le violon*, Paris, 1782.

Michel Corrette, *L'École d'Orphée*, Paris, 1738.

François Couperin, *L'Art de toucher le clavecin*, Paris, 1716. Reprinted as Vol. I of the complete edition of Couperin's works (Paris, 1933; see below under 'Music').

G. B. Doni, *Annotazioni sopra il Compendio de' Generi, e de' Modi della Musica*, Rome, 1640.

Pierre Dupont, *Principes de Violon*, Paris, 1718.

J. P. Eisel, *Musicus Autodidaktos*, Erfurt, 1738.

Georg Falck, *Idea boni Cantoris*, Nürnberg, 1688.

Antoine Furetière, *Dictionnaire universel, contenant généralement tout les mots français tant vieux que modernes*, 2nd ed., The Hague and Rotterdam, 1791.

F. Galeazzi, *Elementi teorico-pratici de musica*, 2 vols., Rome, 1791, 1796.

Vincenzo Galilei, *Dialogo . . . della musica antica et della moderna*, Florence, 1581.

Sylvestro de Ganassi, *La Fontegara*, Venice, 1535. Facsimile reprint, 1934.

Sylvestro de Ganassi, *Regola Rubertina*, Venice, 1542–3. Facsimile reprint, 1924.

Francesco Geminiani, *The Art of Playing on the Violin*, London, 1751. Facsimile edition by David D. Boyden, Oxford University Press, 1952. An abbreviated version, *An Abstract of Geminiani's Art of Playing on the Violin*, printed by John Boyles, Boston, Mass., 1769.

Hans Gerle, *Musica Teusch*, Nürnberg, 1532.

James Grassineau, *A Musical Dictionary*, London, 1740.

José Herrando, *Arte y puntual explicación del modo di Tocar el Violin*, Paris, 1756.

Philibert Jambe de Fer, *Epitome musical*, Lyon, 1556.

Hans Judenkunig, *Ain schone . . . Underweisung*, Vienna, 1523.

Ignaz Kurzinger, *Getreuer Unterricht*, Augsburg, 1763.

G. M. Lanfranco, *Scintille di musica*, Brescia, 1533.

G. Löhlein, *Anweisung zum Violinspiel*, Leipzig, 1774.

Etienne Loulié, *Elements ou Principes de Musique mis dans un nouvel ordre*, Amsterdam, 1698. Original edition with the title change, '*Elemens . . .*' Paris, 1696.

Thomas Mace, *Musick's Monument*, London, 1676. Facsimile reprint, Paris, 1958.

J. F. B. C. Majer, *Neu-eröffneter theoretisch- und pracktischer Music-Saal*, Nürnberg, 1741. First edition with title prefaced by the phrase, *Museum Musicum*, 1732. Facsimile reprint in *Documenta Musicologica*, I, Kassel and Basel, 1954.

Daniel Merck, *Compendium Musicae Instrumentalis Chelicae*, Augsburg, 1688.

Marin Mersenne, *Harmonie Universelle*, Paris, 1636. For an English translation of a substantial part of Mersenne, see Marin Mersenne, *Harmonie Universelle*, 'The Books on Instruments', translated by Roger E. Chapman, The Hague, 1957.

Johann Mattheson, *Das Neu-eröffnete Orchestre*, Hamburg, 1713.

M. Montéclair, *Méthode facile pour aprendre* [sic] *à joüer du violon*, Paris [1711–12].

Leopold Mozart, *Versuch einer gründlichen Violinschule*, Augsburg, 1756. Translated into English by Editha Knocker, *A Treatise on the Fundamental Principles of Violin Playing*, London, 1948, 2nd (corrected) ed., 1951.

Georg Muffat, *Florilegium Primum*, 1695; *Florilegium secundum*, 1698. For details, see under 'Music', below.

Nolens Volens, see Anon., above.

Roger North on Music, edited by John Wilson, London, 1959.

Roger North, *The Musicall Grammarian* (1728), edited by Hilda Andrews, London [1925].

Diego Ortiz, *Tratado de glosas*, Rome, 1553. Reprint edited by Max Schneider, Kassel, 1936.

Stephen Philpot, *An Introduction to the Art of playing on the violin*, London, 1767 (?).

John Playford, *A Breif* [sic] *Introduction to the Skill of Musick for song and viol*, London, 2nd revised ed., London, 1658 (1st ed., 1654; 19th ed., 1730).

Michael Praetorius, *Syntagma Musicum*, Wolfenbüttel, 1618–20. Reprinted in *Documenta Musicologica*, I (ed., W. Gurlitt): Vol. I, 1959; Vols. II and III, 1958. English translation of Vol. II, Parts 1 and 2 by Harold Blumenfeld, New Haven, 1949.

Peter Prelleur, *The Modern Musick-Master*, London, 1731 (some copies are dated 1730).

W. C. Printz, *Musica Modulatoris Vocalis*, Schweidnitz, 1678.

J. J. Quantz, *Versuch einer Anweisung die Flöte traversiere zu spielen*, Berlin, 1752. Facsimile reprint of the third edition (1789), 1953.

François Raguenet, *Comparison between French and Italian Music* (1702), English translation attributed to J. E. Galliard (1709), reprinted in *The Musical Quarterly*, July 1946.

E. F. Rimbault, editor of *Memoirs of Musick by the Hon. Roger North*, London, 1846.

Richardo Rogniono, *Passaggi per potersi essercitare nel diminuire terminatemente con ogni sorte d'instromenti*, Venice, 1592.

Francesco Rognoni, *Selva de varii passaggi secondo l'uso moderno*, Milan, 1620.

Jean Rousseau, *Traité de la Viole*, Paris, 1687.

J. J. Rousseau, *Dictionnaire de musique*, Paris, 1768.

The Self-Instructor, see Anon., above.

Christopher Simpson, *The Division Viol*, London, 1659, 2nd ed., 1665. Facsimile of the 2nd ed., London, 1955.

Giuseppe Tartini, *Trattato di musica*, Padua, 1754.

Giuseppe Tartini, *Traité des Agréments de la Musique* [1771], edited by Erwin R. Jacobi, Celle and New York, 1961. See also the edition of Sol Babitz, published by Carl Fischer, New York, 1958.

Carlo Tessarini, *Grammatica di musica*, Rome, 1741 (?). Translated into English as *A Musical Grammar*, Edinburgh [176–?].

Johannes Tinctoris, *De Inventione et Usu Musicae*, c. 1487. English translation in *The Galpin Society Journal*, Vol. III, 1950.

Pier Francesco Tosi, *Opinioni de' Cantori antichi e moderni*, Bologna, 1732. Translated into English by J. E. Galliard as *Observations on the Florid Song*, London, 1743.

Nicola Vicentino, *L'Antica Musica*, Rome, 1555. Facsimile edition by Edward E. Lowinsky, Kassel, 1959.

Le Cerf de la Viéville, *Comparaison de la musique italienne et de la musique françoise*, Brussels, 3 vols., 1704–6.

Sebastian Virdung, *Musica Getutscht*, Basel, 1511. Facsimile reprint edited by Leo Schrade, Kassel, 1931.

J. G. Walther, *Musicalisches Lexikon*, Leipzig, 1732. Facsimile reprint in *Documenta Musicologica*, I, Kassel and Basel, 1953.

Lodovico Zacconi, *Prattica di musica*, Venice, 1592.

Gasparo Zannetti, *Il Scolaro di Gasparo Zannetti per imparare a suonare di Violino et altri stromenti*, Milan, 1645.

B. SECONDARY SOURCES

Putnam Aldrich, *The Principal Agréments of the 17th and 18th Century*, unpublished Harvard Ph.D. dissertation, 1942.

Willi Apel, *The Harvard Dictionary of Music*, Cambridge, Mass., 1944.

P. O. Apian-Bennewitz, *Die Geige, der Geigenbau, und die Bogenverfertigung*, Weimar, 1892; 2nd ed., Leipzig, 1920.

Sol Babitz, 'Differences between 18th-century and modern Violin Bowing', *The Score*, March 1957.

Sol Babitz, 'A Problem of Rhythm in Baroque Music', *The Musical Quarterly*, October 1952.

Renzo Bacchetta, 'Chi inventò il violino?' in *Stradivari non è nato nel 1644*, Cremona, 1937.

Alberto Bachmann, *Encyclopedia of the Violin*, New York, 1925.

Anthony Baines, 'Fifteenth-century Instruments in Tinctoris's *De Inventione et Usu Musicae*', *The Galpin Society Journal*, Vol. III, 1950.

J. Murray Barbour, *Tuning and Temperament*, Michigan State College Press, East Lansing, Michigan, 1951, 2nd ed., 1953.

J. Murray Barbour, 'Violin Intonation in the 18th Century', *The Journal of the American Musicological Society*, Fall 1952.

Sydney Beck, editor and reconstructor, *The First Book of Consort Lessons Collected by Thomas Morley 1599 and 1611*, New York, 1959.

Gustav Beckmann, *Das Violinspiel in Deutschland vor 1700*, Leipzig, 1918.

Ingmar Bengtsson, *J. H. Roman och hans Instrumentalmusik*, Uppsala, 1955.

Jean Berger, 'Notes on some 17th-Century Compositions for Trumpets and Strings in Bologna', *The Musical Quarterly*, July 1951.

Nicholas Bessaraboff, *Ancient Musical Instruments*, Boston, 1941.

Adolfo Betti, *La Vita e L'Arte di Francesco Geminiani*, Lucca, 1933.

Carlo Bonetti, 'La Genealogia degli Amati-Liutai e il Primato della Scuola Liutistica Cremonese', *Bollettino Storico Cremonese*, Series II, Anno III (Vol. VIII), Cremona, 1938.

Eugène Borrel, 'A propos des Notes Inégales', *Revue de Musicologie*, July 1958.

Eugène Borrel, *L'Interpretation de la Musique Française*, Paris, 1934.

Eugène Borrel, 'Les Notes Inégales dans l'ancienne Musique Française', *Revue de Musicologie*, November 1931.

Charles van den Borren, 'Orlande de Lassus et la musique instrumentale', *Revue Musicale*, May 1922.

David D. Boyden, 'Ariosti's Lessons for Viola d'Amore', *The Musical Quarterly*, October 1946.

David D. Boyden, 'Geminiani and the first Violin Tutor', *Acta Musicologica*, Fasc. III–IV, 1959.

David D. Boyden, 'The Missing Italian Manuscript of Tartini's *Traité des Agrémens*', *The Musical Quarterly*, July 1960.

David D. Boyden, 'Monteverdi's *Violini Piccoli* and *Viole da Braccio*', *Annales Musicologiques*, Vol. VI, Paris, 1958-63.

David D. Boyden, 'Prelleur, Geminiani and Just Intonation', *The Journal of the American Musicological Society*, Fall 1951.

David D. Boyden, 'A Postscript to "Geminiani and the first Violin Tutor"', *Acta Musicologica*, Fasc. I, 1960.

David D. Boyden, 'The Violin and its Technique in the 18th Century', *The Musical Quarterly*, January 1950.

David D. Boyden, 'The Violin and its Technique: New Horizons in Research', *Bericht über den siebenten Internationalen Musikwissenschaftlichen Kongress Köln 1958*, Kassel, 1959.

David D. Boyden, 'When is a Concerto not a Concerto?' *The Musical Quarterly*, April 1957.

David D. Boyden, 'The Violin', a chapter in *Musical Instruments through the Ages* (edited by Anthony Baines), Penguin Books, Harmondsworth, 1961; German translation, Munich, 1962.

David D. Boyden, 'Skordatur' in *Die Musik in Geschichte und Gegenwart*, Vol. XII (1964).

Paul Brainard, *Die Violinsonaten Giuseppe Tartinis*, unpublished Ph.D. dissertation, Göttingen, 1959.

Alexander Buchner, *Musical Instruments through the Ages*, London, [n.d.].

Charles Burney. *A General History*, 4 vols., London, 1776–89. Reprinted, 2 vols., New York, 1935.

Adam Carse, *The History of Orchestration*, London, 1925.

Albert Cohen, 'The *Fantaisie* for Instrumental Ensemble in 17th-Century France', *The Musical Quarterly*, April 1962.

Michael Collins, *The Performance of Coloration, Hemiola, and Sesquialtera (1450–1750)*, unpublished Ph.D. dissertation, Stanford, 1963.

Henry Coutagne, *Gaspard Duiffoproucart [sic]*, Paris, 1893.

Edward Dannreuther, *Musical Ornamentation*, 2 vols., London, 1893–5.

Thurston Dart, *The Interpretation of Music*, London, 1954.

Thurston Dart, 'The Printed Fantasies of Orlando Gibbons' [c. 1620], *Music and Letters*, October 1956.

Thurston Dart and William Coates, *Jacobean Consort Music*, Vol. IX (1955) of *Musica Britannica*, 17 vols. to date, London, 1951–61.

B. Disertori, 'Pratica e technica della lira da braccio', *Revista musicale italiana*, Vol. 45, 1941.

Arnold Dolmetsch, *The Interpretation of the Music of the XVIIth and XVIIIth Centuries*, London [1915].

Robert Donington, *The Instruments of Music*, London, 1949.

Robert Donington, *The Interpretation of Early Music*, London, 1963.

E. N. Doring, *The Guadagnini Family of Violin Makers*, Chicago, 1949.

E. N. Doring (ed.), *Violins and Violinists*, Chicago, April 1938–December, 1960.

M. Dounias, *Die Violinkonzerte Giuseppe Tartinis*, Munich, 1935.

G. Dubourg, *The Violin*, London, 1836, 5th ed., 1878.

Minnie Elmer, *Tartini's Improvised Ornamentation*, unpublished M.A. thesis, University of California, Berkeley, 1962.

Maurice Emmanuel, 'The Creation of the Violin and its Consequences', *The Musical Quarterly*, October 1937.

C. Engel, *Researches into the early History of the Violin Family*, London, 1883.

E. H. Fellowes, 'The Philidor Manuscripts', *Music and Letters*, April 1931.

Ernest T. Ferand, *Die Improvisation*, Cologne, 1956.

Ernest T. Ferand, 'Improvisation', *Die Musik in Geschichte und Gegenwart*, Vol. 6, 1957.

John Fesperman, 'Rhythmic Alteration in Eighteenth-Century French Keyboard Music', *Organ Institute Quarterly*, Vol. 9, Nos. 1 and 2 (Spring and Summer 1961).

F. J. Fétis, 'Du Roi des Violons', *Revue Musicale*, 1827.

F. J. Fétis, *Notice of Anthony Stradivari*, translated by John Bishop, London, 1864.

Ian F. Finlay, 'Musical Instruments in 17th-Century Dutch Paintings', *The Galpin Society Journal*, Vol. VI, 1953.

Francis W. Galpin, *Old English Instruments of Music*, London, 1910.

The Galpin Society Journal, London, 1948–.

R. Giazotto, *Tomaso Albinoni*, Milan, 1945.

Franz Giegling, *Giuseppe Torelli*, Kassel, 1949.

J. W. Giltay, *Bow Instruments*, London, 1923.

Martin Greulich, *Beiträge zur Geschichte des Streichinstrumentenspiels in 16. Jahrhundert*, Berlin Ph.D. dissertation, 1933.

Laurent Grillet, *Les ancêtres du violon*, 2 vols., Paris, 1901 and 1905.

Grove's Dictionary of Music and Musicians, 5th ed., London, 1954.

R. Haas, *Aufführungspraxis*, Wildpark-Potsdam, 1931.

Major Alexander Hajdecki, *Die italienische Lira da Braccio*, Mostar, 1892.

Fridolin Hamma, *Meisterwerke Italienischer Geigenbaukunst*, Stuttgart, n.d. [1931].

Fridolin Hamma, *Meister Deutscher Geigenbaukunst*, Stuttgart, 1948. Translated into English by Walter Stewart as *German Violin Makers*, London, 1961.

Rosamund E. M. Harding, *Origins of Musical Time and Expression*, London, 1938.

Eta Harich-Schneider, 'Über die Angleichung nachschlagender Sechzehntel an Triolen', *Die Musik Forschung*, Jan./März 1959.

George Hart, *The Violin: its famous Makers and their Imitators*, London, 1875. Later editions 1884, 1887, and 1909.

Sir John Hawkins, *A General History of Music*, 5 vols., London, 1776. Reprint ed., London, 2 vols., 1875; also, New York, 1963.

Gerald Hayes, *Musical Instruments and their Music, 1500–1750*, 2 vols., London, 1928 and 1930.

J. A. Herbst, *Musica Moderna Prattica*, Frankfurt, 1653.

Edward Heron-Allen, *De Fidiculis Bibliographia*, 2 vols., London, 1890–4.

Edward Heron-Allen, *Violin Making*, London, 1889.

W. H., A. F., and A. E. Hill, *Antonio Stradivari*, London, 1902.

W. H., A. F., and A. E. Hill, *The Violin Makers of the Guarneri Family*, London, 1931.

Margaret L. Huggins, *Gio. Paolo Maggini: his Life and Work*, London, 1892.

Arthur Hutchins, *The Baroque Concerto*, London, 1961.

Dora J. Iselin, *Biagio Marini: sein Leben und seine Instrumentalwerke*, Hildburghausen, 1931.

Erwin R. Jacobi, 'G. F. Nicolai's Manuscript of Tartini's *Regole per ben suonar il Violino*', *The Musical Quarterly*, April 1961.

A. Jacquot, *La lutherie lorraine et française*, Paris, 1912.

A. Jacquot, *La Musique en Lorraine*, Paris, 1882.

K. Jalovec, *Böhmische Geigenbauer*, Prague, 1959.

K. Jalovec, *Italienische Geigenbauer*, Prague, 1957; original edition (Prague, 1952) in Czech and English.

Journal of the American Musicological Society (1948–).

Lucian Kamiensky, 'Zum Tempo Rubato', *Archiv für Musikwissenschaft*, Vol. I, 1918–19.

Hermann Keller, *Die Bedeutung der Zeichen Keil, Strich und Punkt bei Mozart*, Kassel, 1957.

Hermann Keller, *Phrasierung und Artikulation*, Kassel, 1955.

Otto Kinkeldey, *Orgel und Klavier in der Musik des 16. Jahrhunderts*, Leipzig, 1910.

Georg Kinsky, *A History of Music in Pictures*, London, 1930.

Ralph Kirkpatrick, 'Eighteenth-Century Metronomic Indications', *Papers of the American Musicological Society*, 1938. Privately printed, 1940.

William Klenz, *Giovanni Maria Bononcini of Modena*, Durham, N.C., 1962.

H. Knödt, 'Zur Entwicklungsgeschichte der Kadenzen in Instrumentalkonzert', *Sammelbände der Internationalen Musikgesellschaft*, XV, 1913–14.

W. Kolneder, *Aufführungspraxis bei Vivaldi*, Leipzig, 1955.

Arend Koole, *Pietro Antonio Locatelli da Bergamo*, Amsterdam, 1949.

H. Kretzschmar, 'Allgemeines und Besonderes zur Affektenlehre', *Jahrbuch der Musikbibliothek Peters*, Vols. 18–19, 1911–12.

Max Kuhn, *Die Verzierungskunst in der Gesangmusik des 16. –17. Jahrhunderts (1535–1650)*, Leipzig, 1902.

H. C. De Lafontaine, editor, *The King's Musick*, London, n.d. (preface dated 1909).

Lionel de La Laurencie, *L'École Française de Violon de Lully à Viotti*, 3 vols., Paris, 1922–4.

Murray Lefkowitz, *William Lawes*, London, 1960.

François Lesure, 'La Facture Instrumentale à Paris au seizième Siècle', *The Galpin Society Journal*, Vol. VII, 1954.

François Lesure, 'Le Traité des Instruments de Musique de Pierre Trichet', *Annales Musicologiques*, Vol. III, 1955, Vol. IV, 1956. Also published separately, Neuilly-sur-Seine, 1957.

W. L. v. Lütgendorff, *Die Geigen- und Lautenmacher*, 2 vols., 4th ed., Frankfurt am Main, 1922.

Arthur Mendel, 'On Pitches in Use in Bach's Time—II', *The Musical Quarterly*, October 1955.

Arthur Mendel, 'Pitch in the 16th and 17th Centuries', *The Musical Quarterly*, January–October (four parts), 1948.

Ernst H. Meyer, *English Chamber Music*, London, 1946.

Henry G. Mishkin, 'The Solo Violin Sonata of the Bologna School', *The Musical Quarterly*, January 1943.

Otto Möckel, *Die Kunst des Geigenbaues*, Leipzig, 1930.

Max Möller, *The Violin Makers of the Low Countries*, Amsterdam, 1955.

Andreas Moser, *Geschichte des Violinspiels*, Berlin, 1923.

Andreas Moser, 'Zu Joh. Seb. Bachs Sonaten und Partiten für Violine allein', *Bach-Jahrbuch*, 1920.

A. M. Mucchi, *Gasparo da Salò*, Milan, 1940.

The Musical Quarterly, New York, (1915–).

Die Musik in Geschichte und Gegenwart, Kassel. 11 vols. to date (1949–).

William S. Newman, *The Sonata in the Baroque Era*, Chapel Hill, N.C., 1959.

Henryk Opienski, *La Musique Polonaise*, Paris, 1918.

Stanislao Cordero di Pamparato, 'Emmanuele Filiberto di Savoia, protettore dei musici', *Revista musicale italiana*, Vol. XXXIV, 1927.

H. Panum, *Stringed Instruments of the Middle Ages*, London [1939?].

Marc Pincherle, *Corelli*, Paris, 1935. English version, *Corelli: His Life. His Music*, New York, 1956.

Marc Pincherle, *Feuillets d'Histoire du violon*, Paris, 1927.

Marc Pincherle, *Jean-Marie Leclair*, Paris, 1952.

Marc Pincherle, 'La Technique du Violon chez les Premiers Sonatistes Français (1695–1723)', *Bulletin Français de la Société Internationale de Musique*, August–September 1911.

Marc Pincherle, *Les Violinistes*, Paris, 1922.

Marc Pincherle, *Antonio Vivaldi et la musique instrumentale*, Paris, 1948.

Dragan Plamenac, 'An Unknown Violin Tablature of the early 17th Century', *Papers of the American Musicological Society*, 1941.

Henri Poidras, *Critical and Documentary Dictionary of Violin Makers old and modern*, 2 vols., Rouen, 1928–30.

Newman W. Powell, *Early Keyboard Fingering and its Effect on Articulation*, unpublished M.A. thesis, Stanford, 1954.

Newman W. Powell, *Rhythmic Freedom in the Performance of French Music from 1650 to 1735*, Ph.D. dissertation, Stanford, 1959.

Henry Prunières, 'La Musique de la Chambre et de L'Écurie sous le Règne de François Ier', *L'Année Musicale I, 1911*, Paris, 1912.

Gustave Reese, *Music in the Renaissance*, New York, 1954.

Mario Rinaldi, 'On the Authenticity of the "Chaconne" of Tomaso Antonio Vitali', *La Rassegna Musicale*, April–June 1954.

Julius Ruhlmann, *Zur Geschichte der Bogeninstrumente*, Brunswick, 1882.

Theodore Russell, 'The Violin Scordatura', *The Musical Quarterly*, January 1938.

Curt Sachs, *The History of Musical Instruments*, New York, 1940.

Curt Sachs, *Rhythm and Tempo*, New York, 1953.

Curt Sachs, *World History of the Dance*, New York, 1937.

Henry Saint George, *The Bow*, London, 1896, 2nd ed., 1909.

Walter Salmen, *Der fahrende Musiker in europäischen Mittelalter*, Kassel, 1960.

W. Sandys and S. A. Forster, *History of the Violin*, London, 1864.

Claudio Sartori, *Bibliografia della musica strumentale italiana stampata in Italia fino al 1700*, Florence, 1952.

Max Sauerlandt, *Die Musik in Fünf Jahrhunderten der Europäischen Malerei*, Leipzig, 1922.

Arnold Schering, *Geschichte des Instrumentalkonzerts*, Leipzig, 1905.

Arnold Schering, 'Verschwundene Traditionen des Bachzeitalters', in 'Bachheft', *Neue Zeitschrift für Musik*, September 1904. Expanded in the *Bach-Jahrbuch*, October 1904.

K. Schlesinger, *The Precursors of the Violin Family*, London, 1910 (Vol. II of the *Instruments of the Modern Orchestra*).

H. P. Schmitz, *Die Kunst der Verzierung in 18. Jh.*, Kassel and Basel, 1955.

Georg Schünemann, *Geschichte des Dirigierens*, Leipzig, 1913.

Albert Schweitzer, 'A new Bow for unaccompanied Violin Music', *The Musical Times*, September 1933.

Barbara A. G. Seagrave, *The French Style of Violin Bowing and Phrasing from Lully to Jacques Aubert (1650–1730)*, Ph.D. dissertation, Stanford, 1959.

Walter Senn, *Jacob Stainer der Geigenmacher zu Absam*, Innsbruck, 1951.

Walter Senn, 'Der Wandel des Geigenklanges seit dem 18. Jahrhundert', *Kongress Bericht, Gesellschaft für Musikforschung*, 1957.

Kenneth Skeaping, 'Some Speculations on a Crisis in the History of the Violin', *The Galpin Society Journal*, Vol. VIII, March 1955.

Denis Stevens, 'Seventeenth-Century Italian Instrumental Music in the Bodleian Library', *Acta Musicologica*, Vol. XXVI (1954), p. 67.

The Strad, London, May 1890–.

E. Van der Straeten, *The History of the Violin*, 2 vols., London, 1933.

E. Van der Straeten, *The History of the Violoncello*, London, 1915.

Giuseppe Strocchi, *Liuteria—Storia ed Arte*, Lugo, 1937.

Oliver Strunk, *Source Readings in Music History*, New York, 1950.

'James Talbot's Manuscript', *The Galpin Society Journal* (Vols. I and II), Part I, Anthony Baines, 1948; Part II, Robert Donington, 1950.

Michael Tilmouth, *A Calendar of References to Music in Newspapers published in London and the Provinces (1660–1719)*, R.M.A. [Royal Musical Association] Research Chronicle No. 1, Cambridge, 1961.

Michael Tilmouth, 'Nicola Matteis', *The Musical Quarterly*, January 1960.

Michael Tilmouth, 'Some Early London Concerts and Music Clubs, 1670–1720', *Proceedings of the Royal Musical Association*, 1957–8.

Michael Tilmouth, 'Some Improvements in Music Noted by William Turner in 1697', *The Galpin Society Journal*, May 1957.

Michael Tilmouth, 'The Technique and Forms of Purcell's Sonatas', *Music and Letters*, April 1959.

René Vannes, *Dictionnaire Universel des Luthiers*, 2nd ed., Brussels, 1951, Vol. 2, 1959.

Abraham Veinus, *The Concerto*, London, 1948.

Louis-Antoine Vidal, *Les Instruments à Archet*, 3 vols., Paris, 1876–8.

Violins and Violinists, see Doring.

W. J. Wasielewski, *Instrumentalsätze vom Ende des XVI. bis Ende des XVII. Jahrhunderts*, Berlin, n.d.

W. J. Wasielewski, *Die Violine und ihre Meister*, 6th ed., Leipzig, 1920.

H. Wessely-Kropik, *Lelio Colista*, Vienna, [1961?].

J. A. Westrup, 'Monteverdi and the Orchestra', *Music and Letters*, July 1940.

J. A. Westrup, *Purcell*, London, 1937.

W. G. Whittaker, 'William Young', *Collected Essays*, London, 1940.

Emanuel Winternitz, 'Lira da Braccio', *Die Musik in Geschichte und Gegenwart*, Vol. VIII (1960).

Ariste Wirsta, *École de Violon au XVIIIeme Siècle d'après les Ouvrages Didactiques*, Thesis, University of Paris, 1955.

Johannes Wolf, *Handbuch der Notationskunde*, 2 vols., Leipzig, 1913 and 1919.

Walter Woodfill, *Musicians in English Society*, Princeton, 1953.

C. MUSIC

The following gives bibliographical details of the principal references to music discussed in the body of the book. In no sense is it a complete bibliography of violin music before 1761.

Henricus Albicastro, *Zwölf Concerti A 4*, Op. 7 [*1700–1705*], ed. Max Zulauf, *Schweitzerische Musikdenkmäler*, I, Basel [1955].

Tomaso Albinoni, *Sinfonie e Concerti a Cinque*, Op. 2, Venice, 1700.

Attilio Ariosti, 'Lessons' for viola d'amore, London, *c.* 1728.

Jacques Aubert, *Concerto à quatre Violons, Violoncello et Basse continue*, Op. 17 [*1735*].

Johann Sebastian Bach, *Werke*, edition by the *Bach-Gesellschaft*, Leipzig, 1851–1926; see especially Vols. 9, 19, 21, and 27.

Johann Sebastian Bach, *Sei Solo a Violino senza Basso accompagnato*, facsimile of the autograph, Kassel and Basel, 1950.

Ballet comique de la reine, see *Circe ou le ballet comique de la reine*.

Gustav Beckmann, ed., 12 Sonaten für Violine und Klavier, Berlin and New York [*c.* 1921].

Heinrich Franz Biber, *Sechzehn Violinsonaten* [fifteen 'Mystery' sonatas and 'Passagaglia'], *Denkmäler der Tonkunst in Österreich*, Vol. 25, Vienna, 1905 (reissued, 1959).

G. M. Bononcini, *Arie, Correnti, Sarabande, Gighe, & Allemande A Violino, e Violone, ouer Spinetta*, Op. 4, Bologna, 1671. Ten pieces in Klenz, *Giovanni Maria Bononcini*.

William Boyce, *Twelve Sonatas for two violins, with a bass for the violoncello or harpsichord*, London [1750]. Nos. 2, 8, 9, and 12 published in modern editions by Hinrichsen, London.

G. B. Buonamente, see Alfred Einstein.

J. B. Cartier, *L'Art du Violon*, Paris [1798].

Maurizio Cazzati, *Trio Sonata in d minor for two violins and basso continuo*, in *Hortus Musicus*, No. 34, Kassel. One canzona and three sonatas in Klenz, *Givanni Maria Bononcini*.

G. P. Cima, 'Sonata for solo violin and basso continuo', 1610, in Beckmann, *12 Sonaten*.

Circe ou le ballet comique de la reine [1581], Paris, 1582. Reprinted in *Chefs-d'oeuvres classiques de l'opéra français*, ed. J.-B. Weckerlin, Paris [1882?].

Lelio Colista, *Sonata No. IV in D Major*, ed. Michael Tilmouth, London, 1960.

Lelio Colista, *Trio Sonata A-Dur für zwei Violinen, Violoncello und Basso continuo*, ed. Helene Wessely-Kropik, *Hortus Musicus*, No. 172, Kassel, 1960.

John Coperario, 'fantasia suites'. Two for one violin, bass viol, and organ, and two for two violins, bass viol, and organ, in *Jacobean Consort Music*, ed. Thurston Dart and William Coates, Vol. IX of *Musica Britannica*, London, 1955.

Arcangelo Corelli, *Les Oeuvres de Arcangelo Corelli*, 5 vols., ed. Joachim and Chrysander, London [1891].

François Couperin, *Oeuvres complètes de François Couperin*, 12 vols., general ed., Maurice Cauchie, Paris [1933]. Chamber music in Vols. 7–10.

Archibald Davison and Willi Apel, edd., *Historical Anthology of Music*, 2 vols., Cambridge, Mass., 1946–50.

Denkmäler der Tonkunst in Osterreich, general ed., Guido Adler, Vienna, 1894–.

Denkmaler Deutscher Tonkunst, 65 vols., Leipzig, 1892–1931.

John Dowland, *Lachrimae or Seaven Teares Figured in Seaven Passionate Pavans, with divers other Pavans, Galiards, and Almands, set forth for the Lute, Viols, or Violons* [sic], *in five parts*, London [1604]. Modern versions by Peter Warlock [Philip Heseltine], [London] 1927, and in *Nagels Musik-Archiv*, No. 173, Hannover.

Jules Ecorcheville, ed., *Vingt Suites d'Orchestre du XVIIe siècle francais . . .* Paris and Berlin, 1906.

Alfred Einstein, ed. *Einstein music collection . . . of early vocal and instrumental music*, copied [scored] *by Alfred Einstein at Smith College*, in Smith College Library, Northampton, Mass. This collection contains selections from the works of (*inter alia*) G. B. Buonamente (Ser. II, Vol. 1), B. Marini (Ser. II, Vol. 10), and Salomone Rossi (Ser. II, Vol. 10).

Das Erbe Deutscher Musik, Leipzig, 1935–.

Andrea Falconieri, *Battalla de Barabaso yerno de Satanas*, 1650, in Torchi, *L'Arte Musicale*, Vol. VII.

Carlo Farina, *Capriccio Stravagante*, 1627, in Wasielewski, *Instrumentalsätze*.

Andrea Gabrieli, *Aria della Battaglia*, 1590, in Vol. I, *Istitutioni e Monumenti dell'Arte Musicale Italiana*.

Giovanni Gabrieli, *Sonate für drei Violinen und Basso continuo* [1615], ed. Werner Danckert, *Hortus Musicus*, No. 70, Kassel [1950].

Denis Gaultier, *La rhétorique des dieux* [Paris, c. 1650] *et autre pièces de luth* . . . ed. A. Tessier, *Publications de la Société Française de Musicologie*, 1ᵉ série, Vols. VI and VII, Paris, 1932–3.

Francesco Geminiani, *Sonate a violino, violone, e cembalo* . . . [Op. 1], London, 1716. Second edition, revised by the composer, London, 1739. Modern edition by Ross Lee Finney in *Smith College Music Archives*, No. 1, Northampton, Mass. [c. 1935].

Francesco Geminiani, *Concerti grossi con due violini, violoncello, e viola di concertino obligati, e due altri violini e basso de concerto grosso ad arbitrio* . . . Op. 2, London [1732]. Second edition, revised by the composer, London [1757].

Francesco Geminiani, *Concerti grossi* . . . Op. 3, London [c. 1733]. Second edition, revised by the composer, London [1755].

Louis-Gabriel Guillemain, three sonata movements in Cartier, *L'Art du Violon*.

Georg Friedrich Handel, *Georg Friedrich Händel's Werke*, edition of the German *Händelgesellschaft*, ed. Friedrich Chrysander, 96 vols. and 6 supplements, Leipzig, 1858–1902; see especially Vol. 27 (solo sonatas) and Vol. 30 (*concerti grossi*).

Adamo Harzebski, *Canzoni e Concerti*, 1627. One 'Tamburetta' for violin, two *viole bastarde*, and *basso continuo* in H. Opienski, *La Musique Polonaise*, Paris, 1918.

A. Holborne, *Pavans, galliards, almains, and other short aeirs* [sic] *both grave, and light, in five parts, for viols, violins, or other musicall winde instruments*, London, 1599.

Hortus Musicus, Kassel and Basel, 1936–.

Istitutioni e Monumenti dell'Arte Musicale Italiana, 7 vols., Milan, 1931–41.

John Jenkins, Fancies and Ayres, ed. Helen Joy Sleeper, *Wellesley College Editions*, No. 1, Wellesley, Mass., 1950.

L'Abbé le fils, *Jolis airs ajustés et variés pour un violon seul*, Op. 7, 1763.

Elizabeth-Claude Jacquet de La Guerre, *Sonates Pour le Violon et Pour le Clavecin*, 1707.

William Lawes, 'fantazyas'. One for one violin, bass viol, and organ, in Meyer, *English Chamber Music*; one for two violins, bass viol, and organ, in Lefkowitz, *William Lawes*, under the title 'Sonata No. 8 in D Major'.

Jean-Marie Leclair, *Premier Livre de Sonates à Violon seul avec la Basse continue*, Op. 1, 1723.

Jean-Marie Leclair, *Second Livre de Sonates Pour le Violon et pour la Flûte traversière avec la Basse continue*, Op. 2 [*c.* 1728].

Jean-Marie Leclair, *Troisième livre de sonates à violon avec la basse continue* . . . Op. 5, Paris, 1734.

Jean-Marie Leclair, *Six Sonates pour violon et clavecin ou piano*, ed. Marc Pincherle, Monaco [*c.* 1952]. Contains Op. 1, No. 8; Op. 2, Nos. 1, 11, and 12; and Op. 5, Nos. 1 and 4.

Pietro Antonio Locatelli, *L'Arte del Violino, XII concerti cioè violino solo, con XXIV capricci ad libitum* . . . Op. 3, Amsterdam [1733].

Pietro Antonio Locatelli, *VI Concerti a quattro*, Op. 7, Amsterdam, 1741.

Biagio Marini, see Alfred Einstein. For modern editions, see Schering, *Geschichte der Musik in Beispielen*, No. 183; Davison and Apel, *Historical Anthology of Music*, No. 199; and *Hortus Musicus*, Nos. 129 and 143.

Nicola Matteis, *Ayres of the Violin*, London, Books I and II, 1676; Books III and IV, 1685.

J.-J. C. de Mondonville, *Pièces de Clavecin En Sonates, Avec Accompagnnement de Violon*, Op. 3, Paris and Lille [*c.* 1734]. Modern edition by Marc Pincherle, *Publications de la Société Française de Musicologie*, 1e série, Vol. IX, Paris, 1935.

J.-J. C. de Mondonville, *Les Sons Harmoniques, Sonates à violon seul avec la basse continue* . . . Op. 4, Paris and Lille [*c.* 1738].

Claudio Monteverdi, *Tutte le Opere*, 16 vols., ed. G. F. Malipiero, Asolo and Vienna, 1926–42; see especially Vols. 7 and 8 (madrigals), and Vol. 11 (*Orfeo*).

Thomas Morley, *The First Booke of Consort Lessons*, London, 1599. Modern edition: *The First Book of Consort Lessons Collected by Thomas Morley 1599 and 1611*, reconstructed and edited by Sydney Beck, New York, 1959.

Georg Muffat, *Florilegium Primum*, 1695, and *Florilegium Secundum*, 1698. In *Denkmäler der Tonkunst in Osterreich*, Vols. 2 and 4, Vienna, 1894–5.

Gottlieb Muffat, *Componimenti Musicali*, Vienna, 1726.

Musica Brittanica, London, 1951–.

Nagels Musik-Archiv, Hannover, 1927–.

Giovanni Antonio Piani, *Sonate a violino solo è violoncello col cimbalo* . . . Op. 1, Paris, 1712. Example in Cartier, *L'Art du Violon*.

J. G. Pisendel, *Sonata for violin solo without bass*, *Hortus Musicus*, No. 91, Kassel, n.d.

J. G. Pisendel, 'Violin Concerto', in *Denkmäler Deutscher Tonkunst*, Vols. 29–30.

John Playford, *Apollo's Banquet* . . . London, 1669.

John Playford, *The English Dancing Master* . . . London [1650].

John Playford, *The Division-Violin* . . . London, 1684.

Michael Praetorius, *Terpsichore* . . . *Darinnen allerley Frantzösische Däntze und Lieder* . . . *1612*, in *Gesamtausgabe von Michael Praetorius*, 20 vols., Wolfenbüttel, 1928–40, Vol. 15.

The Works of Henry Purcell, 31 vols., published by the Purcell Society, London, 1878–1928; see especially Vols. 5 and 7 (trio sonatas), and Vol. 31 (fantasias and solo sonata).

Jean Philippe Rameau, *Oeuvres Complètes*, 18 vols., general ed., Camille Saint-Saëns, Paris, 1895–1914. Vols. I and II contain the instrumental music.

J. H. Roman, *Assaggi à Violino Solo* [1730–40], ed. Ingmar Bentsson and Lars Frydén, in *Monumenta Musicae Svecicae*, Vol. I, Stockholm, 1958.

Salomone Rossi, see Alfred Einstein. For modern edition, see *Hortus Musicus*, No. 110.

Arnold Schering, *Geschichte der Musik in Beispielen*, Leipzig, 1931.

J. H. Schmeltzer, *Sonatae unarum Fidium*, 1664, in *Denkmäler der Tonkunst in Osterreich*, Vol. 93, Vienna, 1958.

Heinrich Schütz, *Sämtliche Werke*, 18 vols., ed. Philipp Spitta, Leipzig, 1885–1927; see especially Vol. VII (*Symphoniae Sacrae*, Part II, 1647).

Christopher Simpson, *Months and Seasons*, 1688. One fantasia in Meyer, *English Chamber Music*.

Giuseppe Tartini, *L'Arte del arco*, n.d. Printed in Cartier, *L'Art du Violon*, 1798, 'from a manuscript of the author'.

Giuseppe Tartini, ' "Devil's Trill" Sonata', first published in Cartier, *L'Art du Violon*, 1798.

Giuseppe Tartini, *VI Sonate a violino e violone o cembalo* . . . Op. 1, Amsterdam (1732).

Giuseppe Tartini, *Sonate à violino e basso* . . . Op. 2, Rome [1745].

G. P. Telemann, 'Violin Concerto', in *Denkmäler der Tonkunst in Österreich*, Vols. 29–30, 1905.

Luigi Torchi, ed., *L'Arte Musicale in Italia* . . . 7 vols., Milan [1897–1908?]. Vol. VII contains early seventeenth-century music for strings.

Giuseppe Torelli, *Concerti grossi* . . . Op. 8, Bologna, 1709.

Tremais, *Sonates pour le violon et pour la flûte avec la basse continue* . . . Op. 1, Paris, 1736.

Tudor Church Music, 10 vols., London, 1922–29.

Marco Uccellini, *Arie, Madrigali, et Correnti a 1, 2, 3* . . . Op. 3, Venice, 1620. Several dances in Torchi, *L'Arte Musicale*, Vol. VII.

Marco Uccellini, two *sinfonie* and a canon from Op. 9 (1667) in Klenz, *Giovanni Maria Bononcini*.

Marco Uccellini, *Per ogni sorte de Stromenti musicali Diversi generi di Sonate da Chiesa e da Camera a Due & Quattro* . . . Op. 22, Venice, 1655. Dances, sonatas, and a 'Passacalio' in Torchi, *L'Arte Musicale*, Vol. VII.

Francesco Maria Veracini, *Zwölf Sonaten für Violine und bezifferten Bass, Op. 1* [c. 1720] . . . ed. Walter Kolneder, Leipzig [c. 1958].

Francesco Maria Veracini, *Sonate accademiche a violino solo*, Op. 2, London and Florence [1744].

G. B. Vitali, *Artifici Musicali, Op. 13* [1689], ed. Louise Rood and Gertrude A. Smith, Smith College Music Archives, No. 14, Northampton, Mass., 1959.

Tommasso Antonio Vitali, *Concerto Di Sonate, Opus 4, for violin, violoncello, and continuo*, Smith College Music Archives, No. 12, Northampton, Mass., 1954.

Antonio Vivaldi, [Complete Works], general ed., G. F. Malipiero, *Istituto italiano Antonio Vivaldi*, Milan, 1947–.

Antonio Vivaldi, *L'Estro Armonico. Concerti* . . . Op. 3, Amsterdam [*c.* 1712].

Antonio Vivaldi, *Il Cimento dell'armonia e dell'inventione*, Op. 8, Amsterdam [*c.* 1725].

Antonio Vivaldi, *La Cetra. Concerti* . . . Op. 9, Amsterdam [*c.* 1728].

J. J. Walther, *Hortulus Chelicus*, Mainz, 1688. Two pieces in Beckmann, *12 Sonaten*.

J. J. Walther, *Scherzi da violino solo con il Basso continuo*, 1676, ed. Gustav Beckmann, in *Das Erbe Deutscher Musik*, Vol. 17, Hannover, 1941; also, two pieces in Beckmann, *12 Sonaten*.

Wilhelm Joseph von Wasielewski, *Instrumentalsätze vom Ende des XVI. bis Ende des XVII. Jahrhunderts*, Berlin, n. d., supplement to *Die Violine im XVII. Jahrhundert und die Anfänge der Instrumental-Composition*, Bonn, 1874.

William Young, *Sonatas I, II, and III, for two violins, 'cello, and piano, with optional contrabass* . . .; *Sonatas IV-XI, for three violins, 'cello, piano, with optional contrabass* . . . ed. W. G. Whittaker, London [*c.* 1930–1.]

Glossary

The Glossary is an adjunct to the Index, which includes all the terms defined in the book. For the most part, the terms found in the Glossary are limited to those that have not been defined in the body of the text. Further, words defined in the Glossary are mainly technical words germane to violin playing, not musical terms of a general character unless the definition of such terms is essential to clarify special meanings in the body of the book.

As an additional feature, the Glossary includes a table of the main technical terms for the parts of the violin and bow in English, French, Italian, and German.

'a': open string in French usage. *See* Ex. 161b, p. 407.

Appoggiatura (I): an accented, dissonant note in a melody. In the seventeenth and eighteenth centuries, the appoggiatura was often indicated as a small ('grace') note.

Arco (I): literally, 'bow'. Used after the word *pizzicato* (plucked) to direct the string player to resume playing with the bow.

Arpeggio (I): playing the notes that comprise chords, not as chords, but one after the other in 'harp' style (hence, 'arpeggio').

Articulation: the enunciation of sounds, especially the degree of clarity in enunciating consecutive sounds.

Assimilation: in the particular usage of this book, assimilation refers to transforming dotted rhythms or other duple groupings into comparable triplet rhythms, for example, a dotted eighth plus sixteenth into a triplet group of a quarter plus eighth.

Bouts (of the violin): an inward curve of a rib (or ribs), forming the waist of an instrument of the violin class. On the violin the inward curves of the waist are called the 'middle bouts'. By extension, the upper curves of the violin are called the 'upper bouts' and the lower curves, 'lower bouts'.

Chamber-pitch (*Kammerton*), Choir-pitch (*Chorton*), Cornett-pitch (*Cornett-ton*): before pitch was standardized, different pitches were used: typically, chamber-pitch for instrumental chamber music, choir-pitch for church organ music and sacred choral music, and cornett-pitch for brass instruments played by town musicians. Of the several chamber-pitches in Bach's time, the highest corresponded to modern pitch. Cornett-pitch and choir-pitch were generally higher than chamber-pitch.

Cinquiesme (F): the 'fifth' part of a string ensemble in seventeenth-century France. Variously, viola I or viola III (*see* p. 117).

Con sordino (I): 'with the mute'. Direction to put the mute on.

Consort: an English term of the sixteenth and seventeenth centuries, derived from *concert* (F) or *concerto* (I), to indicate a group of instruments playing together. A 'whole' consort means that all the instruments are of one kind. A 'broken' consort means that they are of different kinds.

Contraction(s): when the player's hand is contracted to less than its normal span, for example, when each finger is playing consecutive semitones (cf. p. 383–4).

Cornett (*cornetto*): the cornett flourished in the Renaissance and gradually became obsolete after 1650. Its body was made of wood or (sometimes) ivory, straight or slightly curved, with six finger holes cut in the sides. The sound was produced by a cup-shaped mouthpiece, as in brass instruments. The cornett was made in various sizes. 'Cornett' should not be confused with 'cornet', which designates a modern instrument of the trumpet family. For 'Cornett-pitch' *see* 'Chamber-pitch' above.

Descant: treble.

Dessus (F): treble or highest part of the string ensemble (French), generally equivalent to violin I.

Détaché (F): a bowing direction to the string player. Literally, 'detached', that is, played short. Also, a single note played by a single bow stroke. In the eighteenth century, synonymous with staccato.

Diminution (figures): refers to breaking up notes into quicker figures or those of shorter duration for purposes of varying the figuration. Diminution often took its starting point from a melody in relatively long notes. Similar to 'Division(s)'.

Discant: English word derived from the Latin term *discantus*, thus, descant, treble.

Enharmonic: a chord, note, or interval that sounds the same as another chord, note, or interval that is written differently. On the piano, A flat and G sharp are enharmonic to each other.

Extension(s): an extending of the hand beyond its usual span. For more specific applications, *see* p. 381–3.

Figuration: stereotyped figures such as arpeggios or running passages of notes.

Fret(s): raised marks on the fingerboard of a stringed instrument to assist stopping the strings and to guide the player's fingers. Usually made of gut loops or ridges of wood or metal (*see* Pl. 3 b).

Frog: the block to which the hair is attached at the heel of the violin bow (*see* Pl. 29c). Also called 'nut'.

Glissando (I): 'sliding'. Rapid scales executed by a sliding movement of the finger or hand, especially on the piano or harp. Cf. *Portamento*.

Grace note: an ornamental note printed in small type to indicate that its duration is not considered part of the measure but part of the note which it generally precedes. So called because 'grace' refers to an ornamental note in general.

Harmonics (on stringed instruments) a note produced by touching the string lightly (not pressing down) at a particular 'nodal' point on the string, producing a light, 'fluty', ethereal sound. Also called 'flageolet' tone. When the harmonic is produced by a single finger, the harmonic is called 'natural'. In 'artificial' or 'two-fingered' harmonics, the first finger of the left hand stops a given note firmly, acting in effect as the nut of the fingerboard, while the second finger of the hand (usually finger 4 or 3) produces the harmonic by stopping the string lightly at the point indicated (cf. Ex. 154, p. 385).

Hatchet head: a type of bow head resembling a hatchet (cf. Pl. 35, No. 7). Used just prior to the modern (Tourte) bow head (cf. Pl. 28a).

Haute-contre (F): the 'counter-tenor' part of a French string ensemble, especially in the seventeenth century. Variously, viola I or viola II (*see* p. 117).

Intonation system(s): collectively, systems of tuning such as meantone temperament, equal temperament, and just intonation.

Klangideal (G): the 'ideal of sound' characteristic of any given period.

Mute (*sordino*): a device for muffling or damping the sound of instruments. The usual mute for strings is a pronged clamp placed on the bridge. *See also* Con sordino.

Nuance: fine shades of expression in general. Used particularly in connexion with subtle gradations of loud and soft.

Nut: (*a*) the fixed ridge, next to the pegbox of the violin, that raises the strings above the fingerboard (*see* Pl. 1); (*b*) the 'frog' (q.v.) of a violin bow.

Obbligato (I): an independent accompanying part.

Open string: a string sounding its full 'open' length without being stopped by the player.

Passaggi (I): passage work. In the art of diminution, which flourished from the sixteenth to the eighteenth century, a generic term for improvised figures of all sorts. Cf. Diminution, Division (for the latter, *see* the Index).

Pike's head: a type of head commonly used on the 'old' bow. *See* the 'Stradivari' bow in Pl. 28a.

Pitch: *see* Chamber-pitch.

Pizzicato (I): to pluck rather than bow the string of an instrument.

Portamento (I): a sliding between two pitches without distinguishing the intermediate tones. Characteristic of the voice, trombone, and strings (especially the violin, as in shifting). *Glissando* distinguishes all the intermediate half steps between two pitches. Thus the piano and harp can play *glissando* but not *portamento*. The voice, violin, and trombone can produce either, but the *glissando* is far more difficult for them. *Portamento* is a legitimate effect whose use is subject to easy abuse. In modern violin playing, *portamento* in shifting is generally avoided.

Portato (I): a bowing in which two or more notes are detached in a single bow stroke. Indicated by dots (or strokes) under a slur.

Position: in string playing, the 'position' of the left hand higher or lower on the fingerbord. In the first (or natural) position, the first finger stops a whole tone above the open string. In the higher positions, the first finger stops the correspondingly higher notes of the diatonic scale. Thus in third position the first finger stops a fourth above the open string.

Purfling: the inlaid border of violins and other instruments. The purfling consists of three small slips of wood, the middle one black, the outer two white (*see* Pl. 1). Sometimes the purfling is double (*see* Pl. 18).

Quinte (F): the fifth part. See *Cinquiesme*.

Saltellando (I): in bounding style. Said of the bow and bowing.

Sautillé (F): a type of bow stroke in which the bow rebounds lightly off the string.

Sordino (I): mute (q.v.).

Spiccato (I): *sautillé*. In the eighteenth century, the same as *détaché*.

Staccato: disconnected. Usually indicated by a dot (or stroke) over (or under) a note. In modern violin playing, *staccato* means a number of *martelé* strokes played rapidly with a single bow stroke.

Table: the top or belly of the violin.

Taille (F): the 'tenor' part of a French string ensemble, especially in the seventeenth century. Variously, viola II or viola III (*see* p. 117).

Tailpiece: the piece to which the strings of the violin are attached at their ends opposite the pegbox (cf. Pl. 1).

Tasti (I): frets.

Temperament: any system of tuning whose intervals deviate from an acoustically 'pure' system. In the latter (such as 'just' intonation), the size of individual half tones varies, and there is similar variety among individual whole tones and other intervals. In equal temperament (used on the piano), each half and whole tone are equal to every other half and whole tone.

Tuner (fine tuner): a device used, especially on the E string of the violin, to get a 'fine' tuning without adjusting the tuning pegs (*see* Pl. 1).

NOMENCLATURE OF THE VIOLIN (cf. Pl. 1)

English	French	Italian	German
Violin	Violon (m)	Violino (m)	Geige (f)
Back	Fond (m)	Fondo (m)	Boden (m)
Bass-bar	Barre (f)	Catena (f)	Bassbalken (m)
Belly (top, table)	Table (f)	Tavola (f)	Decke (f)
Block (corner)	Tasseau (m)	Tassello (m)	Eckklotz (m)
Block (top)	Tasseau du haut	(degli angoli)	Oberklotz
Block (lower)	Tasseau de bas		Unterklotz
Body	Caisse (f) sonore Coffre (m)	Cassa (f) armonica	Schallkörper (m) Korpus (m)
Bouts (upper)		Fasce (f pl) superiori	Oberbiegel (m pl)
Bouts (middle)	Échancrures (f pl)	Fasce centrali	Mittelbiegel
Bouts (lower)		Fasce inferiori	Unterbiegel

English	French	Italian	German
Bridge	Chevalet (m)	Ponticello (m)	Steg (m)
Button (end)	Bouton (m)	Bottone (m)	Knopf (m)
Fingerboard	Touche (f)	Tastiera (f)	Griffbrett (n)
f-holes	Trous (m pl) d'F	le SS (f pl)	F-Löcher (n pl)
Label (ticket)	Étiquette (f)	Etichetta (f)	Zettel (m)
Lining strip	Contre-éclisse	Contro-fascia	Reifchen (n)
Mute	Sourdine (f)	Sordino (m)	Dämpfer (m)
Neck	Manche (m)	Manico (m)	Hals (m)
Nut (of finger-board)	Sillet (m)	Capotasto (m)	Sattel (m)
Peg	Cheville (f)	Bischero (m)	Wirbel (m)
Pegbox	Cheviller (m)	Cassa dei bischeri	Wirbelkasten (m)
Purfling	Filet (m)	Filetto (m)	Einlage (f)
Rib(s)	Éclisse(s) (f)	Fascie (f pl)	Zargen (f pl)
Scroll	Volute (f)	Voluta (f) Riccio (m)	Schnecke (f)
Soundpost	Âme (f)	Anima (f)	Stimme (f) Stimmstock (m)
Stringholder (tailpiece)	Cordier (m) Tirechordes (m)	Cordiera (f)	Saitenhalter (m)
Varnish	Vernis (m)	Vernice (f)	Lack (m)
Vaulting (arching of the belly)	Voûte (f)	Volte (f pl)	Wölbung (f)

NOMENCLATURE OF THE BOW (cf. Pl. 29c)

Bow	Archet (m)	Arco (m)	Bogen (m)
Frog (= nut)	Hausse (f)	Tallone (m)	Frosch (m)
Hair	Crin (m)	Crino (m)	Haar (m)
Head (or point)	Tête (f) Pointe (f)	Punta (f)	Spitze (f)
Screw (of the bow)	Vis (f)	Vite (f)	Schraube (f)
Stick	Baguette (f)	Bacchetta (f)	Stange (f)

Index

'A' (*Aufzug*): 262
'a' (open string): 407 (Ex. 161b)
'A' (up-bow); 403
Abbé le fils: *see* L'Abbé le fils
Abgesetzen: 405
Abgesetzet: 412, 413, 413 n26
Abgesondert: 411, 412
Abgestossen: 411
Absetzen: 412, 413
Absetzung: 412
Abstrich: 403
Accentuation: 287
Accidentals (18th c.): 366
Accordatura: 130, 370
Adler, Guido: 75 n11
Adson, John: 139
Affect: 290, 490
Affections (early 17th c.): 179
'Affects' (18th c.): 338
Affekt: 490
Affetti: 165
  described, 165
  meaning of, 171
  18th century, 338
Affetto: 171, 290, 490
  as a formula of expression, 490
  doctrine developed by theorists, 493
'Afterbeats': 286
'Ag.': 201 n14
Agazzari, Agostino: 90 n34
  on the violin, 89
Agricola, Martin: 9, 11, 29 n44, 40, 45,
  88 n31
  rebec family, 11
  Musica Instrumentalis Deudsch, 24, 28
  tuning instructions, 70
  use of fingernails, 85 n27
  description of vibrato, 91
Agutter, Ralph: 201 n14
Air varié: 337
Airwood (Air.): 201
'Alard' violin (Stradivari, 1715): 317
Albani, Matthias: 199, 242
  violin owned by Corelli, 195
Albani, Paolo: 198
Alberghi, Paolo: 344
Albicastro, Henrico: 350 n35, 352

use of *tremolo*, 267
Albinoni, Tomaso:
  concerto, 332, 333, 342
  Sinfonie e Concerti, 342
  terms in, 446
Aldrich, Putnam: 286 n2
Alembert (d'): on Italian sonatas, 491
Alla breve: 181, 479
  late 17th century, 293
Allam, Edward: 361 n9
Allegro e staccato: 409
'All sorts of instruments': 53, 54, 123, 124
  Rogniono, 89
'Alto': 446
Alto-tenor (*kleine Geigen*): 45
'Alto viola': 446
Amateur instruction: 244
Amateur tradition of violin playing: 365
Amateur violinists: 232, 242
Amati, Andrea: 19, 33, 38, 68, 195, 242
  birthdate revision, 19
  early (three-stringed) violins, 19
  first (?) famous violin maker, 35
  'Charles IX' cello, 35
  'Charles IX' viola, 35, 36, and Pl. 7b
  'Charles IX' violins, 35, 35 n10
  violin owned by Corelli, 195
Amati, Antonio: 36, 108
  birthdate, 109 n3
Amati, 'the brothers': 36, 146, 195
Amati, Girolamo (Hieronymus): 36, 108–
  9
  birthdate, 109 n3
Amati, Girolamo II: 194
Amati, Nicola: 36, 194, 254, 314, 447
  his importance, 109
  first among European *luthiers*, 194
  his pupils, 194–5
  violins described, 195
  'grand' model violin, 195, 197, 202, 281,
    and Pl. 25a
'Amatisé': *see* Antonio Stradivari
Âme (l') [sound post]: 253 n1
Andante allegro: 468
Andante e staccato: 409
Andante larghetto: 468
Andante sciolto: 426

Andante (normal speed): 294
Anet, Jean-Baptiste: 342, 345, 346, 365
Anker (Gurvin and): 199 n10
Anschlagende notes: 474
Antonii, Pietro degli: 218
  solo sonatas, 220
Apel, Willi: 82 n23, 166 n22, 184 n14,
  286 n2
Apollo's Banquet (Playford): 234
Appia, E.: 345 n26
Application: 251
Applicatur: 251, 378
Appoggiatura:
  short (17th c.), 287
  as 'little notes', 340
  in Quantz, 410
  dynamic interpretation of, 455
  18th century, 455
  nuanced, 455
  why written in small notes, 455
  passing, 456
  long (how played), 456
Appuyée: 304
Arbeau, Thoinot:
  quoted, 52
  on *La Volta*, 66
Arcata (= *archata*): 157, 164, 236, 254
Arcata in giù: 403
Arcata in su: 403
Arcate mute: 89 n34
Arcate sciolte: 268, and Ex. 90
  see also *Sciolto(e)*
Arcate sostenute e come sta (Corelli): 256,
  289
Archata lireggiare: 168
Arco:
  defined, see the Glossary
  in Monteverdi, 129
Arger, Jean: 468 n3
Ariosti, Attilio: 375 n26
  'Lessons' for viola d'amore, 250, 352
  special tablature, 352
Aristotle: 98
Arne, T. A.: 352
Arnold, Cecily: 140 n27
Arnold, F. T.: 279
'Arpègemens': 406 n8
Arpeggiando: 225
Arpeggiando con arcate sciolte: 268
Arpeggiato (*harpeggiato*): 246
Arpeggio(s):
  defined, see the Glossary
  in Walther, 268
  as broken chords, 406

18th century, 438ff
  'model' for, 439
'Arp. legato': 268 n23
Arte del Arco: see Tartini
Arte y puntual explicación: see Herrando
Articulation:
  defined, see the Glossary
  in bowing (16th c.), 71
  with the 'Stradivari' bow, 207
  in bowing (17th c.), 263, 268
  in bowing (18th c.), 399
  in Bach, 436
  of 'old' bow, 498
Articulation: 414
Articulées: 414
Artificial harmonics: see Harmonics
'The Art of Bowing': 271
  Mozart on, 400
The Art of Playing on the Violin: see
  Geminiani
Artusi, G. M.: controversy with Monte-
  verdi, 99
Ashmolean Museum (Oxford): 9 n6, 17,
  35, 36, 114, 209, 321 n9, 328 n24
Assaggi: see Roman, J. H.
Assimilation:
  defined, see the Glossary
  in 17th and 18th centuries, 296ff
  Quantz and C. P. E. Bach on, 297
  in Corelli, 298ff
  in J. S. Bach, 300, 482
  observations on, 302
  Leopold Mozart on, 483
  Thurston Dart's rule on, 483
  Michael Collins on, 484 n34
Aubert, Jacques: 345
  stopped unison in, 429
Aufheben: 412, 413
Aufsetzen: in Leopold Mozart, 378
Aufstrich: 403
Aufzug: 262
Auvergne (d'): nuance signs, 486 n37
Avison, Charles: 351
  on double stops, 428
Arkwright, G. E. P.: 139 n22
Ayres: in Matteis, 234

Babitz, Sol: 34, 155 n9, 303 n34, 320 n8,
  431 n5
  on shifting by crawling downward, 155
  (Fig. 5)
  editor of Tartini's *Traité*, 361 n11
  messa di voce bow stroke, 393-4
  on Leopold Mozart's 'Divisions', 395

on Bach's multiple stops, 430
on the short mordent, 454 n3
on *notes inégales*, 473 n15
Baburen, Dirck van (painter): Pl. 17
Bacchetta, Renzo: 505, 506, 507 n4
'Bach' bow: Pl. 40a
  description, 431
  a modern invention, 431
  origin, 432
  historical absurdity of, 433
Bach, C. P. E.:
  assimilation, 297
  slurring, 442
  breaking ties, 443 n24
  appoggiaturas, 456
  double dotting, 481
Bach, J. S.: 316, 332, 334, 365
  owned a Stainer violin, 195
  unaccompanied sonatas, 223, 336, 348
    multiple stops in, 339, 427
  ornamentation, 289
  rhythmic problems, 296
    assimilation, 300, 482–3
    use of *alla breve*, 467
    notes inégales, 477
    double dotting, 481
  tuning of *violino piccolo*, 323
  'Brandenburg' concertos, 336, 349
  Chaconne, 336, 349
    multiple stops in, 440–1
  violin and harpsichord sonatas, 336, 349
  Italian Concerto, 342, 460 n15
  compared to Vivaldi, 343
  Italian influence on, 349
  ritornello form, 349
  solo concertos, 349
  bowings, 404
  bariolage in, 407
  slurred *tremolo*, 422 n43
  notation of multiple stops, 429
  trill in sixths, 429
  articulation, 436
  arpeggios, 439
  following his slurrings, 443
Bachmann, Alberto: quoted, 313
Bacon, Francis: 98
Bailleux, A.: 390
Baillot, P.: 315, 397 n6
  bariolage in, 266 n18
Baines, Anthony: 50 n1, 70 n5, 199 n11
Balancement: 390
Balance point (bow): 328
Baldassare da Belgiojoso: 38
Balestrieri, Tommasso: 319

Ballet: for Polish Embassy (1573), 36
Ballet comique de la reine: 38, 51, 55, 83, 100,
    122
Ballet de cour: 54, 149
Le Ballet Polonais: 55
Balletti: 134
Baltazarini (Balthasar de Beaujoyeulx): 38
  see also Beaujoyeulx
Balthasar (Baltasar) de Beaujoyeulx: *see*
    Beaujoyeulx
Baltzar, Thomas: 144, 234–6, 239
  description of his playing, 142
    by Roger North and Anthony Wood,
    236
Banchieri, Adriano: 116
  tempo markings, 184
Banister (Bannister), John: 202 n15, 230,
    235, 243
Barbieri, G. F. (painter): Pl. 12
Barbour, J. Murray: 186 n19, 219 n8,
    371 n19
Bariolage: 225, 283
  Corelli, 221
  definition (late 17th c.), 265–6
  according to Baillot, 266 n18
  in concerto cadenzas, 334
  18th century, 407
Baroque era: characterized, 99
Bartoli, Cosimo: 90
Bas (of violin family): 31 n2
Baschenis, Evaristo (painter): 109, and
    Pl. 19
Bass (kleine Geigen): 45
Bassani, G. B.: 217
Bass-bars: 110, 201, 204
  measurements, old and modern, 321
Basse: 44, 117
Basse contre: 44
Basse de violon: 324
Bassetschen (Vivaldi): 367
Basso di viola: 60
Batement: 288
  see also Battement
Báthory, Stephen: 40
Battement: 453, 454 n3, 455
  see also Batement
Batterie: 406, 406 n8
Bayonne: 55
'Beat' (mordent): 287, 453, 455
Beaujoyeulx, Balthasar de: 36, 38, 55, 56,
    59, 148
  'best violinist in Christendom', 67
  see also Baltazarini
Beaulieu, Lambert de: 56

Bebung: 389
Beck, Sydney: 58 n18, 59 n19
Beckmann, Gustav: 118 n16, 130 n6, 134
   n11, 163 n17, 224 n14, 224 n15,
   268 n23, 293, 332 n3
Beethoven, Ludwig van: 355
Belem Tower (Lisbon): violin gargoyle,
   12
Belgiojoso (town): 26
Belgiojoso, Baldassare da: 26, 38
Belle qui tiens ma vie (pavane): 52
Beltramin, Antonio: 60
Benda, Franz: 350, 364
Benoit, Marcell: 239 n43
Bengtsson, Ingmar: 336 n9, 352 n40, 358
   n4
Benvenuti, G.: 217 n6, 218
Berger, Jean: 220 n9
Bergonzi, Carlo: 318, 319
Berlioz, Hector: 425
Bertolotti: *see* Gasparo da Salò
Bertolotti, Francesco da: 27
Bessaraboff, Nicholas: 9 n4, 14, 15 n17,
   28, 43 n27, 119
   ranges in *Orfeo*, 119
   violini piccoli alla francese, 119
Besseler, Heinrich: 62 n24
Betti, Adolfo: 336 n9, 350 n37
'Betts' violin (Stradivari, 1704): 198, 317,
   and Pls. 33a and 34
'Beyond the frets': 86
Biber, Heinrich von: 136, 212, 223, 242,
   246, 349, 350 n35
   relation to Stainer violins, 195
   'Mystery' (or 'Rosary') Sonatas, 224
   Passacaglia, 224
   shares technical characteristics with
     Walther, 225
   scordatura, 226
   slurred staccato, 270
Bini, Pasquale: 344
Bishop, John: 397 n7
Le Blanc, Hubert: 395 n5
   opposed to violin, 331
   bow strokes, 392
   playing 'Corelly', 392
   power of violin, 447
   violin sounds, 448
   expression in France and Italy com-
     pared, 490 n48
Bleyer, Nicholas: 136
Blocks (violin), illustrated: Pls. 1 and 34
Blois (painting at): 56 n13
Blumenfeld, Harold: 180 n5

Bocan (Jacques Cordier): 51, 151
   as dance master and choreographer, 149
Bodleian Library (Oxford): 237
Bologna: 18, 217, 218, 319
Bologna school: 220
Bombi: 268
Bonetti, Carlo: 19, 505, 506, 507 n4
Bononcini, G. M.: 217, 238, 279, 289 n6
   scordatura, 131
Bononiensis, Antonius: 18
La Borde, Jean Benjamin de: 491
Bore (Bourrée): 234
Bornet *l'aîné*: 378
Borrel, Eugene: 303 n34, 331 n2
   on *notes inégales*, 306
Borren, Charles van den: 62 n24
Bounding bow (*ricochets*): 265
Bounding strokes: 414
Bourdon (strings): 46
Bourgeois, Loys: 303 n32
Bourrée: 262, 473, 479
Bouts: defined, *see* the Glossary
Bovicelli: 296 n23, 303 n33
Bow change:
   imperceptible, 265 n17
   Leopold Mozart on, 394
   Geminiani on, 398
Bow (description and history):
   nut, 45, 114, 208
   16th century, 45, 68
   description and action, 70
   head, 46, 208
   regulating tension, 46, 112, 327
   lira da braccio, pictured, 47 (Fig. 3)
   early 17th century, 111
   first movable frog, 112
   lengths of old bow, 112, 209–10
   old bow compared to modern bow, 112
   ribbon of hair (Mersenne), 112
   pochette, pictured (Mersenne), 113
     (Fig. 4)
   violin, pictured (Mersenne), 113 (Fig.
     4)
   point, 114
   shape of bow stick, 114, 326
   wood used, 114, 327, 329
   dance bow (French, 17th c.), 149, 210
   late 17th century, 206
   dentated (*crémaillère*), 208
   slot-and-notch (clip-in), 208
   first dated bow (1694), 209
   German bow, 210
   modern, 326–8
   18th century, 324

Tartini's, 324
'Stradivari', 324, 326, 327, 329
Geminiani's, 326
height, 326
Veracini's, 326
balance, 327
first known makers, 328
viola da gamba bow (Walmsley), 138
   n24
pictured, *see* the Plates
nomenclature, *see* the Glossary
Bow, Divisions of: 19th century, 397 n9
Bow (grips):
   viol (16th c.), 73
   violin (16th c.), 73, 75
   early 17th century, 152
   left-handed, 152
   late 17th century, 248
   18th century, 371
   holding above nut, 372
   Italian and French manners described
      (Corrette), 372 (Fig. 6)
   control and power, 373
   pictured (Leopold Mozart), 373 (Fig. 7)
   'old', 499
   see also French grip, Italian grip
Bowing(s):
   indications (16th c.), 78 n18
   discipline (16th c.), 80
   related to number of notes in a measure,
      81, 83, 160
   'replaced bow' (16th c.), 81
   'replaced bow' (17th c.), 162, 259, 262
   related to expression, 91
   early 17th century, 156
   described by Mersenne, 156
   principles formulated (early 17th c.), 159
   syncopated, 165, 265, 407
   in duple and triple time, 259, 401, 419
   in Merck, 260
   in Muffat, 260
   types and their execution (late 17th c.),
      262
   art of, 336
   in Leopold Mozart, 400
   many varieties of (18th c.), 400
   relationship to expression, 400
   related to Rule of Down-Bow, 401
   effect of tempo on, 403
   terminology and signs, 403
   indications (18th c.), 404
   insertions of, 404
   in J. S. Bach, 404
   mixed, 407

slurred, 407
lifted (staccato), 410, 413
   controlled, 411
thrown or *ricochet*, 421
in Vivaldi, 424
'Bowing, The Art of':
   18th century, 400
Bowing discipline:
   formation in Italy, 157
Bow (relation of length to tone): 254
Bow ('soul of the instrument'): 207, 253,
   391
Bow stroke:
   Ganassi's sign for, 77
   single, 78
   long, 156
   description (early 17th c.), 157
   individual (early 17th c.), 163
   Mace on, 253
   Muffat on, 254
   nuanced and sustained (late 17th c.),
      254ff
   number expanded (18th c.), 391–2
   beginning of, 393
   old and modern compared, 394
   non-legato, 395
   speed used to increase volume, 396, 399
   how made (18th c.), 397
   role of fingers, 398
   ordering of (18th c.), 400
   for French dances, 405
   individual, 405
   nuanced (18th c.), 406
   modern terms and notation, 408 n13
   with 'old' bow, 499
Bow (use of lower part): 399
Boyce, William: 352
Boyden, David D.: 43 n27, 132 n9, 246
   n4, 352 n38, 361 n11, 371 n19, 432
   n7
   editor, 350 n37
Boyles, John: 358 n3
Brade, William: 136
Brainard, Paul: 344 n24
Brandel, Rose: 7 n3
Branles: 473
Brantôme (Branthôme): 36 n11, 38 n14,
   55, 59
   La Volta, 66
Brathwaite, Richard: 104–5
Bratsche (Brazzo): 45
Braz. 1 (2, 3): 323
Brazilwood (in bows): 114
Breaking ties: 441

Breaking a tied note (C. P. E. Bach): 443 n24

Bremner, James: 416 n32

Bremner, Robert: 351, 416 n32
  quoted on Corelli's practices, 255–6
  on sustained and nuanced bowing, 255

Brescia: 19, 20, 135
  early makers in, 17
  centre of violin making, 34
  fame of (17th c.), 108
  violin making in, 108
  Maggini, violins of, 198

Brescian school: 18, 41, 194

Briatta, M. A.: 329

Bridge (violin): 200, 202, and *see* the Plates
  low position (16th c.), 34
  17th century, 110
  in low position toward tailpiece, 110
  description *c.* 1600, 110
  Harding fele, 199
  reconstructed, 320 n8

A Brief Introduction (Playford): 245

Brijon: 491

Brissac, Marshall: 38, 56

Brisure: defined, 406

Britton, Thomas: 352

Broken chord passages: 406

'Broken consort': 58–9

Brossard, Sébastien de: 299 n30, 321, 323, 324, 346, 359, 377 n31, 468 n3 & n4
  meaning of *bracio*, 117
  perfidia, 342 n17
  Dictionary, 408, 473 n14
  characterizes violin, 494

Brugnoli: 218

Bruhns, Nicolaus: 223, 365

Bry, Jan Théodore de: 52 n3

Buchner, Alexander: 11 n9, 109 n5, 143 n32

Bukofzer, Manfred F.: 16 n19, 355 n44

Buonamente, G. B.: 135, 143 n32

Burlington, Duchess of: 351, 354

Burney, Charles: 26 n39, 257 n6, 343, 361 n10, 377, 393 n2
  on Veracini, 195
  Geminiani's chromatic fingerings, 381

Buxtehude: 224, 239

C3: *see* Proportional signatures

Caccini, Giulio: 92
  dynamics, 178–9
  free tempo, 184
  expression, 492

Cadence: 464
  double, 287
  'cadence-caprice', 289 n7
  trill, 450

Cadenza: 252, 367, 465
  in Corelli, 221, 334 n5
  defined, 289, 334, 461
  lightly accompanied, 334
  musically integrated, 334
  position of, 334
  may mean 'cadence', 461
  as ornamental device, 461
  written-out, 334
    Vivaldi, 462
  characteristics of, 462
  on tonic six-four, 463
  on dominant, 463
  in Tartini and Locatelli, 464
    distinguished from *capriccio*, 465–6
  how constructed, 464
  Quantz on intent of, 464
  terminology, 464

Calcare: 84

Calista [*sic*]: *see* Colista, Lelio

Cambert, Robert: 235 n35

Cambre: 325, 327

Camilli, Camillo: 319

Campagnoli, Bartolommeo: 397
  enharmonic pairs, 371

Campion, Thomas:
  masque for Lord Hayes (1607), 139

Cantabile: 341
  in fast movements (Vivaldi), 341
  Tartini, 405

Cantare alla viola per recitar: 16 n19

Canzona: 3, 53, 107, 133, 134, 135
  17th century, 123
  description, 134
  in Purcell, 239

Capirola, Vicenzo: 92

Cappa, Goffredo: 198

Capra, Francesca Feraboschi: 507 n3

Capri, Antonio: 344 n24

Capriccio: 134, 334, 464
  Tartini, 465
  = cadenza, 465

Caprices: 334, 461, 464, 465
  Locatelli, 335 n6, 338
    use of fermata, 463
  Paganini, 430

Caracci, A.: 195 n4

Caracci, Lodovico:
  sketch of violin and bow, 37, 75, and Pl. 16

Caravaggio (painter): 34, 37, 109
  violin and bow, 112, and Pl. 11
Carcassi, Lorenzo: 319
Carcassi, Tommasso: 319
Carse, Adam: 129 n5, 446 n29
Cartier, J. B.: 344 n24, 347 n31, 384 n41,
  423 n45, 453 n2, 461, 486 n37,
  489 n44
Casals, Pablo: 275 n26
Castello, Dario: 135, 149, 166
Castiglione, Baldassare:
  Il cortegiano, 16 n19
Castro, D. F. G. de: 240 n44
Castrucci, Pietro: 324, 351, 407
Cateau-Cambrésis, Treaty of: 40
Catherine de' Medici: 21, 36, 38, 55, 56
  n13
Catling: 201 n14
Caus, Salomon de: on violin dynamics, 180
Cavalcabò, Agostino: 505 n1
Cavallino, Bernardo (painter): Pl. 21
Cazzati, Maurizio: 135, 218, 238, 240 n44
Cellier, Jacques: French drawings (*c.*
  1585), 40
Cello: *see* Violoncello
Le Cerf de La Viéville: *see* Freneuse, Le
  Cerf de La Viéville, Seigneur de
Cerone, Domenico Pietro: 143
Cerreto, Scipione:
  on bowing, 82, 82 n24, 158
  on slurring, 164
Chabran: 342, 384 n41
Chaconne: 133, 213, 420
  Lully, 228
  Bach, 336, 349
  Leclair, 345
'Chacony': 232
Chamber music: 141
  17th century, 150
  meaning, 104
Chamber-pitch: 186, and *see* the Glossary
Champier: 12
'Un chant de caprice': 289
'Chanterelle' (the E string of the violin): 32
Chapman, Roger E.: 137 n18
Charles II: 142, 212
  influence on English music, 230
  'detestation of Fancys', 230
  French bias, 231
Charles V (Emperor): 21, 26
Charles VIII: 38
Charles IX: 36, 38, 55, 57, and Pl. 7b
  orders Amati violins, 35, 35 n10
Charles IX violins: *see* Amati, Andrea

Chasse: 337, 345, 491
Chester (town musicians): 58
Chin rest: 152
Chitarrone: 60
Choir-pitch: 204, and *see* the Glossary
Chopin, Frédéric: on *tempo rubato*, 470
Chord breaking:
  Christopher Simpson on, 436
  Quantz on, 436-7
  Leclair on, 437
  Rousseau on, 437
  downward (Rameau), 437
  in practice, 440
Christina of Sweden, Queen: 144
Christine of Lorraine: 60
'Chromatic' (fast playing): 137
Chromatic fingering:
  Geminiani, 375
  contractions, 383
Chromatic scales: 374
  by sliding, 375
Chrysander, Friedrich: 293 n17
Ciaconna: 133
Cicilian, Joanbattista: 86
Cima, G. P.: 134
Cinquiesme: 117, and *see* the Glossary
Circe ou le ballet comique de la reine:
  description, 55
Claew, Jacques Grief de (painter): Pl. 24
Classical flat model violin: 317
Clef: used for violin (17th c.), 117
'Close shake':
  description, 288
  as vibrato, 386, 390
  see also Vibrato
Coates, William: 140 n27
Cohen, Albert: 149 n3
Col arco: 445
Colista, Lelio: 222 n11
  relation to Purcell, 238
Collegium Musicum: 354
Col legno:
  17th century, 130, 132, 171 (defined)
  in Tobias Hume, 172
Colliard, Lucienne: 56 n13
Collins, Michael: 468 n3
  on assimilation, 484 n34
Colophane: 71
Combattimento (Monteverdi): 129, 133
'Combination' tones: 385
Come sta: 458
  significance of, 289
  in Veracini, 486
'Come sta senza passaggi': 127

Compendium Musicae Instrumentalis Chelicae (Daniel Merck): 245
The Compleat Musick-Master: 359 n5
Composer: problem of following intentions of, 357, 495–6
Concert: 345
Concertato: 132 n9
Concerti: of Andrea and Giovanni Gabrieli, 53
Concertino: 280, 332
   18th century, 445
Concerto: 213
   late 16th century, 63
   concerto-like settings (17th c.), 103
   defined, 132 n9, 345
   how performed (Muffat and Torelli), 280
   instrumental, 331
   meaning of the term, 332
   solo concerto (description), 333
   solo concerto (number of movements), 335
   ensemble, 335
   essential principles, 335
   instrumentation, 335
      Geminiani, 351
   'orchestral', 335
   'programme', 337
Concerto grosso: 333
   instrumentation and number of players required, 280
   18th century, 445
   defined, 332
   Corelli, 341
Concert Spirituel: 354
   founded, 348
Concerts Royaux: Couperin, 345
Conducting: according to Quantz, 446
'Conductor': late 17th century, 281
Conegliano, Cima da (painter): 75
Conforto, Giovanni Luca: 177
Confrérie de St. Julien: 346
Con l'arco attaccato alle corde: 426
Consecutive trills: *see* Trill
Con sordino:
   defined, *see* the Glossary
   meaning of (18th c.), 444
   see also Sordino
Consort: defined, *see* the Glossary
'Consort' music: 141
Constantin, Louis: 137
Contractions: 339, 380, 383
   defined, *see* the Glossary
   in Ganassi (16th c.), 88

Coperario (John Cooper): 140–1
   fantasia-suites, 140
Copyright laws: 18th century, 355
Corbett, William: 352
Cordier, Jacques:
   see Bocan
Corelli, Arcangelo ('*il Bolognese*'): 125, 201 n14, 212, 216, 220, 237, 238, 240 n44, 242, 362
   proportional signatures, 182, 293
   passionate expression, 215
   in Bologna, 221
   use of positions, 221, 251
   perpetuum mobile, 221
   concerti grossi, 221, 341
      heard in Rome by Muffat, 257
      evolution of, 332
   solo sonatas, 221, 461
   trio sonatas, 221
   'graces', 222, 289
   influences, 223
   La Follia, 235, 271, 336
   his playing described by Galliard, 243
   discussed by Geminiani, 257
   on sustained and nuanced bowing, 255
   use of *messa di voce*, 255
   vibrato, 255
   bow, 324
   Arcate sostenute e come sta, 256
   long *diminuendo*, 291
   dynamics in his concertos, 292
   assimilation in, 298
   'Cadenza' in, 334 n5
      quasi-cadenza, 462
   impact on 18th century, 341–2
   relation to Herrando, 353
   slurring in, 442
   instrumentation, 279, 445, 446
Corna, Giovan Giacobo dalla: 17
Corna, Giovanni Maria dalla: 17
'Cornets': 139
Cornett: 123, 124, 127, 139
   defined, *see* the Glossary
Cornetto: 62, 124
   in Gabrieli, 68
'Cornett or violin':
   17th century, 123, 124
Cornett-pitch: 186, 204, and *see* the Glossary under 'Chamber-pitch'
Corominas, Don Juan Francisco de: on the violin, 353
Corona: 367
Corona [Corna?], G. G. dalla: 18
Correnti: 134

Corrette, Michel: 347 n32, 406 n9, 444
  picture of violinist, 243, and Pl. 31
  L'École d'Orphée (significance and contents), 359
  holding violin with chin, 368
  scordatura, 370 n17
  Italian and French grip, 371, 372 (Fig. 6), and Pl. 31
  treatise of 1782, 390
  on *staccato*, 409
  notes inégales (description), 472-3
  dynamic effects, 489
Corteccia, Francesco: 24
Cortot, Alfred: 222 n10
Cossetti, A.: 18 n23
Costa, Antonio dalla: 319
Costa, Lorenzo (painter): 12
Costa, Pietro dalla: 319
Coulement droit: 269
Cou'lé-pointé: 304
Coulés: 304
Coup d'Archet Articulé (L'Abbé le fils): 422
Couperin, François ('le grand'): 214, 227 n18, 380 n38, 406 n8
  quoted, 303
  Concerts Royaux, 345
  influence on Corelli, 345
  arpeggios, 438
  use of *croches blanches*, 468 n3
  tempo rubato, 470
  notes inégales, 472
  on dynamics, 485
  on expression, 493
Courante: 262, 346, 420, 473
'Courtiville, Sonata Solo of': 234
Court musicians: advantages in 17th century, 105
Coutagne, Henry: 18 n25
Cozio di Salabue, Count: *see* Salabue, Count Cozio di
Cramer, Wilhelm: 327
Craquer bowing: 262
  defined, 260
  in Muffat, 269
  in L'Abbé le fils, 402, 421
  in Francoeur, 421
  in Guillemain, 423
Craqueter: 270
Crémaillère bow: 208
Cremona: 19, 20, 241, 314
  early reputation for craftsmanship, 17
  centre of violin making (16th c.), 34
  famed as best violins in the world (17th c.), 108, 109, 194

violins at the English Court, 139 n22
  decline of leadership (18th c.), 315
Crescendo: 254
  early 17th century, 178
  long, 180
  in Locke, 292
  serves purpose of description, 290
  18th century, 340
  signs for, 485
Crescendo and *diminuendo*: 291
  long (in Leclair), 488
Crescendo-diminuendo stroke (Babitz): 394
Cristofori, Bartolomeo: 485
Croches blanches: 468 n3
Croches égales (J. J. Rousseau): 476
Croiser: 375 n27
Crome, Robert: 368
Cromwell, Oliver: 142
Cross (+): sign for trill, 450
Cruz, D. Agostinho da: 143 n30
Cudworth, Charles: 229 n22
'Cullin Cliff': 201, 201 n14
'Custos': 91, 367
Czechoslovakia: violins and violinists (17th c.), 143

'D' (*descendre la main*): 378
'd' (*doux*): 403
'd' (down-bow): 262, 403
Dalmatia: violin in, 144
Dance: 135, 214
  style, 149
  French, 241
  pieces (Zannetti), 154
  late 17th century, 213
  England, 232
  France (early 18th c.), 346
  French dance musicians, 346
'Danceries': 54
Dannreuther, Edward: 286 n2
Dart, Thurston: 139 n25, 140 n27
  rule of assimilation, 298, 483
Darwinian theory: applied to art, 313
Davison, Archibald: 82 n3, 166 n22
'Death of St. Hermenegild', painting (Juan de Roelas): 41, and Pl. 10
Degrés-conjoints: 304
Delinet, Sieur: 38
Demancher: 378
Denis: 389 n48
Dentated bow (*crémaillère*): 208
Descant: *see* Discant, and *see* the Glossary

Descartes, René: 98, 100
Descriptive music: 213–14
  France (18th c.), 491
Desplanes: *see* Piani, Antonio
Dessus: 44, 117, and *see* the Glossary
Dessus de viole: 324
Dessus de violon: 55
Détaché:
  defined, *see* the Glossary
  late 17th century, 263
  18th century, 408
  L'Abbé le fils, 409
Détachement:
  17th century, 262
  Muffat, 263
Détacher (17th c.): 305
Détatché [sic]: 414
'Devil's Trill' Sonata: *see* Tartini
'Devisions': 236
Dialogue à 8 (Orlando Lasso): 55 n11
Diatonic scales: 374
Dictionnaire, Brossard: *see* Brossard
Dieupart, Charles: 347
'Differential' tones: 385–6
Dimier, Louis: 56 n13
Diminuendo: 254
  early 17th century, 178–9
  long, 180, 291, 488
  short, 291
  signs for, 485
Diminuer: 396
'Diminutions':
  defined, *see* the Glossary
  Rogniono, 83
  see also Passaggi
Diobono, Pompeo: 38
Direct: 367
  see also Custos
Diruta, Girolamo: 130 n6
Discant: defined, *see* the Glossary
Discantgeig: 116
Discant (Geigen): 45
Discant Viol. (=*viola da braccio*): 116
Disertori, Benvenuto: 90 n35
'Distaccato': 415
'Division': 133, 175
  defined, 3
  technique of (17th c.), 127
  on a ground, 232
    Matteis, 237
  Leopold Mozart (four Divisions), 393,
    395–7
  in Campagnoli, 397
  of the bow (19th c.), 397 n9

  see also Mozart, Leopold; Playford, John;
    Simpson, Christopher
Division-Flute: 234
The Division Violin (John Playford, 1684):
    234, 289
The Division-Viol (Christopher Simpson):
    248, 289
Diziani, Gasparo (painter): 372
Dodd, John (bow maker): 327
  among first to sign his bows, 115, 328
Dodecupla: 219
  Grassineau, 484
Do-it-yourself treatise: 365
  see also Treatise
Dolmetsch, Arnold: 119 n21, 286 n2
  on assimilation, 298
Domenichino (painter): 242, and Pl. 20
Donati, Baldassare: 129 n5
Donedo, G. B.: 18
Doni, G. B.: quoted, 121
Donington, Robert: 199 n11
  on violin family, 100–101
Dorez, Léon: 26 n40
Doring, E. N.: 19 n8, 319 n6, 329 n27
Dot (staccato): 263, 263 n11
Dotted figures:
  lengthening of, 295
  alteration in context of triplets, 296
  methods of playing (Leopold Mozart
    and Quantz), 420
  use of lifted bow, 420
Dotting: double or triple, 295, 478
Dou, Gerard:
  violin bow (painting), 210, and Pl. 22
  picture of violinist, 243, and Pl. 22
'Double Descant' (Purcell): 238
Double dotting:
  French Overtures, 295
  double or triple dotting, 478
  notation, 478
  in dances (Quantz), 479
  in Leopold Mozart, 479
  relative to note values, 479, 480 n29
  in Handel's *Messiah*, 480
  where used, 480
  in C. P. E. Bach and J. S. Bach, 481
  performance in violin music, 481–2
Double sharp (18th c.): 367
Double stops: 90, 155, 168, 220
  defined, 166 n23
  in *lira da braccio* and *lira da gamba*, 90
  'apparent' one in Taverner, 90–1
  unison (17th c.), 131
  in Marini, 135

lozenge form (Matteis), 237
using *tremolo*, 267
finger extension in, 380, 382
18th century, 382, 428
Charles Avison (quoted), 428
L'Abbé le fils, 438
see also Double-stop trill, Multiple stops
Double-stop trill: 341
in Leopold Mozart, 452
in sixths, 429
in L'Abbé le fils, 452
Doubling vocal parts:
violin, 3, 33, 33 n5
Dounias, M.: 344 n24, 465 n31
Doux: 403
Dowland, John: *Lachrimae*, 124, 139
Down-bow:
defined, 79
relative to stress (Cerreto, Ganassi, R. Rognioni), 157-8
terms (17th c.), 262
terms and signs (18th c.), 403
Doyle, A. Conan: quoted, 65
'Drag' (Mace): 294
Dresden:
Chapel, 102
centre of violin music, 350
Dritte Lage: 378
'Drum stroke': 418
Dubourg, Matthew: 351
'graces' to Corelli (ornamented versions), 222, 290, 460
ornamentations, 341
Duc de Joyeuse: see Joyeuse, Duc de
Duchess of Burlington: see Burlington, Duchess of
Duckles, Vincent: 344 n23
Dugdale, W.: 57 n15
Duiffoprugcar, Gaspar(d):
portrait by Woeriot, 14, and Pl. 9
inscription, 31 n1
described, 39
as inventor of the violin, 18
Dupont: 359
Durchgehende notes: 474
Dutch genre painting: 103-4, 239, 242
Dutch violin making: 239
Duval, François: 346
arpeggios, 439
Dynamics:
messa di voce (16th c.), 92
early 17th century, 178-80
late 17th century, 290ff
graded, 291, 485

terraced, 291, 484-5
in Vivaldi, 485
in Leopold Mozart, 487
effects implied, 487
interpretation of appoggiaturas (Tartini), 488
interpretation of consonance and dissonance, 488
in Quantz, 488
18th century, 489

'c' (extensions): 382
'Echo' effect: 129, 291
L'École d'Orphée (Corrette): significance and contents, 359
Ecorcheville, Jules: 138 n20, 228 n20
Editions, modern: violin music, 503
Effect: 490
Effects: descriptive (17th c.), 134
Egan, Patricia: 74 n10
Einstein, Alfred: 90 n36
Smith Collection, 135 n12
Eisel, J. P.:
on Stradivari and Stainer, 317 n3
Musicus Autodidaktos, 360
on long bow stroke, 398 n11
Eitner, Robert: 361 n8, 416 n32
Elizabeth, Queen (England): 39, 41, 44, 57
'Elizabeth-Leicester' picture: 56 n13, and Pl. 14
Elmer, Minnie: 344 n23, 461 n18
Emmanuel, Maurice: 52 n2
Enfler: 396
Enfler le son: 291
England:
violin (16th c.), 41
characteristics of style (17th c.), 102
Engramelle, Père: *notes inégales*, 477
Enharmonic: defined, see the Glossary
Enharmonic notes: 219
distinctions (early 17th c.), 186
Ensemble concerto: see Concerto
Ensembles, string: in 16th century, 43
Entfernet: 413
'*Entrées*': 479
Epitome musical (Jambe de Fer): 15
Equal temperament: 186, 219, 370
Erheben: 412
Erhebung: 418
Esclamazione: 179
Essex, Earl of: 351
Etwas abgesetzet: 412
Europe: map of violin centres, 27 (Fig. 2)

'Evangelista' (painter): 11 n10
Evans, Peter: 233 n33
'Evolution of progress': in art, 313
Exclamation: 287
Experimental attitude: in 17th century, 98
Expression: 178
  related to bowing (16th c.), 91
  aesthetics of (18th c.), 490
  French and Italian attitudes compared
    (18th c.), 490
  expected in violin music (18th c.), 493
    Rousseau, 494
  in modern playing of old music, 502
Extensions: 339
  defined, *see* the Glossary
  in Ganassi (16th c.), 88
  of fourth finger indicated by figure '5',
    154
  in Biber and Walther, 225
  late 17th century, 249, 252
  in L'Abbé le fils, 360
  in Geminiani, 380
  18th century, 381–3
    with double stops, 382
    to avoid formal shifts, 383

Fagott-Geige: 324
Falck, Georg: 360
  Idea boni Cantoris, 245
  scordatura, 246
  holding the violin, 247
  tuning, 247
  French grip, 249
  holding the bow, 249
  use of the positions, 251
Falconieri, Andrea: 132, 185 n17
Fancy: 119, 140, 141
  17th century, 124
  detestation of (by Charles II), 230
  described, 233
Fantaisies: 149
Fantasia: 140, 212, 238
  English, 232
  as cadenza, 334, 461, 462, 464
Fantasias: 142
  Purcell, 120, 231
'Fantasia-suite':
  defined, 140
  of William Lawes, 233
Fantasy: 377
'*Fantazya*' (William Lawes): 140
Fantini: *messa di voce* in, 179
Farga, Franz: 507 n3

Farina, Carlo: 108, 131, 135, 146
  Capriccio Stravagante, 130, 132, 165, 172
  pizzicato in, 172
  sempre più adagio (meaning), 185
Farinel, Michel: 235 n35
  Farinel's Ground, 235 n35
  Farinell's Ground, 239
'Farinelly, Michel': 235 n35
'Faronells Division on a Ground': 234
Fellowes, E. H.: 228 n20
Ferand, Ernest T.: 175 n1, 460 n15
Fermata:
  in concerto, 334, 367
  to indicate cadenza, 462, 463
    on tonic six-four, 464
Ferrara, Alfonso da: 86, 217
Ferrari, Gaudenzio (painter): 19, 20, 26
  'Madonna of the Orange Trees', 7, 16,
    and *Frontispiece*
  fresco at Saronno, 7, 15, and Pl. 2
  viola player described, 74
  bow grips shown, 76
Ferrex and Porrex: 57
Ferrule (bow): 328
Fesperman, John: 303 n34
Festing, Michael: 351, 358 n3
Fétis, François-Joseph: 23, 324, 325, 505
Fiddle: 50, 59
  Renaissance (description), 9, and Pl. 3b
  music, 352
  see also Polish fiddle
Fides: 116
Fidicula: 116
Fifth position: *see* Position
'*Figlin*': 116 n12
Figuration: *see* the Glossary
Filer: 396, 397 n6
Filiberto, Emmanuele, Duke of Savoy: 26
  protection of musicians, 60
  records quoted, 60
Fingerboard: 110
  16th century, 34
  fretted, 250
Fingered chromatics: 339
  Geminiani, 375
Finger extension: Geminiani, 380
Fingering: 379
  open string (16th c.), 85
  use of lowest (G) string, 85
  in Ganassi, 86
  open string (early 17th c.), 153
  late 17th century, 249
  18th century, 339, 374
  indications of, 374 n24

variety of, 379
  legato (18th c.), 380
Fingernail stopping of violin strings: 28
'Finger preparation': 88
Fingers (role in bow stroke and bow change): 398
Finlay, Ian F.: quoted on violin in painting, 103
Fiorentino, Lodovico Lasagnino: 90
'First position' (=second position): 378
  see also Position
Flat model violin: 319
Flatté (vibrato): 390
Flesch, Carl: 418
Florence: 217, 319
Florilegium Secundum (George Muffat): 243, 244
  on Lully bow grip, 432
'Flying staccato': 419
Folia (follia): 213
Les Folies D'Espagne: 235 n35
Folk-fiddler: 11 n9
Follia: 133, 213
Follia, La (Corelli): 221, 222, 235, 271, 336
Fontana, G. B.: 108, 135
Fontenelle: quoted, 214
'For all sorts of instruments': 53, 128
Forcroi le Père: 392
Forte piano (Monteverdi): 179
'For voyce or viol': 128, *see also* 'Voyces and viols'
Fourteenth position: *see* Position
Fourth finger: use of, 374
Fourth position: *see* Position
f-p (or 'f p'): as *diminuendo*, 179, 291, 488
f-p-pp: 291
Fra Angelico: 74 n9
France: dance musicians, 346
Francis I (France): 20, 21, 24, 26, 38, 39
Franco, Francisco: 18 n23
Francoeur, François: *craquer* bowing, 421
  use of thumb, 376
Frederick the Great: 350, 473 n14
French bowing style (Muffat): 261
French Court ballet: 57
French dances and bow strokes (18th c.): 405
French grip: 150, 152, 243, 248, 359
  16th century, 8, 75
  obsolete in Italy before 1700, 153
  described, 371
  by Falck, 249
  18th century, 372
  see also Bow (grips)

French Overture:
  Lully, 229
  double dotting in, 480
French style: 239, 392
  characteristics (17th c.), 102
  described by Lully, 243
French violin clef: 367
Freneuse, Le Cerf de La Viéville, Seigneur de: 214 n1
  on the power of the violin, 447
Frescobaldi, Girolamo: on tempo, 184, 294
Fret(s): 9, 14, 19, 25, 29, 89
  defined, *see* the Glossary
Frog (of the bow): 371
  defined, *see* the Glossary
Frydén, Lars: 336 n9
Fugue: 216
Furetière, Antoine: 292 n13

'g' (*giù*): 403
'Gaasbeck' [*sic*]: *see* Gaesbeck Castle
Gabrieli, Andrea: 53, 129
Gabrieli, Giovanni: 53, 63, 102, 126
  violini = viola, 42
  Sonata Pian e Forte, 53
  usage of 'violin' in, 53
  large viola in, 68
  Sonata for Three Violins, 134–5, 156
Gabrielli, Domenico: 220
Gaesbeck Castle (painting at): 56 n13
Gagliano, Gennaro: 319
Gagliano family (Naples): 198, 319
Gaibara, Ercole (Bologna): 218
Galeazzi: 426
Galen 'Quartet': 12, 13 (Fig. 1)
  holding of violin, 74
Galilei, Vincenzo: 17
Galileo, Galilei: 98, 109
Galliard, J. E.: 203 n17, 471 n10
  on Corelli's playing, 242–3
  quoted, 341
Galpin, Francis: 9 n5, 43 n27
Ganassi, Sylvestro di: 11 n8, 14, 72, 91
  Regola Rubertina (description), 28, 77
  treatises, 76
  bowing discipline, 78 n18, 79, 80, 157
  terminology, 79–80
  down-stroke and *up-stroke* applied to lutanists, 80 n21
  fingerings and positions, 84–88
  shifting, 87
  extensions and contractions, 88
  improvisation, 89

Ganassi, Sylvestro di—*contd.*
  following the score strictly, 89 n32
  multiple stops, 90, 166
  vibrato, 92
  slurs, 164
Ganz Applicatur: 378
Gasparo da Salò (Bertolotti): 12, 18, 19,
    27, 33, 36, 38, 68
  not the inventor of the violin, 18
  origins, 34 n7
  viola in Ashmolean Museum, 36, and
    Pl. 7a
  price of violins, 39
Gaultier, Denis: 278, and Pl. 32
Gavotte: 262, 473, 479
G clef, first line: 367
Geige: 116
Geigen: Polish (*polnische Geigeln*), 29
Geigen (*grosse*):
  = viols, 24
  meaning in Praetorius, 29
Geigen (*kleine*): 24
  Agricola, 28
  meanings, 29
  see also Handgeiglein
'*Geigenwerk*': 179
'Geiger, Anthonj' (Antonio Morari): 62,
    62 n25
Geminiani, Francesco: 232, 288, 316, 324,
    342, 359, 363, 364, 374 n23, 375
    n26, and Pl. 36
  Rule of Down Bow, 163, 401
    against, 258
  quoted, 214, 311
    on Corelli, 257
    on descriptive music, 337
    on 'affecting Discourse', 338
    on holding the violin, 369
    on mordent, 490
    on performance, 493
  ornamentation, 222, 222 n10, 341
    or Corelli, 290
  The Art of Playing on the Violin, 246 n4,
    350, 357
  messa di voce, 255, 486
  dynamic signs, 340, 485
    in *basso continuo*, 485 n36
  life and works, 350–1
  instrumentation, 351, 446
  pupils, 351
  dedications, 354
  vs. John Walsh, 355
  influence, 358
  treatise as prototype, 364

collarbone position, 368, and Pl. 36
chromatic fingering, 375
  Burney, 381
seven positions, 377
fingerings for shifting, 379
finger extension, 380
contraction, 384
vibrato, 386
  sign for, 390
bowing, 397
  variants, 400
  nuanced, 405, 487
  'plain' stroke, 406
  mixed, 424
  staccato, 413
  multiple stops (shifting), 428
  multiple stops (performance), 440
  stopped unison, 428
  arpeggio, 439
  appoggiatura (nuanced), 455
  appoggiatura (long), 457
  'arbitrary' additions, 460
  cadenza, 463
  tempo rubato, 472
  notes inégales, 478 n22
  nuance signs, 486
'Geminiani' grip: 358
  explained, 370
'Genius': according to J. J. Rousseau, 492
Gentileschi, Oratio: 37, 109, and Pl. 8
The Gentleman's Diversion (John Lenton):
    246 n4
Gerle, Hans: 29 n44, 53 n5, 71, 76 n14
German style: characteristics (17th c.),
    102
Gervaise, Claude: 54
Gestossen: 411
Del Gesù:
  see Guarneri, Joseph (del Gesù)
Giardini, Felice de': 342
Giazotto, Remo: 342 n16
Gibbons, Orlando: 141
Giegling, Franz: 342 n16
Gigg: 234
Gigue:
  bowing in Muffat, 262
  rhythmic problems, 296
  dotted rhythm, 299 n30
'Gioan Maria bresiano': 17, and Pl. 4
Girdlestone, C. L.: 347 n30
Giù: *see In giù, In zoso*
Glissando (17th c.): 130, 132
Gluck, Christoph Willibald: quoted, 99
Gofriller, Matteo: 319

Gombert, Nicolas: 33 n5
Gombosi, Otto: 92 n41, 235
Gorboduc (Norton and Sackville): 57, 138
Grabu, Louis: 230, 243
Grace note(s): 488, and *see* the Glossary
'Graces': 222
  in Corelli, 289
Grammatica di musica (Carlo Tessarini): 360
Grancino, Paolo: 195
Grancino family (Milan): 198, 319
'Grand Concertos': *see* Handel
Grande Bande: 227
Grandi, O. M.: 131, 168
'Grand' model Amati: *see* Amati, Nicola
Grassineau, James: 229 n30, 408, 467
  on wire strings, 322
  dodecupla, 484
Graun, Johann Gottlieb: 350
Graun brothers: 350, 364
Greulich, Martin: 80 n21
Grillet, Laurent: 25 n37
Grip, thumb-under-hair: 75
Groppo (17th c.): 176
'*Groppo all'alta*': 177
Groppo di sopra: 177
Groppo di sotto: 177
Grotto, G.: 75 n9
Gruppo (17th c.): 176
G string:
  restricted use, 125
  silver-wound, 203
  passages on, 234
  increased use, 338
  wound (effect on violin sound), 447
Guadagnini, G. B.: 318, 319
Guadagnini, Lorenzo: 319
Gualazzini, Ugo: 505 n1
Guarneri, Andrea: 194, 318
  apprentice of Nicola Amati, 197
Guarneri, Joseph (del Gesù): 198, 314,
  318 n4, 447, and Pl. 33b
  life and works, 318
Guarneri, Joseph Filius Andreae: 318
Guarneri, Peter of Mantua (Pietro
  Giovanni): 318
  maker of bows, 328
Guarneri, Peter of Venice: 318
  death of, 319
Guersan, Louis: 319
Guide: 367
Guignon, J. P.: 342, 346, 365
  the last 'king of the violins', 347
Guilds, Musicians': 106, 354

Guillemain, Louis-Gabriel: 335 n6, 336,
  346, 347, 365
  importance, 347
  craquer, 423
  arpeggios, 440
  trill in sixths, 453
  caprice, 466
Guiones: 367
Gurvin and Anker: *Musiklexikon*, 199 n10

Haas, Robert: 460 n15, 461 n17
Hajdecki, Alexander: 9 n6
Halb Applicatur: 378
'Half' position: *see* Position
'Half shift': 377
Hammerschmidt, Andreas: *tremolo*, 130
Handel, Georg Friedrich: 324, 332, 351,
  352
  Op. 1, 123 n1
  as an accompanist, 350
  'Grand Concertos', 351
  slurred *tremolo*, 422–3
  ornamental additions, 460 n15
  tempo terms, 468
  tempi, 469 n8
  Messiah (double dotting), 480
Handgeiglein: 28
'Hand-grip' notation (*scordatura*): 250
Hapsburg-Valois wars: account of and
  devastation of, 61
Harding, Rosamund E. M.: 291 n10
Harding fele: tuning, 199
Harich-Schneider, Eta: on assimilation,
  298
Harmonics: 337, 444
  defined, *see* the Glossary
  natural, 345, 360, 384, 444
    Mondonville, 339, 375, 384
    L'Abbé le fils, 385
  artificial, 345, 385
    L'Abbé le fils, 339
  'two fingered', 360, 444
  octave, 375
  double stops, 385
  scales, 385
  trills, 385
Harpeggiato (= *arpeggiato*): 246
Harpsichord: used in chamber sonatas,
  278
Hart, George: 19, 201 n13
Harvey, William: 98
Harzebski, Adamo: 52, 144 n33
Hasert, Johann Christian: 317
Hassler, Hans Leo: 136

'Hatchet' head (bow): 208
  defined, *see* the Glossary
'Hatfield House': picture of violin and
  viola, 74
Hausse: 371
Haute-Contre: 117, 323
  defined, *see* the Glossary
Haute-contre de violon: 44
Hautecontre-taille (of violin family, 1556):
  31 n2
Haute-Contre Taille: 117
Haw, Stephan: double stops (Ex. 36), 167
Hawkins, Sir John: 222 n10, 352 n39, 355
  on Stainer, 196
  on bow, 325
Hayden, Hans: 179
Haydn, Franz Joseph: 355
Hayes, Gerald: 20 n30, 43 n27, 114 n8,
  118 n17, 209 n22
Hayes, Dr. William: 428 n2
Heartz, Daniel L.: 54 n7
Heifetz, Jascha: 275 n26
Heinichen, J. D.: 350
'Hellier' violin (Stradivari, 1679): 198
Helmholtz, Hermann Ludwig Ferdinand
  von: differential tones, 386
Hemiola:
  rhythm (Ex. 24), 161–2
  defined, 185
  courante and *passepied*, 346
Henry (Orbus, the German): 167
Henry II (France): 21, 55
Henry III (France): 36, 55, 56 n13
Herabstrich: 403
Herbst, J. A.: 162
  bowing, 159
  trills, 177
  tempo markings, 184
Heron-Allen, Edward: 15 n17, 74 n9,
  359
Herrando, José (Joseph): 240
  significance of, 353
  Arte y puntual explicación (description):
    362
  relationship to Geminiani, 362
  holding the violin, 368
  holding the bow, 371
  on trills, 452
Herschel: 466
Heseltine, Phillip: *see* Warlock, Peter
Hill, Joseph (II): 319, 321, 328
Hill, W. E. and Sons of London: 196, 505,
  506
  quoted on Stradivari, 329

Hill, W. H., A. F., and A. E.: 37 n13,
  109 n4, 195 n4, 318 n5
Hill Collection (Ashmolean Museum,
  Oxford): 209
Hiller, Johann Adam: 378
Hinaufstrich: 403
Hjorth, Arne: 435 n11
Hoby, Sir Thomas: 16 n19
Hoefnagel, Joris: 41
Hoffmann: 317
Holborne, A.: *Pavans, Galliards* . . ., 58
Hopkinson, Francis: 416 n32
Hornpipe (Purcell): 234
Hortulus Chelicus (Walther): 224
Huggins, Margaret L.: 108 n2
Hume, Tobias:
  pizzicato and *col legno*, 172
  two styles of performance, 180
Humphrey, Pelham: 230
Husla: 9
Hutchins, Arthur: 332 n3

Iconography: 19, 34, 76, 112, 138
  as a source for bows, 45, 112
  as a tool, 151
  a source of information (late 17th c.),
    242
Idea boni cantoris (Georg Falck): 245
Idiom (idiomatic): 125
  defined, 121
Idiomatic instrumental music: 3
Imitation of nature: 214
  Leopold Mozart on, 490
  in France (18th c.), 491
  Rousseau on, 491
Improvisation: 4
  Ganassi, Mersenne, and Tinctoris, 89
  16th century, 89
  late 17th century, 288
  violin, 460
  keyboard, 460 n15
  vocal, 460 n15
'In-bow': 79
'In echo': 292 n11
Inequality: *see Notes inégales*
Ingegneri, M. A.: 72
In giù: 79, 403
In Nomine: 124, 141
Instrumental music: development after
  1600, 99–100
Instrumentation:
  Geminiani, 351
  trio sonata and *concerto grosso*, 445
'Instruments of the middle': 11, 117

In su: 79
Intermedi: at a wedding (1589), 60
Intermedio (Italian): 3, 54, 57, 59
  'Psyche and Amor' (1565), 24
Intonation systems: 186, 370
  defined, *see* the Glossary
Introduction to the Skill of Musick (Playford): 238
Involution: 287
In zoso: 79
Iselin, Dora J.: 135 n12
Italian bow grip: *see* Bow (grips) and 'Italian' grip
Italian Concerto (J. S. Bach): 342, 460 n15
'Italian' grip: 90 n35, 150, 153, 242
  described (16th c.), 75, and Pl. 16
  described (18th c.), 371
Italian sonata (in England): 232
Italian style: 392
  characteristics (17th c.), 101-2
  described, 150, 242
Italy: the musical leader (17th and 18th c.), 101

Jacobi, Erwin R.: 298 n28, 324 n20, 361 n10, 361 n11, 389 n48, 405 n7
Jacobs, Hendrik: 109, 194, 199
Jacomelli, Giovan Battista: 71
Jacquot, A.: 20, 35 n10, 39 n20
Jambe de Fer: 15, 19, 22, 23, 29, 34, 38 n14, 51, 72, 152
  on viol and violin, 4
  on first true violins (*Epitome musical*), 15
  quoted at length, 31
  terminology, 42
James I (England): 138
Jannequin, Clément: 129
Jazz: 94, 290
Jenkins, John: 142, 238
  description of works, 233
Jeune, Henry Le: *see* Le Jeune, Henry
Joachim, Joseph: 293 n17
  editor with Moser, 348 n34
Johnson, Marshall: 140 n27
Joseph del Gesù: *see* Guarneri, Joseph (del Gesù)
Joseph, the son of Andrew: *see* Guarneri, Joseph Filius Andreae
Joyeuse, Duc de: 55
  marriage, 66
Judenkünig, Hans: 80 n20, 86 n28
Just intonation: 186

Kamiensky, Lucian: 472 n13

Keller, Hermann: 409 n17
Kelly, Francis M.: 56 n13
Kenilworth: violins at (1583), 57
Kepler, Johann: 98, 100
Kerlino, G.: 18
Kielmannsegge, Baron: 354
'King of Instruments': 151
  Mersenne, 137
'King of the Violins': 137, 354
'King's Musick, The': 41
Kinkeldey, Otto: 60 n21
Kinsky, Georg: 12 n12, 37 n12, 224 n14
Kircher, Athanasius: on strings, 111
Kirkpatrick, Ralph: on metronomic indications, 469 n7
Klangideal: defined, *see* the Glossary
Kleine Geigen: 45, 116
Klenz, William: 136 n14, 217 n5, 289 n6
Klotz, Mathias (I): 199, 319
Klotz, Sebastian (I): 319
Klotz family (Mittenwald): 199
Knocker, Editha: 357 n2
Knödt, H.: 334 n5
Kolneder, Walter: 342 n18, 367 n14, 485 n35
Koole, Arend: 195 n3
Kretschmar, H.: 490 n46
Kreutzer: 315, 397 n6
Kuhn, Max: 89 n33, 296 n23
Kytson, Sir Thomas: 58
  inventory of household instruments, 58

L'Abbé le fils (Joseph Barnabé Saint-Sevin): 316, 347, 359, 363, 369, 375 n27
Jolis airs, 337
  harmonics, 339
  minuet in, 360, 385 (Ex. 154)
Principes du violon, 363
  title page quoted, 73
  importance, 359-60
  as prototype, 365
  on chin-braced grip, 369 n15
  bow grip, 373
  use of fourth finger, 374
  second position, 377-8
  ninth or tenth position, 377
  half position, 378
  fingering for shifting, 379-80
portamento, 381
  extensions, 382, 383
  contractions, 384 n40
messa di voce, 389 n48

L'Abbé le fils (Joseph Barnabé Saint-Sevin)—*contd.*
'bow the soul', 391
bowing, 396
  fingers in bow stroke and bow change, 398
  nuanced, 406
  slurred, 407
  slurred *bariolage*, 407
  détaché, 409
  craquer, 421
  slurred staccato, 422
  on multiple stops, 438
  arpeggios, 440
  ornaments, 450
  short trills, 451
  on double trills, 452
  appoggiatura (nuanced), 455
  appoggiatura (long), 457
  notes inégales, 476
  dynamic effects and signs, 486 n37, 489
  long *crescendo* and *diminuendo*, 489
Lachrimae (John Dowland): 124, 139
Lafontaine, H. C. de: 41 n23, 202 n15
La Guerre, Elizabeth-Claude Jacquet de: 214, 227 n18, 346
  Sonates Pour le Violon et Pour le Clavecin, 347
Lalande, Michel-Richard de: 228
La Laurencie, Lionel de: 227 n18, 240 n44, 345 n25, 346 n28, 347 n32, 423 n45, 489 n44
Lanfranco, G. M.: 17, 24, 42 n26, 116 n10
  tuning of *lira da braccio*, 10 n7
  Scintille di musica (described), 25
Lanier, Nicholas: 243
Largo e puntato: 264 n13
Largo e spiccato: 426
Largo e staccato: 409
Larsen, J. P.: 469 n8
L'Arte del arco: see Tartini
Lasso, Orlando: 55 n11
  Hans Mielich painting of, with Munich Court Chapel, 33, 53, 62, 67, and Pl. 15
  described, 40
  music for ducal wedding, 62
Lavignac, A.: 240 n44
Lawes, William: 141
  '*Fantazya*', 125, 140
  'fantasia-suites', 140, 233
  fantasias, 239
Lazarin: 149, 151
Leap, three-octave: 339

Le Cerf de La Viéville: see Freneuse, Le Cerf de La Viéville, Seigneur de
Le Chesnaye: 56
Lechler, Benedict: *diminuendo* in, 179
Leclair, Jean-Marie: 214, 332, 342, 346, 347, 365, 376 n28
  use of the positions, 251
  his importance, 345
  Chaconne, 345
  slurred *tremolo*, 423
  mixed bowings, 424
  double trills, 429
  sustaining triple stops, 437–8
  chord breaking, 437
  cadenza, 462
  notes inégales, 477
  long *crescendo* and *diminuendo*, 488
Lefkowitz, Murray: 125 n2, 140 n26
  use of term *sonata*, 140
Legato:
  16th century, 92
  fingerings, 380
  slurred *tremolo*, 422
Legrenzi, Giovanni: 217
Leicester, Earl of: 41, 57
Le Jeune, Henry: 127
Lenton, John: 358 n4
  The Gentleman's Diversion, 246 n4
'Lessons for viola d'amore': see Ariosti, Attilio
Lesure, François: 16 n18, 54 n7, 76 n12, 110 n6
Liaison: 265 n17
Lifted bow:
  in staccato, 410, 411, 412
  in Quantz, 417
  in Leopold Mozart, 418
  in dotted figures, 420
Linarola, Ventura: 37
Lira: 29, 44
Lira da braccio: 9 n6, 15, 16, 17, 46, 73
  described, 9, and Pl. 4
  pictured with bow, 47 (Fig. 3)
  holding of, 74
  played at neck, 74 n9
  with long bow, 75
  chord playing (16th c.), 90
  double stops, 90
  hand position and tuning, 90 n35
Lira da gamba: double-stops, 90
Lira-viola:
  Gasparo da Salò, 12
  defined, 36
Lireggiare: 164, 165

Lireggiare affettuoso: described by Francesco Rognoni, 165, 171
'Little notes': appoggiatura, 340
Locatelli, Pietro: 195, 195 n3, 313, 332, 337, 338, 342, 348, 364
  caprices, 335 n6
  use of fermata in, 463
  instrumentation, 351, 446
  in Amsterdam, 352
  bariolage, 407
  mixed bowings, 424
  slurring in, 442
  cadenza, 462, 464
Locke, Matthew: 233
  long *crescendo* and *diminuendo*, 292
  dynamics, 486
Löhlein, Georg Simon:
  on Stainer, 196
  prefers Stainer and Amati violins to Stradivari, 196
  bow, 326
  Anweisung, 358
  vibrato, 390
Lombard figures: 128, 163, 164, 295
  in Quantz, 478
Lombardini, Maddalena: 344, 361
Lombardy: 20
  political fate, 21
Lonati, Carlo Ambrogio: 336 n9
'Long' model Stradivari: 242, 281
Long-short inequality: 305, 473, 477
Lotter, J. J.: 360
Louis XIII (France): 57, 101, 136, 227
  establishes *Vingt-quatre Violons du Roy*, 117
Louis XIV (France): 101, 224, 354
Loulié, Étienne: 303, 305
  quoted on rhythmic alteration, 305
  chronometer, 469
Loure: 420
Louré: 269
Lourer: 17th century, 305
Low Countries: violin paintings in, 108
Lowest string: increased use of, 338
Lowinsky, Edward E.: 19 n29
Lully, Jean-Baptiste: 148, 224, 244, 354
  use of mute, 205 n19, 278
  'test' piece, 227
  founded *Les Petits Violons*, 227
  influence, 227
  operatic pieces for strings, 228
  French Overture, 229
    double dotting, 295
  style of playing (described), 243

source of French style, 257
  use of *trembler*, 267
  banished improvisations, 288
  death, 294
  bow stroke, 392
Lupo, Ambrose: 39, 41
Lupo, Pietro: 38
Lupo, Thomas: 102, 138
Lupot, Nicholas: 315
Lute: in Tinctoris, 50
Lütgendorff, Willibald Leo: 17 n21, 194, 194 n1
Lyon: 12, 55
  violin making (related to Milan), 39
  on trade route from Venice to Paris, 39
Lyonnais wire: 324 n19
'Lyra': 33 n5
  in Lanfranco, 17
Lyra viol: 172

'm' (vibrato): 283, 287, 454
Mace, Thomas: 120, 201 n13, 231, 253
  old and new instruments, 206
  Musick's Monument, 206
  compares music to language, 215
  music related to the universe by, 215
  his 'Perfect Idea of my Living Mistress', 215
  holding the bow, 249
  bow stroke, 253
  staccato, 264
  on the vibrato, 288
Maffei, Scipione: quoted on dynamics, 291
Maggini, Giovanni Paolo: 33, 35, 37, 108, 110, 146, 318, and Pl. 18
  death, 194
  violins of Brescia, 198
Magnificat (Monteverdi, 1610): 133
Majer, J. F. B. C.: 247 n5, 321, 321 n10, 324 n19, 409
  Museum Musicum, 360
Malipiero, Gian Francesco: 117 n15, 425 n46
Mandelli, Alfonso: 507 n4
Manico: 251, 379
Mannheim Court Orchestra: use of long *crescendo*, 489
Mantoano, Rubertino: 86
Mantua: 319
Manuals for amateurs: 242
Marais, Marin: 119, 206, 303
  Pièces, 227
  vibrato, 288
  staccato dots, 306

Marenzio, Luca: *sinfonia*, 60
Maria of Hungary, Queen: 143
Marie Louise, Princess: 239
Marini, Biagio: 108, 135, 146, 149, 168
 figuration, 126
 'Sonata in Echo', 129
 tremolo, 129
 scordatura, 130, 167
 double and triple stops, 131, 169
 works, 135
 Op. 1 and Op. 8, 135
 his term *affetti*, 171
 his *Romanesca*, 183
 '*tardo*' and '*presto*', 185
Markneukirchen: 315
Marlborough, Duchess of: 354
Marpurg, Friedrich Wilhelm: 350 n35,
 357
Martelé: 399, 408 n13, 415, 419
 stroke, 394
 defined, 408
Martellement: 453
Mary Queen of Scots: 55
 Brantôme's description, 59
Mascitti, Michel: 345, 392
Masque: 3, 54, 57, 105, 133, 142, 149
 description, 138–9
 of Ben Jonson, 139
Mast, Herman van der: 56 n13
Matteis, Nicola: 222, 231, 236, 238, 239,
 241, 409, 460
 impression on the English, 143
 'a very long bow', 210
 Ayres, 234, 236
 playing described by North, 236, 248
 n6
 'Division on a ground', 237
 bow grip, 248–9
 second position, 377 n35
Mattheson, Johann: 232, 353 n42
Maugars, André: 119, 137
 in Rome (1639), 148
Mazzaferrata, G. B.: 217
Mazzochi, Domenico: *diminuendo* in, 179
McArtor, Marion E.: 350 n37
Meantone temperament: 186, 219 (ex-
 plained), 370
Médard, Nicholas (III): 199
Medgyes, Parliament of (Hungary, 1855):
 40
Medici, Ferdinand de': 60
Mell, Davis: 142, 235, 236
Memling (painter): fiddle, Pl. 3b
Mendel, Arthur: 182 n11, 186 n18, 240 n18

Mensural C: as triple meter, 183
Mensural division of the notes: 182–3
Menuet: *see* Minuet
Merck, Daniel: 117 n14, 246, 324 n19
 *Compendium Musicae Instrumentalis Che-
 licae*, 245
 Rule of Down-Bow, 258
 bowing, 260
 sign for vibrato, 287
Mersenne, Marin: 108, 113 (Fig. 4), 119,
 121, 133, 137, 138, 149, 168
 five-part ensemble, 44, 229
 improvisation, 89
 characteristic example of new age and
 spirit (17th c.), 100
 strings, 111
 pochette in, 112
 violin bow, 112
 his terminology of the violin, 116
 'instruments of the middle', 117
 on the tone of the violin, 120
 ornamentation, 127
 violin mute, 128
 praise of the violin, 151, 174
 fingering, 154
 on bowing, 156, 66
 on down-bow, 158
 on performing multiple stops, 169–70
 vibrato, 177
 on violin dynamics, 180
 'metronome', 184
 on enharmonic pairs, 186
 mentions mute, 205 n19
 viola parts, 323
Merula, Tarquinio: 134, 135
 tremolo in, 170
Messa di voce: 92, 236, 255, 291, 395,
 396
 defined (early 17th c.), 179
 Corelli, 222
 on long notes, 255
 in North (quotation), 255
 with vibrato, 288
 18th century, 389, 486, 489
 mistranslated from Tartini, 389 n48
 in L'Abbé le fils, 396
 in Veracini, 486
'Messie' violin (Stradivari, 1716): 317,
 321
'Metronomes': 469
Meyer, Ernst H.: 91, 125 n2, 140 n26,
 292 n12
Mezzo groppo: 177
Mezzo manico: 252, 379

Micanzio, Father Fulgenzio: 109
'Midwalders': 199
Mielich, Hans: painting of Munich Court Chapel under Lasso, 40, 62, and Pl. 15
Milan: 20, 159
  under Spanish domination, 21
  center of earliest violin making, 26
  relation to Lyon, 39
Milano, Francesco da: 86
Milton, John: *L'Allegro*, 119
Minuet: 473
  all in harmonics (L'Abbé le fils), 360, 385 (Ex. 154)
Mirecourt: 315
  violin making, 39
Mishkin, Henry: 220 n9
Mitchell, William J.: 297 n25, 442 n23
Mitjana, Rafael: 143 n30
Mittenwald: 315, 319
  violin centre, 27 (Fig. 2), 199
'Mixed' bowings: 424
  18th century, 407
'Mixed' position: *see* Position
Modèle de la batterie: 406
Modena: 217
The Modern Musick-Master: *see* Prelleur, Peter
Möller, Max: 199 n9
Mondonville, Jean-Joseph Cassanea de: 365
  Pièces de Clavecin En Sonates, 336, 347
  an experimentor and innovator, 346
    innovator in the sonata, 346
  Les sons harmoniques, 346
  harmonics, 375
    use of natural harmonics, 339, 384
  use of cross (+), 450
  on imitating nature, 491
Montaigne, Michel de: 60, 60 n22, 319
Montéclair, Michel Pignolet de: 359
  holding the violin, 368
Monter: 378
Monteverdi, Claudio: 102, 108, 135, 146
  portrait, 37
  controversy with Artusi, 99
  violin figuration, 100
  as '*suonatore di vivola*', 108 n1
  on Cremona and Brescia violins, 109
  violini ordinarij da braccio, 118
  violini piccoli alla francese, 118
  violini, 118
  stringed instruments in *Orfeo*, 118
  idiomatic violin parts, 122

Orfeo (violin figurations), 123
  range of the violin, 125
  pizzicato, 129
  use of violin, 132–3
  two finger pizzicato, 172
  diminuendo in, 179
  on dynamics, 180 n8
  'tempo of the hand', 184
  free tempo, 184
  expression, 492
Montichiaro: 17
Morari, Antonio: *see* 'Geiger, Anthonj'
Mordent: 287 (defined)
  early 17th century, 176
  18th century, 453
  performance of, 453
Morley, Thomas: *The First Booke of Consort Lessons*, 58
Moser, Andreas: 116, n12, 134 n10, 136, 154, 348 n34, 413 n10
Moser, Hans Jaochim: 357 n2
Movable nut: 208
Mozart, Leopold: 156, 168, 195, 288, 357, 363, 375, 377
  Violinschule, 246, 316, 357, 361
    described and compared to Geminiani, 364
    as prototype, 364
    arranged in order of difficulty, 364
  shifting, 251
    fingering for, 379–80
  slurred *tremolo*, 269
  quoted on
    slurred staccato, 270
    vibrato, 388
    bow change, 394
    slurred notes, 475
    double dotting, 475
  notation of double dot, 296
  stringing, 322
  standardizing and adjusting violin, 322–3
  bow, 326
  indebted to Tartini, 344, 461
  influence, 358
  teaching attitude, 363
  ways of holding the violin, 369, and Pl. 39
  positions, 370, 376
  bow grip, 372, 373 (Fig. 7)
  dislike of harmonics, 375
  extensions, 382
  'differential' tones, 386
  vibrato, 386, 387

Mozart, Leopold—*contd.*
  bowing
    'small softness' of stroke, 393
    power from index finger, 399
    variants, 400
    insertions, 404
    varieties, 405
    nuanced, 406
    bounding stroke, 414 n28
    in triple time, 419
  'Divisions', 393, 394, 487
    Division 1, 395
    Divisions 2, 3, 4, 396
  sostenuto, 396
  tone production, 399
    manly tone, 447
  Rule of Down Bow, 401
  slurred staccato, 417, 418–19
  playing dotted figures, 420
  sustaining double stops, 428
  trill
    sixths, 429, 452
    accelerating, 451
    consecutive, 452
    double, 452
  arpeggios, 438–9
  pizzicato, 444
  arbitrary additions, 458
  cadenza, 462
  tempo
    inherent, 469
    keeping time and *tempo rubato*, 471
  notes inégales, 475
  assimilation, 483
  dynamic nuance, 487
  short *crescendo*, 488
  imitation of nature, 490
Mozart, Wolfgang Amadeus: 343, 355, 364, 444
  tempo rubato, 472
'Mr' (= mordent): 454
Mucchi, A. M.: 19 n26, 34 n7, 36
Muffat, Georg: 221, 224, 227, 228 n20, 239, 246, 283, 303, 304 n35
  Rule of Down Bow, 158
  minuet bowed in Italian-German and French styles, 163, 261 (Ex. 82)
  on pitch related to thickness of strings, 204
  observer of Lully's style, 224
  description of French style, 243
  Florilegium Secundum (1698), 243, 244
    quotation on Lully bow grip, 432
  tuning, 247

on the bow stroke, 254
on Corelli, 256
significance of his remarks, 257
life, 257 n7
bowing, 260
  related to minuet, 261
  détachement (staccato), 263
  craquer, 269
  slurred staccato, 269–70
defines Italian-German style, 261
on performing concertos, 264, 280
instrumentation of *concerto grosso*, 280 n30, 446
violin ornamentation, 287
'smoothed-out' trill, 286–7 (Ex. 109c)
'inherent' tempo, 293
time-beating, 294
notes inégales, 303, 304
on *battement*, 454 n3
Muffat, Gottlieb: 380 n38
Multiple stops: 90, 166
  in Ganassi (16th c.), 90
  17th century, 131, 167
  defined, 166 n23
  early history, 166–7
  approximate notation, 168, 271ff, 275
    reasons for, 272
    18th century, 429–30
  difficulties of performance, 168–9
    modern ways of playing, 271ff, 275 n26
    playing with 'old' bow, 271–2
  single chords arpeggiated, 169
    their performance (1600–50), 169
  in Biber and Walther, 225
  insertions of slurs, 273, 274
  suspensions in, 273
  duration of notes in, 273
  performance of triple and quadruple stops, 131, 169, 275ff
  according to Simpson, 276
  notation sometimes implies arpeggiation, 276
  in Germany, 283
    18th century, 339, 428ff
  in Bach's sonatas, 427
  in actual practice, 435
    how broken in the 18th century, 435–6
    modern practice of breaking, 436
  no precise system, 443
  see also Chord breaking
'Mummeries': 55
  16th century, 32

Munich: Court Chapel, 33, 40, 67, and Pl. 15
Murillo, Bartolomé Esteban (painter): 143
Museum Musicum (J. F. B. C. Majer): 360
Music as an expression of something: 214
Musical 'wars' (18th c.): 214
Musicians' guilds: 229, 354
Musicians' aims (18th c.): 312
Musicians' Company (1606): 106
Musicians' livelihood: 355
'Musicke of Violenze': 57
Musick's Recreation (Playford): 278
Musicus Autodidaktos (J. P. Eisel): 360
Musikalisches Lexikon (J. G. Walther): 473 n14
Mute:
  defined, *see* the Glossary
  17th century, 128
    in Mersenne, 205 n19
    in ensemble music (Purcell, Lully, Schmelzer), 205 n19
  late 17th century, 278, 283
    in Vivaldi, 339
  material of, 322
  18th century, 443-4
'Mystery' Sonatas (Biber): 224

'N' (*Niederzug*): 262
'n' (*nobilis*): 262
Nachschläge: 286, 450-1
Nagel's *Musik-Archiv*: 216 n4
Nancy: violin making, 39
Naples: 217, 319
Nardini, Pietro: 344, 397 n8
Nationalism: effect on music (17th c.), 101
National style: 366
  of playing, 148
    in 16th century, 72
    late 17th century, 192, 241
    schools, 306
  differences in technique, 212
Natural harmonics: *see* Harmonics
'Natural' position: *see* Position
Natural sign: 18th century, 366
Neck (of the violin):
  16th century, 34
  old style, 110, 197, and Pls. 6 and 26a
Netscher, Caspar (painter): lady playing treble viol, Pl. 5
Nettl, Paul: 377 n34
Newman, William S.: 134 n10, 343 n22, 353 n43
Newton, Isaac: 98

Nichols, John: 57 n15
Nicolai, G. F.: 361 n11
Niederzug: 262
Nobilis: 262
Nolens Volens: 200 n12, 245, 259, 359, 365
Non-legato: 71, 78, 263, 395, 405, 411
  16th century, 92
  18th century, 399
  'plain', 406
Nordberger, Carl: 144 n34
Norman, Barak: 199, 319
North, Roger: 210, 232 n31, 236, 249 n7, 254 n2, 291, 338 n14
  quoted, 232, 495
    on King Charles II, 230
    on Baltzar, 236
    on Matteis, 236, 248 n6
  messa di voce, 255
  beauty of tone, 374
Norton (and Sackville): *Gorboduc*, 57, 138
Norwich (town musicians): 58
Notation:
  conventions of, 366
  triple and quadruple stops, 429
Notes: duration of, 273
Note sciolte: 426
Notes inégales: 263 n11
  late 17th century, 303ff
  'short-long', 304-5, 473, 477
  'long-short', 305, 473, 477
  application of, 306
  in L'Abbé le fils, 402, 476
  18th century, 421, 472
    summary of use, 477
  in Corrette, 472
  in Couperin, 472
  in Leopold Mozart, 475
  in Père Engramelle, 477
  relation to double dotting, 478 n23
Nuance:
  defined, *see* the Glossary
  accompanying vibrato (18th c.), 388
  application to bow strokes, 406
  addition of, 458
  short signs for (18th c.), 486
Nut (bow):
  defined, *see* the Glossary
  movable, 208
  material of, 328
  see also Bow (description and history)

'O' (down-bow): 403
Obbligato: defined, *see* the Glossary
Obbligato parts: violin, 103, 132

Octave:
  broken, 339
  leaps ('Tartini), 340
  trill, 341, 453
Oistrakh, David: 275 n26
Old bow:
  initial 'give' to, 393
  balance, 399
Ondeggiando: 225
  late 17th century, 265
  vibrato, 390
  18th century, 407
Ondulation (vibrato): 390
Ondulé: late 17th century, 265
Open string:
  defined, *see* the Glossary
  late 17th century, 249
  avoided by Quantz, 252
  18th century, 374
  indicated, 374 n24
Opera orchestra:
  17th century, 147
Opienski, H.: 144 n33
Orbus, the German: 167
Orchestra:
  17th century, 146
  opera, 147
'Orchestral' concerto: *see* Concerto
'Orders': 378
Ordre: 378
Orfeo (Monteverdi): 123, 133
Organ: used in church sonatas, 278
Organic relationship between technique, music, and instrument making: 145
'Organo tremolante': 267
Ornaments: 175ff
  early 17th century, 129
  in Geminiani, 222 n10
  'ornament of the Bow' (Simpson), 255
  rationalized, 285
  stereotyped, 285
  cross (+), 286
  use in France and Italy, 449
  indicated increasingly by signs (by 1700), 449
  in L'Abbé le fils, 450
  relation to mood and tempo, 450
  essential and arbitrary, 457
  improvised, 457
  in practice, 457
Orrery, Countess of: 355
Ortiz, Diego: 78
  Tratado, 3
  improvisation, 89 n33

Ostinato forms: 133
  defined, 213
'Out-bow': 79
Oxford (Ashmolean Museum): 321 n9, and *see* Ashmolean Museum
Oxford (Bodleian Library): 237

'p' (*piano*): 403
'P' (*pontare*, or *puntare*): 262
'P' (*poussé*): 262, 403
'P' (up-bow): 158 n14
Padovano, Annibale: 62
Paganini, Niccolò: 313, 314, 315, 338, 339, 360
  Caprices, 430
  caprice in, 466
Pamparato, Stanislao Cordero: 22 n33
Panum, H.: 9 n4, 11 n9
Par-dessus de viole: 73
Paris: 319
  inventories of instrument makers and dealers, 38
  violin making, 39
Parker, Daniel: 319
Parma: 319
'Partia' (Partita): 336 n8
Partitas: 336 n8, 348
Pascal, Etienne: 100
Passacaglia: 213
  Biber, 225
  Lully, 228
Passaggi: 81, 89, 127, 133, 175, 184, 288
  defined, *see* the Glossary
  Rogniono, 89
  Bach, 289
Passepied: 346
Patin, Jacques: 56, 56 n13
Patronage: 354
Paul III, Pope: 26
Paumgartner, B.: 357 n2
Pavia, Battle of: 21
Pegbox (violin):
  16th century, 34
  17th century, 110
'Pellegrino': 18
Peluzzi, Euro: 18
Penshurst Place: painting at, 56 n13, and Pl. 14
Pepusch, J. C.: 352
'Per ballare': 218
'Per camera': 218
'*Percotere la corda*': 84
Perfidia: defined, 342 n17
Performer, freedom of: 356

Peri, Jacopo: 71
Pernambuco wood (for bows): 207, 209, 327
Perpetuum mobile: 221
'Per violino in Tromba' (Vivaldi): 337
'Peter of Mantua': *see* Guarneri, Peter of Mantua (Pietro Giovanni)
'Peter of Venice': *see* Guarneri, Peter of Venice
Pétillement: 269
Petits Violons, Les (Lully): 227, 228 n21
Petrobelli, Pierluigi: 60 n22, 465 n31
Philidor, André: 228, n20, 348
Philidor Collection: 138 n20, 228 n20
Philpot, Stephen: 358
Piacenza: 319
Piani, Antonio (Desplanes): 343, 345
   dynamic signs, 340, 489
   use of *sautillé*, 414
   short nuance signs, 486
Picart (engraver): Pl. 20
Picqué: *see* Piquer
Pictorial music: in Biber and Walther, 225
Pièces à cordes ravallées': 370 n17
Pièces de Clavecin En Sonates (Mondonville): 336, 347
Piedmont: 20
Pierray, Claude: 319
Pike's head (bow): 208, 324, 326
   defined, *see* the Glossary
Pincé: 287, 453
Pincement: 287
Pincherle, Marc: 12 n11, 20 n31, 25 n37, 55 n9, 227 n18, 289 n7, 336 n9, 342 n18, 345 n26, 353 n42, 406, 454 n4
   quoted on Leclair, 345
Pincherle Catalogue: 335
Piquer (*piqué*):
   17th century, 305
   18th century, 408
Pisendel, J. G.: 336 n9, 350, 364, 461, 462, n22
Pitch: 204
   standards (16th c.), 70
   variable standards (early 17th c.), 185–6
Più piano (= modern pp): 291
Pizzicato: 129
   defined, *see* the Glossary
   16th century, 8, 84
   Monteverdi, 129, 133
   17th century, 171, 172
   in Tobias Hume, 172

whole movements
   Biber, 225
   Walther, 277
   late 17th century, 277
'left hand', 278
   Leopold Mozart, 444
   Quantz, 445
   Tremais, 445
'Plain' non-legato strokes: in Geminiani, 406
Plamenac, Dragan: 118 n16, 144, 353 n42
Platner, Michael: 319
Players: number required in *concerti grossi*, 280
Playford, John:
   Introduction, 210, 238, 245
   Apollo's Banquet, 234
   Division Violin, 234, 289
   English Dancing Master, 234
   tuning, 247
   Rule of Down Bow, 258
   notation of multiple stops, 275
   Musick's Recreation on the Viol lyra-way, 278
   proportional signatures, 294
Pluche, N. A.: quoted, 491
Pochette: 112, 119
   pictured with bow (Mersenne), 113 (Fig. 4)
Pochon, Alfred: 420 n38
Poidras, Henri: 207 n20
Point d'orgue: 367, 464
Pointé: 299 n3
   18th century, 408
Pointer:
   17th century, 303, 304, 305
   defined by Rousseau, 476
Polish Embassy: at French Court (16th c.), 36
Polish fiddle: 9, 40, 352
'Polish fiddlers': 40
   vibrato introduced by, 91 n38
Polish *Geigen*: *see* Geigen
Polish violin music: 143
Polnische Geiger: *see* 'Polish fiddlers'
Polyrhythm: 302
Pontar: 16th century, 83
Pontare: 262
Pontare in su: 80
'*Pontar in su*': 158 n14
Portamento: 379, 381
   defined, *see* the Glossary
   17th century, 130
   slides, 375, 381
   in shifting, 380

Portato: 161, 269
  defined, 78, and *see* the Glossary
  in Ganassi, 78, 81
  in Rogniono, 83
  related to slurred *tremolo*, 423
Port de voix: 287
Position:
  defined, *see* the Glossary
  in Ganassi, 85–86
  in Jambe de Fer, 86
  in Zacconi, 88
  in Mersenne, 154–5
  playing
    17th century, 154–5
    late 17th century, 250–1
    18th century, 338
  in Uccellini, 155
  first, 248
    = second position, 378
  second, greater importance (18th c.),
    377
  third, 8, 88, 221
    in England, 234
  fourth, 137, 221
  fifth (in Corelli), 221, 251
  sixth, 110, 125, 250
    about 1650, 86
    L'Abbé le fils, 440
  seventh, 250, 338
    normal limit (18th c.), 377
    Geminiani, 374
  eighth, 250
  ninth and tenth
    L'Abbé le fils, 377
  eleventh (Locatelli), 339
  fourteenth (Locatelli), 338
  reason for use of, 376
  'compound', 378
  'half', 378
  'mixed', 378
  'natural', 378, 379
Potsdam: centre of violin music, 350
'Pouce, Le': 374 n24, 376 n28 and Ex. 133
Pougin, A.: 38 n14
Poussé: 73, 158 n14, 262, 392, 403
Powell, Lawrence Clark: 245 n2
Powell, Newman W.: 78 n17, 296 n24
Power and tone: in Geminiani and
  Mozart, 399
Praetorius, Michael: 25, 100, 108, 119
  n19, 136
  quoted on violin, 1–2
  meaning of *Geigen*, 29
  brass and steel strings, 111

bow, 112
  knobbed bows, 112 n7
  terminology, 116
  Terpsichore, 136
  tuning, 151–2
    lira da braccio, 10
  bowing, 156
  ornaments, 176–7
  crescendo and *diminuendo*, 179
  'Affections', 179–80
  tempo markings, 184
Prelleur, Peter: 320 n7, 455
  The Modern Musick-Master 246, n4, 358
'*Presto*': in Marini, 185
Printz, W. C.: 268 n22
  on 'unequal notes', 306
'Private Musick': 230
'Programme' concerto: *see* Concerto
Programme music: in France (18th c.),
  491
'Progress' in Art: theory of, 313
'Pronation': 372 n21
Proportions: 302
  early 17th century, 182
  signatures, 182, 183
    Playford, 294
  in Corelli, 293
  18th century, 467
Prunières, Henry: 21 n32, 57 n14, 228
  n21
'Psyche and Amor' (Intermedio 1565): 24
Publication of music: 18th century, 354
Public concert:
  17th century, 103
  18th century, 354
Pugnani, Gaetano: 318, 342
Punctus percutiens: 409
Puntar: 16th century, 83
Puntare: 158 n14, 262
Puntato: 409
Purcell, Henry: 222 n11, 230, 237, 238
  use of mute, 205 n19, 278
  on French music, 213
  Fantasias, 120, 231, 294
  Sonnata's of III Parts
    significance, 237
    preface, 279
    part books, 279–80
  two sets of trio sonatas, 238
  solo sonata, 239
  use of canzona, 239
  use of *tremolo*, 267
  use of 'Echo', 292 n11
  tempo terms, 294

Purfling: defined, *see* the Glossary
Purfling, double: 36, 41, 108, 111

Quadruple stops: *see* Multiple stops
Quantz, Johann Joachim: 222, 303, 321,
    365, 374, 379, 473 n14
  'Scotch' snap, 128
  meaning of *mezzo manico*, 252
  playing dotted figures, 295, 420
  notation of double dot, 296
  assimilation, 297
  quoted, 311, 356
    on shifting, 252
    on positions, 338
    on using lower part of bow, 399
    notes inégales, 473–5
  stringing, 322
  cadenza, 334, 462, 464, 464 n28
  studied violin, 350
  bowing, 358, 400
    French dances, 405
    varieties of, 405
  flute treatise, 360
  staccato, 410, 412, 415
    slurred, 416–17
  chord breaking, 436, 440
  slurring, 442
  pizzicato, 445
  conducting, 446
  number of players in orchestra, 446
  violin sound, 448
  trill speed, 451
  battement, 454 n3
  appoggiatura, 456
  arbitrary ornaments, 458
  critical of Tartini and late Vivaldi, 458
    n12
  indebted to Tartini, 460–1
  keeping time, 471
  double dotting, 478, 479
  dynamic directions, 488
  Affetto, 490
Quasi-cadenza: in Corelli, 462
Quinte: 117
  defined, *see* the Glossary
Quinte de violon: 323

'R' (reculer): 378
Rabelais, François:
  on the violin, 68 n4
  on shifting, 88
Rafael (painter): 'The Coronation of the
    Holy Virgin', 74 n9
Raguenet, François: 204, 283, 325

quoted on strings in France and Italy, 203
Rameau, Jean-Philippe: 409
  chord breaking, 437
  'inherent' tempo, 470
Range: limited in French violinists, 137
Reade, Charles: 15 n17
Rebec (*rebeca*, or *ribeca*): 24, 59, 73
  bass, 11
  description, 8–9, and Pl. 3a
  in Agricola, 28
  in Tinctoris, 50
  played at breast or neck, 74 n9
  gradual obsolescence (17th c.), 119
Rebecchino: 29, 44, 116
  = violin, 24
Rebel, Jean-Ferry: 214, 346
Recht abgestossen: 411–12
'*Rechte Discant-Geig*': 116
Recorders: pitch of, 70
Reese, Gustave: 7 n3, 16 n19, 40 n22,
    55 n11
Reformation (Germany): 98
Regale dolce: 62
Regola Rubertina: *see* Ganassi, Sylvestro di
Reichardt, Johann Friedrich: 204 n18
Renée of Lorraine: marries Wilhelm V,
    Duke of Bavaria, 61
Reni, Guido: 152 n6
Rennes: 41, and Pl. 13
  painting at, 56
Replaced bow: *see* Bowing(s)
Restoration (England): 142, 229
Resultant (combination) tones: in Mozart
    and Tartini, 444
Rhythm: 180
  late 17th century, 292ff
  alterations of, 294ff, 472ff
Ribbon of hair (bow): 328
Ricci, Ruggiero: 35 n10
Ricercar: 107
  in Ganassi, 78 n16
Richelieu, Armand Jean du Plessis de,
    Cardinal: 101
Ricochet (bounding bow): 265, 421
Rigaudons: 473, 479
Rinaldi, Mario: 217 n6
Ripieno: 280, 332
Ritornello form:
  defined, 333
  as developed by Vivaldi, 334
  in Bach, 349
Ritournelles: Lully, 228
Rococo music: characteristics of, 364
Rode, Pierre: 315, 397 n6

'Rode' violin (Stradivari, 1722): 317
Roelas, Juan de (painter): 41, 143, and Pl. 10
Roger (Amsterdam publisher): 222 n10
Rogeri, Giambattista: 194
Roger North on Music: 254 n2
  see also North, Roger
Rogniono, Richardo: 78, 158
  discipline of bowing, 82-83
  passaggi, 89
  on slurring, 164
Rognoni, Francesco: 116, 156, 168
  on *passaggi*, 127
  '*ecco*', 129
  on bow grip, 153
  on bowing, 158, 159
  on down-bow, 158
  quoted, 164
  tremolo in, 170
  tone and bowing, 172
  on dynamics, 179
'*Roi des Violons*': 229
Roman, Johan Helmich: 352, 358 n4
  Assaggi, 336
  cadenza, 463, 463 n27
Romanesca: 133
Rome: 216, 319
'Rondeaus': 479
Rood, Louise: 219 n7
Rore, Cipriano de: 62
Rosin: 71
Rossi, Salomone: 135
Rothschild, Fritz: 293 n16
Rouen: 55
Rousseau, Jean: 246, 303
  Traité de la Viole, 227
  on the bow, 253
  defines *tenue*, 265 n17
  description of vibrato, 288
Rousseau, Jean-Jacques:
  defines *batterie*, 406
  on chord breaking, 437
  on *notes inégales* (*pointer*), 476
  imitation of nature, 491
  quoted on 'Genius', 492
  on expression from the violin, 494
Rowe, Walter: 136
Royal band (of Charles I): composition of, 138
Rubato: see Tempo rubato
Rudimenta Panduristae (Wagenseil): 360
  on down- and up-bow, 403
Ruggieri, Francesco ('Il Per'): 195
Rule of Down-Bow: 80, 158, 159, 162
  n16, 163, 257

inspired by dance musicians, 162-3
application to sonata, 163
despised by Geminiani, 258
its essence, 258
Playford on, 258
related to even or uneven number of
  notes in a measure, 258
wide usage, 258
applications and modifications, 259, 402
described by Georg Muffat, 260
late 17th century, 265
effect in multiple stops, 273
18th century, 401
problems in practice, 401
stated by Leopold Mozart, 401
Ruppert, Johann Heinrich: 317
Russell, Theodore: 131 n7

'S' (*su*): 403
Sacchi, Federico: 19 n28
Sachs, Curt: 43 n27, 52 n3, 91 n38, 184
  n14, 472 n13
  on *La Volta*, 66
  on 'small violins', 118
Sackville (and Norton): *Gorboduc*, 57, 138
Saint George, Henry: 326
  on bow, 325
Saint-Sevin, Joseph Barnabé: *see* L'Abbé
  le fils
Salabue, Count Cozio di: 19, 329, 505
Salmon, Jacques: 56
Salò: *see* Gasparo da Salò (Bertolotti)
Saltellando: 165, and *see* the Glossary
Salz, Ansley: Collection at the University of California (Berkeley), 207, 329
Sandberger, Adolf: 62 n25
San Giorgio, Eusebio da (painter): 90 n35
San Petronio Chapel (Bologna): 218
Sarabande: 292 n13, 329 n43, 420, 473
  very fast, 292
Saronno Cathedral fresco: 20, and Pl. 2
  violin family represented, 7
  viola player in, 74
  violinist playing *pizzicato* in, 84
Sartori, Claudio: 135 n12
Sauerlandt, Max: 74 n9
Sautillé: 165, 408, 408 n13, 414
  defined, *see* the Glossary
Savoy:
  House of, 20
  French language used in the province of, 22 n33
Saxophone: 4

Scales:
  chromatic, 250
  diatonic, chromatic, and mixed, 374
  G major favoured, 374
  in harmonics, 385
Scandinavia, violin in: 144
Scarlatti, Alessandro: use of eighth
    position, 250–1
Scheidt, Samuel: 'Imitatio Violistica', 166
Schein, Johann Hermann: 116 n12, 136
Schering, Arnold: 171 n29, 129 n4, 332
    n3, 334 n5, 462 n22
  sinfonia-concerto, 335 n7
  on 'Bach' bow, 432, 433
  bow theory untenable, 434
Scherzi (J. J. Walther): 224
Schindler, Anton Felix: 204 n18
Schleifer: 488
Schmelt, Cor. van: 234, 235
Schmeltzer, Johann Heinrich:
  use of mute, 205 n19
  in Vienna, 223
  slurred staccato, 270
  early concerto, 332
Schmieder, Wolfgang: 348 n34
Schmitz, Hans-Peter: 460 n15
Schneider, Max: 76 n13
Schneller: 451
'School of Nations': *see* Tartini
Schop, Johann: 136, 168
Schrade, Leo: 72 n7
Schröder, Rolph: 431 n6, 435 n11
Schünemann, Georg: 446 n29
Schütz, Heinrich: 135, 136, 182 n11
  as a symbol, 102
  'Tremolant' and 'Tremulus', 170–1
Schwebung: 389
Schweitzer, Albert:
  on 'Bach' bow, 432
  influenced by Schering, 432 n9
Schwermer: 268
Sciolto(e): 268, 425 (Ex. 192), 426
Scordatura: 246, 247, 283, 367, 462 n24
  17th century, 130
  in Marini, 130
  'hand-grip' notation, 130, 250
  advantages and disadvantages, 131
  open string, 153
  for double stops, 167
  in Biber and Walther, 223, 226
  rules of fingering and notation, 250
  in Tremais, 347, 445
  terms for, 370 n17
  18th century, 444

'Scotch' snap: 128
Screw mechanism (for tightening the bow
    hair): 324
  in the 'Stradivari' bow, 207
  in the '1694' bow, 209
Seagrave, Barbara A. G.: 262 n9, 447 n21
Second position: *see* Position
The Self-Instructor on the Violin: 245, 247
  contents, 234
'Self-Instructors': 358
Semitone extension: 154
Senaillié, Jean-Baptiste: 345
'Senior Balshar': 235
Senn, Walter: 39 n18, 196 n8
  experiments, 282
Senz'arco: = *pizzicato*, 277
Seraphin, Santo: 319
Serenata A un Coro di Violini (J. J. Walther):
    225
Serré: 399
Sesquialtera: 181, 468 n3
Seventh position: *see* Position
Sforza, Ludovico, Duke of Milan: 16 n19
Shake: 286, 453
Shift: 378
Shifting:
  in Ganassi, 87
  by crawling downward, 155 (Fig. 5),
    248
  late 17th century, 251
  relative to 'old' violin, 251
  terms for, 251
  in cadenzas, 252
  18th century, 339
  Quantz, 376
  fingerings for, 379
  sequential patterns, 380
'Short-long' inequality: *see Notes inégales*
Signatures:
  tempo, 293
  double, 302
Signs: for *crescendo* and *diminuendo*, 485
Simpson, Christopher: 202, 209, 209 n22
    233, 235
  speculations, 215
  Months and Seasons, 233
  The Division Viol, 248, 289
  fingering, 248
  long bow, 249
  description of bow stroke, 253
  quoted, 254
  on *tremolo* 267 n20
  multiple stops, 275
  on dynamics, 290

Simpson, Christopher—*contd.*
  on nuance, 291
  chord breaking, 436
Sinfonia-concerto: 335 n7
'Singing allegro':
  Vivaldi, 343
Sirmen, Madame: *see* Lombardini, Maddalena
Skeaping, Kenneth: 196 n8, 320 n8
Sleeper, Helen Joy: 233 n34
Slur: 129
Slurred *bariolage*: in L'Abbé le fils, 407
Slurred (legato) groups: 265
Slurred staccato: *see* Staccato, slurred
Slurred *tremolo*: see *Tremolo*, slurred
Slurring and slurs:
  legato (16th c.), 78
  17th century, 128, 164
  Richardo Rogniono on, 164
  problem of adding, 168
  implied insertion of in multiple stops, 273, 441–2
  18th century, 441
Smanicatura: 379
Smith, Gertrude P.: 219 n17
Smith, Thomas: Pl. 38b
Smith William C.: 222 n10
Snakewood ('specklewood'): 209, 327
  in bows, 114
Social position of violin (late 17th c.): 192
Sohlmans Musiklexikon: 199 n10
Solo a Violino senza basso (Bach): 279
Solo concerto: *see* Concerto
Solo sonata: *see* Sonata
Somis, Giovanni Battista: 342, 345
  'holding of a whole note', 393 n5
Sonabile: in Tartini, 405
'Sonades': 408, n8
Sonata: 133, 134, 215, 216
  17th century, 123, 124, 134–5
  for solo violin and *basso continuo*, 132
  trio sonata, 132
    late 17th century, 213
    Purcell, 238
    how performed, 278
    18th century, 336
    instrumentation (18th c.), 445
  types (trio, 'solo', '*senza basso*'), 133
  first solo violin sonata, 134, 220
  origin in canzona (17th c.), 134
  senza basso, 213, 336
  'solo' sonata, 213, 279
    18th century, 336
    type of bow used in, 325

  with written-out harpsichord part, 336
  six unaccompanied sonatas (J. S. Bach), 348
  six sonatas for violin and harpsichord (J. S. Bach), 349
Sonata a tre: defined, 278
Sonata de camera: 134, 140, 213
Sonata da chiesa: 134
  = church sonata, 134
  distinguished from *sonata da camera*, 135
Sonata style: 148 n2, 149
  described, 150
  Italian, 241
'Sonatistes': 214, 372
Son coupé: 409
Sonnata's of III Parts (Purcell): 237, 279
Sonneck, Oscar George Theodore: 24 n36
Sons enflés: 397 n6
Sons filés: 397 n6
Sons soutenus: 397 n6
Sopra il manico tutto: 251–2
Sopranino di viola: 60
Soprano *viola da braccio* (= violin): 45
Sordino (mute): 205 n19, 322
  does not imply soft, 444
  see also Mute
Sorge, G. A.: 385 n42
Sostenuto:
  meaning, 256
  in Leopold Mozart, 396
Sound post: 110, 201, 321
  as 'the soul', 253 n1
Sourdine: 205 n19
Spain:
  relation to violin (16th c.), 40
  violin in (17th c.), 143
'Specklewood': *see* Snakewood
Speer, Daniel: *Grund-richtiger . . . Unterricht*, 246
Spiccare: 84
Spiccato: 208
  late 17th century, 263
  18th century, 399, 408, 408 n13, 414
Spinetta: use in performance, 279
Spitta, Philipp: 196 n5, 411 n22
Spivakovsky, Tossy: triple stops, 275 n26
Spohr, Ludwig: 223, 446
  invention of chin rest, 369
'Stabb' (Roger North): 409
Staccato: 263
  defined, *see* the Glossary
  slurred, 165, 269, 416
    Leopold Mozart quoted, 270
  'flying', 208

in Biber and Walther, 225
late 17th century, 262, 263
signs for, 263, 410
dot (in Walther), 264
in Muffat, 264
described by Mace, 264
staccato-under-slur, 270
violin (18th c.), 408
defined by Brossard, 408
meaning (18th c.), 408
modern meaning, 408
indication for whole movements, 409
general effect of (18th c.), 409
understood without signs (18th c.), 410
performance of individual staccato note,
411
effect of tempo on, 412
in Geminiani, 413
in slurred *tremolo*, 422
Stainer, Jacob: 109, 194, 281, 314, 317,
447, and Pl. 26a
his great fame, 195
his violins owned by Bach, Biber,
Locatelli, Leopold Mozart, and
Veracini, 195
Stainer violin of 1688 described, 196
decline of reputation after 1800, 197
Stamitz, Johann: 350, 364
Stamitz, Karl: 350, 364
Stevens, Denis: 91 n37, 135 n12, 431 n5
Stevenson, Robert: 331 n1, 292 n13
Sticcato pastorale: 416 n32
'*Stile concitato*': in Monteverdi, 129
'Sting' (Mace): 288
'*Stoccata*' (Roger North): 236, 409
Stoccato: 408
Stopped unison: extension, 383
Stradivari, Antonio: 33, 195, 254, 314,
317, 447
obscurities of origins and life, 197
birthdate, 505
marriage, 506
'Amatisé' violins, 197
'Hellier' violin, 198
'Betts' violin, 198, 317, and Pls. 33a
and 34
'Alard' violin, 317
'Messie' violin, 317
'long' model, 242, 281, and Pl. 25b
significance of, 197–8
'classical' model, 317
'Tuscan' viola bridge, 202, and Pl. 27
his significance, 317
earliest date for a Stradivari violin, 506

'Stradivari' bow: 207, 207 n20, 210, 328
playing properties compared to the
modern bow, 207 (cf. Pl. 28)
significance, 208
movable nut, 208
wood used, 209, 327
Stradivari, Francesco: 318
Stradivari, Omobono: 318
Stradivari, Paolo: 328, 505, 506, 507
Straeten, Edmond Van der: 35, 38, 41
n25, 72 n8, 117, 195, 196 n5, 346
Strappato: 426
Stratifario, Antonio: 317
see also Stradivari, Antonio
Strecciate [*sic*]: 426
Stricciate: 426
Striggio, Alessandro: 24, 60, 72, 90
String ensemble: five-part (Mersenne),
229
Strings: 201
of brass and steel (Praetorius), 111
Kircher and Mersenne on, 111
all gut (17th c.), 111
material and thickness, 203
silver-wound, 321
thick vs. thin, 321–2
metal, 322
overspun with copper, 324 n19
'String stop': 320
Strocchi, Giuseppe: 18
'Strohfidel': 416 n32
Stroke: 263 n11
staccato, 263
Strunk, Oliver: *Source Readings* quoted,
72 n7, 90 n34, 447 n30
Strutt, Joseph: 59 n1
Studeny, B.: 336 n9
Sturm und Drang: 473 n14
Su: 403
see also *In su*
Sullivan, Mary: 139 n23
Sul ponticello: 77
17th century, 130, 132, 171 (defined)
Sulla tastiera: 77, 278, 444
17th century, 171 (defined)
'Supination': 372 n21
Suso: see *In su*
'Suspension': in Couperin, 470
Swell:
in Corelli, 255
in Mace, 288
'Sympathetic' stings (*Harding fele*): 199
'Symphonies': 135
Syncopated bowing: 165, 225, 265, 407

Szulc, Prof. Zdzislaw: 353 n42

'T' (*Tirare*): 262
'T' ('*Tirare in giù*'): 158 n14
'T', or 't' (*Tiré*): 158 n14, 262, 403
't' (*tremolo* = trill): 177
't' (trill): 129, 286
Tablatures: 154
  for violin, 117-18
Table (violin): *see* the Glossary
Tactus: early 17th century, 181
Taille: 117, 323
  defined, *see* the Glossary
Taille de viole: 44
Tailpiece: 368
  defined, *see* the Glossary
Talbot, James: 321
  manuscript, 199, 210
Tambourin de village: 55
'*Tardo*': 184
  in Marini, 185
Tartaglia, Nicolo: 18
Tartini, Giuseppe: 271, 332, 343, 379, 458
  n12
  Letter, 255, 244, 361, 378
  Traité des Agrémens, 316, 344, 364, 405
    n7
    dating, 361, 361 n11
    'Bowing Rules', 361 n11
    original Italian manuscript, 361 n11
  L'Arte del arco, 337, 344, 361
  octave leaps, 339
  ornamentation, 341
    arbitrary, 461
    improvised, 461
  importance, 343-4
  manuscripts at University of California
    (Berkeley), 344 n23
  'Devil's trill' Sonata, 344, 452-3
  'School of Nations', 344, 361
  capricci, 465
  second position, 378
  differential tones, 385
  vibrato, 387
  messa di voce, 389
  bow stroke, 393
    articulated, 414
  trill, 450
    three speeds for, 451
    consecutive, 452
  mordent, 454
  dynamic interpretation of *appoggiatura*,
    455
  Adagio, 461

cadenza, 462, 464, 464 n28, 465
Taste and judgement: 184, 356
Tasti: *see* the Glossary
  in Frescobaldi, 184
  role of, 356
Tasto solo: 461
  cadenza, 462
Taverner, John: 91
Teacher: importance of, 246
Tecchler, David: 222, 319
  in Rome, 198
Telemann, George Philipp: 462 n22
  on Polish 'fiddlers', 353-4
Telmányi, Emil: 431 n6, 435 n11
  'Vega' bow, 431
Temperament: defined, *see* the Glossary
Tempi: related to signatures about 1700,
  293
Tempo:
  early 17th century
    markings, 184
    strict and free, 184
    fluctuating, 294
  late 17th century, 292ff, 294
  18th century terms for, 467
  'inherent' tempo
    Muffat, 293
    Muffat and Leopold Mozart, 468-9
    Rameau, 470
  related to time signatures, 467
  denoting mood, 468
  changes in Muffat and Quantz, 468
  terms not very satisfactory, 468
  absolute measure, pulse of the heart
    (Quantz), 469
Tempo commodo: 470
Tempo giusto: 470
Tempo of the hand: Monteverdi, 184
Tempo ordinario: 219
Tempo rubato:
  definitions, 470
  Chopin on, 470
  Leopold Mozart on, 471
  W. A. Mozart on, 471-2
  Tosi on, 471
  Geminiani on, 472
'Tenore': 446
'Tenor viola': 446
'Tenor' violin: 11, 115, 116
Tension: 204
Tenths: in Locatelli, 339
Tenue: 265 n17
Terminology for:
  down-bow, 262

up-bow, 262
  shifting, 378
  vibrato, 389
  bowing, 403
  see also under the term concerned
Terpsichore (Praetorius): 136
'Terraced' dynamics: 291, 484–5
Tessarini, Carlo: 379
  Grammatica di musica, 360
Tessier, A.: 278 n27
Testator il Vecchio: 18
Testore, Carlo Giuseppe: 198
Testore family: 319
Theme and variations: 214
Third position: *see* Position
'Third tones': 385
Thirty Years' War: 102, 136
Thoinan, E.: 137 n17
Thorough Bass: in Purcell, 279
'Thrown' stroke: 408
Thumb, use of: 374 n24, 376
'Thump' ('left-hand' *pizzicato*): 278
Tibia: 33 n5
Tiburtino, Juliano: 90
Tieffenbrucker: *see* Duiffoprugcar,
  Gaspar(d)
Tilmouth, Michael: 201 n14, 222 n11, 231
  n28, 231 n29, 231 n30, 236 n38, 238
  n41
Time:
  beaten audibly, 294
  beaten with the foot, 294
Time signatures: mixed, 296, 302
Tinctoris, Johannes: 67, 166–7 (quoted)
  use of term *viola*, 16
  De Inventione et Usu Musicae, 50, 166
  improvisation, 89
Tintoretto, Jacopo Robusti (painter): 74
Tirade: 270
Tirar: 16th century, 83
Tirare: 262
Tirare in giù: 80, 158 n14
Tiré: 73, 158 n14, 262, 392, 403
Titian (Tiziano Vecellio): 74
Tockieren: 413 n25
Tockiret: 411, 413
Toinon: on 'swelling the sound', 291
Tonal strength: viola, 323
Tone colour:
  Ganassi, 86
  uniformity, 376
Tone production (late 17th c.): 254
Tononi, Giovanni: 319
Tononi family (Bologna): 198

Torchi, Luigi: 132 n8, 136 n14, 185 n17,
  219 n7
Torelli, Giuseppe: 171, 218
  shifting, 251
  on performance, 280
  concerto, 332, 333, 342
  solo concerto, 342
Tosi, Pier Francesco: 471 n10
  on *tempo rubato*, 471
Tourte, François: 70, 114, 115, 211, 316,
  325, and Pls. 28a and 38d
  modern bow, 111, 207, 312
  his achievement and role, 327–8
Tourte *l'aîné*: 327
Tourte *père*: 327, and Pl. 38c
'Tr' (trill): 129, 177, 286
Traité de la Viole (Rousseau): 227
Traité des Agrémens: *see* Tartini
Transport(s): 378
Trasp^{ne}: 378
Transporto dalla mano: 379
Trasposizione: 378
Treatises:
  characteristic of new attitude (17th c.),
    100
  in England and Germany, 244
  for advanced players, 357, 363
  violin (1700–61), 357ff
  level and bias, 363
  as prototypes, 364ff
  'do-it-yourself', 365
Tremais: 365, 444, 453
  use of advanced technique, 347
  on *pizzicato*, 445
'Tremar': 77
Tremblement: 286
  vibrato, 289, 390
  Leclair, 438
Tremblement coupé: 287
Tremblement serré: 389
Trembler: 266
  in Lully, 267
'Tremble with the Bow' (Simpson): 267
  n20
'Tremolant': 171
Tremoletto: 176
Tremolo: 266, 423
  in Monteverdi, 129, 130
    measured, 133
  in Francesco Rognoni, 130 n6
  as trill, 130 n6
  17th century, 170, 176
  in Matteis, 236
  slurred, 266, 269, 422

Tremolo—contd.
   in Leopold Mozart, 269
   18th century, 407
   related to *portato*, 423
   in Leclair
  in Walther, 266–7
  in Albicastro, 267
  in Purcell, 267
  double stops, 267
  as vibrato, 386ff, 390
  unslurred (18th c.), 407
  as repeated notes, 422
  in Leclair, 488
Tremolo adagio: 268
Tremolo spiccato adagio: 266 n9, 267
'Tremulus': 171
Tremulus Ascendens: 177
Tremulus Descendens: 177
Treviso: 319
Trichet, Pierre: 110, 114, 119, 209
  on violin usage, 137
Trill:
  early 17th century, 129, 176
  late 17th century, 286
  18th century, 450
  in thirds or sixths, 167–8
  in thirds, 286
  in sixths
    double stop (Mozart, Bach), 429
    Mozart, 452
    Bach, 453
    Guillemain, 453
  length, 286, 451
  consecutive, 341
  18th century, 352
  double, 341
  minor third, 450
  octave, 341, 453
  in harmonics, 385, 453
  prefix of, 450
  afterbeats of, 450–1
  nuanced, 451
  speed of,
    accelerating (Mozart), 451
    three speeds (Tartini), 451
  syncopated, 452
  vibrato-trill (Tartini), 453
Trillo: 130 n6, 176
Trillo accompagnato (Tartini): 453
Trio sonata: *see* Sonata
Tripla: 181, 219, 292
Triple stops:
  in 17th century, 131, 275ff
  in 18th century, 429

  performance of, 169
  consecutive (Marini), 169
  sustained (Leclair), 437
  see also Multiple stops
Triple time: Leopold Mozart on bowing
  in, 401–2
Triplets: alteration of dotted and other
  figures in context of, 296
'Tripola': 468 n3
Troiano, Massimo: 62 n24
  account of ducal dinner, 62
Tromba marina: 252, 337
Tronco per Grazia: 409 n14
'Tuner' (E string): 109, 322, and *see* the
  Glossary and Pl. 1
Tuning:
  lira da braccio, 90 n35
  'top string as high as it will bear', 186
Turin: 20, 319
  school at, 342
Turn:
  17th century, 176
  18th century, 457
Turner, William: on viol and violin, 231
'Tuscan' viola: 320
  bridge of, 202
'Tut' (staccato): in Mace, 264
Twenty-four Violins of the King: 57, 104, 241
  established by Charles II, 230
  description of dress, 230
  typical ensemble, 230 n24
  see also Vingt-quatre Violons du Roy

'U' (up): 262
'U' (up-bow): 403
Überlegung: 375
Uccellini, Marco: 110, 125, 135, 149, 217
  slurs in Op. 5, 163 n17
Uffenbach, J. F.: 377 n34
  description of Vivaldi's playing, 377
Umstimmung: 370 n17
'Unequal notes': 303, 472
  application of, 306
  see also Notes inégales
Unton, Sir Henry: painting of nuptial
  banquet scene, 58–9
Up-bow: 157, 262
  defined, 79
  terms, 262
'Upper-auxiliary': trill, 450
Use of finger four: 153–4

'v' (*vilis*): 262
'Vanitas' theme: 104, and Pl. 24

Vannes, René: 18 n22, 19 n27, 194 n1
Variation: 133, 213, 216
  Germany (late 17th c.), 224
  England, 232
    history of, 234
  18th century, 336
Vaudemont, Madamoiselle de: 55
'Vega Bach-bow': 431, 435 n11, and Pl. 40a
Veinus, Abraham: 280 n31, 332 n3
Veloce: 184
Venice: 18, 217, 319
  importance of (17th c.), 108
Veracini, Antonio: 217
Veracini, Francesco Maria: 195, 209, 324, 343, 350, 351, 364, 458 n14
  playing the violin, 242, and Pl. 30
  bow, 326
  dynamic signs, 340
  treatise, 361
  holding violin, 368
  bowing signs and terms, 403
  slurred staccato, 417
  slurs over dots, 421
  slurred *tremolo*, 422
  nuanced signs, 486
Verceil: *see* Vercelli
Vercelli: 20, 22
Veronese, Paolo (painter): 37
  'Marriage at Cana' described, 74
Verre cassé (= vibrato): 177
Verstimmung: 370 n17
Versuch einer gründlichen Violinschule: *see* Mozart, Leopold
Vestergaard, Knud: 435 n11
Vibrato: 77, 129, 236, 255, 291
  16th century, 69
    in Agricola, 91
    in Ganassi, 92
  early 17th century, 173, 177
    in Mersenne, 177–8
  combined with nuance, 180, 288
  late 17th century, 282, 287
    sign (*m*), 283, 287–8, 454
  continuous, 288, 386
  in Mace, 288
  in Marin Marais, 288
  in Leopold Mozart, 388
  one finger, 288
  two fingers ('close shake'), 288
  18th century, 340, 386, 395
    double stops, 387
  as ornament, 386
    16th century, 92
  in Tartini and Leopold Mozart, 387

'swelling the sound by Degrees' (Geminiani), 388
  related to *messa di voce* (Tartini), 389
  terminology of, 389
  vibrato-trill (Tartini), 453
Vicentino, Nicola: 19, 92
Vidal, Louis-Antoine: 18 n25, 24
Viéville: *see* Freneuse, Le Cerf de la Viéville, Seigneur de
Vihuela de mano: 50
Vihuela de braco: 25
Vilis: 262
Vinci, Leonardo da (painter): 18, 98
Vingt-quatre Violons du Roy: 116, 136, 146, 227, 228 n21, 243, 346
  names of the five parts, 117
Viol: Pl. 5
  insignificant contribution to violins, 14
  compared to violin, 14, 283
    17th century, 124
  four string and three string, 28
  in Zacconi, 42
  term distinct from violin, 44
  variant spellings, 44
  holding (16th c.), 73
  bowing (16th c.), 79
  Ganassi's fingerings, 84–85
Viola: Pl. 7
  invented, 8
  meaning, 14
  did it precede the violin?, 15
  terminology, 16
  16th century
    need for, 33
    varied in size, 33
    tone, 68
  Tinctoris, 43
  with a bow, 50
  third position, 88
  in alto and tenor sizes (less in demand 1650–1750), 205
  tonal strength, 323
  making, almost died out (early 18th c.), 323
  four distinct parts, 233
  as a bass, 324 n19
Viola (= alto or tenor *viola da braccio*): 115
Viola bastarda: 60
  according to Praetorius and F. Rognoni, 108 n1
Viola da braccio: 16, 29, 33 n5, 116, 188
  meaning, 15
  Zacconi, 42
  17th century, 115

Viola da braccio—contd.
  Monteverdi, 118
  see also Geigen (grosse) and *Geigen (kleine)*
Viola da brazo: 15 n16
'*Viola da brazo senza tasti*': 28
Viola da brazzo: 62, 323
Viola da gamba: 15 n16, 42, 278
  meaning, 15
  Jambe de Fer, 32
  Zacconi, 42
Viola d'amore: *see* Ariosti
Viola in braccio: 16, 16 n19
'*Viola*' (=*lyra da gamba*): 90
'*Violans*': 41 n24
Viol de bracio: 116
Viole d'amour: 203
Viole d'arco . . . con tre corde senza tasti: 19
'*Violenns*': 58
Violeta (Cerone): 25
Violetta: 23, 25, 29, 44, 324
  meaning, 25
  16th century and 18th century mean-
    ings compared, 26
Violetta marina: 324
Violetta picciola: 25, 116
Violette da Arco senza tasti: 25
Violetti: 26, 324
Viole (=viol): 22
Violin (as an instrument):
  defined, 6, and Pl. 1
  early, 6, 7, 14, 32
    combination of rebec, fiddle, and *lira
      da braccio*, 10
    in Agricola, 29
  'true' violin, 6
    after 1550, 29
    description by Jambe de Fer (1556),
      31
    why the fourth string was added, 32
  ancestors, 8
    musical function of, 50
  hybrids, 12
  'inventor' of, 17
  small and large pattern (16th c.), 33
  variations in 'standard' model, 33 n6
  'old' and modern violin compared, 33-
    4, and Pls. 6, 26 and 34
  of five strings, 38 n14
  making
    'in the fashion of' Brescia, Cremona,
      and Venice, 38
    Paris, 39
    Brescia and Cremona, 108
    Cremona, 139 n22

distinction between species and parts, 43
  strings
    how to select, 70
    gut G string, 70
  body arching (17th c.), 110
  description and details of, 199, 200
    17th century, 109
    18th century, 319
  bass bar, 201
  sound post, 201
  tailpiece, 201, 528, and Pl. 1
  fingerboard, 201, 320, and Pls. 1 and 6
  tuning, 247
    18th century, 370
  'classical' (flat) model of Stradivari, 317,
    . 319
  neck, 319, and Pls. 1 and 6
  arched model, 319
  bridge, 320
    tensions on, 321
    proper adjusting (Leopold Mozart), 322
  altering modern instrument, 500
  reducing tension in, 501
  see also the Plates
Violin (music):
  first published music (1582), 51
  dearth of written music (16th c.), 51
  independent musical forms, 103
  idiomatic style
    17th century, 125, 146
    18th century, 338
  Polish (17th c.), 143
  prelude, 213
  duet, 214
  figuration in, 216
  in 'tutors', 232
  expressive performance expected (18th
    c.), 493
Violin (sound of the instrument):
  in 16th century, 67
  sound of 'old' and modern compared,
    69, 173, 497
  in 17th century, 172
    French and Italian, 151
  about 1700, 281ff
  compared to viols, 283
  according to Raguenet and Muffat (*c.*
    1700), 205
  in 18th century, 447
Violin (technique):
  holding the instrument
    across the body, 11 n9
    16th century, 73
    early 17th century, 152

late 17th century, 247–8
18th century, 367–8
on left side of string holder, 369
holding (old' violin), 502
borrowing technique
16th century, 72
16th and 17th centuries, 166
tone production (16th c.), 77
fingerings before 1600, 85
bowing discipline (R. Rogiono, 1592), 82
position(s) and position playing
Zacconi (1592), 88
related to construction of violin in 16th century, 89
17th century, 126
in combinations (17th c.), 103
clef used (17th c.), 117
range of (17th c.), 125
advance in technique after 1600, 145–6
obbligato style, 147
dance style of playing (17th c.), 148
sonata style of playing, 148 n2
treatises
late 17th century, 244
18th century, 357
'tutors' for amateurs, 245 n2
Violin (usage and function):
16th century, 2, 3, 50–54, 139, 147
France, 54
England, 57
Italy, 59
Germany, 61
17th century, 138
in chamber music, 139
England, 141
Spain, 143
in opera and dance music, 147
doubling vocal parts, 147
Italy, 150
Violin (social position):
Jambe de Fer quoted on, 4
16th century, 57
17th century, 104–5
late 17th century, 192
18th century, 365
Violin (miscellaneous):
terms for (16th c.), 29
variant spellings of the term, 44
social and musical roles (17th c.), 102–3
portrayed in Dutch painting (17th c.), 103
pictured with bow (Mersenne), 113 (Fig. 4)

'violin or cornett' (17th c.), 123, 124
a partner of the 'new' music, 124
adaptable to temperament, 186
bow, the 'soul' of, 207
increased vogue (late 17th c.), 213
adopted by amateurs (late 17th c.), 245
amateur tradition, 365
Hawkins' opposition to, 331
Violin: *see also* Bow, Bridge, Fingerboard, and Neck
Violin (=*viola da braccio*): 188
Violin family:
emerges, 151, and Pl. 2
distinguished from viol family, 31
complete about 1550, 33
terminology and tuning (theorists), 115
terminology (music), 118
'Violini in Tromba Marina': Vivaldi, 337
Violini Milanesi: 26, 52
Violini ordinarij da braccio: Monteverdi, 118
Violini piccoli alla francese: Monteverdi, 118
Violinist:
left handed, 147 n1
education of (late 17th c.), 246
Violinista: 20 n31
Violino: 20, 22, 23, 42
first appearance as a term, 26
in personal records, 27
meanings (16th c.), 29, 44
in Zacconi, 42
16th century, 43
in Marenzio, 60
in Gabrieli (=viola), 68
17th century, 115
in Monteverdi, 118
Violino da braccio: 17th century, 115
Violino da brazzo: 83, 116
Violino de concerto: Albinoni, 446
Violino piccolo: 37, 323
16th century, 44
17th century, 115
tuning in Bach, 116 n11
Violino primo: Albinoni, 446
Violino scordato: 323
Violinschule: *see* Mozart, Leopold
Viollon (=violin, in England): 22
'*Viollons*': of Francis I, 25
'Viollons de Thurin': 26
'*Violn de Bracio*': 116
Violon: 20, 29
etymology, 22
confused with *Violone*, 23

Violoncello: 234
　invented, 8
　etymology, 44
　reform by Stradivari, 323
Violon da braccia: 15 n16, 32, 42
'Violon da braccia ou violone': 23
Violon discordée: 347
Violon(e): meaning (16th c.), 22
Violone: 32, 278, 324
　meaning, 15
　　16th century, 44
　as double bass only, 23
　= *violono*, 23
　use in performance, 279
Violone da braccio: 23
Violone-cello: 44
Violoni: meaning, 25
Violoni da tasti & da Arco: 25
Violons: 42
　in Emmanuele Filiberto, 60–61
Violons du Cabinet: see *Petits Violons, Les*
'Violons ordinaires de la chambre du Roy': 57
Viotti, Giovanni Battista: 211, 314, 315, 344
　introduces Stradivari violins to Paris, 198
　role in modern bow, 327
Virdung, Sebastian: 29 n4
Virchi, Girolamo: 18
Virtuosity:
　rise of, 306
　in solo concerto, 333
Virtuoso: 341
Vitali, Giovanni Battista: 217, 218, 219 n7, 220, 238
　Chaconne, 217 n6
　Artificii Musicali, 218
　Passagallo, 219
Vitali, T. A.: 217
Vivaldi, Antonio: 313, 332, 334, 344, 348, 349, 458 n12
　concerto, 332, 333
　　number of, 336
　　'programme', 337
　Concerto in G minor, 335
　Il Cimento (Op. 8), 337
　'Spring' Concerto, 337
　significance in concerto, 342
　'singing allegro', 343
　style of his music, 343
　scordatura, 370 n17
　playing described, 377
　extensions, 383
　bariolage, 407

　bowing variety, 424, 425
　instrumentation, 446
　cadenza, 462
　dynamics, 485
　　diminuendo, 488
Vivola: 116
　according to Praetorius, 108 n1
Vivola da brazzo: parts in Monteverdi, 117
La Volta: 57, 74, and Pls. 13 and 14
　description, 66
'Voyces and viols': 53
　see also 'For voyce or viol'
Vuillaume, Jean-Baptiste: 315, 321 n9, 328 n23, and Pl. 26b
Vyollon: 22
Vyollons de Verceil: 22

Wagenseil, G. C.: 360, 403
'Waits': 54 n6
Walmsley, Peter: 319
　stamped bow, 328 n24
Walsh, John: 222 n10, 350, 355
Walther, Johann Gottfried: 164 n20, 323, 324
　quoted on staccato, 409
　Musikalisches Lexikon, 473 n14
　bow in, 326
Walther, Johann Jakob: 136, 212, 223, 242, 246, 271, 291, 349, 350 n35
　Hortulus Chelicus, 224
　　Serenata A un Coro di Violini, 225
　Scherzi, 224
　technical characteristics shared with Biber, 225
　staccato dot, 264
　tremolo, 266–7
　arpeggio, 268
　slurred staccato, 270
　pizzicato, 277
Warlock, Peter (Phillip Heseltine): 139 n24
Wasielewski, W. J. von: 132 n8, 134 n10, 136 n14, 137 n19, 183
Weber, Carl Maria von: 446
Wechsberg, Joseph: 56 n12, 432 n9
Weigel, Johann Christoph: 326
Weigel bow: 210, and Pl. 37
'Welschen' (*Geigen*): 28
Wendish fiddle: 9
Wessely-Kropik, Helene: 222 n11
Westhoff, J. P. von: 246
　in Dresden, 224
　diminuendo in, 292
Westrup, Jack Allan: 118, 238 n41
'White cromes': 468 n3

Whittaker, W. G.: 237 n40
Wilbye, John: 58
Wilhelm V, Duke of Bavaria: 61
  description of nuptial banquet, 62
Wilhelm, Wolfgang: 135
Willaert, Adrian: 76
Wilson, John: 236 n37
Winternitz, Emanuel: 7 n3, 9 n6
Wirsta, Aristide: 360 n7
Woeriot (painter): 14, 18, 31 n1, and Pl. 9
  portrait of Duiffoprugcar described, 39
Wolf, Johannes: 118 n16, 162 n16
Wood, Anthony: on Baltzar, 236
Woodfill, Walter: 39 n18, 57 n16, 58 n17,
    103 n2, 104 n4, 105 n5, 106 n6, 138
    n21, 139 n22
  on 'waits', 54 n6

Young, William: 140, 142, 238
  sonatas, 237

Zacconi, Lodovico: 25, 34, 116
  viole da braccio (three registers), 42
  terms in, 42–3
  positions in (1592), 88
Zanetto (da) Montichiaro: 17
Zannetti, Gasparo: 162
  violin tablature, 118
  use of figure '5', 154
  use of tablatures, 154
  Il Scolaro, 154, 154 n7
  scheme of ensemble, 154 n7
  his significance, 154 n7
  dance pieces, 154
  ensemble for violin, two violas, and
    cello, 154 n7
  on bowing, 159
  example of down-bow and up-bow,
    160–1
Zusammenschlag: 455

Set in Monotype Van Dijck by
W. & J. Mackay & Co. Ltd.,
Chatham
and reprinted lithographically by
Latimer Trend & Co. Ltd.,
Whitstable